A Chinese Rebel beyond the Great Wall

James A. Millward, Series Editor

The Silk Roads series is made possible by the generous support of the Henry Luce Foundation's Asia Program. Founded in 1936, the Luce Foundation is a not-for-profit philanthropic organization devoted to promoting innovation in academic, policy, religious, and art communities. The Asia Program aims to foster cultural and intellectual exchange between the United States and the countries of East and Southeast Asia, and to create scholarly and public resources for improved understanding of Asia in the United States.

Gifts in the Age of Empire: Ottoman-Safavid Cultural Exchange, 1500–1650
Sinem Casale
Published 2022

Daemons Are Forever: Contacts and Exchanges in the Eurasian Pandemonium
David Gordon White
Published 2021

The Compensations of Plunder: How China Lost Its Treasures
Justin M. Jacobs
Published 2020

Geocultural Power: China's Quest to Revive the Silk Roads for the Twenty-First Century
Tim Winter
Published 2019

Islam and World History: The Ventures of Marshall Hodgson
Edited by Edmund Burke III and Robert J. Mankin
Published 2018

A Chinese Rebel beyond the Great Wall

The Cultural Revolution and Ethnic Pogrom
in Inner Mongolia

TJ CHENG, URADYN E. BULAG,
AND MARK SELDEN

The University of Chicago Press
Chicago and London

The University of Chicago Press, Chicago 60637
The University of Chicago Press, Ltd., London
© 2023 by The University of Chicago
All rights reserved. No part of this book may be used or reproduced in any manner
whatsoever without written permission, except in the case of brief quotations in critical
articles and reviews. For more information, contact the University of Chicago Press,
1427 E. 60th St., Chicago, IL 60637.
Published 2023
Printed in the United States of America

32 31 30 29 28 27 26 25 24 23   1 2 3 4 5

ISBN-13: 978-0-226-82684-4 (cloth)
ISBN-13: 978-0-226-82686-8 (paper)
ISBN-13: 978-0-226-82685-1 (e-book)
DOI: https://doi.org/10.7208/chicago/9780226826851.001.0001

Support for this publication was generously provided by the Henry Luce Foundation.

Library of Congress Cataloging-in-Publication Data

Names: Cheng, Tiejun, 1943– author. | Bulag, Uradyn E. (Uradyn Erden),
    1964– author. | Selden, Mark, author.
Title: A Chinese rebel beyond the Great Wall : the Cultural Revolution and ethnic
    pogrom in Inner Mongolia / TJ Cheng, Uradyn E. Bulag, and Mark Selden.
Other titles: Cultural Revolution and ethnic pogrom in Inner Mongolia | Silk roads
    (Chicago, Ill.)
Description: Chicago : The University of Chicago Press, 2023. | Series: Silk roads |
    Includes bibliographical references and index.
Identifiers: LCCN 2023001495 | ISBN 9780226826844 (cloth) |
    ISBN 9780226826868 (paperback) | ISBN 9780226826851 (ebook)
Subjects: LCSH: Cheng, Tiejun, 1943– | Political persecution—China—Inner
    Mongolia—History—20th century. | Political activists—China—Inner
    Mongolia—Biography. | Dissenters—China—Biography. | Inner Mongolia
    (China)—Politics and government—20th century. | China—History—Cultural
    Revolution, 1966–1976. | Inner Mongolia (China)—Ethnic relations. |
    LCGFT: Autobiographies.
Classification: LCC DS793.M7 C482 2023 | DDC 951.7/705—dc23/eng/20230130
LC record available at https://lccn.loc.gov/2023001495

♾ This paper meets the requirements of ANSI/NISO Z39.48-1992 (Permanence of Paper).

Contents

Maps and Figures

Maps

Figures

This book has been long in the making, its origins dating to 1978, when Cheng Tiejun and Mark Selden met in Raoyang county, Hebei, where Tiejun was teaching high school English and Mark was researching rural China for the book *Chinese Village, Socialist State* (published in 1993). The project started in 1986, when Tiejun began his doctoral research on China's household registration (*hukou*) system under Mark's supervision at Binghamton University. At that time, Tiejun introduced the experience of transferring his household registration from the poor North China rural county of Raoyang to Hohhot, the capital of Inner Mongolia, in 1959 and back to Raoyang in 1972, as well as the anti-Mongol pogrom he witnessed in Inner Mongolia in 1968–1969. It was not, however, until the mid-1990s that they began to record Tiejun's life history in the form of an oral account centered on the fierce conflicts of the Cultural Revolution in Inner Mongolia.

The three authors began their collaboration in 1998, when Bulag joined them, having taken up a teaching position at Hunter College in New York. Not only had he grown up as a child in Inner Mongolia during the Cultural Revolution; he was then starting his own research on Ulanhu, the founder of the Inner Mongolia Autonomous Region and, for two decades, from 1947 to 1966, its leader. His book *The Mongols at China's Edge: History and the Politics of National Unity* was published in 2002. The three authors agreed to focus the work on China's interethnic history and the Cultural Revolution in the borderlands. Bulag provided background information on the history of Inner Mongolia and rebel-loyalist clashes from Red Guard tabloids and pamphlets collected in Inner Mongolia, while Mark analyzed the borderland experience in the framework of the twentieth-century Chinese revolution and Tiejun recorded his experience in Inner Mongolia from 1959 to 1972 as a student, a Red Guard, and a journalist on the borderlands of Inner Mongolia, Mongolia, and the Soviet Union.

In 2003, Tiejun began working as coauthor of a memoir of Gao Shuhua, Inner Mongolia's foremost rebel activist, whose big-character poster on June 2, 1966, at Inner Mongolia Teachers' College set off Inner Mongolia's rebel movement. Their friendship dated from Tiejun's college years, when Gao was his teacher, and Tiejun became one of Gao's staunchest followers in the rebel movement that eventually propelled Gao to membership in the Standing Committee of the Inner Mongolian Revolutionary Committee. Following Gao's untimely death, Tiejun completed the memoir, which was published in Chinese in 2007 as *Neimeng Wenge Fenglei: Yiwei Zaofanpai Lingxiu de Koushushi* (*The Cultural Revolution in Inner Mongolia: The Oral History of a Rebel Leader*), highlighting the role of the rebels in Inner Mongolia's politics during the Cultural Revolution. This perspective led us to reconsider the parameters of our own book. Instead of a personal memoir of a rebel, it dawned on us that the value of our manuscript might lie precisely in rethinking the perspective of the rebels, a much-maligned group that, in the wake of Mao's death, had been blamed for the Cultural Revolution–era violence and tragedies throughout China, including Inner Mongolia.

We agreed that our book would not be an attempt to exonerate the rebels but rather would seek to explain the rationale behind their rebellion, the nature of the conflicts between rebels and loyalists over the decade of the Cultural Revolution, and the conflicts within rebel ranks as they sought to adapt to new signals from Mao and the Central Cultural Revolution Group under the leadership of Zhou Enlai. In particular, we set out to analyze the meaning of rebellion in the borderlands, an interethnic social milieu in which the primary targets of rebellion were Mongols in the *wasu* repression directed by General Teng Haiqing. The challenge was to bring together a personal memoir with an understanding of the changing dynamic of Chinese-minority relations in Inner Mongolia and eventually throughout China.

China's heavy-handed policy toward Xinjiang since 2017 was a turning point in China's post–Cultural Revolution ethnic policy and in global understanding of Chinese nationality relations. The incarceration of an estimated one million or more Uyghurs and other minorities in Xinjiang, accompanied by fierce repression of their cultural and religious heritage, prompted an international outcry. Notable in recent criticism of Chinese human rights abuse are new charges of genocide and crimes against humanity. In 2020, the introduction of a new policy in Inner Mongolia phasing out Mongolian-language-medium instruction of key subjects at Mongolian schools lent urgency to our effort to complete the manuscript, deepening recognition that the Inner Mongolian story we are relating here is part of a larger pattern of nationality policy. In this context, we revisited the notion of pogrom, an organized massacre or expulsion of a specific ethnic group, to describe the tragedies we unearthed in Inner Mongolia. This led to the decision to write a substantial coda on the significance of the Cultural Revolution in Inner Mongolia to understand the nature of the interethnic violence by building a framework that engages critically the conceptions of genocide and settler colonialism for understanding China's ethnic policy.

This, then, has been a project that took three decades to complete in an attempt to offer a new understanding of China's ethnic politics that spans the violence of the pogrom of the Mongols in Inner Mongolia in the Cultural Revolution and various contemporary assaults on minority nationality rights, notably those of the Uyghurs, the Tibetans, and the Mongols.

We are deeply grateful for the support of family members and colleagues over the three decades that were required to complete this work. We regret only that Kyoko Selden, who enthusiastically encouraged the early stages of the project, sharing in the excitement and humor of Tiejun's vivid narrative, did not live to see its fruition. Here we offer our gratitude to two generations of family members, particularly Quin, Peng, and Hui Cheng; Mei and Annabelle Bulag; and Lili, Ken and Yumi Selden for their support even as they wondered, "Will it ever end?," over the duration of the project.

We would like to thank Mary Al-Sayed, acquisitions editor for anthropology and history at the University of Chicago Press, and James Millward, series editor, for suggestions that improved the analysis and for including the book in the Silk Roads series. The series offers a unique platform for bringing our findings to a wider audience to help understand and seek solutions to the ongoing challenges confronting China's ethnic borderlands and its multiethnic population. Katherine Faydash admirably turned our text into a model of Chicago style, and PJ Heim's meticulous indexing has no rivals anywhere.

The sensitive nature of the contents meant that we kept the writing to ourselves, never showing any chapter to anyone for comments before its completion. The only people who have read the manuscript were the two anonymous reviewers whose critical but supportive comments sent us back to extensively revise the manuscript. The constructive comments of Robert Barnett, who has agreed to reveal his identity, proved exceptionally useful in revising the coda that reflects our comparative and theoretical ambitions in probing China's ethnic relations, for which we are profoundly grateful.

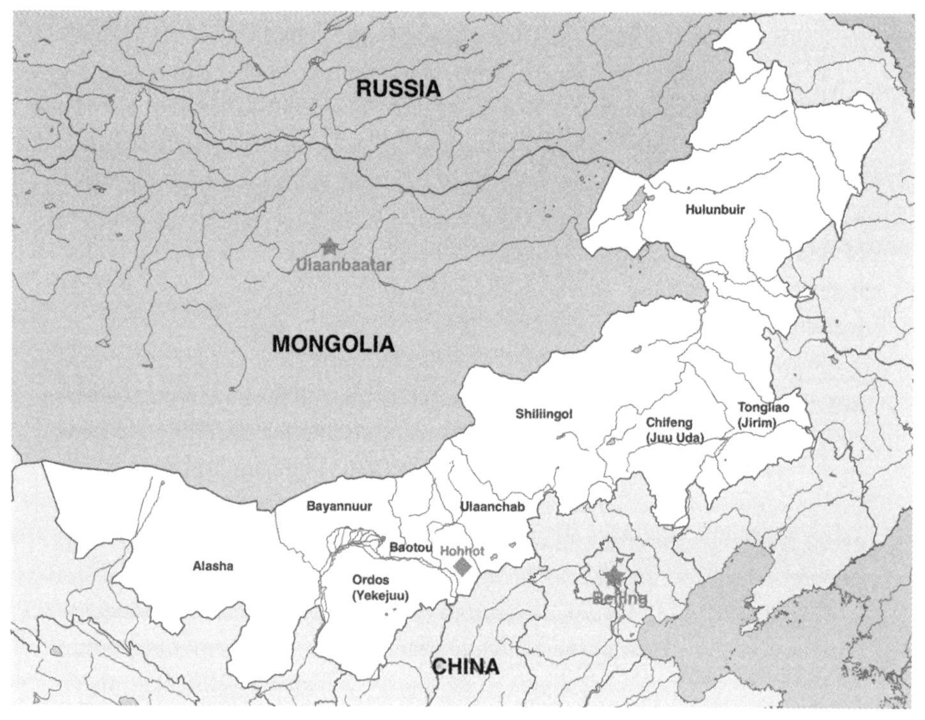

MAP 1 Map of Inner Mongolia

Introduction

It was 1959, one year into the Great Leap Forward, one of the twentieth century's boldest, yet most disastrous, utopian experiments. The Mao Zedong–initiated Leap sought to accelerate China's economic growth and transform its society with the creation of communes in order to swiftly surpass the prosperity of the United States and the United Kingdom in a new socialist order. Instead, the Leap resulted in one of the deadliest famines humanity has ever seen. In the summer of 1958, in rural Hebei, as in much of rural China, the agricultural fields were deserted as many able-bodied men and women, and even middle school students, were dispatched for industrial work far from their villages. The primary task for most was to smelt iron, the symbol of scientific communism, not in giant factories but in homemade stoves scattered throughout the countryside. Heaps of useless jagged metal were produced while famine devastated rural communities as crops were left standing in the fields. Between 1959 and 1961 thirty million or more Chinese villagers died of hunger.

Cheng Tiejun, the protagonist and coauthor of this book, was fourteen years old, a junior middle school student living with his mother and brother in a poverty-stricken North China village in Raoyang county, one hundred miles south of Beijing. His parents had divorced, and his father worked as a truck driver in Hohhot, the capital of the Inner Mongolia Autonomous Region (IMAR). With sharp cutbacks in middle school education in the countryside during the famine, his mother decided that Tiejun would fare better by moving to live with his father. At that time, hundreds of thousands of famine refugees also set their eyes on the Mongolian steppe to the north beyond the Great Wall on the Mongolian-Soviet borderland. The Chinese state turned back many. However, with an official letter from his commune and school, he was among the last to resettle in IMAR.

Over millennia the region now called Inner Mongolia has been a point of intersection for the peoples of the Steppe and the Chinese, most of whom inhabited agrarian regions and cities to the south. With the rise of the Mongol world empire in the thirteenth century, China came under Mongol rule, and the area subsequently became part of the Mongol heartland following the building of a new Great Wall by the Ming dynasty (1368–1644) to prevent the Mongols' reconquest of China. From the mid-seventeenth century to 1911, the Mongols were incorporated into the Qing Empire as subordinate allies of the Manchu rulers, but not without being divided into two conglomerations that eventually became Outer Mongolia and Inner Mongolia. From the late nineteenth century, Inner Mongolia became a destination for Chinese famine refugees and government-sponsored settlers who quickly outnumbered the native Mongol inhabitants. By 1949, at the founding of the PRC, with the Mongols constituting only about 14 percent of the region's population, Inner Mongolia was a Chinese settler colony.

In 1946, the post–World War II international settlement of the "Mongolian Question" included the Republic of China's formal recognition of independence of the Mongolian People's Republic (MPR, formerly Outer Mongolia), and Inner Mongolia was incorporated into China. With the founding of the PRC in 1949, Inner Mongolia was reconstituted as an autonomous region of China, tracing its origin to a Chinese Communist Party–led Mongolian autonomy established in 1947. In the early 1950s, the IMAR was a model for the system of nationality regional autonomy (*quyu minzu zizhi*), the PRC's most important institution in the governance of the 60 percent of its territories inhabited by non-Han peoples including Uyghur, Tibetan, Hui, and Zhuang among the largest minority nationalities recognized by the Chinese state.

Communist internationalism and Inner Mongolia's geopolitical location initially produced high expectations for its political and economic prospects. Throughout the 1950s, it was a beneficiary of China-MPR-Soviet cooperation and aid, its steel industry, military industry, and urbanization all advancing rapidly along with agriculture and the pastoral economy. With a savvy and stable Mongol-centered leadership under the veteran Communist Ulanhu that enjoyed access to the highest Party leaders in Beijing, Inner Mongolia in the seventeen years from 1949 to 1966 was the PRC's flagship experiment in promoting amicable interethnic relations and cooperation. This was the land where Cheng Tiejun arrived in 1959, and where he spent thirteen eventful years in what he called his second home.

Inner Mongolia was not, however, immune from China's intensified class-struggle-oriented political culture, especially in the wake of the Anti-Rightist Campaign (1957–1959). At school, Tiejun's class status as a poor peasant was questioned because of his father's experience of working for the Nationalists during the war, and his criticism of the famine he experienced in Raoyang in 1959 found its way into his personal dossier. This dark spot in his record repeatedly thwarted his effort to join the Chinese Youth League, essential for any young person aspiring to Communist Party membership and a leadership position.

Tiejun completed his secondary education in Hohhot and in 1963 entered Inner Mongolia Teachers' College, one of the region's key colleges, to study English. During his college years, which coincided with the Socialist Education Movement (1963–1966) guided by Mao's dictum "Never forget class struggle," Tiejun was repeatedly singled out for harboring rightist thoughts, a dangerous position that was tantamount to being classified as an enemy of the revolution. Meanwhile, with mounting Sino-Soviet tensions in the early 1960s, the position of Mongols in Inner Mongolia and their relations with the Soviet-allied MPR, many Mongolian students and faculty at his college were targeted as splittists, that is, supporting the MPR.

For students and young intellectuals like Tiejun, the opening salvos of the Cultural Revolution (1966–1976) in Inner Mongolia and throughout the nation held out the promise of social justice and opportunity to participate in shaping the nation's future. In the summer of 1966, they eagerly seized the chance that beckoned when Mao issued the clarion call to the newly formed Red Guards: *Zaofan youli!*, or "it's right to rebel!" To them, the enemies of the Cultural Revolution were those revisionists in power opposing Mao's revolutionary political line. It was a rebellion against an oppressive Party apparatus, which Mao was then attacking for betraying the revolution. Indeed, Mongols as well as Han were among those who enthusiastically embraced the call to revolution.

Tiejun's experience as a rebel activist would have been unremarkable, indistinguishable from that of millions of others in inland China, had Inner Mongolia been just another Chinese province. The campus rebellion against college leaders and the rebellion among sectors of the industrial working class coincided with Party- and army-led moves to destroy the Mongol-centered autonomous polity led by Ulanhu. The fall of Ulanhu and his colleagues at the start of the Cultural Revolution, the first leading group among all provinces and regions to be ousted, and the subsequent onslaught against the Mongols, spelled the demise of the PRC's system of nationality regional autonomy in practice, if not in name.

For three years, from 1967 to 1969, beginning with high hopes among the many young people spurred by the call to revolution, Inner Mongolia descended into a living hell—by official count, 16,222 lives were taken, and 87,188 were crippled or maimed. A total of 346,653, including many of Cheng Tiejun's personal friends and associates, were persecuted on trumped-up charges. Many more were not recorded in this official toll. The overwhelming majority of the victims were Mongols, the native inhabitants of the land. Their tormentors, overwhelmingly, were Han, with the military taking the lead and with the backing of three hundred thousand sent-down Chinese youth relocated to Inner Mongolia fresh from Red Guard activism in North China cities. The Inner Mongolian casualties and deaths were by far the largest number recorded in any province or autonomous region during the Cultural Revolution, and local accounts suggest that the official figures are gross underestimates.

Nor were these the only consequences of the Cultural Revolution for Mongols and for the region. From July 1969, for ten years, large swaths of Inner Mongolia were partitioned among four neighboring provinces (Heilongjiang, Jilin, Liaoning, and Gansu) and the Ningxia Hui Autonomous Region. Only the central area retained the name IMAR. In short, the very "autonomy" of the Mongol region was shattered by administrative fiat in the wake of the 1966 dismantling of the Ulanhu leadership. The remaining fragment of the IMAR was placed under martial law in December 1969, with the highest levels of Party and military leadership then, and to this day, firmly in Han hands. The ability of Mongols, the titular population, to exercise autonomy and authority, as they had to a considerable extent in the years 1947–1966, was broken.

*

This book introduces a tumultuous era that would leave its stamp on China's future, particularly on Chinese relations with the Mongols and other minorities in the contested Chinese-Mongolian-Russian borderland region and across the nation. Indeed, the very nature of Chinese society, particularly Chinese-minority relations, and China's position in the world, would be transformed. It draws in part on the observations and actions of a Han Chinese rebel Red Guard—Cheng Tiejun—who experienced, participated in, and observed the Sturm und Drang of the era both as a Cultural Revolution activist and a reporter traveling throughout the region including remote border areas, gaining unique perspectives on the fractious Chinese-Mongol relations of the period. It also confronts the complex position of the rebels, a few of whom were co-opted into the highest political echelon as standing committee members of the IMAR Revolutionary Committee and participated in the anti-Mongol pogrom that devastated the titular minority. By *pogrom* we refer to the onslaught of dominant forces in state and society directed against minority populations leading to large-scale marginalization, eviction, torture, and appalling numbers of deaths.

This book is a product of collaboration among three authors: Cheng Tiejun, Uradyn Bulag, and Mark Selden. Over the years, we have come to recognize that this is not simply the story of a bygone era in a single borderland region, one that Chinese authorities have sought to bury. Half a century later, the legacy of the Cultural Revolution not only weighs heavily on Inner Mongolia but also profoundly affects the entire Inner Asian borderland, notably including Tibet and Xinjiang, as well as other regions with significant minority populations. Our account invites readers to rethink the nature of revolutionary change and the place of minority nationalities in the People's Republic in light of some of the darkest episodes in its history.

A political activist from his college years and throughout the Cultural Revolution, Cheng Tiejun was subsequently trained as a social scientist both in China and in the United States. As a prominent student rebel and a reporter for the *Inner Mongolia Daily*, he left Inner Mongolia in 1972 for his home province of Hebei and subsequently completed an MA in political economy in Beijing before leaving for the United States for an MA in economics at the University of Massachusetts at Amherst and a PhD in sociology at Binghamton University. Following the Tiananmen repression of 1989, he continued his activism in the United States in support of the Chinese democracy movement and subsequently as a professor and researcher on Chinese society at the University of Macau.

Uradyn Bulag, born in 1964 and raised in rural Inner Mongolia, was a child during the Cultural Revolution. Like Cheng Tiejun, he graduated from the Foreign Languages Department at Inner Mongolia Teachers' University (the college was upgraded to university in 1983) before completing a PhD in social anthropology at Cambridge University. Though too young to experience many of the events described here, he grew up at a time when the Mongols, including family members and neighbors, were being ravaged by the Cultural Revolution. He brings to bear extensive experience in researching the historical and contemporary trajectories of both Inner Asian and Chinese societies and serves as a professor of social anthropology at Cambridge University.

Mark Selden is a longtime student of the Chinese revolution, including the anti-Japanese resistance of the 1930s and 1940s in North and Northwest China, as well as the Cultural Revolution and the geopolitics of the Asia-Pacific region. Professor emeritus of sociology at Binghamton University, he was the founding editor of the *Asia-Pacific Journal*, from 2002 to 2022. China's borderland experience in the long twentieth century provides opportunities for him to reexamine contentious issues of settler colonialism, nationalism, revolutionary violence, and ethnicity in the borderlands and beyond.

Told through both the eyes and the experiences of Cheng Tiejun and drawing on a close examination of the documentary historical record of the transformation of Inner Mongolia and China, the book recounts some of the most poignant and little-known events of the Cultural Revolution and the nation as Inner Mongolia became the site of the bloodiest pogrom anywhere in China, devastating the Mongol population. Tiejun's extraordinary photographic memory, capable of evoking vivid details, reinforced by diaries and documents covering many of the events recorded here, and his knack for storytelling, together with the three authors' close examination of the documentary record of the era, including government and Party records and the official and Red Guard press, make it possible to vividly convey the narrative and significance of the Cultural Revolution in Inner Mongolia and beyond.

This is, then, an experiment in collaboration that brings together different perspectives, experiences, and expertise, weaving them into a coherent account of the Cultural Revolution in China's troubled Inner Mongolian borderland, with implications extending across the landscape of Chinese-minority relations to the present. The main chapters are narrated in the first person even as they are written collectively, supplementing Cheng Tiejun's personal narrative with contributions drawing on the research of the three authors. The final chapter offers a theoretical framework to capture the historical events of multiple transformations in Inner Mongolia throughout the long twentieth century to explore the changing character of contemporary Chinese-minority relations in the Xi Jinping era, notable for deepening ethnic conflicts involving Uyghurs in Xinjiang, Tibetans in Tibet, and Mongols in Inner Mongolia—and beyond. It affords an opportunity to transcend the immediacy and details of the narrative to engage the regional, national, and international consequences of the events recorded here.

*

The heavy toll in the form of Mongol injuries and deaths at the hands of Han, with the Party and army leading the way during the Cultural Revolution, together with the territorial partition of Inner Mongolia and the destruction of the region's autonomy, raise sensitive questions about the nature of the Cultural Revolution in the borderland as well as about the character of China's nationality relations. Indeed, events described here raise questions about the legacy of the socialist transformation and the future trajectory of China as a multiethnic state: How did the initial rebellion proclaiming a cultural revolution turn into an ethnic onslaught targeting the Mongols? Indeed, how did an ethnic pogrom occur in a region long touted as the exemplar of interethnic friendship and unity? What did rebellion, framed as a struggle for social justice, mean in a borderland region with Mongols, who supposedly held a leadership position, while the Han, the overwhelming majority, enjoyed the privilege of their position as an "advanced" and "chosen" people? How did the region's entrenched settler colonial structure, rooted in the hegemony of Chinese leadership and prerogatives associated with a Chinese majoritarian democracy and the repression of the Mongols in the wake of the fall of Ulanhu, give rise to the violence?

These questions guiding the writing of the book ultimately compel us to ask further difficult questions: What role did the Chinese state, the Party, the People's Liberation Army, and the Central Cultural Revolution Group in Beijing play in launching and directing the pogrom during the Cultural Revolution in the borderlands? And what is the contemporary legacy of the pogrom in Inner Mongolia and throughout China? We are, of course, also keenly aware of racial and nationality conflict in the United States and Europe, where the Black Lives Matter movement and the shock of multiple racist attacks on African Americans and diverse immigrant populations, alert us to the fact that the issues of racial and nationality conflict addressed in this book have important contemporary ramifications of global scope.

We also assess the responsibility that rebels in Inner Mongolia bear for the Mongol tragedy, which was concurrent with their eventual brief rise to a position of shared power in the autonomous region. Post–Cultural Revolution assessments diverge sharply on the role of the rebel Red Guards. The official Chinese verdict holds them and Cultural Revolution radicals, notably the "Gang of Four" and Kang Sheng, but not Mao Zedong, Zhou Enlai, or the military, responsible for the violence and repression that took so heavy a toll on the nation. For their part, many rebels, looking back on the era, would celebrate their antiestablishment activities as the dawn of pro-democracy activities while distancing themselves from the disasters that followed. The account in this book supports neither of these positions. This leads us to a rethinking of the class-inflected categories emphasized by all camps during the Cultural Revolution.

Cheng Tiejun's work as a journalist at the *Inner Mongolia Daily*, the Party's leading newspaper in the region, allowed him to travel widely throughout Inner Mongolia to investigate instances of torture and murder conducted in the name of the Cultural Revolution by rebel as well as loyalist forces, and above all, by the Chinese Party and army authorities in Inner Mongolia and in Beijing. With a fresh interpretation particularly of the role of Premier Zhou Enlai and the military in shaping Cultural Revolution outcomes, Tiejun's experiences and observations offer multiple insights into the nature of the Cultural Revolution in the borderland and beyond.

The most difficult challenge this book confronts is how to characterize the ethnic pogrom that took so heavy a toll in Mongol lives in the name of waging a cultural revolution. There is a consensus among Mongols, a view increasingly shared by many international scholars, that the anti-Mongol pogrom of the Cultural Revolution period constituted genocide against the Mongols.

Indeed, since 2020, the terms *genocide* and *cultural genocide* have come into common (but not uncontested) usage in the West to refer to the suppression led by the Chinese Party-state of the rights of ethnic or religious groups, notably the Uyghurs and other minorities in Xinjiang, but also the Tibetans, and the Mongols, with policies including large-scale roundups of the Uyghur and Kazakh population in Xinjiang reeducation camps, illegal land grabs and "Sinicization" of Buddhism in Tibet, and attacks on Mongolian-language-medium instruction in Inner Mongolia.

The story of Inner Mongolia's Cultural Revolution is, however, not one of pure ethnic conflict that can be captured by the overarching concept of genocide. It is one in which the Chinese Communist state attacked one of its own "basic systems," namely nationality regional autonomy, by waging a "people's war," mobilizing its military, government agencies, and, above all, Han settlers against the Mongols. It is a story of challenging the Mongols' political loyalty at the height of geopolitical contention between China and the Soviet Union and its ally, the MPR, and concluding, in the absence of any significant evidence, that many were guilty of treason. The goal, however, was neither to drive the Mongols out of China nor to eliminate them physically in toto, the primary goals of genocide. Rather, it was to destroy their ethnic, political, and cultural identity and assimilate them into a Han-dominated nation.

The coda to this book presents an alternative concept of politicide to recast understanding of the Cultural Revolution in a new framework of settler colonialism, competing nationalisms, and China's intensifying ideological conflict with the Soviet Union and the MPR, one that resulted not only in scapegoating of the Mongols but also in huge losses of life and intense pressure on surviving Mongols. Our argument that the Cultural Revolution violence against the Mongols destroyed their capacity and will to organize "politically" is critical for understanding China's renewed attacks on minorities in the borderlands involving Uyghurs, Tibetans, and Mongols in the new millennium.

As we concluded this volume, intensified Chinese ethnic oppression and state-directed attacks in Xinjiang, Tibet, Inner Mongolia, and Hong Kong borderlands have come to center stage within China at a time of mounting US-China conflict that is redefining the international relations of China, the Asia-Pacific, and the world. How China treats its borderlands and its ethnic and other minorities is no longer a domestic issue; it has become a global benchmark that tests China's resolve both to establish its growing global presence and to respond to mounting international challenges at a time of a weakening of the global power of the United States. And it takes new forms in the wake of the Russian invasion of Ukraine and a potential deepening of Russian-Chinese alliance in the face of a US- and NATO-led coalition of forces, a situation that poses the risk of global nuclear war.

As China and the United States and its allies gear up for a new era of conflict that threatens to lead to hot war, with China's borderlands and its peoples entering the strategic calculations of both sides, readers will gain new perspectives and insights on the Cultural Revolution in Inner Mongolia and its legacies in the contemporary era that this book explores.

1

A North China Country Boy
Travels beyond the Great Wall

A Wartime Childhood

The year 1943 was a momentous one for the world and for me. The year saw the Cairo Declaration issued by the Allies in World War II setting goals for the postwar order, and my birth in Lanzhou, the vast sprawling capital city of Gansu province in Northwest China. I was too young to remember the war, except for hiding in a small bunker with my mother and my younger half brother Ruijun, listening to the gunshot sounds, like firecrackers on New Year's Eve. Danger was never far off. As a strategic transfer point for channeling Soviet military aid for China's resistance against Japanese invasion, and as the headquarters of China's Eighth War District, responsible for defending the northern provinces of Gansu, Qinghai, Ningxia, and Suiyuan, Lanzhou was a frequent target of Japanese air raids from 1937 to 1943. My father, Cheng Dehua, was a truck driver working for a transportation company based in Lanzhou. However, my fate would be tied not to this city, where I had spent the first seven years of my life, but to Inner Mongolia, where my father moved in 1950, a year after the founding of the People's Republic of China.

My native place (*jiguan*), that is, the residence of my paternal ancestors, was Raoyang county, a rural backwater a hundred miles south of Beiping (today's Beijing) in central Hebei, where the family owned land. From the age of seventeen, my father was apprenticed as a truck driver in Zhangjiakou (a.k.a. Kalgan)—the most important border town separating inland China from the Mongol steppe to the North—which became the administrative seat of Chahar province, one of several Chinese provinces established on Mongol land by the Chinese Nationalist government in 1928. In 1936, as the Japanese Kwantung Army and Mongolian nationalist forces controlled northern Chahar and encroached on Zhangjiakou, Father returned home and married Sun Wenhua. Soon, he went to work in Lanzhou, where the Chinese government had begun to build a rear defense base. He left his newlywed wife behind to care for his parents. Young, literate, and patriotic, Sun headed the village women's association. When Japanese forces began mopping-up operations to root out Communist-led resistance in central Hebei, Sun's contacts advised her to divorce and join revolutionary forces in the Taihang Mountains of neighboring Shanxi province. Her brother, however, pressed her to stay and care for her in-laws. She stayed.

After several years without contact, my father returned in 1943 to Raoyang and then took his wife back with him to Lanzhou. En route, he informed her that he had taken a second wife, Dong Xiuying, from suburban Lanzhou, and had a son with her. That was me. Polygyny was common during the Republican era. Many drivers, working away from home for years at a time, had concubines. Refusing to live with my father's second wife but unable to return to Raoyang in the face of stepped-up Japanese military campaigns, Sun Wenhua moved to Pingliang, an important trading town on the ancient Silk Road between Lanzhou and Xi'an, the ancient Chinese capital.

In 1943, within weeks of my birth, my birth mother abandoned me and returned to her village. Father then brought me to Sun Wenhua in Pingliang. A year later, my birth mother reconciled with my father and returned to Lanzhou. My parents demanded my return. I was not yet two years old, but it seems that I struggled fiercely against being separated from the woman I knew as my mother. I won and continued to live with Sun, who treated me as her own son. In 1947, she gave birth to my half brother, Ruijun.

By 1947, as Communist-led People's Liberation Army forces advanced in the Civil War against the ruling Nationalist Party (Guomindang), government forces were in retreat all across North China. In 1948, Father was conscripted to drive for Fu Zuoyi's army. Fu had risen under the warlord Yan Xishan, who was the ruler of Shanxi province. In 1931, Chiang Kai-shek, China's president, had appointed Fu governor of Suiyuan province in western Inner Mongolia.[1] During the Anti-Japanese War, Fu became a Chinese national hero by resisting the Japanese and their Inner Mongolian allies. In early August 1945, the Soviet Union entered the war and, with its ally, the Mongolian People's Republic (MPR), defeated the Japanese army and its puppet Mongolian forces in Manchuria and Inner Mongolia. In January 1949, Fu surrendered Beiping, and in September 1949, he surrendered Suiyuan to Chinese Communist forces and their Mongolian allies who had secured control of the frontier of Inner Mongolia and North China and proceeded to unify the nation without a costly battle. Fu was rewarded for his negotiated surrender by appointment as minister of water conservancy under the People's Republic. His soldiers, as "uprising elements" (*qiyi renyuan*), were demobilized and settled in Suiyuan.[2]

My destiny, then, would be intertwined with Suiyuan and Inner Mongolia because of my father.

With the founding of the People's Republic in October 1949, Father lost his job as a military driver and bought a truck to start a private business in Guisui (present-day Hohhot), then capital of Suiyuan province. In 1950, when I was seven, he picked up my Raoyang mother and my half brother Ruijun and me in Pingliang, where we were living, and set off for Raoyang in northern Hebei. The plan was to drive to Tianjin and then on to Raoyang, where we were to live while he returned to Guisui to work. But en route, my parents decided to leave me in Tianjin with my father's younger sister, to take advantage of better schooling.

A year later, mother and Ruijun came to Tianjin to bring me home. We took a small boat. In 1951–1952, many Raoyang villagers still had private boats. They would float downstream to Tianjin to sell produce and crafts, returning with manufactures, sundries, and dried seafood. Fighting the current and the wind, several men would pull the boat by rope. It took three or four days, starting on the Grand Canal and eventually plying the Hutuo River.

We talked a lot on the boat. I felt so close to mother. Although I was not her biological son, people always said that we were especially close, closer than her biological son, Ruijun. I asked many questions about home. From her face, I could see that life was difficult.

When we arrived, mother said, "This is your *laojia*," your hometown, meaning my father's native village of Zhangcun. The Cheng lineage, with seventy households, was the largest in the village. Father's thirty-five-member extended family lived in three interconnected courtyards, each with four houses. During the land reform in Raoyang (1946–1948), the family owned twenty-five *mu* of farmland, but since that was below the maximum allowance of five *mu* per person, and because family members cultivated their own land having no hired labor, the family was classified as "poor peasants." Nonetheless, owning land and with the remittances my father and my uncles working in Tianjin during slack seasons sent, we were quite prosperous compared to other villagers.

With the implementation of the new marriage law passed in 1950 that banned polygamy, my father divorced my birth mother in 1953, and in 1954, he divorced my independent-minded Raoyang mother. Two years later he married a local woman in Hohhot. After the divorce, with a decent salary as a senior driver in a state company, Father supported his three children—a daughter in Lanzhou and two sons in Raoyang. He would return home from Hohhot, the newly minted capital of the Inner Mongolia Autonomous Region, once a year, bringing us pictures and books whose photos of the grass-lands introduced me to the Mongolian borderlands.

Fleeing the Great Leap Famine in Rural North China

The year 1958 was a turning point for all China, myself included. I was four-teen years old, a second-year junior middle school student boarding in the combined Raoyang Middle School in the county seat.

In the summer of 1958, instead of a vacation, the seven hundred students built three small factories on the school grounds. The physics teacher Zhou Futian directed us in building a coke factory, an iron and steel factory, and a cement factory. It was our contribution to the Great Leap Forward, the mass campaign then sweeping the nation. The countryside was to move to the fore with the production of the industrial symbols of the era: steel and cement. The promise was instant prosperity for all.

The year 1958 was also one of bumper crops both in summer and in fall in Raoyang and throughout much of the country. But in June there was a se-vere labor shortage. Nearly all able-bodied Raoyang men had been mobilized to work at iron and steel and other factories that were being constructed in Chengde county. Chengde, the summer retreat and capital of the Qing em-perors, was located over one hundred miles northeast of Beijing, north of the Great Wall.[3]

In August, a stunning announcement came down from the Communist Party leadership of Hengshui prefecture. Scientific research had proved that sweet potatoes were far more productive than corn. The corn was already three feet high, but we were ordered to cut it down and plant sweet potatoes. Never had the Party intervened so directly to violate farmers' wisdom. Every-one knew that it was necessary to plant in June to harvest a sweet potato crop. When villagers ignored the order, the militia moved in with sixteen-foot-long ropes, dragging them through the fields to destroy the corn. Villagers' hard work was cast to the winds, and of course, the sweet potato crop was stillborn.

The Great Leap Forward also promised dramatic expansion of education for all. Indeed, in 1958 the number of middle schools in Raoyang increased from one to six. In winter of 1958–1959 I shared a dormitory in the single middle school in the county seat with thirty boys, ten to a room and five each to a large bunk bed.

But with hunger intensifying and industries failing, enrollments were slashed and schools closed. In June 1959, the Raoyang Middle School princi-pal ordered the student body to *zhandui*—queue up in two long lines—and count off: one, two, one, two. We then learned that all even-numbered students would continue their schooling. Odd-numbered students were dismissed on the spot. There was no favoritism or privilege, not even discrimination against children of landlord families, certainly none that we students were aware of. Even some cadre children were sent home. Some schools repeated the lottery several times, each time cutting enrollment.

My number came up even. But it was hardly an occasion for rejoicing. In 1957, out of thirty-five students in my primary school class, seven had gone on to middle school; by the fall of 1959, all but three had returned to the village. One transferred to a senior middle school near Chengde; another joined the People's Liberation Army (PLA) and eventually became an officer; I was the third. In 1959, with schools slashing enrollments, mother feared that my schooling, and any future prospects, would be dashed. The future seemed bleak.

Father had often tried to persuade me to live with him and attend school in Hohhot. In 1956 he had married his third wife, who was twelve years his junior. In early 1959 he wrote contrasting Raoyang, a poor rural county, with Hohhot, a provincial capital in a rapidly industrializing region. The good life he described became irresistible at the height of famine.

"I don't want you to live with your stepmother," Mother said, "but education is the most important." At her suggestion, I would attend the Hohhot No. 5 Middle School (Wuzhong) close to the Hohhot Transportation Company, where father drove trucks.

Wuzhong required a letter of certification of school transfer (*zhuan xue zheng*) from my middle school. I made several trips to the commune center and the Raoyang county seat to get that and two more essential documents: household registration transfer (*hukou qianyi zheng*) and grain transfer certificate (*zhuan liang zheng*). The former changed my official residence from my mother's village to Hohhot; the latter guaranteed that I would receive government grain rations as the dependent of a state worker. The Chinese state attempted to control access to the cities from 1958, but the Great Leap Forward overwhelmed such attempts, and in 1958 and 1959 tens of millions of rural migrants found work in burgeoning urban industries and less devastated rural areas throughout the country. In 1959 it was the last time it was possible to obtain permission to take up residence in a city. The following year, as China's economy crashed, migrants were turned back at provincial borders.

Mother saw me off to Hohhot at the riverbank north of our village. Carrying a small bag on my back, I started at dawn before Ruijun woke up, because I feared he would cry. Following me on the winding path, Mother urged me to study hard and avoid conflict with my stepmother. Her words were repeatedly interrupted by a cough from pulmonary emphysema, one of many

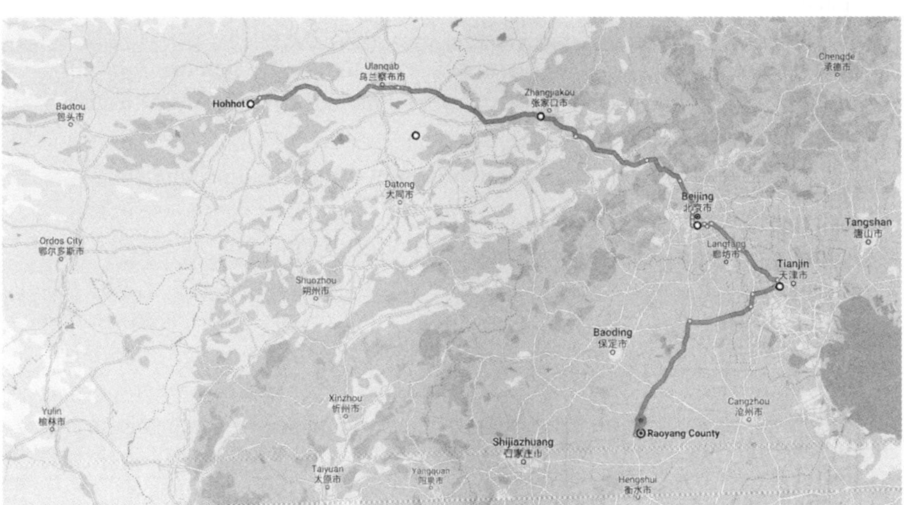

MAP 2 Cheng Tiejun's route from Raoyang to Hohhot via Tianjin and Beijing

afflictions rampant in a time of hunger. Fighting tears, I begged her to return home. As her thin figure faded in the morning fog and her cough dissolved behind a grove of trees, I finally burst into loud crying.

It was the first time I had left home alone. The prospect of leaving my mother to live with my father and a stepmother I had never met weighed heavily on me. But at sixteen I was keen to study and to see the world.

A Country Boy in Hohhot

I arrived in Hohhot in August 1959 to find a rapidly growing regional capital. Hohhot was a railroad hub with links to Beijing, Tianjin, and Northwest China, and a cultural and educational center. In a way, I was disappointed, for it had little of the exotic or ferocious frontier quality I had fantasized. Mongols were predominantly herders or farmers. In Hohhot, the Mongol presence was scarcely visible, except through the signs of the work units and shops written bilingually in Mongolian and Chinese and occasional cheerful herders walking the streets. Few in number and wearing colorful Mongol gowns, they stood out, rather like Native Americans in a nineteenth-century American frontier town. For me, though, the large Han presence was reassuring. I would not need to struggle to adapt to a different way of life or learn a new language.

Hohhot, located on the Tumed plain at the southern foot of the Daqing Mountains, consisted of two towns.[4] The Old Town, a market town formerly called Guihua (meaning "submission"), had long been inhabited by Mongols, Muslims, and Han. The New Town had originated in the eighteenth century as a Manchu military encampment named Suiyuan ("pacification"). Father's apartment was in the Old Town.

Father worked for Inner Mongolia's biggest transportation company. Each time he returned from a trip he took me to the grandest bathhouse in town, where we soaked in hot water in the big pools. But most of the time he was cold toward me. Nor could I warm to him, despite my efforts. My stepmother, Xue Yuzhen, was a Han from Tuoketuo, a rural county to the southwest of Hohhot. Her tiny feet were just four inches long. In Raoyang, I had often seen bound feet, but they were much larger than four inches. Mongols never bound their feet.[5] While many men were casting off traditional brides in the aftermath of the Civil War, my father again chose a bound-footed woman. My birth mother, unlike my Raoyang mother, also had bound feet.

In 1959, when I first met Xue Yuzhen, she was in her midthirties and was busy caring for an adopted three-month-old baby girl named Yingdi, which means "beckoning a younger brother," a tradition holding that a boy was the source of happiness and security. Like my father, she was cold to me from the start. I struggled to understand why.

Our apartment consisted of one room, about fifteen feet by twenty-five, with a small attached kitchen that took up about a quarter of the space. Two-thirds of the room was taken up by a *kang*, a raised mud platform that provided "air-conditioning" throughout North China and the borderlands. The *kang*, introduced by the Jurchens long ago, was used as a sofa for sitting and eating; at night it served as a bed that could be heated. The apartment was terribly cramped.

In the spring semester of 1960, I moved into the student dormitory at Wuzhong. I never again stayed overnight at my father's house. During summer vacations I returned to Raoyang to see my mother and brother and to work in the fields, earning work points that translated into higher rations for them.

The first decade of the People's Republic brought about the transformation of the Old Town through curbing the scope of many cultural and religious activities associated with Mongol and Muslim life. Temples and monasteries were hit particularly hard. Among the few religious sites that remained open, I often visited Hohhot's two biggest Buddhist temples, known respectively as Da Zhao and Xilitu Zhao.[6] There were only about a dozen lamas. Some Mongols visited, but few dared to worship openly. I was drawn to a shop that sold goods catering to Mongol tastes, including brick tea, brocade gowns, saddles, and snuff bottles. In the early 1960s, many Mongols, urban dwellers and especially those coming in from the grasslands, wore Mongol dress and

FIGURE 1 The New China Boulevard and the building of the Inner Mongolia government (left), Hohhot, late 1950s

leather boots. Their language, mannerisms, and facial structure marked them as not Han.

Shortly after arriving in Hohhot, the man I called "Uncle," Xue Guicheng, my stepmother's brother, took me on the back of his bicycle to visit the New Town. The year before my arrival, most of the older buildings in the New Town, as well as the city wall, had been torn down to make way for the new government center. South of the New Town, a large area had been cleared for several new universities including Inner Mongolia University, Inner Mongolia Teachers' College, Inner Mongolia Agriculture and Animal Husbandry College, and Inner Mongolia Forestry College. Higher education had expanded rapidly in Hohhot during the first decade of the People's Republic. The new buildings were built in the Russian style: bulky, gray, and solid.

The streets were wider in the New Town and had recently been planted with willow and pine trees. A statue of a flying horse soared atop the newly built Inner Mongolia Museum. A modern theater, built in the Tibetan style close to Wuzhong, was named Wulanqiate (Ulaan Tyater in Mongolian)—Red Theater.

By August 1959 when I left home, Raoyang and many other parts of North China were experiencing food shortages, and within the year, millions were starving to death. But food was more plentiful in Inner Mongolia. While Beijing and Tianjin residents had a daily vegetable ration of 250 grams, in Hohhot, our ration was 500 grams. While Beijing vegetable sellers would cut an

FIGURE 2 Inner Mongolia Museum with a camel caravan passing by, Hohhot, circa 1959

eggplant or squash in half to keep the ration within the quota, Hohhot sellers gave the customer the benefit of the doubt in going over the quota. And many work units (*danwei*) obtained additional food through unofficial channels. The prescribed ratio in Hohhot was 40 percent fine grain (wheat) and 60 percent coarse grain (millet, sorghum, corn, rye, and naked oats).[7]

Inner Mongolia suffered far less than most parts of China during the Great Leap Forward. Although the Leap triggered the expansion of agriculture at the expense of pasture, the Inner Mongolian leadership insulated the agrarian and pastoral sectors from the most extreme manifestations of Great Leap frenzy. In fact, in 1960 alone, as requested by Mao Zedong and Zhou Enlai, Inner Mongolia shipped 550 million kilograms of food grain to Beijing, Shanghai, and Liaoning, to ease food shortages there. That equals 60 kilograms on average (about two or three months of rationing) from each Inner Mongolian resident.[8] Still, Inner Mongolia was also drawn into the craze of building backyard iron-smelting furnaces in response to the call of the Party Central Committee—or the Center—to double the steel and iron output in

1958.[9] The Qing dynasty–era walls of Suiyuan city were mostly dismantled in 1958, with the bricks and stones used to build small furnaces for making iron and steel.

Just two weeks after I reached Hohhot in 1959, instructions had come down banning rural-to-urban migration. In 1960 a Central document ordered Inner Mongolia to send back the large number of immigrants who had arrived without official authorization during the Leap. Still they came. In 1960, nearly 1.3 million immigrants arrived, most fleeing famine on the North China plain. In 1961, the Inner Mongolia authorities allowed just two thousand people to settle, mainly girls who had married local men, while sending away 436,700 migrants.[10]

A document entitled "Urgent Notification from the Central Committee of the Chinese Communist Party and the State Council to Stop Blind Outflow of Rural Laborers," dated March 11, 1959, was posted at every railway and bus station and throughout every city. Those castigated as the "blind flow" population (*mangliu*), meaning all migrants not dispatched by the state, were detained by police. Since Inner Mongolia was better off than surrounding provinces and Hohhot a relatively prosperous city, migrants continued to arrive.

My school was close to the Hohhot Railway Station. I often saw armed police carting migrants to the suburban detention center. They were sent back to their hometowns with warnings, and sometimes beatings, to drive home the point that they were not to return.

Poem on Glass in the No. 5 Middle School

About half the students at Wuzhong were recent immigrants. Many had come to Hohhot in 1958 and 1959, when their parents, intellectuals and skilled workers, were reassigned from Tianjin, Shenyang, and other industrial cities of North and Northeast China to state enterprises, government offices, or schools in Hohhot. In my class, I alone was from rural Hebei.

The students and teachers were predominantly Han. There was only one Mongol student in my class. The only Mongol teacher was in physical education. Not only did Mongols comprise a small percentage of the Hohhot population; most Mongols attended ethnic schools, such as the Hohhot Mongolian Middle School or the Tumed Middle School, whose language of instruction was Mongolian. Some Mongols attended the elite No. 2 Middle School and the middle school attached to Inner Mongolia Teachers' College, which also had two classes taught in Mongolian.[11]

My teachers in Raoyang had been dedicated, and some were outstanding, but Hohhot teachers had superior training. All were college graduates, compared with only one-third of teachers in Raoyang, where most middle school teachers were graduates of the county normal school. I later learned that many of my teachers had been sent to Hohhot after speaking out during the Hundred Flowers Movement of 1957, when the Party had briefly invited suggestions and critique. Ulanhu, Inner Mongolia's leader, eagerly recruited the best teachers from Beijing, Shanghai, Tianjin, and beyond. Driven by the desire to improve education and modernize Inner Mongolia, he provided them with good housing and salaries regardless of the political problems they faced elsewhere.

During the semester that I lived at home, I was always the first to arrive at school. I entered as soon as the gatekeeper opened the gate, even at dawn. I was also the last to leave. After class, I stayed for evening self-study and then helped clean the school. I always tried to help in this and other work as I was seeking Youth League admission. My attitude and behavior (*biaoxian*) were rated excellent. I was a "five good" student, meaning good in ideology, studies, physical education, physical labor, and nonacademic activities.[12] Two of the Youth League branch leaders supported my membership application. But the head teacher (*ban zhuren*), Su Yueqing, blacklisted me and my application was rejected.

One day in November 1959, Teacher Su called a meeting of the entire class. Clearly something important was about to happen, as the classroom had been sealed off before the meeting.

Teacher Su stepped to the platform.

"This morning something unusual was found on our windowpane."

"What was it?" everyone asked.

"We cannot tell you yet. If anyone did anything or saw anything, report to me immediately."

No one had any idea what was amiss. People divided into groups to discuss the situation.

"What happened last night? Who left last?"

"I did." A girl, another boy, and I had all left together after the others and walked home.

We three were called to Teacher Su's office.

"What were you doing last night?"

"After self-study, we cleaned the classroom."

"Did any of you write anything on the window?"

I remembered that I had scratched a message on the frosted windowpane, to vent my home sickness.

"I did."

"What did you write?"

"A poem."

Teacher Su's face turned ice cold.

"Can you remember it?"

"Give me a piece of paper."

I wrote down the poem:

> Born in a rural family, now I feel sadness
> Twinkling stars in the western night sky.
> Burning midnight oil, I continue reading Lu You's book
> Wolf smoke rising from a post fire near Cangzhou.[13]

Teacher Su, a mathematician, could make neither head nor tail of the poem. "What does it mean?"

"The first two lines expressed my feelings. The last two lines evoked ancient times and faraway places. I was born in rural inland China far from here," I answered.

"Why were you sad?"

"I was missing my mother and brother in Raoyang."

In 1959, with the Great Leap Forward in full swing, everything was politicized. The Pull Out the White Flag (*ba bai qi*) movement had ended the semester prior to my arrival. The movement was closely related to the criticism of Peng Dehuai, China's defense minister, whom Mao toppled after Peng obliquely criticized the excesses of the Great Leap Forward and, implicitly, the Chairman himself. In Hohhot, the campaign even reached down to middle school students, where it was framed by the question, What is watermelon and what is sesame? Peng Dehuai had allegedly said that China's achievements in steel making during the Great Leap were those of a sesame seed, but we lost a whole watermelon, meaning that crops were destroyed and people starved when the harvest was left standing in the fields while farmers produced useless iron in their backyard furnaces.

Middle school students in Hohhot had just been taught that the Leap's great advance was the watermelon, and the losses were as insignificant as a tiny sesame seed. Of course, it was not permissible to mention famine, or even hunger. Even junior middle school students were alerted to the importance of drawing the line between the red and the white flag, between revolutionaries and reactionaries.

I had arrived in Hohhot in August 1959. By the time I left, rural Raoyang had not conducted a Pull Out the White Flag campaign among its middle school students, so I was unaware of the watermelon and the sesame seed. In class discussions in Hohhot I had expressed confusion at the disparity between the propaganda of the Leap and the fact that crops had been left rotting in the fields in summer 1958 when villagers were ordered to make steel. Back home in Raoyang, no one would have made a fuss about my remark. Everyone had experienced hunger, and villagers were painfully aware of the crop losses caused by the steel campaign and the disastrous consequences of government orders to cut down the corn crop to make way for sweet potatoes. But in Hohhot, to pose questions, or even to express lonesomeness, was tantamount to "attacking the Three Red Banners": the General Line, the Great Leap Forward, and the People's Commune.

Teacher Su said, "You didn't know about the campaign, but you should never write anything on the pane."

I explained that I had read Lu You's poem, written in the Southern Song dynasty at the time of the Jurchen attack on Cangzhou, near my hometown. Chinese patriotic poems often rehearse ancient conflicts between Steppe peoples and Chinese. However, the issue of the poem was not ethnic but political. In the Leap, China could be portrayed only as red and good. Even a hint to the contrary invited censure and punishment. "Don't write anything. If you feel lonesome, talk to the Party," he said.

To my relief, Teacher Su said that I was a good student. The matter was dropped. But unbeknownst to me, Su, an aspiring Party member, reported it to the school's Party branch. I later learned that the principal had sent a photographer to photograph the poem on glass before erasing it. Recorded in my personal dossier, the case would accompany me throughout my school years and subsequent work life.[14]

I was sixteen years old then. That blemish on my record cast a dark shadow over my future. I was a "five good" student, but I could not join the Youth League. The Youth League meant not only acceptance but also the opportunity to participate in and lead extracurricular activities. It was the first step toward Communist Party membership, a key to success in most careers. Everyone coveted a Youth League badge with its gold stars, red flags, and hammer and sickle. It was a sign of approval and a promise of the future. After that window event, though, whatever I did, I would always be told that I needed more tempering. I agonized over why I couldn't be accepted by the Youth League.

Attending Hohhot's Elite Middle School

It was the summer of 1960, the eve of my graduation from junior middle school. I was eager to attend senior middle school, the route to higher education.[15] As an aspiring Youth League member, however, I knew that my choice of school and career was a political test. So, like all my classmates, I expressed willingness to go wherever I was needed after graduation. Despite my political problem, perhaps because my entrance examination score was high, I was admitted to No. 2 Middle School (Erzhong), the top school in Hohhot. I was elated, especially knowing that my mother would take pride in my achievement.

Hohhot's elite school was across the street from the New Town Guesthouse, which hosted visiting dignitaries to the autonomous region. In 1960, high-cadre children and others with outstanding test scores attended Erzhong. The No. 1 Middle School, Yizhong, located in the Old Town and formerly Suiyuan Middle School, was a second top school. Admission to both schools was by examination. Yizhong was reserved mainly for students from a working-class background. In part because of its location in the New Town, which was dominated by Party and government offices, in part because it was the school of choice for cadre children, Erzhong had the aura of being modern and advanced. Both would be officially designated among Inner Mongolia's eleven key point schools (*zhongdian xuexiao*) on June 30, 1962. But before that time, everyone knew that Erzhong was the school of choice for children of leading cadres as well as top achievers.

There were 1,200 students in Erzhong, 600 each in the three-year senior middle school and the three-year junior middle school.[16] The standard curriculum was taught in Chinese, and Han students received no instruction in Mongolian language or culture. Beginning in the fall of 1955, however, nationality classes (*minzu ban*) had been introduced. These classes were comprised exclusively of Mongol students who received Mongolian-language instruction in addition to the standard curriculum taught in Chinese. To promote nationality education, the government increased the size of scholarships for Mongol students, increasing them above the level of financial support for Han students.[17] We could hear students in the Mongol classes reading aloud in Mongolian and in Chinese.

In 1962, the Inner Mongolia Autonomous Region issued a directive on the fifteenth anniversary of its founding encouraging all cadres and students to learn both Mongolian and Chinese, the two official languages of the region.[18] The Mongol parents of some of my classmates responded enthusiastically, and some of their children began taking classes in Mongolian language, culture, and history. But not a single Han classmate studied Mongolian. I bought the elementary *Mongolian Language Textbook* and began self-study through the radio, which broadcast a teaching program. After a few months, however, when my schedule conflicted with the program, I gave up. It was essential for urban Mongols and others seeking to rise to positions of leadership to master Chinese, but Han had few incentives to learn Mongolian. In Hohhot, where

Han outnumbered Mongols by approximately fifteen to one in 1962, the dominant language was Chinese in offices, schools, and especially on the streets.[19]

The overwhelming emphasis in most urban and higher-level schools, was on Chinese education, particularly after the anti-rightist movement in 1957–1958, when Mongol "local nationalism" was denounced and pressures mounted on Mongol students to integrate with the Han majority. In 1963, however, when I graduated, quotas were introduced to increase the numbers of both Mongols and cadre children (in the name of political and class criteria), and the number of Mongol students at Erzhong rose to approximately 20 percent.

Han students were aware of the increasing number of children of high-ranking Mongol officials, and some bridled at the privileges these Mongol cadre children enjoyed. In the early 1950s, the majority of Mongol cadres were working in Ulaanhot (Red City) in eastern Inner Mongolia, where the autonomous government had been founded in 1947. With the seat of Inner Mongolia moving to Guisui in 1952, and with its original Mongolian name, *Hohhot*, restored two years later, almost all the new Mongol immigrants were associated with the Party, government, army, or educational institutions.

Erzhong traced its origin to the school that Guomindang General Fu Zuoyi established in 1942 at his military base in Shanba, west of Baotou city. Fu used the Suiyuan Private Struggle Middle School (Suiyuan Sili Fendou Zhongxue), as it was then called, to cultivate patriotic Chinese military and civilian officials. The first Mongols were recruited in 1954, when it was renamed Hohhot City No. 2 Middle School. With its prime location and government support, Erzhong became the school of choice for children of Communist leaders, Han and Mongol alike.[20]

The elite presence at Erzhong was clear. At Wuzhong, I had never seen a car parked on the playground. But at Erzhong, every Saturday afternoon a few chauffeured cars arrived, their windows curtained against prying eyes. A daughter, Ulaanchechig, and a son, Sönid, of Inner Mongolia Party Secretary Ulanhu, were among those picked up by limousine on weekends. They rode bicycles to school most weekdays. Erzhong was a boarding school. More than 80 percent of students lived on campus. Many children of the highest cadres, however, lived at home.

In the early 1960s, students believed that school entrance was based on test scores, not parental rank or class status. High-cadre children didn't look down on working-class children and relations among classmates were very good. We respected high-cadre children, and many of them seemed ready to learn from working-class children.

As a "five good" student, I wanted to perform well, and one way was to show leadership by becoming the class monitor (*banzhang*) or one of the four members of the class committee (*weiyuan*) elected at the beginning of each fall semester. Nominations came through two channels. One was the Youth League. Students also nominated candidates, with five signatures required for nomination. In a meeting chaired by the outgoing class monitor, students voted by secret ballot, writing down the name of the preferred candidate for class monitor or committee member in charge of studies, literature and art, physical labor, and sports. In hindsight, there was a high degree of democratic process in electing middle school class leaders, perhaps because, from the perspective of the authorities, little was at stake. Still, being elected a class monitor was an honor and a sign of activism that often paved the way for membership in the Youth League.

Wang Qingxian was the committee member for cultural activities. She had grown up in the Yellow River area of northwestern Inner Mongolia. She was hardworking and able, but not a top student. As the cultural committee member, she organized festivals and performances. Each class held a competition to choose performers. I still remember her song and dance duet *Xiong-mei Kaihuang* (Brother and Sister Open the Wasteland). It was a eulogy to the Nanniwan experience of military self-sufficiency in the Shaan-Gan-Ning Communist-liberated area during the Anti-Japanese War.[21] Qingxian was one of four sisters, all fine performers. Sometimes they performed together. She was pretty, and many boys admired her singing and dancing. She often invited friends to her home on weekends for parties or to study together.

Qingxian later became my wife, but back then, we had no special relationship. Middle school students rarely dated (*lian'ai*). I was in fact a bit jealous because she became a Youth League member while I remained excluded from the ranks of the chosen. She had struggled to overcome a suspect family background. Her father had been a colonel in Fu Zuoyi's Fifth Cavalry Division of the Thirty-Fifth Army, which had surrendered to the Communist side in 1949. At first those who came over were treated well, in recognition of their contributions to the peaceful liberation of Beiping. They were "uprising elements," praised for having thrown support to the Chinese Communist Party (CCP). But later they were viewed with suspicion, like others who were formerly associated with the Guomindang or the warlords.

To become a Youth League member, Qingxian had to criticize her father. During a grueling two-hour meeting, she denounced her father's "black history" in serving the Guomindang army after attending a military academy in Nanjing. Qingxian provided the Youth League with a detailed family history.

Eventually, after two or three rounds of discussion, she passed. Her father's background of poor peasant origins helped. In my class, seven students were inducted into the Youth League during senior middle school. Some others had joined earlier, so there were about fifteen members.

I was elected committee member for physical labor, in charge of work in the fields and cleaning up on campus. But the poem I had scratched on the frosted windowpane in Wuzhong and my father's Guomindang association because of his work as a driver for Fu Zuoyi's army continued to thwart my aspirations to join the Youth League. I tried to improve my *biaoxian*, or performance, working harder and longer than others, and taking on the harshest jobs when we went to labor in the countryside. But no matter how hard I tried, there was no change in the leaders' attitudes toward me.

All but four of my fifty-one classmates at Erzhong were Han, many of them children of officials or intellectuals. Some, like Qingxian and myself, as well as several who were from landlord families, had problems because of our parents' class origins or political histories. Yet at the time, it was still possible for students with suspect or even tainted class or historical backgrounds to overcome obstacles, to assume leadership roles, and to go on to higher education.

Social Investigation in the Countryside

From 1958, China's population registration and control (*hukou*) system formally divided residents into urban and rural, agricultural and nonagricultural, populations. From 1959, the state, which assumed responsibility for feeding and providing health care, pensions, and other benefits for the nonagricultural population, closely regulated entry to the cities. As late as 1957, the ratio of agricultural and herding population to nonagricultural population in Inner Mongolia was 3 to 1. But by 1960, with migration to the cities from within and outside, the nonagricultural population increased from about 2.3 million people to 4.5 million, and the ratio of agricultural to nonagricultural dropped to 1.7 to 1. The explosion of the urban population placed heavy financial pressure on the system as the state not only built urban housing and infrastructure but also fed increasing numbers of city residents. As famine deepened in many parts of China in 1959–1960, food rations for urban residents everywhere were reduced.[22]

Facing a hunger crisis, authorities throughout China acted to ensure stability in major cities by reducing the urban population. Reversing the recent rapid urbanization of Inner Mongolia and elsewhere, the state transferred millions of urban people to the countryside in 1960–1961. Whereas urban residents received subsidized food and many also received housing and welfare benefits, those who were sent to the countryside were responsible for producing their own food in the collective economy. Hard-pressed communes and brigades had to guarantee the rations for those sent down (*xiafang*), including city youth, workers, and their families. Conditions in Inner Mongolia were better than those in many other autonomous regions and provinces, but even Inner Mongolia suffered the negative consequences of the Great Leap Forward.

From 1960, entire urban work units collapsed, including many that had expanded during the Leap. The Hohhot Steel Plant was one high-profile unit that closed. Many others cut large numbers of personnel. Individuals who had political problems were particularly vulnerable to being "sent down" to the countryside.

Middle school students who failed to pass college examinations had to join their families in the countryside, including two of my classmates, Zhao Yongyi and my friend from martial arts Zhang Rong. Overall, by 1962, nearly 1.5 million urban residents in Inner Mongolia had lost their food ration privileges and were forced to leave the cities.[23] Throughout China, the urban population dropped by 20 million in the years 1960–1961, increasing the burden on the countryside to provide food and jobs.[24]

I caught glimpses of life in rural Inner Mongolia in the wake of the Leap. Every year our entire school went to the countryside to work for one or two weeks. Physical labor was meant to instill appreciation for labor and emulate the Party's revolutionary history, as well as to help bring in the harvest when labor was at a premium. My class went to Dataishi village, Qiaobao commune, in a suburb east of Hohhot. The village had seventy or eighty households, rather large by Inner Mongolia standards. The villagers had more land than they could farm, so during the three famine years (1959–1962), they allocated a plot of land for our school to grow vegetables.

We walked close to four hours from our campus to the village for labor training. As a labor committee member, I was in charge of all work arrangements and led the group. Such classes also provided opportunities for investigation and research (*diaocha yanjiu*), a tradition initiated by Mao Zedong in the late 1920s and relaunched nationwide in late 1960. The year 1961 was designated "a year of investigation and research."[25]

The villagers treated us well. Viewed through my own eyes as a country boy from Hebei, two aspects of Inner Mongolian agriculture surprised me. One was the wasteful land use. Land was so abundant and labor so scarce compared with densely populated agrarian China. The result was that land productivity was low. The second thing was that in Han villages in Inner Mongolia, almost no women worked in the fields. Most married women stayed at home caring for children and carrying out domestic tasks. By contrast, in rural Hebei and in Mongol communities in the autonomous region, most women worked in the fields. On the grasslands, Mongol women were the main workforce, tending to both livestock and household chores.

During our social investigation class, I investigated why there were so few Han girls and women in the countryside. The answers I discovered confirmed the continued existence of female infanticide and discrimination against girls. In hungry times, girl infants and children were more likely to starve and less likely to receive medical care. Mongols, however, never practiced infanticide.

Ulaan, the charismatic Mongolian chairwoman of the Inner Mongolia Women's Association and a heroine of the anti-Japanese resistance, publicly criticized Han marital practices in Inner Mongolia. Speaking at Erzhong, she told a story of two families that were unable to agree on a bride price. Finally, the worth was determined on the basis of the bride's weight, just like a pig. By contrast, she praised Mongol practices, which she said involved no bride price. We all laughed at this story that lashed out at the high bride price paid by Han rural households in Inner Mongolia. Ulaan's point was that many customs demeaning to women were coming back with the Great Leap famine. We students had believed that "feudal" practices such as bride price and dowry had disappeared for good in the revolutions of the 1950s.

Our class conducted household surveys, delving into family histories, income and labor. Having studied Mao Zedong's rural household surveys conducted in the Soviet areas of Jiangxi province in the 1930s, we tried to emulate them. The school gave us forms to work with. We learned from the village Party secretary about families that had arrived as part of the official migrant population and others that the Chinese state described as part of the "blind flow" of migrants from across North China who fled rural famine. One migrant family had four girls and one boy, the oldest being seventeen. They had taken refuge in a small temple at the edge of the village. In the summer of 1961 many other migrants had been driven away, but this household with four girls, one of whom was already approaching marriage age, was welcomed to settle.

Social investigation for middle school students primarily consisted of holding meetings for *suku* (speaking bitterness) and *yiku sitian* (recalling bitterness and reflecting on sweetness) to listen to the peasants tell about their miserable lives in the old society and the happy days since liberation.[26] Of course, some old peasants who had no education and didn't know how to lie would occasionally say that their bitterness in the past didn't compare with the hardships of the 1960 famine. Then the organizer would correct the error, and politically correct stories would follow. The rural class struggle was not yet intense, so the speaker's error could pass unpunished.

We also worked in Nanxiaoying, a village close to Ulanhu's home area, Tabu, which lent its name to Tabu commune in Tumed banner. It was called Tabu, meaning "five," because the village originally consisted of five families, Ulanhu's and their four Han tenant families. In 1964 the village would be renamed Tabusai (Tavansain in Mongolian), meaning "five good," signifying ethnic amity and echoing Ulanhu's nationality policy for Inner Mongolia. The City Education Bureau sent a truck to bring us. The village had about forty Mongol and five Han households. Almost all the Mongols were named Yun, the surname in Chinese of Ulanhu, who grew up using his Chinese name, Yun Ze, and, like many Tumed Mongols, speaking and reading no Mongol. He changed his name to Ulanhu (red son) in 1947, when he became chairman of the Inner Mongolia Autonomous Government.

Tumed had constituted a powerful federation (*tumen*, or "ten thousand") in the sixteenth century, one of six *tumen*s of central Mongolia ruled by Chinggisid princes. Given their resistance to the Manchus, in the seventeenth century the Chinggisid chiefs were stripped of their noble titles, and the Tumed became professional soldiers serving the Qing dynasty. For their service, each soldier was allocated *hukoudi* (household land). However, because men were soldiers and women were herders, there was never enough labor to cultivate the land. As Han flooded into the Tumed region as early as the sixteenth century and continuing through the twentieth century, Mongols rented their land to the migrants. Villages then formed around each Mongol household, which led to a unique ethnoscape in the Tumed region: Mongols became landowners and Han migrants became tenants.

The fertile Tumed plain along the Yellow River was thus highly Sinicized. Not only were there numerous Han immigrants, but by the early twentieth century, the Tumed Mongols had lost much of their power. Han land brokers leased land from impoverished Mongol households at low prices and sublet it to landless Han or new immigrants. Land was frequently bought and sold by so-called second landlords (*er dizhu*), or Han land merchants.[27] The Tumed Mongol population by the twentieth century had adopted the Chinese language and lost many distinctive Mongol cultural traits, including living in mud-brick houses rather than yurts.

Handing in My Heart to the Party

As China began to recover from the Great Leap famine, and as I struggled with my personal problems, a storm was brewing. Unbeknownst to me, in 1962 a movement had just been launched called Hand in Your Heart to the Party (*xiangdang jiaoxin*), in response to nationwide famine and subsequent demoralization. The Party responded to the failures of the Leap by demanding displays of Communist loyalty. It was a moment of being tested.

During my years at Erzhong, the repeated rejection of my Youth League application had led me to seek inspiration in biographies and autobiographies. One book that had a great impact on me was Li Rui's *Comrade Mao Zedong's Early Revolutionary Activities*.[28] I was impressed by Mao's ability to analyze issues and his sympathy for people's distress. I tried to follow his example. But the more I tried to emulate him, the more people thought I was a dangerous element.

Frustrated and isolated, I poured my thoughts into letters to my old friend Liu Wang, who was in the air force in Gansu. His father, Liu Ke, who had joined the Communist forces in Raoyang during the anti-Japanese resistance, eventually rose to direct the Industrial Bureau in the industrializing city of Shijiazhuang, Hebei. Liu had been my middle school classmate in Raoyang. We had painted landscapes together, and both of our mothers were divorced. After he joined the army in 1960, we exchanged letters. He was the only person I could open my heart to.

I had recently begun self-study of political economy with F. V. Konstantinov's text that circulated widely in China in the 1950s and Yu Guangyuan's *Socialist Political Economy*.[29] At that time, many publications classified as "internal distribution" (*neibu faxing*) could be found in the New China Bookstore in Hohhot. I bought Tito's writings and a text on the Yugoslav-Soviet polemics, though not Djilas's hard-hitting criticism of Tito, which was available only in a highly classified translation. So as a middle school senior, I read and thought about political economy and philosophy. Liu Wang and I exchanged views on political theory and the Great Leap Forward.

Some months passed during which we exchanged several letters. Gradually I became aware that the school Party secretary and Youth League secretary were very cold toward me. I knew that something was wrong, but not what. Then one day, the class counselor Lü Aimin told me to see the school's Party secretary Yang Zhongxin after school.

Secretary Yang told me that she had received my Youth League application many times.

"You are a good student. You are plain living and hard working." She treated me politely. Then she asked, "Do you have anything deep in your heart that you want to report to the Party? You should tell the Party everything. If anything troubles you, we can help."

"My only problem is that my application for Youth League membership has been held up for more than two years. That is my mental burden," I replied.

"You have a long way to go. There are many things on your mind that you haven't told the Party." Her face turned cold. Then she asked, "Do you have a friend in the military?" Her eyes looked like two daggers.

"Yes. How did you know?"

"We know everything if we want to know. The Communist Party leads everything, everywhere."

Suddenly I realized that my letters to Liu Wang had been read by others. There was no point in trying to conceal the relationship. I immediately told her everything, convinced I had done nothing wrong.

"Do you blame our Party's Three Red Banners?" She pressed on like a police interrogator.

I said that I did not blame the Party, explaining that I sought answers to China's problems in reading more of Marx, Lenin, Stalin, and Mao.

"You come from the countryside. You didn't experience political movements that were conducted in the city. Two years ago, we had a movement to pull out the white flags. You are young and can't understand many things. Chairman Mao and the Party are always correct. If you want to write or discuss some of your thoughts, we can exchange ideas." Her attitude seemed friendlier at last.

I told Secretary Yang that I wanted to write my deepest thoughts. We talked many times before I wrote. If the Party secretary spent this much time with someone who was not even a Youth League member, it meant that there was a serious problem. Rumors flew that I was suspected of being a spy. In my eagerness, I was oblivious to the dangerous course I had embarked on in discussing my deepest thoughts, first with my friend Liu Wang and then with the Party secretary. I was a country bumpkin, after all, when it came to ideological struggle. I was only eighteen years old.

Later, in the Cultural Revolution, students checked my dossier and transcribed the letter that the military had written to the school authorities: "You have a student Cheng Tiejun who is constantly writing letters to one of the soldiers in this unit, discussing important political issues. From what he wrote, we sense serious political mistakes. Both you and we should emphasize education to avoid their taking a very dangerous road." They drew no official conclusion, nor did they quote the letters or name Liu Wang. But a letter from the political department of a military unit was a very serious matter.

Four years later, Liu Wang was demobilized. Because of the letters, he was never admitted to the Party or promoted as an official. He worked in the Raoyang county government printing shop until retiring in 2003.

In applying for Youth League membership and in applying for college, everyone wrote a one-page autobiography with basic facts. But because of the problems I faced, I decided to "hand in my heart to the Party." I said to Secretary Yang: "I have an outline. Would you like to read it?"

"You can talk about it or write it up. It's up to you." After hesitating for two weeks, in late spring of 1963, as I was preparing for college admission, I decided to write.

On four consecutive Sundays, from morning to night, I sat alone in a classroom writing and revising my autobiography. I hoped that this would alleviate the leaders' suspicions. I explained everything. I wrote some forty pages and twelve thousand characters on Chinese writing paper drawn in squares. I must have broken a record: how on earth could a middle school student write such a long autobiography?

I was determined, though, to "turn in my heart to the Party." The result was *Cheng Tiejun Zizhuan* (The Autobiography of Cheng Tiejun). I began by telling about my family and the reason I came to Hohhot for education. I explained my interest in studying political economy, my desire to become a Marxist-Leninist and to emulate the young Mao, as well as my esteem for the fine experiences of model youth. My experience had raised many questions about understanding my family situation, as well as conditions in my home county and the nation. I listed many questions that I was struggling with: How to view the Great Leap Forward? Was the famine a natural or man-made disaster? In the spring of 1959, when I was sixteen my brother had begged for a bowl or two of corn flour from neighbors. When I returned to Raoyang in 1960, I had seen people selling children and wives, and others begging. How to view this, the dark side of the bright society?

I decided to open up everything. Yes, I was naive. But I was also stubborn and committed to beliefs that drew both on my personal experience in the countryside and a reading of Maoist and Marxist classics. It was impossible not to be deeply concerned by famine conditions that threatened the very survival of my village in Raoyang, and that of my mother and my brother.

After revising the autobiography, I copied it in my best calligraphy, writing very small. I had never written anything so long or concentrated so hard in writing.

Both the Party and league secretaries at the school levels were women: Yang Zhongxin was Party secretary; Zhang Meirong was league secretary. They shared an office. Both had talked with me. Thinking about it now, both must have been astonished by the autobiography. After I submitted my autobiography, nothing happened. They did not approve my league membership, nor did they apply pressure on me. It was as if I had never written anything at all. Life at school went on.

Rumblings:
Prelude to the Cultural Revolution

Going to College: One Red Heart and Two Preparations

In the spring of 1963, I asked the school Party and Youth League branch secretaries whether I should plan to go to the countryside, work in a factory, join the army, or enter college by examination after graduation. *Yike hongxin, liangzhong zhunbei*—one red heart and two preparations—was their stock answer. Be prepared to serve, whether as a college student or in other assignments. The Party knows best.

Going to college was far from straightforward. Not only was it necessary to be prepared to accept other assignments, but certain subjects involved levels of secrecy or political sensitivity that posed an insurmountable challenge for me.

I later learned that Wei Shiyu, the academic director (*jiaodao zhuren*) of Erzhong, wrote in my graduation appraisal: "This person's thought is rather complicated. His family background needs further investigation and clarification. He is unsuitable for secrecy-rated subjects but can apply for ordinary subjects." My autobiography and other documents in my dossier had begun to exert their power. Still, I was lucky, as in 1959 I had migrated to Hohhot just before opportunities to migrate closed. In 1963, test scores still weighed heavily. From the following year and for years to come, political evaluation, political background, and class origin would become the determining factors in college acceptance.

I passed the college examination in July. My first choice was the political economy program at Nankai University in Tianjin, one of China's leading universities. This was the logical extension of my personal study of Mao's writings and of Marxist political economy. But I was rejected on political grounds. My second choice was Inner Mongolia University. I applied to the department of Chinese language and literature. This was a nationally ranked university, and although it was located in a minority region, it had some leading professors. I thought that if I could not be admitted in political economy, it was wise to choose another field that might lead to middle school teaching. My application, again, was unsuccessful.

The third choice was the Inner Mongolia Teachers' College English program. I had studied Russian, the only foreign language offered at most senior middle schools in Inner Mongolia. From 1960, with the Sino-Soviet rupture and the withdrawal of Soviet technicians from China, English began to replace Russian as the primary foreign language, but no middle school in Inner Mongolia had begun to teach English! Teachers' College planned to enroll forty students in English, the third year that English was offered. The test, however, was given in Russian.

In the end, nineteen out of forty-five graduating students in my class at Erzhong entered college. Three joined the army before the exams. The remaining twenty-three went to work. Of the nineteen students, most went to colleges in Hohhot. Three, including myself, attended Inner Mongolia Teachers' College, three the Medical College, three the Industrial College, two the Agricultural and Animal Husbandry College, and three the Forestry College.

After the college entrance exam and before the results were posted, the academic director Wei Shiyu asked me to deliver a speech representing our school at a three-day conference of senior middle school representatives organized by the Hohhot Education Bureau, the Youth League, and the Party. Ironically, I had been selected to speak on the basis of the writing ability I demonstrated in my autobiography and my speaking ability. My speech must have been satisfactory, because I was asked to speak as the student representative at a subsequent mass meeting of all Hohhot senior middle school graduates.

"If I succeed in the examination, I will try to serve the country as a student. If I fail, I will go wherever the Party sends me," I solemnly pledged on behalf of my fellow students, before almost five thousand people, including school graduates, their families, and officials.

Deputy Mayor Chen Bingyu, a Tumed Mongol, then spoke. Guo Yiqing, Party secretary and deputy president of Inner Mongolia University, spoke eloquently, with a thick Henan accent. Other speakers represented farmers, workers, and family members. This was the best memory of my middle school years. I was critical of certain Party practices, and deeply disturbed by the Great Leap famine, but speaking in front of officials, teachers, and fellow students gave me a feeling of accomplishment—and hope.

I later reported to an assembly at Erzhong about the three-day meeting. Friends quipped, "You climbed onto the *kang* without passing through the kitchen," joking that I, who had been barred from the Youth League, seemed to be leaping directly to the Party. However, the route to the Party was via the Youth League, and my application remained in limbo.

F I G U R E 3 Senior middle school graduation photo taken on July 30, 1963, with Cheng Tiejun (second from left in the front row) and Wang Qingxian (third from right in the second row)

College Life

I had never discussed college choices with my father. He simply said that if I passed the exam, it would be OK to attend college; otherwise, he suggested that I enroll in truck-driving school and become a driver like him. When I was admitted to Inner Mongolia Teachers' College, he said nothing. But my stepmother grinned, saying in her backcountry accent: "That means you'll become a teacher! It's better than being a peasant, you won't have to work outside in sun and rain." Her smile meant, among other things, that there would be no fees to pay. Teachers' College students were often called *chifan* (eating) instead of *shifan* (teacher training), a pun indicating that their education was completely subsidized, including food. This tradition dated from the late Qing period. The state subsidized all higher education in the People's Republic, but only teachers' colleges and military and police academies were completely free, including room and board.

The college year began in September 1963. There were two English and two Russian classes, each with more than twenty students, and all together more than eighty students in my grade. Most of the thirteen departments enrolled about forty each. A few, such as our department and the Chinese language and literature department, which had two specializations, Chinese and Mongolian, had eighty. There were more than 600 first-year students and 2,500 in all at the college. Many were villagers; some were from poor urban families. I liked students from rural backgrounds, finding them honest and direct (*hanhou*). They joked in a particular way that urban students might think vulgar, but I enjoyed it, because like draws like.

The students and faculty at Teachers' College included Mongols and other minorities. Han students constituted well over half of the student body. Minority students, who accounted for a third of the student body, were categorized by those whose classes were taught in Chinese and those enrolled in Mongolian-language courses. Not only was Mongolian language and literature offered in Mongolian, but from 1962 Mongolian-language-medium instruction was also offered in mathematics, physics, chemistry, biology, and history. Students in the Mongolian-language track included Mongols, Daurs, and a small number of bilingual Han.[1]

My good friend Chöji Jalsan, a Mongol with a Tibetan name who came from Hulunbuir league,[2] was one of the top mathematicians in the college. He was also the son of a landlord who was beaten to death during land reform; his mother brought up three boys and three girls by washing laundry, eventually sending four of them to college. One sister became a doctor and another a nurse.

Most Mongol students enrolled in the Mongolian-language track, and many of them hailed from the grasslands. Their first language was Mongolian, and their previous education had been conducted in Mongolian.

An affirmative action program aided minority students. Mongols applying to programs that were taught in Chinese had fifteen points added to their test scores. This slightly increased the number of Mongols in the Chinese track. It was irrelevant, however, to students whose education had been exclusively or primarily in Mongolian, including many from the grasslands. The result was essentially a two-track system in which the majority of Mongols were enrolled in courses in the Mongolian-language track and did not compete with those studying in the Chinese track. Except for Mongolian language and literature, the content in the two tracks was the same.

Language was a contentious issue for Mongol students, then and now. Because Chinese was the second language for most Mongol students, the dominant pedagogy held that it would be counterproductive and burdensome for them to learn an additional foreign language, as they already had to learn Mongolian and Chinese. Only those who had been educated in Chinese rather than Mongolian were allowed to study foreign languages. In short, despite their political predominance, Mongols, especially those who received Mongolian education, were effectively denied access to certain university programs in Inner Mongolia at a time when assimilationist policies were rapidly eroding the linguistic and symbolic foundations of their culture. There were few Mongol students in our department, and none in my class.

Han and Mongol students received the same living stipend. Mongol students were eligible to receive extra meat and dairy products, which they paid for out of their stipends. There was no separate student dining hall for Mongol students, but those who could afford it went to the faculty dining hall, where special food was served for them. A canteen for Muslims served no pork.

Dormitory accommodations were arranged on the unit (*danwei*) principle. This meant that the few Mongol students in programs such as Russian language shared dormitories with their Han classmates. Overall, however, there was de facto housing separation, as most Mongols were enrolled in overwhelmingly Mongolian-focused programs, such as Mongol history and literature and a range of other academic subjects taught in Mongolian. Each program had its own accommodations. Separation was reinforced by the fact that many students in all-Mongol programs spoke poor Chinese and few Han students spoke any Mongol. There was thus little interaction at school between Han and Mongol students, except in departments with mixed Han and Mongol students and in activities such as sports that brought them together.

I and many of my classmates respected Mongols highly, including their intelligence. Those Mongols whom Han students looked down on usually had difficulty in the Chinese language. But of course, while very few Han had mastered even a smattering of Mongolian, many Mongols spoke, read, and wrote excellent Chinese, and some, including students at our college, were fully conversant in both Chinese and Mongol society and culture.

A number of Daur and Mongol faculty taught at Teachers' College. The director of the Marxist-Leninist Mao Zedong Thought Department was a Daur, whose Chinese name, Xinsi (1929–1989), meant "new thought." His Mongolian name was Has'erdeni, meaning "jade treasure." He was an outstanding teacher of the history of the Communist International, Marxist philosophy, and classics of philosophy. He taught in both Mongolian and Chinese and published widely. I admired his teaching style and knowledge. Another teacher, Tuomusi (Tömös), a fine-arts teacher trained in Beijing, was a Tumed Mongol.

In 1960, the Treaty of Friendship and Mutual Assistance between the People's Republic of China and the Mongolian People's Republic was signed. The MPR had the only foreign consulate in Hohhot. Around this time, with the rupture in Sino-Soviet relations, most technical experts returned to the Soviet Union, and the Soviet aid program was terminated. In Inner Mongolian universities, a few Soviet teachers and technical specialists remained for several years. Ala, an instructor of Russian at Teachers' College, was a single mother with a young daughter. She was a highly regarded teacher. Although the Soviet polemics had reached a fever pitch, she continued to teach, living simply in her own apartment. Her daughter attended the affiliated primary school and spoke with the language students in Russian and with her schoolmates in fluent Chinese.

Studying English in Inner Mongolia

Not a single student in our English class had studied English. All had studied Russian. We used Xu Guozhang's introductory English textbook, the same text that was used at Beijing University and the most influential textbook in China.

I vividly remember the story of Gorky's mother from this textbook: "Pavel was arrested. That day Mother did not light the stove. Evening came and a cold wind was blowing. There was a knock at the window. Then another. Mother was used to such knocks, but this time she gave a little start of joy. Throwing a shawl over her shoulders, she opened the door." We had no recordings, only the book. In our third year, Beijing sent some large reel-to-reel tapes featuring people such as Dr. George Hatem (an American public health specialist known as "Ma Haide" in China), the New Zealand writer Rewi Alley, and the American journalist Anna Louise Strong—as well as a few other international "friends of China" with many years of experience in China associated with the Communist movement. We also listened to Radio Beijing and discussed the broadcasts in English.

The teachers were dedicated. Zhang Naijun was the very best; he had been the interpreter for Liu Ningyi, head of China's labor federation. He learned English at Fu Jen University in Beijing from American and British teachers, graduating in the early 1950s. Zhang taught translation. Over six feet tall, he looked every inch the intellectual. Liu Qingrong, our class counselor, graduated from the Liaoning University English Department. Pang Hongbin graduated from Heilongjiang University. Pang, who had a long scar on his dark-brown face, looked more like a gangster than an intellectual. He later married my classmate Zhang Hongying.

He Qichao, who taught English pronunciation, was an Oxford graduate who also taught music. He had studied in the United Kingdom in the early 1940s and returned to China in 1947 with a DPhil in music theory. He spoke

English slowly and with a musical emphasis. He wanted to make us aware of English as a musical language.

The eight students from Fengzhen middle school had problems with pronunciation. We always joked with Wang Zhen. There was a unit called "Wang Qing gets up," and we learned "brushes his teeth," "goes to class," and so on. We delighted in imitating his pronunciation. Of course, it was easier to mock someone else's errors than to improve our own pronunciation. An exasperated Professor He implored us, "Don't speak Fengzhen English anymore!"

Unlike the Russian-language students who had a native-speaking Russian-language teacher, Ala, we English students were not so lucky. And we were expressly prohibited from talking with the few foreigners who visited Hohhot. The only experience of a student speaking English with a foreigner in early 1966 precipitated police intervention.

My classmate Yang Chengzhi, the shortest boy in the class, was shopping in the biggest department store, Lianying Shangdian. Suddenly an English-speaking tourist took out his camera to take a picture of a shabbily dressed little boy. Alerted by socialist education campaigns, Yang recognized the man as an imperialist out to humiliate socialist China by showing a poorly dressed boy in an expensive department store. So he stepped in, covered the visitor's lens, and said in English: "No, no! You cannot do that. Why don't you take pictures of those beautiful products and customers? You are not respectful of the Chinese people!"

Yang was detained by the Hohhot police and interrogated for hours. Did he know the visitor? Was he passing intelligence or disclosing state secrets by speaking in English to a foreigner without official permission? Eventually, the police called the security department of the college to take him back to school. No one was allowed to speak English to foreign visitors without a special permit!

On January 5, 1964, Inner Mongolia's Party and government departments dispatched 17,600 cadres to agricultural regions to conduct the Socialist Education Movement, also known as the Four Cleanups. Specialized work teams were then sent to agricultural, pastoral, and industrial sites throughout the year.[3] Teachers' College faculty and students in the humanities led work teams in localities across rural Inner Mongolia. Those in the sciences followed. Only foreign-language students remained on campus. Premier Zhou Enlai and Foreign Minister Chen Yi, we learned, had urged Mao to exempt language students from participating on the practical grounds that we would quickly forget the language we were learning. China, they argued, could ill afford the loss of language skills necessary for foreign affairs at a time when the nation faced simultaneous conflicts with the Soviets and the Americans.

My classmates vigorously debated the issue. Most supported the directive to continue our language studies to improve skills essential for our future work. It was encouraging that national leaders saw our work as important. A few political activists, however, angrily denounced our exclusion from a historic movement. If the Socialist Education Movement was so important, they asked, why should we be excluded? Foreign-language study could always be made up, but the opportunity to participate in class struggle was a once-in-a-lifetime opportunity. Only one student, Ma Wenyuan, countered: "Hey, what's the hurry? There'll be plenty of chances for class struggle. If the Socialist Education Movement doesn't go smoothly, we'll all go sooner or later. The whole college might even close." At that time, of course, no one had an inkling of the Cultural Revolution that lay ahead. Two years later, we teased Ma playfully and called him *San nian zao zhidao*, extolling his foresight in anticipating three years in advance what was to come. As for me, I knew that participating in the struggle was an opportunity to learn about society. But as a political target, I knew that I too would be criticized.

The Socialist Education Movement

The immediate stimulus for the Socialist Education Movement was the attempt to restore morale and strengthen the Party's credibility in the wake of the Great Leap famine that had devastated rural areas and strained the nation's resources and morale. The campaign to root out corruption among rural officials and punish their crimes and brutality sought to restore grassroots support for the Party and direct anger away from the disastrous errors committed by national leaders. In Inner Mongolia, the movement took on a volatile ethnic and class character whose roots can be traced to the land reform of 1947–1948 and to earlier land conflicts.

In eastern Inner Mongolia in 1947–1948, immediately after the founding of the Inner Mongolia Autonomous Government, the CCP led Han tenant farmers in the overthrow of Mongol landowners in ethnically mixed agricultural areas. Land reform was a key CCP strategy to mobilize Han peasant support in the Civil War with the Nationalist government by providing poor peasants and tenant farmers tangible benefits. Neglecting the specificity of pastoral society and Mongol-Han relations in the newly liberated area under the jurisdiction of the autonomous government, land reform cadres, many of them dispatched from the CCP Northeast China Bureau, acted on the assumption that intra-Mongol and Mongol-Han class problems in Inner Mongolia could be resolved by implementing policies identical to those used with landlords and tenants in rural North China. In Inner Mongolia, however, Mongol land was often distributed to Han peasants, and even small Mongol landholders were frequently labeled "landlords" and "Mongol traitors" (*Mengjian*) because of their earlier association with Japan's semicolony Manchukuo.[4]

Land reform teams in pastoral areas even took livestock ownership as the equivalent of land ownership. Land reform in Inner Mongolia not only decimated herds, as herders slaughtered their livestock in desperate efforts to avoid reclassification as herdlords, but also led to Mongol deaths, exacerbated Han-Mongol conflict, and upended the fragile pastoral economy. In February 1948 more than two hundred Mongols staged a rebellion and sought refuge in the Mongolian People's Republic, thereby adding an international dimension to the conflict over land reform and threatening the security of Inner Mongolia at the height of the Guomindang-CCP Civil War.

In Hulunbuir league, a small landlord by local standards with 120 *mu* of land who had served as a magistrate under Japanese rule was detained and tortured. His legs were bound, and he was dragged through the dirt streets from village to village. By the time he was sent home, he was near death. His second son was Chöji Jalsan, my schoolmate at Teachers' College, who recalled that his father's wife and six children held his bloody head, sobbing, until he expired. Then they buried him.

Responding to the polarizing land reform and to calls to jump-start the economy after decades of warfare, Ulanhu initiated a policy, "three nos and two benefits" (*sanbu liangli*), for governing ethnic and class relations in the autonomous region: no class struggle, no redistribution of property, and no class labeling of Mongols; mutual benefit for herders and herdlords.[5] Ethnic harmony would establish foundations for economic development and mutual prosperity. After the founding of the People's Republic in 1949, this policy was implemented in varying degrees in pastoral areas throughout China, including Tibet, Qinghai, Xinjiang, and Suiyuan. Under Ulanhu's influence, in the land reform carried out in ethnically mixed agricultural areas such as Suiyuan in 1951, different criteria were used to determine class designation for Han and Mongol farmers. In general, Han farmers were treated more leniently than their counterparts in inland Chinese provinces, and as far as the Mongols were concerned, a more flexible policy was implemented whereby a variety of factors were considered: size of land owned, size of land rented to a so-called second landlord (*er dizhu*, or a rich Han farmer), amount of rent income, actual labor force of the household, experience in farming, and so on. For instance, Baatar's household had two people, both of whom had lost the ability to do farmwork. They rented out three thousand *mu* of land, and their annual rent income was ten *dan* (equal to 310 kilograms) of grain. Because their actual living standard was lower than that of a "middle peasant," they were designated "poor peasants." Moreover, to reduce ethnic tension, designation of "landlord class" label to Mongol farmers in Suiyuan province had to be approved by the Inner Mongolia Party Committee.[6]

Ulanhu's brand of land reform, while widely appreciated by pastoral Mongols, had produced divergent responses among rural Han of various classes and communities in Inner Mongolia. In the ethnically mixed area of Tumed banner, Ulanhu's hometown, Han farmers were dismayed to receive higher class labels than their Mongol neighbors. But my classmates Zhao Xilan, a girl from Hulunbuir league, and Bai Heling, a boy from Jirim league, from mixed ethnic areas in semiagricultural, semipastoral regions of eastern Inner Mongolia, told me that Han in these communities highly appreciated Ulanhu's "three nos and two benefits" policy. That was because it brought stability and prosperity compared with nearby agricultural counties where violent class struggle and radical redistribution polarized Mongols and Han and hampered economic recovery. Nevertheless, class and nationality conflicts remained latent even where land reform proceeded smoothly.

The Socialist Education Movement of 1963–1966 reopened issues of land and class conflict fifteen years after land reform. The North China Bureau of the Party designated Linhe, a Han-dominated county of Bayannuur league, as a key point for investigation.[7] A storm was gathering. I learned about the campaign and the conflicts that it ignited from schoolmates who participated in it.

Linhe and the adjacent area west of Baotou city in western Inner Mongolia was a prime agricultural area. Opened to farming in the early twentieth century, it benefited from the building of canals diverting water from the Yellow River. During World War II, Shanba was the headquarters of Fu Zuoyi's Guomindang forces. It was also one of the key centers for Mongol-Han conflict over land, and well into the 1950s, offshoots of Fu's army put up resistance to the PLA. As a key point for the Socialist Education Movement, it attracted a powerful contingent of North China Bureau and Inner Mongolian cadres led by Xie Xuegong, who had risen as a radical proponent of the Great Leap Forward in Hebei to become Party secretary of Tianjin and secretary of the North China Bureau Secretariat, with close ties to its leader Li Xuefeng. The highest-ranking local participant from the autonomous region was Gao Jinming, secretary of the Inner Mongolia Party Secretariat.[8]

Students from Teachers' College set off for the countryside to join the Socialist Education Movement singing a song that had been composed by music students at the college. I remember the words and tune as if it were yesterday, because those of us who remained on campus rallied to see them off at the campus gate. We sang together:

> Eight hundred *li* plain in the Yellow River bend
> It's the Jiangnan [fertile area south of the Yangtze River] of Inner Mongolia
> Irrigation network is like a spiderweb
> Yellow River water makes all the land fertile.
>
> Work team comes to the countryside
> The poor and middle peasants' smiles welcome it
> The class line redraws class distinctions
> Keep the revolution red for ten thousand generations.

Qingxian, the Erzhong classmate I began to date in 1964, then a medical student, was dispatched in late 1965 as part of a work team to Dongsheng county of Yekejuu league, also known as Ordos. South of the Yellow River and not far from Baotou, the area was very poor. The population was predominantly Han. Teams of twelve to fourteen members were assigned to each people's commune.[9] One-third of the members were college students, another third were local officials, and the final third were officials from the Inner Mongolia Autonomous Region.

For almost ten months, the work teams interviewed cadres and villagers to collect evidence of corruption and crime. Cadres in this desperately poor area, as everywhere, were forced to confess to crimes of theft, however petty, and provide restitution. The campaign also publicly humiliated powerless former landlords yet again.

Badrangui, a Mongol friend who majored in Mongolian history at Teachers' College, was a native of Bayannuur. He was sent to Shiliingol league, a pastoral zone in central Inner Mongolia near the border famous for its lush grass and fine horses. Few brigade meetings were held there because it was a four-hour horseback ride from a production or herd group to brigade headquarters. Even a truck took up to three hours to go from commune headquarters to a brigade. A brigade had only forty scattered households, so there were no teams.

Two brothers tended the commune's five hundred sheep and sixty cows. Their greatest pleasure was drinking the local hot sorghum spirits, and they would carry a bottle while riding herd. Every day they brought back stories from the Soviet Union and the MPR culled from listening to shortwave radio. Once a week, they met their brother, who lived across the border in the MPR. They were among the many families that were divided between Inner

Mongolia and the MPR. In August 1945, in the wake of the Soviet-Mongolian declaration of war against Japan, following the call for unification of the Mongols, many Mongols from Ujumchin and Sönid banners had migrated to the MPR. Even after people on both sides were forced to withdraw from the border when Sino-Soviet and China-MPR relations worsened in the early 1960s, the brothers continued to meet each week. Knowing the precise schedule both of the MPR and PLA border patrols, they simply crossed right after the soldiers passed.

The stories I heard reinforced the generally peaceful image of the early stages of the Socialist Education Movement in much of Inner Mongolia, in line with Ulanhu's long-standing efforts to mute the class struggle and conflicts among nationalities. But as the movement wore on, tensions deepened. Local zealots and North China Bureau leaders challenged Ulanhu's "three nos and two benefits" policy of the earlier land reform, initiating a new round of class struggle.

The scale of the movement can be gleaned from the experience of one banner in Bayannuur—Urad Front banner—an ethnically mixed banner between Linhe and Baotou. In 1965, the Socialist Education Movement was carried out in seventeen communes involving more than four hundred members of the work team that consisted of cadres from the autonomous region's government, Bayannuur league's government, and the banner's government, as well as more than nine hundred instructors of the Socialist Education Movement (*fudao duiwu*). A total of 2,318 local cadres became targets of the campaign. Of them, eighty-five were severely punished: two commune cadres (one commune leader and a deputy secretary) were ordered to stop work (*tingzhi*); thirteen brigade cadres were dismissed from posts (*chezhi*), three cleansed (*qingxi*); twenty-four team cadres were dismissed, ten cleansed, twelve denounced in public meetings (*pidou*), and eleven deprived of Party membership in a full-scale attack on local leaders.[10]

In the agricultural areas, the old class labels fixed in 1947–1948 (in eastern Inner Mongolia) and in 1951 (in Suiyuan) during land reform were reexamined. Many households had been reclassified from rich peasant to landlord, or from middle to rich peasant, and attacked as class enemies. The situation in some ethnically mixed banners, such as Tumed near Hohhot, was particularly volatile. With Socialist Education Movement work teams fanning the flames, Han farmers in some villages accused Mongol leaders of corruption and denounced Mongol villagers for enjoying privileges at the expense of their Han neighbors.

Ulanhu tried to prevent attempts by outside cadres to reclassify Mongols, particularly to exclude them from the newly formed Poor and Lower Middle

Peasant Associations, by insisting that nationality issues should not be conflated with class issues. But with the whiff of class struggle in the air, and the North China Bureau's Li Xuefeng pressing the attack, Ulanhu's opponents denounced him for violating Mao's slogans: "Never forget class struggle" and "The nationality struggle in the final analysis is the class struggle." Insisting that the immediate challenge was to improve economic conditions in the wake of the Great Leap famine, in the fall of 1965 Ulanhu sought to redirect the focus of the North China Bureau work team leaders from class struggle to education, production, and irrigation, in order to improve the livelihood and unity of rural communities. Again, he was denounced for sabotaging the campaign. For the first time, under the North China Bureau's prodding, Ulanhu's authority was challenged by local Han leaders who fanned resentment among predominantly Han farmers discontented with the earlier land reform.[11] Meanwhile, storm clouds of criticism were gathering at Teachers' College and beyond as tensions grew between Mongols and Han throughout Inner Mongolia.

Down with Tömörbagan!

Inner Mongolia had two famous twentieth-century men named Tömörbagan. One was a former Inner Mongolia People's Revolutionary Party (Nei Menggu Renmin Geming Dang—Neirendang, for short) leader who served as chief justice of the Inner Mongolia Supreme Court from 1954 to 1965. In 1925, he and Ulanhu had joined the Neirendang while studying in Moscow. He joined the Soviet Communist Party before returning to eastern Mongolia under Comintern order in 1929, when Ulanhu, a CCP member, returned to Hohhot to carry out underground work against the Guomindang. In 1947, he was instrumental in supporting Ulanhu's effort to establish the Inner Mongolia Autonomous Government under CCP leadership.[12]

In late 1964 and early 1965, another Tömörbagan, the former Party secretary of Teachers' College, drew attention.[13] Soon after I enrolled at Teachers' College, he was transferred to the Inner Mongolia Education Department. But I had one experience that led me to think well of him. Lights in the dormitory were turned off every night at ten, when students were supposed to sleep. If students wished to mend clothes or write a letter, they had to work outside under the streetlights. I often went out late at night to read. It was hard on the eyes, and in winter the bitter cold made it almost impossible. I petitioned in late 1963 that a room be provided so students could work at night. I suggested that some unnecessary streetlights could be turned off, but students needed access to a lighted room after ten o'clock. Tömörbagan's secretary called me to the office, saying that they appreciated the spirit of my letter but that going to bed at ten was mandatory. Students had to be fresh for morning physical exercises at six, so they would turn off the lights on the road. My proposal had only made things worse, depriving us of outdoor lighting. But at least, I thought, Tömörbagan had responded, if only through his secretary. Given the unwritten rule of hierarchy, a lowly person like me rarely received any response.

Before the criticism of Tömörbagan, I, and many of my classmates, knew virtually nothing about Mongol-Han political relations at the college. The faculty of the Foreign Languages Department was almost exclusively Han, except for Ulanhu's son Lishake, and two other outstanding Russian-language teachers, Meng Chuan (Mongolian name "Enkhe") and Meng Surong, who were brother and sister.[14] They were Daur, born in 1941 and 1942, respectively. They grew up with Russians and Mongols in Hulunbuir.

Nationality conflict in the borderlands came to a head in China in 1964 not over Inner Mongolia but over Tibet. Following the 1959 flight of the Fourteenth Dalai Lama to India, the Ninth Panchen Lama had emerged as the leading Tibetan official in whose name "democratic reform" and other Chinese state policies were promoted in Tibet and in neighboring provinces inhabited by Tibetans, including Qinghai, Gansu, Sichuan and Yunnan. In the years 1960–1963, the Chinese state pressed Party building in Tibet, combined with a sharp attack on the monasteries, which singled out leading monks as exploiters. In May 1962 the Panchen Lama met with Mao and presented his seventy-thousand-character petition to the Central Committee through Zhou Enlai.[15] The petition argued that the accelerated social and economic development strategy associated with the Great Leap Forward and the democratic reform (*minzhu gaige*) undermined the rights of the Tibetan nationality, that the population was declining, that Buddhism had been virtually annihilated, and that numerous young people had been arrested. In September 1964, the Panchen Lama was charged with plotting revolt and subjected to mass criticism, physical violence, and public trial. In December, Zhou Enlai announced that the Panchen Lama had been stripped of his post as acting chairman of the Preparatory Committee for the Tibetan Autonomous Region for organizing counterrevolutionary activities. He retained a minor post at the Preparatory Committee and other ceremonial positions. On December 17, 1964, the State Council in Beijing for the first time publicly denounced the Dalai Lama as a traitor and dismissed him from the positions of chairman of the Preparatory Committee for the Tibetan Autonomous Region and vice-chairman of the National People's Congress.[16]

The Tibet question was inextricably linked with Inner Mongolia not least because Tibetans and Mongols shared the same Buddhism. In 1958, Ulanhu had opposed a military crackdown on the Tibetan rebellion in the Sichuan-Qinghai-Tibetan borderlands.[17] Sympathetic to the Panchen Lama's petition, Ulanhu may have been instrumental in persuading the Chinese leadership to respond positively to it. On May 15, 1962, three days before the Panchen Lama's submission of his report to Zhou Enlai, the *Report on the Nationality Work Conference* was issued, signed by Ulanhu, Li Weihan, Xu Bing, and Liu Chun on behalf of the United Front Department and the Commission of Nationality Affairs, and endorsed by the Party Center. The report criticized so-called Great Han Chauvinism and acknowledged errors in nationality affairs.[18] However, with the start of the Socialist Education Movement campaign, and with the denunciation of the Dalai Lama and the Panchen Lama, Ulanhu was thrown on the defensive. Nationality conflict coincided with intra-Party divisions centered on the Socialist Education Movement in 1964–1966 as Ulanhu sought to consolidate his position in Inner Mongolia.

At Teachers' College, as the Socialist Education Movement intensified, the authorities announced an investigation of Tömörbagan, the former Party secretary of the college. In his late thirties, articulate and energetic, Tömörbagan was a Horchin Mongol from eastern Inner Mongolia and the son of a landlord. After heading a land reform team in 1947, he served as education director of a county in Liaoning province. When the Inner Mongolia Autonomous Government was established, he became a division head of the Education Department. After serving in various educational capacities under Hafenga, who, until 1961, was concurrently deputy chairman of the Inner Mongolia Autonomous Region and head of the Education Department, Tömörbagan rose to head the Administrative Office of the Education Department and, in 1961, became Party secretary of Teachers' College. In June 1964 he was appointed deputy director of the Inner Mongolia Education Department.

The investigation of Tömörbagan grew out of mounting official concern about nationality separatism (*minzu fenlie zhuyi*, literally "nationality splittism"). He was suspected of having links with Mongol separatists, a new vocabulary then emerging inspired both by fears of Tibetan separatism and by China's rising tensions with both the Soviet Union and the MPR.

A work team appointed at the level of the autonomous region investigated Tömörbagan in June 1965. The work team was led by Cholmon, deputy propaganda head of the Inner Mongolia Party Committee and a Tumed Mongol. Members of the work team included Ji Zhi, a Han from Hebei who had succeeded Tömörbagan as Party secretary of Teachers' College in 1964; Yun

Shiying, a Tumed Mongol who was a deputy head of Inner Mongolia Public Security; and Han Ming, a Han from Shanxi province who was Party secretary and director of the Education Department.

Cholmon called a mass meeting in the Teachers' College dining hall that was attended by 1,500 students and the entire faculty. Ji Zhi chaired the meeting. Tömörbagan entered, walked to the front of the stage, and sat on a stool at a small desk. From beginning to end, he was not allowed to say a word in his defense, only to take notes.

Cholmon presented the charges. He listed Tömörbagan's problems, including his family background as a landlord; his revisionist views on class struggle, land reform, education, and nationality policy; his corrupt lifestyle; sexual misconduct; and the most serious allegation, foreign espionage. The first to criticize was Ji Zhi. Ji, a leading Russian specialist who had served as director of higher education in the Ministry of Education in Beijing in the early 1950s, had been transferred to Teachers' College in 1959 as punishment for allegedly having confessed to his Communist Party membership under Guomindang torture when imprisoned in the 1930s. At Teachers' College he became Party secretary in January 1964. Ji joined the chorus of Tömörbagan's critics: "After working with him for several years, I find that, far from being a revolutionary, he is a class enemy. His problems are political behavior, political beliefs, and national separatism. He is a corrupt bourgeois element. Instead of drawing a clear line between his landlord father and himself, he tried to change his father's landlord label."

Staff from the Teachers' College Political Office (*zhengzhi chu*) rose one after another to denounce Tömörbagan. One charged that Tömörbagan had brought his landlord father Gombolkhan to Hohhot to try to change his class label. The most damaging testimony came from Tömörbagan's ex-wife, Shang Chai, a Han who was a graduate of Beijing Normal University and taught Chinese literature at the middle school affiliated with Teachers' College. Shang vividly described how he had kicked her in the stomach while she was pregnant in an effort to kill the baby and then divorced her and married a young student from the Agriculture and Animal Husbandry College. That aroused people. Tömörbagan was not only a chauvinist nationalist but also a chauvinist husband! The fact that Shang was a highly educated Beijing intellectual who had come to Inner Mongolia to support socialist reconstruction made Tömörbagan's abuse particularly reprehensible to the students. People yelled, "Down with Tömörbagan!" They demanded that he stand and bow, a symbolic gesture of admitting crime. He did.

The physics student Hao Guangde was particularly active. A Han from

Chifeng city in eastern Inner Mongolia, he wore a stylish leather jacket. Hao led the slogan shouting and directed singing from the platform. Students sat in columns by class and sang revolutionary songs. Hao would come to play a large role in Inner Mongolia's politics in the coming decade.

As deputy director of the Inner Mongolia Department of Education, Tömörbagan had tried to increase stipends for Mongol students. This opened him to accusations of providing preferential treatment for Mongols at the expense of Han. He was accused of discriminating against Han in hiring faculty and of being so tempestuous that his Han subordinates feared him.

More serious accusations were leveled by a Han staff member of the college's Political Education Department for spurring division among nationalities (*minzu fenlie*), quoting Tömörbagan's words from a dossier on the 1947 land reform and his self-criticism in the 1957 anti-rightist movement. People criticized Tömörbagan's mishandling of nationality issues, his work as a land reform team leader, and his attempt to expunge his father's label of "landlord." Tömörbagan's work as deputy director of the Inner Mongolia Education Bureau was criticized, particularly his protection of rightists during the 1964 Socialist Education Movement.

One of the most damaging charges centered on Tömörbagan's role in the case of Mandakhchi, a student in the middle school attached to Teachers' College. In 1962, when Mandakhchi attempted to flee to the Mongolian People's Republic, police detained him. Tömörbagan sent a representative to bring him back to school, and he subsequently resisted attempts to punish the student for the crime of flight. Rumors swirled that Mandakhchi had sought to win support in the MPR for unification of all Mongols. The following year, Mandakhchi entered Teachers' College as a physics student. In August 1963 three Mongol students from the college escaped to the MPR, and Mandakhchi was later implicated in the case. As de facto Party secretary of the college at that time, Tömörbagan was held responsible for the defection.

During the fall 1964 investigation of Tömörbagan, the police carried out a high-profile arrest of Mandakhchi, sending a squad car and armed police to arrest him as a thousand students looked on. It was a means of highlighting Tömörbagan's culpability. Watching the students closely, I could see that while most Han were curious, Mongols were sad, sympathetic, or angry.

Tömörbagan's diaries were checked for evidence of nationalist or splittist opinions linking him to the MPR, but no damning evidence was discovered. Although he had already moved to work at the Inner Mongolia Education Department, he was brought back to Teachers' College for an investigation into incidents that had taken place over the preceding six years. In March

1965, Tömörbagan became the highest official in Inner Mongolia to be targeted in a special investigation movement (*zhuan'an yundong*).

To press the campaign, Teachers' College and its affiliated middle school stopped classes in June 1965. The criticism of Tömörbagan went on every day for three weeks. Morning and afternoon sessions each lasted for about three hours. Just over five feet tall, he was rotund, but conveyed an aura of intelligence and energy. After each session there was a department meeting, then each class discussed the issues. Throughout the entire proceedings, Tömörbagan remained unflappable, impeccably dressed in a woolen Mao suit.

Every student was required to write a criticism report. For this purpose, we received many basic documents on nationality policy, including classics by Lenin, Stalin, and Mao. We studied their speeches and writings on nationality affairs. I was particularly interested in Lenin's concept of national self-determination. Reading these documents and listening to discussions, for the first time I began to think seriously and sympathetically about the need to recognize the rights of minorities. The right of self-determination, including independence, had simply never occurred to me. Reading Lenin's, and especially Stalin's, writings on national self-determination, as well as Mao's Yan'an writings, I became more aware of inconsistencies between the Party's earlier and later nationality policies. This was the intellectual foundation for my growing sympathy toward the Mongols. Of course, given my own political trouble, I could not speak publicly or even hint at the real issues that were at stake in the criticism report that each of us submitted to the Party secretary. Having recently been subjected to criticism, I was learning to hide my thoughts while continuing to study.

I talked privately about the nationality documents with my friend Zhang Daren, who, like me, had been criticized. Zhang said: "I'm not a Mongol, but if I was, I'd go to the independence camp." Of course, we Han thought in terms of our own national history. China was a semicolony that had been attacked and invaded by Europeans, Americans, and Japanese, so it seemed natural that strong nationalism was generated in the fight for independence. Why, then, should Mongols and other nationalities be denied the same opportunity to fight for their rights?

At the end of the third week of struggle, Tömörbagan was told to stop work and wait for the decision of the Party Committee. The Inner Mongolia government did not, however, have the power to remove him from his posts. The Inner Mongolia government could only appoint or remove county-level cadres. Department- or prefecture-level cadres were appointed or removed by the North China Bureau or the Party Center. He formally remained deputy director of the Education Department until February 1966.

The case of Tömörbagan heralded the unfolding of a campaign targeting Mongols, which would soon culminate in the tragedies of the Cultural
Revolution.

Nasanmönkh's Suicide

Several Mongols were implicated in the Tömörbagan case: Adia, the director of
the Personnel Department of the college; Tumen, the chair of the Mongolian
language division who had received postgraduate education in the MPR; and
Nasan, the deputy principal of the middle school affiliated with the college. Each
was charged with being a Mongol nationalist and a follower of Tömörbagan.

The case of Nasanmönkh, an accountant at the college, was poignant. His
daughter Narangoa had married a Soviet expert in Hohhot, then settled with
her husband in Leningrad and become a Soviet citizen. In 1965, when the
Sino-Soviet polemics heated up, Nasanmönkh was repeatedly ordered by the
security chief of Teachers' College to report what his daughter had asked him
to do when she came home to visit a year earlier. He denied that she had attempted to recruit him as a Soviet agent, saying that she had just returned for
a family visit.

Nasanmönkh came from Khorchin Left Rear banner of Jirim league in
eastern Inner Mongolia. His elder brother Dawa Odsor was a prominent Mongolian scholar-politician. A graduate of Peking University in the 1930s, Dawa
had been governor of Khorchin Left Rear banner during the Manchuguo period (1932–1945) and in 1946 drafted the Eastern Mongolia Autonomy Law
(Dong Meng Zizhi Fa) of the Eastern Mongolia Autonomous Government.[19]

Nasanmönkh had a less celebrated career than his elder brother. A classmate
of Hafenga, the foremost eastern Mongolian nationalist leader, at the Northeast
Mongolian Banner Normal School, he later worked as a police section chief in
Manchuguo. After 1945, he was deputy magistrate of Kailu county, before being
sent to study at the Second College of the Inner Mongolia Military University
(Nei Meng Junda Eryuan). His acknowledgment of having been a Guomindang Party member led to his arrest and reform through labor (*laogai*) for three
years. In 1949, on his release, he found employment at Teachers' College cutting
stencils and later in the financial department of the College.[20]

During and after Tömörbagan's denunciation sessions, Nasanmönkh was
publicly humiliated for refusing to confess to spying for the Soviet Union.
One night in mid-June 1965, the college's security again demanded that he
confess. He was criticized and struggled (*pidou*) for four hours before being released. Instead of going home, Nasanmönkh climbed the hundred-foot
chimney used for heating the campus and jumped.

Not content with Nasanmönkh's death, Party Secretary Ji Zhi ordered the students to compose a song set to the tune of "Andai," a Mongolian shamanic song meant to expel illness, which became a popular Mongolian song and dance in the 1950s to celebrate the first harvest while dancing around a fire and waving a handkerchief. I still recall the refrain:

> Nasanmönkh, counterrevolutionary
> Suddenly at midnight thought of climbing the chimney
> Lost his life by jumping to the ground
> How hateful committing suicide to hide his crimes.

His daughter in Leningrad could not return. Another daughter was in Hohhot. His act was branded reactionary, suicide being deemed a deliberate rejection of the Party, so no funeral was allowed. Only his wife and brother were allowed to pick up his corpse. It was taken to an unmarked burial mound south of Hohhot between the Da Heihe and Xiao Heihe rivers and buried without ceremony.

On many later occasions, Ji Zhi mentioned the suicide to illustrate the sharpness of class struggle on our campus. Several friends and I saw it as a tragedy. Anyone with a heart should at least have felt sympathy for his family. But many students simply joked at his expense.

"Marx's Beard Is Like My Pubic Hair"

In the fall of 1964, pressure mounted to target struggle objects among students in the urban counterpart of the rural Socialist Education Movement. A document issued by the Central authorities, "The Socialist Education Movement in Higher Education Institutions" (Gaoxiao Shejiao Yundong), ordered struggle sessions for reactionary students.

Li Guixian, a senior Russian-language student we called "Da Gui," was denounced for demeaning our revolutionary ancestor Karl Marx. A Han from Chifeng city in eastern Inner Mongolia, Da Gui was said to have said, "Marx's beard is like my pubic hair [*qiumao*]." If this seems ludicrous, the charges were deadly serious.

Here's what actually happened. One day, the Russian class Youth League Branch Secretary Zhao Decheng, while shaving, with white bubbles covering his face, looked admiringly in the mirror and asked aloud, "With this beard, do I look like Marx?" Da Gui, who happened to be at his side, responded irreverently, "Your beard looks like my pubic hair." In the supercharged political atmosphere of the Socialist Education Movement, this mockery of the secretary's pretensions was turned into a counterrevolutionary attack on

Marx. Zhao convened a class meeting to humiliate Da Gui. One classmate after another criticized him, pointing to his rich peasant class origins, his disdain for the Party, and his grumbling that political study interfered with language learning. Da Gui was expelled from the college.

We Will Collectively Help Comrade Cheng Tiejun

During the Socialist Education Movement, a plan for criticism in each class was drawn up at the department level by the faculty in charge of the Youth League, Liu Pu and Gao Shuhua.[21] But most events were organized below their level. In April 1965, the class's Youth League Branch Secretary Wang Yumin (the only Party member in our class) set a two-week period for struggle and self-criticism. "Tomorrow," she would announce, "we will collectively help Comrade So-and-So." In the Party's lexicon, one subjected to being "helped" was considered low in ideological consciousness or as having committed errors. Wang Yumin, a Hebei native, targeted five people: Wang Jinglin, Zhang Daren, Liu Dongsheng, Liu Luxi, and myself. Luxi was the only girl in the cohort. Our supposed errors ranged from petit bourgeois individualism and liberalism to hewing to petit bourgeois values. I was the main target.

Wang Yumin had arranged for politically reliable, ambitious, and vulnerable students to spy on the "backward" elements. She had Zhao Xilan report on Zhang Daren. Later Xilan and Daren fell in love and almost married! Luxi was assigned to shadow me. Luxi and I had good impressions of each other. Some classmates suspected (wrongly) that we were dating. But we were friends.

If the pettiness of the charges today seems ludicrous, the potential to destroy careers and lives was anything but laughable. The expulsion of Da Gui made clear the stakes.

Criticism meetings were held in our large classroom in April 1965. The desks were arranged in a circle. The main speaker spoke from the rostrum to the forty students in attendance. The first four days went quickly as each of the accused confessed and was admonished without serious punishment. In my case alone, teachers were also present. In addition, Liu Pu and Gao Shuhua, the department's student Party branch secretary and the deputy secretary, both attended, lending weight to the case.

Wang Yumin chaired. She announced the purpose, outlined the process, and stated the charges:

In our class, reflections of the class struggle are manifest. Already four classmates have been criticized and made self-criticisms. This will further our revolutionary cause and help students to improve. The final case is that of Cheng Tiejun. His problems have accumulated over many years. He has many mistaken ideas about the Three Red Banners. All of us participated in the Great Leap Forward. We know that it contributed greatly to our nation's advance. But Cheng Tiejun does not share our view. Not only does he have deviant thoughts himself; he also tries to win others to his ideas. He must make a self-criticism.

After Wang Yumin presented the case, I criticized myself for having insufficiently studied Mao's writings; I had one-sidedly looked at the shortcomings of the Three Red Banners, underestimating the achievements of the Great Leap Forward. But I insisted that I had never opposed the Party line and Mao Zedong Thought. Proof of my sincerity lay in the fact that I had voluntarily provided my exhaustive autobiography to the Party secretary.

I summarized the problems addressed in my autobiography, taking a whole day, morning and afternoon. I alone spoke during this time. The room was tense. During the lunch break, not a single classmate dared speak to me.

The four students who had previously been criticized were ordered to attack me first. At least two of them tried to minimize the damage. The other two were a bit harsher, but I understood that everyone had to say something.

After others criticized my attitude, Liu Pu spoke. His tone was sharp. "We have long sought to help Cheng Tiejun, but he has refused to confront his problems. He remains skeptical about the achievements of the Three Red Banners. He is very cunning. From middle school to college, he has always resisted the Party line."

Gao Shuhua's criticism was more sophisticated, drawing on his training in Marxism. He said that my errors reflected the general class struggle on campus and beyond. He cited my letters to show the necessity for self-criticism. Gao also cited my case as a reflection of the class struggle in our college, but his tone was less harsh than that of Liu Pu. Listening to the criticisms, I was surprised to have no fears, but I was amazed that people would raise such petty things to the level of higher principle, accusing me of alienating myself from the league and the Party.

Luckily, although I was singled out as having the most serious problems in my class, no formal punishment was meted out. I was never labeled a class enemy or expelled or locked up.

Following the criticism, I tried to perform better (*biaoxian*) and show loyalty to the Party, or at least that I was a good person. But I was depressed. I tried to find release. Whenever I could, I went to the library to read English and Chinese novels. I read Dickens's *David Copperfield* and Mark Twain's *Tom Sawyer*. I was particularly moved by Harriet Beecher Stowe's *Uncle Tom's*

Cabin and even translated it for friends. I continued to read Marxist classics. I also tried to steel myself through physical labor. I felt that I had been unjustly criticized. But I also believed that I could improve myself by "serving the people."

It was the summer of 1965, and a new wave in the campaign to "Learn from Comrade Lei Feng," the martyred PLA hero promoted by Mao as a model citizen in 1964, had begun. The masses were encouraged to emulate his selflessness and devotion to Mao by performing good deeds. I don't know whether I was subconsciously imitating Lei Feng, but I asked to work on a small flower garden that had fallen into disarray to improve the look of the campus. By working and chatting with the other workers and the manager, I established good relations with them. They provided seeds and bushes and taught me how to plant them. I did this for a year from summer 1965 to summer 1966. Eventually, the pole in the middle of the garden became the loudspeaker's broadcast center. Later, during the Cultural Revolution, people sat there surrounded by flowers listening to directives from the Party Center or the latest quotation from Chairman Mao. Feeling that I had made a modest contribution, I recalled the Chinese saying: previous generations plant trees, later generations enjoy the shade—*qian ren zhong shu, hou ren cheng liang.*

As I sought to find a place for myself on campus and in society, the mood of struggle was deepening in Hohhot and throughout the country, with the most intense fighting taking place in Beijing. As the Tang poet Xu Hong put it, the wind blows before the approaching storm—*shanyu yulai feng man lou.*

3

The Hour of Rebellion:
The Cultural Revolution Comes to
Inner Mongolia

Ulanhu's Troubles

Each morning throughout the spring of 1966, the Teachers' College loud-speaker broadcast a joint editorial by the *People's Daily*, the *Liberation Army Daily*, and *Red Flag*, the latter the Party's theoretical journal. This was how we first learned of the criticism of writers Deng Tuo, Wu Han, and Liao Mosha (branded the "three-family village," or *san jia cun*), then of the rising chorus of attacks on Beijing Party secretary, mayor, and Politburo member Peng Zhen, along with Luo Ruiqing (PLA chief of staff), Lu Dingyi (director of the CCP Propaganda Department), and Yang Shangkun (head of the CCP General Office).[1] As early as 1962, we students in the borderland area had become aware of the public polemics between China and the Soviet Union. In 1966, for the first time, we recognized clearly that the stakes were high and the divisions sharp not only in international affairs but also in charting China's domestic future.

In May, these ranking veteran leaders were denounced as an "anti-Party clique" and stripped of their positions. The fall of Peng, Luo, Lu, and Yang, "the four-family shop" (*si jia dian*), orchestrated by Lin Biao and Mao, was the prelude to a full-scale attack on revisionism at the highest level of the Party. Beginning with a critique of Soviet revisionism formulated during the Chinese-Soviet polemics of the early 1960s, in the course of the Socialist Education Movement, Mao focused the attack on Khrushchev-type revisionism in China. This meant ousting those at the highest levels of the Party and army who were "taking the capitalist road" and ensuring the cultivation of revolutionary successors.[2] A storm was brewing that would sweep across the nation and recast my future.

The increasing military tension with the Soviet Union and the MPR in the midst of US escalation in the Vietnam War had profound implications both for China's military and for its Inner Mongolia borderland. In October 1964, during a three-level cadre conference (region, league or city, and banner or county), while Ulanhu was in East Germany leading a Chinese friendship delegation, Li Xuefeng, first secretary of the CCP North China Bureau, came to Inner Mongolia for three days and addressed senior cadres and military officers. Li harshly criticized Ulanhu without naming him: "Inner Mongolia is like a pool of stagnant water, its leader is like a walking dead man, never emphasizing class struggle." At one point, he insulted the Mongols by asking, "What does the word *Meng* in *Nei Menggu* [Inner Mongolia] mean? Doesn't it mean muddle headed?" He then pressed, "Don't be *meng* anymore, rise up and fight!"[3]

Under Li's prodding, most of Ulanhu's senior Han colleagues, including the secretaries of the Inner Mongolia Party Secretariat, Wang Duo and Quan Xingyuan, and many members of the standing committee of the Inner Mongolia Party Committee, began to distance themselves from, and even actively undermine, Ulanhu's authority. Some sent secret reports to higher authorities about Ulanhu's alleged Mongol nationalist activities. The attack on Ulanhu was spearheaded by senior Han Party and military officials who had long served the Ulanhu administration. Ulanhu was accused of not only protecting Mongol herders from becoming targets of class struggle but also, and more seriously, for oppressing the Han.

Facing mounting pressures, in January 1966, Ulanhu created the Acting Party Standing Committee (*dai chang wei*), appointing his most trusted allies to key positions—nine Mongols (six of them members of his own Tumed "tribe" and including his wife, son, and other relatives) and three Han. In February, he streamlined government departments into five large committees. Four were led by Tumed Mongols, including his eldest son, Buhe, who headed the Culture Committee. He also appointed Hao Fan, a Tumed Mongol from the Central Nationalities Institute in Beijing as deputy secretary-general of the General Office of the Party Committee; Yun Liwen, his wife, as acting director of the Policy Research Office of the Party Committee; Yun Shiying, a Tumed Mongol, as deputy director of the Political and Legal Team of the Party Committee; and Chen Bingyu, a Tumed Mongol, as acting director of the Organization Department of the Party Committee.

In addition to the Party Committee and the departments at the autonomous region level, most municipal and league Party Committee leaders were reshuffled and controlled by his protégés.[4] Inner Mongolia's familial politics exceeded even those of the Central exemplars, Mao Zedong, Lin Biao, and Liu Shaoqi, all of whose wives and close relatives held high positions in the Party. Unlike the Center, however, in Inner Mongolia, the politics of family was entangled with ethnicity, which would play out in new ways as tensions rose and loyalty took on meanings of life or death.

Ulanhu drew on both his Mongol and his Han allies and associates to strengthen his position in the face of serious challenges. The Tumed Mongol officials he appointed had come of age in Yan'an, where many spent the years from 1939 to 1945. Ulanhu's strategy revealed fault lines among Mongols. In Ulanhu's view, Mongol officials from eastern Inner Mongolia were tainted by their association with Japan-dominated Manchuguo and had weaker Communist credentials than his Tumed colleagues. Some who hailed from agricultural and semiagricultural regions and had experienced the land reform of 1947–1948 did not fully appreciate Ulanhu's insistence on the "three nos and two benefits" policy that had been implemented in the pastoral region. Influenced by Mao's concepts of class struggle and egalitarianism, some Eastern Mongol leaders supported the demand of Han farmers for equal land rights that had been put forward during the land reform and reiterated during the Socialist Education Movement. Rejecting Ulanhu's "three nos," they insisted that pastoral society also be governed by class relations and principles of class struggle. This might have been unproblematic if Inner Mongolia was monoethnic, but unlike Ulanhu, who made efforts to shield the pastoral Mongols from the class struggle in a multiethnic Inner Mongolia, their class sensibility played into the hands of the North China Bureau, which was looking for every piece of evidence to prove Ulanhu to be anti-Mao.[5]

Ulanhu's effort to restore and protect Inner Mongolia's original territory also prompted criticism. Although the Inner Mongolia Autonomous Government was founded in 1947, it had taken seven years, until 1954, to incorporate the former Suiyuan province and two more years before Alasha and Ejine banners were brought into the autonomous region. Meanwhile, large areas of Mongol land were lost to other provinces: Liaoning (Harachin West and Mongoljin banners), Jilin (Gorlos Front banner), and Heilongjiang (Gorlos Rear and Dürved banners, the latter of which hosted the Daqing oil field).

In the early 1960s, however, domestic border clashes multiplied as some neighboring provinces began to challenge the raison d'être of Inner Mongolian territorial autonomy. To land-hungry Chinese provinces, especially in the wake of the famine, the size of Inner Mongolia appeared illegitimate. In a desperate attempt to halt land grabbing at the expense of Mongols, at a December 1965 preparatory meeting to mark the twentieth anniversary of the founding of the Inner Mongolia Autonomous Region in May 1967, Ulanhu ordered reprinting of Mao's 1935 "Proclamation of the Central Soviet Government to the People of Inner Mongolia" and distributed a copy to each participant. Mao's proclamation was Ulanhu's answer to questions of why Inner

Mongolia had such a large territory. The following passages from the proclamation raised many eyebrows:

1. We maintain that the six leagues, twenty-four sections, and forty-nine banners of Inner Mongolia, Chahar, the two sections of Tumute, as well as the whole area of the three special banners in Ningxia, whether they have changed their status into counties or have been designated as grassland, should be returned to the Inner Mongolian people as part of their territory. The titles of the three administrative provinces of Re[he], Cha[har] and Sui[yuan] and their de facto administrative offices should be abolished. Under no circumstances should other nationalities be allowed to occupy the land of the Mongolian nation or expropriate it under various pretexts.

2. We maintain that the Inner Mongolian people have the right to solve all their internal problems themselves, and no one else is entitled to interfere by force with the life, customs, religion, morality, and other rights of the Inner Mongolian nation. At the same time, the Inner Mongolian nation can organize in whatever way it pleases. It has the right, in accordance with the principle of independence, to shape its own life and set up its own government; it has the right to form federal ties with other nations, and it also has the right to remain completely separate. In a word, a nation is deserving of respect, and at the same time all nations are equal.[6]

Ulanhu argued that Inner Mongolia's territoriality was a restoration of historical Mongolian land and that it had been promised by the supreme leader Mao at a time when support of the Mongols was critical to Communist victory in the first Guomindang-CCP Civil War and the subsequent anti-Japanese resistance.[7] In January 1966, 1,250 copies of the text were distributed to Party and government organizations at the banner or county level and above.[8] Mao was being quoted everywhere throughout China at this time, yet Ulanhu's act aroused suspicions among North China Bureau authorities and among many non-Mongol officials in the autonomous region who saw it as an aggressive Mongol assertion of autonomy.

From the time of the Socialist Education Movement, Gao Jinming provided secret reports to the North China Bureau detailing Ulanhu's "nationalist deviation." Gao, an ethnic Manchu from Liaoning province, had come to Inner Mongolia in the 1940s, eventually rising to become a secretary of the Inner Mongolia Secretariat, equivalent to a deputy Party secretary of Inner Mongolia.[9] In early 1966, as the executive secretary (*changwu shuji*) of the Party's secretariat, he felt slighted by Ulanhu. Quan Xingyuan, another disgruntled secretary, and a Han, also filed secret reports. He clashed with Ulanhu in a speech to the Socialist Education Movement Work Corps at the Medical College in 1965. These reports provided useful information for Li Xuefeng, first

FIGURE 4 Cartoon depicting Ulanhu's alleged encroachment on territories of neighboring provinces, 1967

secretary of the North China Bureau. Though second secretary of the North China Bureau, Ulanhu was in fact Li's superior in the Party hierarchy, as he was an alternate member of the Politburo, while Li was not. Ulanhu's protection of Inner Mongolia from the North China Bureau's intervention in the Socialist Education Movement had angered Li.

On April 30, 1966, the North China Bureau sent an investigation team led by Xie Xuegong, the Tianjin Party secretary and an executive secretary of the North China Bureau, to investigate Ulanhu.[10] Xie, who was a close ally of Li Xuefeng with strong ties to Jiang Qing, Mao's wife, had risen to power during the Great Leap Forward. In 1958 Xie had introduced Mao to the Great Leap Forward model county of Xushui, in Hebei, and he had recently led a Socialist Education Movement work team in Inner Mongolia.[11]

Investigators ordered the Inner Mongolia Party Committee to submit the entire dossier of Ulanhu's documents, records, publications, and speeches, an enormous file including all major statements since the 1947 founding of the Inner Mongolia Autonomous Government. Leaders of Inner Mongolia were summoned to Beijing to review the situation in the autonomous region at this critical moment of inner-Party conflict.

An enlarged Politburo meeting held in Beijing between May 4 and 24 exposed the depths of the divisions at the highest levels of power.[12] Peng Zhen, Politburo member and mayor of Beijing, who had been under attack since April, was the focal point of criticism. The "May 16th Circular," revised by Mao, summed up the condemnation of Peng and established a new Central Cultural Revolution Group (Zhongyang wenhua geming xiaozu, or CCRG) led by Chen Boda with Kang Sheng as adviser and Jiang Qing and five of her associates among its members. From its formation to its abolition in April 1969, the CCRG was Mao's executive arm that ran the Cultural Revolution, working closely with Premier Zhou Enlai. Zhou was not formally a member, but he attended CCRG meetings and even chaired many of them. The CCRG denounced as revisionists "those representatives of the bourgeoisie who have sneaked into the Party, the government, the army and various cultural circles."[13]

Warning in a May 18 speech of "the smell of gunpowder in the air," Defense Minister Lin Biao charged four senior leaders with conspiring to overthrow Mao and his radical lieutenants. The four—Peng Zhen, Lu Dingyi, Luo Ruiqing, and Yang Shangkun—were vilified and dismissed from their posts.[14] In attacking them, Lin extolled Mao's genius: "Every sentence of Chairman Mao's works is a truth; one single sentence of his surpasses ten thousand of ours.... Whoever is against him shall be punished by the entire Party and the whole country." A storm was brewing again, now at the highest levels of the Party, government, and army.

From May 22, the North China Bureau convened a marathon conference at the Qianmen Hotel in Beijing. The conference featured sessions focusing on specific provinces and metropolises within the North China region. Ulanhu was responsible for organizing the Inner Mongolia session, and Gao Jinming was charged with running its day-to-day affairs. For the first few days, the Inner Mongolia session "studied" the documents issued by the Center, such as the "May 16th Circular" and Lin Biao's speech on May 18 discussing plots and coups within and outside China, setting the ideological ground for the subsequent attack in Inner Mongolia and throughout the country.

The First Big-Character Poster at Teachers' College

On May 18, two days after the release of the "May 16th Circular," Ji Zhi presided over a mass meeting in the Teachers' College dining hall. The Party secretary and president called on students and faculty members to participate in the Cultural Revolution by studying the documents emanating from Beijing. The campaign seemed safely distant, more political brouhaha from the capital. No one suggested criticizing local leaders or even local intellectuals or blacklisted elements, the ritual whipping boys of earlier campaigns. We students were unaware of the struggle at the top involving the North China Bureau and Ulanhu. But no one could remain oblivious to the mounting political tensions in the weeks and months that followed.

On June 1 at eight in the evening, Mao broadcast to the nation his euphoric personal endorsement of the first big-character poster by Nie Yuanzi, Party secretary of Peking University's philosophy department, whose May 25 broadside ignited the Cultural Revolution at Peking University. The same day, a *People's Daily* editorial broadcast called on people to break with the "four olds" who had created the old ruling classes and "sweep away all monsters and freaks." On June 2, a *People's Daily* commentator denounced the Peking University leadership as a "die-hard anticommunist fortress" and published Nie's poster with an article praising it.

The Teachers' College leadership immediately grasped the implications of the events at Peking University. On the afternoon of June 2, Party Secretary Ji Zhi and Zhang Xueyao, director of the Department of Political Education, summoned Gao Shuhua, Russian-language instructor and acting Youth League secretary of the Foreign Languages Department, to the office. A few days earlier, Gao had criticized their leadership at the foreign languages faculty meeting. The leaders asked Gao to monitor the students' state of mind and activities and promised to promote him to Youth League secretary of the college at the conclusion of the movement. They also warned Gao pointedly not to repeat the errors of the bourgeois rightists of 1957, who fell after criticizing the leadership during the Hundred Flowers Movement. They had not gauged their man.

In the foreign languages faculty office, four colleagues awaited Gao's return from the meeting. Gao quickly drafted a big-character poster. Three of them, Liu Pu, Liu Zhen, and Lou Jili, like Gao all young faculty members, agreed to sign their names with him. The fourth, Wang Lü'an, the department chair and Party secretary, declined to join them.[15]

On the morning of June 3, walking to class after breakfast, I saw a big-character poster on the Foreign Languages Department's billboard.

Just nine hundred characters long, the poster was written in Gao's bold hand on three pink sheets to form a six-foot-long document. Seeing a big-character poster for the first time since my arrival in Inner Mongolia, I noted its resemblance to the large death-sentence verdicts I had seen posted on city walls with red crosses through the names of the criminals. The title barely hinted at its explosive contents: "Comments on Ji Zhi's May 18 'Mobilization Report.'"[16]

"On May 18 Ji Zhi delivered a 'mobilization report' to teachers and students of our college." The poster went on, "Whether this report was to mobilize or to pour cold water on the revolutionary masses requires some research." Demolishing the speech for its lackluster support for the Cultural Revolution, it concluded:

> The numerous facts noted above eloquently prove that, during the Cultural Revolution, Ji Zhi is pursuing a revisionist line, a line that is in opposition to that of the Party Center and Chairman Mao. We resolutely oppose it!
>
> All revolutionary comrades should bravely stand up, hold high the great red banner of Mao Zedong Thought, defend the Party Center, defend Chairman Mao!
>
> At the same time, we should also be one hundred times more vigilant of all conspiracies of the ghosts and monsters beside us, not giving them a chance to fish in troubled waters.
>
> Sweep away all cow monsters and snake spirits [*niugui sheshen*]! Carry the Great Proletarian Cultural Revolution to the end!

The message packed a punch. Faculty and students were being misled. Sitting passively in class studying or reflecting on distant intellectual debates, we had forgotten to examine the political situation on campus. The poster sharply criticized Ji Zhi, branding his speech, which was ostensibly to mobilize students to participate in the Cultural Revolution, an effort to suppress the movement by channeling it into the study of documents.

Tall and charismatic, Gao Shuhua was from a railroad worker's family in Hohhot. A 1958 graduate of Erzhong, and in 1962 of Inner Mongolia Teachers' College, he became a Youth League member at age fourteen and a Party member at nineteen. At twenty-five, he was a rising star in Inner Mongolian politics and cultural criticism. In 1965 he had published criticism of the Soviet writer Mikhail Sholokhov's *And Quiet Flows the Don*, and the Inner Mongolian writer Malchinhuu's *On the Vast Grassland* (*Zai Mangmang de Caoyuan shang*), closely following the Party line in denouncing the Soviet and Inner Mongolian writers as revisionists whose writings masked class struggle. Grasping the significance of the change of political winds, Gao was one of the first in Inner Mongolia with the courage to act boldly on this recognition.

Gao's poster set off a tidal wave that started at Teachers' College then coursed throughout the Autonomous Region.[17] Like many others that appeared across China at this time, it was modeled on Nie Yuanzi's May 25 poster at Peking University. Encouraged by cultural radicals—including Kang Sheng; his wife, Cao Yi'ou; and others close to Mao and Lin Biao—Nie and six of her colleagues had denounced the Peking University mobilization speech by Lu Ping as suppression of the masses (*zhenya qunzhong*), not allowing the people to lift the cover of the Party Committee (*jiekai dangwei de gaizi*). Nie's poster had immediately drawn fire from supporters of the Peking University

FIGURE 5 Russian-language training class graduation photo, July 18, 1961: Gao Shuhua (left in the back row), Liu Pu (right in the middle row), and Zong Fuhua (second left in the front row)

Party Committee and higher Party officials, only to be silenced by Mao's June 1 radio message heralding her poster as "a declaration of the Paris Commune of the sixties of the twentieth century."[18]

Gao had impeccable establishment credentials, and he had personally criticized me and other teachers and students during the Socialist Education Movement. This made all the more dramatic his initiative to launch the rebel movement on campus. As he later explained, he found Ji Zhi's attempt to buy him off with the promise of promotion mixed with threat and the order to spy on the students profoundly immoral. He sensed that Teachers' College was no different from Peking University and Ji Zhi was just like Lu Ping as denounced in the *People's Daily* editorial who "as the 'Party Secretary' of Peking University, in the name of 'organization,' threatened students and cadres who had risen in revolution, saying that if they did not obey the order of this handful of people, they violated discipline and they were opposed to the Party." Gao Shuhua "shuddered at" this thought, and "realized the gravity of the situation."[19]

Within hours of its posting on the morning of June 3, the college was in turmoil. Hundreds of students and faculty pressed into the main corridor of the foreign languages building to read the poster, shouting at those ahead of them to move quickly so that others would have a chance to read.

I observed two very different responses to the poster among faculty, who were overwhelmingly Han. Many younger teachers were excited by the call to arms. But experienced teachers, often survivors or victims of earlier campaigns that targeted intellectuals and "rightists," looked anxious. In fact, many were terrified. Reading the poster, their faces turned white. Meanwhile, scores of students, younger faculty, and staff rushed to find paper, ink, and paste to write their own posters. When the supply of colored paper was exhausted, people turned to old newspapers.

That day, and in the months and years to come, no one would teach and no one would listen. In June, college and middle school classes across the country halted so that faculty and students could devote their full time to the Cultural Revolution. This was an extension of the work during the Socialist Education Movement, when many faculty and students left campus to redirect the countryside toward revolution. This time, however, the primary targets were the Party leaders of the college, Hohhot city, and Inner Mongolia: those in authority taking the capitalist road, those who insisted on production, on work rather than implementing Mao's instruction to engage in class struggle. I was in my third year of college, but from that moment to the day I graduated in July 1967, I never took another class. It would be a decade or more before many colleges and universities resumed regular classes.

At this time, unbeknownst to us, almost all the top Inner Mongolian leaders were in Beijing for the investigation of Ulanhu. The Inner Mongolia Party Committee had been left in the hands of two secretaries of the Party Secretariat, Biligbaatar and Wang Yilun, the former a Tumed Mongol and the latter a Han.

The principal leaders of the Culture Committee (Wenwei), the umbrella organization in charge of universities in Inner Mongolia—Buhe (Ulanhu's eldest son), Zhao Gerui (a Tumed Mongol), Han Ming, and Sun Peiqing—were in Hohhot. They came to Teachers' College on June 3, advising Ji Zhi to remain calm and to handle the situation firmly but tactfully. That same day, Gao Jinming called Hohhot from Beijing twice to transmit Li Xuefeng's instruction that student and faculty activity be contained within the campus.[20] For the time being, the Party was firmly in charge. But would it be the party of Ulanhu who had dominated Inner Mongolian affairs for two decades or the party of his challengers led by Li Xuefeng?

Ji Zhi responded to the poster attack by halting all classes and issuing orders to the administrative office to dispatch a truck to bring all paper from the bookstore for poster making. Brushes and ink were provided and cooks supplied their entire flour reserve to make paste for mounting posters in a huge cauldron. Everything was free. The big-character poster was the newest weapon in the ideological struggle that Mao personally endorsed. Big-character posters had developed throughout the long twentieth century. In the Cultural Revolution, however, they became omnipresent, suggesting the possibility of a new form of expression with protodemocratic and mobilization potential. Rather than the anonymous ballot cast on behalf of a candidate or party every several years as in democratic countries, people began to express their views and reach out to others with posters of their own creation. This meant the emergence of a politics that could, under certain circumstances, challenge the Party's monopoly on power from below. But it was also one that could be manipulated by Party and army leaders to suppress dissent. At a time of fracturing of the Party, no political figure could assume that the Party's imprimatur provided a guarantee of security.

The college's Party secretary who had sought to channel the movement in safe directions by quieting protest now sought to place himself in its vanguard. Within hours, the campus was plastered with posters. That afternoon, some third-year students in the Chinese language and literature department raised the slogan "Defend the College Party Committee," followed by posters by students from departments of mathematics, political education, and Chinese language and literature, supporting Ji Zhi.[21] But many others mirrored the original Gao Shuhua poster or Nie Yuanzi's poster that had inspired it. Reading the *People's Daily* and listening to radio broadcasts, it was clear that Mao supported the attack on the Peking University Party leadership that had been touched off by Nie's poster. Everyone looked to Beijing for cues.

In Hohhot, Teachers' College took the lead, but within days every campus was awash with posters. As space became scarce, campus workers came up with the brilliant idea of setting up posts in the courtyard and connecting them with wires from which posters could be hung. Between the main building and the administrative building, a hundred wires went up, each fifty feet long.

One tragedy occurred at this time. The college electrician fell from his stepladder while setting up posts, installing power lines, and putting up lights; students carried him home, but his head had struck the cement during the fall and he soon died. Xiao Zhang, who was in his late twenties, left a wife and young son. He was the first, and perhaps most innocent, victim in the frenzy of the Cultural Revolution in Inner Mongolia. His funeral on campus was one of the last acts supported by people across the political spectrum.

The hour of rebellion was at hand.

The First Political Cartoon

What to do? I felt as if a war were unfolding around me. Despite—or perhaps because of—the criticism I had received, I found it impossible to take no position. My response was to put my artistic skill to practical use. I drew the first

FIGURE 6 Reproduction of a 1966 cartoon based on memory. © Cheng Tiejun 2020

cartoon lampooning the college Party secretary, portraying Ji Zhi as a policeman standing on a box at a crossroads directing traffic with four long arms. Each wielded a baton on which was written "go this way" or "go that way."

My classmates Zhai Ximin and Zhang Daren watched in amusement as I drew, contributing ideas such as the cow monsters and snake spirits writhing beneath Ji's feet. These monsters were the people Ji sought to protect, directing people to look everywhere except at conditions in our college. My friend Zhang Daren accepted my invitation to join me in signing it.

I was proud of the artistic skill that I had been honing since childhood. After graduating from No. 5 Middle School I had briefly considered studying fine arts in college until one of my teachers put an end to my fantasy.

Many similar drawings followed my cartoon. Fine-arts students produced more sophisticated cartoons. But people remembered mine not only because it was the first but also because I had recently been attacked as a politically "backward" student during the Socialist Education Movement. Naive to the possible consequences of my action, I was emboldened by the fact that Gao Shuhua enjoyed strong support on campus and his initiative seemed aligned with signals coming from on high in Beijing.

The cartoon was a political statement that also let me vent personal grievances. I was far from alone in feeling discontent with officially orchestrated repression. There were numerous scapegoats, such as Da Gui, the Russian-language student expelled for his alleged quip "Marx's beard is like my pubic hair." Mao's call to attack the Party Committee, as filtered through the Nie Yuanzi and Gao Shuhua posters, was exhilarating to many who felt oppressed and silenced. The process underway seemed to open a path to push aside "reactionary" Party Committees to carry on the revolution (*tikai dangwei nao geming*). It seemed natural to us to rebel. I didn't think much about the personal or political consequences in the event of a U-turn.

On June 5, the *People's Daily* published the editorial "To Become Proletarian Revolutionaries, or Bourgeois Royalists?" (*Zuo Wuchan Jieji Gemingpai, Haishi Zuo Zichanjieji Baohuangpai?*). Students, intellectuals and workers throughout the country promptly declared themselves "proletarian revolutionaries." For many people like myself, this was an invitation to air long suppressed grievances against arbitrary authority and abuses of power. In the passion of the moment, many dared to criticize official policies that flouted popular interests. However, the Party organizations saw us as troublemakers, rebelling (*zaofan*) against authorities, not least because many of us had troubled backgrounds as rightists or bad elements and had been criticized in political movements. To us, however, rebellion was quintessentially revolutionary, sanctioned by Mao himself as in a 1939 comment: "There are innumerable principles of Marxism, but in the final analysis they can be summed up in one sentence: 'To rebel is justified.'"[22]

At this stage, we called ourselves "revolutionary leftists"; it would be another two months before *rebel* became a positive factional term openly supported by Mao.

The messages from the Center were by no means unambiguous. The *People's Daily* published two important pieces of information on June 4. The first announced the reorganization of the Beijing Municipal Party Committee. Li Xuefeng, the new Party secretary, replaced Peng Zhen, who had been Ulanhu's powerful ally. Li, the main force seeking to topple Ulanhu and to suppress the rebellion on campus, was also elevated to alternate membership in the Politburo. The second relayed the decision by the new Beijing Party Committee to sack Peking University President Lu Ping, who had been the main target of the Nie poster, and to send a work team to the university.

On June 5, loudspeakers informed students that the Inner Mongolia Party Committee and the Culture Committee led by Buhe were dispatching a work team to each of the seven colleges in Hohhot to strengthen Party leadership. All revolutionary students were ordered to welcome the teams. Meanwhile, rumors flew not only about what had happened on Beijing campuses but also about the meetings that were in progress that would determine the fate of Ulanhu and his associates in the Inner Mongolia leadership.

Central Radio was the source for the latest political ideas from Beijing, and with the Party apparatus apparently paralyzed, it seemed to speak directly for Mao. When the voice of the broadcaster grew stern, people gathered below the loudspeaker hanging high above. Many also enjoyed the flowers in the garden and the peach trees behind the science building. As people gathered, I was reminded that I had made a modest contribution in planting the garden.

The Work Team in Command

After the big-character posters criticizing the Party and other leaders surfaced in the first few days of June 1966, the Party organization threw its formidable power into the counterattack against its critics. Liu Shaoqi, China's president, who had led the early Socialist Education Movement in the countryside, was responsible for guiding the movement during Mao's absence from the capital. He sought to criticize revisionism (meaning mainly rightist intellectuals) and bring under Party control a movement that threatened the Party leadership. With Party leadership on the defensive in the wake of Nie's poster, Liu authorized the dispatch of more than four hundred work teams with more than ten thousand members to Beijing college campuses and key government agencies charged with finance, trade, industry, and communications. Everywhere they reasserted Party leadership by bringing student and other rebel movements under control.

Hohhot quickly followed suit. On June 7, a twenty-member work team arrived at Teachers' College. Students who initially supported the Gao Shuhua poster warmly welcomed them, anticipating support for our cause. Their leader Gu Dong, a Shanxi native and a Han, was president and deputy Party secretary of the Inner Mongolia Industrial College. In his midforties, he was unsmiling in a Mao suit and leather shoes. Gu had been deputy director of a Socialist Education Movement work team in the countryside.

On June 8, a rally held in the Foreign Languages Department denounced Ji Zhi and Wang Lü'an for persecuting Gao Shuhua and his three colleagues.[23] Within hours, the Inner Mongolia Party Committee, bent on bringing the campus under control, sent in reinforcements. Chen Juesheng, deputy director of the Hohhot Culture Bureau, arrived with nineteen people to become the deputy leader of the enlarged team under Gu Dong.[24] The work team immediately convened a collegewide rally to announce that Ji Zhi had stopped work in all his official posts inside and outside the Party. This appeared to be a huge victory for activists, who had criticized Ji and the Party Committee beginning with the Gao Shuhua poster. It was the first case in Inner Mongolia in which a college Party secretary was brought down by protest from rebellious teachers and students.

However, the work team had not come to support the critics, or even to investigate their charges, but to crush the rebellion and restore Party authority. Calling themselves firefighters (*xiaofangdui*), they set out to squelch the flames of criticism. In fact, the firefighter trope had been used by Liu Shaoqi and Deng Xiaoping in a meeting on June 3 that issued the directive to send work teams to school and college campuses that had become rebel strongholds. The work teams hewed to the Eight Central Points (*Zhongyang Ba Tiao*) issued by Liu and Deng in Beijing: "Differentiate inside from outside," "take care not to reveal secrets," "big-character posters must not go out into the street," "do not parade," "do not seek to make connections" (*chuanlian*), "do not organize large-scale denunciation sessions," "do not surround the residence of black gang members," and "do not beat or slander people." In the words of a July 13 Politburo resolution concerning Beijing's middle schools, the central task of work teams was to "restore the leading role of the Party branch."[25]

The work team, having put Ji Zhi aside, openly warned the students: "Watch how you jump; you are newborn calves, unafraid of tigers (*chusheng niudu bupa hu*). But do you know what happened in 1957? This movement is like that one!" The 1957 anti-rightist movement had consolidated Party power in the wake of popular protest. Many students grew fearful as work team members entered departments and began compiling lists of names. They classified students in three categories: revolutionary leftists who supported the Party Committee and denounced Gao Shuhua and his colleagues; middle elements who blindly followed Gao Shuhua but did not attack the Party Committee strongly; and reactionary rightists who were die-hard followers of Gao Shuhua including some such as Cheng Tiejun and Zhang Daren, who had been criticized for a rightist tendency during the Socialist Education Movement.

During the weeks following the appearance of the Gao Shuhua poster, 90 percent of Teachers' College students and faculty had mounted posters. Under work team pressure, however, many students and faculty renounced everything they had said in their original poster. Student after student repented, criticizing themselves first and then other poster writers, especially the original four.

To sharpen the attack, the work team circulated damning information about the class backgrounds and families of the remaining die-hard students.

Naturally, they targeted me because of the cartoon I had drawn, attacking its message and deriding my claims to "poor peasant" class origin based on my father's class status.

Each student's family background had been checked during the college admission process, so all records were available. The work team circulated details about my father's service under General Fu Zuoyi. I found this all the more irritating because I was distancing myself from my father. In fact, I had criticized him in my autobiography. Now I was forced to suffer because of his personal history. The Communist credentials of my mother Sun Wenhua were also questioned because she had not maintained active contacts with the CCP organization during the period when Raoyang was under Japanese occupation. Known as *zixing tuodang* (giving up Party membership of her own accord), this meant that my family background had a "black mark." I came to hate the blood pedigree theory (*xuetong lun*) that the work team repeatedly used to discredit critics on the basis of the class status of parents and relatives.

As in Beijing and throughout the country, work teams assigned "revolutionary leftist" students from each department to secretly copy posters to secure evidence against "reactionary rightist" students as in the 1957 antirightist movement. They kept a notebook, recording the most incriminating passages in wall posters, placing them in the student's file, as evidence of anti-Party activity. Under pressure, most "revolutionary leftists" recanted.

The North China Bureau's Attack on Ulanhu

From June 2, 1966, the North China Bureau Conference attacked Ulanhu and his supporters. Xie Xuegong, who led the North China Bureau work team, denounced Inner Mongolia for having abandoned class struggle principles in the Socialist Education Movement, instead targeting Han chauvinism. Xie did not mention Ulanhu by name, but the criticism was unmistakable.[26]

For two days, on June 5 and 6, Xie Xuegong, Wang Zaitian (a.k.a. Namjilseren, a Khorchin Mongol, secretary of the Inner Mongolia Party Secretariat), Quan Xingyuan (secretary of the Inner Mongolia Party Secretariat), Lei Daifu (member of the standing committee of the Inner Mongolia Party Committee), and others criticized Ulanhu. These senior leaders had been marginalized or threatened with demotion in the recent administrative reshuffling to strengthen Ulanhu's position. The most serious charges centered on Ulanhu's order to print Mao's 1935 proclamation on Inner Mongolia. This was branded as a "nationality splittist" activity.[27]

In response, some Tumed Mongol supporters rallied to Ulanhu's defense: Chen Bingyu, Li Wenjing, and Yun Rui. A few Han officials in Inner

Mongolia, including Li Gui, also supported the veteran leader. Li Gui, Party secretary of the Hohhot Municipal Party Committee, stated unequivocally, "As far as Hohhot is concerned, Han chauvinism exists objectively, and it is the main (problem); even some children are Han chauvinists."[28]

On June 7, at the Inner Mongolia Party Standing Committee conference at the Qianmen Hotel in Beijing, Li Xuefeng delivered a scathing assault on Ulanhu, charging him with sabotaging the Socialist Education Movement by suppressing class struggle, encouraging nationality splittism, and attempting to establish an "independent kingdom," a phrase Mao had used to attack Peng Zhen. Why, he asked, did Ulanhu emphasize the study of the 1935 proclamation but ignore Mao's March 1958 Chengdu Conference criticism of Ulanhu for discriminating against Han cadres in Inner Mongolia?

The Chengdu Central Committee Conference on March 8–26, 1958, had been an important first step in launching the Great Leap Forward. After Ulanhu's report to the conference, Mao had commented:

> Explain clearly that you should be intimate with the Han nationality, believe in Marxism, and all nationalities should trust one another. Make Mongols and Han cooperate. No matter what nationality, we should look at on whose side the truth is. Marx was a Jew, Stalin was a minority nationality. Chiang Kai-shek is a Han, but very bad, so we should oppose him resolutely. Power doesn't have to be held by people from the same province; regardless of where one is from, be it south or north, this nationality or that nationality, we only ask who is for communism. If Marx becomes a party secretary, will you support him or not? He is not a local. Han chiefs [*touzi*] should explain this clearly to minority nationality cadres. . . .
>
> We should look at China's nationality question historically. Eat nationalist food or Communist food, local food or Communist food? First eat Communist food. We want nationalities, we want localities, but we do not need isms.[29]

Highlighting Mao's remark "Marx was a Jew, Stalin a minority nationality and Chiang Kai-shek a Han," Li Xuefeng insisted that the critical issue was not nationality but whether one was a Communist. More was at stake than Ulanhu's leadership or the ethnic composition of the Inner Mongolia bureaucracy. Li's attack posed the fundamental question of the legitimacy of the concept of regional autonomy and, ultimately, whether the powers of appointment of leaders in the autonomous region lay in Inner Mongolia or with the Center.

Things went from bad to worse for Ulanhu. On June 8, a North China Bureau work team of twenty-three members took charge of the conference on Inner Mongolia.[30] Xie Xuegong, executive secretary of the North China Bureau, headed the work team with Zhao Han, deputy head of the Party's

Central Organization Department, as his deputy. Its members included Liu Chun, who had earlier worked in Inner Mongolia and was deputy head of the Party's United Front Department and deputy commissioner of the State Nationality Affairs Commission, and Li Shude, director of the financial office of the North China Bureau.[31]

On June 8, the acting standing committee of the Inner Mongolia Party that Ulanhu had created was abolished, starkly revealing the conference's real purpose. Hao Fan, Ulanhu's main confidant in Hohhot was ordered to hand over his gun, and the telephone was removed from his house. On June 10 he was ordered to stop work. The first victim of the conference, Hao Fan, a Tumed Mongol, had recently been appointed deputy secretary-general of the General Office (*Bangong ting*) of the Inner Mongolia Party Committee.[32] One after another, Ulanhu's protégés faced angry denunciations. On June 14, Ulanhu made his first self-criticism. He admitted, however, only to having nationality bias, a trivial criticism that further infuriated his tormentors.

Ulanhu's alleged nationality splittism was dramatized during the Qianmen Hotel Conference. One Tumed Mongol army officer, Yun Chenglie, assistant chief of staff of the Juu'uda League Military Subdistrict and Ulanhu's nephew, became agitated when he heard that Ulanhu was under attack in Beijing. After consulting a few Tumed officials in Hohhot, he went to Beijing on June 16 and was alleged to have sent a message to Ulanhu telling him, "Revolution is permanent, we will carry on the revolution even if it means fighting a guerrilla war in the Daqing Mountains," an allusion to Ulanhu's anti-Japanese guerrilla days.[33] Whatever its truth, this information was cited by Ulanhu's enemies as proof that he was plotting to split off Inner Mongolia from China.

With Lin Biao warning of the dangers of a coup d'état, attention turned immediately to an Ulanhu plot to rebel in Inner Mongolia. Liu Shaoqi and Deng Xiaoping immediately ordered the North China Bureau to convene a meeting of the Inner Mongolia Party Committee behind Ulanhu's back. That meeting made several key decisions: leaders of the Inner Mongolia Military Region in Beijing were to return to their bases immediately to control their units, all senior officials sent down for the Socialist Education Movement were also to return immediately, and Quan Xingyuan was to take control of the Inner Mongolia Party Committee.[34] A wave of anti-Mongol activity swept through Inner Mongolia. All Tumed Mongol military officers were arrested, and most Tumed civilian officials were sacked. Ulanhu's power base, constructed over two decades of leadership, collapsed under the assault.

On June 17, the conference made three decisions about Ulanhu's administration: to investigate every member of the Inner Mongolia Acting Standing

Committee, to seize power from the Hohhot Party Committee, and to dismiss Chen Bingyu as acting head of the Organization Department, Yun Liwen as acting director of the Party Committee's Policy Research Office, and Gao Ni, as deputy chief of the General Office of the Party Committee.[35] On June 18, Buhe and his deputy Zhao Gerui, labeled as Ulanhu's "black gang" (*heibang*), were sacked from their leading positions in the Culture Committee.

The term *heibang*, designating leading cadres and their network, first appeared in an editorial in the *People's Daily* on June 2, 1966, "Hail to the First Big-Character Poster of Peking University." Denouncing the municipal Beijing Deputy Party Secretary Deng Tuo, deputy mayor Wu Han, and propaganda chief Liao Mosha as a "black gang," it called on the people to rise up and destroy the "black gang, black organization, and black discipline." The June 16 *People's Daily* editorial "Go All Out to Mobilize the Masses to Thoroughly Overthrow the Reactionary Black Gang," labeled all "anti-Party and antisocialist elements," "bourgeois representatives," and "demons and monsters" as a "black gang" and demanded that they be overthrown. The editorial propelled the country into an orgy of "overthrowing the black gang."[36] In Inner Mongolia, the prime target of attack was Ulanhu's associates.

On June 19, Quan Xingyuan, who had led the attack on Ulanhu among Inner Mongolia officials in Beijing, returned to Hohhot to lead the Cultural Revolution in Inner Mongolia.

Gao Shuhua Is Denounced as a Black Gang Member of the Ulanhu Clique

The Hohhot campus turmoil had no effect on the downfall of the Inner Mongolian leadership. Ulanhu fell under an attack from the Party Center, including Mao, Lin Biao, Liu Shaoqi, Deng Xiaoping, and Li Xuefeng, backed by critics in the Party, government, and army in Inner Mongolia.

However, Gao Jinming and Quan Xingyuan closely monitored the campus from Beijing. Learning that Gao Shuhua was very close to Ulanhu's son Lishake, who was once a teacher in the Foreign Languages Department, Gao Jinming and Quan suspected that Lishake was behind Gao Shuhua's poster to distract attention from the attack on Ulanhu in Beijing. Mistakenly thinking that Shuhua was a female name, Gao Jinming even suspected that Lishake might have had a special relationship with Gao Shuhua. The work team sent into Teachers' College investigated Gao's connection with Lishake.[37]

As Ulanhu's Mongol-centered administration crumbled, the work team exercised power on campus, serving a new leadership led by self-proclaimed leftist secretaries (*zuopai shuji*) Gao Jinming, Quan Xingyuan, Wang Duo, and Wang Yilun: a Manchu who passed as Han (Gao) and three Han. This ended the two decades during which Ulanhu's leadership and his ability to work effectively with Mongol and Han colleagues made possible a certain level of Mongolian autonomy and relative peace between Mongols and Han in Inner Mongolia.

We students had not the faintest awareness of the significance of ethnic issues at the time, caught up as we were in class-struggle conceptions framing conflict on campus. Nevertheless, the change in leadership gave us an opportunity to turn the tables on the work team at Teachers' College and elsewhere. This was because the crumbling of Ulanhu's regime threw Inner Mongolia into turmoil with officialdom at every level of Party, government, and army divided into antagonistic camps, each vying to outdo the other in denouncing the former leader and all distancing themselves from his associates. Ulanhu's fall precipitated a tirade of criticism of the former leader in ways that transformed an ostensibly class struggle issue into an attack on Mongol nationalism.

Since Chen Juesheng had been sent to campus by Buhe and Zhao Gerui, we began to attack him for being a "black gang member," that is, an associate of Ulanhu. We demanded that Chen be dismissed as the deputy leader and the work team be reconstituted.[38]

On June 24, some work team members denounced Chen Juesheng because of his close relationship with Hao Fan, deputy secretary-general of the General Office of the Inner Mongolia Party Committee.[39] Gao Shuhua attacked the work team as "a counterrevolutionary commando of the 'Hao family yard' black gang" in a poster on June 28 signed with his three comrades Liu Zhen, Lou Jili, and Liu Pu.[40]

Unbeknownst to Gao, on June 18, Ji Zhi's private secretary, Chen Hanchu, director of the college president's office, had written a letter to Su Qianyi, a secretary of the North China Bureau, detailing the special relationship between Gao Shuhua and Ulanhu's son Lishake.[41]

For over a year from March 1963, Gao Shuhua had shared a dormitory room with Lishake, the third son of Ulanhu who had returned from graduate study in nuclear physics in Moscow. Having declined offers of positions in China's nuclear project that would have required working in the hinterlands, Lishake taught Russian at Teachers' College between 1961 and 1964. In late 1964, Lishake participated in the Socialist Education Movement in Dalad banner, Yekejuu league, then at the No. 2 Wool Textile Factory in Hohhot. But his formal position was at Teachers' College. Every month, Gao Shuhua would deliver Lishake's salary to the house of his elder brother, Buhe, where he stayed.[42]

In the final week of June, Gao and the work team crossed swords repeatedly as an avalanche of anti-Lishake posters appeared on campus. By this time, Lishake and over a hundred members of the "black gang" had been captured and brought to Teachers' College to face denunciation and undertake labor reform under the work team. Leaders of the Foreign Languages Department and other departments denounced Gao's ties to Ulanhu, particularly through Lishake and through Ulanfu's wife, Yun Liwen.

On July 6, the political department of the Culture Committee put up the poster "Who is Gao Shuhua's backstage boss?"[43] For the first time, Gao Shuhua was labeled a "black gang" member whose boss was Cholmon, former deputy propaganda head of the Inner Mongolia Party Committee. The great majority of students and faculty sided with the Culture Committee and supported the work team, shouting slogans and mounting posters like "Down with black gang member Gao Shuhua!" To most, it seemed the safest course in the midst of the tornado that was ripping through Inner Mongolia and the university.

Gao's supporters in the Foreign Languages Department were placed under surveillance and faculty and students were barred from entering or leaving campus, effectively imposing martial law.[44] The rebellion at Teachers' College was on the verge of defeat.

Those Who Refuse to Confess Will Be Expelled

Under work team pressure, everyone worried about the future—their own future and that of family and friends, but also that of the nation. Fearful of becoming targets of another anti-rightist movement, many who initially supported the rebels confessed their errors and began to criticize Gao Shuhua and his allies. A few people changed their tune many times in a single day with each new pressure from the work team and counterthrust from rebel classmates. Many were hopelessly confused. A number of tragicomic episodes unfolded on campus. Li Xiulan, a second-year English-language student and a Youth League candidate from eastern Inner Mongolia, was terrified that she would be punished for following the wrong faction: "I beg for punishment from Chairman Mao!" One moment Xiulan said she supported Gao Shuhua; the next moment she changed her mind. After further criticism, she changed her mind again. People joked, "Don't follow Li Xiulan, she confessed twelve times in one day." Still, Xiulan was hardly alone in racing to recant under pressure.

Bayanmönkh, a fourth-year Mongol student in Mongolian language and literature who had recently studied classical Chinese, wrote a big-character poster. Finding no prime wall space left to post it, he placed it on the sidewalk where everyone would see it. Bayanmönkh wrote: "Tigers and wolves block our way; China is dying" (*Hulang dangdao, zhongguo xiuyi*). His intention, of course, was to spur us to fight the reactionaries. But mechanically copying the classical phrases he had worked so hard to master, he unfortunately ended up in deep trouble. At first people just laughed and asked, "Why did he write that?" This is, after all, the era of Mao's leadership. But some Han students pounced on the poster, insisting that since Chairman Mao was in charge, such sentiments were reactionary. Bayanmönkh was terrified. "Sorry, sorry, I didn't mean anything, my Chinese is poor," he cried, tears in his eyes.

But smelling blood, the conservatives wouldn't let him off so easily.

Mongol students and some Han students leaped to his defense: "He's a Youth League member and a good person. His intentions were good."

Fortunately, the incident was not pursued, but people laughed nervously about it long after.

Many of Gao Shuhua's early supporters deserted him. He had been the deputy Party secretary in charge of student Party members. Those who wanted to join the Party had fawned on him. Later, when he was in trouble, many of those, especially his model student, Wang Yumin, the class Youth League branch secretary, were harshest toward him.

The work team organized the Arts Department to draw cartoons mocking Gao and his supporters. One cartoon depicted a huge tree. Gao's name means "tall tree," and we also nicknamed him "Da Shu" (big tree). The tree was rooted in "bourgeois soil," giving rise to a rotting, half dead tree. There were monkeys on the branches, each with the name of a die-hard student, including myself. The cartoon's motif was inspired by a popular saying: "When the tree falls, all the monkeys flee" (*shudao husun san*). It depicted us as long-tailed monkeys deserting the tree, our faces immediately recognizable. People long remembered this cartoon. I admired the artistry and the humor. But I could not accept the message.

As for me, I was stubborn. I was not one to easily change views or betray friends and comrades. Why did I follow Gao Shuhua? When a friend advised me not to support him, recalling that he had once persecuted me, I lashed back: You don't know how to separate personal feelings from the general orientation! The Cultural Revolution doesn't claim that all past work was wrong. It doesn't say that the Three Banners were wrong. I can't say that Gao's criticism of me was entirely baseless. Anyhow, he followed the orders of the Party Committee. Gao isn't attacking Ji Zhi personally. This is a matter of the general orientation of the revolution and Chairman Mao's call.

Under pressure from the work team, eventually I was one of only five die-hards among my classmates in the third-year English class who refused to renounce Gao Shuhua, along with Wang Jinglin, Zhang Daren, Zhai Ximin, and Bi Wuqing.

Rumors flew that those who refused to confess would be expelled. Zhang Daren, who had joined me in signing the cartoon, said, "I'm ready to go home." Facing the possibility of arrest and jail, we remained firm, but we also worried. Unable to sleep, we met on the playground to discuss the situation late each night.

As work team pressures mounted, on July 8, a small group of students from departments including Foreign Languages, Chinese, Physical Education, and Arts painted a huge slogan on the second story of the main classroom building: "Support Comrade Gao Shuhua. See through the schemers who persecute the left." Each character was two feet high. The work team responded by organizing a few hundred students from physics, biology, and other conservative strongholds to shout slogans—"Down with counterrevolutionaries!" "Down with reactionary student Han Tong!" "Down with reactionary student Liu Hongyin!"—referring to the two students who mounted the banner.

Seeing their danger, I sought help from the physical education students. I knocked on their doors: "We need your help!" Many of them had suffered at the hands of work team officer Liu Qingxiao, who had mobilized the department to denounce students and young faculty members who criticized Ji Zhi. When I returned, I found that Han Tong had been injured, and Xue Yongchang, a third-year Chinese literature student, had been captured and forced to bow down before Mao's portrait. When the strong physical education students arrived, we were able to release Yongchang.

Eventually, the work team and its supporters mounted a huge banner that read "Sternly punish black gang element Gao Shuhua and his lackeys." They also forced Han Tong, Liu Hongyin, and others to climb ladders to scrub away their original slogan, with hundreds of students keeping watch below. It was total humiliation for us.

Ulanhu's Capitulation

On July 8, Gao Shuhua and seven student leaders escaped from campus and traveled to Beijing to report to the North China Bureau and the CCRG on the Cultural Revolution at Teachers' College and the activities of the work team.[45] The marathon conference at the Qianmen Hotel was still in session. Ulanhu's opponents continued to demand that he confess to all his "crimes."

Ulanhu's resistance finally crumbled on July 2, 1966. Over the next week, Liu Shaoqi and Deng Xiaoping took his case to the highest levels of the Party, echoing the North China Bureau's charges, denouncing Ulanhu's local nationalism, revisionism, and refusal to engage in class struggle. They criticized point by point Ulanhu's major achievements, including the land reform policy of "three nos and two benefits," and especially his criticism of Han chauvinism during the Socialist Education Movement.[46]

Liu Shaoqi asked: "Has Han chauvinism ever oppressed you? Now, Inner Mongolia is not under oppression, rather it is equal inside the country. Using the nationality question to substitute for the question of the class struggle is the line of the bourgeoisie. It represents the interest of the Mongol landlords, herdlords and bourgeoisie, not the interests of Mongolian workers, peasants and poor herders."

Ulanhu's refusal to criticize the Mongolian People's Republic was another focus of the criticism.

For example, Deng Xiaoping: "Since the second half of last year, at the height of our struggle to denounce Soviet revisionism and its anti-China activities, you lowered the flag of antirevisionism."

And Liu Shaoqi: "Xinjiang is rebuking Soviet radio, but Inner Mongolian radio is no longer rebuking Outer Mongolian radio."

Challenging Ulanhu's self-criticism that his local nationalist thought dated to the twentieth anniversary of the founding of Inner Mongolia, in 1965, Deng roared, "You consistently leaned to the right with respect to the 1955 suppression of rebellion, the 1956 socialist reform, and subsequent suppression of rebellions. . . . You have never given up your wrong viewpoint."

Kang Sheng shrieked: "Just where are you leading the Inner Mongolian people? . . . Are you raising the flag of socialism and Mao Zedong, or the flag of Ulanhu and nationalism?" Kang was referring to the acting Standing Committee that Ulanhu had appointed without the Center's approval.

From July 7–10, Ulanhu made a humiliating self-criticism, admitting to all the charges. It was not enough. Guo Yiqing, one of thirteen acting Standing Committee members of the Inner Mongolia Party Committee, in an effort to save his own career, shouted at Ulanhu to "surrender by giving up his weapons." Denunciation followed denunciation of Ulanhu.

On July 14, the participants recommended that the Party Center strip Ulanhu of all his Party posts, and all posts in Inner Mongolia and the North China Bureau. On the following two days, Gao Jinming accused him of the ultimate crime of seeking to "unify Inner Mongolia with Outer Mongolia to create a Great Mongolian State, and to become a modern day Chinggis Khan!" On July 18 and 19, a week before the Qianmen Hotel Conference ended, Xie Xuegong delivered the final verdict, confirming all charges against Ulanhu. Summing up, he said, "Our struggle against Ulanhu is a serious political struggle; after two months, we have achieved decisive victory!"

This was an extraordinary verdict for a leader who had played a critical role in preserving Inner Mongolia within China by integrating former independent-minded members of the Inner Mongolia Revolutionary Party (Neirendang) into the Chinese Communist Party and presiding over an Inner Mongolia administration that unified Mongols and Han for decades of peaceful development and attention to both Mongol and Han interests.

A month later, Liu Shaoqi and Deng Xiaoping, who led the attack on Ulanhu, would become the two highest Party leaders to fall.

Gao Shuhua had sought North China Bureau support for himself and the rebels. But with the meeting on Ulanhu in full swing, no one in the North China Bureau was willing to allow Gao to explain, still less to support, his position. He received a warmer reception, however, from Nie Yuanzi, his counterpart at Peking University. Nie encouraged Gao to continue the struggle, informing him that Mao had just returned to Beijing and would surely support their rebel cause throughout the country.[47]

Gao Shuhua's Triumph

Every morning, on waking up, we listened to the radio for the latest instructions from Mao. We learned to our joy that Mao was calling on all organizations, and on workers, peasants, soldiers and students, to struggle against injustice of all kinds and against "those in authority taking the capitalist road." Suddenly Mao was openly at odds with the Party committees and work teams that claimed to restore order in his name. These broadcasts strengthened our determination to hold to principle.

Gao Shuhua's secret trip to Beijing was not discovered until July 10, when several posters denounced it as a counterrevolutionary act.[48] On July 12, forty Russian-language students posted a telegram from Gao in Beijing charging that the work team had committed a serious "mistake of line" (*luxian cuowu*) at Teachers' College.[49] Many students who had been forced to recant mounted posters reiterating their earlier position. But on July 14, my classmate Wang Yumin and three others posted a "strong demand" that Gao be brought back to Hohhot for punishment.[50]

With some students and faculty continuing to resist, the Inner Mongolia Party Committee sent another work team, led by Quan Jiafu, to Teachers' College. They entered on July 17, the day Gao Shuhua returned from Beijing. A Han from Ulaanhot in eastern Inner Mongolia, Quan had been appointed by Ulanhu to the State Nationality Affairs Commission.[51] After serving as a member of the Socialist Education Movement work team sent by the North

China Bureau to work in Inner Mongolia, he was appointed to lead the expanded team at Teachers' College. In addition to the twenty original members, twenty new members arrived. Our hopes for rehabilitation were dashed, as the new work team labeled Gao Shuhua a "black gang" member and on July 23 placed him under house arrest in the faculty dormitory.

Gao's supporters were denounced in posters and interrogated by the work team. One of the team's most effective methods was to visit the parents of student supporters, pressuring them to persuade their children to change their position before it was too late. By July 24, Gao's supporters had ostensibly been completely crushed, including the three colleagues who signed the first poster with him. No one dared oppose the work team openly. Covertly, however, many students and faculty members, mainly in the Foreign Languages Department, continued to resist.

On July 26, the *People's Daily* published a report on Mao's Yangtze River swim of July 16. It was a call to arms for us, inspired by the Chairman's vigor. That day Mao demanded the recall of all the work teams that Liu Shaoqi had dispatched to schools: "The work teams know nothing. Some work teams have even created trouble.... Work teams only hinder the movement.... [Affairs in the schools] have to be dealt with by the forces in the schools themselves, not by you, me, or the provincial committees."[52]

Sensing that the tide was turning, on July 26 Gao Shuhua again attempted to go to Beijing to report, but he was caught at the train station and returned to campus. Gao Shuhua, Liu Pu, Liu Zhen, and Lou Jili were put under stricter round-the-clock surveillance.[53] All of Gao's followers were forced to write self-criticisms. Only five students in the third-year English class, in the Foreign Languages Department, refused to write self-criticisms, including Zhang Daren, Zhai Ximin, and myself.

Mao's order to disband the work teams was announced in Beijing on July 27, but we did not learn of it until nine o'clock at night on August 1, when reports by Liu Shaoqi, Zhou Enlai, Deng Xiaoping, and Li Xuefeng were broadcast on Hohhot campuses. We were so moved that we cried. We couldn't sleep that night, shouting "Long live Chairman Mao!"[54]

We thought that the work team's withdrawal was imminent. But we were wrong. The work team trumpeted the claim that it had unearthed a "several-hundred-person anti-Party clique," labeling the rebels "counterrevolutionaries" and "reactionary students." Finally, on August 4, the Inner Mongolia Party Committee announced the withdrawal of the work teams from all universities but stipulated that the work team would remain at Teachers' College and a few other campuses to act as liaison between the colleges and the Party Committee.

The August Debates

After Mao's August 1 broadcast criticizing the decision by Liu Shaoqi and Deng Xiaoping to send work teams to the universities, attitudes toward Gao Shuhua began to change. The students who were assigned to keep watch on him began to call him "Teacher Gao."

On August 5, the *People's Daily* published Mao's first big-character poster, "Bombard the Headquarters":

China's first Marxist-Leninist big character poster and Commentator's article on it in *Renmin Ribao* (*People's Daily*) are indeed superbly written! Comrades, please read them again. But in the last fifty days or so some leading comrades from the central down to the local levels have acted in a diametrically opposite way. Adopting the reactionary stand of the bourgeoisie, they have enforced a bourgeois dictatorship and struck down the surging movement of the great cultural revolution of the proletariat. They have stood facts on their head and juggled black and white, encircled and suppressed revolutionaries, stifled opinions differing from their own, imposed a white terror, and felt very pleased with themselves. They have puffed up the arrogance of the bourgeoisie and deflated the morale of the proletariat. How poisonous![55]

This was a complete vindication of Gao Shuhua's view and his big-character poster of June 2, 1966. Good news came twice for us. On August 1, Mao had distributed to the Eleventh Plenum of the Eighth Central Committee, held August 1–12, two big posters from the Red Guards of the Middle School affiliated with Tsinghua University, "Long Live the Revolutionary Rebel Spirit of the Proletariat" (June 24), "Once Again On Long Live the Revolutionary Rebel Spirit of the Proletariat" (July 4), along with his "Letter to the Red Guards of the Middle School Affiliated with Tsinghua University." Mao reiterated his 1939 slogan, "To rebel is justified," thereby officially inaugurating an era of rebellion.

In the wake of Mao's big-character poster, and with support of the Party Committee and North China Bureau representatives in Inner Mongolia, the Inner Mongolia University faculty and students immediately organized a three-day debate to refute the work team's "counterrevolutionary" labeling of those who called themselves revolutionary leftists (*geming zuopai*).

The conflict pitted the university's leadership against the rebels, notably Vice President Yu Beichen, against Jia Guotai, a second-year physics student, who had posted Inner Mongolia's first big-character poster. Like Gao Shuhua, Jia had been sharply criticized and persecuted by authorities. On June 30, university authorities detained him and the next day sent him to the Public

Security Bureau. I attended the debate at Inner Mongolia University and saw Yu Beichen and his official associates crushed by Jia Guotai and his partner (later his wife) Miao Xiuying, a third-year physics student and an outstanding debater.

Encouraged by this change of wind at Inner Mongolia University, from August 8, 1966, victims of the work team at Teachers' College mounted big-character posters criticizing the work team. That day the Eleventh Plenum of the Eighth Central Committee approved the sixteen-point "Decision of the CCP Central Committee on the Proletarian Cultural Revolution." It endorsed Mao's version of a Cultural Revolution whose goal was to "change the mental outlook of the whole of society." Mao and the Party called on the nation to "struggle against and overthrow those persons in authority who are taking the capitalist road, to criticize and repudiate the reactionary bourgeois academic 'authorities' and the ideology of the bourgeoisie and all other exploiting classes, and to transform education, literature and art, and all other parts of the superstructure not in correspondence with the socialist economic base." Mao's call for the Cultural Revolution inspired rebels who were convinced that the Chairman supported them.

Gao Jinming, a secretary of the Inner Mongolia Party Secretariat whose secret reports to the North China Bureau had been instrumental in bringing down Ulanhu at the Qianmen Hotel conference, came to see Gao Shuhua and his supporters on campus on August 8. He was surprised to find that Shuhua was a man, not a woman! Ever sensitive to the changing political winds, Gao Jinming and many other Party leaders in Inner Mongolia had begun to reassess their support for the work team in light of signals from Mao and the CCRG in Beijing.

On August 10, Gao Jinming returned to Teachers' College to plan a debate on the work team and Gao Shuhua, which eventually extended over seventeen days from August 10 to 27. Even in the wake of Mao's intervention and the counterattack on the work teams, at Teachers' College a presidium was elected, with eighteen people supporting the work team styled as representing the majority view (*duoshu guandian*), and six opponents representing the minority view (*shaoshu guandian*). The student Han Tong, the Gao Shuhua supporter who had mounted the banner high on a campus building, was elected executive vice president of the presidium. That evening, Wang Zaitian, Gao Jinming, Quan Xingyuan, and Wang Yilun, and members of the North China Bureau investigation team, attended the debate. Quan Xingyuan made a preliminary report on behalf of the Inner Mongolia Party Committee. Stating that the work team had made mistakes of direction and line, he ordered that all confession materials of students be destroyed in public.

We demanded access to our personal dossiers to see how we had been slandered. Just then, however, an order from the Center stated that to avoid factional fighting, material confiscated from the work team was to be burned publicly, with all students and faculty in attendance.[56] Before the files were taken for burning, however, my intrepid friend Zhang Daren broke into the office and found three sets of files, one for revolutionary leftists, another for reactionary rightists, and a third for middle elements. The revolutionary leftists were to be promoted, the middle-of-the-roaders were to be tested (many were applicants for Party and league membership), and the reactionary rightists were to be punished as black elements.

My personal file was nearly four inches thick. Having been labeled a bad element before the movement began, I was under surveillance from the start. The work team had assigned three students to track me. They had recorded everything I posted and even kept records of what I said. The thought of this sophisticated surveillance still sends chills up my spine. But at the time, learning the contents of my dossier strengthened my resolve.

Over the next two weeks, Gao Jinming, Quan Xingyuan, Wang Yilun, and Shen Xinfa frequently attended the debate. But the struggle was not confined to debate. Gao Shuhua supporters captured Han Ming and Sun Peiqing and struggled them, while work team supporters captured Lishake at the No. 2 Wool Textile Factory and paraded him around campus. An alleged culprit would be seated while receiving verbal abuse and sometimes physical torture. During the Cultural Revolution, *pidou* (criticism and struggle) was differentiated as *wendou* (civilized struggle) and *wudou* (violent struggle), the former referring to verbal criticism, the latter including beating and torture. At this stage, our struggle was rather civilized.

The debate ended on August 27 with no agreement on how to assess the work team and Gao Shuhua. The majority faction held that the work team was mainly good despite having made some mistakes. Despite the "Sixteen Points" and Mao's statement criticizing the work teams, they branded Gao Shuhua an anti-Party and antisocialist schemer and careerist. The minority faction charged the work team with serious mistakes of line and direction, of suppressing the Great Proletarian Cultural Revolution at Teachers' College. Gao Shuhua, they insisted, was an exemplary revolutionary comrade. I regularly attended the debates but never took the stage. I was cautious. Wang Mengqiu, a chemistry student, was the majority faction's top debater. I could not but admire her debating skill—slowly, carefully, she built up a case that highlighted the loopholes and distortions in her opponents' arguments.

In this supercharged political atmosphere young people experienced unprecedented personal freedom as the everyday structures of classes and organizational discipline collapsed. The debate provided an occasion for the two camps to present their views systematically. For us, this brought legitimation after protracted isolation and relentless criticism. It did not, however, substantially change the balance of forces.

On campus there was a half-completed building with walls and doors but no ceiling. So, boys and girls could go inside together. No one paid any attention. One day after a sudden downpour several dozen people ran out from inside. Everyone saw them and laughed. Huang Zhigao recited a classical poem: "Black clouds arrive suddenly, and rainfall drives the love birds everywhere"—*Turan yipian tongyun zhi, yuda yuanyang daochu fei.*

Even in those days, there was life beyond political struggle.

4

Red Guards on the March

Red Guards, Red August, and the Attack on the Four Olds

The Eleventh Plenary Session of the Eighth Central Committee of the CCP, held August 1–12, 1966, three months after the launch of the Cultural Revolution, was a monumental event. The session marked the start of Mao's showdown with Liu Shaoqi. The Politburo was reshuffled, recruiting Xu Xiangqian, Nie Rongzhen, and Ye Jianying, three serving marshals, strengthening the military presence in China's highest political organ. With Lin Biao replacing Liu as number two in the Party and anointed as Mao's closest comrade-in-arms (*qinmi zhanzhou*), Mao signaled his intention to rely on the army to carry out the Cultural Revolution. The communiqué of the Eleventh Plenary Session on August 12 issued this call: "Industry learns from Daqing, agriculture learns from Dazhai and the whole country learns from the People's Liberation Army."

On August 18, Mao presided at a rally of one million young people at Tiananmen that launched the Red Guard movement. It was the first of eight massive Red Guard rallies in Beijing's Tiananmen Square paying homage to Mao and strengthening the political grip of Lin Biao's army and the Central Cultural Revolution Group. The Red Guard movement institutionalized Mao's dictum that "to rebel is justified," creating a new nationwide paramilitary structure for use against his enemies within the Party. When a girl student placed a Red Guard armband on the aging leader, the signal instantly reached youth across the country. Not only did Red Guard organizations spring up immediately in schools and factories; millions of young people took advantage of their sudden empowerment to travel. Logistical support provided by the army made possible transportation by train to Beijing and throughout the nation, with housing, food, and logistical arrangements provided at state expense.

The Inner Mongolia Party Committee immediately issued a notice directing campuses and factories to set up Cultural Revolution Committees.

The first Red Guard organization was formed in Hohhot the next day at the No. 2 Wool Textile Factory, eventually becoming known as Geming Zhanshi (Revolutionary Soldier). Within a week, students at every college and middle school in Hohhot had established Red Guard organizations. At Teachers' College, the earliest Red Guard organization was the Mao Zedong Thought Red Guard General Headquarters.[1]

Students at Teachers' College, as elsewhere, were divided. Although all vowed to support Mao and the Party's proletarian line, interpretations of Mao's goals for the Cultural Revolution differed. Those rebelling against the work team understood their enemies to be corrupt officials or revisionists within the Party, whose evil was manifest in their own experience of political persecution and what they saw as the corrupt behavior of officials. The majority of students, however, targeted traditional enemies of the Party: rightists, intellectuals, teachers, landlords, capitalists. The result was the splintering of Red Guard organizations and others into two camps: loyalists (*baoshoupai*) and rebels (*zaofanpai*).[2]

Even those of us who were among the original "rebels" were divided. Many Party and Youth League members and candidates distanced themselves from people who had been criticized before the Cultural Revolution. Most rebel groups initially barred people like Gao Shuhua and me to avoid suspicion that they were harboring black elements. Thus, it would be more than a month before some of us joined or organized our own Red Guard organizations. This delay would have important ramifications for Inner Mongolia.

At a Hohhot mass rally on August 22, Inner Mongolia Party leaders Gao Jinming and Wang Duo called on people to "follow Chairman Mao to carry out revolution, smash the old world and build the new world." This was a reference to the first point of what was known as the sixteen-point "Decision of the CCP Central Committee on the Proletarian Cultural Revolution," issued on August 8, which called for destroying the "four olds" and building the "four news": "Although the bourgeoisie has been overthrown, it is still trying to use the old ideas, culture and customs, and habits of the exploiting classes to corrupt the masses, capture their minds, and endeavor to stage a comeback. The proletariat must do just the opposite: it must meet head-on every challenge of the bourgeoisie in the ideological field and use the new ideas, culture, customs, and habits of the proletariat to change the mental outlook of the whole of society."[3] A nationwide destructive rampage followed.

Tens of thousands of college students and officials in Hohhot pledged to carry the Cultural Revolution to the end, as proposed by Red Guards in Beijing on August 20. Student activists demanded the destruction of "feudal culture," including the eradication of superstition and the burning of all reactionary and bourgeois books. At Teachers' College, library workers prepared lists of poisonous books to be removed from shelves and burned. Some activists opposed book burning, but it was difficult to prevent it at a time when everything feudal and capitalist was under attack.

There was a huge pile of books from the library on the playground, more than twenty-five thousand. Records were thrown on a separate pile. It wouldn't do to burn several thousand records because of the fumes. So these were chopped to pieces, with poles wielded like baseball bats. The book burning began after dinner. The books continued to burn until the next morning. People picked up some books, shouting: "This book needs special criticism! Don't burn this one; it can be used to expose poisonous weeds." Hundreds of students watched and cheered as the pyre burned. Luckily, the library staff had prepared well to protect the precious heritage from destruction. Rather than wait for rampaging students to seize the books, the librarians had taken the lead in selecting "poisonous weeds" to be burned. This allowed them to choose what to burn and what to save, making sure that at least one copy of each work was preserved.

Every twist and turn of the movement marked a rite of passage, a test of one's *biaoxian*, or basic attitude toward revolution. No one, regardless of how they felt at heart, could escape the necessity to perform repeatedly. Many who had been handicapped by their suspect class origins or political labels were particularly desperate to display revolutionary zealotry. Nevertheless, at Teachers' College, the cruelest, most violent, and mindless acts in such campaigns as the attack on "the four olds" were conducted by students with "good" class backgrounds.

The destruction was not limited to campus or to books. My friend Guo Weilin, fearful because of his "landlord" class label, joined a night raid with a group of Red Guards to destroy "the four olds." The group targeted all the old temples in the vicinity of Hohhot and burned all the precious books and cultural items they could find. They also ransacked people's homes vigilante-style, burning or stealing books, paintings and other family treasures. One activist who had earlier followed Gao Shuhua in campus rebellion was famous for the ten gold rings that adorned his fingers. Of course, they had been "confiscated."

At one inn serving carters in the Southern Firewood Market in the Old Town (Jiucheng nan chaihuo shi), people were sleeping thirty to a room on two big *kangs* when Red Guards drove a truck inside the gate and kicked open the door. Guests were forced out of bed and lined up in the fall cold. After two hours of questioning and harassment, the students finally allowed the travelers to return to rest. "I felt so sorry," my friend later told me. "Why did we treat those innocent working people like that?" At the end of the interrogation, he said to one old man, "Please go back to your *kang* and rest, we are sorry." The man turned back and said, "Don't mention it. You are much better than the Japanese," alluding to Japanese treatment of Chinese in the resistance war.

Red Guards rushed to destroy all buildings and art that had local, ethnic, or historical character. To eliminate the old, the feudal, or the capitalist was to usher in the new and revolutionary. Hohhot's two ancient Buddhist temples, Dazhao and Xiaozhao, suffered heavy damage at the hands of high school red guards. Red Guard Action Days (*Hongweibing huodongri*) were devoted to raiding all suspected of having bourgeois, landlord, or "feudal" backgrounds. Numerous organizations sprang up with military names like "fighting corps" and "headquarters" as local Red Guards copied militant practices that originated in Beijing.

The campaign to destroy the four olds also unleashed Red Guard violence against teachers, resulting in many deaths. The first recorded beating to death of a teacher by Red Guards took place at Beijing Normal University's Affiliated Girls' High School. On August 5, 1966, Bian Zhongyun, the female Party secretary and vice principal was beaten to death. Among the student activists who were rumored to have been responsible for her death were Song Binbin, a daughter of Song Renqiong, Party secretary of the Northeast CCP Central Bureau, and her classmate Deng Rong, a daughter of Deng Xiaoping. When on August 18 Binbin placed a Red Guard armband on Mao on the Tiananmen rostrum, igniting the Red Guard movement, the Chairman suggested that she change her name from Binbin (meaning "polite and cultured") to Yaowu (meaning "quest for the military"), and she proceeded to make the change.[4]

If Beijing took the lead in violence, terrible things soon took place at Erzhong, my alma mater, whose students included many children of high cadres. Cadre children were the first to organize as Red Guards. Many middle school students sought to exact "class revenge" for the crimes allegedly committed by bourgeois and feudal elements. Class revenge also involved students acting on personal grievances toward teachers.

Some Red Guards kicked and beat teachers, capping with high dunce hats all who were vulnerable or who had angered them. They tortured not only the faculty but also those branded black elements among the students, girls and boys. Capping an enemy was employed earlier by Hunan peasants against landlords and gentry as celebrated by Mao in his March 1927 report: "At the slightest provocation they make arrests, crown the arrested with tall paper hats, and parade them through the villages." "A revolution," Mao wrote, "is not a dinner party, or writing an essay, or painting a picture, or doing embroidery; it cannot be so refined, so leisurely and gentle, so temperate, kind, courteous, restrained and magnanimous."[5] Red Guards took up this method that had been perfected in waves of subsequent social movements, especially land reform in the years 1947–1953.

Red Guard activists tortured to death three teachers at Erzhong. Four more committed suicide to preempt such a fate, including the best Russian-language teacher, Lü Wei. Another victim was a fine pianist who had taught the warlord Zhang Xueliang's family in Manchuria in the late 1920s. Red Guard students pressured her to confess to having had an affair with Zhang. Incarcerated, tortured, and subjected to humiliation and physical abuse, she was finally forced by the students to perform a loyalty dance on top of upside-down stools. They eventually tortured her to death.

My future brother-in-law Wang Zhengping was one of five students in his class at Erzhong who were locked up by student Red Guards headed by Wang Jiyan, Wang Duo's son, and Wang Jianhua, Wang Yilun's son. Both Wang Duo and Wang Yilun were secretaries of the Inner Mongolia Party Secretariat. Zhengping was detained for six weeks in a makeshift prison (a converted classroom) and whipped mercilessly, leaving him with permanent scars on his back. Red Guards ransacked the family home. Qingxian, then a medical student, was active in the early days of the rebel movement. After her brother's arrest and torture, she withdrew, not daring to speak or to act.

One of her younger sisters and all students of dubious class background in her middle school class were forced to line up daily to bow to Mao and sing the "Ox Demon Snake Devil Song" (*Niugui Sheshen Ge*) that was widely circulating at the time:

> I am an ox demon snake devil,
> I am a cow demon snake devil,
> I am guilty, I am guilty!
> I am guilty before the people,
> The people exercise dictatorship,
> I bow my head and admit guilt . . .
> If I speak and act in a wholly irresponsible way,
> Crush me to pieces!

It was a ritual of degradation. More than half a century later, she can still sing the song.

Compared with the torture and killing at the middle school, the struggles at Teachers' College were rather civilized. Zhang Naijun, the best English teacher, became a target after putting up a poster supporting Gao Shuhua. When ordered to accept labor reform, he hung his shirt on a tree and worked bare chested. At the peak of forced labor, all the victims were forced to wear high paper hats, but only Zhang made his own, with his name on it. People on the road laughed.

Party Secretary Ji Zhi was the top Teachers' College power holder. With the fangs of the work team pulled, several hundred students who had been victimized in the earlier campus rebellion dragged him from his office and put a big cap on him. He grabbed the hat and ripped it off. "As a Party member, I will only bow to the truth, not to force," he shouted. In the subsequent scuffling between opposing Red Guard groups, with a white paper hat on his head, Ji was marched back and forth across campus until he collapsed. But he was not beaten or killed.

The early Red Guards in late August 1966 responded to Mao's call for rebellion but did not achieve the destruction of his enemies in the Party throughout the country. In Inner Mongolia, as elsewhere, Red Guards largely focused on destroying the four olds, both the cultural heritage of the nation and the alleged agents of the past including aristocrats, landlords, Guomindang members, and rightist intellectuals. For Mao, they were the *luoshuigou*, dogs who had fallen in the water, no longer posing any real danger. "New" Red Guards would soon emerge, distinguishing themselves from these "old" Red Guards.

Students to the Rescue: The Lanzhou Incident

Immediately after the convening of the Eleventh Plenum of the Eighth Party Congress, the educational leadership in Hohhot decided to send a "study" delegation to Beijing. Delegates were elected by each college. On the evening of August 5, 1966, the same day that Gao Shuhua was released from detention, twenty-five Teachers' College students were elected as leftists (*zuopai*) to join the delegation. All represented the former majority faction. One criterion for a leftist was whether one opposed Gao Shuhua.[6] The delegation, including Wang Yumin, the only Party member in our class, left for Beijing the following day. Inner Mongolia's *dachuanlian*, or great liaison, had begun.

On August 16, upon learning of the Central Committee's decision to strip Ulanhu of his posts as first secretary of the Inner Mongolia Party Committee and second secretary of the North China Bureau, the delegation returned to Hohhot, proclaiming that it was "bringing back the strong atmosphere of revolutionary rebellion of the capital's masses to ignite an upsurge of struggle against the black gang." Students and faculty who had previously clashed on almost every issue now sought to outdo one another in attacking Ulanhu and his "black gang." One remaining contentious issue, however, was the future of Gao Shuhua: while many branded him a confederate of Ulanhu, his followers like me viewed him as a hero in inaugurating the Cultural Revolution at Teachers' College and throughout Inner Mongolia. There was no longer any open support for the fallen leader Ulanhu. Suddenly, in Inner Mongolia, the targets were mostly Mongols who had fallen from power. The rebellion was led by the Inner Mongolia Party Committee, in the hands of Han Party secretaries who were the earliest Party rebels against their former boss Ulanhu.

That day, rebel faculty and students at the medical college rushed to the cultural committee to seize Buhe, Ulanhu's eldest son, and to the Inner Mongolia Party Committee to capture Hao Fan, acting secretary-general of the General Office of the Party Committee. We rebels at Teachers' College also organized a meeting to struggle black gang members, capturing Han Ming and Sun Peiqing, who had written the poster attacking Gao Shuhua for his relationship with Lishake. Han and Sun had become the top leaders of the Culture Committee by targeting Buhe and Zhao Gerui as Ulanhu's black gang members. Now rebels denounced them as Ulanhu's black gang members. Throughout Hohhot, Red Guards, regardless of factional differences, captured and struggled Ulanhu's closest associates and family members.[7] On the evening of August 16, Lishake was detained and paraded on campus. By the following day, rebel faculty and students had arrested and paraded all the "big and small ox demon snake devils." Ji Zhi, Wang Lü'an, Tömörbagan, Möngön, and Jirimtu were among the many who were detained and struggled.[8]

During this period, compared with colleges and universities in many provinces, most Inner Mongolian students treated their leaders with a certain "civility," for although severely abused and humiliated, no one was killed on the college campuses. In contrast, between June 21 and early September, at least seven college presidents or vice presidents were killed or committed suicide throughout the country; thirteen more died in the next four years.[9]

The Lanzhou incident electrified students, transforming the situation in Inner Mongolia and throughout the nation. In early June, a work team sent by the Gansu Provincial Party Committee criticized the chancellor and Party secretary of Lanzhou University, Jiang Longji, for suppressing the Cultural Revolution. On June 25, he was found dead, reportedly committing suicide by drowning after the Gansu Provincial Party Committee publicly sacked him at a large rally. As in all such instances, the fine line between murder and suicide was impossible to establish. Nor was he entirely innocent. As vice president of Peking University in 1957, he was directly responsible for persecuting 526 student and faculty "rightists."[10] Two days after his death, on July 11, the *Gansu Daily* published an editorial enumerating Jiang's alleged crimes.

Li Guizi, a fifth-year history student, played a leading role in supporting the work team in the struggle that led to Jiang Longji's suicide. However, as Mao began to oppose the work teams, Li Guizi and some leaders of the Gansu Provincial Party Committee also turned against them. Touted as Lanzhou University's Nie Yuanzi, that is, an outstanding rebel leader, Li was appointed director of the Lanzhou University Cultural Revolution Preparatory Group despite not being a Party member. For over two months Li unleashed a reign of terror, during which 658 of 2,577 students were beaten, or 26 percent of the student body. Two students committed suicide, twelve attempted suicide, thirty-one fled the university, and one went missing; 380 faculty or staff were beaten, out of 1,157. Four faculty or staff committed suicide, seven attempted suicide, seven fled, and two went missing.[11]

Li Guizi's atrocities came to the attention of the Party Center in Beijing from mid-August when visiting Red Guards from Tsinghua University issued the big-character poster "Measuring the Gansu Provincial Party Committee against Mao Zedong Thought." Their attack touched off a storm of criticism of Gansu provincial leaders. Executive Party Secretary Pei Mengfei and secretary of the Party Secretariat Ma Jikong were sacked with the approval of the Party Central Committee on August 22 and subjected to struggle by students.[12] On the previous morning, August 21, Li Guizi fled.

News of the clashes in Lanzhou reached Hohhot in the third week of August, when students from Beijing forwarded an SOS. We had had no direct contact with Lanzhou students, but when their leaflets arrived by train, we reprinted them on our mimeograph machine and distributed them widely. Activists from Teachers' College and other campuses called an emergency meeting at the gate outside Inner Mongolia Party Committee headquarters to respond to the death of the Lanzhou students and teachers. Some six hundred college students, the largest contingent coming from Teachers' College, attended the meeting and demanded that Inner Mongolia help the embattled Lanzhou students. Confronted with the murderous atrocities in Lanzhou, Hohhot students overrode factional differences, for the first, and perhaps the last, time.

The Inner Mongolia Party Committee had come to be dominated by Gao Jinming, Quan Xingyuan, Wang Duo, and Wang Yilun. Thousands of students from all seven Hohhot colleges rallied before Party headquarters. We demanded that the Party Committee provide funds to carry out a rescue mission to Lanzhou. Students sat peacefully in lines, singing revolutionary songs, chanting slogans, and demanding that the leaders negotiate. With our sit-in entering its third day, a group of students began a hunger strike. One hundred demonstrators vowed to continue the strike until the Party Committee accepted our demands, and the numbers soon grew. Around this time, we received news that Li Guizi, the murderer, was at large, and a nationwide manhunt began.

Eventually, after four hours of bargaining, the Inner Mongolia Party authorities agreed to send student representatives to Lanzhou. Each college would send five representatives and the Inner Mongolia Party Committee would send two representatives to provide logistical support including train tickets and hotel accommodations.

The students were overjoyed on learning of these unprecedented arrangements in response to the growth of student power, above all the legitimation of our mission together with the pledge to provide full public funding. As soon as the agreement was announced, the Inner Mongolia Party Committee sent in a big cauldron with porridge, rice, and vegetables. It was close to midnight when loudspeakers announced to students in the square: "Revolutionary students, you have won! Now you must eat! We will then send you home in government cars and buses."

This was my first car ride. It was a Soviet-made Volga, almost the only brand available in China for government agencies at the time. The compact car was pretty nice. It felt wonderful to return home in style savoring our victory. The Party Committee brought in all available vehicles to clear the square: two buses and eight cars from Party headquarters and several buses and trucks from the seven colleges brought all three hundred participants who remained in the square to their campuses.

The next evening, August 23, a Hohhot student delegation was organized to support the Lanzhou "revolutionary teachers and students." Teachers' College sent five representatives: Guo Shihai, Li Fusheng, Dong Yuhua, Zhao Zongzhi, and Wei Jinguang. All except Wei were rebels. The Hohhot delegation was to leave by train immediately. The Lanzhou incident was one landmark event in a process that sent student activists all over the country in the coming months.

In Hohhot, many who were not selected as delegates were determined to go, too. Hundreds of students, I among them, swarmed the railway station only to find students with Red Guard armbands standing guard to prevent interlopers from boarding the train. Not expecting to be able to board, I had prepared nothing. I was wearing shorts, a T-shirt, and plastic sandals. I had my student ID in a wallet with only six yuan.

As I approached the train, a powerfully built student stopped me. He was Ruoxi, a member of my martial arts club, a Mongol first-year student in fine arts. Before the Cultural Revolution, we had practiced martial arts under Liu Enshou, a famous kung fu master. Since Ruoxi was a junior member, I often corrected his moves and treated him like a younger brother. When he asked for a ticket, I just said, "Forget it, get out of my way," and he let me climb aboard. Personal friendship was not entirely tarred by factional strife at that time.

The train, which had originated in Beijing, was jammed with students. Some lay on overhead luggage racks. Even the toilet was packed. Of the hundreds who had rushed to the station, only about twenty boarded in addition to the official delegation. Five of us eventually got together, three foreign-language students and two Chinese literature students: Zhai Ximin, Zhao Lanke, Cao Jun, Huang Zhigao, and me. We were all "bad elements," and we were all rebels protesting against Ji Zhi. We agreed to travel together. But how to eat during the trip, and where to stay in Lanzhou? I had six yuan, another had ten yuan. The other three didn't have a cent. So, among us we had sixteen yuan.

On the train, we learned just how "backward" we were. Beijing students had been traveling across the country exchanging "revolutionary experiences" for some time. We were the first from Inner Mongolia. The Beijing students received stipends from their universities, both grain coupons and cash, and they quickly learned how to travel for free. With student travelers garbed in the revolutionary virtue of their Red Guard armbands, conductors dared not demand fares. None of the Beijing students had obtained an official travel permit! It is difficult to exaggerate the sense of liberation we experienced at this opportunity.

Students from Inner Mongolia, except the official delegates whose expenses were paid, received nothing from the government or from our schools. We were embarrassed to learn that others had money or coupons for food when we did not. We were revolutionaries, so we didn't want to beg. As Chinese revolutionaries were fond of saying *ren qiong, zhi bu qiong*, although financially poor, we were not spiritually poor. But we had to eat. The dining-car manager explained that he was not authorized to give food away without payment. However, we soon hit upon a solution. We would show our ID cards, and he would write down our names and send the bill to our college. A new form of revolutionary credit was established with this novel solution. As the number of students traveling spiraled, the strains on both transportation and the economy would become acute.

I learned that if you really want to do something, you should dare to do it! We would eventually travel forty days, living and eating well without so much as having our tickets checked. Chairman Mao had opened the door for us, saying that "a free ride for students is good." The short-lived communism for students spread like wildfire. Students in the millions rode far and wide as government reception centers provided free food and lodging to traveling Red Guards and students. All trains, buses, and boats applied this policy. Airplanes were the exception, but even that exception proved partial. In Chengdu, Sichuan province, posters signed by Zhang Guohua—the Party, government, and military leader of Tibet—announced that the Tibet Autonomous Region's leaders not only welcomed Red Guards but also would provide free air tickets.

By the time we reached Lanzhou, the work team sent to Lanzhou University had withdrawn and the provincial Party and government were in disarray. What counted politically were Mao's latest directives, which were published in the press and broadcast again and again. Under pressure from the Central Cultural Revolution Group in Beijing, the Lanzhou students had been freed and their persecution ended, but the black materials on them remained on file. No directive addressed the persecuted faculty, many of whom remained in makeshift jails. And no murderer had been brought to justice. Everywhere big posters attacked Gansu's Party and state leaders and their running dog Li Guizi: "Down with Pei Mengfei and Ma Jikong!" and "Arrest and execute murderer Li Guizi!"

Lanzhou was a huge city, much larger than Hohhot with a population of approximately two million in 1966. I was excited about returning to the city where I was born. But I had no time for nostalgia. I dimly felt that my birth mother and sister were still living in Lanzhou but didn't even know their names. I had no memory of my birth mother. My love embraced the Raoyang mother who had nurtured me from infancy.

During our stay in Lanzhou, each day tens of leaders of various work units were paraded with their hands tied, wearing tall paper hats. Their names were crossed out with big red *X*s (the historical symbol of imminent execution, each additional X indicative of a higher degree crime) and their faces were painted. As outsiders unfamiliar with local conditions, we had no way to judge the merits of the case when we saw public confessions, struggle meetings, and assemblies. Thousands of students from all over China arrived to investigate. Posters lined the campus and students from each faction vied to tell their story to each new group. So, we read posters, listened to student leaders and activists, and attended public criticism mass assemblies. It was like a festival. Everywhere there were drums, cymbals, and people shouting slogans. There was a sense of liberation. Lanzhou's situation resembled Hohhot's, but Lanzhou's factional fighting was more acute. I began to think about what might happen if factional fighting produced large-scale bloodshed and even civil war throughout China.

On the Road

It was the end of August 1966 and the newspapers were beginning to publicize student travel (*dachuanlian*). Following Mao's August 18 reception of one million students in Tiananmen, *dachuanlian* was encouraged at the highest levels of Party, government, and army as a new way to make revolution by strengthening the bonds between revolutionary youth and the leader. Millions of students were inspired by a sense of mission to go to Beijing to link both to the Chairman and to their generation of revolutionaries. They were also keen to see and experience the "world" they had learned about in their history and geography classes, in novels, and through folk traditions. Millions of students set off across the country, released from the tight fetters of family and education and given the opportunity for free revolutionary tourism.

I suggested to my companions in Lanzhou that we continue on to Xi'an, the capital of Shaanxi province, rather than return immediately to Hohhot. We were attracted to it as the scene of the 1936 Xi'an incident in which Guomindang leader Chiang Kai-shek was captured by warlord generals Zhang Xueliang and Yang Hucheng and forced to accept an alliance with the Communists to resist Japanese invasion. Xi'an was also a former imperial capital emblematic of China's eminence in the Tang dynasty.

Xi'an was just a night-train ride from Lanzhou. We stayed in the Northwest Hotel and visited the Xi'an Communications University, a leader in science and technology, the Shaanxi Teachers University, and the Xi'an Foreign Language Institute.

The city was full of student travelers. Posters and slogans described how Liu Lantao, the first secretary of the Northwest Bureau, and Shaanxi Provincial Party Committee, had sent work teams to suppress the students and teachers who criticized school leaders, just as at Peking University and Inner Mongolia Teachers' College.

From Xi'an we decided to return to Hohhot via Zhengzhou, the capital of Henan province, and Beijing. In Zhengzhou thousands of students were traveling to Beijing from all over China while others visited Xinjiang. Cao, Zhai, and I decided to continue south to see Jiangnan, an area south of the Yangtze River famed for its beautiful landscape. It seemed the chance of a lifetime. Zhao Lanke and Huang Zhigao headed north to Beijing, where Mao was receiving Red Guards. We reasoned that there would be later opportunities to visit Beijing. But when would we have the opportunity to visit south China for free again?

From Zhengzhou we took a train to Changsha in Hunan province. We visited the Hunan provincial library and the normal school where Mao had studied. Rather than his birthplace in Shaoshan, the main attraction for most visitors, we decided to visit other universities after learning that it was necessary to stand in line for six hours before receiving a five-minute tour of Mao's home.

Our next stop was Chongqing in the southwestern province of Sichuan. Red Guards with swords, spears, and knives were patrolling on motorcycles. In demonstrations in Chongqing, people marched, goose-stepping like soldiers, while workers carried tools or big knives.

Campus divisions at Chongqing University were deep in early September, but people were not yet using guns. They still used their fists. One year later, in the summer of 1967, some of the Cultural Revolution's fiercest combat would take place in Sichuan, turning the rivers red with blood.

From Sichuan we proceeded to Guilin in the Guangxi Zhuang Autonomous Region. Arriving at almost midnight on September 7, we found rebel faculty and students of Guangxi Teachers' College confronting the city Party Committee. Party work teams had been driven out of the college and the rebels demanded self-criticism by the authorities and rehabilitation of all who had been labeled. The Party Committee refused.

We had come to Guilin for its magnificent scenery of mountains rising above the Lijiang River, the finest under heaven—*Guilin shanshui jia tianxia*—as the saying had it. But as we exited the station, we saw a huge slogan: "Welcome all revolutionary students from across the country. Join our hunger strike."

If we had been a little more experienced, we would have gone to a restaurant first to prepare ourselves. We had already traveled by train eighteen hours without eating, anticipating a good meal on arrival. But it seemed shameful to eat under the circumstances.

"We should support them," Lao Cao said excitedly, knowing nothing of the particulars of the local struggle. There were about five thousand people in the square in front of the government building, including students, families, workers, and some cadres. People were lying or sitting on the lawn, under trees, or in the square. Hospital ambulances lined up as the hunger strike was in its third day. The government provided big buckets with salt water and free food, but no one touched the food. On seeing this scene, our blood began to boil. I took out a pen and wrote a message: "You have comrades here from Inner Mongolia. . . ."

When that was broadcast to the square, there was a buzz of excitement. No one had come from so far north to this southern outpost. It was a mild early September night. Once our message was broadcast, there was no standing down from supporting the hunger strike. We stayed three full days and nights, sleeping under the trees. At first, I could get up to drink salt water. But after a day and night without food, I was too dizzy to move.

The hunger strike centered on Guangxi Teachers' College. The majority of the students and faculty opposed the work team and dared to challenge the Guilin city authorities directly. After the work team was withdrawn on August 18, spurred on by Red Guards from Beijing, the Guangxi Teachers' College rebels stormed off campus to rally people to oppose the capitalist roaders, that is, city authorities. Branding the Beijing Red Guards troublemakers, the city authorities organized local Red Guards and workers to drive them away. Undaunted, on September 7, over one thousand students launched a hunger strike, demanding that the city authorities retract labels such as "rightists" and "counterrevolutionaries" that had been applied to rebels, and stop attacks on the Beijing Red Guards.[13]

Broadcasts informed us of the progress of negotiations with the city Party Committee. Premier Zhou Enlai reportedly urged the city to compromise, warning that if any student died, the local Party Committee would be held responsible.

When victory was announced around 10 p.m. on September 10, Guilin residents organized to carry the weak but triumphant students home. Perhaps as many as one thousand students, including supporters from all over China, had joined the hunger strike. Thousands of residents supported the student rebels. Two men carried me on the twenty-five-minute walk to the college where we were to stay.

There were forty wooden barrels filled with thin rice porridge in front of the campus gate. We were told to drink it little by little, then lay down to rest. Some of the hunger strikers required treatment, but two servings of porridge were enough for us to recover. The following day, a splendid breakfast was served with rice, *mantou* (steamed bun), and two dishes with vegetables and braised pork.

After the rebel victory, we spent several days enjoying the beautiful scenery and swimming in the Lijiang River. I had never seen such clear water—in the north all the rivers were yellow. I could see the river bottom and the fish swimming. We visited the famous Elephant Trunk Mountain and rowed bamboo barges on the river.

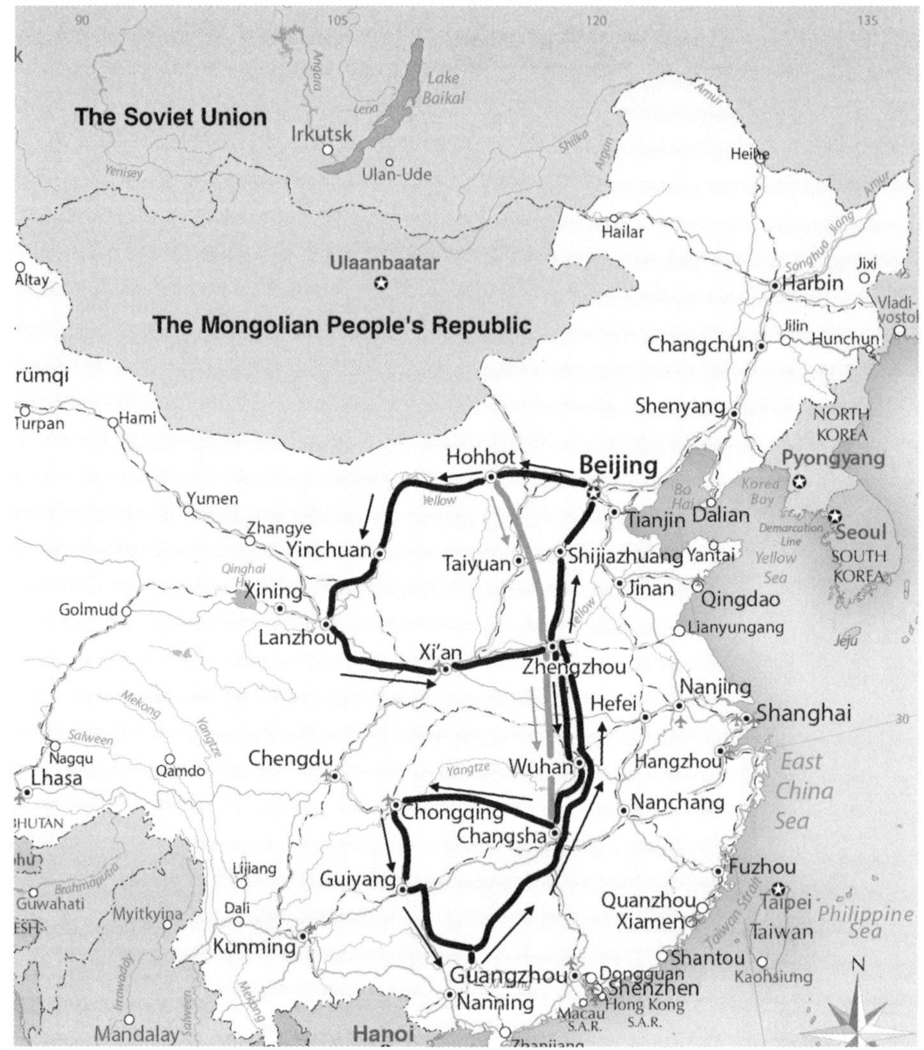

MAP 3 Cheng Tiejun's Long March routes

Inspected by Chairman Mao

Exhausted, but with a rare sense of accomplishment, we returned directly to Beijing in late September 1966. The trains were jammed. Hundreds of thousands of students from all over China were hoping to arrive at Tiananmen in time for National Day on October 1. Previous receptions were held on August 18, August 31, and September 15. Students poured into Beijing as "Chairman

Mao's guests," where they received free accommodations and food courtesy of Lin Biao's military.

The August 31 Beijing reception for Red Guards had been a dramatic one for Inner Mongolia. Ulanhu had been stripped of his high Party posts on August 16. The news was announced in Inner Mongolia on the afternoon of August 30 when Gao Jinming denounced Ulanhu's anti-Party, antisocialist crimes, and explained the Center's decision to strip him of his positions as second secretary of the North China Bureau and first Party secretary of Inner Mongolia.[14] Xie Xuegong, a secretary of North China Bureau Party Secretariat, was appointed the first Party secretary of Inner Mongolia, with Li Shude and Kang Xiumin as secretaries of the secretariat. They were all ranking members of the by then disbanded North China Bureau.

That same day, rebels mounted a huge banner with just three characters atop the main building at Teachers' College: Song wen shen (Away with Pests). It was the title of Mao's 1958 poem celebrating the drive to eliminate the dread disease schistosomiasis. Everyone knew the poem. A group of several dozen rebel students moved to humiliate the work team on campus. Raiding work team living quarters, they threw their belongings out the window onto the street. Rebels set off firecrackers to celebrate and loudspeakers blasted Mao poems and revolutionary songs far into the night. About a dozen work team members quickly packed and left campus.

Ulanhu lost positions in the Party, but he was still nominally the chairman of the government of the Inner Mongolia Autonomous Region, commander and political commissar of the Inner Mongolia Military Region, and president of Inner Mongolia University. Suddenly, on August 31, Mao and the Party Center allowed him to appear on the Tiananmen Rostrum. This shocked both rebels and loyalists, who were competing to outdo one another in denouncing the fallen leader. At the same reception, Jia Guotai, the Inner Mongolia University rebel, author of the first big-character poster in Inner Mongolia, made a brief speech on the rostrum, representing the faculty and students of North China visiting Beijing.[15] The presence of both Ulanhu and Jia Guotai on the rostrum revealed that Ulanhu's fate remained undecided.

When I arrived in Beijing on September 28, I learned that students were to register with their own school through the Inner Mongolia Liaison Office (Nei Menggu Zhujingban). It was housed in an elegant compound in the city's eastern district, close to the Forbidden City, which was originally the home of a Qing-dynasty Mongolian aristocrat. Many students from Inner Mongolia would arrive shortly, including my girlfriend Wang Qingxian.

In preparing for Mao's October 1 reception, the Party and government of Inner Mongolia had sent staff to handle logistics. Ulaan, chair of the Inner Mongolia Women's Federation, headed the group. I vividly recalled her speech attacking mercenary marriages in which villagers sold their daughters by weight. I also respected her achievements as a heroine in fighting the Japanese.

I tried to telephone Qingxian, but failing to reach her, I turned to Ulaan for help and eventually her office located Qingxian. Her willingness to help a student who she did not know personally left a deep impression on me.

I met Qingxian at the Central Nationalities Institute. When I asked about her family, she cried and told me about her mother's and brother's torture and her father's house arrest. The ugliest incidents had occurred at Erzhong, my alma mater, where teenagers beat classmates and teachers and tortured several teachers to death. I told her what I had seen in other parts of China and my fear that Chairman Mao and the Center were losing control of the country: "If they cannot stop the fighting and torture soon, the whole country will collapse in anarchy, even civil war." I had never before shared with her my pessimism about China's future.

On the eve of National Day, October 1, we went to bed at 4 p.m. At 1:30 a.m. officials woke us. After breakfast, we lined up for food rations: two *mantou*, one moon cake, two eggs, and two apples to last us until six that evening. We started walking to the square at 3 a.m. It was pitch black. We carried the Little Red Book and our food. Nothing else. One million students were proceeding on the five mile walk to the square from different parts of the city in ten long lines. It was dawn when we arrived.

Along Chang'an Boulevard tiles were pulled up at regular intervals revealing large cement ditches with water flowing. About every hundred yards there was a huge WC walled by reed mats with separate entrances on each side.

At 10 a.m. the march halted. Loudspeakers brought Lin Biao's high-pitched, morbid voice from the rostrum: "*Tong—zhi—men!* Comrades, little Red Guards, and all comrades in arms of proletarian revolutionaries! Now begins the celebration of the seventeenth anniversary of the People's Republic of China!" There followed the national anthem and brief speeches by Li Xuefeng, the newest member of the CCRG and mayor and Party secretary of Beijing, by Premier Zhou Enlai, and Jiang Qing. Zhou led the crowd in chanting slogans: "Firmly carry the Cultural Revolution through to the end!" "Learn from Comrade Jiang Qing!" "Good health forever to Vice-Chairman Lin!" "Long live, long, long live Chairman Mao!" We felt a bit disappointed that Mao did not say a single word. It was a sentiment that could only be conveyed to close friends.

After the speeches, around 11 a.m., Red Guards and students started their march for Mao's inspection. The human waves flowed through the huge Tiananmen Square. My heart skipped a beat. I was right in front of the rostrum, but I was so far away that the figures were too small to be identified. With everyone wearing the PLA uniform, I couldn't distinguish Mao, Lin Biao, Zhou Enlai, Jiang Qing, or anyone else. Still, everyone in the marching lines cried and screamed.

"Chairman Mao, Chairman Mao, long live Chairman Mao!"

The girls especially wept. Probably their feelings were real. But everyone had to shout and cry at the top of their lungs.

I shouted and cried along with all the others. As a rebel enthusiastically responding to his call to overthrow corrupt Party authorities, under whom I had suffered, I saw him as the greatest revolutionary leader in the world. But even as I shouted his praise, I felt torn by conflicts resulting from my own experience at school, the chaos and violence I encountered on the road, the poverty I had witnessed during the Great Leap and on my Long March, and above all the news about the tragedies that had befallen Qingxian's family. I shared my mixed feelings with Qingxian that evening. She was frightened by my thoughts, although I could see from her face that she agreed with me. "You'd better not tell anybody else about your true thoughts. It is very dangerous," she warned me.

Becoming a Red Guard

Following the rally in Tiananmen on October 1, 1966, Gao Shuhua, who was also in Beijing, met with his rebel friend Kuai Dafu, a chemical engineering student who spearheaded Tsinghua University's rebel movement. Kuai urged him to set up his own Red Guard organization at Teachers' College.

Kuai Dafu's rise to prominence closely mirrored that of Gao Shuhua. In early June 1966, the new Beijing Party Committee sent a 528-member work team into Tsinghua University. Its size and elite composition was a measure of its importance. Liu Shaoqi's wife, Wang Guangmei, who had previously led the nation's top Socialist Education Movement work team in Taoyuan Brigade in Hebei, joined the Tsinghua University work team from June 19 to August 3.

Kuai Dafu dared to attack Jiang Nanxiang, the powerful Tsinghua University Party secretary, and the work team sent in by Liu Shaoqi to quell the rebels and protect the university leadership. Kuai, whose parents were party members, was a member of the Youth League. Between June 24 and July 17, the work team organized numerous struggle meetings labeling him as a counterrevolutionary. Kuai responded by launching a hunger strike. On July 22,

Wang Li, a leading member of the CCRG, met him and on August 4, Zhou Enlai personally rehabilitated Kuai, who had been stripped of Youth League membership and placed under house arrest, and the Center disbanded the work team at Tsinghua.

With support from the CCRG, on September 24 Kuai organized his own Tsinghua University Jinggangshan Red Guards, named after Mao's 1927–1930 guerrilla base in Jiangxi province. In late September, he brought together rebel university student Red Guard organizations from other universities to form the Red Guard Third Headquarters.[16] We were attracted to Kuai, not only because of our shared experience as rebels who had faced work team repression, but above all because his Third Headquarters had been endorsed by the CCRG and showed signs of becoming a major force. Jinggangshan published its own newspaper, *Tsinghua Jinggangshan*, initially a weekly, then a daily, reportedly publishing several million copies at its peak.

With a letter of introduction from Gao Shuhua, together with two rebel student leaders from the Chinese language and literature department, Li Fusheng and Guo Shihai, we sought out Kuai Dafu to seek his advice on building a Red Guard organization in Hohhot.

Kuai was twenty-one, two years younger than me. Wearing black-framed glasses, he spoke slowly and very politely but with determination and with a slight Jiangsu accent. After a one-hour conversation he said: "Fear nothing. As long as you support Chairman Mao, just do it [*ni jiu gan*]!"

He urged us to organize our own Third Headquarters in Hohhot where the First and the Second Red Guard Headquarters had already been established.

"But it's difficult to organize in Inner Mongolia. It is so conservative. Where could we have our own stamp and armbands made?" I lamented.

"Stamp?" Dafu smiled, "Just find an art student to carve one. That was illegal before the Cultural Revolution, but now it's OK. . . . The armband is even easier. Just use ours. How many armbands do you need? We can help."

"Perhaps five hundred," Guo Shihai responded modestly.

"Oh, take a thousand," he replied magnanimously, giving us a whole bag of armbands inscribed "Jinggangshan Hongweibing" (Jinggangshan Red Guard). We were inspired to start our own Jinggangshan Red Guards in Hohhot, emboldened by ties to an ally who was winning victories in the nation's capital and attracting the attention of Chairman Mao.

Red Guard Organizations in Hohhot

In early October, I returned from Beijing to find that the Cultural Revolution had reached every urban unit, office, college, factory, even middle and primary school, in Hohhot. Classes had stopped, but students came to school to participate in the movement. Mao had proclaimed support for the so-called four bigs (*si da*): speaking freely, airing views freely, writing big-character posters, and holding great debates (*da ming, da fang, dazibao, da bianlun*). Every work unit was split into opposing camps, and internal divisions within the camps paralyzed many units. Workers had particularly severe problems. Those who criticized leaders were persecuted, lost income and housing, and were driven out of their units. Rebel workers, under attack and frequently isolated, regularly came to Teachers' College to seek help. Above all, Red Guard organizations sprung up everywhere.

Before leaving for Lanzhou in late August 1966, I and a few dozen students had talked with Gao Shuhua about organizing our own Red Guards. At the time, Red Guard organizations were starting to appear in Hohhot following Mao's inspection of the Red Guards on August 18. They rampaged through the city destroying the four olds and beat teachers. On August 31, during my absence, Dongfanghong Zhandou Zongdui (The East Is Red Fighting Column), a Teachers' College rebel organization known as Dongzong, was formed, with an initial membership of about three hundred, of which over two hundred were from the Foreign Languages Department. But Gao Shuhua, who had initiated it, was barred from joining Dongzong because of suspicions about his relationship with Lishake. Also barred were about a hundred of Gao's staunch supporters.[17]

Dongzong was one of the first two rebel Red Guard organizations (the other being Dongfanghong Hongweibing, or the East Is Red Red Guards) to emerge at Teachers' College. Both were formed by a so-called minority faction, in opposition to the majority's Nei Menggu Shiyuan Mao Zedong Zhuyi Hongweibing (Inner Mongolia Teachers' College Mao Zedongism Red Guards). Dongzong established a branch in each department and a combat team in each class. Our class combat team was called Quanwudi (Invincible), a phrase from a Mao poem.

In early September 1966, three Red Guard headquarters were established in Beijing after Mao's August 31 inspection of Red Guards. In Hohhot, Red Guard organizations also began to consolidate into three headquarters.

Initially, it was difficult to differentiate Red Guard organizations in Hohhot as all pledged fealty to Mao and all denounced Ulanhu. But the victims of the work teams designated their own Red Guard organizations "rebel" and all others as "loyalist." The distinction on the ground was far from clear cut, but for narrative convenience, we will adopt this rebel-centric terminology while noting its factionalist roots.

On September 5, a "Maoist Red Guard Provisional Headquarters of the Hohhot City Institutes of Higher Learning" was set up.[18] Headed by Fu Rong, a fourth-year chemistry student, who was head of the loyalist Teachers' College Mao Zedongism Red Guards, this organization involved both loyalists and rebels, including Teachers' College's Dongzong, and the loyalist Red Guards of Erzhong, my alma mater, who had been active in destroying the four olds. Known as Huyisi—the Hohhot First Headquarters—it was wracked with conflicts between loyalists and rebels.

Intense competition between rebel and loyalist Red Guards in Hohhot was a microcosm of a nationwide phenomenon. In a September 25 speech in Beijing, Chen Boda exhorted children of high-ranking cadres to resign from their Red Guard leadership positions. The following day, September 26, Red Guards from Erzhong led by Wang Duo's son Wang Jiyan and Wang Yilun's son Wang Jianhua withdrew from the First Headquarters and proclaimed the establishment of "the Mao Zedong Thought Red Guard Headquarters of the Colleges and Schools of Hohhot,"[19] also known as Hu'ersi, the Hohhot Second Headquarters.[20] These high-cadre children vowed to honor their "proletarian fathers."[21] Dongzong also broke with Huyisi, leaving it a much weakened force.

The rebel Red Guards were initially in disarray, without an umbrella organization. But on October 6, Central leaders including Zhou Enlai, Chen Boda, Kang Sheng, Jiang Qing, and Zhang Chunqiao attended a mass meeting at the Beijing Workers' Gymnasium. Zhang read the "Emergency Instruction regarding the Great Proletarian Cultural Revolution in Military Universities and Colleges" issued by the Central Military Affairs Commission and approved by the Party Center the previous day. The document announced the rehabilitation of all those persecuted by university Party committees or work teams labeled as counterrevolutionary, anti-Party, rightist, and "false leftist, real rightist." The majority of the victims, it said, were revolutionary. Zhou Enlai added that this instruction applied to all colleges throughout the country.[22] I attended the meeting before returning to Hohhot that day.

Armed with this new weapon, I applied to join Dongzong only to receive a cool reception from Dongzong leaders who called me unqualified for Red Guard membership. I was also dismayed to learn that our class combat team Quanwudi was led by Meng Dianxian, who had earlier picked up my letter and forwarded it to the Party secretary. Undaunted, I and others decided to organize our own Jinggangshan Red Guard group aligned with Kuai Dafu's Jinggangshan in Beijing.

Gao Shuhua returned from Beijing in early October. He was invited into a large classroom on the first floor of the Teachers' College main building that housed the Foreign Languages Department. Dongzong was holding a meeting chaired by Han Tong, a popular rebel leader. Han urged fellow leaders to accept Gao Shuhua as a revolutionary leftist. Gao's earlier exclusion had been to protect Dongzong, he said, but now that Gao's situation had been clarified, Han Tong proposed Gao as the leader of Dongzong. He also asked Gao not to build a rival Jinggangshan and suggested that all Jinggangshan members join Dongzong. Gao was deeply touched and joined Dongzong then and there, becoming one of its key leaders. But he did not agree to disband Jinggangshan, insisting that the two organizations could become allies.[23]

After this meeting, Teachers' College Jinggangshan was founded. Initially thirty students, at its peak there were 120 members. Jinggangshan maintained its own organization while working in alliance with Dongzong.

I became one of seven executive committee members of Jinggangshan. The leading group (*qinwu zu*) of Jinggangshan comprised three activists: Li Fusheng, Guo Shihai, and Chen Fuyu. Li, a fourth-year Chinese-language student, was the first chairman. Guo, who had been labeled "backward" for several years, was an excellent speaker, a shrewd debater, who spoke with a dialect from Northeast China. Many active Jinggangshan members were from Chifeng in Eastern Inner Mongolia, an area with superior education, but also one tainted by its association with Japanese rule in the years 1932–1945.

Chen Fuyu, a political education student from Baotou, had a flair for bold initiatives. We acted immediately on his suggestion to requisition the office of Ji Zhi, the disgraced Party secretary. Ji continued to collect his salary but performed supervised physical labor each day as a black element. Ji's large office contained a red line telephone with direct access to Inner Mongolia Party and government offices.

I ran the Jinggangshan office at first as rebel workers and students from all over Inner Mongolia sought our help. Requests poured in from schools, factories and offices. We staffed the office twenty-four hours a day to deal with emergencies.

Throughout the struggle, Jinggangshan membership, especially its leadership, was overwhelmingly Han with relatively few Mongols. Han and Mongols participated on both sides. Since the population of Hohhot was 90 percent Han and Han comprised the majority of college students, and since Han tended to be more active on national issues, they led all Red Guard organizations in Hohhot and Inner Mongolia. No organizations, however, were all Mongol or all Han, either in principle or in practice, and the majority of Mongols were rebels.

Gao Shuhua's association with Ulanhu through his son Lishake continued to dog the rebels, allowing the Party Committee and its loyalist allies to accuse Dongzong and Jinggangshan of supporting Ulanhu. Meng Chuan and Meng Surong, the sibling Russian-language instructors, who were also Daur, were very close to Gao Shuhua and to most rebel Russian-language students.

They joined Dongzong from the very beginning. Since they also had very close relations with Lishake and often spoke Russian with him, some people suspected that they might have a special relationship with the Ulanhu circle.

The rebels grew stronger as a result of drawing lessons from the October 1966 meeting that I had attended in Beijing. By mid-October, Dongzong had become the most powerful Red Guard organization at Teachers' College, its membership quadrupled, swelling from three hundred to well over one thousand, claiming three-fourths of the students and faculty. It was on the verge of becoming a major political force in Hohhot and throughout Inner Mongolia.

The Rise of Husansi and the Split in the Party Committee

After the fall of Ulanhu, Gao Jinming became director, and Quan Xingyuan deputy director, of the Inner Mongolia Party Committee Cultural Revolution Group, which was established on August 4, 1966, with Li Shude, and Guo Yiqing as members. Xie Xuegong, who had been a ranking figure in the North China Bureau, became the new first Party secretary of Inner Mongolia. However, he remained in Tianjin and sought to control Inner Mongolia through Gao Jinming and the Cultural Revolution Group.[24] Gao Jinming was the most powerful leader in Inner Mongolia, while his fellow secretaries Wang Duo, Wang Yilun and Liu Jinping were marginalized.

In the following months, these self-proclaimed leftist secretaries began to split. By wearing a Red Guard armband in Tiananmen Square, Mao had sent an unmistakable message linking the Red Guards to the Chairman and revolution. The problem, however, was that in Inner Mongolia three opposing Red Guard organizations emerged: First, Second and Third Headquarters all claimed to defend Mao. As the Party secretaries sought to restore Party authority, they found themselves on a collision course with rebel Red Guard organizations who responded to Mao by challenging all authorities. From the beginning the secretaries were divided: Wang Duo, Wang Yilun, and Liu Jinping treated the First and Second headquarters as their constituencies whereas Gao Jinming and Quan Xingyuan, who were more astute in sensing trends in Beijing, aligned themselves with the Third Headquarters.[25] The subsequent clashes among Red Guard organizations further split the Party leaders, with devastating consequences for Inner Mongolia.

The split was sparked by a dispute over the Party Committee's plan to direct the Cultural Revolution in Inner Mongolia. On October 7, Wang Duo delivered a report at a region-wide conference of Party Committee units on behalf of Gao Jinming who was attending a meeting in Beijing. It stated that of the three stages of the Cultural Revolution—*dou, pi, gai* (struggle, criticism, and transformation)—Inner Mongolia had basically completed the first two. It urged all directly affiliated units of the Party Committee to complete the first two stages within a month and enter the final stage—*gai* (transformation). The report also called for restoration of Party and league organizations that had collapsed in the recent turmoil.

The report could not have been more untimely. By then it was clear that Mao sought to intensify the Cultural Revolution, not bring it to a close. Rebels, who were battling with work teams dispatched by the Party, attacked the plan for conspiring to terminate the Cultural Revolution.[26] Dongzong rebels posted slogans and dispatched propaganda trucks denouncing the report. On October 10 Dongzong rebels, led by Gao Shuhua and our newly established Jinggangshan, stormed into the Party Committee compound and forced General Office director Zhang Lu to surrender his report tape.[27]

With the trend in Beijing favoring the Third Headquarters and radical rebel forces, it became necessary to reexamine the Gao Shuhua question in Inner Mongolia, particularly at Teachers' College. On October 23, Quan Xingyuan and Kang Xiumin came to Teachers' College and spoke on behalf of the Inner Mongolia Party Committee to rebel and loyalist organizations. Now on the defensive, they examined the mistakes made by the Party Committee in the Cultural Revolution and rehabilitated Gao Shuhua.[28]

With the tide turning in their favor, Gao Shuhua, Hao Guangde, and other rebel leaders met on October 29 in Red Theater to proclaim the founding of a new umbrella rebel organization: "The Revolutionary Rebel Headquarters of Red Guards of Colleges and Schools of Hohhot,"[29] popularly known as Husansi—The Third Headquarters of Hohhot. We again borrowed an organizational name from our Tsinghua allies led by Kuai Dafu. Husansi brought together seventeen rebel organizations from thirteen colleges and schools. Its core was Dongzong of Teachers' College.[30] With the establishment of Husansi, rebels, as a faction, became institutionalized and would soon enter politics and leave their imprint on Inner Mongolia and beyond.

Requests poured into Husansi from all over the city to send a representative to help, as if we were saviors. Hao Guangde was a master at recognizing which way the wind was blowing and at grasping power. Suddenly, even cadres and workers courted him, calling him Commander Hao (Hao Siling). As chairman of Husansi, Hao could dispatch people to support rebels throughout the city. With a single phone call and a broadcast announcement, he could mobilize five hundred trucks and ten thousand people. His supporters and allies could be found in every unit, including the police and the PLA. He was instrumental in making Husansi the strongest faction in Hohhot.

Husansi even began to achieve national prominence. Its most powerful allies were reporters from Xinhua News Agency, *People's Daily*, the *PLA Daily*, and *Red Flag* stationed in Hohhot and at key educational institutions, including Peking University, Tsinghua University, Harbin Military Engineering College, and Shanghai Military Medical College. These connections provided information and powerful allies. Kuai Dafu's ally Ning Kuixi (we nicknamed him "Ning Zuo," or "would rather be on the left"), the leading representative of Tsinghua Jinggangshan in Inner Mongolia, was the top adviser to Hao Guangde and Gao Shuhua. Most Husansi strategies came from him or won his approval.

Husansi's organizational network spread quickly to schools and work units throughout the autonomous region. One secret organization, the River West Company (Hexi gongsi), was directly controlled from Beijing. It was the external name for the Academy of Rocket Motors Technology (a.k.a. Academy 4) of the Seventh Ministry of Machine Building. Founded in 1964, from 1965 it operated in the Daqingshan Mountains outside Hohhot, in an area several hundred square miles in size. Academy 4 built rocket motors and its refineries processed solid fuel.[31] Villagers were warned to say nothing about their work. River West had fifty thousand employees, all skilled demobilized PLA soldiers or highly educated technicians. With privileged access to information from Beijing and familiar with Mao's support for the rebels, 80 percent supported the rebels. River West Company's rebel organization 8.18 was led by technician Wang Zhiyou and became more powerful than the company's official leaders.

Among members of Husansi were also Huochetou (Locomotive) of the Hohhot Railway Bureau (headed by train driver Liu Litang), Jinggangshan of Inner Mongolia Huajian Construction (headed by truck driver Huo Daoyu), and Red Flag Headquarters, an umbrella organization encompassing rebel organizations from the Party Committee units and the *Inner Mongolia Daily* (headed by Li Feng, a cadre from the Propaganda Department).

Opposing Husansi were three large loyalist organizations: Gongnongbing, Hongweijun, and Wuchanzhe.[32] Organized on December 30, 1966, the core of Gongnongbing was retired and demobilized soldiers headed by Fan Junzhi, a former bodyguard of Huang Hou, deputy commander of the Inner Mongolia Military Region. Hongweijun, formed on January 1, 1967, was an Inner Mongolia–wide organization supported by Party secretaries Wang Yilun and Liu Jinping. Its leader was Zhang Sanlin, a technician at the Hohhot Rubber Factory. Wuchanzhe, formed in early January, was headed by Zhang Qisheng. Its core were workers, and it claimed a membership of thirty-five thousand in Hohhot alone. Other powerful loyalist organizations included Kangda

Bingtuan from Teachers' College, formed on October 18, 1966, and Hongse Zaofanzhe Lianmeng (Alliance of Red Rebels), formed in early 1967, which comprised cadres from the Inner Mongolia Party Committee work units and college teachers.[33]

These loyalists, allied with Wang Duo, Wang Yilun, Liu Jinping, and the Inner Mongolia Military Region, vowed to uphold Party rule and resolutely opposed Gao Jinming and Quan Xingyuan, who were sympathetic toward Husansi.

The stage was set for bloody battles between rebel and loyalist forces in the months ahead. Although initially much weaker due to their relatively small student base, with support from workers, rebel strength grew rapidly.

The rebels' greatest weapons were Mao's latest pronouncements and their "correct" reading of the trend of the Cultural Revolution. When the rebels targeted Wang Duo, his comrades began to distance themselves from him. The Party Propaganda Department forced Wang to make a self-criticism on October 28. Wang admitted only to having "unconsciously" implemented the bourgeois reactionary line while seeking to shift responsibility for his errors to the Inner Mongolia Party Committee.

On October 31, rebels from *Shijian* (Practice), a Party Committee journal, and six affiliated units of the Party Committee, organized their own organization, Geming Zaofan Zhandoudui (Revolutionary Rebel Fighting Corps), led by Nasanbayar, a mid-level Mongol cadre. Their first big poster, "A Bourgeois Reactionary Line Ran through the North China Bureau's 'Qianmen Hotel Conference,'" singled out Wang Duo, Wang Yilun, and Liu Jingping for protecting Ulanhu. This was a devastating attack on the three, who had sought to protect their careers by criticizing Ulanhu at the conference. The poster was widely copied all over Hohhot and beyond. The Party Committee was facing rebellion from within its own ranks, as well as from rebel students.[34]

The poster led to the convening of a three-level cadre conference beginning on November 4. On November 10, Husansi organized a rally pledging to attack the bourgeois reactionary line. The Inner Mongolia Party Committee leaders and all the representatives participating in the three-level cadre conference attended the rally. Rebels denounced Wang Yilun, forcing him off the platform.

On November 24, Husansi organizations, including Dongzong and a dozen other rebel organizations, staged a bold action, "kidnapping" Wang Duo and taking him to Beijing to debate Inner Mongolia issues before the leaders in Beijing.[35] Meanwhile, armed clashes erupted in Hohhot, spurred by loyalist Hongweijun forces that received strong support from Wang Yilun.[36]

In late December, Gao Jinming, attending a conference in Beijing, learned that the CCRG had sided with the Third Headquarters. Returning to Hohhot, he proclaimed that Husansi held the Great Flag of Mao Zedong Thought in the criticism of the bourgeois reactionary line. Gao Jinming's move saved his career.[37] It also precipitated an open split among Party leaders, with Gao Jinming and Quan Xingyuan as well as Kang Xiumin, Guo Yiqing, Li Shude, Li Zhi, and Wang Zaitian supporting the rebels while Wang Duo, Wang Yilun, and Liu Jingping hewed to the loyalists.

Gao Jinming and his close associates' support for Husansi and Dongzong initiated an alliance of the rebels with a group of Inner Mongolia's Party leaders that would soon plunge the region into profound political crisis.

My Long March

Soon after its founding in October 1966, I had become an active member of Jinggangshan. But as the political debate and sharpening organizational struggles in Hohhot and Beijing continued, I became less interested in building a rebel network on campus than in setting out once again on a Long March. The *People's Daily* editorial from October 22, titled "Red Guards Are Not Afraid of the Long March," touched my soul. From the second half of August 1966, many students, I among them, had been investigating and sometimes participating in local struggles, forging alliances, and seeing the country.

Student activists from Haiyun (Maritime) College in Dalian proposed that Red Guards march to Tiananmen on foot to ease the burden on the railroads and learn from the Red Army, linking students to the tradition of the Long March. At a joint meeting of Dongzong and Jinggangshan in Hohhot there was vigorous debate as to whether this was the time to set out on a Long March. Cao Jun, Huang Zhigao, and I proposed setting out. Hao Guangde, however, responded: "We can't go now. Every school and work unit is asking rebels from Teachers' College for support. Every day people invite us to speak about our struggle experience in expelling the work team. How can we abandon the struggle to begin a Long March at a time like this?" Gao Shuhua and Guo Shihai agreed that it was critical that rebels run the office, but they felt that it was fine for some to go.

Cao Jun and I prepared to set off leaving Guo Shihai and Li Fusheng responsible for the Jinggangshan office while Hao Guangde and Gao Shuhua prioritized building the new umbrella rebel organization Husansi.

Some people, including my father and some close friends, criticized me: "You helped to organize the rebel faction and you were the most determined. But now, with victory at hand, suddenly you want to travel. After all, you're scum; you won't see this through to the end."

FIGURE 7 Wang Qingxian in Yan'an, December 1966

I was eager to test myself by undertaking a Long March on foot. I wanted to learn what was happening all across the country. Walking would be very different from traveling by train and staying in guesthouses in terms of understanding the lives and thoughts of ordinary people, especially villagers and mountain people.

At that time, Qingxian and I were pretty close, and I tried to convince her to join me and others on a Long March. I planned to hike a thousand miles from Hohhot to Shaoshan in Hunan, and eventually to Jinggangshan in Jiangxi, home to the original soviet, before returning. But Qingxian decided to join another team of fifteen people to march from Hohhot to Yan'an, Mao's wartime revolutionary capital. "The shorter distance might be more suitable for me," she said. We were both shy. Besides, the revolutionary atmosphere prohibited any open manifestation of love, lest it pollute the purity of revolution.

I set off with Cao Jun, Zhai Ximin, and Zhao Lanke. We were all from Teachers' College, all Jinggangshan, and we had been together on an earlier expedition by train. The trip, more than two thousand miles each way, was a pilgrimage to the source of revolutionary origins and an opportunity to learn what was happening across the countryside and to link up with other rebels.

To prepare, we each bought a Mongol knife, fourteen inches long. In the past, such knives served multiple functions, including fighting and eating, since Mongol cuisine featured boiled lamb or beef. Each of us bought a huge fur hat, leg wrappings, rubber boots, and a quilt. We had a first-aid kit, a field cauldron, chopsticks, bowls, a wash basin, a compass, Red Guard certificates, and a letter of introduction provided by Jinggangshan headquarters of Teachers' College. Each carried one hundred Mao badges and fifty Little Red Books of Mao quotations. I also had thirty huge Mao portraits. This time the college logistics office provided grain tickets and money in advance for food, as well as all necessary supplies at no charge.

On November 18, the day of our departure, we ceremonially bowed to Mao's portrait and vowed to travel on foot to Shaoshan, to disseminate Mao Zedong Thought, and to learn from the poor and lower middle peasants. We planned to arrive in Hunan in about three months, perhaps taking three additional months returning via Jinggangshan and Beijing to Hohhot. But with the country in a state of anarchy, the whiff of smoke was in the air, and many talked of civil war.

We had good maps with clear road markings for each province. Each day we walked eight to ten hours, a minimum of twenty-two miles. Our record was thirty-four miles. Sometimes we stayed a few days in one place.

The first four to five days were hardest. After that there was no feeling in our feet; they were just numb. We always ate and slept well. We avoided big cities, staying in poor rural and remote mountain areas to learn how the revolution had transformed the poorest rural areas. From Hohhot to Datong in Shanxi province was a four to five days' walk. We passed through Datong, a huge coal-mining city, staying just long enough to buy a red silk Jinggangshan flag.

On the first day, for the first three hours we laughed and talked as we marched. After that we just walked in silence. We noticed suddenly that Zhai was missing. Retracing our steps, we finally found him under a tree. He complained that we were walking too fast. He was the tallest in our group, but we comforted him like a little brother. Finally, he agreed to go on.

During this first leg of the journey, we started to quarrel. "Chairman Mao called on us to go on foot, but look how full the trains are. Why not go faster?" Zhai said. Seeing his low morale, I encouraged him: "Come on, Lao Zhai, you

FIGURE 8 Gao Shuhua (second left), Han Tong (third left), and their "Long March" team, December 1967

need physical training." With much coaxing, he agreed to continue. But on December 12, Zhai decided to return by train to Hohhot via Hebei, leaving three of us to continue our Long March. He tried to persuade me to go with him to our hometown, Raoyang, but I refused.

On December 18, we stayed overnight in the guesthouse of Xiyang county, famous for the Dazhai Brigade, the national model village. When the manager saw our Jinggangshan flag, he told us that another group of Red Guards had stayed there a few days earlier. Their record book revealed that Gao Shuhua and sixteen other Teachers' College rebels had recently arrived.[38]

Two months later, when we returned to Hohhot, Gao Shuhua told me that the Inner Mongolia Party Committee had asked Teachers' College to organize a model Long March team. Gao then led a seventeen-member team (two women and fifteen men), including Han Tong, Huang Zhigao, Ren Zuolin, and Guo Shihai. They took the train to Taiyuan, then set off on foot to Dazhai and the coal-mining city of Yangquan. In late December, arriving in Beijing, they learned of the loyalists' attack on rebels in Hohhot and returned in mid-January 1967.

We reached Dazhai on December 20 to find it packed with students. After lunch in a reception station to provide for the thousands of daily student visitors, we lined up to visit the cave of Dazhai leader Chen Yonggui. His wife Hu Ni was at home, working on the *kang*. Chen was attending a meeting in Beijing. Hu was in her forties, healthy and strong. Each family in the village had identical two-story homes. The first was a deep cave with one door and two windows. The caves were neat and clean, with portraits of Chen wearing a white towel on his head, or of Mao or Zhou Enlai. None showed him working in the fields. The village had electricity, rare at the time, particularly in the mountains. The second floor was for storage, the first for living.

The stonemason Jia Jincai told us that the stone he had worked on in the course of a lifetime could reach to the moon. We touched his hand, which was as hard as wood. Jia showed us the seven ditches, eight gorges and one hillside—*qi gou ba liang yimian po*—the terraces they built right up to the top of the mountain. No forest was left. Other mountain villages were similar. In the mountains, rarely were pieces of land more than a fraction of an acre, and some were barely the size of a table.

We saw the army stationed a mile from the village—a camp in the valley. Villagers told us that one battalion of soldiers, a construction unit, was permanently stationed there with heavy equipment—diggers, tractors—to help Dazhai build terraces, the village having been designated as a national model in 1964. In Duzhuang village, a mile and a half south of Dazhai, an old man said pointedly: "We did the same as Dazhai. The only difference is that we received no outside help."

After spending a few days in the coal-mining town of Yangquan in southern Shanxi, where we found the life of miners exceedingly hard, we moved into northern Henan in late December. Hejia county was the hometown of my companion Zhao Lanke. At the reception station we talked about the famine that had devastated Henan in the Leap. We were told that 15 percent of the villagers had died. Most of Lanke's family had moved to Inner Mongolia in the 1950s, before the famine.

On January 8, 1967, in Zhengzhou, the capital of Henan province, my two remaining companions decided to follow the railroad to Changsha. This meant that they could arrive in Shaoshan earlier, then return to Inner Mongolia by train. I decided to continue on foot alone to see more of the countryside and to test myself. My martial arts experience and the big knife I carried made me confident of my ability to travel alone.

FIGURE 9 Cheng Tiejun in Shaoshan, February 1967

On January 19, I was walking along the road from Zhengzhou to Nanyang after dark when a truck stopped and invited me in. We were in an area famous for the battles of the Three Kingdoms period, including the hometown of the warrior Zhuge Liang. I said to the driver that I could walk. But the driver insisted. It was the only time I rode in a vehicle during the trip, riding four miles to the seat of Xinye county in southern Henan. The driver asked if I'd heard about the recent murders of Red Guards reported in the local newspaper and warned that it wasn't safe to walk alone after dark. I continued my journey.

After crossing Hubei, I reached Hunan on February 3, 1967. At Yuanjiang in southern Hunan, PLA and militia units were everywhere, armed with rifles with bayonets. Posters ordered a crackdown on Xiangjiang Fenglei, the Xiang River Storm, one of the largest rebel organizations. It was February 5, and martial law had been imposed throughout the province. At every crossroads a reception table took confessions from reactionary organizations, that is, rebel organizations. Anyone higher than a team leader (in charge of thirty people) was required to confess or be arrested. Many people had their hands tied, wearing paper dunce caps, and having placards hung on their necks with their names inscribed with red *X*s. I was shocked to see so many soldiers mobilized to arrest rebels, forcing them to run with hands tied tightly behind their backs. The feeling was of bringing the arrested to execution.

Arriving in Shaoshan in Hunan on February 12, I encountered my friend Pang Naiwu, a rebel primary school teacher from Hohhot's southern suburb. At the start of our Long March, I had spent a night at his primary school. I had asked whether he could join us, but he replied that the Hohhot education authorities would not allow teachers to go. One month later, the policy changed.

We decided to return to Hohhot together via Shanghai by train, dropping my original plan to walk from Hunan to Jinggangshan, the early revolutionary base in Jiangxi province. The Center had publicly terminated *dachuanlian* on February 3, 1967, eliminating free food and lodging.[39] Returning on foot would therefore have been difficult. But we could not return without seeing Shanghai, the leading center of rebel activity in the Cultural Revolution and China's great industrial city.

5

The First PLA Murder of a Red Guard

Murder

I had embarked on my Long March from Hohhot on November 18, 1966, and reached Shaoshan, Mao's birthplace in Hunan province, eighty-six days later, on February 12, 1967, having traversed six provinces on foot. Pang Naiwu and I then took a train from Ningxiang, Hunan, to Nanchang in Jiangxi province, then on to Shanghai.

Shanghai was at the center of the storm then sweeping the country. Following their challenge of the Shanghai Party Committee and government in late 1966, Zhang Chunqiao and Yao Wenyuan, with the support of the Shanghai Workers' Headquarters, and with strong backing from Mao and the Central Cultural Revolution Group (CCRG) in Beijing, led the first and most acclaimed of many power seizures throughout the country.

On January 31, 1967, the *People's Daily* published an editorial "On the Proletarian Revolutionaries' Struggle to Seize Power" extolling Mao's characterization of Nie Yuanzi's big-character poster as a manifesto of the people's commune: "Chairman Mao wisely and ingeniously foresaw that our state organ will take a brand-new shape." On February 5, they proclaimed the Shanghai People's Commune, styled after the Paris Commune, referencing the first short-lived communist revolutionary victory in 1871. Although Mao initially approved of the new name, he later told Zhang and Yao that "it better be renamed a revolutionary committee" (*haishi jiao geming weiyuanhui hao*).[1] Mao apparently thought that the Paris Commune principle was too anarchistic and that some kind of revolutionary governance was necessary.[2] Renamed the Revolutionary Committee of Shanghai Municipality on February 24, China's first Revolutionary Committee was presented as a national model. Soon revolutionary committees, which comprised representatives of the Party, the PLA, and the people, were springing up throughout the nation at provincial, city, county, and commune levels, challenging and replacing the Party apparatus.[3]

Arriving in Shanghai almost at midnight on February 19, we took a bus from the station to an old inn assigned to us by the Shanghai Red Guard Service Center. As the bus turned onto the boulevard, we saw walls overflowing with posters signed by Hong Zong (Red Guard Headquarters) from Shanghai No. 2 Military Medical University describing events in Hohhot.

"Martyr Han Tong will live forever!"

"Strongly demand that the Center try the murderers!"

"People who gun down Red Guards will have no peace!"

Some of the characters were the color of blood.

Unable to control my feelings, I burst out, "My God! Han Tong was murdered!" Passengers turned and stared at me.

"Who is Han Tong?" Naiwu asked.

"He is a fourth-year English student at my college."

A native of Inner Mongolia, he was born into a poor Han family in Getuyin village in Tuoketuo county south of Hohhot in 1942. He spoke with a heavy Shanxi accent, his village close to the Shanxi border. Tall and handsome, he was active in the performing arts, performing beautifully in a two-person opera form called *er'rentai* popular in Shanxi and western Inner Mongolia.

At the time of the Gao Shuhua poster that touched off the Cultural Revolution in Hohhot, Han Tong and I joined the rebels and became close friends. I was a member of the student union propaganda team in charge of the bulletin board in the department, and he was in the performance team. We also shared scissors, clippers, and razor to provide free haircuts for our classmates. He later became a leader of the rebel umbrella organization Dongzong in charge of propaganda, drafting, printing, and distributing leaflets. It was he who invited Gao Shuhua to join Dongzong, after months of exclusion by other rebel leaders.

That night I read dozens of posters describing Tong's political activities in the days before his murder. The issues centered on military involvement in the Cultural Revolution in Hohhot. The posters denounced the Inner Mongolia Military Region (IMMR) for supporting the loyalist camp in the factional struggles that had intensified during my absence. I could see that the Party Committee was divided into two camps. One was denounced by its critics as "a handful of powerholders taking the capitalist road" and the mass organizations, including Red Guard organizations, supporting them as either *baoshoupai* (conservatives or loyalists) or, worse, *baohuangpai* (royalists). The other camp proclaimed itself "revolutionary leftist," and its supporters styled themselves "revolutionary leftists" or "rebels" (*zaofanpai*). Following the national trend toward civil war that I had observed during my Long March, the two sides in Inner Mongolia were now in open confrontation. The difference was that in Hohhot the PLA had opened fire on rebel students. This was particularly distressing because Mao had called on the PLA to actively support the revolutionary left a month earlier, on January 21, 1967. I realized the magnitude of the event, but reading these first accounts of a PLA murder of a rebel student, I couldn't figure out whose side Mao and the Center were on.

It was too late for us to return from Shanghai to Hohhot that night. The next morning, February 21, we tried but failed to book train tickets for that day (tickets were free with a student or faculty ID). Finally, we got two tickets for the first train to Beijing on February 22. In Shandong province, local factional fighting caused a twelve-hour delay; then, in the southern suburbs of Tianjin, a rail accident caused a further ten-hour delay.

Arriving in Beijing early in the morning of February 24, we read more posters describing the murder and detailing the role of the military in suppressing the Cultural Revolution in Inner Mongolia. We learned that Zhou Enlai and the Central Cultural Revolution Group (CCRG) had convened an emergency meeting to discuss the situation. At that time, Inner Mongolia representatives, including Husansi rebels Gao Shuhua and Hao Guangde, were in Beijing. I tried, but failed, to contact them through the rebel leader Kuai Dafu at Tsinghua University. Kuai told me over the phone that they were prohibited from making contact with outsiders. Even he could not see them unless Zhou Enlai asked him to join the discussion. "You'd better get back to Hohhot quickly; there will be more fighting ahead," he said.

Rebel Power Seizure

Han Tong's death was the consequence of fighting between warring Red Guard and mass organizations and the Inner Mongolia Party Committee, with divided Party secretaries mobilizing different factions. The conflict erupted on November 24, 1966, shortly after my departure on a Long March, when Gao Jinming and Quan Xingyuan threw their support to the rebel Husansi and Dongzong for their action in kidnapping their fellow Party secretary Wang Duo. In early 1967, Gao Jinming and some of his fellow Party leaders demanded that the Party Committee immediately stop the work of Wang Yilun, another Party secretary.

Mass organizations were also divided: rebel organizations such as Husansi and Dongzong supported Gao Jinming, whereas the loyalist mass organizations Wuchanzhe and Hongweijun stood by Wang Duo and Wang Yilun. Wuchanzhe, with membership drawn from writers and journalists from the Party

Committee's *Agriculture Team Bulletin* and the Party School, became the theoretical force defending Wang Duo and Wang Yilun, as Hongweijun became more militant.[4] A civil war was unfolding in Inner Mongolia and many other parts of the country.

In this war, the rebels, confident of support from the highest authority in Beijing, moved aggressively. Inspired by the Shanghai rebels' power seizure, and Mao's support for the action, on January 11, rebels at the *Inner Mongolia Daily*—Dongfanghong Zaofan Zongbu (The East Is Red Rebel Headquarters)—seized control of the press and published a new edition of the paper that it styled *Nei Menggu Ribao, Dongfanghong Dianxun* (*Inner Mongolia Daily, East Is Red Dispatch*), preparatory to publishing a new *Inner Mongolia Daily*. Changing the format of a provincial-level Party news organ without the approval of the Party Center was unprecedented. Although the rebels claimed that the Party Committee supported their action, the Party Committee was divided. Approval might have been given by Gao Jinming or another Party secretary supporting the rebels. The loyalist *Daily* leaders quickly called in militant Hongweijun workers to expel the rebels. The rebels for their part called in Husansi rebels from Teachers' College, who repulsed the Hongweijun attack and took control of the *Daily* building. The ensuing clash between loyalists and rebels turned Hohhot into a battlefield, with thousands of people on each side proclaiming themselves "revolutionary leftists." The rebel attack was further fueled and legitimated by a January 21 *People's Daily* editorial titled "Proletarian Revolution Must Create a Grand Alliance to Seize Power from Those in Authority Taking the Capitalist Road."

In the new political jargon of the time sanctified by the CCRG and Mao, *geming zuopai* (revolutionary leftist) and *zaofanpai* (rebel) were deemed politically correct. Their opponents, dubbed *youpai* (rightist), *baoshoupai* (conservative), or *baohuangpai* (royalist), were criminalized as "counterrevolutionary elements" or "reactionary organizations." These were not random labels of little significance. They determined whether one was a supporter of Mao or of his enemies. One who was labeled as an enemy would become a pariah or lose even the most basic right to live as a human. The enormous stakes involved in label designation informed the vehemence in the fight. Many rebels, including myself, had been denounced as "bad elements," "rightists," or "backward elements," becoming targets of political campaigns. Becoming rebels in June 1966 gave many a new political life. But their fate hinged on the outcome of new political battles.

The stakes were equally high for the Party secretaries of Inner Mongolia. They proclaimed themselves "revolutionary leftist cadres" by denouncing Ulanhu and labeling his associates a "black gang" in summer 1966. Now many had become swept up in the next round of Mao's campaign against the Party bureaucracy. Having become "power holders" with the seizure of the *Inner Mongolia Daily*, were they still revolutionary leftists, or were they taking the capitalist road? In the political struggles that followed, political lines were ephemeral as everyone sought to claim a place in the ranks of revolutionary cadres. The careers, and even the lives, of many political leaders and activists, hung in the balance.

There was little difference between the two camps in terms of policy issues. Their difference was more of degree than substance. Wang Duo and Wang Yilun were more inclined to prioritize stability in implementing the Cultural Revolution and to maintain some continuity in the cadre ranks. Gao Jinming and Quan Xingyuan were intent on demonstrating their revolutionary credentials by sweeping aside all they deemed insufficiently radical in supporting Mao. Rebel Red Guards, especially those from Teachers' College who became radicalized in their fight against work team suppression, were critical of all authority in Inner Mongolia. This common political orientation led college rebel Red Guards and radical leftist Party secretaries to mutual support.

On January 22, 1967, Hongweijun, Wuchanzhe, and Geming Zhanshi, loyalist forces associated with a base among industrial workers and Party and government work units, advanced on the *Inner Mongolia Daily* compound with more than thirty trucks and buses. They came to stop the publication of the first issue of the new *Inner Mongolia Daily* by the rebels, which loyalists viewed as a conspiracy by Gao Jinming and Kang Xiumin to control all Inner Mongolia. At 4:50 p.m., loyalist activists stormed the printing house of the *Daily*, cutting the power lines and destroying machines. When rebels throughout the city rushed to aid their comrades, heavy fighting ensued.[5] With the Inner Mongolia Party Committee paralyzed, Hongweijun and other loyalists appealed to the army for assistance.[6] Hohhot was in virtual civil war.

The Inner Mongolia Military Region originated with the Inner Mongolia Self-Defense Army on June 3, 1946. It merged Ulanhu's soldiers with the Eastern Inner Mongolian Autonomous Army. Ulanhu was the commander and political commissar; Asgan and Wang Zaitian became deputy commanders. In January 1948, during the Civil War, this army was incorporated into the CCP-led People's Liberation Army and was renamed the Inner Mongolia People's Liberation Army of the IMMR, and in May 1949, the IMMR was placed under the command of the North China Military Region. In May 1955, the IMMR was elevated to become one of twelve newly structured Large Military Regions (*da junqu*) with the same rank as the Beijing Military Region (formerly the North China Military Region).[7] Ulanhu was the commander and political commissar. However, with the merger of Inner Mongolia with the

Suiyuan Military District in 1952, numerous Han officers took up important positions in the Inner Mongolian army. It was no longer a Mongol-dominated army.

The IMMR leadership had been decimated in the initial rounds of the Cultural Revolution. Ulanhu, commander and political commissar, Kong Fei, deputy commander, Ting Mao, deputy political commissar, Tala, deputy chief of staff, and Buyanjab, deputy director of the political department, almost the entire top Mongol echelon of the IMMR, were sidelined in the aftermath of the Qianmen Hotel events.[8] With their demise, the IMMR was controlled by first deputy commander Liu Huaxiang, deputy commander Xiao Yingtang, deputy commander Huang Hou, chief of staff Wang Liangtai, deputy commissar Liu Chang, and Zhang Degui, deputy director of the political department. All were Han, and the military was firmly in control.

From the beginning of August 1966, Generals Liu Huaxiang and Xiao Yingtang led an attack on Mongol generals Kong Fei, Ting Mao, and Tala, denounced as nationality splittists and black gang members of the Ulanhu Anti-Party Treasonous Group (Wulanfu fandang panguo jituan), that is, plotters for Mongolian secession and unification with the Mongolian People's Republic. In mid-September, the Central Military Affairs Commission approved the IMMR's decision to sack these Mongol officers and investigate their crimes. From November, struggles intensified, and in January 1967, they were taken from one struggle session to another, their arms tied behind their backs, followed by kicks with heavy military boots. Kong Fei suffered several broken ribs.[9] Most of the torture sessions were supervised by Generals Liu Huaxiang, Xiao Yingtang, and Wang Liangtai.

The only Mongol survivor in the Center's purge of the IMMR was Major General (shaojiang) Wu Tao, the first political commissar, who saved himself by distancing himself from Ulanhu during the conference at Qianmen Hotel. He, too, would suffer under the Han officers. Although he had support from Marshal Ye Jianying, vice-chairman and secretary-general of the Central Military Affairs Commission, and was sent back to head the Leading Group of the Cultural Revolution in the IMMR, Han commanders attacked him for being a black gang member of the Ulanhu group. This, despite repeated interventions from the Central Military Affairs Commission and the army's General Political Department, which insisted that he was opposed to Ulanhu. From July 1966, his home telephone was cut off, car confiscated, bodyguards removed, and he was put under surveillance.[10]

Although this attack on the Mongol generals including Wu Tao was ethnically based, from late January 1967, things began to develop in a different direction. On January 23, the IMMR organized a special struggle session against Wu Tao, during which he was stripped of his military uniform and forced to wear a placard denouncing him as a *sanfan fenzi*, or a "three anti" element (anti-Party, anti-socialism, and anti–Mao Zedong Thought). He was accused of supporting radical leftist Party leaders Gao Jinming, Quan Xingyuan, and Li Shude, and he was identified as the backstage master directing Husansi's attack on loyalist Party leaders Wang Duo and Wang Yilun. He was subsequently forced to stop all work and write repeated self-criticism reports. From January 23, he was subjected to torture, repeatedly slapped in the face, kicked in the stomach, and forced to kneel on hard wood for hours.[11] The Han generals' physical torture of Wu Tao coincided with the Center's decision to involve the PLA in the seizure of power that was raging throughout the country.[12]

By this time, PLA leaders in Beijing were divided over PLA participation in power seizures; many preferred to maintain law and order while the whole nation descended into anarchy. When beleaguered loyalists appealed to the IMMR for military intervention on January 22, Xiao Yingtang consulted the Cultural Revolution Group of the PLA in Beijing about whether to support the loyalists. Marshal Xu Xiangqian, director of the group, reportedly instructed Xiao to "carry out investigation to determine the situation by all means. . . . Stand on the side of the revolutionary leftists. The army must not use force, but it can mediate."[13] The instruction left it to Xiao and his fellow commanders in IMMR to figure out who the revolutionary leftists were. In the face of widening anarchy, many in the army, as the Party's security apparatus, were inclined to support the Party leadership to maintain some semblance of stability. Indeed, by this time, the IMMR leaders had already recognized Wang Duo and Wang Yilun in the Inner Mongolia Party Committee as the revolutionary left. It identified the mass organizations such as Hongweijun, Wuchanzhe, and Gongnongbing, which supported the two Wangs, as revolutionary left organizations because most of their members were workers, peasants, demobilized soldiers, and lower-ranking cadres who had good class backgrounds. They regarded rebel organizations such as Husansi, 8.18, and others as "counterrevolutionary organizations" bent on "wrecking the Party, wrecking the Army," stating that 60 percent of members had family backgrounds of "landlords, rich peasants, counterrevolutionaries, bad elements, and rightists," all enemy categories. Gao Jinming, Quan Xingyuan, and Li Zhi in the Party Committee were identified as controlling these rebel organizations from behind the scenes and supporting the bourgeois reactionary line.[14] Marshal Xu Xiangqian's instruction thus firmed up the IMMR's determination to support those they believed to be the genuine revolutionary leftists.

At 11 p.m. on January 22, the IMMR dispatched an armed company to stop the fighting at the *Inner Mongolia Daily*. Arriving at 12:30 a.m., on January 23, the company supported the loyalist leaders of the *Daily* against Husansi. Cordoning off the compound, the army issued a three-point directive: secure military control of the *Inner Mongolia Daily*; cleanse the personnel of the *Daily*, allowing people to go out but not come in; and leave the fate of the *Daily* to be determined later.[15]

The IMMR's action to control the *Daily* brought the army directly into the factional fighting in Inner Mongolia, a phenomenon that was occurring throughout the country. In fact, on January 15, the army had already taken control of the Inner Mongolia Radio Station, following the Central directive "On the Question of Broadcast Stations," which placed radio stations under military control. The military's support for the loyalist leadership of the *Daily* was tantamount to treating Husansi as a counterrevolutionary organization. This was the greatest insult to the rebels, who fervently believed that they had Mao's support.

Husansi by this time had become a powerful citywide rebel alliance consisting of sixty-five organizations. When it demanded that top commanders of the IMMR come to the office in person to explain their decision to send troops into the conflict at the *Daily* and to crush rebels and support loyalists, Liu Chang, deputy commissar and Gao Bi, deputy director of the mass work department appeared at 5 a.m. on January 23. Explaining that the army had been sent in to protect the building and to prevent factional fighting, they agreed to withdraw their troops.

But the rebels were not satisfied. They invited Liu and Gao to Teachers' College, the rebel stronghold, at ten o'clock that morning to provide a public explanation. After a fierce debate with Husansi at Teachers' College, Liu Chang admitted that it had been a mistake to send armed soldiers. He agreed to go to the *Daily* to apologize the following afternoon.

That day, with the withdrawal of the army from the *Daily*, Husansi published a black masthead *Inner Mongolia Daily* (New No. 1)—Party newspaper mastheads were usually in red, denoting revolution. In addition to changing the color, the rebels also took out the Mongolian masthead that accompanied the Chinese. This was a bold symbolic action because the five Chinese characters *Nei Meng Gu Ri Bao* were written by Mao. Nevertheless, the convention of eliminating the Mongolian masthead continued into 1969.[16] The rebels at this stage, for all their struggle against illegitimate authority, had little respect for Mongol rights as the titular nationality of Inner Mongolia, or for the autonomous region as a special polity. This was not surprising given the rebels' alliance with the radical Han Party secretaries who took over the leadership of Inner Mongolia after taking down Ulanhu. As they were drawn into the region's increasingly contentious ethnic politics, the rebels became more vocal in their attack on Ulanhu and Mongol nationalism. The rebel attack in Red Guard tabloids was often fiercer and more unequivocal than the more restrained official attack.[17] This rebel radicalism was less informed by any knowledge about ethnic relations in Inner Mongolia than by a competitive urge to demonstrate ideological loyalty to Mao and to challenge Mao's alleged enemies. This was the beginning of the rebels' departure from their original position in opposition to authoritarian rule.

Husansi's bold action could not have been better timed. As noted, on January 23 the Central Committee, State Council, and Central Military Affairs Commission called for a mass seizure of power from "those in authority taking the capitalist road." The same decision called on the PLA to actively support "the broad masses of revolutionary leftists in their struggle to seize power" and "resolutely suppress counterrevolutionary elements and counterrevolutionary organizations that oppose the proletarian revolutionary left."

Responding on January 24, the new *Inner Mongolia Daily* controlled by Husansi published an article entitled "Proletarian Revolutionary Groups throughout the Country Act Immediately to Forge Great Alliances and Seize All Kinds of Big Power from Bottom to Top." The Xinhua News Agency reported power seizures all over China, highlighting the replacement of the Shanghai Municipal Party Committee and Government by the rebel-led Shanghai Revolutionary Rebel Liaison Headquarters one day earlier. It later changed its name to Revolutionary Committee.[18]

Facing mounting violence and the Center's demand that the army support the revolutionary left, army leaders in Inner Mongolia confronted the question of apologizing to Husansi. On January 24, the IMMR Party Committee decided that it would not apologize, insisting that the army had not supported any particular faction and that its military intervention and subsequent withdrawal was correct.[19]

Infuriated by the army's refusal to apologize, in the late afternoon of January 25, thirty-nine Jinggangshan rebels from the industrial college marched into the IMMR headquarters compound, demanding that Liu Chang issue a public apology. The army promptly detained them. That evening, Dongzong and other rebel organizations sent representatives to intensify pressure on Liu Chang. Hundreds of slogans posted on the southern wall of the military compound denounced Liu.

The military in Hohhot, as elsewhere, was deeply split along factional rather than ethnic lines, the Mongol officers having already been purged. The IMMR's Cultural Troupe was particularly supportive of the rebels. It formed an organization called Hongse Zaofantuan (Red Rebel Corps), many of whose members were women, and called on the Inner Mongolia Party Committee to mediate.[20] The next day, Gao Jinming and Li Zhi came to military headquarters asking that the students be released and that the army support Husansi, but the generals remained adamant.[21] The IMMR and the Party Committee led by Gao Jinming were in open confrontation.

The army charged that Gao Jinming and Li Zhi were behind-the-scenes supporters of Husansi in a bid to discredit them. Under pressure, Red Flag, a rebel organization of the Inner Mongolia Forestry College withdrew from Husansi.[22] To bring discipline to its ranks, on January 27 Husansi decommissioned all Husansi armbands and issued new ones together with a Red Guard certificate for each member. Henceforth, no member of Husansi could represent the organization without an official letter.[23]

PLA Shooting

The rebels' political fortunes suffered a setback from January 28 when the Central Military Affairs Commission published an Eight-Point Order that prohibited any group from storming a military organization.[24] The PLA's participation in factional fighting during power seizures had not only failed to bring about law and order but also made it the target of the faction that it opposed. As many commanders and military headquarters throughout the country began to be attacked by Red Guards, the marshals running the Central Military Affairs Commission successfully appealed to Lin Biao and ultimately to Mao to restore order in the military and to protect the PLA from Red Guard assaults.[25]

Emboldened by this order, the IMMR immediately fortified the headquarters compound and prepared to defend it against attack, with machine guns if necessary. It also organized armed patrols and even staged a military parade. Still, the military remained under pressure from rebels to heed Mao's instruction to support the rebels.

Amid growing threats of nationwide violence, on January 29 a delegation from a rebel organization called Hong Zong (Red Guard Headquarters) from the Shanghai No. 2 Military Medical University arrived in Hohhot. They were on a linking-up action, *dachuanlian*. Clad in military uniforms, the Hong Zong delegates provided support to the embattled Hohhot rebels facing military pressure.

On that day, rebel organizations including Dongzong, 8.18 of the River West Company, Hohhot Railway Bureau's Huochetou (Locomotive), Hongqi (Red Banner) of the Party Committee, and Dongfanghong Lianshe (East Is Red Associated Organizations), agreed to form an alliance to confront the loyalists. The alliance demonstrated rebel support among workers, the military, and government as well as students. Wang Zhiyou, the head of 8.18, was the commander based on his military experience.[26]

On the night of February 2, Gao Shuhua led more than a dozen rebel Red Guards to the military compound to deliver a letter of appeal, calling on the army to support the rebels as the "leftists." They waited through the night for an answer, but none came.

At that time, the army started beating and dragging away student rebel protesters throughout the city. The army detained the army rebel leader Wang Jianping and raided the offices of Hongse Zaofantuan. All but three army rebels were detained. These, however, escaped to Beijing to report the army's crackdown.

On the afternoon of February 2, Hongweijun arrived at the south gate of the IMMR compound in a dozen trucks and clashed with Husansi students. Hongweijun was a loyalist mass organization that comprised mostly workers and a few cadres. Numbering thirty-five thousand, the core came from the Hohhot Rubber Factory. Hongweijun was backed by Wuchanzhe (Proletarians), which included cadres, university and middle school students, workers, and some villagers. On that day, the loyalist Wuchanzhe detained Gao Jinming, Quan Xingyuan, and Kang Xiumin, the Inner Mongolia Party leaders most sympathetic to the rebels.[27]

Around 9 p.m., sixty-four rebel students from the industrial college launched a hunger strike in front of the military compound.[28] Supporting the hunger strikers, thousands of rebels staged a sit-in before the south gate of the military compound as temperatures dropped to twenty degrees below zero Celsius.

On February 4, the *Inner Mongolia Daily*, under rebel control, published articles about the January 22 and January 25 clashes at the newspaper office, mentioning by name several generals. It was pouring oil on fire. That noon, the IMMR responded to rebel demands for support. A military officer in a command car came out to invite one hundred representatives from the various rebel organizations to meet the commanders. Gao Shuhua, who headed Dongzong, immediately organized the One-Hundred-Person Delegation to Meet Liu Chang. As soon as the delegation entered the compound, two trucks blocked the gate and several hundred soldiers began to beat the rebel representatives. To rescue them, rebels from outside the compound climbed in and the soldiers retreated suddenly at an order, allowing the detained delegates to leave. On the morning of February 5, the military leadership issued a three-point ultimatum proclaiming that Husansi was counterrevolutionary, that the

FIGURE 10 Han Tong, the first rebel Red Guard killed by the PLA on February 5, 1967

sit-in hunger strike was counterrevolutionary, and that the students had to disperse or they would be severely punished. The rebels defied the ultimatum. The sit-in continued.

Han Tong, a fourth-year Teachers' College student, holding a battery speaker in front of the south gate of the compound, was urging the crowd to be patient and follow discipline not to cross the cordon.[29] Two shots rang out from inside the compound and Tong fell. It was 12:15 p.m. on February 5.[30]

The first few rows of rebels in front of the gate were workers of 8.18 from the River West Company, whose fifty thousand workers were involved in building missiles. As soon as the shots rang out, the workers in front, most of whom were demobilized soldiers, realizing the danger of a bloodbath, stood up and pressed backward, pushing the several hundred students behind them fifty yards to the rear. This action undoubtedly saved many lives by preventing a riot.

According to information later released in Beijing meetings held to discuss the incident, hundreds of soldiers lay in wait beyond the gate with four machine guns hidden behind trees and bushes, ready to mow down rebels who entered the compound. At that moment, Chief of Staff Wang Liangtai was standing on the roof of military headquarters watching and Deputy Commander Xiao Yingtang was in the command post waiting for the rebels to charge the gate.[31]

Following the shooting of Han Tong, the army encircled the rebels with armed soldiers and commandeered the hostel where the rebels were staying. Recognizing that the nature of the conflict had changed in essence, that evening the rebels halted the hunger strike and sit-in and withdrew from the army hostel, preparing to take their case to Beijing. Han Tong was rushed to a hospital, where he died at 5:40 p.m. The rebels had their first martyr.

Han Tong was the first student killed in cold blood by the People's Liberation Army during the Cultural Revolution in all of China. The event would set off far-reaching changes in Inner Mongolia, across the nation, and in my own life.

The Qinghai Incident

The explosion of violence in Inner Mongolia was also taking place in many parts of China. The New Year's 1967 editorial of the *People's Daily*, *PLA Daily*, and *Red Flag*, followed by Shanghai's "January Storm," emboldened rebels to attempt to seize power from "those in authority taking the capitalist road," notably loyalists in the Party and the military. Shanxi was the first to emulate Shanghai. Rebel forces there declared on January 14 that they had seized power from the "Old Regime"; on January 24, Qingdao rebels declared victory, followed by Guizhou on January 25 and Heilongjiang on January 31. Power seizures swept the country. After the killing in Inner Mongolia, news came from Qinghai Province of more PLA killings of rebels. The events unfolding in Qinghai would impinge on Inner Mongolia and vice versa.

Qinghai province was established, along with Ningxia, Suiyuan, Chahar, and Rehe, in 1928, when Chiang Kai-shek completed his northern expedition to unify China. Known as Kokonuur (blue lake) in Mongolian and Amdo in Tibetan, the area had long been contested among Mongols, Tibetans, Hui Muslims, and Han.

The Cultural Revolution in Qinghai followed a familiar course. In this multiethnic province with no titular minority nationality, Han dominance was secure and ethnicity was not a compelling political issue as it was in Inner Mongolia. As the Cultural Revolution unfolded, as elsewhere, Qinghai's top leaders split.

In late September and early October, two opposing Red Guard factions emerged: the rebel 8.18 Red Guard Headquarters and the loyalist Headquarters of Qinghai University and Middle School Red Guards (known as Red Guard Headquarters). The dispute concerned the two leading Qinghai Provincial party secretaries. The 8.18 faction supported the first Party secretary and first political commissar: this was Yang Zhilin, a Han revolutionary veteran hailing from the Tumed region of Inner Mongolia. After working many years in Inner Mongolia as one of the most important subordinates of Ulanhu, Yang was dispatched by the Center to Qinghai in 1962 to clean up the mess created by the great famine. His daughter was my schoolmate who left after graduating from Erzhong in 1964. The loyalist Red Guard Headquarters supported Second Secretary and Governor Wang Zhao.

As in Hohhot, the two factions fought for control of the *Qinghai Daily*. On January 4, 1967 the loyalist Red Guard Headquarters sealed *Qinghai Daily*, which had been under the control of the rebel group 8.18. By January 11, the PLA had taken over the *Daily* and on January 12, 8.18 took over the offices. Instead of relaying reports from Beijing and throughout the country, as was the practice of other Party newspapers, the new *Qinghai Daily* under rebel control reported only local news and rebel editorial comments and criticism of their opponents, just as the new *Inner Mongolia Daily* did under rebel control. Seeing the situation out of control, both Party secretaries, Yang Zhilin and Wang Zhao, left Xining, and the warring factions each appealed for support to the Qinghai army.

The Qinghai army was in a very difficult situation, receiving conflicting and changing orders from the army's high command in the Lanzhou Military Region and Beijing and, like so many other organizations, it was internally divided. On January 24, deputy commander Zhao Yongfu supported the loyalist Red Guard Headquarters and seized power within the army by arresting Commander Liu Xianquan who supported the rebel 8.18. After a month of scuffles with the rebels occupying the *Qinghai Daily* but failing to gain support from the Lanzhou Military Region, on the morning of February 23 Zhao commanded the army to storm the *Qinghai Daily*. At one o'clock that afternoon, Zhao ordered the troops to open fire on the unarmed rebels, killing 169 and wounding 178.

The CCRG initially kept silent on the Qinghai incident. But the rebels wrote bloodstained letters accusing the local army of atrocities and in March, following two investigations ordered by Mao, the Center supported the rebels and arrested Zhao Yongfu. On March 24, 1967, the Party Center, the State Council, the Central Army Committee, and the CCRG issued "The Decision on the Qinghai Question," which accused Zhao of staging a military coup and suppressing the masses. He was jailed, other army and local party leaders were punished, and 8.18 was declared a revolutionary mass organization. Liu Xianquan was rehabilitated to lead the PLA Qinghai Province Military Control Committee set up on April 3. The province was placed under military control. With this verdict, Liu crushed his opponents in the army, government and mass organizations. His ruthlessness in restoring order was appreciated by the Center, and he was subsequently appointed to bring order to the fractious Inner Mongolia. Liu, however, remained in Qinghai. The job of pacifying Inner Mongolia would fall to another general.[32]

The Center Intervenes

The shooting of Han Tong in Hohhot focused the attention of Mao, Zhou Enlai, and the CCRG on the critical role of the army in the Cultural Revolution. Up to that point, the PLA had generally supported power holders in the Party and government, the work teams that they dispatched, and the loyalist Red Guards who backed them. However, Han Tong's death at the hands of the military in opposition to a campaign authorized by Mao shook the PLA and the CCRG. As the unfolding events show, many of the power seizures, far from being anarchic, were controlled by Mao and the CCRG, as localities were required to gain official endorsement from higher levels, and provinces from the Center, to retain power and pursue their transformative agendas. Of thirteen known seizures of power in December 1967, however, the central media acknowledged, and thus implicitly supported, only four in two municipalities and two provinces—Shanghai (December 14), Qingdao (December 24), Guizhou (December 25), and Heilongjiang (December 31). Shanghai had set the precedent, as Mao, Lin Biao, Zhou Enlai, and other Central leaders in the CCRG sought to dominate by reviewing and approving new structures of Revolutionary Committees and the leading personnel of Party, state, and army. But with the nation in turmoil, the ability of the Center to control was mixed, at best. Inner Mongolia is a notable case in point.

Han Tong's murder plunged Inner Mongolia into a deepening crisis as confrontation sharpened across the country. Both rebel and loyalist groups in Hohhot had links to Beijing. The military, Party, and government of course had direct institutional ties to power centers in Beijing, as did loyalists through ties to these institutions. Rebel links to the Center were through Tsinghua University's Jinggangshan, which maintained a liaison in Hohhot. The CCRG also had two representatives in Hohhot, *Red Flag* correspondent Yu Shunchang and PLA news correspondent Song Xiekong, as well as the Inner Mongolian branches of the *People's Daily* and the New China News Agency. These reporters immediately cabled news of Han Tong's murder to Beijing, making cover-up difficult, in this respect differentiating Inner Mongolia from Qinghai.

One day after the shooting, on February 6, Zhou Enlai urgently cabled in the name of the State Council and Central Military Affairs Commission, directing all parties to take no further action and to send representatives to Beijing to discuss the situation. This gave the rebels a seat at the table with the political and military authorities and their loyalist supporters. The urgency of the situation was emphasized by the fact that Zhou provided two chartered planes to bring the representatives to Beijing. Zhou's instruction issued in a telegram read:

> The incident that occurred at the IMMR should stop immediately, and the situation must not get worse. The four sides—the IMAR Party Committee, the IMMR, the Third Headquarters of Hohhot and Hongweijun of Hohhot— please send three to five delegates each to Beijing to solve the problem through consultation. We will send airplanes on February 6 to Hohhot to pick up your delegates.
>
> We learn that a student from Teachers' College was shot to death in the vicinity of the Military Region; if this is so, then the perpetrator and the instigator (*zhihui zhe*) must be hunted down and punished when found. Also, the family of the deceased should be offered condolences and given a pension.[33]

Since the telegram was sent in a plain code, Husansi published the full text in their tabloid the next day and the story was immediately picked up and reported on the radio of the Mongolian People's Republic.[34]

Although three of the four groups ordered to send representatives to Beijing were in the loyalist camp, the military resisted participating. Huang Hou reportedly said, "It is disgraceful to negotiate with Husansi."[35] The army countered that the Center should either send a delegation to investigate the affair in Inner Mongolia, or that an official delegation, comprised of Party and military leaders, be dispatched to Beijing to report on the crimes of Husansi. The army insisted on branding Husansi's "storming" of the IMMR headquarters a counterrevolutionary activity. In fact, the result of self-proclaimed power seizures in many provinces was to reinforce existing power structures with the army almost everywhere supporting loyalist Party, government and mass organizations. Mao and the CCRG would eventually label and seek to reverse this February adverse current (*eryue niliu*). A protracted four-party negotiation followed with far-reaching consequences for Inner Mongolia.

Inner Mongolia's military leaders in the end yielded to pressures from the Center to enter four-party discussions. On the afternoon of February 8, the planes Zhou Enlai had dispatched returned to Beijing with twenty representatives, five each representing the Inner Mongolia Party Committee, the IMMR, rebel Husansi, and loyalist Hongweijun.[36] All representatives were Han. In the wake of the fall of Ulanhu and his group, not a single Mongol was involved at the initial stage of negotiating the fate of the Inner Mongolia Autonomous Region at the highest level of national power.

Husansi prepared thoroughly. The key rebel organizations associated with Husansi—8.18 of the River West, Huochetou of the Railway, Red Flag of the Party Committee, and rebel organizations of the Forestry College, Agriculture and Animal Husbandry College, and Teachers' College—met to prepare a strategy and elect representatives. Hao Guangde, as head of Husansi, and Gao Shuhua, head of Dongzong, whose members included Han Tong, were selected along with Liu Wenyan, who taught in the Political Education Department at Teachers' College and was knowledgeable in Marxist theory, along with Chen Yonghua and Zhou Jianmin, recommended by the Industrial College rebels, comprised the rebel delegation.

Gao Shuhua dispatched rebel Red Guards to find out who had killed Han Tong. A few hours before boarding the airplane, reports from army rebels revealed that Liu Qing was the murderer.[37]

On February 5, Dongzong reported Han Tong's death to the Inner Mongolia Public Security Bureau and asked that a forensic doctor conduct an autopsy. However, police loyalists refused to act. At General Wang Liangtai's order, the Police Bureau finally sent a jeep to Teachers' College to conduct the autopsy. When Gao Shuhua learned that Wang Liangtai had ordered the police to act, he realized that the intention was to destroy Han Tong's corpse. The rebels therefore refused to allow the autopsy.[38]

On February 10, Premier Zhou and Xiao Hua, the political commissar of the army, met the representatives at the Great Hall of the People. No side was able to present conclusive evidence to prove who had killed Han Tong. Husansi representative Hao Guangde told Zhou Enlai that the military had attempted to seize Han's corpse to suppress evidence, but that Husansi was protecting the body. Gao Shuhua sent a letter to Zhou stating that the murderer was Liu Qing.[39]

The military denied responsibility for the death, saying they only heard two firecracker sounds. Its case was weakened, however, by its refusal to examine the guns and ammunition of the soldiers on duty to see if they had been fired.[40]

Learning this, Zhou Enlai dispatched Zeng Shan, minister of internal affairs, together with two forensic doctors to conduct an autopsy.[41] The autopsy, conducted on February 12, revealed that two bullets (of a Model 59 handgun) lodged in Han Tong's lung. Penetrating from the front, the bullets passed through the fifth rib and cut his lung artery. Zeng also confirmed that Colonel Liu Qing, deputy director of the Military Training Department, was the killer.[42] This was officially accepted as proof that Husansi's story was correct and the military had lied.

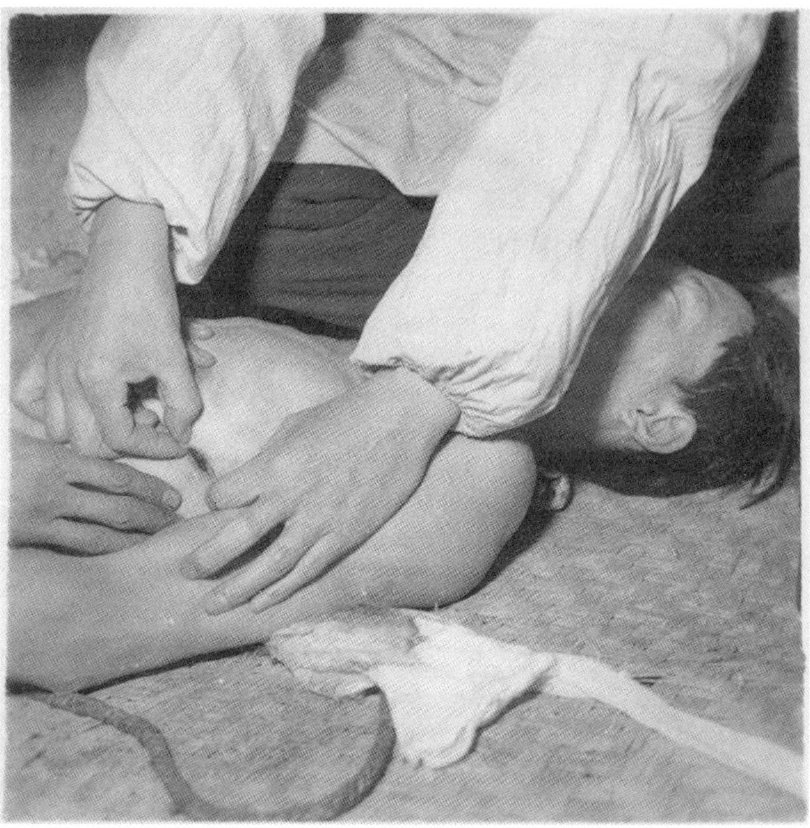

FIGURE 11 Han Tong's autopsy, conducted by Dr. Tian Guang under supervision of Zeng Shan in March 1967

In Beijing each camp maneuvered to increase its representation at the center of power in Hohhot. Zhou Enlai ordered army deputy commander Liu Huaxiang to free Gao Jinming and Quan Xingyuan, whose attempts to mediate had precipitated their arrest. After Zeng Shan returned from Hohhot on February 13 with evidence from the autopsy, marathon meetings began in Beijing with the addition of Party Committee members Gao Jinming and Wang Yilun, a representative from the army's Red Rebels and Ning Kuixi of the Tsinghua University Liaison Station in Hohhot. Zhou Enlai then called for additional rebel representation. They included two Mongols: Nasanbayar, from the Education Department, and General Wu Tao, the sidelined first deputy political commissar. They were the only two Mongols participating in the meeting that would shape the fate of the IMAR in the post-Ulanhu era, but they played almost no role in the negotiations.[43]

In Inner Mongolia the military and its loyalist supporters maintained pressure on the rebels. Even with negotiations proceeding in Beijing, on February 12 Husansi was forced to vacate the *Daily* building.[44]

On February 16, Zhou Enlai, General Xiao Hua, and Zeng Shan received the delegations for the second time. Husansi was immediately thrown on the defensive because its newspaper had published Zhou's telegram mentioning the death of Han Tong and many articles criticizing the IMMR for committing murder. Zhou said that Mao and Lin Biao felt "very anxious" after reading it. Although the military was guilty of Han Tong's murder, Zhou nevertheless criticized Husansi, stating that surrounding the army compound was unacceptable because the army was the core of the Cultural Revolution. Ignoring the role of the military in repressing the rebels in Inner Mongolia, Zhou held that rebel forces should rely on it in attempting to seize power. Zhou was concerned about more than the PLA's reputation: "Of course, you had numerous reasons, but the telegram sent by the Center was an internal document. Nevertheless, you published it in a newspaper. Once published, it will spread abroad, and Outer Mongolia will obtain it immediately. After I read it, I regretted it greatly. . . . Students, young as you are, how can you not care about our PLA?"[45]

The Husansi representatives immediately apologized for their indiscretion. With no criticism of the military for the murder, Husansi appeared outflanked and on the defensive. The Center's stance underlined the strategic sensitivity of Inner Mongolia on the Mongolian-Soviet border at a time of sharp border conflicts with the Soviet Union and MPR.

Even as negotiations proceeded in Beijing, the military consolidated its power in Hohhot by arresting the two journalists from Beijing who had reported Han Tong's death. It also waged a massive propaganda campaign, attacking the hunger strike and the new *Inner Mongolian Daily* published by Husansi. Supporters of the military staged armed parades commandeering more than fifty trucks and shouting: "Down with the counterrevolutionary Husansi!" They insisted that Han Tong was killed not by the military but by Husansi and 8.18.[46]

The meeting ended with a four-point instruction from Zhou Enlai: stop verbal attacks through newspapers and radio, stop mutual fighting, stop mutual kidnapping, and stop mass meetings and demonstrations.

The instruction, even-handed in tone, dealt a blow to rebel forces: first, because it affirmed the authority of the PLA, whose power remained unimpeachable and above criticism; second, because it deprived rebels of their sole source of influence, the ability to mobilize for mass actions; third, because it made no mention of who had killed Han Tong despite the finding of the autopsy that he was killed by the military. Nor was that all. The Central Military Affairs Commission ordered the Shanghai military college rebels and other outsiders who supported the rebels to return to their units. By February 28, all nonlocal Red Guard organizations in Hohhot, including Tsinghua Jinggangshan, had left Hohhot, leaving local rebels without key external support.

At the end of the meeting, Zhou Enlai ordered the representatives of each group to return to Hohhot to enforce the four points. He specifically directed Gao Shuhua not only to draft a self-criticism on behalf of the rebels for blackening the image of the PLA but also to cool rebel hostility toward the PLA. Recognizing the difficult environment the rebels faced, Zhou also warned military leaders that they must guarantee Gao's safety: "Your people may not kidnap or attack him, he is my guest."[47]

Zhou may have thought that the meeting had restored peace in Inner Mongolia. Nothing could have been further from the truth.

The Army's Counterattack

Pang Naiwu and I arrived in Hohhot from Beijing on the morning of February 25. Not realizing that things could be so serious, we were shocked to find soldiers with rifles and bayonets out in force everywhere. Machine guns were mounted atop the railroad station. The atmosphere was tense, with key points tightly guarded.

At Teachers' College, soldiers were walking in groups or riding motorcycles. It felt like martial law. On campus I met Li Zhenrong, a classmate and a member of Jinggangshan. Telling me what had happened, tears ran down her cheeks. She had been there. After the murder, student rebels had hidden Tong's body. "His body is still in the gym," she told me.

"May I see him?"

"Of course! Let me go with you."

She got the key and we entered the gym. Students stood guard outside around the clock to prevent the army from seizing his body and destroying the evidence of the murder.

Inside the gym, paper flowers were piled high like mountains. We moved the flowers aside to reach his body, displayed on a high platform of four desks covered with a red Dongzong rebel banner that was emblazoned with the hammer and sickle, like the Chinese Communist Party flag. He wore the long military overcoat and military hat he had been wearing when he was shot. His body was frozen stiff from the cold February air. His face had already shrunk a bit. Some makeup had been applied to preserve his color.

"I still remember what you said, what you sang, what you thought. I remember the day we parted. You said that we should take care of ourselves and that you would travel to Yan'an," I recalled. I cried for almost half an hour, and so did Li Zhenrong.

I had practiced martial arts and Tai Chi in this gym. Now my friend's corpse was there. Han Tong's death provoked the first tears that I had shed since becoming an adult.

After mourning Han Tong, I immediately joined the rebels struggling to protect our campus. The main teaching building was the last stronghold for rebels facing loyalist attack in Hohhot.

One afternoon in late February 1967, Guo Shihai and Dong Yuhua, the two leading members of Dongzong, called a meeting of rebel activists. Guo told us that Premier Zhou had sent Gao Shuhua back to Hohhot to report on the Beijing meeting with his four-point instruction to the rebels.

On the morning of Gao's arrival, Dongzong organized about one hundred rebel students riding bicycles and brandishing our flags to welcome him at the train station. When our bicycle lines, accompanying Gao on the way back to campus, arrived at the New China Square, one hundred more bicycles, organized by Husansi joined us. On passing Erzhong, a further hundred bicycles, organized by the school and the nearby Inner Mongolia University, joined the procession. Before reaching Teachers' College, there were more than five hundred bicycles.[48] It was a grand spectacle, welcoming back our rebel leader on a mission to determine our fate. Emblematic of people's power by the rebels, it was designed to show defiance to the heavily armed military.

That day, a crowded meeting in the first-floor lecture hall in our main building welcomed Gao Shuhua. His vivid story about the meeting in Beijing helped boost rebel morale. But as rebel organizations hewed to Zhou's principles and avoided antagonizing the military, the army, and loyalist organizations stepped up their attack on Husansi, Gao Jinming, and Quan Xingyuan. The army set about eliminating the rebels and assuring that the Center would recognize their loyalist Revolutionary Committee.

On March 1, the Inner Mongolia army moved to crush the small rebel opposition in its own ranks. It sent armed troops to Beijing, arrested sixteen soldiers who were members of the army rebel organization Hongse Zaofantuan, and took them back to Hohhot for punishment. The Hohhot steel plant, Hohhot railway bureau, *Inner Mongolia Daily*, and other units that had been in rebel hands, were captured by Hongweijun. With army support, former leaders of these units who had been overthrown by rebels resumed power. Husansi and other rebels were harassed, beaten, and arrested by the army and Hongweijun.

With the city under virtual martial law, one after another, rebel branches were sealed off by the military and police. The army branded Husansi a counterrevolutionary organization and set out to destroy it.

On the evening of March 7, some ten thousand loyalists affiliated with Hongweijun and Wuchanzhe, with trucks, motorcycles, and jeeps, encircled Husansi Headquarters in the Inner Mongolian General Trade Union building, which also housed headquarters of six other rebel organizations. Storming the building, Hongweijun and Wuchanzhe arrested staff members. The following day, remaining Husansi and other rebel activists regrouped to Teachers' College. Armed PLA soldiers and Hongweijun immediately attacked the last remaining Husansi stronghold, which had been the center of rebel strength in Hohhot from the outset. Even at Teachers' College, only the main building remained under Husansi control.[49]

State of Siege

I joined the fight along with other embattled Husansi rebels. Rumors flew that the military and the loyalists were preparing a final assault. Their slogan was "It's easy to move a mountain; it's hard to move the PLA!" (*Han shan yi, han jiefangjun nan*) Their loyalist backers added "Whoever opposes the PLA is our enemy!"

The rebels gamely fought back with the only resources we had, mounting posters to inform people and bolster morale. Our poetic slogan was "Green pine, never aging; Third Headquarters never overturned!" (*Qingsong bulao, sansi budao*).

But the loyalists countered: "If Third Headquarters can't be overturned, we'll burn it. If the green pine doesn't age, we'll use shovels to uproot it!" (*Sansi budao, yonghuo shao. Qingsong bulao, yong gaopao*).

Facing military pressure and the defeat of one rebel unit after another, every individual was forced to choose: whether to support the PLA and the loyalist groups it endorsed, or the embattled Third Headquarters. Of course, most people said, "we support the PLA." The prestige of the military was high and its power was growing. The power holders and loyalists, with PLA backing, were riding high. Still, in each unit a few people persisted. They had to flee or face arrest, beatings, or criticism. Hundreds had already been jailed by the military or the police.

On March 8, three Inner Mongolia Party leaders Quan Xingyuan, Kang Xiumin, and Lei Daifu came to Teachers' College to lend support to the rebels, declaring: "If we have to die, we will die with you; if we live, we will live with you!"[50] This lifted our morale. What made it possible to persist in these dark times was that as long as negotiations in Beijing continued, there was a ray of hope. The possibility of victory in the negotiations hinged on the credibility of the rebels' reports on the army, including the killing of Han Tong and continuing Hongweijun atrocities. We were determined to inform the Center that the loyalists were grossly violating Premier Zhou's four-point instruction by repressing rebel forces everywhere.

I was part of a Dongzong group of fifty couriers who collected information and forwarded it to our representatives in Beijing. I picked up information from rebel informants in the military who deposited it at a secure mailbox and forwarded it by train messenger to Beijing. The rebel backbone was the 8.18 workers and locomotive drivers and engineers. I contacted railroad rebel leaders who were locomotive drivers on the train between Hohhot and Beijing. After the military took control of the railroad on February 8, we disguised a rebel leader as a train worker to break the blockade.

Twice I carried information directly to Beijing and stayed at the Shijin Huayuan, the Inner Mongolia office, a grand complex with five courtyards. I met privately with Hao Guangde and Gao Shuhua, who stayed at the State Council Guest House to assess documents and prepare reports. At our first meeting in late February 1967, they spoke optimistically about the negotiations. They had met with Zhou Enlai twice and his liaison Zhao Gang five times. By the second meeting in mid-March, however, they were pessimistic as the IMMR and the loyalists cracked down relentlessly on the rebels. The dilemma was this: if we acted in self-defense, loyalists could utilize it as evidence that the rebels were anti-PLA, resulting in more criticism of Husansi from the Center.

During my second trip to Beijing, I brought photographs of each of the nearly one hundred rooms in the classroom building that served as Husansi's new headquarters, showing everything we had. Altogether, a few dozen people made about one hundred trips carrying materials to Beijing, providing information to substantiate rebel interpretation of the struggle.

The premier's main office was in Zhongnanhai, the ancient imperial garden that served both as residence and office complex for the country's top leaders. But we dealt directly with staff members in the North China Group of the CCRG whose offices were in the Diaoyutai State Guest House in Beijing's western suburbs, which hosted President Nixon and other international figures in the 1970s and after. At a March 9 meeting between Zhou and Husansi representatives, Hao Guangde reported on our desperate situation in Hohhot.

Approximately one thousand people from schools and work units had joined forces inside our besieged classroom building at Teachers' College. Another one thousand activists were working outside prepared to defend. There were about one hundred classrooms and small offices in the building. Each room was crowded, people barely having a space two feet wide to lie on. There were no beds or pillows. Most people slept on newspapers on the cold cement floor in winter with outside temperature often below 25 degrees Celsius at night. But there was heating inside the building and cold running water. For weeks, people didn't bathe or change their clothes, so there was unbearable body odor and lice. My girlfriend stayed for a few days before being driven out by the stench.

For the first week or two, I came and went every day to the main building. I and other leaders, however, did not stay overnight to avoid capture in the event of an attack. Instead, we slept in the dormitory next to the campus garden and farm. The Husansi flag flew from the besieged classroom building fortified against attack while our opponents tightened the noose.

Rumors flew that Husansi had prepared chemical weapons, guns, and ammunition to resist an assault. Of course, we had nothing but a few training rifles without ammunition. Our weapons were bricks, rocks, slingshots, and baseball bats. Could these defend against the armed PLA attack that appeared imminent? Our hopes hinged on being able to hold out long enough to win Beijing's support. We barricaded the building with sandbags and prepared fire extinguishers and food. Hao Guangde's girlfriend, Zhou Bohua, my secondary schoolmate, was in charge of broadcasting. Loudspeakers broadcast revolutionary songs and poems to boost morale. The cooks kept us well supplied with food. Three meals a day, and sometimes, there was tea. But at times when too many people arrived to reinforce the building, leaving no time to cook enough food, we had to eat cold *mantou* (steamed buns) and *wowotou* (corn meal bread) washed down with cold tap water. Expecting to have the electricity cut momentarily, we readied generators and candles as well as kerosene lanterns.

As time passed conditions worsened. Everyone was exhausted and on edge. Old people and pregnant women were among those inside. The stronger students, especially physical education and martial arts students formed the first line of defense with two hundred people standing outside the gate. When I was on campus, I joined the second line with three hundred more people in front of the building, leaving the weak inside.

Three or four times, soldiers tried to break into our stronghold without firing. One day we captured seven young soldiers; they were terrified, believing we were reactionaries and monsters, and that we had a lot of weapons. We didn't beat or torture them but tried to win them over. After serving them food and drink, we released them.

On March 12, army propaganda trucks paraded inside the college, blaring, "Leniency to those who confess their crimes and severity to those who refuse!" On the streets outside the college, loyalist slogans proclaimed, "Bombard Dongzong; Flood Husansi with blood!" (*Paoda Dongzong, Xuexi Sansi*).[51]

Finally, the emergency situation with the potential to produce heavy casualties led Zhou Enlai on March 14 to dispatch Hao Guangde back to Hohhot to report on what was happening. He went to Teachers' College and the Forestry College and reported to rebels on the negotiations in Beijing, encouraging them to continue to resist. That day, the IMMR, having received instructions from the Central Military Affairs Commission to take control of the River West missile facility, arrested 156 members of 8.18, the most important rebel labor organization.[52] Our isolation at Teachers' College was almost complete.

We remained on high alert. When we went to bed, we didn't even undress so that we could defend instantly when called. Late on the night of March 15, 1967, thirty truckloads of attackers using tanks and tractors broke down our north gate wall. Our strongest fighters rushed to repel the attackers. Miraculously, the defenses held. But the next day, the army and Hongweijun returned. This time, in heavy fighting, they seized control of the first floor of the classroom building. Their attempt to occupy the second floor, however, was repelled.[53] But we were cut off from food and water. When other rebels tried to deliver food and water to the second floor, Hongweijun cut the rope, sending the buckets tumbling. To boost our spirits, we sang "Raising our heads to look at the Big Dipper / We Miss Chairman Mao in our heart" (*Taitou wangjian beidouxing, xinzhong xiangnian Mao Zhuxi*). This was from the song and dance epic *Dongfanghong* (The East Is Red), describing the difficult years of the Red Army under attack by Nationalist forces in the 1930s. We pasted Chairman Mao's portraits on windows and hung out a huge banner, "Defend Chairman Mao with blood and life."

Some military and government officials in Hohhot supported the rebels, but most Party leaders at the highest levels sided with the military and the loyalists. Gao Jinming, Quan Xingyuan, Kang Xiumin, and Lei Daifu, among ranking party officials, supported Husansi at this time. They became targets of the loyalists. While Gao Jinming participated in the negotiations in Beijing, Quan, Kang, and Lei were forced to flee loyalist persecution. They hid in our college, protected by Husansi students. But how to disguise leaders who wore woolen Mao suits and leather boots? We dressed Kang Xiumin and Lei Daifu like old workers and hid them in the printing factory building. They slept in the worker's dormitory at night and stayed in the print shop during the day. Quan Xingyuan was too tall (six foot two). We could not find a suitable worker's uniform. The one uniform that fit was for a worker in the college's boiler room. Wearing it he shoveled coal during the day, returning to our dormitory at night.

I often joked with them and their secretaries. Kang Xiumin, a native of Shenxian county, Hebei and the former Party secretary of Shijiazhuang Prefecture, loved flowers, birds, and poetry. His passion was classical literature. He was sent from Hebei to Inner Mongolia after the Qianmen Hotel Conference to serve as a secretary of the Inner Mongolia Party Secretariat and later became a standing committee member of the Revolutionary Committee.

Quan Xingyuan, a native of Wanxian county, Hebei, was a member of the revolutionary generation who had risen with Ulanhu. At the time of the Qianmen Hotel Conference of 1966, however, he had harshly denounced Ulanhu, thereby securing his own position.

Eventually, Hongweijun captured Quan Xingyuan, Kang Xiumin, and Lei Daifu. They were struggled on March 16, the day the army and Hongweijun stormed Teachers' College.

Power seizures brought more and more units under military control. By March 17, with the army in ascendance, and with Wang Duo and Wang Yilun's support, the army announced that a Revolutionary Committee would be formed in Hohhot the following day.

A shocked Zhou Enlai called deputy commander Liu Huaxiang at one a.m. ordering him to cancel the announcement.[54] The Center required the provinces to secure approval prior to finalizing the composition of revolutionary committees. Its sovereign authority was at stake.

The attack on Husansi headquarters led Zhou to convene another session with representatives of the four factions at 3:20 a.m. on March 18, 1967. Hao Guangde, who had returned to Beijing after two days in Hohhot, cried as he reported on the military attack on Husansi. When Hao reported that the IMMR authorities had dispatched forces to arrest army rebels who had fled to Beijing on March 1, the atmosphere grew tense. Zhou Enlai and Kang Sheng were furious that the army dared to enter the capital with arms and ammunition without the knowledge of, and permission from, the Center. Kang lashed out at the generals: "How could you send soldiers to capture people in the place of Chairman Mao and the Party Center?"[55]

The Inner Mongolia command had gone too far. Zhou dispatched a Central Investigation Team to review the incident at Teachers' College. It was led by the deputy chief of staff Admiral Li Tianyou and Wu Tao. Wu had once worked under General Xiao Hua in Beijing's Central Military Affairs Commission. In 1959 he was appointed first deputy political commissar of the IMMR. Soon after the Qianmen Hotel Conference, he was dubbed a "Three-Anti Element" by leading Han generals in IMMR. On March 18, learning that Wu Tao had been "illegally" deprived of power by other generals in the IMMR, Zhou ordered restoration of Wu's position as first deputy political commissar and Party secretary of the IMMR.[56] Zhou and the Center would use Wu Tao to control the IMMR. From this time on, Wu was virtually the only high-ranking Mongol to play a role in Inner Mongolia's Cultural Revolution. However, his role appears to have been symbolic at best.

The Central Investigation Team set off from Beijing by plane at 8 a.m., arriving at the military airfield in Hohhot two hours later. March 18 was a sunny day in Hohhot and the day seemed all the brighter to embattled rebels when campus loudspeakers announced that Premier Zhou was sending a representative to inspect our stronghold. The military and Hongweijun, knowing this in advance, had already left. At 2 p.m., five vehicles arrived: a car, three jeeps, and a truck filled with local soldiers armed with rifles. People crowded the windows of our stronghold to watch. You could see their unshaved faces and long hair. All across the campus people shouted "Long live Chairman Mao! Long live the PLA!"

Admiral Li Tianyou in a long navy blue coat was followed by a uniformed, powerfully built bodyguard with cartridges on his chest, an automatic rifle on his back and two pistols at his side. Everyone shouted "Welcome Comrade Li Tianyou, Chairman Mao's Representative." The front gate opened. I followed the Admiral and Wu Tao as they strode into the building. Li inspected one floor after another.

Then he asked the rebel leaders: "Do you have chemical weapons?"

"No."

"Do you have arms and ammunition?"

"No."

The admiral's query about weapons was not an idle one in light of the tragedy in Qinghai on February 23. From March 13 to 24, the CCRG met four times with leaders from the Qinghai Party, government, army and mass organizations involved in the Qinghai army's massacre of rebels. Zhao Yongfu had justified his order to shoot to kill by falsely claiming that the rebels inside the *Qinghai Daily* had amassed large numbers of weapons and fired first.

The admiral inspected every room. People had nothing but their shabby personal belongings. Some women, with nowhere else to stay, had brought their children. He walked around, talking, asking questions, and shaking hands with many people.

"You must trust the Central Committee and Chairman Mao. The Central Committee will give you an appropriate answer. You must love the PLA."

Li reiterated Zhou's four-point instruction, urging all parties to stop fighting. He also ordered Husansi to dismantle its defenses. Li Tianyou and Wu Tao stayed in Hohhot for three days, meeting with military, Party, and rebel leaders. They ordered the Hongweijun loyalist Red Guards to free imprisoned

Party leaders Quan Xingyuan, Kang Xiumin, and Lei Daifu. From Li's attitude, especially the fact that he had come directly to Husansi headquarters from the airport without even consulting the Inner Mongolia military commanders, we sensed that the situation was hopeful.

On March 21, Quan Xingyuan and Kang Xiumin, as well as General Wang Liangtai, the chief of staff of the Inner Mongolia Army, accompanied the Central Investigation Team back to Beijing to join the marathon meetings that would determine the fate of Inner Mongolia and the rebel resistance. In Beijing, the situation turned against the IMMR and two key members of the Inner Mongolia Party Committee: Wang Duo and Wang Yilun. On March 23, six weeks after the murder of Han Tong, Zhou ordered the arrest of Colonel Liu Qing, branding him a counterrevolutionary assassin. The following day, Zhao Yongfu, the deputy commander of the Qinghai army, was detained for further investigation following the passing of the Center's "Resolution concerning the Question of Qinghai." But Inner Mongolia's issues would prove more difficult to resolve.

6

Rebel Victory and the Military Takeover of Inner Mongolia

The Center's Verdict

Late on the evening of March 30, 1967, Zhou Enlai and top leaders of the CCRG, including Jiang Qing, Chen Boda, Kang Sheng, Zhang Chunqiao, and Yao Wenyuan, met the Inner Mongolia Party Committee representatives participating in discussions in Beijing: Gao Jinming, Quan Xingyuan, Wang Zaitian, Li Shude, Kang Xiumin, Li Zhi, Guo Yiqing and Zhang Lu, on the rebel side, and Wang Yilun, and Wang Duo on the loyalist side.

With Zhou Enlai chairing, the Central leaders supported the rebels and their Party backers. Wang Yilun and Wang Duo would be criticized for supporting the IMMR's action against the rebels including the murder of Han Tong during a sit-in at a military base in Hohhot.

Kang Sheng immediately jumped on Wang Yilun's March 2 tape report, pressing him to say whether he had endorsed the terror waged by the military and its supporters against the rebels. Wang remained calm. Saying that he had telephoned home expressing disapproval of fighting, he addressed Kang as Comrade Kang Sheng. That was too much for Jiang Qing. She exploded: "We are interrogating you! What do you mean by saying 'Comrade Kang Sheng,' mouthing one phrase after another. . . . You are terribly disrespectful of Kang Lao, very arrogant!" In the CCP protocol, addressing each other as comrades (*tongzhi*) is a way of conveying equality and shared values.[1] However, used by a junior to a senior leader, the term could also imply disrespect. The adjectives *lao* (old) or *xiao* (little) are commonly used before a surname to indicate seniority between individuals, but when *lao* is used after a surname it implies admiration and respect. During the Cultural Revolution, Kang Sheng was one of very few CCP veterans who was often addressed by others, including Mao, as "Kang Lao" (Kang, the Senior), even though he was five years younger than Mao. Jiang Qing always addressed Kang Sheng as Kang Lao.

Zhou Enlai lashed out at Wang Yilun: "You stubbornly follow the Liu-Deng line, and you are also Ulanhu's man. Ulanhu protected you."

Zhou also attacked Wang Duo's opposition to Husansi. Zhou labeled the two Wangs' refusal to apologize unequivocally as the "stance of landlords and the bourgeoisie." When Kang Sheng said their behavior was a counterattack by the bourgeois reactionary line, Zhou followed: "This is an Ulanhuist counterattack without Ulanhu, an Ulanhuist restoration without Ulanhu."

Kang, who headed China's secret police, pressed the attack on Wang Yilun, calling into question his credentials as a Party member. When and where, he asked, had Wang joined the Party? When he answered that he had joined while studying in Moscow, Kang said that he had examined the records of every Moscow party member but found no mention of Wang.

Wang Duo and Wang Yilun were not allowed to attend the fourth meeting with representatives of the four factions on April 4. The rebels cited more atrocities committed by the army and reported that the army still held many people in custody. Zhou Enlai ordered the IMMR to apologize, but, with an eye to the region's sensitive international position as well as its critical position in Chinese politics, he again insisted that the rebels had to protect the reputation of the army in Inner Mongolia, in China, and above all internationally:

> In our meetings, you are allowed to make strong criticism. But don't make any propaganda outside, don't transmit the news to people outside Inner Mongolia who have no need to know. Don't propagandize, don't make phone calls, don't send out loudspeaker cars, don't broadcast, and don't distribute pamphlets, otherwise, once this spreads to Hong Kong, Outer Mongolia, America, and Japan, our enemies everywhere will be pleased, it will delight them. Inner Mongolia has a problem of nationality unity, and a problem of fighting against revisionism. China has a twelve hundred mile antirevisionist frontier, so you should be particularly careful.[2]

On April 13, 1967, at midnight Zhou Enlai convened the sixth and final meeting to resolve the Inner Mongolia imbroglio. Present in the Great Hall of the People, in addition to Zhou and Inner Mongolia representatives, were Chen Boda, Kang Sheng, Wang Li, General Xiao Hua and Admiral Li Tianyou. The CCP Central Committee, the State Council, the Central Military Affairs Commission, and the CCRG issued a joint eight-point directive meant to settle matters in Inner Mongolia.

Zhou delivered a long speech explicating Central Document (67) 126: "The Chinese Communist Party Central Committee Decision on the Problem of Inner Mongolia." He admonished the army for a mistake of line (*luxian cuowu*) in failing to support the rebels after February 5. Zhou said that the army had been too rash. Rejecting the army's claim that Husansi had stormed its positions, Zhou styled the event a sit-in, a demonstration that sought the trust and support of the army, believing that, in the wake of the decision by the Center, the army would support the rebels. But the army panicked, and an officer fired two shots killing Han Tong. Instead of apologizing, the army denounced Husansi as a counterrevolutionary organization and brutally suppressed it, arresting many people. Zhou further said that although Ulanhu had been pulled off his horse, he still had supporters in Inner Mongolia, naming Wang Yilun and Wang Duo as Ulanhu's agents (*dailiren*). The army's basic mistake lay in supporting those in authority taking the capitalist road in opposition to the revolutionary rebels.

Zhou noted that the IMMR had arrested Inner Mongolia Party secretaries Gao Jinming and Quan Xingyuan, who were in fact their superiors since the army was under the leadership of the Inner Mongolia Party Committee. Most serious—indeed, more serious in the eyes of the Central authorities than the cold-blooded murder of a student—was the fact that the army had sent soldiers to Beijing to arrest rebels, thereby usurping the authority of the Center.

Zhou further noted that the army not only refused to accept responsibility for killing Han Tong, it even detained and tortured Tian Guang, the forensic doctor who conducted the autopsy for Zeng Shan, detaining her for thirty days. Zhou accused the army of boasting that the marathon meetings in Beijing constituted a "Chongqing Negotiation," referring to Mao's and Zhou's 1945 negotiation with Chiang Kai-shek in Chongqing that shaped the outcome of the subsequent civil war. This implied not only that the army had attempted to negotiate on an equal plane but also that it treated Mao and Zhou as opponents rather than as their superiors. Issues of status, above all the status of the Party Center, were paramount in the verdict.

Zhou placed the main responsibility for the Inner Mongolian incident on Wang Yilun and Wang Duo, followed by military leaders. However, to protect the reputation of the PLA, the document criticized no generals by name or unit. In failing to specify what should be done with respect to the generals, or to hold any of them specifically responsible for Inner Mongolia's problems, Zhou left intact intractable problems that future leaders in Inner Mongolia would have to confront.

Han Tong, whose death had touched off the turmoil in Inner Mongolia, finally won high honors. Zhou approved a funeral for Han Tong: "Han Tong's death has enabled the Inner Mongolian proletarian revolutionary forces to unite and seize power! He is reborn! He was 'born a great birth, died a glorious death.'"[3]

Zhou also clarified the Center's attitude toward Ulanhu. Ulanhu, who formally remained Chairman of the IMAR, despite having been stripped of all other posts, was not to be openly criticized in Inner Mongolia, including in the press. This decision, Zhou stated, was primarily driven by "strategic priorities, mainly in consideration of the problem of Mongolian Revisionists and Soviet Revisionists." When Hao Guangde proposed to take Ulanhu back to Inner Mongolia for struggle, Zhou demurred, saying that this could be done later. But Wang Duo would be sent back for mass struggle and criticism. Wang Yilun's problem was more serious, and Zhou announced that he had been arrested that night. The Center remained divided over what to do with Ulanhu who was bereft of power, disgraced, and under heavy attack by both rebels and loyalists. Yet he remained a powerful symbol for many Mongols at home and abroad, a centerpiece of the Party's nationality policies. Concern at the highest levels of the Party and Army pivoted above all on international reaction to Ulanhu's fall at a time of high tension in the Chinese-Mongolian-Soviet borderlands.

Zhou announced that Liu Xianquan, the Qinghai army commander, would take charge of Inner Mongolia. However, since Liu was busy with Qinghai matters, he would be temporarily replaced by a deputy commander of the Beijing Military Region, Teng Haiqing. Teng and Mongol general Wu Tao were charged with organizing a preparatory team of the IMAR Revolutionary Committee including Gao Jinming, Quan Xingyuan and Kang Xiumin.

Although Inner Mongolia was not immediately put under total military control, as eight provinces had been between March and May 1967, this opened the door to eventual military control by the Beijing Military Region. This followed the national pattern of army commanders leading the newly emergent revolutionary committees which combined the functions of the Party, government and army in one body. The so-called April 13 decision thus followed the spirit of the Central Military Affairs Commission's decision issued on March 19, 1967, which called on the army to "support the left, support the peasants, and support the workers, and to implement military control and military training," popularly known as the "three supports and two militaries." The priority of the "three supports" was "support the left," and that of the "two militaries" was "military control."[4]

If Zhou and the CCRG calculated that the verdict would restore peace in Inner Mongolia, they could not have been more wrong. The verdict deepened the divide between opposing factions, institutionalizing the opposition between loyalist and rebel forces. The opposing factions remained on a collision course. It was a fight to the death to prove who could wield power to what

FIGURE 12 Cartoon representation of the "Ulanhu Kingdom" listing key members and crimes, 1967

ends in a fractious borderland region. The immediate effect of the decision was to plunge Inner Mongolia deeper into turmoil.

Rebel Victory

Zhou Enlai was the Central leader who was most instrumental in determining the fate of Inner Mongolia in the early years of the Cultural Revolution, largely through his leadership of the Central Cultural Revolution Group (CCRG). Zhou's dominance of the CCRG, and his impact on Inner Mongolia and other regions of China during the Cultural Revolution, is a story that remains largely untold. From its establishment in May 1966 as Mao's executive arm in running the Cultural Revolution, the CCRG gradually replaced the CCP Politburo as the highest Central administrative organ. Initially headed by Chen Boda with China's spymaster Kang Sheng as its adviser, from February 1967 the CCRG directed the Center's administrative work, and Zhou Enlai became its de facto head, chairing its daily meetings attended by relevant Party, army, and government officials and bringing Party and military leaders as well as some rebel activists to Beijing to resolve critical issues. Lin Biao, although the No. 2 leader after Mao, mainly concerned himself with military matters, delegating the running of the Center's day-to-day affairs to Zhou Enlai.[5] Zhou determined who should attend the meetings and signed off on every single document issued in the name of the CCRG. In short, from its formation in May 1966 to its dissolution in May 1969 when a new Politburo was formed at the Ninth Party Congress, Zhou Enlai was involved in drafting and signing off on all Central decisions regarding Inner Mongolia and other embattled provinces. For three critical years, 1966–1969, "Chairman Mao and the CCRG" were the embodiment of the Proletarian Revolutionary Line, with Zhou Enlai playing a decisive role.[6]

The night before Zhou issued the eight-point verdict on Inner Mongolia on April 13, 1967, he ordered the Beijing Military Region to send a small military force to take control of the Hohhot railway, securing transportation between Hohhot and Beijing. The army arrived at 12:14 p.m. the following day, April 14. With the Inner Mongolia military still siding with the loyalists and on collision course with the rebels and the Center, the incoming PLA soldiers were fully armed. Notified in advance of their arrival by rebel representatives in Beijing, more than forty thousand rebels and supporters gathered at the railway station from 5 a.m. to welcome the arriving troops, shouting "Long live the PLA! Long live, Long, long live Chairman Mao!" and setting off firecrackers. They cheered and cried, overwhelmed by the prospect of their changing fortunes.[7] Rebels saw this as the advance party of a military that they hoped would shift the balance from repression of rebel forces to supporting their new legitimacy.

Throughout the day, we celebrated our victory. The whole city seemed to be on holiday, in any case nobody worked. Many rushed to Teachers' College as if it was a tourist site. In fact, it had some of the qualities, for the moment, of a revolutionary shrine. Rebel survivors shouted slogans from the windows, crying and praising Chairman Mao for saving their lives while thousands visited to pay homage.

My father had never once come on campus during my college years. With the decision by the Center affirming the legitimacy of the rebel movement of which I was a part, he came to campus for the first time. He arrived by bicycle at around 11:00 a.m. to find the whole campus like a bazaar. He wore his Mao style uniform and the medals he had received as awards for his work. He was a model truck driver in his transportation company and a model technician in Hohhot city for conserving fuel. He had accumulated a dozen different awards and medals over the decades. He only wore a Mao style uniform and his medals on holidays and for important events. Now he thought Husansi's victory was one of them. He asked many questions about my Long March and the struggles at Teachers' College. When I mentioned the death of Han Tong, and the fact that his brother Han Zi had become mentally deranged after Tong's death, he expressed regret for the family tragedy. He knew Han Zi personally, having trained him and other truck drivers in the IMMR to conserve fuel. His first visit to campus would also be his last.

Taking advantage of the protection afforded by the Beijing Military Region troops, the rebels took the offensive using the Center's verdict as a weapon to crush their opponents. Mass rallies celebrated the victory. On April 16, over one hundred thousand rebels and supporters gathered at Teachers' College for a rally followed by a huge parade. At the rally, a chastened army deputy commander Xiao Yingtang publicly apologized for the IMMR's mistakes and vowed to support Husansi.

However, other army generals and loyalists did not passively accept the verdict. They were angered and humiliated by the directive, particularly by the deployment of troops from Beijing. Although the verdict named no individuals, local commanders had clearly been branded as opposing the Party Center. The appointment of Teng Haiqing and Wu Tao as the acting commander and commissar, especially Wu Tao's return, signaled that the careers of some officers could be destroyed.

Wuchanzhe and a number of other loyalist organizations sent delegations to Beijing to protest in direct violation of the Center's orders. Army leaders implicated in the event, Huang Hou and Liu Chang, cried when they read the April 13 verdict to soldiers in Inner Mongolia. The soldiers had never seen their commanders so humiliated. Some shouted: "Down with Gao Jinming! Down with Wu Tao!" and even shredded the documents. Many soldiers took to the streets to protest. They accused Husansi of fabricating the verdict. The document, they insisted, did not have the usual two characters written by Mao: *Zhao Ban* (act accordingly). The rebels, however, embraced it ecstatically, proclaiming that the document was "personally ratified by Chairman Mao and Vice-Chairman Lin."

The loyalist red guards, long dominant in Hohhot politics and bolstered by the military, were equally dismayed. As losers in this political war, they would be deprived of their right to lead the Cultural Revolution and their organizations banned. Indeed, Zhou Enlai regarded them as opponents of the CCRG, but he said that only a few leaders should be punished. Suggesting that the Preparatory Group of the Revolutionary Committee of the IMAR would later determine who were "reactionaries" to be punished, Zhou ordered that the leaders be sent back to their original work units. Better elements among them would be welcomed to join "mass organizations," that is, rebel organizations, in their own work units.[8]

FIGURE 13 New leaders of Inner Mongolia from May 1967 to May 1969: Lieutenant General (*zhongjiang*) Teng Haiqing (left) and Major General (*shaojiang*) Wu Tao

The loyalists would not give up without a fight. Hongweijun leaders set up two bastions to resist the Center's decision. The first was the labor union building, which had become the headquarters of Hongweijun after Husansi was expelled. The second was the Hohhot steel plant.

In Beijing, Teng Haiqing and Wu Tao, the new leaders of Inner Mongolia, met with rebel representatives on April 14 and 15 to discuss establishing the Preparatory Group of the Revolutionary Committee of the IMAR. They prepared a provisional list of names for the Center's approval.[9] Nine in the long list were rebel leaders. The list included two Mongols, Wu Tao, and Nasanbayar. Four others—Gao Jinming, Quan Xingyuan, Kang Xiumin, and Li Shude—were leading Party officials who had supported the rebels. This followed a historical pattern in China: winner takes all.

With this change of power at the highest level in Inner Mongolia approved by the Center, most of the rebel representatives in Beijing returned to Hohhot on April 17, with Wang Duo as their trophy. Wang Yilun, however, had been placed under arrest in Beijing due to his confrontation with Kang Sheng, so rebels had no access to him.

The Center's April 13 decision, made by the CCRG with Zhou Enlai at the helm, instead of bringing order, sent Inner Mongolia deeper into turmoil. Unlike the first round of persecution, in which the Mongol victims accepted their fate with minimal resistance, in this second round of punishment, the victims were Han and they were military. They would not give up without a fight. The intensity of their anger and their desire to be recognized for loyalty to Mao and the Party led them to take extreme measures.

Teng Haiqing and the Descent into Civil War

Lieutenant General Teng Haiqing, the newly appointed acting commander of the IMMR, arrived in Hohhot from Beijing along with Wu Tao, Quan Xingyuan, Gao Jinming, and a few bodyguards on April 18, 1967. Far from welcoming them, the IMMR aggressively protested. For three hours, they were trapped inside the plane without food. It required Beijing's intercession before they could deplane and drive downtown.

Unable to move into the IMMR headquarters, Teng was forced to go to the government guest house, the *Xincheng Bingguan*. When loyalists learned where he was staying, several hundred soldiers and loyalists surrounded the building and beat his guards. Eventually, with the protection of rebels, Teng set up his headquarters in the railroad building since the railroad was under martial law control by Beijing.

Having formerly commanded the Twenty-First Army stationed in Baoji, near Xi'an in the Northwest, and served as deputy commander of the Beijing Military Region under the Central Military Committee, Teng faced his most severe challenge in Inner Mongolia.

Born in 1909, Teng hailed from Jinzhai county, Anhui. Said to have been a coal miner in his youth, he joined the Red Army in 1930 and the Chinese Communist Party the following year. He joined the Long March in 1933 and rose in the New Fourth Army in Northern Jiangsu in the 1940s. Short and brawny, he was known to be extremely obstinate.

The day after his arrival, all the winning factions and the military sent representatives to hear Teng convey the orders from the Center. Teng would meet representatives of the losing factions later. I participated in that meeting not as a representative of the rebels but as a reporter for the Teachers' College paper *Dongfanghong Zhanbao* (The East Is Red War Bulletin), one of the voices of rebel forces in Hohhot. Following Teng's arrival, another paper *Husansi* (The Hohhot Third Headquarters) was created as the official voice of the rebels, and many *Dongfanghong Zhanbao* staff members transferred to the new paper.

On April 18, the day that Teng arrived, to assure that the authority of the Center was recognized, Zhou Enlai, in one of the grander technological tours de force of the Cultural Revolution, sent helicopters to distribute a three-point instruction from the CCRG and the Army Cultural Revolution Group, confirming that the decision was ratified by Mao. The helicopters flew overhead for four days.[10]

On the following days, I saw three helicopters and one plane leafleting the city. As the leaflets fell, rebels raced to pick them up. Two documents were included: the April 13 decision by the CCRG and a letter to soldiers. There were three main points in the letter: First, the Center's decision is genuine, and it was "ratified" by Chairman Mao and Vice-Chairman Lin Biao. Second, open your eyes and don't be fooled by a few bad elements. Target your spear to attack the biggest capitalist roader and his Inner Mongolia followers. The reference was to the unnamed Ulanhu, and to Wang Duo and Wang Yilun, who would bear the brunt of the attack. Third, it stated that the Center had correctly resolved the Inner Mongolia problem and ordered soldiers who had gone to Beijing to protest to return to Inner Mongolia immediately. The directive called on people not to block transport or impede production and barred protesters from going to Beijing.

The loyalist soldiers, however, insisting that the April 13 verdict did not have the usual Mao seal of approval *Zhaoban*, continued to send people to Beijing to protest. Meanwhile, rebels trying to propagate and celebrate the verdict confronted thousands of well-armed opponents. On April 22, Hongse Gongren (Red Workers Alliance), a new loyalist labor federation that included Wuchanzhe, brought more than one hundred truckloads of people to Teachers' College to confront Dongzong, beating rebel activists and capturing four. On the same day, over three hundred army rebels from the Infantry School and army Cultural Troupe took to the streets to proclaim the verdict only to be beaten by loyalist troops, their trucks and broadcasting equipment smashed. It was civil war but without shooting.

Leaflets and posters appeared denouncing the verdict as a Zhou Enlai conspiracy. Soldiers and loyalists shouted: "Down with Gao Jinming! Down with Wu Tao!" and ripped the eight-point verdict to shreds. Loyalist resistance peaked on April 25 when soldiers harassed Teng as he delivered a speech in the military auditorium. Teng had to be hospitalized following an attack of his old hypertension. Rumors were rife that Teng's car had crushed someone to death.

Meanwhile, Inner Mongolian soldiers and Wuchanzhe loyalists streamed into Beijing. They staged a sit-in outside the front gate of Zhongnanhai for six days and nights in late April to protest the April 13 decision and demand that the Center annul it. An angry Mao and Lin Biao ordered Zhou Enlai to organize another meeting on April 27.

Zhou, Chen Boda, Kang Sheng, Xie Fuzhi, Xiao Hua, Zhang Chunqiao, Wang Li, Guan Feng, and Qi Benyu, all associated with the CCRG, as well as Wu Tao and Liu Huaxiang from the IMMR, met in the Great Hall of the People with three thousand protesting soldiers and Wuchanzhe loyalists supported by several thousand people from the Beijing loyalist organization Hongdaihui and a few dozen Husansi supporters from Beijing. There were no rebel representatives from Hohhot. When the protesters refused to let Zhou speak, clapping their hands rhythmically in a show of discontent, Kang Sheng shouted at them to get out. Eventually, however, Zhou patiently explained the Decision despite repeated interruption by slogan chanting: "We miss Chairman Mao."[11] They deeply distrusted Zhou and the CCRG. In response, Kang Sheng doubled down saying that the meeting was held to implement Chairman Mao's line on the Great Proletarian Cultural Revolution, to implement the eight-point decision on Inner Mongolia approved by the Chairman.[12]

Liu Huaxiang then read a written self-criticism on behalf of himself, Xiao Yingtang, Liu Chang, Huang Hou, and Wang Liangtai, all leading generals from the IMMR.

After the meeting, the PLA General Political Department issued another instruction insisting that soldiers obey orders and not join demonstrations. But protests in Beijing and Hohhot continued.

The heart of the problem was the very absolutism of the decision, which divided the mass organizations and the people of Inner Mongolia unequivocally into revolutionary (rebel) versus loyalist forces in Party, army and mass organizations, leaving no middle ground or ambiguity. To be labeled as "loyalist" was tantamount to being denied any shred of legitimacy to participate in the ongoing Cultural Revolution then at fever pitch and occupying center stage in Chinese politics.

In Hohhot, on the morning of April 29, rebels went to the labor union building to try to persuade the loyalists to disband and return to their original units only to be greeted by a fusillade of bricks, stones, and desks, driving them off and injuring many. The rebels captured Cheng Jilun, the leader of Hongweijun, on the evening of April 30.

On May 4, Teng Haiqing, on the instruction of the State Council and the Central Military Affairs Commission, placed the *Inner Mongolia Daily*, Inner Mongolia Radio Station, Public Security Department, and Hohhot Telecommunication Bureau and Public Security Bureau under martial law. The following day, a fight between loyalist and rebel soldiers left forty soldiers severely injured, and fourteen hospitalized, most of them outnumbered rebels. When Teng Haiqing's secretaries and four journalists visited the injured in the Railway Hospital in the small hours the following morning, they too were attacked and severely injured.

Anarchy reigned. A frustrated Teng Haiqing flew back to Beijing on May 6 to report on his work in Inner Mongolia. The Central Military Affairs Commission decided to convene a cadre conference of the IMMR. It was a bad omen for the Inner Mongolia army.

With continuing disorder in Hohhot, Zhou Enlai issued an emergency instruction on May 7: "From today, factions from the Party, government, army, people and schools are forbidden to demonstrate in the streets." Yet again, the premier was whistling in a storm. The loyalists stepped up their attacks. That day, Hongse Gongren and Liandong (United Action), a loyalist organization of the *Inner Mongolia Daily*, occupied the New China Bookstore in Hohhot.

By this time, along with a number of rebel students from Teachers' College, I had been assigned by Gao Shuhua to work as a journalist at the *Inner Mongolia Daily*, part of a postvictory sharing of spoils by the rebels. I started work immediately after the May Day rally. As a novice reporter, in the first few days I tried to learn the trade, working mainly at night and sleeping during the day as the civil war raged.

Just after midnight, in the small hours of May 11, 1967, having finished the night shift at the *Daily*, I was about to go to bed when the loudspeaker atop the *Daily* building announced an emergency meeting, summoning everyone who was not working to attend. A fight was in progress at Inner Mongolia Party Committee headquarters. We rebels were called on to support the besieged comrades there. On May 10, Hongse Gongren, Wuchanzhe, Hongtie Zhanshi (Red Railway Worker Fighters), and Liandong organized several thousand people to rally at the Racetrack (*saimachang*) in the northern fringe of the city. Their aim was to capture Gao Jinming and smash the Party Committee rebel organization Red Flag. After destroying rebel defenses at the Financial College nearby, they stormed the Inner Mongolia Party Committee building, occupying the first floor and setting fire to the wooden staircase leading to the second floor where more than two hundred rebels dug in to defend against attack.

When the rebels inside the Inner Mongolia Party Committee building called Zhou Enlai directly for help, Zhou was in discussion with Teng Haiqing, Wu Tao, Huang Hou, Liu Chang, and others who were in Beijing attending the IMMR meeting attempting to bring the autonomous region under control. Urging the rebels to continue to resist, Zhou dispatched military forces from outside Hohhot to break the siege.

At 3 a.m. on May 11, Unit 4928 of the IMMR came to the aid of the rebels. With 8.18, Husansi, Huochetou, and other rebels, the army recaptured the Party Committee headquarters and arrested loyalist leaders Zhang Sanlin and Cao Wensheng. At 5 p.m., the army and rebels surrounded the New

China Bookstore building. By midnight, the bookstore had fallen. But loyalists continued to occupy the labor union building.

The loyalist headquarters was in the heart of the new city in the six-story
labor union headquarters. They stored bricks and rocks to defend the premises as rebel sharpshooters using slingshots took out the higher windows.

I was sent by the *Daily* to report on this incident, but we were no longer
allowed to report factional fighting publicly in the paper. Reports were only
published in the internal edition circulated for Party and government offices
and high-ranking officials.

Zhou Enlai and the Center decided to crack down on the Inner Mongolian army. On May 13, the State Council and the Central Military Affairs
Commission ordered the Sixty-Ninth Army of the Beijing Military Region to
take control of the Baotou Railway Office and Baotou Train Station. Unit 8696
of the IMMR was ordered to station troops in the IMMR headquarters, Army
guesthouses, and Inner Mongolia's 253 military hospital. They replaced the
Inner Mongolia Guards Battalion that had been implicated in the Han Tong
murder and had strongly resisted the Center's verdict. The PLA leadership also
ordered each squad of the Guards Battalion to send a representative to Beijing.

From this moment, Husansi and Dongzong would play an important role
in Inner Mongolian politics. Dongzong's *Dongfanghong* newspaper published
an editorial on May 7, entitled "Resolutely Ferret out Inner Mongolia's Black
Headquarters," pointing to the existence of an underground loyalist headquarters. A few days later, Husansi rebels called on the army to crush "counterrevolutionary reactionary organizations."

Rebels surrounded the labor union building while Unit 4928 of the Inner Mongolian army, which had helped take the Party Committee building,
maintained order and prevented bloodshed. A battle of loudspeakers ensued
with both sides blaring songs, shouting slogans, and broadcasting articles.
The building was surrounded twenty-four hours a day, telephone and electric
lines were cut, and the defenders were denied food from outside. But their water was not cut. Periodically, the doors opened and helmeted loyalists rushed
out to try to capture some of their rebel attackers and force them inside. My
good friend Ouyang Ruchen was captured on the morning of May 12. Those
captured were threatened and tortured, and forced to renounce their views and
accept their captors as revolutionaries. After their "confessions" were broadcast, they were released. The rebels had done the same in defending against
the earlier siege. Ruchen steadfastly refused to confess or bow to his captors.

Ouyang Ruchen, a senior Russian student at Teachers' College, met a tragic
end. He had migrated with his parents from Hunan and graduated from high

FIGURE 14 Ouyang Ruchen, a rebel martyr beaten to death in May 1967

school in eastern Inner Mongolia. Ruchen was quiet, partly because of the inhibiting effect of his family's landlord classification. An outstanding student of Russian language and literature, he became a member of Dongzong.

On the evening of May 18, Dongzong issued a statement, demanding that the loyalists ensure Ruchen's safety and free him immediately. Teng Haiqing's office also warned that he must be released. But Hongse Gongren refused. To prevent escalation of the event and avoid endangering Ruchen, the rebels refrained from further action.

We found Ruchen the next day. His body, already cold, was left on the floor, covered by newspapers in the hospital mortuary. An autopsy conducted at the hospital revealed that his stomach was empty except for some tobacco. Denied food, he had picked up a few butts from the floor and swallowed them. His face, swollen and bloody, was unrecognizable.

Learning of Ruchen's death, in tears, we vowed to smash the enemies. Some Dongzong rebels from the Year 4 Russian Class in the Foreign Languages Department formed an Ouyang Ruchen Fighting Squad.

Final Victory?

On May 16, Central leaders and Inner Mongolian army representatives met in Beijing. Zhou Enlai, Kang Sheng, Jiang Qing, Ye Qun (the wife of Lin Biao) and Marshals Xu Xiangqian and Nie Rongzhen met with 2,700 military protesters from the IMMR. The protesters shouted: "We want to see Chairman Mao!" "Teng Haiqing, get out of Inner Mongolia!" They still refused to believe that Mao had signed the April 13 Decision. Zhou's statement that certain (unnamed) leaders of the IMMR had made mistakes of line stirred a commotion in the hall. Taking the onus away from the military, Zhou stated that the army's problem was caused by the deception of Party leaders Wang Yilun and Wang Duo: "You are not responsible, you are innocent," he wooed the recalcitrant troops.

Both Jiang Qing and Ye Qun made speeches trying to convince the soldiers that, as wives of the two top leaders, they could guarantee the authenticity of the April 13 document. But in the absence of Mao and Lin Biao, their arguments fell on deaf ears.

On May 18, Zhou summoned Party leaders Gao Jinming, Quan Xingyuan, Kang Xiumin, and major leaders of various rebel organizations to come to Beijing for a second meeting with Central leaders. Zhou's patience had run out. On May 21, Zhou ordered a special train to send all the protesting soldiers back to Hohhot in line with the Center's directive. "If anyone continues to disobey orders, they must be treated as deserters. Then the Beijing Military Region and the Beijing Garrison Command will take action." Zhou was particularly impatient with the inability or unwillingness of the generals to control the soldiers: "We trusted you, so we didn't deploy the [outside] army, but [our] patience is limited."[13]

Many finally returned to Inner Mongolia, but some troops still lingered in Beijing. On May 24 at a farewell party organized by the General Political Department of the PLA for the Inner Mongolian soldiers in Beijing, the soldiers read a five-point statement calling on the Center to reverse the April 13 Decision and remove their "loyalist" caps. They quarreled with the generals and pressed Wu Tao to sign and endorse their demand. When he refused, one hundred soldiers stormed the platform. Wu was severely beaten.[14]

This time, the soldiers had gone too far, angering the Central leaders, including Mao. On May 25, Teng Haiqing and Wu Tao issued an order that all Inner Mongolia soldiers in Beijing and elsewhere must return to their units by the end of May or be treated as deserters. To add authority to the order, the Central Military Affairs Commission issued an instruction on the order, and Mao added his stamp of approval *Zhaoban*.[15]

On May 26, the Central Military Affairs Commission issued Document (67) 12, "Decision on the Problem of the Inner Mongolia Military Region." Deputy Commander Huang Hou and Chief of Staff Wang Liangtai were detained and ordered to criticize themselves. Liu Chang, deputy political commissar, and

Zhang Degui, deputy director of the political department, were ordered to stop work and conduct self-examination. All Inner Mongolia soldiers who continued to protest were arrested and sent to study. The restless Guards Battalion and other recalcitrant Inner Mongolian army units including an anti-aircraft battalion, a topographic battalion, and part of the communications battalion were transferred out of Inner Mongolia.

Most importantly, the IMMR lost its status as a supra-provincial "large military region" (*da junqu*), being demoted to become a provincial-level military district under the jurisdiction of the Beijing Military Region. The Center ordered the dispatch of a large force to Inner Mongolia: the 578 Regiment of the Sixty-Fifth Army, Eighty-Third Battalion, Eighty-Fourth Battalion, one regiment of the Eighty-Second Battalion, and the Fifty-Second Regiment of the railway engineering corps of the Sixty-Ninth Army to form the advance command (*qianzhi*) of Hohhot.[16] On May 27, Zheng Weishan, a deputy commander of the Beijing Military Region, arrived in Hohhot at the head of the Sixty-Ninth Army. Zheng would later play a pivotal role in Inner Mongolia.

One day in early June, bicycling past the gate of the Inner Mongolia Museum, I was surprised to find that the soldier on guard with a rifle was a friend from my hometown, Zhangcun village in Raoyang county, Hebei. I learned that two friends—Shan Jinquan and Qi Guoye—from the same village had been sent to Hohhot with the Twenty-Eighth Division of the Sixty-Ninth Army. Subsequently, we often met to talk. Qi was a squad commander.

I learned that the Sixty-Ninth Army of the Beijing Military Region had been stationed in Datong, Northern Shanxi Province. Their orders came cloaked in secrecy. Told only that a serious situation existed on the border, the troops boarded freight trains at night on May 24 with loaded rifles and ammunition boxes. The cars were open and in late May the night air was frigid. Each soldier was issued a sheepskin coat. They squatted on top of their luggage and ammunition boxes, covering themselves with the fur coat. They were warned not to stand up since it was a secret mission. They traveled almost ten hours. By the time they were allowed to stand, many could no longer move their legs. Rumors flew that they would soon be fighting Soviet troops on the border. But their mission was to bring Inner Mongolia under the control of the Party Center. In Hohhot troops occupied every high building, including the radio station, railway bureau, the newspaper, police headquarters, and military headquarters.

To distinguish themselves from local soldiers, each member of the Sixty-Ninth Army wore a large glass-framed portrait of Chairman Mao on his chest when on patrol. The talisman, which distinguished them from local soldiers who opposed the Central government decision, was an ingenious form of protection. People might try to push them around, but no one dared break the glass, thereby desecrating Chairman Mao. The first day they showed up, you could see the difference. Local soldiers were slovenly; they cursed, drank, and more. The Sixty-Ninth dressed smartly and, touting Chairman Mao, were all business. No one smiled.

The Inner Mongolia Military District, under the direct command of the Beijing Military Region, sent a unit to surround the labor union.[17] They informed the defenders inside that their commanders Huang Hou and Wang Liangtai had been detained for investigation. Facing strong military and political pressure, some defenders on the second floor staged an "uprising." Soldiers and rebels then stormed the building, capturing the holdouts. It was May 30. The last loyalist stronghold had fallen. Hohhot now appeared to be in "our" hands! But at a huge cost. In the armed violence lasting more than a month after April 13, more than a dozen people lost their lives and over 1,300 people were wounded, 300 heavily.[18]

The arrival of the Sixty-Ninth Army was good news for the rebels. Numerous rallies celebrated our victories. We little realized that the price we paid was destruction of the autonomy of Inner Mongolia.

Then, on June 17, 1967, as news of the successful explosion of China's first thermonuclear bomb reached us, the whole city exploded with pride. It was a rare event that cut across the loyalist-rebel divide, underlining the nationalism that drove both camps, heralding China's arrival as a world power, and its ability both to achieve independence from the Soviet Union and to confront bullying by the United States. A New China News Agency report published on the front page of the *Inner Mongolia Daily* celebrated the event claiming that no country would again be able to humiliate a China armed with the hydrogen bomb.

The following day, at 5 p.m., the founding of the Preparatory Group of the IMAR Revolutionary Committee was announced. One hundred and fifty thousand people rallied on the Xinhua Square, cheering both the hydrogen bomb explosion and the establishment of the new regime.

Teng Haiqing, acting commander of the Inner Mongolia Military District (IMMD), chaired the Preparatory Group of the Revolutionary Committee. The two deputy chairs were Wu Tao, the Mongol major general and Huo Daoyu, a truck driver who had risen high as a rebel worker at the North China Construction Company whose one hundred thousand workers worked on projects all across North China. Standing committee members were Gao Jinming and Quan Xingyuan. Both secretaries of the Inner Mongolia Party Secretariat under Ulanhu, they had successfully distanced themselves from Ulanhu and then, at a critical moment, had thrown support to the rebels;

Kang Xiumin, a Hebei native who worked in the North China Bureau and was assigned to Inner Mongolia in late 1966 after the Qianmen Hotel Conference that toppled Ulanhu; and Nasanbayar, a Mongol official in the department of education who became the leader of government rebels; Gao Shuhua, the Teachers' College Dongzong rebel leader whose poster had touched off the Cultural Revolution in Inner Mongolia; and his rebel colleague Hao Guangde, commander of Husansi.

The composition of the Preparatory Group of the Revolutionary Committee reflected a new political order based on a three-in-one combination (*san jie he*) that was to bring together three groups of people: leading revolutionary cadres of the Party and government, ranking army officers, and leaders of the revolutionary mass organizations to provide leadership in each unit and at each level of administration throughout the country. This structure was introduced on February 2, 1967, in an editorial of the *People's Daily*, but in Inner Mongolia, implementation had been delayed because of the turmoil. In fact, as in most provinces at this time, the new Inner Mongolia leadership was dominated by the military although Party secretaries led by Gao Jinming and rebel leaders including Gao Shuhua and Hao Guangde of Teachers' College each had a place in the preparatory group. The domination of the military would become clear when the Revolutionary Committee was formally established on November 1, 1967.

A Reporter under Partial Military Control

Following the arrival of Teng Haiqing in April and the formation of the Preparatory Group of the Inner Mongolia Revolutionary Committee in June 1967, all major government agencies were reorganized. Because Teachers' College rebels had been at the center of the Cultural Revolution in Inner Mongolia, the rebel victory opened numerous job opportunities for activists there as the Verdict of the CCRG offered them a new lease on life and a seat at the table.

On the morning of May 1, 1967, during a rally at the New China Square to celebrate the twentieth anniversary of the IMAR and implement the Center's eight-point decision, Zhang Peiren handed me a note from Gao Shuhua, inviting me to meet with a few others at the Dongzong office at Teachers' College to discuss strengthening the *Inner Mongolia Daily*. Gao told us that Teng Haiqing's office had mandated that rebel students be sent to reinforce the Inner Mongolia radio station, newspaper, and the Hohhot public security bureau.

Gao offered me several choices including working for public security, the radio station and the *Inner Mongolia Daily*. All three were directly controlled by PLA personnel appointed by Teng Haiqing. I chose the *Daily*, having already begun to gain experience and a reputation as a writer for the rebel newspaper and the Teachers' College paper. I saw reporting as an opportunity to learn about developments in other parts of Inner Mongolia and the hotly contested borderlands with the MPR and the Soviet Union.

Rebel headquarters assigned more than twenty people from different universities to work at the newspaper, which the Center had placed on a martial law footing. Six were from Teachers' College. All had been active with rebel newspapers. Eventually, more than sixty rebels were assigned to the *Daily*, including about twenty reporters for the Mongolian edition.

I was deputy head of this student group, which was headed by Zhang Peiren, a fourth-year Chinese literature student and an experienced rebel journalist. Teng Haiqing's office formally appointed each of us as newspaper staff members and in the next two days we moved into the paper's dormitory. On June 18, 1967, the formal document finalizing the assignment was issued as part of the official announcement of the establishment of the Preparatory Group of the Inner Mongolia Revolutionary Committee.

Several Mongolian language graduates of the Central Nationalities Institute in Beijing, none of them Mongols, were assigned to work in the Mongolian Editorial Department in late 1967 to early 1968. Two were from Shanxi, three from Hebei, and two from Jiangsu, and all were Communist Party members. I was surprised to learn that the Central Nationalities Institute trained Han as well as minority students. They said that when they sat for the college exams, Party officials asked if they would be willing to work in a minority region. At the Party's urging, they applied to the Nationalities Institute. The same was true of other minority language majors, especially Tibetan and Uyghur. All such students were selected from Han localities, not regions with substantial minority populations.

The *Inner Mongolia Daily* was at the center of Inner Mongolian politics. Li Yulou and Qiao Tong, both rebels, were the senior editors. The new reporters received a warm welcome from them and from other rebels. The former chief editors, Zhuang Kun (Chinese edition) and Delger (Mongolian edition), had been detained earlier. Rebels, including newcomers like myself, thought that we would control the paper. Within a few days, however, the Inner Mongolia Military Command and the Preparatory Group of the Revolutionary Committee announced military control of the press, radio, and public security.

The newly appointed leaders of the *Daily* were Shi Ke and Jin Feng. Shi was an Eastern Mongol, former chief editor of the weekly *Zhanyou Bao* (Comrades in Arms) of the Inner Mongolia Military Region. Jin, also an eastern Mongol who had been a reporter for the *Liberation Army Daily*, had long been stationed in Hohhot in charge of military news about the IMMR. Educated in eastern Mongolian schools, both were bilingual, excelling in reading and writing in Chinese and Mongolian.

The chain-smoking Jin, with his professorial air and the habit of writing at night and sleeping days, handled editorial matters. A real newspaper man, he was rail thin and used to work from seven at night to six in the morning, then sleep all day. He often corrected my writing. He wasn't at all like a PLA cadre, more like a professional writer. He had supported Husansi from the very beginning of the Cultural Revolution. His daughter Saihan, an attractive student majoring in painting in the Art Department at Teachers' College, was a dedicated Dongzong member.

Shi Ke, quiet and intense, hardly ever spoke, and almost never smiled. In contrast to Jin Feng's liberal and intellectual aura, he was military to the core. Always buttoned, very precise and formal, he handled the administrative side. Both wore military uniforms, but we could laugh and joke with Jin, never with Shi. When Shi and Jin talked between themselves, they often spoke in Mongolian rather than in Chinese, presumably for reasons of privacy.

The two military men worked closely with Teng Haiqing's office, popularly known as Tengban. When Teng wanted to disseminate a policy, he summoned an editorial writer and spoke while the writer took notes (we had no tape recorder). After the writer drafted the editorial, Jin Feng would read and correct it. After a second draft, Jin would approve the text, sign it, and send it to Tengban. If it was urgent, the writer biked to Tengban, where Li Shude, who ran the office, would read and approve it. In important cases, Teng himself would read and sign. Only then could the editorial be published.

Shi Ke and Jin Feng imposed rigid guidelines for running the paper. For national news, we relied exclusively on Xinhua, whose Inner Mongolia branch occupied a corner of our building. We knew most of the Xinhua staff. All were rebels. We received Xinhua news dispatches from Beijing by shortwave telegram. Even major Inner Mongolia news, which was drafted by the Xinhua people in the same building, had to be sent to Beijing for editing before coming to us via Beijing. The *People's Daily* also had a Hohhot office. Xinhua news came with detailed instructions: a specified article to be placed on page 1, in column 1, and even the size of the title. Visiting the editorial office of the *Gansu Daily* in the summer of 1968, I learned that this was a national policy that enabled the Center to tightly control information.

The most important assignments at this time went to rebels. Many loyalist reporters fled when the paper was reorganized, but eventually they came back to work and did what they were told to do. On the night shift, editors of all four pages were rebels; loyalists only did proof reading.

My first job was to cover political and law enforcement news on the night shift. After a few weeks of sleeplessness, we got used to the hours. The longest time I worked the night shift was three months. Sun Panshi, my roommate at the *Daily*, and a first-year physics student at Teachers' College, worked the night shift for more than two years. We nicknamed him night owl.

While peace reigned in our office, in the early months fierce factional fighting reverberated throughout Inner Mongolia. This made us very cautious about what could and could not be reported. News was an important factional weapon. Even the slightest language mistake could lead to political suspicion. We were given an impossible guideline: bring no factional slant to reporting but follow Chairman Mao's revolutionary line!

Armed guards secured the premises at the *Daily*, even setting up artillery in our courtyard. Five huge artillery pieces were deployed in the courtyard along with a platoon of forty soldiers. They conducted daily military exercises and artillery practice. Two soldiers with rifles and bayonets guarded the gate at all times. I never got used to it.

The newspaper compound, located in the New Town, had two courtyards. One contained the huge editorial building, the other our dormitory and the telegraph station. They were three minutes apart by bicycle. Each time we entered either courtyard we had to stop, dismount, and salute. This absurd ritualized access to important premises was ubiquitous across China. The soldiers from the Sixty-Ninth Army who guarded the premises, most hailing from rural North China like me, were unsmiling. My friend Zhao Zongzhi once asked a soldier: "Why do we bicycle riders have to dismount, while officials in cars do not?" The young soldier just stood still, impassive.

The military regime brought Cultural Revolution–style ritual to the office: the staff began each day by lining up to ask for instructions from Chairman Mao. In the evening we lined up again to report on our work to him, each time waving the Little Red Book of Mao quotations and asking for his instructions. The relaxed tone of the usual newspaper office, with people coming and going early and late depending on their own schedule, was eliminated. Still, we joked a lot among ourselves. But the moment the military entered everyone rose. We bowed to Mao's portrait, waved the Little Red Book and wished the Chairman a long life, a long, long, long life, not forgetting to wish good health, good, good health, to Vice-Chairman Lin Biao. The military stood in front with Shi Ke leading this ritual. We writers were in the back.

Zhao Zongzhi was the Shandong-born son of a high military commander who had died before 1949. Confident in his military background, he poked fun at this ritual. He and I always stood as far back as possible, snickering, or sometimes escaping to the bathroom.

The Funerals of Ouyang Ruchen and Han Tong

All modern political regimes mark their victory by honoring fallen comrades. On June 8, 1967, after the IMMD was firmly under Teng Haiqing's control, the Ministry of Internal Affairs, chaired by Zeng Shan, recognized both Han Tong and Ouyang Ruchen as martyrs.[19]

Four days earlier, on June 4, rebels had staged a big ceremony for their fallen comrade Ouyang Ruchen. His sister, brother and sister-in-law, but not his parents, who were still intimidated by their landlord label, traveled from Chifeng to Hohhot for the funeral. Ruchen was cremated and the urn with his ashes was brought home.

The funeral was held on the sports ground of Erzhong, the Hohhot No. 2 middle school. Forty thousand people honored him in the campus auditorium. All rebel organizations sent wreaths and made speeches. The Foreign Languages Department of Teachers' College published a memorial booklet commemorating the two students who had sacrificed their lives.

The biggest honor was reserved for Han Tong, the rebels' first martyr whose death had touched off monumental changes in Inner Mongolia. As the central symbol of the rebels' struggle for justice, his funeral was perhaps ten times the size of Ruchen's.

The funeral took place on June 20, two days after the formation of the Preparatory Group of the Inner Mongolia Revolutionary Committee. From the beginning, the event was shrouded in controversy. Zhou Enlai had stated that Han Tong had died a martyr's death, but Teng Haiqing insisted that the funeral be kept to less than one thousand people and one hundred vehicles. Teng's strictures were ignored. Every unit sent representatives. And many people went spontaneously. The first of more than seven hundred vehicles, including all Teachers' College cars and trucks, had already arrived in Han Tong's village when the last set out on the twenty-mile journey from Hohhot.

The road was clogged with vehicles decked with flowers and wreaths made and donated by people in each unit. The speakers were Inner Mongolia's two leading rebels, Gao Shuhua, Tong's teacher, and Hao Guangde, his school-mate. Han Tong's father simply thanked everyone during a brief speech. People encouraged his mother to speak, but she could not utter a word through her tears. His brother, who had gone crazy under military torture, was also unable to speak, alternately laughing hysterically and crying.

The gravestone, about three feet high, had finely wrought characters engraved in gray stone: "Revolutionary Martyr Han Tong Will Be Remembered Forever." He was buried in the village cemetery, his ashes carried in a box by his brother Han Zi in military uniform, with Gao Shuhua and Hao Guangde

FIGURE 15 Han Tong's funeral, held in his hometown in June 1967

flanking him. The box was placed in the grave, then the stone was erected and firecrackers set off. Thousands of people lined up to pay respects to his parents at home. It took an entire day for the line to pass.

Even loyalist classmates attended the funeral. Han Tong had been liked by everyone, and he had sacrificed his life. Only Wang Yumin, the former league secretary and my tormentor during the Socialist Education Movement, did not attend. After the Center's verdict on Inner Mongolia was issued, the loyalist group that she led, Kangda Bingtuan of Teachers' College, was disbanded. Wang Yumin was among about a dozen most-wanted loyalist leaders who were on the run. The list was issued by Dongzong, with the approval of the Preparatory Group of the Inner Mongolia Revolutionary Committee. It was almost a year before she came out of hiding and returned to school as a student.

The New Regime Conducts an Execution

In the early summer of 1967, I had just begun work as an editorial writer at the *Daily* when Jin Feng dictated an editorial hailing the newly established authority of the Revolutionary Committee, specifically its role in suppressing counterrevolutionary activities. I took notes. I was simply a writing machine. I did some work on the draft and he corrected it. He and Shi Ke both signed the editorial. There was no place for my signature. The text was brought to Wang Zaitian (Namjilseren), a Preparatory Group member who chaired the Political and Legal Subcommittee, which had important public security functions. Wang was a Mongol with revolutionary credentials dating from the anti-Japanese resistance. A long-term associate of Ulanhu and a specialist in legal affairs, he had survived in 1966 by joining the attack that toppled Ulanhu. After working all day writing three drafts, I made an 11 p.m. appointment to see Wang, together with Bao Jingguo, the editorial director and a rebel leader at the *Daily*.

Bao was a Beijing University journalism graduate whose mother worked at *People's Daily*. Bao and I went to Wang's residence and office in a two-story red-brick building with about ten rooms and attractive gardens; it was located in the same neighborhood as the Inner Mongolia government compound. We drank milk tea while Wang read the draft. After changing one or two phrases, he signed it.

The editorial stated that thirty-two people would be jailed and one would be executed. But the trial was not scheduled to take place until the next day.

Why, I asked Bao, was the editorial written *before* the trial?

"You're so naive. It's always done this way."

"But why execute someone right after establishing a new authority? Throughout history," I added, "when a new emperor ascended the throne, the court usually announced a general amnesty and stay of execution for most criminals. Isn't that true?"

"You can't just copy the old ways, Little Cheng. That was feudalism. It won't do for our proletarian dictatorship. It's been like this ever since Yan'an days. This was true in Inner Mongolia in 1947 at the inauguration of the Autonomous Government and in 1949 at the founding of the People's Republic. It has been true ever since. It's a matter of killing the chickens to scare the monkeys."

The next day I cycled to the mass trial at the Hohhot Workers' Stadium. As a reporter, I received a ribbon for identification. Carrying a camera and notebook, I joined a dozen other broadcast and newspaper reporters seated on the platform where I could see everything.

This was a criminal trial, but it was thoroughly politicized as a mass meeting to criticize the so-called antirevolutionary adverse current. All the surviving Ulanhu clique criminals and other "bad elements" were brought before the crowd. All together there were about twenty black elements, including

Ulanhu's son, Buhe and his wife Julanchechig, who had been Party secretary and director of the Inner Mongolia Film Studio; Zhang Sanlin, the loyalist leader who occupied the Party Committee building and was captured by PLA rebel forces; and Liu Qing, the PLA murderer of Han Tong. Each stood with head bowed, a big signboard on his or her chest.

That day, I was seated behind Ulaan, the former leader of the Inner Mongolia Women's Association. I felt miserable seeing her in these circumstances; she had helped me find my girlfriend in Beijing only months ago. Now she was charged as an Ulanhu black gang member.

Two soldiers held the prisoner's arms behind his back. Slogans denouncing the Ulanhu clique rang out.

"Uphold the unity of the nationalities, oppose national splittism!"

"Firmly support the newly established red authority!"

"Carry through the Great Proletarian Cultural Revolution to the end!"

"Down with Liu Shaoqi and Deng Xiaoping! Down with Ulanhu!"

"Resolutely suppress all counterrevolutionaries!"

"Long live the red revolutionary authority! Long live Chairman Mao!"

That day, two hundred thousand of Hohhot's three hundred thousand people were reportedly mobilized. It was the first event staged by the newly formed Revolutionary Committee. Those who could not crowd into the stadium listened by loudspeaker at points set up around the city. Heavily armed soldiers and police were everywhere.

Ge Zhisheng chaired the meeting. A Political Department staff member from Teachers' College, he became a rebel leader and rose to become deputy director of the Hohhot Revolutionary Committee.

Teng Haiqing, in his PLA uniform, spoke first, setting the guidelines and tone for the meeting. Then came a deputy director of the Hohhot Revolutionary Committee and the chair of Hohhot Public Security Military Control, Ma Boyan, a Hui Muslim, also in PLA uniform. He announced the new regime's first public trial. Thirty-three criminals, both active counterrevolutionaries and ordinary criminals such as burglars, were to be tried. The crowd roared its denunciation of one criminal after another, faithfully playing its part in the orchestrated drama.

Burglars got three to four years, and two historical reactionaries were dragged out yet again and given fifteen-year sentences.

Finally, Ma denounced the "counterrevolutionary murderer" in a crime of passion, village electrician Xin Erhuan from Dongtaishi village in the suburban Qiaobao commune. Xin was strong and stubborn. He had persisted against pressure from both his own and his lover's family, all of whom opposed his plan to divorce his wife. Finally, his lover decided to terminate their relationship. One night, when villagers were watching a movie, he asked to say his parting words. The lovers met in a nearby forest. They quarreled, and he strangled her. The body was found a few weeks later, and Xin was convicted of rape and murder.

The chief justice of the Hohhot People's Court announced the verdict: execution. The moment the sentence was pronounced, policemen changed the handcuffs from the front to behind his back. Xin fought furiously, shouting, "I'm not a rapist. It's a lie."

The whole stadium buzzed. Ma Boyan struck the table and shouted, "Bring the prisoner to the back."

Four policemen carried him out. In the back of the platform, right behind where I was sitting, they smashed his head on the ground, twisted his arms behind his back, and bound his wrists tightly with a thin rope. Then they pulled back on the rope, breaking his shoulder joints. You could hear the snap. That way your arm could reach to the back of your neck. They tied his arm around his neck. These were thin ropes with a handle in back to hold. If the prisoner attempts to shout, tightening the rope on his throat silences him.

Following the police to the back, Ma Boyan ordered, "Inject him." Two needles injected anesthesia into his neck to prevent any shouting. Xin was then brought to the front, bound and silent.

The judge delivered the execution decree, which required the criminal's fingerprint to complete the process. A policeman brought ink and printed it with Xin's hand behind his back. Another policeman put a sign in front with the name covered with red crosses. On his back, his name and an arrow reaching up over his head signified execution. It was a form used in the Qing dynasty.

Heavy leg irons were on Xin's feet. His head had been shaved. Xin and all other prisoners were driven around the city. He was in the first truck filled with soldiers and police with rifles. All other criminals followed, ending with the black elements, in a caravan of two dozen trucks.

My friend Yang Yongsheng, a radio reporter, called me to the first truck with the convict awaiting execution. This was a privilege, made possible because he knew Ma Boyan, the police chief, well. I hesitated. I had never witnessed such an event. Curious but fearful, I mounted the truck. From the worker's stadium the procession wove its way through the new city, passing the main government buildings, the museum, and newspaper headquarters, through the major streets to the old city.

Old men and bound-footed women whispered, "Such a young man to be put to death."

After a parade of an hour and a half, the procession exited through the south gate of the old city, heading toward the Big Black River. Thousands of people had gathered in a circle at the execution ground on the riverbank, about one hundred yards from a pit. They were stopped by armed soldiers, but I was among about a dozen people permitted to follow the prisoner into the execution ground. I was just eleven yards away from the pit and five yards from the executioner.

The truck stopped about 150 feet from the hole. Four policemen pulled Xin Erhuan down from the truck. He was wearing a white shirt and black trousers. He was barefoot, having lost his shoes. They dragged him to the hole, then a policeman kicked his knees so he fell to them on the ground. The police moved away and a soldier lifted his rifle. Another soldier waved two red flags. Two shots were fired from twenty-five feet and Xin fell facedown.

I could see that the soldier's hand shook and his face was white as he fired.

I felt as if I were being executed.

Although Xin fell, his body was still heaving and he continued to groan.

Ma Boyan cursed the soldier: "You botched it. Fire again!"

The soldier went up to Xin and fired two more shots at point blank next to his head. Still, he did not stop groaning.

Ma Boyan kicked the body with his black leather shoes so that Xin's face turned up. His face was bloody, but he was still heaving.

Ma shouted to another soldier: "Shoot him in the neck. This time use a dum-dum."

The soldier changed bullets and shot twice in the throat, his gun almost touching the victim.

Xin's head exploded and the red blood and white brain spilled out into the ditch.

Two more police took off the leg irons and threw them on the truck.

A soldier waved the flag once more and the soldiers withdrew.

Suddenly, a wave of people rushed toward the ditch to gain a closer look at the body. Some hoped to collect the brain and blood for medicinal purposes. It was just like the episode in Lu Xun's 1919 story *Yao* (Medicine), which described how a Chinese revolutionary martyr's blood was turned into a bun and sold as medicine.

As we were leaving, I saw Xin Erhuan's uncle leading a small donkey cart with a straw pallet rolled up and a rope. He had come to collect the body.

Another policeman came up: "Old Xin, your nephew has been executed. Tell family members not to cry or have a funeral, just bury him. Now, you must pay the bullet fee."

"How much?"

"Your nephew wasted five bullets, but we'll only charge you for one: thirty-seven cents." The old man gave him the money, muttering, "Thank the government" (*xiexie zhengfu*).

This was the only time that I observed an execution up close. The horrifying image lingered in my mind for weeks, interfering with eating, working, and sleeping. It took on special meaning for rebels who had fought against powerful odds in the service of justice now that we sometimes found ourselves exercising power at the highest levels of Inner Mongolia state and society.

7

The *Wasu* Movement and My Career as a Journalist

A Reporter on the Grasslands

After about three months of writing editorials and working the night shift from May 1967, growing discomfort with office rituals, salutes to soldiers, and the formalities of official writing, but above all the desire to learn what was happening beyond Hohhot, led me to request assignment to report from the grasslands. Since coming to Inner Mongolia in 1959, I had traveled far and wide to Lanzhou and Xi'an in the Northwest, to Mao's birthplace in Hunan, as far southwest as Guilin and on to Shanghai and Beijing. But I had never traveled in Inner Mongolia beyond the agricultural villages to the east of Hohhot. To be sure, I met Mongol herders on the street and saw the grasslands from the window on the train to Beijing and back, but what was life like for herders on the grasslands? The northeastern, central, and western parts of Inner Mongolia boast China's largest grassland, where herders concentrate, but I had seen none of that. I was also eager to move beyond the regional capital to take the political pulse elsewhere. In late July I was sent to Hulunbuir league, the northeastern tip of Inner Mongolia. Bordering the Soviet Union to the north and the Mongolian People's Republic to the west, it was strategically important.

Hulunbuir, far from being a remote no-man's-land as it appeared on a map, was a meeting ground of both ethnic groups and ideologies. One of the original birthplaces of the Mongols, Hulunbuir became the fiefdom of Chinggis Khan's brother Hab Hasar in the thirteenth century. Beginning in 1727, it was garrisoned by the Qing when the Treaty of Kyakhta was signed between Imperial Russia and the Qing Empire to regulate their relations. After December 1911, the last days of the Qing, when Outer Mongolia proclaimed an independent Mongolian state, Hulunbuir came to be hotly contested between Mongols and Han. It also became a major destination for thousands of Buryat Mongols from the Chita region of Siberia fleeing the Russian civil war in 1917–1919. In 1924, a young Daur intellectual called Merse (a.k.a. Guo Daofu) who was working in the Chinese Ministry of Foreign Affairs in Beijing organized the Inner Mongolian People's Revolutionary Party (Neirendang) with the Kharachin Mongol Bai Yunti from the Josotu league of Inner Mongolia. Merse became its first secretary-general and wrote the Party's program and other key documents.[1]

Under Manchuguo, the semicolonial state dominated by Imperial Japan from 1932 to 1945, Hulunbuir initially enjoyed a special status thanks to the enthusiasm on the part of Mongol and Daur aristocrats for Manchu-Mongolian independence. But in 1939, the western border of Hulunbuir became a battlefield pitting Japanese (and Manchuguo) forces against the Soviet army (and MPR cavalry). This became known as the Nomonhan battle or Khalkhyn Gol battle (as it is called in the Soviet Union and the MPR). With the loss of one hundred thousand troops (half killed in battle, the rest taken prisoner) by the combined Soviet and MPR armies, Japan was forced to abandon efforts to occupy the MPR and attack the Soviet Union. It focused instead on China and Southeast Asia, and two years later, in 1941, it attacked the United States.[2]

Coming under the jurisdiction of the Inner Mongolia Autonomous Government in 1947, Hulunbuir was a pastoral region. Ulanhu's policy of "three nos and two benefits," formulated in 1948, centered on protecting pastoral Mongols in Hulunbuir, and his closure of many of Wang Zhen's military farms in the area in 1962 won him enormous popularity among pastoral Mongols. I was eager to learn how the Cultural Revolution unfolded in this land of complex history and proximity to both the Soviet Union and the MPR.

The train trip from Hohhot to Hailar, the capital of Hulunbuir, took five days through Beijing and all three northeastern provincial capitals (Shenyang, Changchun, Harbin), with changes in Beijing and Harbin. I could take the Number 1 international train from Beijing to Moscow with my journalist ID to save a day of travel. But I decided to see the northeastern provinces, making more stops and meeting people on the train.

One of the crimes that Ulanhu had been charged with was the attempt to link western and eastern Inner Mongolia directly by rail and provide rail connections for more border towns and cities. His critics would now label that nationalist splittism. It was sheer stupidity to attack the attempt to provide transportation links to integrate Inner Mongolia's vast grasslands and its cities! But with deepening China-Soviet conflict, the charges undermined Ulanhu's credibility.

Our *Inner Mongolia Daily* station was a one-man office in Hailar, occasionally supplemented by visiting reporters. Mandahu, a Mongolian-language editor, and Buyan, a Mongol reporter for the Mongolian-language edition, periodically came to the station. Stationed there for years, they had a deep familiarity with the region.

Mandahu and Buyan introduced me to officials, including leading members of rebel and loyalist groups, and helped as interpreters in Mongol-speaking areas. Before leaving Hohhot, Jin Feng had repeatedly warned me not to become involved in factional fighting. He urged me to listen to all views and try to uncover any positive news about the economy; *Zhua geming, cu shengchan* (Grasp revolution, promote production) was a slogan of the time: "If you encounter any serious factional conflict, report to me, and I will pass it along to the Preparatory Group."

The *Inner Mongolia Daily* had a comfortable apartment with an office and two bedrooms behind the league Party Committee. We also had two bicycles and a telephone that allowed us to make long-distance calls. The Party Committee office would provide a jeep or a car to visit nearby towns and villages. In an emergency, we could ask for a police vehicle from the military subdistrict.

My classmates on campus envied my high income based on subsidies for those working outside Hohhot, and the ability to travel, with our Russian-made Gif camera and Meiduo shortwave radio allowing us to listen to the news while working in the grasslands.

I began listening to foreign broadcasts in Chinese, including Radio Moscow and Red Star Radio (the Soviet military station). Of course, listening to foreign broadcasts (the official term was *di tai*, or "enemy radio") at that time was a crime. We were close to Soviet territory, so reception was much clearer than in Beijing or Hohhot. The Soviet Chinese broadcasts ran around the clock. I also occasionally listened to Chinese broadcasts from Taiwan as well as the BBC, Voice of America, and broadcasts from France and Australia. The *English 900* program on Voice of America helped me to review my rusty English.

My reporter's ID card with photo and military committee chop in a green hardcover booklet allowed me to go anywhere, including into Party, government, and military meeting rooms, if they were open for reporting. Another important document was a dark-blue hardcover booklet (Telegraph ID) with our charge number for telegraph use anywhere in the country. It could be used only to telegraph the office of the *Daily* in Hohhot without payment.

Remote from Hohhot though it was, Hulunbuir could not escape the political turmoil then sweeping Inner Mongolia. Hulunbuir league Party secretary Qi Junshan, a Tumed Mongol, was the first to fall as an Ulanhu black gang member. Those who survived the initial purge fell after the Center's April 13 decision of 1967 that proclaimed the rebel victory over the Inner Mongolia Military Region. Rebels began to attack Mongol leaders such as the governor Jirgal and deputy Party secretary Butgegchi as agents of the "Inner Mongolian February Adverse Current." In late May 1967, Butgegchi and Gombojab, another deputy Party secretary, were caught fleeing to Beijing to report on the league's troubles and were dragged back to Hailar for struggle. They lost consciousness several times during repeated physical tortures. Butgegchi was airlifted to Hohhot by the IMMD for emergency treatment.[3] He survived, but his comrade died in July at the hands of the rebels.[4]

Soon after my arrival, I set off to travel beyond Hailar. One day I went to the border town of Manzhouli. Near the bustling railway station, a few Russian-style edifices (the Border Gate, Railroad Hospital, and Garrison Headquarters) testified to the Russian influence over the preceding centuries through the 1950s Sino-Soviet friendship. Every passenger got off the train and waited for about two hours while the train changed wheels to suit the broad track on the Russian side. Across the border was a small Russian town called Zabaikalsk. But even with my reporter's ID, I could only look at it from an observation tower. The Russian houses—white walls of solid brick and stones or wood, and roofs covered with iron sheets—were colorful and shining, in sharp contrast to the gray bungalows of Manzhouli.

After the Soviet army moved into the MPR in 1966, Soviet and Mongolian military airplanes sometimes flew over Hulunbuir to monitor Chinese defenses. I sensed that war with the Soviets might break out soon.

The trip to Nomonhan, on the border between the MPR and Hulunbuir league, took about two hours from Hailar.

PLA Colonel Jambal, a Mongolian director of the New Barga Left banner's Department of the People's Armed Forces (*wuzhuang bu*), escorted me in his jeep to the vast Nomonhan battlefield of 1939. Three decades later it remained filled with craters, massive graves littered with remnants of dead bodies, scattered broken parts of weapons and equipment, rusted cannonball shells, and bullet shell cases. The site of the battle that had transformed the World War II in the Far East was deserted. It had never been memorialized, since no Chinese forces were involved.[5]

Under the blue sky and white clouds, flocks of sheep, cows, and cattle, peacefully grazed. Larks flew high in the sky, with pink lilies and white peonies in bloom below. Reflecting on life and death, on peace and war, I silently prayed for the souls of the dead, hoping there would never again be such killing in this beautiful land. But other conflicts loomed in Beijing, Hohhot, and the remote grasslands.

Storm Clouds Gather

A phone call one mid-September afternoon in 1967 from Jin Feng, the number two military representative in our editorial office at the *Inner Mongolia Daily*, ordered Mandahu and me to return to Hohhot immediately.

"Why the rush?" I asked.

His voice was stone cold: "Don't ask too much. You'll learn the reason when you arrive."

We decided to fly back. The next day was Wednesday, the only scheduled flight day each week.

This was my first flight. The plane was a small Soviet-made AN24 with twenty-two seats and five small round windows on each side. There were only eight passengers (the other six men appeared to be cadres), with two pilots and an attendant. I was excited to look down at the grasslands below, with several tiny white yurts and flocks of sheep and goats. Four hours later we arrived at Hohhot, after refueling at Shiliinhot Airport.

As Mandahu had suspected, the urgent summons had come from Teng Haiqing's office (Tengban). The Preparatory Group was organizing teams to dispatch to different leagues (including Hulunbuir) to investigate the factional fighting erupting everywhere. A Revolutionary Committee preparatory group was to be established in each league on the basis of the investigation. I was assigned to a five-member investigation group to be dispatched to Hulunbuir. Li Zhidong, the head of the group, was a member of the rebel Red Flag of the Inner Mongolia Party Committee; Chidaltu, the only Mongol and deputy head of the group, from Tengban. A rebel leader in the Inner Mongolia Geological Bureau, Chidaltu was a Hulunbuir native who had graduated from the Hailar No. 2. Middle School. The PLA Captain Luo Shulin was a Russian-language interpreter and a graduate of the Beijing Foreign Language Institute who worked in the Political Department of the IMMD; and Song Guoqing was a rebel student from the Inner Mongolia College of Agriculture and Husbandry.

Jin Feng later told me that I was selected for the team for two reasons: first, having worked briefly as a reporter in Hulunbuir, I had some familiarity with the area; I was also recommended by Gao Shuhua and Gao Jinming. Jin Feng had also recommended Mandahu because he had been stationed there and had good relations with many Mongolian officials. He was not, however, included. After learning that his nomination had been vetoed, Mandahu confided to me: "You know why, Little Cheng? Tengban doesn't want many Mongols in the group."

Two days later, the members attended a morning meeting at Tengban. Gao Jinming chaired. After studying the documents issued by the Preparatory Group, including the directive from Beijing to accelerate formation of revolutionary committees at all levels and Teng Haiqing's instructions to implement the Center's directive, the group discussed its division of labor.

We set off in late September 1967, traveling by train to Beijing, then changing to the international train from Beijing to Moscow.[6] It was my chance to ride a Soviet train and to encounter Russians and Europeans.

The international train had soft sleeper carriages, with ten compartments in each car, each with two upper and two lower berths. The two heads, Li Zhidong and Chidaltu, occupied one compartment; we three occupied another. We were in a Soviet-run car. The attendant, Andrei, spoke Russian only. I had studied Russian in middle school, but after switching to English, I could barely communicate with him in my simple Russian.

Andrei told us that the train had ten to twelve cars at the peak of Sino-Soviet friendship. But now, with few passengers, there were five cars, including two managed by China (with Chinese attendants), two managed by the Soviet Union (with Soviet attendants), and one dining car (with Chinese cooks and a waitress). The locomotive with its Chinese engineer ended its service at the border city of Manzhouli, where a Soviet locomotive and Soviet engineers replaced it. During the two-day trip, we met four British tourists (two elderly couples) in the dining car. It was the first time I communicated with foreigners in English. Following a ten-day China tour, they wanted to see Siberia and Moscow.

Arriving in Hailar, we met with top league officials and leading members of Party, government, military, and mass organizations to explain our mission. We then split up, with each investigator taking two banners or cities. I investigated Hailar city and New Barga Right banner in the triangle between the Soviet Union, MPR, and China.

After two weeks of individual investigations, the group met in the Hulunbuir league guesthouse in mid-October 1967 to discuss our group report. Li Zhidong, the investigation group leader who had been a writer in the Propaganda Department of the Inner Mongolia Party Committee, drafted the report.

Our major disagreement focused on Shang Min, political commissar of Hulunbuir Military Subdistrict. All group members except me favored Shang Min as chair of the new Hulunbuir League Revolutionary Committee. I had submitted several internal reports to the Inner Mongolia authorities through the *Daily* detailing his crackdown on rebel students during the February Adverse Current,[7] and his persecution of Mongol officers and family members.

There was information detailing his harassment of deputy commander Ölji-dalai, chief of staff Nima, and others, often stopping their work and searching their homes without authorization from above. My personal interview with him revealed that he knew almost nothing about the history of Inner Mongolia from the 1920s to the 1950s. I concluded that he would be unable to handle nationality relations sensitively and work effectively with Mongol officers, soldiers, and local people. Chidaltu agreed with my view privately but dared not speak. He encouraged me to persist in my view.

Soon after preparing our report, all investigation group members as well as Party and military leaders from Inner Mongolia, were summoned to Beijing to meet with Teng Haiqing. We were housed in the gray brick buildings of the Beijing Military Region Guest House in Beijing's Dongcheng District. The meeting lasted four days, even continuing on October 1 (National Day).

Mongolian PLA officers described their persecution by Shang Min. Suddenly, Teng Haiqing rudely interrupted: "Chairman Mao teaches us: Revolution is not a dinner party. If you have evidence of Shang Min's political crimes, reveal it. I don't want to listen to chicken feathers and garlic skins (*jimao suanpi, popomama*)," that is, old wives' tales. Teng's interjection terrified everyone. No one dared speak.

I stood up and, firmly but politely, said: "Commander Teng, Chairman Mao also teaches us to allow people to finish speaking. If we do not let people speak, heaven will fall sooner or later. Please let the Mongol officers finish speaking. I heard many similar stories from family members of soldiers. You can read these in my internal reports." Perhaps because I came from Husansi and dared to speak in this way, he controlled his temper and asked the three Mongol officers to finish speaking. Neither their complaints nor my internal reports, however, prevented Shang Min's appointment as the top leader in Hulunbuir league several months later when revolutionary committees formed throughout Inner Mongolia.

I wondered why Teng Haiqing didn't even want to listen to the reports on Shang Min. Was he acting on higher-level directives from the Center on the danger of Ulanhu and Mongol splittism? From the outset, Teng, having been sent in to bring a fractious province under the control of the Center, was suspicious of and hostile toward locals, Mongols in particular. He had been briefed by Zhou Enlai and other leaders to beware of hidden Ulanhuist remnants in the Party, government, military, and mass organizations. Who then could be trusted? The resistance that Teng encountered in the early months of his assignment deepened his suspicions. But as an outsider, he knew little about the divisions within the Inner Mongolia polity and between Party and people beyond the fact that there was an "Ulanhu black gang," the capitalist roaders, and that some local generals were hostile to him as an outsider imposed by the Center with a mandate to place their rebel foes in power.

In late October, I returned to Hohhot with the delegation. The next morning Jin Feng showed me a document titled "Look at the Behavior of the Inner Mongolia Daily Black Reporter Cheng Tiejun in Hulunbuir." Drafted by a Shang Min staff member, it was submitted to Tengban and the PLA Military Control Committee of the *Daily*. The 120-page document investigated my reporting in Hulunbuir, particularly focusing on my secret meetings and interviews with Mongol officers. The major allegation was my lack of political consciousness, which led me to sympathize with these die-hard nationalist elements and their splittist activities.

The allegations sent a chill down my spine. After reading it carefully, I returned the report to Jin Feng and asked: "Director Jin, do you believe this? Do you really think I am a splittist?"

Jin inhaled deeply on his cigarette and smiled: "Xiao Cheng, if we [meaning Shi Ke and himself] had any suspicions about you, I could not show you the report. You are a young Han rebel with no family ties to Mongols. How could you possibly support splittism? We trust you; therefore, we explained that to Tengban."

Jin Feng sighed, then continued: "Xiao Cheng, you are a good comrade who wants to understand our Mongols, and I appreciate this. Since Shang Min is prejudiced against you, you'd better not return to Hailar. We can assign you to Bayannuur league. Most of the population there is Han and you won't need Mongolian interpretation. Our senior reporter Lu Yonglong is working there and can help you. Take a break for a week, then study with us every morning for several weeks. You need to know what's going on in Hohhot. I have scheduled your transfer to Bayannuur in late November."

Jin's words and his order to transfer me to Bayannuur meant that I was no longer trusted. I felt banished. With hindsight, however, I cannot thank Jin Feng enough for saving me from persecution by Shang Min.

"Ferreting Out Traitors" and the Beginning of *Wasu*

Before leaving for Bayannuur league in western Inner Mongolia, I took a one-week break, visiting my father at the transportation company, my girlfriend Qingxian at Medical College and schoolmates at Teachers' College. They were interested in my adventures in Hulunbuir and Beijing and concerned about the meeting with Teng Haiqing and the report condemning my sympathy for the Mongol PLA officers. Meeting rebel friends at Teachers' College and elsewhere, and gathering inside information, I realized that another round of class struggle was gathering momentum. This time it would be more serious.

I met with Gao Shuhua twice, once in his office and once at his home. He told me that, in early October 1967, an organization called Ferreting Out the Traitor Clique Liaison Office (*Jiu pantu jituan lianluo zhan*) headed by a Mongol called Ulaanbagan submitted the "Brief Report on the Big Treasonous Group Harbored by the Ulanhu Black Clique" to the Preparatory Group for the Revolutionary Committee. The report described the alleged traitorous activities of many Mongol leaders, including Hafenga, Tegusi (Tögös), Wang Zaitian (Namjilseren), Wangdan (Vandan), Mulun (Mörön), and Yidaga (Yatga). Some rebels at Teachers' College supported their call to ferret out more Mongol enemies. Gao Shuhua, however, noted that both Tegusi and Wang Zaitian were on the list to be approved by the Center to join the Inner Mongolia Revolutionary Committee. "If they are enemies, both Teng Haiqing and the Center have made big mistakes. If they are comrades, then Ulaanbagan must be a pernicious enemy who is attacking the Revolutionary Committee," he said. From the start of the campaign, both Gao Shuhua and I were skeptical of Ulaanbagan's claims.

Ferreting Out Traitors was a movement launched on March 16, 1967, with the Central document "Materials on the Treachery of 61 Persons, Including Bo Yibo, Liu Lantao, An Ziwen, and Yang Xianzhen, Who Had Pleaded Guilty to the Enemy." We were told that "these traitors have long been hiding within the Party, usurping important posts in the leading Central and local Party and government organizations." The exposure of the sixty-one traitors was the work of a Nankai University rebel organization called 8.18. Praised by Mao and Kang Sheng, 8.18's action galvanized a nationwide frenzy of "ferreting out traitors."[8]

In Inner Mongolia, the campaign started later than in the rest of the country because of the turmoil in the first half of 1967, which led to the victory of the rebels and the arrival of Teng Haiqing. However, after the founding of the Inner Mongolia Revolutionary Committee Preparatory Group on June 18, 1967, some politically astute rebels began to take action. In July, with Gao Jinming's approval, and with the tacit support of Teng Haiqing and the Center, an organization called Ferreting Out the Hafenga Liaison Station captured and struggled Hafenga, the former deputy chairman of the Inner Mongolia Autonomous Region government and a member of the Standing Committee of the Chinese People's Political Consultative Conference in Beijing.[9]

In August, inspired by the Ferreting Out Hafenga Liaison Station, two Mongol intellectuals, Ulaanbagan (deputy chairman of the Inner Mongolia

Writers Association) and Erdeni-Uul (a rebel colleague who became the director of the Political Department for the Mongolian Edition of the *Inner Mongolia Daily*) organized a Ferreting Out the Traitor Clique Liaison Office, comprised of fifty Mongol and Han members, all rebels from the Inner Mongolia Federation of Literary and Art Circles, *Inner Mongolia Daily*, Inner Mongolia Language Committee, Office of the Inner Mongolia Revolutionary Committee, the Inner Mongolia Military District, Teachers' College, and Inner Mongolia University, among others. The organization and its membership were approved by the Party leaders of the Inner Mongolia Revolutionary Committee Preparatory Group, Gao Jinming, Quan Xingyuan, and Kang Xiumin. Teng Haiqing at this time was preoccupied with border defense, preparing for what seemed like an inevitable clash with the Soviet Union and the MPR.

The initial objective of the Ferreting Out the Traitor Clique Liaison Office and similar organizations was to investigate Ulanhu and Hafenga's treason, tracing their crime to the Inner Mongolia People's Revolutionary Party founded in 1925 and revived in 1945. Among the targets was an organization called Inner and Outer Mongolian Terminology Committee, which was established in 1957, with forty-three members from both Inner Mongolia and the MPR. The Terminology Committee was a product of the CCP Center's 1953 decision on language reform. Following its spirit, Inner Mongolia planned to adopt the Cyrillic script used in the MPR to replace the classical Mongolian script. The organization was disbanded in 1958 when China, following the deterioration of Sino-Soviet relations, decided to adopt Latin script to replace the classical Mongolian script. Now this organization, in the eyes of the rebels, offered evidence of Ulanhu and Hafenga's conspiracy to unify with the MPR. Crucially, the key Party leader in charge of the Terminology Committee was Tegusi, the deputy propaganda chief of the Inner Mongolia Party Committee, who had become a member of the IMRC Preparatory Group.

Not every rebel accepted these charges. Gao Shuhua and I privately concluded that the new policy of targeting those intellectuals was a case of blowing individual mistakes out of proportion. We both respected Tegusi highly. However, in the tense atmosphere, we could do nothing.

The Ferreting Out the Traitor Clique Liaison Office, led by Ulaanbagan, submitted "Brief Report on the Big Treasonous Group Harbored by the Ulanhu Black Clique" to the Preparatory Group on October 3, 1967. Ulaanbagan then started telling the following story everywhere:

> Just before May Day in 1966 five masked men entered my house. They tied up
> my family, blindfolded and gagged me, and pushed me into a jeep. Although

I could see nothing, I suspected that we were climbing the Daqing Mountains. We soon left the paved road and continued up. When we stopped, I was
ushered into a cave. When they uncovered my eyes, I saw hundreds of workers and herdsmen carrying burning torches and lanterns. Their leader was a
strong man with a full beard.

"Fellow Mongols," he said, "today we meet secretly in this cave. As descendants of Chinggis Khan, let's sacrifice for the Mongol nation, cutting our
fingers and drinking this brew of fermented mare's milk mixed with the blood
of all (*shaxue weimeng*). We brothers will fight for Mongol independence and
overthrow the Han oppressors."

When they finished taking the oath, they took me back in the jeep, saying
"You are our kin and a famous writer. Having witnessed this act, we hope you
will join us. The choice is yours. But if you divulge our secret to anyone, we
will kill you."

Back in town they released me. I was told to face the wall with my hands
raised and not to move or they would shoot. Finally, when the sun began to
rise, I saw that I was close to my courtyard. I went home, not daring to tell
anyone what had happened.[10]

This was a reference to a mysterious incident that occurred in 1963. An
envelope containing two letters was intercepted in Jining, the capital of
Ulaanchab League on February 6, 1963. One letter was addressed to a certain Oidovdorj in the MPR, and the other to the Mongolian People's Revolutionary Party, the presidium of the People's Great Khural, and the Council of
Ministers. The sender was Zhao Jinhai from the Nationality Middle School
in Jining city; the school was nonexistent. The first letter asked Oidovdorj to
deliver the second letter to the MPR government, explaining the founding of
the Mongolian People's Revolutionary Party. The main letter was seven thousand characters long and was written in classical Mongolian on the back of
a picture of the Beijing opera virtuoso Mei Lanfang. Dated February 4, 1963,
it stated that on November 26, 1961, twenty-two representatives attended the
first congress of the Mongolian People's Revolutionary Party. It claimed that
forty-three representatives of 2,346 members attended the second congress,
held on February 3, 1962. Attacking the Chinese Communist Party's nationality policy, it called for unification between Inner and Outer Mongolia before
May 1, 1966.[11]
The intercepted letter was forwarded to the Inner Mongolia Party Committee and the Inner Mongolia Public Security Bureau, and then to Beijing.
Ulanhu instructed Wang Zaitian, a Mongol secretary of the secretariat in
charge of security, to investigate. A secret region-wide hunt targeted all suspected of having relations with the MPR and all critics of nationality policy.

The case terrified many Mongols who were desperately trying to prove their loyalty to the Chinese state and who bore the brunt of the secret crackdown that the case set off. Both Beijing and Hohhot investigated the so-called 206 Special Case (the message having been intercepted on February 6), but no evidence of a plot was found. Gao Jinming later told me that it might have been a KGB plot to inject chaos into Inner Mongolia on the Chinese-Mongolian-Soviet border. What was certain was that three years of investigation by the Ministry of Public Security produced no evidence of any splittist activity.

Everyone was familiar with the Inner Mongolia People's Revolutionary Party (*Neirendang*) and knew that Ulanhu, Hafenga, Tegusi, and other Mongol leaders had been members of that party before its dissolution, with its members joining the Chinese Communist Party in 1947. Moreover, nothing happened on or around May 1, 1966, the putative day of unification between Inner and Outer Mongolia. What was ominous was the charge that some Mongol leaders who had survived the 1966 purge of Ulanhu's black gang and joined the new leadership after Mao's May 22 Directive in 1967 had been secretly recruiting new members for the Neirendang since 1961. Now, Ulaanbagan used the 1963 letters as evidence of the revival of the Neirendang. Curiously, the name mentioned in the letters—Mongolian People's Revolutionary Party—was renamed Inner Mongolian People's Revolutionary Party, adding the word *Inner*. Because the letter claimed that the party held its first congress on November 26, 1961, this party was called the New Inner Mongolian People's Revolutionary Party. This was the purported birth of the so-called Xin [New] Neirendang.

On November 1, 1967, the Inner Mongolia Revolutionary Committee was formally established, with leadership as follows:

Director: Teng Haiqing

Deputy directors: Wu Tao, Gao Jinming, Huo Daoyu

Standing committee members: Quan Xingyuan, Li Zhi, Li Shude, Xie Zhenhua (Sixty-Ninth Army Commander), Yang Desong (Independent Division Commander, IMMD), Kang Xiumin, Guo Yiqing, Hao Guangde, Gao Shuhua, Wang Jinbao, Wang Zhiyou, Liu Litang, Yang Wanxiang, Nasanbayar, Li Feng, Zhou Wenxiao, and Zhang Guangyou (Sixty-Ninth Army deputy commander)

The three PLA members of the standing committee never attended meetings: Xie Zhenhua, Yang Desong and Zhang Guangyou. The only Mongols were Wu Tao, one of three deputy chairs, and Nasanbayar, one of nineteen standing committee members. Tegusi, Wang Zaitian, Bayantai, and a few other Mongols were among the eighty-five committee members.

FIGURE 16 Poster celebrating the establishment of the Inner Mongolia Autonomous Region Revolutionary Committee

A new concept emerged after Teng Haiqing's speech at the mass meeting inaugurating the Inner Mongolia Revolutionary Committee. Teng said, "The task of the Revolutionary Committee is to lead the people of the whole Region's various nationalities in further digging up (*wa*) Ulanhu's black line and cleansing (*qing*) Ulanhu's pernicious influence." According to Qi Zhi, Gao Jinming felt that the term *qing* was not forceful enough. He preferred *su* to *qing*, as *su* implied more thoroughgoing punishment. Teng Haiqing accepted his suggestion; thereafter, "Digging up (*wa*) Ulanhu's Black Line, Eliminating (*su*) Ulanhu's Pernicious Influence" or *wasu* for short, became the standard formulation of the Inner Mongolia Revolutionary Committee.

Ulanhu's black line—that is, the targets of *wasu* in Teng's conception—were three forces (*sangu shili*). The first included Ulanhu's old associates, notably Tumed Mongol officials and some Han such as Wang Duo and Wang Yilun; the second was Hafenga's associates, including Soviet-Mongolian, Japanese, and Guomindang spies, Mongol feudal lords, herdlords, and bandits; and the third was those who sneaked into the Party after Suiyuan was incorporated in Inner Mongolia in 1954.[12]

Just as the leaders were planning to implement the *wasu* campaign, Jiang Qing's speeches of November 9 and 12 warned of alleged enemies: "We should be steady, accurate and harsh—towards our enemy."[13]

On November 27, 1967, Jiang Qing called for "cleansing the class ranks" (*qingli jieji duiwu*): "In the process of reforming and building the Party . . . we must cleanse out traitors, spies, and those unrepentant people who have committed mistakes."[14]

Cleansing the class ranks is widely known as the cruelest movement of the Cultural Revolution. According to Ding Shu, throughout China, thirty million people were struggled and half a million people died during the cleansing of the class ranks. This was "the stage of the Cultural Revolution that incurred the most deaths. Except for the war and the great famine of 1959–1960, never had so many innocents died unnatural deaths."[15]

MacFarquhar and Schoenhals argue that "cleansing the class ranks" from late 1967 and reaching most parts of China by the summer of 1968, provided those in power with an opportunity to get rid of opponents.[16] In Inner Mongolia the targets were mostly Mongols who had survived earlier cleansings and were recently appointed to new revolutionary committees at various levels.

Late at night on November 24, rebel leader Jin Yonghong, from the Hohhot Sports Committee and a member of the Hohhot Revolutionary Committee, led ten cadres and workers in kidnapping Tegusi, former deputy director of the Propaganda Department of the Inner Mongolia Party Committee and a member of the newly established Inner Mongolia Revolutionary Committee.

Behind the kidnapping was a new organization, Ferreting Out the Black Hands Liaison Station (*Jiu heishou lianluo zhan*), headed by Liu Wenyan, a rebel from Teachers' College who enjoyed the support of Hao Guangde, the legal affairs chief of the newly established Inner Mongolia Revolutionary Committee, Gao Jinming, and Guo Yiqing, and that of Teng Haiqing and his powerful Tengban.[17] They relied on information provided by Ulaanbagan and Erdeni-Uul's Ferreting Out the Traitor Clique Liaison Office.

Teng Haiqing later noted, "Ferreting out Tegusi was the first shot fired to deepen the thorough criticism of Ulanhu's black line, pushing the Cultural Revolution to a new stage . . . an important marker of its determination to wage a people's war of '*wasu*,' starting with literary and artistic circles."[18]

Tegusi was a leader of the Inner Mongolia Revolutionary Youth League in the late 1940s. However, in 1947, on the eve of the founding of the Inner Mongolia Autonomous Government, he switched allegiance from his political patron Hafenga to Ulanhu, the new top leader of Inner Mongolia. Tegusi was the chief editor of the *Inner Mongolia Daily* in the early 1950s and deputy director of propaganda in the Inner Mongolia Communist Party Committee until the beginning of the Cultural Revolution.

In 1966, during the Qianmen Hotel Conference, Tegusi's report on the "four cleanups" in the pastoral region documenting class conflicts among herders furnished crucial evidence for Li Xuefeng to attack Ulanhu. Having emerged as a revolutionary leftist leader, Tegusi was pro-rebel during the confrontation with the Inner Mongolia Military Region and became a member of the Inner Mongolia Revolutionary Committee, established on November 1, 1967.

Ulaanbagan, born in 1929 in Jirim league, worked at our *Daily* from 1948 to 1956 as an editor, after having been a soldier in the Inner Mongolia Autonomous Army. He was captured by the Guomindang and eventually released. The Communist leadership viewed his surrender as treasonous and his release as evidence of perfidy. Ulaanbagan was punished by Tegusi, who was the director of the Inner Mongolia Party School where Ulaanbagan studied as a probational Communist Party member. His probational Party membership was annulled, depriving Ulaanbagan of all hopes for a political career. His writing skill nevertheless earned him entry into the Propaganda Department of the Inner Mongolia Party Committee in 1956; there he rose to prominence as a famous novelist after the 1958 publication of his *Caoyuan Fenghuo* (Flames of War on the Grassland). In 1964, he became deputy chairman of the Inner Mongolia Writers Association and deputy chairman of the Inner Mongolia Federation of Literary and Art Circles. A rising literary star, he was supported by Ulanhu.

In the early stage of the Cultural Revolution, however, Ulaanbagan was denounced as an Ulanhu black gang member. Tegusi ordered the attack. After further humiliation under the work team sent by the Inner Mongolia Party Committee to the Inner Mongolia Federation of Literary and Art Circles, Ulaanbagan established his own rebel organization called Dongfanghong, the East Is Red, in December 1966.

In June 1967, after the establishment of the Inner Mongolia Revolutionary Committee Preparatory Group, finding that Tegusi was still in power, Ulaanbagan determined to pull him down.

Erdeni-Uul was born in 1933 in Jaraid banner of Hulunbuir. He entered the *Inner Mongolia Daily* at the age of fourteen and soon become an editor and journalist of the Mongolian edition. Like many other intellectuals, he had been punished during the anti-rightist movement of 1957–1959. In 1959, while studying at the Party school, his critical comment on the wasteful iron-smelting campaign would cost him opportunities for promotion.

He was also a victim of Tegusi at the beginning of the Cultural Revolution. In June 1966, a work team led by Tegusi moved into the *Inner Mongolia*

Daily, denounced Erdeni-Uul, and stripped him of his position as director of the Politics and Culture Department. After the Qianmen Hotel Conference, he was attacked for another crime—as a member of the Ulanhu black gang.

Thus, Ulaanbagan and Erdeni-Uul were both victims of work teams led by Tegusi. The expulsion of the work team and Mao's May 22 Directive exhilarated them, but Tegusi's continued presence in the leadership was infuriating. They would combine forces to destroy their common foe.[19]

I knew Erdeni-Uul, but not well. On November 10, 1967, eight organizations held a citywide meeting in Hohhot's Red Theater to "dig up the Neirendang." He had asked me to attend, but I found a pretext to excuse myself. The disconcerting experience of being attacked as a black element in Hulunbuir led me to keep a distance.

Assignment to Western Inner Mongolia

In late November, as the *wasu* movement began to unfold, I took the westbound train from Hohhot via Baotou to Bayangol, the capital of Bayannuur league, formerly Sanshenggong, a famous trading town on the western bank of the Yellow River.

The natural environment in Bayangol was strikingly different from that of Hailar in eastern Inner Mongolia. In Hailar, the green of grass and trees between May and October gave way to the white of snow and ice during the winter months from November to April. By contrast, in Bayangol, yellow sand, yellow river water, and barren mountains dominated the landscape year round. Most of the area is desert, with only small patches of arable land along the irrigation networks, which stretched from near Bayangol in the west almost to the industrial city Baotou in the east. In summer, the fields and trees along the Yellow River banks and irrigation channels were green. But after the harvest, sandstorms covered everything with yellow, from windowpanes to people's faces.

Our *Daily* station in Bayangol was on the first floor of the League Government Building. Lu Yonglong and I occupied one room each, combining bedroom and office. Four years my senior, Lu grew up in a fishing village in Zhejiang's Zhoushan Islands. A 1959 journalism graduate of Fudan University, he knew most of the local leaders and prominent intellectuals. It took him several weeks to introduce me to all his friends and connections in the Party, government and military units that we turned to in preparing reports.

As soon as I could handle the work independently, Lu was transferred to the editorial office in Hohhot. I was left alone to run the station. Fortunately, Lu's friend Li Shijun, a local rebel cadre, and director of the propaganda office of the Bayannuur League Revolutionary Committee, often accompanied me to visit local VIPs and scenic spots on evenings and weekends. On weekends, I rode one of our station's two bicycles. Sometimes, Li Shijun borrowed a Chinese-made Shengli (Victory) motorcycle for me, allowing me to visit nearby towns and villages, mines and factories, and the Sanshenggong Dam.

On the west side of the government building in Bayangol, there was a square compound, with a gray, brick-walled courtyard surrounding a beautiful classical garden and three houses with palatial architecture, resembling Beijing's summer palace. The larger gate on the south side, which was often locked, had a paved driveway connected to the garage attached to one of the smaller houses. I asked Li Shijun what the buildings, with their armed guard, were for. A mysterious smile flickered across his face, and he said, "That is probably the last princely residence built for the last prince of Alasha banner, Dalizhaya (Darijiya) and his Manchu wife Aisingoro Yunhui (Jin Yuncheng)."

Prince Darijiya was born in 1906 in the westernmost Inner Mongolia banner of Alasha. Educated in Beijing, in 1925 he married his cousin, a daughter of Zaitao, uncle of the last Qing emperor Aisingoro Puyi. Their marriage was the last example of the Manchu-Mongol marital alliance that had been designed to secure loyalty of Mongol princes to the Qing imperial family. After his father Prince Ta passed away in 1931, the Chinese Nationalist government appointed Darijiya, who was heir to the princely throne, to serve as the *jasag* (ruling prince) of Alasha banner. During the Civil War, he supported the CCP and the PLA, and for his loyalty, he was appointed governor of the Bayanhot Mongolian Autonomous Prefecture and deputy governor of Gansu province. In 1956, when the Mongolian prefecture merged with the IMAR, he was appointed governor of Alasha banner, governor of Bayannuur league, and deputy chairman of the IMAR.[20]

In the early stage of the Cultural Revolution, Darijiya was labeled as a black gang element, but Zhou Enlai gave the couple permission to stay in their home in Beijing. In the winter of 1967, at the time of "cleansing the class ranks," after Ulanhu was publicly denounced, Darijiya and his wife were forced to return, as members of the Ulanhu black gang, to their residence in Bayangol to accept "the people's criticism."

"They currently live there under house arrest, on orders from both the Central Cultural Revolution Group and Tengban. Now, the Darijiya palace has turned into their prison," Li Shijun observed.

One day, I bumped into the couple in the government dining hall. They looked familiar. I recalled that during the fifteenth anniversary of the IMAR on May 1, 1962, when we middle school students marched through New China Square in downtown Hohhot, I saw Darijiya and his wife standing next to Ulanhu and his wife in the center of the platform. The princely couple caught people's eyes not only because of their colorful Mongolian gowns (many other VIPs wore the same) but also for the lady's Manchu hairstyle, resplendent with jewels.

By late 1967, they had fallen. They were carrying their own aluminum lunch boxes, standing in line to buy their meals. Two uniformed guards followed and watched them at a distance. Darijiya wore a dark-blue Mao suit and a long black wool coat. His wife wore a yellow-green cotton soldier coat. No shining silk Mongolian gown or splendid jewels could be seen, only faces covered in sadness and gray dust.

I tried to interview Darijiya and Aisingoro Yunhui, but the security guards said that there could be no interview unless authorized by Tengban. I called Jin Feng to ask whether he could apply for a permit on my behalf. Jin told me that Tengban had issued an internal directive to the *Daily*: "during the early stage of the *wasu* campaign, the media should keep hands off these special cases," including the Darijiya case. I lost the chance to interview the most prominent Mongol prince who was still alive.

Mass Dictatorship

Having little to do in a small town, I wondered what was happening in Hohhot. My best source was Zhang Peiren, my *Daily* colleague and rebel friend from Teachers' College. At the end of November, I called and he told me that Ferreting Out the Black Hands and Ferreting Out the Traitors, along with forty-five other mass organizations, held a rally in the government auditorium to criticize Tegusi, along with Wang Duo, Wang Yilun, Hafenga, Buhe, and Julanchechig (Buhe's wife). About thirty thousand people attended rallies in nine locations.

While many rebels, both Han and Mongol, had private reservations, it was extremely difficult to challenge the campaign. A few leading Mongol rebels led by Nasanbayar (standing committee member of the Inner Mongolia Revolutionary Committee) and Bayantai (committee member), the primary and secondary leaders of the Lu Xun Army Corps, courageously challenged the detention of Tegusi. They headed the leading rebel organization of Inner Mongolia representing cultural and educational institutions with thousands of Mongol and Han intellectuals.[21]

Mongol rebels raised questions at meetings and in posters: "Tegusi is a member of the newly established Revolutionary Committee and the adviser of our rebel organization. Who approved the Ferreting Out the Black Hands campaign to arrest Tegusi? What is the evidence that he is a bad element?

Why didn't the authorities [Tengban] notify other standing committee members when raising such an important matter? Don't we need procedures for arrests and other actions taken against committee and standing committee members in our new revolutionary authority?" Tegusi remained under arrest.

I later learned that in late December 1967, the Inner Mongolia Revolutionary Committee directed Gao Shuhua to establish the Inner Mongolia Culture and Art Revolution Office after the fall of Tegusi. Gao was the chair and Alta, a female Mongol rebel student from the Inner Mongolia Art School, the deputy chair.

Ulaanbagan and the Han dancer Sun Lingling from the Inner Mongolia Song and Dance Troupe spearheaded the *wasu* forces in literary and artistic circles, maintaining close relations with Tengban. Teng's chief secretary, the director of Tengban, Li Dechen, sent orders to "ferret out the black hands" without even contacting the Culture and Art Revolution Office under Gao Shuhua's leadership.

On January 6–18, 1968, the second plenary session of the Inner Mongolia Revolutionary Committee convened at the Hohhot guesthouse. Its proclaimed task was eliminating alleged rightist conservatism represented by two leading Mongol members of the Inner Mongolia Revolutionary Committee, Nasanbayar and Bayantai, through the deepening of the *wasu* campaign. The two Mongol rebel leaders who had dared to question Tegusi's detention were subjected to intense criticism, even from Han rebels. The *Husansi Weekly News* posed this question: "What led to the demise of the Lu Xun Army Corps? It was the rightist conservatism of its leading members!"[22] Husansi was divided, with many excited at participating in the new *wasu* campaign. This division ran along ethnic lines, but not quite.

During the plenum Li Dechen, the director of Tengban, warned Gao Shuhua against being too rightist—that is, insufficiently aggressive—in the *wasu* and cleansing the class ranks campaigns. Gao reportedly responded to Li Dechen that Ulaanbagan's stories about class enemies in Inner Mongolia were too histrionic to be trusted. In his view, they were either products of Ulaanbagan's novelist imagination, or he himself must be a member of Neirendang. No outsider could possibly possess such information. However, the craze continued.

With the sidelining of the two Mongol rebel voices, the *wasu* campaign gained momentum. Gao Shuhua's office was ordered to investigate the song and dance troupe and the film company. Checking the list of staff members, they discovered that all the leaders had been labeled reactionaries, and all prominent singers, actors, and directors had been forced to stop work or sent to labor camps.

Because Gao Shuhua failed to actively pursue the suppression of new class enemies among the remaining performers, mainly young people in their twenties, Tengban criticized him as a rightist. When I met Gao in Hohhot during the Lunar New Year of 1968, he told me that he would rather be labeled a "rightist" than repeat the errors of the work teams and the IMAR Party Committee in the summer of 1966.

On January 15, 1968, the Hohhot Mass Dictatorship Headquarters (Huhehaote Qunzhong Zhuanzheng Zhihuibu) was established with support from the Ferreting Out the Black Hands, Ferreting Out Hafenga, and Ferreting Out Ulanhu liaison stations. It was led by Ge Zhisheng. Ge, a Teachers' College cadre, was a rebel leader who had been in the forefront of challenging the Military Region leadership in spring 1967. However, the real power behind the scenes was Tengban. Its armed personnel could arrest, detain and torture anyone at any time. Hohhot citizens whispered of being "unafraid of being sentenced and imprisoned, but afraid of dealing with the Hohhot mass dictatorship!" (*Bupa panxing zuojian, jiupa hushi qunzhuan*).

Mass dictatorship was the form of Mao's people's democratic dictatorship proposed in the 1949 article "On the People's Democratic Dictatorship."[23] It was modeled after the political system established by the Paris Commune in which administration, legislature, and judiciary would merge, and dictatorship of the masses would replace a standing army and police.[24] In the summer of 1967, in a letter to Jiang Qing, Mao expressed distrust of the PLA, which he believed would support the right, and called for mass dictatorship. In October, the Center issued "Important instructions issued by the Chairman during his inspections of North China, Central South China, and Southeast China." It contained the following instruction: "Dictatorship is the dictatorship of the masses. It is not a good idea to rely on the government to arrest people. The government should only arrest a very small number of people at the request and with the assistance of the masses."[25]

Far from an anarchist conception, however, Mao's mass dictatorship frequently pivoted on "power-seizures in public security organs and the courts."[26] It was, moreover, according to Michael Schoenhals, "the outsourcing by the supreme state leadership of selected surveillance, inquisitorial and other violent tasks."[27] In Inner Mongolia, the driving force of the *wasu* movement remained the Revolutionary Committee and the military—that is, Tengban—which led the mass dictatorship to expand the campaign into an all-out "people's war."

The *wasu* activists included former rebels such as Liu Wenyan, Ge Zhisheng, and Hao Guangde from Teachers' College. Many other rebels, such as

Gao Shuhua and Qin Weixian, exhausted in the protracted struggles against heavy odds, eventually tried to distance themselves from repressive political campaigns. Still others, such as Nasanbayar and Bayantai were not only sidelined but also threatened with becoming *wasu* targets. Some previous loyalists joined the new groups, whether to demonstrate fealty to the new power center, to show enthusiasm for the class struggle, or to take revenge on rebel foes at a time when some rebels who had ascended to positions of power were singled out as new targets of struggle. With the rise of mass dictatorship organizations, rebel organizations such as Husansi, which still ran a small office and a newspaper, were marginalized and attacked.

Teng Haiqing criticized the Husansi leadership for alleged "rightist attitudes toward the *wasu*." Under pressure from Tengban, on January 18, 1968, *Husansi News* published the front-page editorial "Mass Dictatorship Is Very Good." Infuriated, I called Lei Shanyuan, a third-year Russian-language student who edited the paper. "Shanyuan," I asked, "do you really think the mass dictatorship is good?"

"Of course, it's no good! Only a bastard would think so. But what choice do I have if I don't want to be attacked by Tengban?" he replied honestly. Lei, who hailed from a Hebei peasant family, had become class Youth League secretary at Teachers' College. As a rebel activist and Gao Shuhua's student, he had accompanied Gao to the negotiations in Beijing and later, after Hao Guangde's promotion to the Inner Mongolia Revolutionary Committee, became second in command at Husansi.[28]

One week before the Lunar New Year, on January 23, 1968, three members of the Inner Mongolia Revolutionary Committee—Li Shude (member of the Standing Committee), Li Dechen (director of Tengban), and Hao Guangde (deputy director of the Legal Affairs Committee)—took charge of the investigation of the Neirendang. Since each had *De* in their name, meaning "virtue," people ironically called them the Three Virtues Group (*San De Xiaozu*).

Shortly before the Lunar New Year (January 30, 1968), I returned to Hohhot. On January 28, Lu Yonglong told me the shocking news that Wang Zaitian, another Mongol member of the Inner Mongolia Revolutionary Committee who was in charge of law enforcement, had been singled out as a suspected Ulanhu black gang member. I remembered Wang reading and signing my article in his study on June 27, 1967. It seemed inconceivable that such an old Communist veteran could be a deeply entrenched class or ethnic enemy. My suspicion was that Tengban wanted the last Mongol leader in the Inner Mongolia Revolutionary Committee out of the way so it could launch a deeper and wider *wasu*.

That same day, the Hohhot Mass Dictatorship Headquarters launched its official journal: *Joint Battle Report* (*Lianhe Zhanbao*). Its front-page headline thundered "What We Want Is Exactly Mass Dictatorship!"

On the eve of Lunar New Year and New Year's Day (January 30 and February 1) I spent a day at home, enjoying dumplings with my father, stepmother, and stepsister. As usual, we had a small party at my girlfriend Qingxian's home with her parents, brother, three sisters, and several high school classmates. Qingxian's father, fearful that the *wasu* might get out of hand, refused to drink. He told us that among the two dozen cadres who had been detained at his work unit (Inner Mongolia Department of Animal Husbandry), only one was Han. He had been ordered to write yet another self-criticism on his own Guomindang history but was allowed to go home.

"If the campaign continues like this, I fear that nationality relations will be destroyed." Whatever the common sense of ordinary people, the momentum of the *wasu* campaign continued to grow.

The Campaign against the New Neirendang

While directing the mass organizations to go after *wasu* enemies who had sneaked into leadership positions, on January 10, 1968, the Inner Mongolia Revolutionary Committee established a special case office (*zhuan'an ban*) to investigate the Neirendang. It took charge of all "ferreting out" organizations and outsourced tasks to them for investigation.

Ulaanbagan and Erdeni-Uul's Ferreting Out the Traitor Clique Liaison Station was its prime agent. On December 12, 1967, Gao Jinming approved funding. The station then sent out personnel to make investigations, but instead of reporting to the Special Case Office, it reported directly to Teng Haiqing and Gao Jinming. With about fifty members, mostly writers, university teachers and students, the station obtained materials from "ferreting out traitor stations," revolutionary committee organizations and rebel organizations throughout Inner Mongolia. By May 1968, the station had processed more than 1,800 collections of materials and written 127 reports.[29]

On February 4, Teng Haiqing and Li Shude went to Beijing to report on Inner Mongolia's *wasu* and mass dictatorship campaigns. They were met by the leaders of the CCRG. As usual, Zhou Enlai chaired. Jiang Qing praised Inner Mongolia for digging out bad people in literary and artistic circles and exposing bad people and reactionary party organizations. Applauding the "great achievements" in Inner Mongolia, the spymaster Kang Sheng instructed: "Ulanhu's influence is big, his poison deep. First purge it in the army. On the one hand, criticize and struggle against Ulanhu, but simultaneously expose and denounce Wang Yilun and Wang Duo, so the masses will know that we are not against the Mongol people. [Let] Mongols mobilize the Mongolian masses to ferret out and struggle."[30]

The remarks reveal Kang's intuitive grasp of the ethnic character of the campaign and his ability to exploit Han-Mongol tensions. With leadership in Inner Mongolia almost entirely in Han hands, Kang stressed the need to criticize Han as well as Mongols, encouraging Mongols to take the lead in ferreting out and struggling fellow Mongols.

In this meeting, the CCRG endorsed Teng Haiqing and Li Shude's report and promoted broadening the attack on the Neirendang. Although Kang Sheng issued the main instruction, Zhou Enlai chaired the meeting and set the agenda. MacFarquhar and Schoenhals say of Zhou's role in the CCRG: "Such was the extent of the premier's power over the CCRG that he himself, when he deemed it prudent, intervened directly and extensively in local disputes of a factional nature in the name of the CCRG."[31] Zhou, more than any leader at the Center, was responsible for the April 13 decision in 1967 that sent Inner Mongolia into chaos and promoting the *wasu* campaign against the Neirendang. Thousands of suspected enemies were dug out in the campaign's first weeks. Most were from Hohhot, Baotou, and a few other cities.

One day after the Center's leaders endorsed Teng Haiqing and Li Shude's report to ferret out the Neirendang in the next stage of *wasu*, Teng Haiqing's secretary Li Liang summoned Ulaanbagan, Erdeni-Uul, and Rash (the three most active Mongol members of the Ferret Out the Traitor Clique Liaison Station) to Beijing. On February 5 they reported on their work. Li promised increased support.

On February 6, Teng Haiqing, Wu Tao, Gao Jinming, Quan Xingyuan, Kang Xiumin, Li Shude, and Hao Guangde met to discuss the Neirendang issue in Beijing. All agreed that, after the Chengde Conference of April 3, 1946, when the Neirendang officially disbanded, it secretly continued its activities. As the "New Neirendang," the strategy for attacking it was finalized.[32]

On February 13, the core group (*hexin xiaozu*) of the Standing Committee of the Inner Mongolia Revolutionary Committee was established, with Teng Haiqing as its chair, and Wu Tao and Gao Jinming deputy chairs. Members included Quan Xingyuan, Li Shude, Yang Yongsong, and Li Zhi.[33] All were Han, except the deputy chair Wu Tao, a Mongol, and Gao Jinming, a Manchu who passed as Han. And all were Party and military leaders. No rebel leader was among them. Li Shude was in charge of the *wasu* campaign, working closely with Li Dechen, director of Tengban. The core group immediately began to implement the instructions of the CCRG. In other words, the official launch of the attack on the New Neirendang was authorized by the CCRG led by Zhou Enlai, Chen Boda, Jiang Qing, and Kang Sheng. Kang played a key role in guiding the movement.

With the New Neirendang identified as the primary target of *wasu*, the core group set to work. Ulaanbagan obtained permission from *Tengban* to access the archives of the Department of Public Security to collect evidence of a pervasive New Neirendang.[34]

Gao Jinming played a key role in attacking the New Neirendang. He divided Neirendang history into three stages: from its inception in 1925 to its dissolution in the 1930s; from its revival in 1945 to its formal abolition in May 1947; and from May 1, 1947, when it went "underground," to the present.

The "New" Neirendang had allegedly been active underground for two decades beginning in 1947. The proof of recent Neirendang activity was Case 206, which surfaced in 1963. Gao insisted that the target of *wasu* should be the Neirendang in the third stage.[35]

An all-out attack was unleashed from the leadership to the grassroots, extending to the entire Mongol population of Inner Mongolia and beyond to the three small minorities of Daur, Evenki and Orochon in Hulunbuir, who were closely associated with the Mongols. Many Han were also attacked for being sympathetic with or related to Mongols.

The Inner Mongolia Revolutionary Committee and the grassroots organizations of mass dictatorship officially joined hands to unleash China's biggest ethnic pogrom during the Cultural Revolution against a hapless minority.

"Down with the Bogus Foreign Devils"

In mid-February, I returned to Bayannuur league. On February 26, the *Inner Mongolia Daily* published a front-page commentary, "Down with the Bogus Foreign Devils" (*dadao jiayang guizi*), which was jointly drafted by editorial writer Li Baoyi and *Tengban* staff. Referring to Lu Xun's *True Story of Ah Q*, it called on previous loyalists (Ah Q) to rebel against the previous rebels (the bogus foreign devils) who prevented Ah Q from participating in revolution. It was a call to mobilize the former loyalists who had stood in the wrong queue, that is, had made the mistake of supporting the Inner Mongolia Military Region in spring 1967 to join the *wasu* and overthrow the former rebels who held leadership positions. It was also a call to strip former rebels of their ties to Gao Shuhua to save themselves before it was too late.

The earliest signal of the attack on Gao Shuhua was a "friendly talk" by the "core group." In early March 1968, Teng Haiqing, Gao Jinming, and Quan Xingyuan terminated Gao Shuhua's work at Wenyi Ban (Culture and Art Revolution Office) and assigned him to the Long Live Mao Zedong Thought

Exhibition, whose tasks included making Mao badges. He was sent to Guangzhou and Shanghai to learn how to organize the exhibition. Gao's rebel friends joked that he was a *bi ma wen* (the title in the classic novel *Journey to the West* given to the Monkey King when demoted to take care of the Jade Emperor's horses). Rumors spread that Gao was internally labeled as a rightist in the *wasu* campaign.

On March 12, the Inner Mongolia Revolutionary Committee held an Extended Standing Committee Meeting to deepen the *wasu* campaign. Gao Jinming phoned Gao Shuhua to return from Shanghai to attend the meeting. His tone roused Gao Shuhua's suspicion, so he phoned rebel friends at Teachers' College. They told him that Hao Guangde, Liu Wenyan, and Qin Weixian— all leaders of Dongzong—were preparing to attack him again for his relationship with Lishake, Ulanhu's son. Their plan was supported by Gao Jinming and Guo Yiqing, with the endorsement of Teng Haiqing behind the scenes.

On March 15, en route to Hohhot, Gao called Zhang Zuowen, Zhou Enlai's secretary in Beijing, informing him of developments in Hohhot and Inner Mongolia. "We will do our best to avoid violent infighting among rebels," he said. "Please pass my materials on this issue to Premier Zhou." Zhang promised to forward his report.

On March 18, Qin Weixian, a Dongzong leader, established a March 18 Case Group (*3.18 zhuan an zu*) in the Agriculture and Animal Husbandry School in Hohhot. The group interrogated more than a dozen Ulanhu family members, including Lishake, to disclose his special connections with Gao Shuhua.

Then, in a five-day meeting with members of the Hohhot and Baotou revolutionary committees attending and Gao Jinming as chair, Hao Guangde and Liu Wenyan led the attack targeting Gao Shuhua's relations with Lishake. Some participants insinuated that Gao Shuhua was Ulanhu's "Fifth Column" within the Inner Mongolia Revolutionary Committee, a point that Gao Jinming had previously made on numerous occasions.

For five days, the participants debated, some attacking Gao Shuhua, some defending him. Gao Shuhua kept silent throughout while sending materials to Zhou Enlai reporting on the meeting.

Gao Shuhua's strategy paid off. In Beijing, after reading Gao's report and materials on the internal fighting among rebels, Zhou Enlai intervened by phoning Teng Haiqing, who, with Wu Tao, was attending a meeting in Beijing. When Zhou criticized the attack on Gao Shuhua, Teng immediately ordered Gao Jinming to end it.[36]

Zhou's intervention saved Gao Shuhua from the attack. Having known him as a young rebel in Inner Mongolia from the days of four-party negotiations

FIGURE 17 Top Inner Mongolia leaders (Teng Haiqing, second from right; Gao Jinming, fourth from right; Wu Tao, first from left) visiting the Mao Zedong Thought Exhibition organized by Gao Shuhua (first from right), summer 1968

in the spring of 1967, Zhou did not accept the charges that Gao Shuhua was an Ulanhu black gang member. This did not mean, however, that Zhou rejected the *wasu* campaign. This event marked the open split among rebel leaders, some becoming *wasu* activists, while others like Gao Shuhua refused, or were reluctant, to participate in *wasu*.

A Journey to Remote Ejine Banner

In late April 1968, Jin Feng assigned me to collect information in Bayannuur league on the *wasu* and anti–New Neirendang campaigns. Mönkh, the political commissar of the Ejine banner border station, told me, "From 1949 to now, the *Inner Mongolia Daily* never sent a single reporter to visit our banner."

Ejine banner is located in the remote northwestern corner of Inner Mongolia, bordering the MPR. There were two routes to Ejine, one by truck or bus across the Gobi northwestward, and the other by train to Jiuquan or Qingshui in Gansu and then across the western part of the Badanjilin Desert, making a big loop toward the township of Dalaihubu, the capital of Ejine banner, close to the China-MPR border. I learned that there was a train line to Ejine, but it was monopolized by the Central Military Affairs Commission for missile and nuclear weaponry personnel. Without special permission to enter the "forbidden zone," it was not possible to travel by that route. Although assigned by the *Inner Mongolia Daily* to investigate the *wasu* campaign, with a photo ID stamped "PLA Military Control" and letters from the Political Department of the IMMD and the commander of the Bayannuur Military Subdistrict, and most important my assignment to investigate the locality in terms of the Tengban priority, the *wasu* campaign, I was nevertheless denied access to the forbidden zone.

I started in the evening of April 30, bound for Ejine through Inner Mongolia, the Ningxia Hui Autonomous Region, and Gansu province. The train arrived in Lanzhou on the morning of May 1, 1968. My interview with the editor in chief of the *Gansu Daily* the next morning went smoothly. He gave me materials (both external and internal) concerning the Cultural Revolution in the province's minority Tibetan, Mongolian, and Hui regions, which I forwarded to Jin Feng by registered express mail.

I was forced to wait until May 15 for one of the two trips each month to Ejine. I visited the nearby Jiayuguan (Jiayu Pass), at the western end of the "Great Wall." I still remember the Chinese saying we recited in Raoyang Middle School about travelers' impressions on going through this pass: "Once going west of the Jiayu Pass, tears won't dry in the eyes; ahead is the great Gobi, behind is the gate of hell" (*Xichu Jiayuguan, Liangyan leibugan, qiankan gebitan, houwang guimenguan*).

After touring for a few days, I was ready to begin the hard journey to Ejine banner. I got up at 6:00 a.m. to catch the bus, an old Russian-made GS-69 four-wheel-drive open truck with not a single seat. I stood on one side of the truck, holding on to the wooden cargo box. There were about twenty passengers, most of them Mongol herders or cadres, who were returning home from medical treatment in Jiuquan.

Early in the afternoon of the third day, our truck arrived at the shabby "bus station" of the transportation company of Ejine banner. The PLA officer Mönkh, political commissar of the Ejine banner border station, picked me up in his military jeep. From the accent of his spoken Chinese, I judged that he came from eastern Inner Mongolia. "Yes," he said, "my hometown is a village south of Ulaanhot. I joined the Inner Mongolia Self-Defense Army in the cavalry in late 1948. After battles with the Tibetans in Qinghai in 1959, and one year of training in the Infantry School of the Beijing Military Region in Shijiazhuang, I was promoted to major and transferred here."

He had prepared a nice guest room in his border station headquarters.

It was a guarded square yard with five rows of red-brick houses. Each row had about twenty rooms. Mönkh's job was to patrol the border to prevent smuggling and border crossings. In the following days, he accompanied me in his military jeep to the famous Juyanhai Lake. Composed of twin lakes, it is located at the outer edge of the Heihe (Black) River, which formed a large inland delta between the Qilian Mountains in the south and the Gobi Altay Mountains in the west.

Crossing the lakes, we could faintly see the grassland and hills on the Mongolia side. This border region also required a special passport to enter. Tensions among the Soviet Union, Mongolia, and China throughout the 1960s had placed the area on high alert. But as Mönkh told me, conflict did not seem imminent. The MPR and Chinese military officers had regularly scheduled meetings each month, mainly handling security issues concerning cross-border herds or smugglers.

On the gravel road back to town, the sunset painted the sky purple. I asked Mönkh about the *wasu* and anti-Neirendang campaigns in Ejine banner. What he said really surprised me:

> I have been nominated as the chair to prepare for the banner's Revolutionary Committee by the Bayannuur league and Tengban. If nothing unusual occurs, our Revolutionary Committee should be established in mid-July 1968.
>
> After discussion among committee members, we submitted an outline for the two campaigns. Since this banner had just finished a rigorous campaign to cleanse class ranks in 1965–1966, under the supervision of the Lanzhou Military Region for improving security in the "forbidden zone," all suspicious personnel had already been transferred elsewhere. From 1966 to the present, the Center asked us not to follow other places in launching the Cultural Revolution. We had no rebels, loyalists, or factional fighting. As part of the IMAR, we still participate in *wasu*, but we do so by asking people to study Chairman Mao's works and party documents. We pay attention to any new signs of class struggle but we have no plan to detain anyone for interrogation. Our plan has been approved by the higher authorities.

I had never heard of such a situation! Could one banner be allowed to escape the bloody *wasu* and anti–New Neirendang campaign that was sweeping the IMAR? After reading their official documents on this special arrangement, I called Jin Feng to confirm the facts. He told me it was true, with final approval coming from the Center, that is, from Mao Zedong and Zhou Enlai. They didn't want their nuclear project threatened. But this borderland peace would soon shatter, as many Mongols were persecuted as elsewhere in Inner

Mongolia. My brief visit simply did not allow me to detect the undercurrents of what lay ahead.

In late May I took a similar truck ride from Dalaihubu and returned through the east route crossing the Gobi to the coal city of Wuda before taking the eastbound train back to Bayangol. On resuming my regular job in the station in early June, I would have to face the *wasu* issue again.

Wasu and the Rebels

Deepening the *Wasu* Movement

Ejine banner was a Shangri-la, blithely immune from the ruthless struggles gathering momentum throughout Inner Mongolia. While I was there, I heard nothing about developments in Bayangol and Hohhot. Long-distance calls were not only expensive but also sensitive. And no official media even mentioned the bloody events in progress throughout Inner Mongolia. During my brief absence from Bayangol and Hohhot, much had happened in the *wasu* and anti–New Neirendang movements. As the Chinese saying has it, *Dongzhong cai shu yue, shishang yi qian nian* (only months had passed in the cave, but in the outside world a thousand years had already passed).

On April 14, before my trip, Teng Haiqing had met with the standing committee members and staff of Husansi, the largest rebel student organization, which existed in name only by that time. Teng criticized the organization for holding back from the *wasu* campaign, saying: "In the *wasu* struggle, some units of [Hu]sansi have played a pioneering role, but as far as [Hu]sansi as a whole is concerned, I have not been satisfied. . . . The Cultural Revolution all along has centered around the struggle between two classes, two roads and two lines . . . Is [Hu]sansi following Chairman Mao's revolutionary line or is it standing at the crossroads?"[1]

Teng praised rebels from Medical College and Industrial College. Jinggangshan of Industrial College acquired the nickname of Teng Haiqing's "royal army" for strongly supporting *wasu* activist Ulaanbagan. Teng hinted that if other rebels failed to play an active role in *wasu*, they too would be targeted for struggle.

That day, Guo Yiqing, former Party secretary of Inner Mongolia University and former Propaganda Department chief of the Inner Mongolia Party Committee, then a member of the IMAR Revolutionary Committee, achieved a "breakthrough." Under his order, rebels from Inner Mongolia University tortured Batu (vice president of the university) to confess. He named sixteen high-ranking Mongols as members of the New Neirendang, including Buyanjab, deputy director of the Political Department, Inner Mongolia Military District; Erdenitogtoh, deputy director of the Language Commission; Öljinaran, vice director of the Economic Commission; and Tegusi, deputy chief of the Propaganda Department, among others. All were immediately jailed in isolation.

By the end of April, following Batu and Buyanjab's torture confessions, Li Shude and Li Dechen set up ten key cases to deal with Buyanjab, Batu, Tegusi, Mörön (president of Inner Mongolia Medical College), Töbshin (vice president of Inner Mongolia University), Öljinaran and Saishinga (Baotou Steel Factory), and Sainbayar, Vandan, and Erdenitogtoh. All were leading Mongols, and all were forced to name more names. By this time, Inner Mongolia had dug out many class enemies through torture and forced confessions.

On the basis of these confessions, on April 26, the core group submitted a report to Chairman Mao, Vice-Chairman Lin, the CCP Central Committee, the State Council, the Central Military Affairs Commission, the CCRG, and the Beijing Military Region: "Report on the Treason Case of 'The Inner Mongolia People's Revolutionary Party.'" Drafted by Li Dechen, director of *Tengban*, and signed by Gao Jinming, deputy leader of the core group, on behalf of the Revolutionary Committee, the report used the term *Inner Mongolia People's Revolutionary Party* for the first time officially in describing Case 206 of 1963 by adding *Inner* (*nei*) to Mongolian People's Revolutionary Party, which was mentioned in the intercepted letters.[2]

Several days later in May, the Inner Mongolia Revolutionary Committee set up a new office, the Second Special Case, charged with the responsibility to ferret out the New Neirendang. A pogrom was unleashed that would penetrate every nook and cranny of the region, targeting Mongols but touching everyone and transforming the relations between Han and Mongol that formed the center of Inner Mongolia politics and society.

In Bayangol, the number of detentions increased from dozens in the spring to hundreds in the summer. With the exception of Prince Darijiya and his wife, other Mongol leaders in the League revolutionary committee and local PLA units, including Ölji and Batubagan, were locked up for interrogation. I occasionally heard screams of torture and weeping late at night. The jails were guarded by PLA soldiers.

Initially, the Inner Mongolia Revolutionary Committee was unclear who to attack in the next stage of *wasu*. The original formulation of Ulanhu's black line targeted three categories of people: Ulanhu's followers, Hafenga's followers, and followers of Guomindang generals Fu Zuoyi and Dong Qiwu. The problem was that they had all been identified and punished. Indeed, that was also the question confronting Gao Shuhua when his Culture and Art Office was first set up. He was sidelined for failing to identify any new enemies, and the office was closed after only three months.

On July 5, the Third Enlarged Plenum of the Inner Mongolia Revolutionary Committee met in Hohhot to discuss *wasu* and New Neirendang issues. On July 20, the plenum passed two key documents: "Opinion on the Treatment of 'the Inner Mongolia People's Revolutionary Party'" and "Opinion on the Treatment of 'the Inner Mongolia People's Revolutionary League.'"[3] They were distributed throughout Inner Mongolia as *Document from the Inner Mongolia Revolutionary Committee (68) No. 351 and No. 352*. The two documents established policies for screening black elements. The plenum charted the anti–New Neirendang Campaign.

The documents were drafted by Li Shude in the spirit of Gao Jinming's earlier "theoretical" presentation and Ulaanbagan's theory of four evolutions: Inner Mongolia's CCP evolved from the Neirendang; Inner Mongolia's PLA evolved from the Neirendang's autonomous army; Inner Mongolia's cadres evolved from Neirendang cadres; and Inner Mongolia's Chinese Communist Youth League evolved from the Neirentuan, the Inner Mongolia People's Revolutionary Youth League.

The first document presented Neirendang history in three stages. It basically affirmed the work of the Neirendang during the first stage in the 1920s, presenting it as a "bourgeois nationalist political party" that "opposed imperialism, feudalism, and national oppression, and supported national independence, and freedom." Denouncing the Neirendang in its second stage as a "local nationalist political party," it severely criticized Ulanhu's 1947 "political quid pro quo" with Hafenga and Tömörbagan in which core elements of the Neirendang were recruited into the Communist Party. These were described as traitors, puppet Manchuguo officials of the Japanese, and bourgeois intellectuals. It accused Hafenga and Tömörbagan of seeking to undermine CCP leadership in Inner Mongolia in March and April 1947 by attempting "to split and betray our country." The document concluded that, far from disbanding, the Neirendang had "gone underground after May 1947." The following were the guidelines for assessing and punishing Neirendang members who joined at different historical stages:

1. All who joined the Neirendang from 1925 to 1936, and from August 1945 to May 1, 1947, should not be regarded as having joined a reactionary organization.

2. All who joined the Neirendang between August 1945 and May 1, 1947, should be treated as having ordinary historical problems, but they must make a clean breast. Chinese Communist Party members and state cadres who conceal this part of their personal history, must be severely punished.

3. Mongol traitors, spies, herdlords, landlords, reactionary feudal upper echelon elements, and other counterrevolutionary elements who dodged the people's punishment under the shield of the Neirendang, must be punished in accordance with relevant Party policies.

4. After May 1, 1947, the Neirendang and its mutant organizations were counterrevolutionary organizations.

Its members must register at designated units within one month of receipt of this document; any who fail to register will be severely punished.

Members of branch committees and core elements at higher levels who have no official posts but were backbone members should be treated as counterrevolutionaries. Those who thoroughly confess and expose and renounce their counterrevolutionary activities will be treated leniently. Those who render outstanding service [i.e., disclose the names and activities of Neirendang members] may be treated as other than counterrevolutionaries.

Ordinary members will not be treated as counterrevolutionaries, but if they refuse to confess or expose others, they must be severely treated.[4]

With this document, the campaign against the New Neirendang targeted followers of Ulanhu and those of Hafenga and Tömörbagan.

The second document classified the Inner Mongolia People's Revolutionary Youth League as a progressive organization before May 1, 1947. In the campaign that followed, however, many of its members would be subjected to imprisonment and torture.

In addition, the plenum issued "Policy Regulations for Categorizing and Cleansing Class Elements in the Pastoral Areas (Draft)."[5] The new directives officially negated Ulanhu's "three nos" policy of "no struggle, no division of property, and no class designation" and the "two benefits" policy of "mutual benefit between herders and herdlords" that had governed Inner Mongolia's treatment of pastoral Mongols after 1948. The document posited two antagonistic classes, which were further divided into six ranks, the first two being designated as exploiting classes: herdlord, rich herder, upper-middle herder, middle herder, lower-middle herder, and poor herder. Herdlords, rich herders, and those designated as "feudal upper echelon" and "religious upper echelon," that is, nobles and senior Buddhist monks, would be stripped of their positions and their property. The core policies that Mongols and some others had welcomed for bringing peace to the grasslands two decades earlier became the crimes of Ulanhu and his lackeys. Most important, this opened the way for targeting rural Mongols in the *wasu* campaign.

As tensions rose between China and the Soviet Union, Lin Biao called for a political border defense (*zhengzhi bianfang*). Large numbers of Mongol herders living close to the Sino-Mongolian and Sino-Soviet borders were removed from the border areas to ensure that they would not collaborate with the Soviets or the MPR.[6]

From July 1968, digging up the New Neirendang became a region-wide movement led by revolutionary committees at every level. That campaign marked a new phase of the Cultural Revolution in Inner Mongolia, one that screened *every single Mongol*, including many herders and farmers with no history of association with the Neirendang, or indeed of any political involvement. This campaign was taken up by activists who had once fought one another on behalf of the loyalist and rebel causes but now united in a campaign of terror that targeted the Mongol population.

Mongol commanders and soldiers in the Inner Mongolian army were primary targets of the new campaign. The top Mongol commanders had almost all been punished or sidelined in the first stage of the Cultural Revolution, immediately after Ulanhu's fall. The army was then briefly in the hands of Han commanders, men who were not beholden to Ulanhu, including several brought in from outside Inner Mongolia. But in the wake of the Han Tong murder, many Han commanders were transferred out of Inner Mongolia. Some Mongol generals who had fallen early in the Cultural Revolution were rehabilitated after Teng Haiqing's arrival. But in nearly all cases, not for long. Wu Tao was the only ranking Mongol military leader who survived Teng's murderous witch hunt, whether because of the strength of his long-term intelligence ties to the Central Military Affairs Commission in Beijing, because of his consistent allegiance to Teng Haiqing throughout the *wasu* campaign, or so that the movement would not appear to be a pogrom against Mongols.

The first to be charged as a New Neirendang element who had infiltrated the army was Buyanjab, a deputy director of the Political Department of the IMMD. Under torture, he produced a list of prominent Mongol leaders who he claimed were New Neirendang members. A vicious assault was then launched on the New Neirendang in the PLA. According to Tumen and Zhu, 3,567 people in the IMMD were accused of being New Neirendang members. This included 160 people at military headquarters, 217 in the logistics department, and virtually the entire political department, 195 out of just over 200 people.[7]

FIGURE 18 Parade in Hohhot, carrying caricature posters: at left "Down with Liu [Shaoqi], Deng [Xiaoping], Tao [Zhu]"; at right "Thoroughly Destroy the Ulanhu Family Kingdom," 1968

During the *wasu* movement, Mongol military cadres were subject to particularly cruel tortures by soldiers from the IMMD Band, Guard Battalion, and Division 30. The torture was led by Wang Jizhuang, a deputy secretary-general (*fu mishuzhang*) of the Political Department of the IMMD who arrived after the IMMD was subordinated to the Beijing Military Region. An outsider, he was a master at inventing tortures that drove many to commit suicide.

Chas was one of the Mongol military cadres who suffered deeply during the *wasu* campaign. A poor peasant from Ulaanhot, he was a member of the Neirentuan who joined the Chinese Communist Youth League after 1947 and fought in Lin Biao's army all the way from Manchuria in the Northeast to Guangdong in the South. Rising through the ranks as a cavalry commander, he was eventually transferred to Inner Mongolia where he served as political commissar of the border patrol in Eastern Ujumchin banner in the years 1966–1968 before being sent to Shiliingol League Military Subdistrict. Targeted during the *wasu* campaign, he was tied up and hung from the ceiling just above hot stoves. After the *wasu* campaign, he was transferred to Raoyang county in Hebei, and we eventually became good friends. He recalled of the torture: "During the war, not even war criminals were treated like this. They were worse than the Guomindang."

His torturers, led by a Han militia head, whipped him with leather belts. That was the first day of interrogation. "When I woke up, I was lying on the ground on straw, thinking that I would soon die."[8]

I asked him what other torture methods were used. Chas answered simply: "*Laohudeng*, the tiger bench. They tie your feet to a bench with ropes, then put bricks under your feet, adding bricks until the ropes break. My back and legs were permanently damaged. I was tempted to confess that the commander of the Shiliingol League Military Subdistrict was a Neirendang leader, but I gave up the idea, deciding that I'd rather die than lie."

From October 1968, "cleansing the class ranks" was the battle cry throughout China. In many towns and villages of Inner Mongolia, no trials were conducted. Rather, any hint of suspicion was grounds for arrest. Each unit from schools, factories, and offices on up to Inner Mongolia Military Headquarters and the Inner Mongolia Revolutionary Committee, created its own makeshift jail. This system extended to the villages. In the leading rebel-dominated units, like River West Company and Northern China Construction Company, loyalists attacked and incarcerated rebels.

Wasu at the *Inner Mongolia Daily*

In the summer of 1968, I was called back to the editorial office to work the night shift. I edited page 2 of the paper, which carried the Inner Mongolia news, responsible for everything from the selection of news items to editing and printing.

The *Inner Mongolia Daily*, with a staff of approximately one thousand, incarcerated sixty people in its makeshift jail. This was a modest number, because there were fewer Mongols compared to many larger factories and schools each having hundreds of prisoners. Many were held for periods of months and even years, often under intolerable conditions.

Everyone who was accused was arrested, questioned, and tortured. Some prisoners sought to retaliate by accusing Ulaanbagan of involvement in the conspiracy that he claimed to uncover. In speech after speech, Ulaanbagan told stories of how Mongols killed Han and shouted slogans to avenge Han deaths. Such accounts of Han-hating orgies by Mongols coming from the lips of a Mongol of considerable social standing was exactly what Teng Haiqing needed.

There were nine targeted as former Neirendang and about twenty former Neirentuan members at *Inner Mongolia Daily*. Zhuang Kun and Delger were the first journalists to be targeted. Zhuang, the former chief editor of the Chinese edition and a Han, and Delger, a Mongol former chief editor of the Mongol edition, were placed under house arrest. Delger was targeted as a Neirendang element. Zhuang had worked on the old *Inner Mongolia Daily* printed in Zhangjiakou in 1947, under the leadership of Tegusi. In the Ulanhu years, the two had controlled the press. Now branded Ulanhu followers, they were held at the *Inner Mongolia Daily* and pressured to confess.

The "jail" at the *Inner Mongolia Daily* consisted of four classrooms that held up to twenty prisoners each. From the newspaper's dormitory, beating and moaning could be heard late into the night. The interrogators and assailants were not reporters or staff, but young Han, as well as Mongol workers and militia members from the printing factory.

I asked one of the print workers about the beatings. He explained that assailants "turned off all the lights so that no one could identify who had beaten whom." The director of the *wasu* office ordered confessions, and it was the assailants' job to get them.

From the fall of 1968 to spring of 1969, the anti–New Neirendang campaign mainly focused on alleged Mongol nationalism, but other class enemies, including Han and other nationalities, were also targeted. *Wasu* was after all a campaign to "dig out (*wa*) Ulanhu's black line and eliminate (*su*) Ulanhu's pernicious influence"; it extended to Han Communist leaders such as Wang Duo and Wang Yilun, and to Guomindang spies. One victim was my Han colleague Zhou Zhiyun, or Xiao Zhou, as we called him.

One late evening in November 1968, an incident occurred that would cast a shadow over our work from that time forward. I was working in Baotou but was called back to the *Daily* to participate in criticizing Gao Jinming. Zhou Zhiyun had been a Youth League group leader in the printing shop and was active in the rebel organization. Twenty-three and always smiling, he had recently married a sent-down Beijing-educated girl. Returning after a honeymoon trip from Beijing, he went to work typesetting news stories. The work was done by hand, and it had to be done quickly to meet deadlines. A thousand-character article had to be finished in thirty to forty minutes.

The names of important Party leaders were kept together so they could be found easily. This was convenient because their names came up frequently, especially, of course, Mao Zedong's. At this time, the political situation was changing rapidly. Leaders rose and fell. That night, Zhou set type for an important article denouncing Liu Shaoqi who had just been stripped of all his positions, expelled from the Party, and publicly denounced as a "renegade, traitor and scab" and "lackey of imperialism, modern revisionist and Guomindang reactionaries." Inadvertently, he placed all the black labels on Mao rather than Liu.

Working in the print shop, we always printed a sample to check for errors, so mistakes could be corrected before any damage occurred. Usually two typesetters worked together in this; but this time, a PLA platoon leader Song had been asked to stand in for a sick typesetter. Ever alert to any signs of "class struggle," the moment he saw the proofs he telephoned the police, then summoned the entire office: "Look at these proofs! What is the nature of this 'mistake'?"

The moment people saw it, the color drained from their faces.

Just then Shi Ke arrived with three police detectives. They photographed the evidence, interviewed witnesses, handcuffed Zhou, and drove him away. The next day, everyone on the night shift was summoned for an important meeting. The process began of investigating every aspect of Zhou's class background, his factional affiliation, and his work.

No one dared speak out to protect or support him. But secretly, many people were sympathetic. Who could not see himself in Zhou's shoes, a career and a life destroyed for committing one careless error? Moreover, the article had not even been published.

This incident deeply affected work at the newspaper. One consequence was to reduce the speed with which we produced the paper. More or less overnight typesetting went from thirty to forty minutes to two hours for each thousand-character article. Typesetters checked their work as if their lives depended on it. Indeed, Zhou Zhiyun's case made plain that it did. There was a remarkable reduction in the number of typographical errors in the paper.

The mockup had to be finished by midnight. Then the editor signed it, releasing it to the photographic workshop to prepare for the printer. The printing had to be finished by 5 a.m. so the paper could go out to the entire region by train. As a result of this incident, however, we couldn't bring out the paper until afternoon. We joked that the *Inner Mongolia Daily* had become the *Inner Mongolia Evening News*.

Zhou was detained. Police asked the newspaper staff to recommend sentencing. No one wanted to say a word, but everyone privately blamed the error on Xiao Zhou's exhaustion from his honeymoon trip.

The case went up to Teng Haiqing's office, Tengban, for a decision. Finding little evidence of criminal motive on the part of Zhou, and fearing that continued delay in publishing the *Daily* would be criticized by the Central leaders in Beijing, Teng personally signed the case off as a "political incident," not a crime, suggesting that Xiao Zhou be released but receive administrative punishment. Xiao Zhou spent two months in jail before being released. He did have one piece of good luck. Had he been caught by one of the mass dictatorship organizations rather than by the army and the police he might have been beaten to death. Xiao Zhou could also thank his lucky stars that he was not a Mongol.

Job Assignment after the Four-Facing Principles

From July 1968, the Party Center sent military and worker propaganda teams (*jun xuan dui* and *gong xuan dui*) to discipline rebellious youth; tens of millions of middle school graduates were transferred to the countryside to receive reeducation from the poor and lower middle peasants or the workers, that is, to labor in communes or in factories or mines. They became so-called sent-down youth (*zhiqing*). College students were also dispatched to work in factories, mines, state farms, and communes, many of them in remote mountainous and frontier regions.

Inner Mongolia quickly implemented the Four-Facing Principles (*Sige mianxiang*): facing the countryside, facing the grass roots, facing the frontier, and facing the factories and mines. The college graduating class of 1966 had already been assigned jobs in late 1967 and early 1968. The central documents stipulated that the class of 1967, my class, be assigned jobs in the summer of 1968; and the classes of 1968, 1969, and 1970 would receive assignments in late 1968 to early 1969. There were then no students on campus until 1970, when college doors gradually opened to "worker, peasant, and soldier students" selected from their work units without entrance examinations or educational credentials.[9]

Because the central documents stipulated that all college graduates would receive formal job assignments, the Inner Mongolia Revolutionary Committee terminated the "temporary employment" of rebel students at the *Inner Mongolia Daily*, the radio station, the Public Security Bureau, and other institutions. Before we returned to our colleges for job assignments, Jin Feng and Shi Ke called a meeting of the more than forty students at the *Daily*. Jin said: "During months and years of working here, you have contributed greatly to the *Daily*. Deep in our heart, we don't want you to leave. However, you must return to school to comply with state guidelines. When the *Daily* needs your services, and state policy allows us to do so, we will try to arrange your transfer." Because of this promise, I continued to keep a working diary until I left Inner Mongolia in 1972.

Everyone then returned to college for job reassignment. Because we had studied English and the Center had ordered all middle schools to change their foreign language from Russian to English, English teachers were in demand. We were welcomed by middle schools despite the fact that, after more than two years of class interruptions, most of us had forgotten much of what we had learned, and none of us had completed the upper-level courses required for the degree. Still, we thought we could handle beginners learning the ABCs.

Of the forty-seven students in my class (English grade 3, class of 1967), seven students volunteered to return to their home leagues to become first generation English teachers, having been assured that they would be assigned to the league capital city. That left forty students to be dispatched to the two major cities in Inner Mongolia. I was assigned to Baotou, to start in September 1968.

On the evening of August 15, 1968, before our departure, all employees of the *Inner Mongolia Daily* were called to the auditorium to listen to Teng Haiqing's speech to the *Daily* and the Inner Mongolia Radio Station. Jin Feng asked me and my roommate Sun Panshi to attend the meeting. This was the last time that I would face Teng Haiqing at the *Daily*. Seated in the audience close to the platform, I could clearly see Teng's round red face. While reading his speech from a text in his right hand, his left hand held a large cigar. Panshi told me that our colleague Li Baoyi had drafted the speech. Li was transferred from another rebel organization to become a leading editorial board member at the *Daily*. Because of his thick beard, we called him Beard Li. He had close relations with Tengban, particularly with its director Li Dechen and Teng Haiqing's secretary Chen Xiaozhuang. Whenever Teng had some ideas he wanted to convert into official policy, he would call in the three to listen to his idea and then direct one of them to prepare an article draft, with the other two suggesting improvements. Then, after his final reading, the draft would be printed as his speech or would appear as an article on the front page of the *Inner Mongolia Daily* and in other publications.

Teng Haiqing spoke for two hours. The speech was in three parts: The first called for deepening the *wasu* campaign:[10] "Our *wasu* struggle started in literary and artistic circles last November [1967] beginning with the speech of Comrade Jiang Qing to literary and artistic circles in Beijing . . . From January 17 of this year our *wasu* struggles have been conducted throughout the region . . . Revolutionary criticism has now entered a period of all-out people's war."

The second part analyzed the struggles between two political lines, especially within the newly established revolutionary committees. Warning against rightist deviations that took "the form of war-weary emotions, thinking that enough enemies have been dug up, so we should stop," Teng shouted, "Down with two-faced counterrevolutionaries!" He punctuated the last slogan by thrusting his fist vigorously in the air.

The third part of his speech was crucial. Teng criticized reactionary *zichan jieji de duo zhongxin lun* (bourgeois multicentrism), which, he charged, led to "factionalism, sectarianism, divisionism, and independent kingdoms." "At the end of the day, it is a matter of 'power,' the matter of 'political power,'" he emphasized.

Teng's speech hinted at the power struggle underway at the Inner Mongolia center. The main target of his speech was Gao Jinming. The conflict between Teng and Gao Jinming was soon revealed.

Whither the Rebels?

Reviewing the two and a half years of the Cultural Revolution in Inner Mongolia, as in many other regions, it is clear that no sooner did the rebels achieve victory than their leaders were ordered to join newly created revolutionary committees at all levels from the autonomous region to the grass roots. There, as part of a so-called three-in-one combination of revolutionary cadres, military representatives, and mass organization activists, shorn of the support of rebel organizations that were everywhere disbanded, rebel representatives frequently found themselves marginalized or unable to compete effectively with their experienced and institutionally rooted political and military foes.

Many of the revolutionary committees created throughout the country in 1967–1968 were dominated by the very power holders in Party, government, and army who had been deposed and denounced in the early phases of the Cultural Revolution and who had long provided the backbone of loyalist forces. In most provinces and autonomous regions, including Inner Mongolia, the dominant force was the military. What was distinctive about Inner Mongolia, however, was that military power was directly imposed by the Center through the transfer of Teng Haiqing and his forces from outside the autonomous region.

By the summer of 1968, the number of college students on campuses in Inner Mongolia and throughout the country had been sharply reduced. The graduates of 1966 left for jobs by the end of 1967; the graduates of 1967, among whom I numbered, having lost their senior year educational experience to the Cultural Revolution, would leave school at the end of the summer of 1968. For these former students, being put on the state payroll was certainly a good thing. Moving all students—rebels and loyalists—off campuses meant reducing dissonant voices as "Red Guards," "rebels," and "loyalists" all largely disappeared.

One day in late August 1968, Xue Yongchang, a third-year Chinese-language student who had been a member of our martial arts team, called and asked to see me at Teachers' College. When I entered the small garret under the stairway of the main building, about a dozen people were crowded inside what had once been a storage room, including Gao Shuhua. Wang Aixue, a first-year chemistry student, chaired the discussion. He said: "Today we gather to speak from the heart, as we did in previous years. I believe there is no informant among us. We can say anything we want, and when we walk out of the room, we can forget everything that was said."

Our discussion focused on one point: whether Red Guards and rebels had been used as tools to serve a new dynasty. Someone said that the truth might be worse than that. Everyone should carefully read Yao Wenyuan's recent article "The Working Class Must Exercise Leadership in Everything."[11] We might be just like a dishcloth to be discarded, even destroyed, after being used.[12]

In September 1968, we 1967 college graduates set off for new jobs. I was among fifty-two recent graduates from all over Inner Mongolia dispatched to the Baotou Municipal Experimental Orchard by the Baotou Municipal Education Bureau to carry out manual labor in the name of "receiving reeducation from the peasants." The highway linking Baotou and Hohhot passed through our hundred-acre orchard, with the Daqing Mountains to the north and the Yellow River to the south.

There were only about twenty "worker" households. The *hukou* status of the villagers had been changed from "peasant" to "urban dwellers" after their land was nationalized and made a state-owned orchard. The orchard was classified as a "scientific experiment," to see whether fruit could grow there. The fruit was not sold in the market; it was given free to city leaders and institutions to secure their political and financial support.

We arrived during the harvest season for apples, pears, and grapes. To pick the fruit before the frost, we had to work in the fields more than ten hours a day. We were sternly warned never to taste the fruit, except on the final day of the harvest, when Party Secretary Zhang generously offered each of the graduates one apple, one pear, and ten grapes. Secretary Zhang asked the "workers" in the orchard to keep close watch on the "bourgeois intellectuals who needed reeducation from the poor and lower middle peasants."

After about one month, by late October, when all work in the fields had been completed, Zhang ordered us to cut down the dead trees and dig big holes to plant new trees in the spring. He set a daily quota: each male to dig three holes and each female to dig two holes, each a foot and a half in diameter and five feet deep. In summer, that would not have been a big problem, but with the soil frozen, even one hole was difficult. We set out to remedy the situation.

Attentive to power relations, we elected Zhao Lu (from Inner Mongolia Teachers' College) and Zhen Cheng (from Tongliao Teachers' College) as our representatives to lobby the Baotou city authorities to change our work unit. Zhao's elder sister Zhao Yun was director of the Planning Commission, and Zhen Cheng's father was a high-cadre in the Baotou Revolutionary Committee in charge of cultural and educational affairs. The two drafted a petition on behalf of the fifty-two graduates and submitted it to Li Jinbao, Zhen Cheng's former middle school classmate, a prominent rebel student leader who had become a standing committee member of the Baotou Revolutionary Committee. With Li Jinbao's quick approval of our petition, and even quicker action by the Baotou Planning Commission, an official introduction letter was issued to Zhao and Zhen authorizing them to contact the dozens of Baotou state factories to see whether one would sponsor the graduates in their work or reeducation programs. Most factories were happy to receive many working hands free. All they had to provide was dormitory rooms. They didn't have to pay salaries because, as future middle school teacher candidates, the Baotou Municipal Bureau of Education paid our modest salaries.

With this letter in hand, we eventually selected the Baotou Electric Machinery Plant, which had moved from Tianjin to Baotou a few years before the Cultural Revolution, in line with Mao's "Third Front" strategy of war preparation against possible attacks by US and Chinese Nationalist forces from Taiwan. We were impressed by their technology and management, but it was the quality of the dining room that trumped other factors. After a lunch sampling the variety of Tianjin-style dishes, we agreed on this factory. We could not wait to tell the orchard authority, with feigned regrets, that the government had ordered a change from "education by the peasants" to "education by the working class." A city truck picked up our luggage, and a bus transported all the graduates. Leaving the orchard, we smiled at the sight of Secretary Zhang and a few employees standing about looking disgruntled.

In this way, we began life in a new environment. With about 800 employees, including 50 cadres, 150 technicians, 500 certified skilled workers, and 100 unskilled workers, the major products were electrical motors for tanks and artillery.

With the deterioration of the Sino-Soviet relationship in the early 1960s, China sought to establish its own independent technology and parts supply system, replacing Soviet technology with domestic manufactured machinery, plus some imported Japanese and German equipment. Because Baotou was one of the few places that produced artillery (Baotou No. 1 Machinery Plant) and tanks (Baotou No. 2 Machinery Plant) to supply the Vietnam War, the plants had moved from Tianjin to serve the two big arsenals.

The leadership treated the graduates like their own junior apprentices, beginning with an orientation to the dozen shops and inviting us to apply for the kind of work we wished to learn. I applied to become a lathe operator in Shop 107 (for machinery repairs). My master was Sun Shilin, a thirty-eight-year-old, fifth-degree lathe operator (the eighth degree being the highest). Like other apprentices, we wore uniforms and worked all three shifts in rotation: early shift from 7 a.m. to 3 p.m., middle shift from 3 p.m. to 11 p.m., and night shift from 11 p.m. to 7 a.m., eight hours per day, six days a week, with Sunday off and longer hours if production fell behind schedule.

Wasu on the Factory Floor

Among the fifty-two students sent to Baotou were former loyalists and rebels who had fought one another tooth and nail. In the new location, our former conflicts remarkably dissolved. We graduates were classified as bourgeois intellectuals being reeducated by the working class. This did not mean that we were exempt from politics. Indeed, we were confronting a new kind of politics that made our former conflicts look like child's play.

In fall and winter of 1968, *wasu* and anti–New Neirendang campaigns spread to every corner of Inner Mongolia including Baotou and our Electrical Machinery Plant. In fact, Teng Haiqing paid particular attention to Baotou both politically and economically. Politically, Baotou's highest authority was Li Zhi, Gao Jinming's longtime associate from the Qianmen Hotel Conference, which had targeted Ulanhu in the spring of 1966 to the Cultural Revolution in Hohhot. Teng suspected Li and his wife Yang Hongwen (deputy director of the Hohhot Revolutionary Committee) of being part of a Gao Jinming clique that secretly resisted the *wasu* and anti–New Neirendang campaigns.

Baotou was Inner Mongolia's most important national defense industrial center and one of the most important in all China. With the launch of the *wasu* and anti–New Neirendang campaigns, industrial production slowed. In mid-February 1968, Teng Haiqing and Li Shude conveyed a directive from the Center's leaders.[13] They promoted two models for "making revolution and promoting production": the Baotou Steel Mill and the Second Metallurgical Construction Company (Baogang Erye).

From the summer to the fall of 1968, Tengban organized dozens of meetings in the two model companies, and tens of thousands of people studied their "advanced experiences." The Baogang Erye experience can be summarized in two points: First, "revolution" meant "mass dictatorship." Every employee was compelled to confess their involvement in any activity being investigated during the *wasu* and anti–New Neirendang campaigns. Anyone who did not confess and was exposed risked torture. Second, "production" meant intense pressure to increase output without access to more advanced machinery or equipment. Some workers summed up the Baogang Erye experience this way: "If everyone was to pass the gate of *wasu*, it would mean doubling the production quota" (*Renren yaoguo Wasu guan; shengchan biding fanyifan*). But would political repression boost productivity?

After Tengban and the Baotou Revolutionary Committee popularized the Baogang Erye experience, most factories, schools, and other work units quickly set up detention centers to lock up victims.

A biochemical firm, the Baotou Fine Bone Glue Factory, with only three hundred employees locked up more than forty suspected New Neirendang members and other counterrevolutionaries. We often heard torture victims screaming late at night. Rumors circulated of murder and suicide.

When Sun Panshi, my *Daily* colleague and roommate, visited Baotou, he told me that his friend Zhang Yuanxi, a young worker in the Fine Bone Glue Factory nearby, had been detained for some counterrevolutionary misdeed. He asked whether we could do anything to free him.

Zhang's father was a second lieutenant who had served under General Fu Zuoyi, the warlord general whose uprising made possible Beiping's peaceful liberation. The factory had sent an investigation letter to the school where Yuanxi had been a student to inquire whether he had shouted slogans in 1952 praising President Truman and criticizing China's forces in Korea. Yuanxi's personal file contained the allegation written by his primary school teacher. The family had futilely appealed to remove the allegation.

Sun explained that when Yuanxi was eight years old a group of neighborhood boys imitated the political war games they often saw on the street. Yuanxi had a large nose, so he was often chosen to play Truman, while other boys played the Chinese soldiers. Finally, in frustration, he refused to play the American villain, shouting: "I am not a bad man, I am a good man. You are the bad guys!" That story, reported to their teacher, became the basis for the political allegation. According to Sun Panshi, the real reason for his misery was his father's historical background. During the political campaigns from the early 1950s to the mid-1960s, especially in the early stage of *wasu*, all Fu Zuoyi soldiers and lower-ranking officers in Inner Mongolia were subjected to attack, and their children also were often targeted.

I discussed Yuanxi's case with Zhao Lu, Zhang Daren, and Zhao Zongzhi. Eventually, we came up with a scheme to save him. Sun Panshi and I first contacted Wu Zhenye, a rebel student who was in charge of foreign affairs and investigations at the Baotou Police Bureau. He also sympathized with Yuanxi. He phoned the factory, saying that the *Inner Mongolia Daily* had sent two reporters to Baotou to investigate the case and write an internal report.

The next morning, Sun and I arrived at the Bone Glue Factory. After showing our photo ID for the *Daily*, with the military committee chops on them, the factory leaders were very polite to us. They were anxious to show us all the records and answer our questions. After carefully examining the dossier, we said that we would write an internal report for the editorial office and the military control committee.

"May I ask you why you are interested in Zhang Yuanxi's case? Would your internal report hurt our factory's reputation?" The boss was worried.

"We're just following our leaders' orders," Panshi replied. "We don't know the background of the case."

About a week after our visit to the factory, someone knocked on our dormitory door looking for me. It was Zhang Yuanxi. With smiles, he came to thank everyone who had helped him. Looking at him, I noticed that his nose was indeed higher than that of most Chinese. No wonder he had been forced to play Truman!

He told me that after our visit, the factory leader, fearful of negative repercussions, decided to close his case and free him, even giving him a one-week vacation to visit his parents in Hohhot.

I asked whether he had been tortured during detention. He said that the security guards had treated him fairly because most of them had played on the same basketball team. But the forty-five detainees, including eight Mongols who were labeled New Neirendang members, were tortured badly. The favored method was to turn off all the lights at night. Five people then beat up one tied victim using a rubber belt with a metal spring inside. The beating, which could seriously damage the internal tissues, left few scars. When finally released, one Mongol cadre was wounded so severely that he could no longer eat or speak.

By the time the *wasu* campaign ended in May 1969, five lives had been lost, including three Mongols and two Han at this site. Two were beaten to death, and three committed suicide.

The Baotou Electric Machinery Plant also had detentions and torture, but nothing comparable to our neighboring factory. Since the factory had moved to Inner Mongolia from Tianjin just a few years before the Cultural Revolution, and there were no Mongols, it was hard to find suspected New Neirendang. Also, the authorities had closely screened politically suspect people since the factory was engaged in military production.

The second reason was related to the character of leading members of the plant. Xu Chunshan and Jiang Shengquan, the chair and deputy chair, were peacemakers, eager to avoid conflict and struggles in the factory. Wang Shulin (we called him Wan Wen, or "Cultural Wang"), the propaganda chief, wrote beautiful articles for the bulletin board of "revolutionary criticism" at the entrance of the plant, making it very attractive, but he had no interest in actual class struggle. Only Lü Chunlai (we called him Lü Wu, "Martial Lü"), the security chief, tried to promote the *wasu* and anti–New Neirendang campaign in our plant. My master, Sun Shilin, told me that as someone with little education and no special skills, Lü saw struggle as the route to promotion. Before our arrival, Lü had labeled a dozen people as new "class enemies," including his close colleague Li Wenxiu. They had entered the plant together as apprentices in Tianjin in 1958. Li was soon promoted to a higher technical level while Lü turned to the political path. After joining the Party in 1960, he rose quickly as a cadre in charge of security. During the early stage of the Cultural Revolution in Baotou, a case of a "reactionary slogan" occurred in the No. 105 workshop. Someone had drawn a cross through the revolutionary slogan "Resist America, Support Vietnam," which was painted on one of the packing boxes ready to ship to Vietnam.

After weeks of investigation, Martial Lü insisted that it must have been Li Wenxiu. Baotou's public security bureau never accepted the verdict because of a "lack of evidence." Nevertheless, Li Wenxiu, the primary "counterrevolutionary element," remained locked up in the factory's detention center with seven other bad elements, including the highest senior technician Ma Lianbi (labeled a *fandong jishu quanwei*, or "reactionary technological authority"), and five so-called *yezhu* (business owners) or *zibenjia* (capitalists).

After the establishment of the factory's Revolutionary Committee, the detention center was closed, and the detainees were allowed to go home. But Martial Lü insisted that each wear a white label with his or her name on it. This was one of the things that had disturbed our group of college graduates. Zhang Daren said, "Fuck Martial Lü. Why should he be able to torture these people constantly? Even big black gang members, like Ulanhu's associates, were only forced to wear high paper hats for a few hours. Why should these people be forced to wear the labels every day?"

When our criticisms reached Lü's ears, he challenged these "smelly bourgeois intellectuals" who were at the factory to be reeducated. As director of the *wasu* office in the plant, he ordered the graduates to join the daily meeting with other workers for self-criticism and confession. But he was overruled by Xu Chunshan and Jiang Shengquan, chair and deputy chair of the Revolutionary Committee. They said that only the five graduates who were on their payroll could be included in the regular daily activities. The other fifty-two graduates remained under the jurisdiction of the Baotou Education Bureau. They pointed out that this violated the city's official position that the factory should give positive education to the new graduates, not screen them one by one, unless special cases had been exposed.

In late November 1968, the plant received a request to check on the political performance of the three Mongols in our group. It was an opportunity for Martial Lü to dig out some New Neirendang elements. Investigations were underway everywhere. The Baotou Education Bureau had previously checked their personnel dossiers and evaluated them positively. Martial Lü drafted a letter and asked some workers to sign on behalf of the working class of the factory without showing them the letter. When Cultural Wang privately passed the information to us, Zhao Lu and I drafted a protest on behalf of the student group, and everyone signed it. After receiving our letter, Xu Chunshan and Jiang Shengquan on behalf of the Revolutionary Committee called a public meeting of the workers as well as the graduates to discuss the performance of the three and their behavior was highly assessed. Martial Lü had failed again.

Compared to many other factories and institutions in Baotou, this factory had relatively humane ways of treating "class enemies." During the rest of our stay, there was no detention center, no torture, no suicide, not even a single struggle meeting.

Unfortunately, however, we were unable to help in Li Wenxiu's case, which had been filed with the Baotou Police Bureau. Poor Wenxiu and seven other black elements were not rehabilitated until after Mao's death in the late 1970s.

The Fall of Gao Jinming

In the early stage of *wasu*, Teng Haiqing, a newcomer to Inner Mongolia, relied heavily on Gao Jinming and Guo Yiqing, both of whom had worked in Inner Mongolia for decades and knew the political ropes and nationality issues. That knowledge proved lethal as the two pinpointed their targets with precision. Teng appropriated their achievement as his merit to show to his superiors in Beijing. But with the advance of *wasu* and the shift to uprooting the New Neirendang, especially in the wake of the fall of his close colleague Guo Yiqing, Gao Jinming's enthusiasm for pressing the campaign diminished.

Guo Yiqing, a Henan native, had once been a trusted subordinate of Ulanhu, who had promoted him to be Party secretary of Inner Mongolia University (Ulanhu was the president, one of many hats that he wore, in addition to heading the IMAR Party, government, and army over nearly two decades). But at the Qianmen Hotel Conference, Guo saved himself by turning against Ulanhu, and in November 1967, he was appointed to the Standing Committee of the Inner Mongolia Revolutionary Committee. From the outset, he hounded Gao Shuhua, also a Standing Committee member of the Revolutionary Committee, by supporting Gao's rival Hao Guangde, and attacking

Gao for links with Ulanhu's son Lishake, ultimately marginalizing Gao in the region's high politics. He then became Ulaanbagan's enthusiastic patron in the *wasu* campaign. Having gained Teng Haiqing's trust by feeding him trumped-up conspiracy theories on New Neirendang activities, he too fell victim to the Ferreting Out Traitors movement, not in Inner Mongolia, but in his home province of Henan.

After receiving damning materials about Guo Yiqing from Henan via the Beijing Military Region, in August 1968 the core group suspended his positions as a Standing Committee member and director of the Political Department. Guo was sent to a study class for investigation, though not released to the mass dictatorship organizations for struggle.[14] By this time, Kang Xiumin, another Standing Committee member, was undergoing investigation by mass organizations in his hometown of Shijiazhuang, Hebei. This was the beginning of the disintegration of the post-Ulanhu Inner Mongolia leadership, culminating in the fall of Gao Jinming, the most important civilian leader of the Inner Mongolia Revolutionary Committee.

On August 26, 1968, Yao Wenyuan published "The Working Class Must Lead Everything" on the front page of the *People's Daily*, emphasizing "struggle, criticism, and transformation (*dou pi gai*)." It called for sending worker propaganda teams to campuses to lead and reeducate students: "If students refuse to be reeducated, the working class should impose dictatorship on them." Immediately, worker propaganda teams, poor and lower middle peasant propaganda teams, and PLA propaganda teams were dispatched to universities, middle schools, and primary schools throughout the country.

Sensing a change of wind in Beijing, or perhaps concluding that the campaign had gone too far and needed to be reined in, Gao Jinming found in Yao's article a signal that the Center was calling for a shift from the primacy of class struggle to transformation of the social order. In analyzing the article, Gao concluded that "transformation is the result and the test of the struggles and criticism."[15] Teng, however, continued to press ahead with the struggle and criticism that were the essence of the *wasu* movement. As a result, Gao and Teng clashed over the new stage of struggle and its presentation in the editorials of the *Inner Mongolia Daily*.

On August 30, Gao Jinming vetoed a draft editorial entitled "The Worker Propaganda Team Must First Focus on the *Wasu* Struggle." Unbeknownst to Gao, the *Daily* editor brought the editorial to Teng Haiqing for his inspection, and he approved it. Publication of the editorial on August 31 dismayed Gao, who vowed to dig out the black hand at the *Daily*. On September 20, at Gao's instruction, the *Daily* published the editorial "Meeting the National Day Celebration with Great Achievements of Struggle, Criticism, and Transformation," emphasizing transformation (*gai*) and downplaying the struggle (*dou*) and criticism (*pi*) priority of *wasu*.[16]

Gao was determined to bring *wasu* to a halt, fearing that he and his comrades might be the next targets. On September 25 Gao spelled out both his priorities and his anxiety in a speech to Inner Mongolia Party and government employees: "Overall, in most parts of Inner Mongolia, the Anti-Party Traitors Clique of Ulanhu has been completely defeated. The great majority of traitors, special agents, capitalist roaders, and national separatist elements have been exposed. . . . If we continue to dig deeper, it will target our own people."[17]

The September 20 editorial and Gao's speech on September 25 touched off a huge reaction throughout Inner Mongolia. Big-character posters denounced the earlier editorials approved by Teng for deepening the *wasu*. Demonstrations staged by rebel organizations were notable for shouting slogans criticizing Teng. There were even calls for rehabilitation of the *wasu* victims. Gao Shuhua and his close rebel supporters opposed Gao Jinming.[18]

Teng vowed to deepen the *wasu* movement in the spirit of Mao's call to "carry the revolution to the end." He was boldened by the Enlarged Twelfth Plenum of the Eighth Central Committee, convened in Beijing October 13–31, 1968, which branded Liu Shaoqi a "renegade, traitor, and scab." Stripping the former president of all posts, it expelled him from the Party, touching off a frenzy of activity to root out capitalist roaders throughout the country.[19]

On October 18, 1968, a "public notice" posted on all important roads and buildings in Hohhot again ordered all who had joined the Neirendang after May 1, 1947 to register by November 21, 1968, or face severe punishment.[20] Trucks with loudspeakers blared the order day and night on the streets, terrorizing residents, Han and Mongol alike.

On October 21–25, Teng Haiqing and Wu Tao, while attending the Enlarged Twelfth Plenum in Beijing, asked Tengban director Li Dechen to transmit their "opinions" to leading Revolutionary Committee members in Hohhot emphasizing that the direction of *wasu* and uprooting the New Neirendang was absolutely correct.[21] They now had the Center's full support. Upon returning to Hohhot, in a speech on November 18 during the Fourth Meeting of the Inner Mongolia Revolutionary Committee (Extended) in Hohhot, Teng launched an open attack on Gao Jinming's "rightist opportunism," blaming him for wreaking havoc on *wasu*.[22]

In suggesting that the *wasu* campaign had gone too far, Gao Jinming had opened himself to charges of adhering to Liu Shaoqi's theory of "the dying out of class struggle" (*jieji douzheng ximie lun*). In the final months of 1968, throughout China many senior cadres were attacked and some ousted for historical associations with Liu Shaoqi or, in Inner Mongolia, his "agent" (*dailiren*) Ulanhu. Loyalist and rebel as well as working-class activists, many of whom had demonstrated their revolutionary fervor during the *wasu* campaign, were inducted into revolutionary committees in line with Mao's injunction to "spit out the old and take in the new" (*tu gu na xin*). In Inner Mongolia, the attack on the right, which had been redefined to include not only all who were formerly associated with Ulanhu but also many rebels who criticized the *wasu*, led to accelerating the *wasu* movement. The terror reinforced Teng Haiqing's grip on power.

Following Teng's attack, the Fourth Meeting halted Gao Jinming's work and subjected him to mass public struggle.

On November 3, Tengban called the Baotou Revolutionary Committee and ordered Zhao Zongzhi and me to return to the *Inner Mongolia Daily* to participate in the struggle to "expose and criticize Gao Jinming." As one Tengban officer said, "These two former reporters and rebel students from Teachers' College had close relations with Gao Jinming and will know more about his black activities." Because many rebels associated with Gao Shuhua were known to have clashed with Gao Jinming, we were considered useful allies in exposing Gao Jinming. But I was not privy to the conflict between Gao Shuhua and Gao Jinming that started in March 1968 since I was in Bayannuur. My impression of Gao Jinming remained positive, since he had supported the rebels in the fight against the military in spring 1967.

On the train from Baotou to Hohhot, I asked Zongzhi: "Do you think we should criticize Gao Jinming as Tengban directed?" "Well," Zongzhi replied, "I don't think Gao Jinming has done anything wrong in trying to bring the political movement under control. Teng Haiqing is making major mistakes by locking up so many innocent Mongols and causing so many deaths. But if we openly align ourselves with Gao Jinming, Tengban will persecute us. We should convince Tengban that we have no personal relationship with him. Our only relationship with him is through our work, including the Cultural Revolution at Teachers' College and reporting for the *Daily*. What do you think?"

"After returning to the *Daily*, let's see what Jin Feng and Shi Ke advise," I responded. When we arrived at nine the next morning, Jin Feng was waiting for us in his smoke-filled office. We asked about the "campaign to criticize Gao Jinming." Smiling wryly, Jin said:

Neither Comrade Shi Ke nor I, nor other leading comrades of the *Daily*, know what's going on at the upper level. Gao Jinming, one of the core leaders of the autonomous region, has suddenly been targeted as an enemy but there are no official documents explaining the case. However, as military officers, we can only follow orders from Tengban. You are here at the order of Tengban to participate in the campaign. We have arranged your room and board, and you can attend meetings and write posters. As far as Gao Jinming is concerned, Tengban still calls him a comrade, not a class enemy, so you should do just as Chairman Mao says: "Uphold unity, seek truth from facts, learn from past mistakes to avoid future ones, and cure the disease to save the patient" (*Weihu tuanjie, shishi qiushi, chengqian bihou, zhibing jiuren*).

His tone suggested that he was sympathetic toward Gao Jinming.

After meeting with Jin Feng, we saw Zhang Peiren, who was still working in the main editorial office. He brought us to his home in the *Daily* courtyard. While his wife was cooking lunch, Peiren angrily lashed out at Teng Haiqing: "Since you left in September, Teng Haiqing and his army of running dogs are going crazy targeting so many people as New Neirendang members. Now he even labels Gao Jinming as a rightist to be struggled. In the eyes of these PLA officers who know nothing about Inner Mongolia and Chinese history, it seems that no one in Inner Mongolia can be trusted. If Chairman Mao and the Party Center don't stop the craziness of Teng and his officers, disaster will befall Inner Mongolia, even all China!" Zhang's animated tone and high-pitched voice scared his wife, who repeatedly came into our room asking him to lower his voice.

On November 5, at the Fourth Revolutionary Committee meeting, Teng Haiqing directed the *Inner Mongolia Daily* to organize a meeting to criticize and attack Gao Jinming. About thirty-five people attended, including Gao Jinming and two officers from Tengban. Zhang Peiren, Zhao Zongzhi, and I were also invited to attend. Gao Shuhua sat in a far corner, maintaining a very low profile. He silently waved in greeting to us, his former students and rebel colleagues.

After Shi Ke announced the beginning of the meeting at 9 a.m., five representatives (three Han and two Mongols) criticized Gao Jinming, who sat in the middle of the room taking notes. Li Baoyi, Li Yulou, Qiao Tong, Erdeni-Uul, and another young Mongol from the print shop spoke. The criticisms focused on Gao Jinming's order to the *Inner Mongolia Daily* not to publish the editorial of August 31, "The Workers' Propaganda Teams Should First Focus on the *Wasu* Struggle." Gao Jinming was denounced for attempting to slow down the *wasu* in Teng Haiqing's absence. They further criticized his speech of September 25 and labeled his activities as the Secret Current of September, or *Jiuyue anliu*.

Erdeni-Uul, the leading *wasu* activist at the *Daily*, dug deeply into Gao's previous history in eastern Inner Mongolia in the 1940s. "Comrade Gao

Jinming should dig out the dirty thoughts behind his own current conservatism and link it with his conservatism in the 1940s. If he does not change his
viewpoint completely, the revolutionary masses should expose him as a class
enemy."

We later learned that Ulaanbagan and Erdeni-Uul had scoured the his-
torical archives of the 1940s in eastern Inner Mongolia, where Gao had been
an undercover Communist agent. But after learning about their activity, Gao
Jinming had stopped their work and ordered the closure of their Ferreting
Out Traitor Clique Liaison Station, along with the Ferreting Out Black Hands
Liaison Station, the Mass Dictatorship Headquarters, and other *wasu* activist groups. As director and deputy director of Ferreting Out Traitor Clique
Liaison Station, Ulaanbagan and Erdeni-Uul had strong incentives to take
revenge on Gao Jinming.

Throughout the morning session, Gao Jinming was not allowed to say
one word. I felt it strange that Jin Feng and Gao Shuhua said nothing. Zongzhi and I kept silent, too.[23] At lunch in the *Daily* dining hall, I asked Gao
Shuhua why he didn't speak during the meeting. He said, "Many people think
I should hate Gao Jinming because he and Guo Yiqing tried to label me as an
Ulanhu black gang member. But his idea to slow the *wasu* campaign is not
wrong. So, I rejected Tengban's invitation to criticize Gao but agreed to attend
the proceedings."

The meeting to criticize Gao Jinming at the *Daily* had been confined to
a small circle and the atmosphere, while tense, maintained a certain civility.
This soon changed. On November 25, 1968, in a speech at the North China
Construction Company, Teng Haiqing stated that mass organizations could
bring Gao Jinming to their meetings for public criticism.[24] I subsequently attended several mass meetings.

One struggle meeting was organized by *wasu* activists in the auditorium
of the Inner Mongolia government compound in late November 1968. All
two thousand seats were filled with representatives from government agencies, institutions, and enterprises. Most were *wasu* and anti–New Neirendang
activists.

When I walked into the great hall a young man was angrily attacking Gao
Jinming. Above their heads, a giant banner hung on the dark purple velvet
curtain: "Expose and Criticize Gao Jinming's Right Opportunist Line and
Achieve Greater Victory in the Movement to Dig Up the Neirendang!"

Gao was seated at a small student desk, taking notes in his small black
notebook. But after three or four speeches, some attendees angrily ordered
him to stand up in front of the platform. Gao slowly rose and moved to
the center at the edge of the platform. Under the lights, his dark-gray Mao

suit and light-gray hair were clearly reflected. His arms were sagging, like a schoolboy who had made mistakes.

At the end of each speech, the speaker shouted slogans: "Thoroughly criticize Gao Jinming's right opportunist line! Carry the *wasu* and anti-Neirendang campaign to the very end! Let Gao Jinming perish if he doesn't surrender!"

The slogans reminded me of the most difficult time for our Husansi in the winter of 1966 and spring of 1967, when powerful loyalist organizations labeled him as the black hand behind the rebel students. At that time, loyalists seized Gao Jinming and Quan Xingyuan and publicly humiliated them. However, given his appointment by the Party Center, no armed guards forced Gao Jinming to bend his head or beat him.

I soon lost interest in watching the farce of the so-called criticism of Gao Jinming and left the auditorium.

Cleansing the "Little Gao Jinmings": Deepening *Wasu*

After the Fourth Revolutionary Committee meeting, which centered on criticizing Gao Jinming as Inner Mongolia's exemplar of rightist opportunism, every league or city, banner or county, people's commune, enterprise, PLA division, military subdistrict, university, and school set up Mao Zedong Thought study classes. These were in fact detention centers that used torture to force detainees to confess.

The campaign unleashed a new power struggle. At the regional level, Teng curbed the power of Lei Daifu, Zhang Lu, and other close associates of Gao Jinming in the Revolutionary Committee while pressing them to criticize him publicly. Most city- and league-level revolutionary committee leaders were labeled New Neirendang elements, or as Gao's associates.

In Hohhot, Ma Boyan, deputy commander and political commissar of the Hohhot Military Subdistrict, attacked almost all leaders of the Hohhot Revolutionary Committee including Gao Zenggui (director), Yue Ziyi (deputy director), and Yang Hongwen (deputy director). In late November 1968, Ma sent armed *wasu* activists to publicly humiliate them in mass assemblies. All three officials had long careers in Hohhot dating from the 1950s. During the Qianmen Hotel Conference in early 1966 and the Cultural Revolution in late 1966 and early 1967, they had joined Gao Jinming in attacking Ulanhu and supporting the rebel student movement. Now all of them had fallen.

Many rebel leaders in the revolutionary committees were soon labeled "Little Gao Jinmings." They lost their positions, further reducing the possibility of any attempt to moderate Teng Haiqing's anti–New Neirendang campaign.

For instance, in the Jining Railroad Agency, among the sixty-five revolutionary committee members from rebel organizations, twenty were persecuted, of whom eight were labeled "Little Gao Jinmings" and expelled, thirty-four were labeled "New Neirendang members" and locked up, and eleven more were placed on the "suspicious list" to be taken care of later.[25]

At Teachers' College, the former rebel stronghold, more than one hundred faculty members, mainly Mongols, were labeled New Neirendang members, including rebels who had served on revolutionary committees at the college and department levels.

Following the fall of Gao Jinming and the onslaught against the rebels in revolutionary committees, in late 1968 Teng Haiqing asked the Beijing Military Region to transfer two hundred Han officers at battalion and regiment levels or above to Inner Mongolia, to "reinforce revolutionary committees" to spearhead his anti–New Neirendang campaign policy.[26] Most were from Hebei and Shanxi. Subsequently, the *wasu* campaign was almost entirely led by the PLA, with the assistance of civilian activists. The key military activists were as follows:

1. Shang Min, commander of Hulunbuir Military Subdistrict
2. Zhao Yuwen, commander of Jirim Military Subdistrict
3. Zhao Derong, commander of Shiliingol Military Subdistrict
4. Zhou Fayan, commander of Ulaanchab Military Subdistrict
5. Wu Shangzhi, commander of the Fifth Cavalry Division
6. Wang Xirong, commander of Juu'uda Military Subdistrict
7. Ma Boyan, deputy commander and political commissar of Hohhot Military Subdistrict
8. Li Dechen, director of Teng Haiqing Office (Tengban)
9. Chen Xiaozhuang, secretary of Teng Haiqing.

On November 23, 1968, the Military Control Commission of the Hohhot Public Security Bureau, chaired by Ma Boyan, issued Notice No. 2, ordering all "New Neirendang" members to turn themselves in and register at nearby police stations by December 23 or face severe punishment.[27]

At the same time, it publicized twenty-three slogans for suppressing those nonexistent enemies, such as "Leniency to those who confess, severity to those who resist," and "If the New Neirendang won't surrender, we will annihilate it." Shock brigades for uprooting New Neirendang (*Wa Xin Neirendang Tujidui*) were deployed to force thousands to register. Four tactics were used to secure registrations throughout Inner Mongolia: *wudou*, or violence; *chelun*, or the use of several interrogators taking turns to wear down a single target; *bigong*, or extortion; and *kongbu*, or terror. The *Inner Mongolia Daily* editorial of November 24 set the tone: "If we are not relentless to enemies it is useless to talk about being 'firm' and 'accurate.'"

One day in the dining hall when I was eating with Zhao Zongzhi, Li Baoyi, the author of the editorial, sat down at our table. I said: "Baoyi, you said that 'ruthlessness' is the key. If we are not ruthless to enemies, it is useless to talk about being 'firm' and 'accurate.' Do you mean that we should support physical torture to treat suspects ruthlessly? In my view, accuracy is more important than ruthlessness in order to screen good people from bad ones. What do you think?" His sharp eyes glanced at me and he smiled: "Actually, that language was copied exactly from Teng Haiqing's words." "Does Teng really suggest using violence to interrogate detainees?" Zongzhi asked. "Well," Li continued, "according to the experiences reported by the *wasu* activists in Ulaanchab league, we could only touch the souls of die-hard Neirendang elements by touching their skin and flesh. They did not use the words violent struggles, but you can guess what that means."

On December 2, 1968, the *Inner Mongolia Daily* published the editorial "Broadly Develop the Cleansing of the Class Ranks in Agricultural and Pastoral Areas," which called for digging out the New Neirendang. The editorial pushed each township and village to establish detention centers to extort confessions through torture.

In December 1968, Tengban director Li Dechen drafted the "Report Outline on the Neirendang Issue" for Teng Haiqing's report to the Center's leaders in Beijing. It became the famous "December Report Outline" (*12 yue huibao tigang*).[28] According to this outline, by December 10, 1968, some 10,911 Neirendang members had been dug out from two cities (Hohhot and Baotou) and four leagues (Ulaanchab, Shiliingol, Yekejuu, and Juu'uda), and those numbers did not include Hulunbuir, Jirim, and Bayannuur.

In his "December Report Outline," Teng and the Revolutionary Committee claimed that in digging out the New Neirendang, they succeeded in "cleansing the motherland's northern frontier of a hidden peril." This report, issued at the peak of tensions over war with the Soviet Union and the MPR, named Ulanhu as the general chief (*zong toumu*) of the Neirendang and listed sixty-eight leaders and core members of the New Neirendang. All were Mongols, except one Han (Shi Guanghua, Ulanhu's son-in-law), and one Daur (Guo Wentong, brother of Guo Daofu, or Merse). All were former top leaders of the Inner Mongolia Autonomous Region.

9

"Inner Mongolia Has Gone Too Far"

Wu Tao, the Last Mongol

After attacking Gao Jinming's associates—mostly Han, and a few surviving Mongol officials—Teng Haiqing and his associates went after the only Mongol who retained a position at the highest level in the Inner Mongolia Autonomous Region who might pose an obstacle to further witch hunt targeting of Mongols: Major General Wu Tao.

If the second phase of the *wasu* campaign starting from July 1968 was notable for Han torturing and killing Mongols, the third phase following the Twelfth Plenum of the Eighth Central Committee of October 1968 targeted both Han and Mongols. Teng Haiqing turned on his former collaborators, including ranking leaders Gao Jinming and Quan Xingyuan, just as the earlier campaign against Ulanhu and his associates had eventually targeted ranking Han officials Wang Duo and Wang Yilun, as if to prove that the attack was not ethnically driven.

Teng made explicit the broadening of the sphere of activities of the Neirendang campaign in a commentary on December 7, 1968:[1]

> Some people think that the "Neirendang" is a historical relic. Wrong! It is an active counterrevolutionary party; it is the largest anti-Party treasonous group and spy organization. It has never ceased its counterrevolutionary activities and recruitment of party members. It has a complete force and ammunition and sound organization. It has a black command headquarters at the highest level, and below it has grassroots party cells. It has not only officers but soldiers, and it has woven a web from Hohhot to every league and even to every banner and county. Its party chief still usurps some power in the Party, government, treasury, culture and army, and it has sneaked into some hearts.

Then, in a stunning revelation, Teng exposed Wu Tao, the highest-ranking Mongol in the Inner Mongolia military, as the new party chief of the Neirendang, with Gao Jingmin and Quan Xingyuan as his deputies styled as the second- and third-generation princes (*erdai wangye, sandai wangye*). Ulanhu was, of course, the current prince (*dangdai wangye*). Here Teng transplanted a Mongolian feudal title from a Mongol to a Manchu (Gao Jingmin) and a Han (Quan Xingyuan), charging both with conniving to restore Ulanhu's Mongol kingdom.

Their greatest crimes were hindering the *wasu*, indeed, almost killing it prematurely. They were, perforce, "rightists," and "traitors."

Although Wu Tao had maintained good working relations with Gao Jinming since Zhou Enlai freed both of them from the custody of loyalists in spring of 1967 and asked them to work together to help Teng Haiqing establish the IMAR Revolutionary Committee, Wu could hardly be identified as a Gao Jinming associate. Both before and during the Cultural Revolution, Wu mainly focused on military affairs in the IMMD and was seldom involved in civilian affairs.

Although appointed as the second highest leading member in the Inner Mongolia Revolutionary Committee, Wu seldom expressed his own views, but closely followed Teng Haiqing's lead. Most Central decisions and meetings were attended by Teng and Wu and the pair (*Teng Wu Shou Zhang*) frequently signed off on them, suggesting that Wu was privy to major decisions, and, at a minimum, performed an affirming role. Nonetheless, throughout the *wasu* campaign, Wu Tao had maintained a very low profile. During the first half of 1968, the first phase of the *wasu* campaign, he was in the 301 Military Hospital in Beijing with kidney problems.[2]

With the deepening of the *wasu* campaign targeting the New Neirendang, Wu faced mounting personal contradictions between his loyalty to the Party and army on the one hand and his ethnic identity as a Mongol familiar with the history of the Neirendang on the other. Wu Tao suffered from insomnia and eventually had several heart attacks. From late 1968, he carried his small medicine bottle everywhere.

After months of internal struggle, the tone of Wu's speeches gradually changed, subtly distancing himself from Teng Haiqing. For instance, his speech on January 21, 1969, to an audience of ten thousand in Hohhot conveyed dissent: "In the past twenty and more years, Mao Zedong Thought has been predominant in Inner Mongolia. . . . The broad revolutionary cadres and people of all nationalities love Chairman Mao, love the CCP and the socialist country, and support Mao Zedong Thought. Therefore, more than 95 percent of cadres and the masses are trustworthy. This is the basis for policy making . . . Chairman Mao teaches us: '[We] should rely on evidence, investigation and research, and strictly prohibit forced confessions through torture.'. . . It does not work to use torture to force confessions."[3]

With this statement, Wu Tao finally broke the "one voice" (*Teng Wu*) status quo after the fall of Gao Jinming. Although this failed to dampen Teng Haiqing's insistence on deepening the *wasu*, it at least established a compelling alternative to Teng's reading of Inner Mongolian political history. Bayantai described Wu Tao's speech as "the most magnificent page of Wu Tao in the ten-year Cultural Revolution. Wu himself was in danger. All of his close associates had already fallen. He had little time left, so he threw caution to the winds and made his last shout."[4]

Teng Haiqing turned on Wu Tao at a February 4, 1969, meeting with the leaders of the CCRG, including Zhou Enlai, Chen Boda, Kang Sheng, Jiang Qing, and other Central leaders.[5] The Central leadership affirmed Inner Mongolia's "great accomplishments" while issuing six points of attention:

1. The Inner Mongolia situation is good;
2. It is inevitable that a few bad elements have sneaked into our revolutionary committees after their establishment. You should handle it carefully;
3. The Neirendang is a counterrevolutionary organization. We have to destroy its organization and discredit it politically;
4. The issue of Neirendang members in the PLA is serious, and we should pay attention to it. Army cadres must be reshuffled, and the army must be securely in our hands;
5. Gao Jinming's mistakes are very serious, and he has to receive a good check;
6. We should promote some workers, poor and lower middle peasants, and herders to the revolutionary committees, including training young cadres from minority nationalities.[6]

Encouraged by the Center's support, Teng Haiqing reportedly said, "Wu Tao is no longer reliable, he is a member of the Ulanhu anti-Party clique."[7] Zhou Enlai, however, was determined to protect Wu, whom he had personally rehabilitated in the April 13, 1967, verdict on Inner Mongolia. This time, Zhou observed, "Some people still gather materials to attack Comrade Wu Tao, calling Comrade Wu Tao an Ulanhu element, a 'Neirendang,' and demanding that the Center annul Wu Tao's status as a delegate to the Ninth Congress. This is wrong."[8]

Teng nevertheless determined to proceed against him.

Ma Dianyuan, one of Teng's Neirendang hunters in the Political Department of the Inner Mongolia Military District, tortured two Mongol military cadres to implicate Wu Tao as a Neirendang member. One, Saish, a Mongol

officer at the Propaganda Department, later described how he was tortured
to expose Wu:

> I entered the study class on November 13 last year [1968] and was isolated on
> November 28. There were four people in charge of my special case: two from
> the Propaganda Department, and two assigned from the field army. The team
> leader was Zhong of the Propaganda Department, who was the department's
> "real revolutionary." . . .
>
> After being forced to admit that I was a Neirendang member, from De-
> cember 11, they demanded that I tell them my position in the Neirendang and
> expose political commissar Wu. . . .
>
> On the morning of the 12th [of December], Zhong ordered that I expose
> political commissar Wu's problems . . . At the time, I confessed that Wu was
> the key to reversing the verdict on Ulanhu. When I confessed, Tong recorded
> in earnest. . . .
>
> On December 16, Tong came to find me again, saying, "When the tree
> falls, the monkeys flee. Do you say that the tree of the Neirendang in the Mili-
> tary District has fallen?" I said, "Yes, the Neirendang chief in the Military
> District is Buyanjab; he was ferreted out in December 1967." Tong said, "Is
> Bu[yanjab] the tree? Does he have such great capacity? Why didn't the mon-
> keys disperse after the fall of Bu? You must say who the tree is." . . . Tong said,
> "Speak out. First, we will not cap you; second, we will be responsible for your
> personal safety." I said, "The tree of the Neirendang in the Military District is
> Wu Tao." . . .
>
> On April 1, the "Ninth Congress" convened . . . I then fabricated that Wu
> Tao was the main member of the coup leadership team of the Inner Mongolia
> Autonomous Region, and the military team leader of the coup organization.
> After this, Tong said, "This is still not enough, you must confess the details
> of the process of planning the coup. Only that will show that you have really
> broken with him."[9]

Saish's account vividly conveys the combination of torture and incentives
that forced confessions. Teng had fabricated "evidence" about Wu Tao, including the forced confession from Saish, and had repeatedly asked the Center in Beijing to eliminate Wu Tao from the Inner Mongolia power center. But
Zhou Enlai and other central leaders continued to recognize Wu's symbolic
ethnic value for the *wasu* campaign and blocked Teng's moves to unseat him
in the runup to the Ninth Party Congress of April 1969.

Throughout Inner Mongolia, hundreds of thousands of people, the overwhelming majority of them Mongols, were arrested in the late 1968 sweep.
This pogrom was by far the largest crackdown and mass detention of an ethnic minority carried out anywhere in China during the Cultural Revolution.
It was conducted overwhelmingly by Han in the Mongols' homeland. In con-

trast to the earlier Red Guard violence and the initial stage of the *wasu* campaign, the organized violence and ruthless efficiency of the state and military were directly brought to bear against a single virtually defenseless minority group. Tens of thousands of Mongols—political and military cadres, but also ordinary workers, peasants, and herders—were tortured to force confessions and to disclose other "coconspirators." Some died under torture. Many more eventually told their torturers whatever they wanted to hear, anything to stop the torture. The list of "coconspirators" grew. The net inexorably widened. So did the number of those who took their own lives to end the torture. By late 1968, in Inner Mongolia, violence driven by the Party-state and army organized through the new revolutionary committees at all levels, spun out of control, extending across the countryside targeting areas with predominantly Mongol populations.

A Matter of Torture

On January 1, 1969, the *People's Daily*, *PLA Daily*, and *Red Flag* published a joint editorial, "Using Mao Zedong Thought to Command Everything," which sought to reduce the disruption of class struggle. It carried Mao's newest directive: "In cleansing class ranks, first act quickly, second pay attention to policy." It also emphasized: "In treating reactionaries and people who made mistakes, we must pay attention to policy; the scope of attack should be narrow and the scope of education should be broad. We must emphasize evidence, emphasize investigation, while the use of extorted confession as evidence must be prohibited." By this time, Mao's directives had lost their power; local leaders frequently ignored them even while quoting his words. Certainly, Teng Haiqing did in this instance.

In early January, the Beijing Military Region reportedly informed Teng Haiqing that the slogan "encircling and suppressing the Neirendang" was wrong and forcing Neirendang members to register within a limited period of time was inappropriate. This directive was verbally transmitted by lower officials by telephone, so Teng simply ignored it and carried on as usual. This was the earliest notice from Beijing warning that Inner Mongolia had gone too far in *wasu* and the anti–New Neirendang campaigns.

In every village, school, factory, and agency, meetings continued where people were forced to admit that they were Neirendang members. My father's unit, the Hohhot Transportation Company, with five hundred trucks and one thousand drivers, had only ten Mongols. It didn't matter. There could be no stopping until every alleged conspirator had been rooted out. He told me that a typical meeting went like this:

The *Wasu* Office director had a piece of paper with new victims' names inscribed. "We already have information on Neirendang elements. You must confess. Today is the last chance." Then activists and those who had already confessed pressured others to confess.

"You have ten minutes to confess. Nine, eight, seven. . . . three. . . ."

As the director walked around, people trembled.

"Time's up."

Those whose names were on the list were surrounded by militia members. Four militia men would drag one victim by the collar or the hair to the platform. They were beaten and forced to bow. Around their necks was a sign: "New Neirendang Element," or "XXX Class Enemy."

"Look at their ugly faces. These are the hidden elements. Like Khrushchev time bombs beneath our beds. Today we succeeded in digging them up," the *wasu* director announced in a loud voice.

"Down with XXX! If the enemies won't surrender, we'll dig them out," the participants of the meeting shouted.

After the meeting, the victims' arms were locked behind their backs and the torture began.

These attacks lasted from the winter of 1968 to the spring of 1969. Under psychological and physical torture, some victims died without medical attention while others committed suicide in detention or after going home.

Hohhot's No. 2 Wool Textile Factory was renowned for producing high-quality material for cadre uniforms. Women workers, who arrived in 1958 from Shandong, Henan, and Hebei after receiving a year of training at the Qinghe Wool Textile Factory in Beijing, comprised roughly one-third of the workers. Later, younger Mongols from the grasslands were added. Ulanhu had long dreamed of building up a Mongol working class. He recruited young Mongol women who knew both Mongolian and Chinese, sent them to Qinghe for training, then brought them back to the No. 2 factory. All the machinery and technology came from the Soviet Union.

The campaign set about digging up Neirendang members from the ranks of Mongol women workers. I knew one of these women well. Her name was Sechen. Her younger brother, Chöji Jalsan, was a close friend, a rebel from the math department at Teachers' College. Another sister, Narangoa, also my good friend, was an immunology researcher in Hulunbuir league. An elder brother, Ölji, was a doctor in the Hohhot New Town Hospital.

Their father, a Japanese-educated intellectual in Jaraid banner in Hulunbuir, was a landlord and a banner magistrate during the Manchukuo era. He was beaten to death in 1947 in a land reform struggle meeting when Lin Biao's army arrived.

FIGURE 19 Cheng Tiejun's Mongolian friends Sechen (left in front row), Narangoa (right in front row), Ölji (left in back row), Chöji Jalsan (right in front row), in Hohhot, summer 1970, after their rehabilitation

One night, Sechen called from the factory on a public phone asking to meet me. We met in the woods north of Inner Mongolia University. It was nine at night. Seeing her dressed in her best woolen clothes, I feared she would commit suicide. She told me that in her factory nearly one hundred people had been locked up, and her elder brother Ölji in Hohhot and elder sister Narangoa in Hulunbuir had been detained as New Neirendang suspects. She feared that she would soon be singled out as a Neirendang element.

Every evening that week meetings were held in the factory and people arrested. Each time, two or three women workers dragged the victim by the hair to the platform to confess their crimes and name coconspirators. Under torture people named others, often randomly, in desperate hopes of stopping the torture.

Tears in her eyes, Sechen told me that she was prepared to be dragged up to the platform as a New Neirendang element. I asked: "When might that happen?"

She stopped crying, replying in a cold but calm voice. "Anytime, tomorrow or the day after tomorrow."

"What might they do to you?"

"Anything, from torture to killing." A bitter smile crossed her face, her eyes, reflecting the moonlight streaming through the black pine branches.

She said that two bodies had been carried away from the detention center the previous week. No one knew whether they were killed or committed suicide.

I tried to comfort Sechen. "This is insane. Try to survive. Don't lose hope. This can't last long."

She cried. "I don't want to survive like an animal. Why not die?"

We talked for about two hours in the forest. "I'll wear my best clothes, so if they beat me to death, at least I will have good fabric to bring to my coffin," she said, tears rolling down her face. I could do nothing but encourage her to be strong and not lose hope.

Two days later she disappeared. I knew that something was wrong when she didn't call. I asked my roommate Sun Panshi and my classmate Zhang Daren to look into the situation through connections in the factory. They learned that five people, including Sechen, had been jailed the previous day. Sechen's brother Chöji Jalsan was teaching in Yekejuu league, so there was no one to help her. We wanted to bring some food to her, thinking that a small gift from friends might encourage her to try to survive.

Zhang Daren found a back door: "Sunday evening, when people are off work, we can go and ask for Luan Zhenping. She has been Sechen's apprentice." Through Luan, we delivered a small package with some cakes and a note: "Small cakes will give you energy. Wear warm clothes in winter and spring will come soon."

There was no news until the end of the *wasu* campaign, when the surviving prisoners were released. Sechen dressed up again and came to the editorial office to visit. She had not yet been rehabilitated.

I asked how much torture she had suffered. She smiled and said, "Just a little," refusing to tell me the details.

That factory had few men, so beatings were less severe than elsewhere. I asked how many had been jailed. When the order from Beijing finally ended the nightmare, about 100 of 1,500 workers had been jailed, among whom 11 died and several dozen were maimed. This tragedy made several of us close friends. Sun Panshi and Sechen, and Zhang Daren and Luan Zhenping, fell in love. After dating for months, both couples married.

Compared with the most horrendous units, this torture seemed almost civilized. There were reportedly homemade detention centers in virtually every department of the Inner Mongolia Military District, and 90 percent of the detainees were Mongol officers.

A few days later after New Year's Day 1969, I happened to meet Gao Shuhua at the northern gate of Teachers' College. He invited me to his home in the dormitory near the college. After being promoted to the IMAR Revolutionary

Committee Standing Committee, he was offered better housing, but he had refused.

I asked about rumors of detention and torture in the Military District. He said, "Tiejun, although I am a member of the Standing Committee with access to confidential documents, those matters circulate only among the core group members. I tried not to believe that physical torture was occurring, at least in the government and PLA system. But unfortunately, I was wrong." He then confided the following:

> Last Sunday, I was invited to a wedding at a friend's home in the Military District Headquarters. Leaving the dormitory at about 11 p.m., I heard sounds of beating, shrieks, and screaming in the neighboring building. My friend explained that the Political Department was extorting confessions by torture from Neirendang suspects. Ma Dianyuan, the rebel leader of the Military District, was in charge.
>
> Instead of going home, I went directly by bike to the Duty Room in the Tengban Office to report the case. An officer dialed Ma Dianyuan's number, but Ma denied any torture. I took the phone and questioned him: "I've just passed your building and heard the screaming with my own ears." Ma then admitted to the beatings, but insisted, "There's nothing wrong with beating a few bad people!" He also ridiculed me saying that I had become so righteous that I now almost stand on the side of enemies.[10]

If serious torture and forced confession like this occurred in Hohhot, right under the nose of Teng Haiqing and his office, conditions were likely far worse in remote rural and pastoral regions. The military adamantly denied torture but never restrained it.

Gao Shuhua had just returned from a trip to Bayannuur league. I asked him about the situation. His answer made my blood run cold. Darijiya, the old prince and League chairman, had died during a public criticism and humiliation meeting in Dengkou county on November 8, 1968.

The news about Ejine banner was even worse. At the start of the Cultural Revolution, the banner had been spared political turmoil because of its location adjacent to the national missile center. But after October 1968, the Center approved the request from Beijing and Lanzhou Military Region to change the original lenient policy to one prioritizing the cleansing of class ranks. A military work team was sent there to reinforce the *wasu* and the campaign to uproot New Neirendang. After detention and torture, most cadres from eastern Inner Mongolia were labeled New Neirendang members, including my friend Mönkh. Even more sinister, they claimed to have discovered a so-called Torghut Party among the local Torghut Mongols. This small tribe, with a population of about two thousand, had hundreds jailed. Nearly two hundred died; many were tortured to death.[11]

Atrocities took place almost everywhere, especially in places having Mongol cadres, teachers, workers, farmers, or herders, many of whom were detained, tortured, killed, or forced to commit suicide.

In the summer of 1968, Li Dechen, director of Tengban, Wang Jinbao, a rebel student from Industrial College, and Liu Wenyan, a faculty member from Teachers' College and an IMAR Revolutionary Committee member, reported on the violence in Yekejuu league after attending a conference in Dongsheng county. They were shocked to see their roommate, a director of a banner armed force, marching with his arms bound, accused of being a New Neirendang member.

To get some relief from the tense atmosphere, they visited the Buddhist temple Wang'aizhao (Mongolian: Vangiin Juu) in Dalad Banner. Whenever people saw their jeep, they fled. Liu Wenyan met a former student who told him that people from the banner often came to the villages to arrest "Neirendang members," and that anyone arrested was taken away by jeep to be beaten by people of the Mass Dictatorship. Seeing the jeep, local people fled.

The three leading members who had been active in promoting the *wasu* had become frightened at what they had unleashed. After returning to Hohhot, they submitted an "urgent report" to Teng Haiqing. The arrests and torture, however, continued, despite the fact that one of the signers was Li Dechen, director of Tengban, Teng's office.[12]

Because the objects of attack were overwhelmingly Mongols, Teng Haiqing brought in Han outsiders to run the campaign in predominantly Mongol rural areas. Traveling groups dispatched to every township explained how to extract confessions: each variety of torture was given a revolutionary, even a poetic, name. In the countryside the method of choice was called warmly helping (*reqing bangzhu*). Rural Mongols heat their homes with animal dung burned in a special stove. Investigators would set up three or four large stoves, burning red-hot, in a single room. The victim would be placed in the midst of the stoves wearing a heavy fur coat and questioned and criticized for hours until a confession was secured. A victim who fell against a stove would be burned severely. Some died. At a certain point, if the victim became weak or lost consciousness, interrogators would pull off the coat and force the victim to kneel outside in the snow without clothes. This too had a name: *lengjing sikao*, meaning "thinking it over while cooling off." Many victims were permanently disabled as a result of the sudden change from intense heat to ice cold.

These exquisitely named tortures derived from the feverish imaginations of sent-down Han youth sent all over the region to secure confessions. Four decades before the tortures designed by US military inquisitors in Iraq and Afghanistan, these Han youth, driven by Teng's *wasu* campaign, were every whit as macabre and inhumane.[13]

Hundreds of thousands of sent-down youth, many coming from Tianjin, Beijing, and other North China cities and regions, were working in the Inner Mongolia Construction Corps, on state farms, in villages, and in animal husbandry production teams. Most were high school graduates who had been sent "Up to the Mountains and Down to the Countryside" (*shangshan xiaxiang*), a movement launched by Mao in December 1968. With universities closed and factories not recruiting new workers, sixteen million urban youth were dispatched to the countryside as the Party and the military began to think about restoring stability, especially to the borderlands, and preparing for war with the Soviet Union.[14]

Inner Mongolia was the most important frontier destination for sent-down youth. Half of the three hundred thousand youths settled in agricultural villages and pastoral production teams. The others joined the Inner Mongolia Production and Construction Corps under the Beijing Military Region, which, in early 1969, took over remote state farms and labor camps.[15] The Construction Corps combined production and semimilitary training under the control of uniformed PLA officers. Knowing nothing about Mongol politics, society or culture, speaking no Mongolian, many deeply prejudiced toward the Mongols, their heads filled with tales of conspiracy and heroism, and eager to prove themselves politically, these young people took charge of cleansing the class ranks in many rural areas.

Bao Qingwu, a journalist at the *Inner Mongolia Daily*, sent a report to the Inner Mongolia Party Committee on July 27, 1978, describing some of the torture conducted during the *wasu* campaign in Yekejuu (Ordos) in southwestern Inner Mongolia:

> Scorch with burning green willow twig: Women herders were stripped naked and then scorched in the bellies and abdomens with burning green willow twigs. The intestines were exposed. Then vaginas and vulvas were destroyed, making them look neither like women nor men.
>
> Lash with wolf-teethed whip: a leather whip was tightly wrapped with nails and iron wire. Each lash bit into the flesh. After twenty lashes, the skin and flesh on the back were stripped away, exposing the bones. Large patches of flesh then rotted and stank.[16]

Yekejuu was among the leagues hardest hit by the campaign, as it is home to the Chinggis Khan shrine, a symbolic center for Mongol nationalism.[17] It had also been the military base for the Neirendang in the late 1920s. Shine

Lama, a rebellious lama who had joined the Neirendang and led its army, became a martyr who inspired Mongols to fight for a Mongol homeland against Han settler land grabbing. During World War II, the region was Ulanhu's operational base against the Japanese. This history made Ordos Mongols particularly vulnerable during the *wasu* campaign. Its people then became victims not only because of a special relationship with Ulanhu but also because many had been old Neirendang members.

After November 1968, when the Inner Mongolian Revolutionary Committee intensified its movement targeting the New Neirendang for destruction, the Yekejuu League Revolutionary Committee set up the No. 2 Special Case Office, in charge of digging out the New Neirendang. The hunt started on December 7, 1968, when numerous Mongol cadres and ordinary people were sent to "study classes" or were subjected to "mass dictatorship." By one estimate, more than 150,000 people were targeted, 21 percent of the entire population of Yekejuu league. Then 1,260 people were killed, 2,322 were maimed, and 5,016 injured.[18] If the 150,000 figure is at all accurate, not only most Mongols but also many Han were targeted. The Mongol population then was a mere 70,000, about 10 percent of the total Yekejuu population. What is certain is that the Mongols bore the brunt, and ordinary herdsmen suffered most.

Tug commune in Ushin banner, an almost purely Mongol commune, was designated the "black lair of the New Neirendang." The local Party, Youth League, militia, poor herders' association, and production teams were all designated New Neirendang organizations. Of the 2,691 people in the commune, 1,200, or 70 percent of the adult population, were accused of being New Neirendang members. Forty-nine were killed, and 270 seriously maimed and disabled. Semchu, the commune Party secretary, had five people in his family. Only a nine-year old daughter who was away survived.[19] The pogrom was conducted by sent-down Han youth in the commune and Han farmers from nearby villages.

The *wasu* campaign in Sönid Right banner, Shiliingol league, a pastoral community, was exemplary. Teng Haiqing promoted it throughout Inner Mongolia with three reports published in the *Inner Mongolia Daily*. Located in central Inner Mongolia, and bordering the MPR, the pastoral area was almost eight thousand square miles, similar in size to Albania, with a population of about one hundred thousand. It was the home banner of Prince Demchugdonrub, the Mongol nationalist leader who led Inner Mongolian autonomy with Japanese support in the 1930s until 1945.

On June 14, 1969, a petition group (*shangfang tuan*) from the banner submitted a "report" to the core group of the Inner Mongolia Revolutionary

Committee stating that more than thirty reactionary organizations had been dug out. Neirendang members accounted for about 14 percent of the total population of the banner. Mongols accounted for about 87 percent of the total number dug up. "If the digging continues, even the cattle and sheep would be dug up": "All 'study classes' or 'workshops' are equipped with cells, interrogation rooms, which are actually confession rooms. More than one hundred methods have been applied for interrogation, such as 'pressing by thick stick,' 'electric chair,' 'fire cupping,' 'stove burning,' 'hot boiling water,' 'plug-in bamboo sticks,' 'finger clamping,' 'hair hanging,' etc."[20]

The Inner Mongolia Revolutionary Committee received another report concerning tragedies in the banner's Bayanhan commune from the Appeal Group of Bairin Right Banner, Juu'uda League. This pastoral commune had nearly three thousand Mongols, almost half the total population. The report, submitted on June 10, 1969, stated that during the *wasu*, the Mongols were forbidden to speak Mongolian and were subjected to "hanging, beating, pressure by thick stick, tying with thin ropes, squatting on stools, etc., in all about 40 methods." The result was harrowing: "Of the eight Mongols in the fourteen-member Revolutionary Committee, seven were labeled Neirendang members. Among the ninety-five cadres and staff in the commune, forty-eight (52 percent) were dug out as Neirendang. For Mongols, the percentage was 64 percent, for Communist Party members, the percentage was 47 percent. In ten households all family members were labeled Neirendang. Two Communist Party branches were marked as Neirendang branches."[21]

The data reveal some of the "glorious achievements" of Teng Haiqing and the military as well as the role of Han cadres and sent-down youth and a few Mongol cadres and citizens driven by revolutionary zeal, fear, and torture, to wage a pogrom directed overwhelmingly, though not exclusively, at the Mongol population.[22]

"Teng Haiqing, What Do You Really Want to Do?"

The earliest resistance to Teng Haiqing's extreme policy on *wasu* and the anti-Neirendang campaign again came from Teachers' College. This time it was not initiated by the faculty in our Foreign Languages Department, but by Qin Weixian, a former cadre in the Political Office, who became deputy chair of the newly established revolutionary committee of the college and was a standing committee member of the rebel organization Dongzong. Qin, a Han, was also a member of the Inner Mongolia Revolutionary Committee. In March 1969, after a quarrel with Teng Haiqing, Qin openly challenged Teng's extreme policy by organizing his own group, Jiu Wu Liandui (United

Team to Ferret Out Ulanhu). He also organized the rescue of detained Mongol PLA officers and soldiers in the Cavalry Fifth Division stationed in Jining, Ulaanchab league.[23] The newly freed PLA soldiers escaped to Beijing, together with family members and relatives. Carrying papers and evidence of torture, they sought justice from the Center. Stories circulated that some of them bared their chests, thrusting Mao badges into their bloody flesh to display loyalty to the great leader. Of course, no media reported on their action.

Three months had passed since Zhao Zongzhi and I were called back from Baotou to the *Inner Mongolia Daily* to criticize Gao Jinming and his "rightist opportunism." After witnessing so many tragedies, however, far from wishing to join in criticizing Gao Jinming, we both wanted to criticize Teng Haiqing's leftist adventurism and Great Han Chauvinism. I discussed the possibility of writing a poster with Zhao, but he seemed preoccupied with dating his girlfriend. Under the intense political pressure of the time, it was necessary to proceed with caution because of the great trouble that a poster or protest could cause. My old friend Zhang Peiren fully supported my idea of criticizing Teng Haiqing and was willing to share the risk. "We have been labeled as reactionaries many times already, so who cares about one more time?" After all we were rebels.

We decided on the title "Teng Haiqing, What Do You Really Want to Do?" to catch people's eyes. The title was borrowed from the big-character poster that had touched things off at Teachers' College in 1966. After discussing the outline, Peiren suggested that I write the first draft, and he would refine it. He also asked me to collect at least three or four signatures to increase the impact.

While my roommate Sun Panshi worked the night shift, I completed the draft on February 23, 1969. Showing Panshi my draft, I feared that he might be frightened by my bold plan. In my eyes, he was somewhat self-centered. Being the only boy at home, his parents had greatly spoiled him.

To my surprise, Panshi was completely supportive. "Fuck Teng Haiqing!" he said angrily. "He discriminates against us rebels and Mongols too much. We should have taught him a lesson long ago. I fully support what you said. Have you discussed this with Peiren? Great, I'll also sign my name. You know, Zhang Daren has returned to Hohhot. Why not ask him to join us?"

I knew that Panshi's determination on this matter was closely related to his personal feelings toward Sechen. He had been falling in love with her all the more deeply since she was locked up.

Zhang Daren was easily convinced to join us. When we lived and worked together at the Baotou Electric Machinery Plant, we often cursed Teng Haiqing. So, after a few meetings, we polished the language and signed our names.

Our poster started with the standard practice of quoting a Mao epigraph: "To whom should the fruits of victory in the War of Resistance belong? It is very obvious. Take a peach tree for example. When the tree yields peaches, they are the fruits of victory. Who is entitled to pick the peaches? Ask who planted and watered the tree. Chiang Kai-shek squatting on the mountain did not carry a single bucket of water, yet he is now stretching his arm from afar to pick the peaches."[24]

Taken from Mao's speech delivered at a 1945 cadre meeting in Yan'an, "The Situation and Our Policy after the Victory in the War of Resistance against Japan," it not only added eloquence but also lent unimpeachable authority to what followed. We wrote of Teng Haiqing as an outsider who made no contribution to the rebel victory marked by the April 13 decision in 1967. We charged that, although we had trusted him initially, as he had been sent by Chairman Mao and the Center, he "disappointed the Inner Mongolian people of all nationalities, failing to live up to the trust of the Center." We continued:

> After collecting all important policy-making powers in his hands, Teng Haiqing first dismantled the rebel organizations and their publications, calling on loyalists to take revenge on the rebels. Teng then forced leading rebel members of the Inner Mongolia Revolutionary Committee to step down, either marginalizing them or driving them out of power, without legal procedures approved by the Center. Comrades Gao Jinming, Quan Xingyuan, Li Zhi, Gao Zenggui, Yang Hongwen, Tegusi, Wang Zaitian, and many others, were forced to stop work. In recent days, it is said that even Comrade Wu Tao, the only remaining Mongol in a leading position in Inner Mongolia, has become a New Neirendang suspect. Teng Haiqing should be held responsible for destroying the Inner Mongolia Revolutionary Committee. In Teng Haiqing's mind, few if any local revolutionary cadres are worthy of trust. He trusts only his secretaries and a few military personnel in his office.

We went on to criticize Teng's ignorance of the history of Inner Mongolia and the Party's correct policy on nationalities in his *wasu* campaign to uproot the alleged New Neirendang. Citing the atrocities he had committed as a result of extreme leftist adventurism, we concluded, "You are responsible for destroying nationality unity and harmony in Inner Mongolia."

We urged the Central leadership to dispatch a Central inspection delegation to Inner Mongolia to investigate and halt Teng's torture-driven *wasu* campaign. We also urged the Center to issue a document to correct the errors of anti–New Neirendang activists "who have committed crimes by obtaining confession through force responsible for causing deaths and disabilities. After the campaign ends, those criminals should be tried in court. In our opinion, only such a serious Central document or administrative order may be strong

FIGURE 20 Gao Shuhua (second right in back row) with the Inner Mongolian delegation before departure for Beijing to attend the Ninth Party Congress, March 1969

enough to stop the out-of-control anti–New Neirendang campaign and prevent Inner Mongolia from falling beyond redemption."

After completing the poster, we discussed where to post it, what size paper to use, and how big the characters should be. My first plan was to place it on the bulletin board at the entrance of the dining hall of the *Daily*, where all staff members, including military personnel, would immediately see it.

But Sun Panshi had a better idea: "Let's post it on the much larger board at the entrance to the *Daily* compound facing New China Boulevard where many more people will see it." The board was fifteen by eighteen feet.

At that time, representatives to the Inner Mongolia delegation to the Ninth Party Congress in Beijing were staying at the New Town Guesthouse for a month-long training session in preparation for the congress. Gao Shuhua was among them. We all agreed that the delegates would not miss the board, which was not far from the guesthouse.

I immediately sat down to copy the poster on papers, each piece the size of a fully opened newspaper. I had studied traditional painting and calligraphy from middle school and big-character poster writing during the Cultural Revolution. But this poster was special, not only because of its higher risk but also because the large size required use of an extra-large brush to copy the text.

By 11 p.m., I had finished twenty-five pages. I hoped to complete it the next morning and mount it on the big board that afternoon.

By morning I had almost completed all forty-two pages. After lunch, Zhang Peiren and Zhang Daren rushed into our dormitory room. Peiren, his face pale, said in a low voice: "Guys, hold everything, don't write anymore! A disaster is imminent!"

"Why?" Panshi and I asked with one voice, "What's happening?"

"Gao Shuhua asks us to stop immediately. This would give Teng Haiqing a pretext to arrest all of us and to label our poster as a counterrevolutionary act," Daren said.

He had seen Gao Shuhua that morning and told him about our poster. I stopped my brush reluctantly, and we discussed why Gao Shuhua, the author of the first big-character poster at Teachers' College, wanted to stop us. We agreed that this was a sensitive time with the Party's Ninth Congress imminent, and recognized that if we attacked Teng Haiqing, it would have serious political consequences for Gao Shuhua because of our close association with him. His political opponents, such as Hao Guangde, would definitely consider this firm proof that Gao was Ulanhu's agent. Hao Guangde, who was unhappy about not being selected as a Party representative for the congress, might use this to undermine Gao Shuhua's delegate status.

Peiren recalled that Gao Shuhua planned to report on the Inner Mongolia situation directly to Zhou Enlai and other central leaders on behalf of the rebels. My spirit lit up at this. Why not ask Gao Shuhua to pass the information in our poster to Premier Zhou? All agreed.

We decided to drop our big-character poster, rewriting it on letter-size paper and asking Gao Shuhua to submit it to the Central leadership. The following Sunday, Peiren and I met at his home. Dressed in a new PLA uniform, Gao appeared in high spirits. When we told him that we had agreed to give up the poster, he smiled and said: "That's great! I can now sleep peacefully. You know I am one hundred percent supportive of your opinion but putting up a poster at this moment would be regarded as challenging the Revolutionary Committee and would precipitate a crackdown."

I asked him, "Would you be willing to pass it on to the Center through Premier Zhou or his secretary?" I took out the ten-page document from my bag and handed it to him.

After quickly glancing over the pages, the smile disappeared from his face and his voice became serious: "Comrade Li Shude has announced the discipline for the delegates, one of which is that we are not allowed to pass any information to the Center without the approval of the Inner Mongolia Revolutionary Committee leadership. If I were to do this, I would have to submit the text to Li Shude and Teng Haiqing for approval first. But suppose we try this: I will pretend not to know of the existence of this text. It could be something inserted by one or another student. When we arrive in Beijing, I will assess the situation and decide when and how to pass it on to higher levels. Would that be OK?"

We could only reluctantly agree and thank him for his suggestion.

Returning to our dormitory at the *Daily*, I couldn't sleep. The aborted poster still weighed heavily on me. My original purpose was not to submit a memorial to the throne but to issue a warning to the *wasu* activists and to let people know that not everyone supported Teng Haiqing's disastrous policy. I also could not rule out the possibility that the Center was clearly aware of what was going on in Inner Mongolia and allowed, even connived, in it. Viewed from this angle, our poster idea was a failure.

Of course, from the perspective of personal safety, Gao Shuhua's suggestion provided relief for all four of us. When my girlfriend Qingxian learned that we had given up our poster plan, she responded, "You should thank Gao Shuhua, not feel disappointed. He has helped you greatly. I don't want to see you behind bars and tortured. Now, I'll be able to sleep better," she said.

Suddenly it was March. It was turning warmer, and light green started to cloak the willow trees in front of New China Boulevard. Zongzhi and I decided to return to our factory in Baotou.

"Inner Mongolia Has Gone Too Far"

The thirty-six-member Inner Mongolia delegation, with Teng Haiqing, Wu Tao, and Li Shude departing ahead of it, arrived in Beijing for the Ninth Party Congress in late March 1969. If Mao's revolutionary line had decisively defeated the so-called revisionist line of Liu Shaoqi and Deng Xiaoping, what would be the next step in China's "continuous revolution"? For the Inner Mongolian people, the overriding preoccupation of both Han and Mongols, activists and victims alike, was the anti–New Neirendang campaign that was devastating the region.

Returning from Hohhot, Zhao Zongzhi and I resumed our factory jobs. During mealtimes, we often discussed the political situation in Baotou, Hohhot, and Beijing. In addition to concern about the future of China and Inner Mongolia, I was also preoccupied with the fate of our document that Gao Shuhua had promised to submit to Central leaders.

The Ninth Party Congress convened in Beijing from April 1 to 24. From early April, the factory revolutionary committee often called meetings to convey "important Inner Mongolia Revolutionary Committee documents," mainly the messages sent back from Beijing by "Chiefs Teng & Wu" (Teng Wu Shouzhang). In Beijing, Teng and Wu found that the political winds had shifted and were no longer favorable to *wasu*. From mid-March to early April 1969, Teng and Wu, sometimes with Li Shude, sent letters and telegrams, or made phone calls, to Hohhot every three to five days. A shift was notable with the resumption of power first by Quan Xingyuan in January 1969 and then by Gao Jinming in mid-April during the congress.[25]

The following letter from Teng Haiqing, Wu Tao, and Li Shude to Quan Xingyuan and the Standing Committee, dated April 4, 1969 (three days after the opening of the Congress), illustrates the changes (our clarifications in square brackets):

> Comrade Quan Xingyuan and other standing committee members:
>
> You must be prepared to comfort those good comrades [reference to Gao Jinming and his followers] who have been criticized. Those who have been reviewed and checked [that is, suspected class enemies] should not blame the masses. They should understand the positive achievements of the campaign and mass movement. . . . For some people who stumbled while participating in "the [New] Neirendang" [those who were detained and tortured], the masses' review of them is entirely reasonable. . . .
>
> Today, under Chairman Mao's proletarian line, we liberate them, and they should be devoted to Chairman Mao, be grateful to the revolutionary masses, and should not have any conflict [with their persecutors]. Concerning class enemies who incite riots [alluding to victims who revolt and seek justice], we should never relax vigilance.[26]

Suddenly, it was the *wasu* activists who felt confused: "If the *wasu* is so successful, why stop prematurely?" Their negative reaction and spontaneous resistance to Teng and Wu's new call was logical within the framework of the *wasu* movement.

The ostensible goals of the Ninth Party Congress were to bring the Cultural Revolution to a victorious conclusion and forge reconciliation among antagonists on the basis of new Revolutionary Committee structures that would consolidate the military in its position of primacy and anoint Lin Biao as Mao's successor. Teng Haiqing, learning that a major policy shift would be announced at the congress, was prepared to bring Inner Mongolia's chaotic situation under control to avoid becoming a victim of the Center's latest tack. However, it was too difficult for the speeding anti–New Neirendang express to make a sudden U-turn.

At the Ninth Party Congress, the Inner Mongolia delegates began to face their own problem of *wasu* and New Neirendang. On April 15, 1969, a small-group discussion was held in Beijing's Western Guesthouse (Jingxi Binguan). Kang Sheng attended. Seated next to Gao Shuhua and smoking a Panda brand cigarette, Kang conveyed Mao's supreme directive (*zuigao zhishi*) on Inner Mongolia for the first time: "Inner Mongolia has already gone too far during the cleansing of the class ranks" (*zai qingli jieji duiwu zhong, nei menggu yijing kuoda hua le*).[27]

These restrained words, "gone too far," far from capturing the massive injustices, atrocities, and deaths inflicted on the Mongol people and other victims, nevertheless reverberated throughout Inner Mongolia's supercharged political milieu. Mao's muted signal to slow the campaign created panic among the officials and activists, whose political judgment was keyed to taking their cue from Mao.

After that, Kang Sheng ordered Teng Haiqing, Wu Tao, and Li Shude to conduct self-criticisms. Gao Shuhua recalled that Li Dechen, director of Tengban, who was secretary of the Inner Mongolia team at the congress, immediately changed his attitude toward Teng Haiqing, ridiculing Teng's self-criticism. Disgusted at his quick about-face, Gao Shuhua snapped at him: "Director Li, you've also been active in digging out Neirendang and cleansing Ulanhu!" Li responded, "I've long known that this had gone too far." Gao retorted, "So you knew it before Chairman Mao!" Gao concluded sarcastically, "You would have become a hero now if you had stood up earlier saying no to Teng's mistakes."[28]

Mao's call was not limited to Inner Mongolia. On April 16, Zhou Enlai conveyed Mao's directive to North China delegates from Hebei, Shanxi, Beijing, Tianjin, and the Beijing Military Region.

On April 19, "Self-Criticism from Three Comrades Teng Haiqing, Wu Tao, and Li Shude" was addressed to Mao and the Center in a desperate attempt to mitigate punishment. The self-criticism constituted a U-turn from Teng's earlier position on the *wasu* and on Gao Jinming, who was confirmed as "having been correct in warning against the excesses of the campaign."

Appealing obsequiously to Mao, they wrote: "Our mistakes are concentrated on a single point. That is, in doing everything, we failed to follow Chairman Mao's words, failed to follow Chairman Mao's instructions, and poorly implemented Chairman Mao's most recent instructions on Inner Mongolia. This shows that we have been disloyal (*buzhong*) to Chairman Mao." The self-criticism continued: "By the Fourth Revolutionary Committee meeting [in November 1968], 130,000 people had already been dug out in Inner Mongolia; at that time, it was discovered that some work units had engaged in armed struggle and forced confession. . . . From November last year [1968] to March 15 this year, 250,000 more were dug out (including more than 68,400

Neirendang members). Of these, a tiny minority are bad people, but mistakenly many good people, including Mongol cadres and masses, have been deeply hurt, leading to a relatively tense situation in nationality relations."

They acknowledged that the majority found to be Neirendang were discovered under torture. In one government study class with fewer than 200 people in Jining city, for instance, 144 Neirendang members were dug out, 80 percent of whom were cadres and Communist Party members who had been born extremely poor. They even reported that 80 percent of Mongol cadres in the IMMD Headquarters, the No. 5 Cavalry Division and No. 2 Independent Division had been labeled "Neirendang."

While glossing over tortures, murders, suicides, and atrocities, the self-criticism detailed specifics of the *wasu* campaign by authorities at the highest levels of army and Party. The chief "mistake" was said to have been Teng Haiqing's taking of a "leftist" position, insisting on opposing "rightism" even after the meeting in early February 1969 with Central leaders in Beijing.[29]

For all these "mistakes," however, on April 25 Teng Haiqing and Wu Tao were elected to membership in the Ninth Central Committee. Teng and his associates were rewarded for their leadership of the *wasu* campaign and their mild self-criticism was accepted. Nothing was said of Teng Haiqing's recent attempts to purge Wu Tao, who was saved yet again by intervention of Zhou Enlai and the CCRG.

The Center's May 22 Verdict on Inner Mongolia

In Beijing, the pressure from the Inner Mongolian victim petitioners grew, forcing the Center to formally address the question of Inner Mongolia. Zhou Enlai, chairing the Central leadership group, on May 13 and May 16 received Inner Mongolia delegates, including four civilian cadres (Gao Jinming, Quan Xingyuan, Li Shude, and Li Zhi) and six military officers (Teng Haiqing, Wu Tao, Xiao Yingtang, He Fengshan, Liu Shuchun, and Li Dechen). On May 16 the meeting continued for twelve hours.[30]

The intensity of the meetings underlined the urgency of the situation in Inner Mongolia. Li Dechen drafted a report titled "Several Opinions on Resolutely Carrying Out the Center's Directive on Current Work in Inner Mongolia" and submitted it to the CCP Central Committee on May 19 in the name of Teng Haiqing, Wu Tao, Gao Jinming, Quan Xingyuan, Li Shude, and Li Zhi. The self-criticism of Teng Haiqing, Wu Tao, and Li Shude accompanied it.

On May 22, the Central Committee briefly commented on the report: "The Central Committee agrees with your report, wishing that you hold high the great flag of Mao Zedong Thought, carry on the spirit of the Ninth Party

Congress, unite to face common enemies, quickly correct the excesses in previous work, correctly handle two contradictions with different characteristics, stabilize the situation in Inner Mongolia, summarize lessons, implement policies, and work toward greater victories."

Three documents (a six-person report, a three-person self-criticism, and the Center's brief comment) were issued as a package as CCP Central Committee Document (69) 24 for implementation. Lest there be any doubt, Mao added his personal "Act Accordingly" (*Zhaoban*) imprimatur. The instruction, distributed nationwide, became known as Mao's "May 22 Directive."[31]

The report by the core leadership of the Inner Mongolia Revolutionary Committee affirmed Teng's "contributions": "Comrade Teng Haiqing has been closely following Chairman Mao's great strategic plan since arriving in Inner Mongolia in April 1967; he has done a lot of work, making new contributions." His mistake, the report stated, hewing closely to and quoting Mao's mild criticism, lay in his failure to heed the Center's warning about excesses in the cleansing of class ranks after November 1968: "During the cleansing of class ranks, he exaggerated Ulanhu's influence in Inner Mongolia, overestimating the enemy's situation, and, especially in the work against the Neirendang, he made serious mistakes of obtaining confessions by compulsion and giving them credence, as well as enlarging the scope of the campaign."

The report criticized the core group of the Inner Mongolia Revolutionary Committee for dragging the PLA into this morass, destabilizing its internal unity and stability, leading "some comrades to make certain mistakes in their work," emphasizing learning from the PLA so as to consolidate the unity between army and government, and between army and people.

Glossing over the systematic torture and killing by the Party over the preceding year, the report blandly and with exquisite understatement called for interethnic unity based on rehabilitation of victims who had been wronged or injured: "During the cleansing of class ranks in the preceding period, some Mongolian and other minority nationality cadres and masses were mistakenly hurt. They should be resolutely and thoroughly rehabilitated and trusted."

The Center would affirm the essential correctness of Teng's leadership even while mildly criticizing a campaign run amok with tragic consequences for the Mongolian people and the future of interethnic relations. In sum, the *wasu* policy was endorsed in fundamentals while acknowledging "excesses" in implementation.

The Center could not acknowledge that a mistake of line had been committed at the highest level because that line was Mao's, and it was endorsed and implemented by the CCRG under the leadership of Zhou Enlai and Kang Sheng. According to Tumen and Zhu, Teng Haiqing and his fellow leaders left Beijing in a fury on May 21 without notifying the Center. Teng left a self-criticism letter with Zhou Enlai, saying that he had made a "line mistake." The following morning, Zhou scolded Teng through a phone hotline: "I told you not to write about making a line mistake. . . . Don't criticize yourself in this way!"[32]

The timing of the Chinese leaders' change of heart concerning the anti-Mongol pogrom is striking. The Sino-Soviet conflict reached peak intensity in 1968 and 1969, including frequent border clashes. Teng Haiqing was severely criticized for creating an opportunity for the Soviet-MPR camp by creating chaos and division on the sensitive border that was Inner Mongolia. Kang Sheng and Zhou Enlai's order that Teng criticize himself noted that "Inner Mongolia has made such a serious mistake, and many good people among the masses have been hurt. However, none of the masses there fled to Outer Mongolia. Their heart is toward the Chairman [Mao], toward Beijing; they love their motherland, love socialism; this is the advantageous condition whereby you correct your mistakes." In short, the Inner Mongolian authorities were urged to "unite, correct mistakes, sum up experiences and policies, stabilize the situation and confront the enemy together."[33]

Zhou Enlai had praised Mongol loyalty to China in a bid to strengthen that loyalty at a time of international tensions, but in the eyes of the Center, Mongol loyalty did not warrant reversal of the pogrom. Neither then nor later would the perpetrators of the Mongolian pogrom, notably Teng Haiqing and ranking leaders of the PLA and the Inner Mongolia Revolutionary Committee who implemented it, but on up to Mao, Zhou Enlai, Lin Biao, and the Central Cultural Revolution Group in Beijing, be held accountable for these immense crimes against humanity and the devastating toll in human lives leaving devastated Han-minority relations in Inner Mongolia and beyond.

The Center's May 22 Directive on Inner Mongolia sent ambiguous signals to both assailants and victims in the Autonomous Region. There would be no blanket rehabilitation since the leadership asserted that the line had always been correct: the Neirendang not only existed but also continued to threaten national unity at a time of Sino-Soviet ideological and geopolitical conflict. The document neither ended the virulent conflicts in Inner Mongolia nor brought succor to hundreds of thousands of brutalized victims, including those who had lost their lives, and the families of victims. Inevitably, new factional divisions and power struggles erupted. Chaos reigned throughout Inner Mongolia as authorities under the leadership of Teng Haiqing continued to persecute victims.

Inner Mongolia under Martial Law

Criticizing Teng Haiqing

Mao's supreme edict on curbing the *wasu* and anti–New Neirendang campaigns had the effect of transforming the victims' resistance from scattered small fires into a blazing prairie fire. As *wasu* activists beat a hasty retreat, hundreds of thousands of released victims, and in many cases family members, rushed into Hohhot, and some moved on to Beijing, appealing for justice.

Following the Ninth Party Congress in April 1969, the Inner Mongolia delegation returned to Hohhot. When Gao Shuhua led a group of five workers and peasants to Baotou to report on the congress in late May, Zhao Zongzhi and I went to see him at the Kundulun Hotel. Gao was in fine spirits, buoyed by the recent turn of events.

After greeting us, he turned immediately to our poster. He said that he had handed it to Premier Zhou's secretary Zhang Zuowen before the opening of the congress. Zhang was reluctant to accept it at first, but after hearing that it concerned the Neirendang issue, he agreed to deliver it to the premier. Zhang told Gao that Zhou's office had received hundreds of letters and materials on Inner Mongolia in recent months. One letter, drafted in December 1968 by rebel students in the Jining First Middle School, listed ten problems with Teng Haiqing's policy on *wasu* and the anti-Neirendang campaign.[1] "The Center has been aware of this problem, and will shortly have some specific solutions," Zhang told Gao.

Gao Shuhua said to us: "Your assessment of Teng Haiqing's leftist adventurism was absolutely correct. Now, Mongol victims have rushed to Hohhot and Beijing demanding punishment for the murderers and rehabilitation for them and their loved ones. Liaison Stations for Criticizing Teng Haiqing (*Piteng lianluozhan*) are mushrooming everywhere. They may soon appear here in Baotou. People are concerned about how to end the disasters created by the anti-Neirendang campaign."

A few days later, Qi Jinglin, a standing committee member of the Baotou Revolutionary Committee, also a Mongol from Yekejuu league who was said to be a direct descendant of Chinggis Khan and had been labeled a Neirendang suspect, raised the question of his purge during the *wasu* campaign. Li Jinbao, another standing committee member and a Teachers' College graduate, also came to our factory. Qi and Li turned to our student group for support since most of us were former Husansi rebels.

After several meetings, we agreed to cooperate in establishing "the General Liaison Station of Baotou East River District for Criticizing Teng Haiqing" (*Baotoushi Donghequ Piteng Lianluo Zongzhan*). We organized more than twenty substations in Baotou, mainly in local middle schools and factories with Neirendang victims.

With the support of the two leading members and former rebels, we were assigned a nice suite on the first floor in the government-run East River Guest House, with three bedrooms, an office and a conference room with two telephones, three mimeograph machines, and a sound truck converted from an old bus. There were five members working full-time, including Zhao Lu, Zhao Zongzhi, and myself.

When Zhao Lu and I reported our plan to the plant's Revolutionary Committee, Director Xu Chunshan supported us: "We should criticize Teng Haiqing for his mistakes. Let us know if you need practical support." Xu ordered the plant's vehicle team to provide gas and maintenance for our sound truck. From June 1, 1969, the station began formal operation.

Zhao Zongzhi and I were responsible for editing and printing leaflets of letters of protest sent from our substations. In addition to broadcasting, we distributed leaflets to pedestrians.

The summer of 1969 may have been the most difficult time of Teng Haiqing's life. With the Center's verdict, he not only had to criticize himself in one mass rally after another throughout Inner Mongolia, facing thousands of angry and aggrieved victims; at night he had to direct the region's crumbling Revolutionary Committee.

While we former rebels mobilized to criticize Teng, *wasu* activists were divided into two factions, the Pi-Teng (criticize Teng Haiqing) faction and the Bao-Teng (protect Teng Haiqing) or May 22 faction, which took its name from the Center's May 22 Directive. The Pi-Teng faction demanded that Gao Jinming replace Teng as representative of the correct revolutionary line, whereas the May 22 faction held that the Neirendang mistake was made collectively. They insisted that, although Teng bore heavy responsibility, other leaders, including Gao Jinming, were not innocent. Simply put, the former favored Gao Jinming, and the latter Teng Haiqing.

From late May 1969, Mongol victims of *wasu* poured into Hohhot seeking justice. Many mass organizations, even government agencies, turned their offices into "Criticize Teng Haiqing Liaison Centers," or "Pi-Teng Stations," demanding that the Center punish Teng and other *wasu* activists and restore Gao Jinming and his supporters' positions to establish order and rehabilitate the victims. Most government departments were paralyzed or totally ceased to function. Teng Haiqing and other standing committee members could not even find a peaceful place to meet.

The main problem viewed from Beijing was how to quickly implement policies to prevent Inner Mongolia from experiencing further chaos. Under the circumstances, no sustained efforts were made to care for and rehabilitate the victims or to reassess their cases. In fact, the *wasu* campaign continued as Teng Haiqing and the military continued to press it. On May 28, 1969, one week after the May 22 Directive, ten New Neirendang members were arrested in Jirim league, and on May 31 a New Neirendang suspect was beaten to death there. The Inner Mongolia Revolutionary Committee sent an investigation team, only to find the telephone lines in the hotel rooms cut. They were watched day and night on orders of Zhao Yuwen, the commander of Jirim League Military Subdistrict, a key *wasu* activist.[2]

Gao Shuhua, with fresh memories of how Gao Jinming, once his close friend and ally, had tried to label him as an Ulanhu black gang element, refused to side with Gao Jinming and join the Pi-Teng faction. Although highly critical of Teng, he did not think Gao Jinming should be exonerated for initiating the anti–New Neirendang movement even though Teng Haiqing had marginalized him for trying to terminate *wasu*. Gao Shuhua ended up joining the May 22 faction.

My work in Baotou's Pi-Teng Station lasted only a few weeks. In mid-June 1969, the *Inner Mongolia Daily* again summoned Zhao Zongzhi and me to return to Hohhot. This time it was to criticize Teng Haiqing. Zhang Peiren had passed our poster draft to Jin Feng, who summoned us to provide information about Teng's manipulation of the newspaper. With Teng Haiqing still in power, on the train to Hohhot we discussed the situation and decided to play it safe: we would publicly discuss only our work at the newspaper, not our private views about the *wasu* and anti–New Neirendang campaigns.

Hohhot was in chaos; so was the *Daily*. Jin Feng asked Zhao Zongzhi and me to investigate and write internal reports on what we observed. Two days after our arrival in Hohhot, on June 18, we attended a Criticize Teng Haiqing assembly in the Railroad Auditorium. As we entered the hall, a young Mongol widow mounted the stage, carrying a baby in her arms, to describe how her husband was beaten to death. Turning to Teng Haiqing she shouted, "Return my husband! Return my boy's father! How malicious you are! . . . . How can we survive as widow and orphan?" When the infant began to cry, she tried to hand him to the embarrassed general: "This man killed your father. Go ahead, ask him for your father!"

Above the platform, a big white banner hung from the ceiling: "Implement Chairman Mao's May 22 Directive; Criticize Teng Haiqing's Errors of Going too Far." After several victims spoke, Teng Haiqing began his self-criticism: "It is correct for Comrades Gao Jinming, Qin Weixian, and others to criticize my mistakes on Neirendang. Even I do not know where the New Neirendang is to be found, and what the evidence is." Hearing this, the audience exploded in fury, and many tried to jump onto the platform. A woman with disheveled hair rushed at Teng and boxed his ear. Teng was quickly protected by staff members of the railroad Pi-Teng Station.

Mongol Victims Seek Justice

For all its limitations, the Center's May 22 Directive, particularly Mao's endorsement of it, sparked a ray of hope in victims that wrongs would be righted and justice done. Once it became clear that their tormentors remained in power and their grievances were unaddressed, however, some victims sought personal revenge, directing their fury at Teng Haiqing and his henchmen. Inner Mongolia began to fragment into pro- and anti-Teng camps. The anti-Teng camp consisted primarily of Mongol victims of the *wasu* witch hunt, while the pro-Teng camp centered on Han military and civilian followers, who saw this as the best hope for maintaining their personal power and defending themselves against reprisals from Mongol and other victims. This division, as well as the earlier division between Pi-Teng and May 22 factions and the Center's continued support for Teng despite criticisms of his policies, left rehabilitation an empty promise. Violence and confrontation continued. Not even Teng was safe from pursuit by victims and their families. For some weeks, Teng changed his residence daily. Once he was discovered and dragged out of an air-raid shelter, but his guards enabled him to elude capture. It was déjà vu of his experience in April 1967 when he first arrived in Hohhot, except this time, he was hounded not by Han soldiers of the Inner Mongolia Military Region but by Mongol victims.

The Mongols were no longer the warriors they had once been, whether as world conquerors in the thirteenth century or as a military force supporting the Qing dynasty in the seventeenth through nineteenth centuries. Not even as forces fighting for autonomy in the 1920s and 1930s or supporting the CCP in the Chinese Civil War in the late 1940s.

Even when subjected to brutal and degrading torture, the evidence suggests that Mongols made no attempt to escape to the MPR, as Zhou Enlai concluded. According to Bayantai, between 1964 and 1974, 25 people escaped from Darhan-Muumingan banner to the MPR, not a single one of them Mongol. This was remarkable because out of a total of 10,800 Mongols in the banner, 831 were dug out as New Neirendang members and 266 were killed during the *wasu* campaign.[3] Thus, Beijing was the only place they could take their case against out-of-control local officials who were then subject to criticism from the Center. After Mao's supreme directive, no one had the authority or the will to stop victims from pleading their case to Beijing.

Most of the petitioners did not speak Chinese, so translators came from the Central Nationalities Institute. Although the premier did not personally receive them, rumors spread that even Zhou Enlai, on hearing of their stories, cried. Such an image pandered to the popular imagination that only local hooligans were to blame, while Central leaders, notably Mao and Zhou, cared deeply for the pain of minority people. What is certain is that at least since 1966, Zhou Enlai—working with Kang Sheng and other members of the Central Cultural Revolution Group—was the primary Central official monitoring the situation in Inner Mongolia, from his critical role in the Beijing military takeover of Inner Mongolia through support for the *wasu* and the anti–New Neirendang campaigns, to a belated recognition that the mass torture and killing of innocent Mongols threatened the ability to govern.

In the summer of 1969, emboldened by official admission of errors and a halt to the pogrom through the Center's order, a group of fifty Mongol widows (*Wushi guafu shangfangtuan*) appealed to the Inner Mongolia authorities for redress. Each had lost a husband to torture. Traveling from the grasslands of western Inner Mongolia to Hohhot, they demanded that the Inner Mongolia Revolutionary Committee send representatives to the locality to arrest those responsible for the persecution, torture and murder, and rehabilitate their husbands. The two women we saw on June 18, 1969, at the platform in the Railroad Auditorium, one carrying a baby and another trying to attack Teng Haiqing, belonged to this group.

Many arrived in Hohhot with babies in their arms, carrying their meager belongings. They set up stoves on the roadside to cook and slept overnight on the steps of the main government building. At first guards tried to drive them away with bayonets. But they appealed for justice, showing their husbands' bloodstained belongings. They had also brought some torture instruments with them. Showing these instruments, they appealed to all who would listen to them on the streets in the heart of the city. Thousands gathered to hear their story, many cursing Teng Haiqing.

Hohhot residents, who had themselves suffered during the campaign, had no inkling of how much worse the situation was in the countryside. Now they would learn through these vivid personal accounts. Many of the fifty were widows of cadres, and some were themselves cadres, so they could speak Chinese, enabling them to communicate with Hohhot's predominantly Han population.

At this time, Teng Haiqing's office, Tengban, located in Ulanhu's former mansion behind the IMAR Party Headquarters in New Town, was in chaos, fearful both of censure by the Center and of violent revenge by Mongol victims. Teng therefore ordered guards to use restraint and try to mollify the protesters. As soon as the widows discovered that the guards would not shoot or arrest them, they burst through the gate and occupied Tengban. When Zhao Zongzhi and I interviewed them, kids were running around the office and defecating on the carpet. The place was a mess.

Soon after the arrival of the widows, a delegation of one hundred orphans appeared. These children who had lost both parents were organized by a newly formed General Coordination Body to Criticize Teng Haiqing headed by Qin Weixian (a Han from Teachers' College), Jargal (a Mongol from Inner Mongolia University), Wang Jianxi (a Mongol from the Inner Mongolia Labor Union), and Nasanbayar (a Mongol from the Inner Mongolia Revolutionary Committee). They were all former rebel leaders. Some of the victims were very young (five to six), some came with sisters and brothers. Many had traveled by train with no money and no grain coupons. Unlike the Red Guards during the *dachuanlian* of 1966, who had basked in the support of Mao and the army, however, to survive, these children had to beg en route to Hohhot. The coordination offices tried to help the widows and orphans by providing shelter and food. After all, the hotel and guesthouse rooms had been filled, so the Inner Mongolia Revolutionary Committee agreed to open the luxurious New Town Guesthouse to the victims.

We wrote internal reports for the *Daily*, interviewing victims who could speak Chinese. The orphans described their persecution and isolation. When their parents were jailed or killed, many children were left without food or assistance. Schoolmates beat them and cursed their parents. They were forced to wear a patch on their clothes saying *gouzaizi* (son of a bitch), that is, a son of class enemies. Neighbors dared not come to their aid.

The widow's delegation displayed a Mongol-style horse whip with a two-and-a-half-foot-long handle and a raw leather rope, seven feet long. The whip was encrusted with human blood and flesh. People instantly recognized it because the identical whip was displayed in the class struggle museum before the Cultural Revolution. The display explained that owners had used it to beat slaves on the Mongol grasslands before "liberation" in 1949.

"The same whips tortured our husbands who devoted their whole lives to the revolution," three widows told rapt audiences. They showed fingernails torn off by torture and explained that youthful Han torturers pushed sharp knives into the nails until the whole nail was lost.

Teng Haiqing and his followers, aware of the explosiveness of the situation, retreated. They quickly closed all *wasu* offices, and many people who had been prominent in the campaign fled or went underground. Sent-down youth disappeared from the localities where they had committed atrocities, but it was more difficult for local cadres and activists to leave. Eventually, Teng Haiqing transferred hundreds (if not thousands) of PLA officers who had engaged in torture to new positions in Hebei and Shanxi. An estimated eight hundred *wasu* activists among PLA officers were transferred and continued their careers smoothly.

The Inner Mongolia Revolutionary Committee sought to prevent victims from settling scores in a new wave of vengeance. The Revolutionary Committee's directive stated that no files could be opened to the public. The Inner Mongolia Revolutionary Committee and Inner Mongolia Military District jointly issued Document No. (69) 165: "It is essential to thoroughly and completely liberate anyone who was mistakenly labeled as a "Neirendang member" (including a member of other reactionary organizations). According to regulations, the fabricated materials about them must be destroyed."

Urging reason and moderation, it called on people to forget old grievances and look forward to the "bright future." Victims and persecutors were told to unite for a "new Inner Mongolia."[4] But the wounded, the tortured, and the bereaved could not forget the murder, injuries, and degradation that they and their loved ones had suffered. They could not forget that the torturers remained in power while relatives and colleagues, including those who had died or suffered torture, remained condemned as traitors and without restitution of any kind.

The Inner Mongolia Revolutionary Committee proclaimed that all *wasu* files would be burned publicly under police guard. Each unit was ordered to burn all its files. No one was permitted to read or take them. Within about a week, each unit's files were burned. The entire staff witnessed the files taken from the cabinet and burned in front of the *Inner Mongolia Daily* editorial building. Under the eyes of PLA guards with rifles, fifteen sacks of documents were piled high and set ablaze. The Inner Mongolia Revolutionary Committee thus destroyed the crucial evidence of its crimes, depriving victims of future opportunities to seek justice.

Shi Ke and Jin Feng, the military representatives who had run the paper and led the *wasu* campaign there, tried to shake hands with their recent victims. But their gestures were spurned, as in the case of Jargal, the former deputy editor who had been jailed. Among the cultural units directly managed by the Inner Mongolia Revolutionary Committee, the *Inner Mongolia Daily* was one of the units least affected by the *wasu* pogrom. If the antagonism between persecutors and victims was still so deep even at our *Daily* where torture was relatively rare, we can imagine the situation in hard-hit units and places.

Teng Haiqing Retreats

Husansi, Hohhot's preeminent rebel organization in the years 1966 and 1967, was another casualty of the *wasu* campaign. A few of its leaders had risen high, but it ceased to be a force to be reckoned with in Inner Mongolia politics. By the summer of 1968, the Red Guards and other rebel organizations had been disbanded. Most former Red Guards were sent to the countryside while a small number were assigned jobs by the new leadership following the Center's intervention. The few rebels who assumed positions in revolutionary committees were outnumbered and overwhelmed by military officers and former Party and government officials, most of whom had supported the loyalists in earlier struggles. The most prominent Husansi leaders who were co-opted into the Inner Mongolia Revolutionary Committee were Gao Shuhua, Hao Guangde, and Wang Jinbao. All became Standing Committee members under Teng Haiqing, but none was a member of the core group that wielded power. Some activists like myself secured positions in organizations throughout the region as a result of Husansi's 1967 victory. But that victory, far from bringing Husansi to power, simply allowed a few former activists to survive within a politics that Teng Haiqing and the military charted along the path of pogrom at the expense of the Mongol population.

The conflict between Gao Jinming and Teng Haiqing after November 1968 set Husansi on a collision course with Teng and the military. When Gao Jinming was subjected to criticism, many Husansi rebels were attacked as "Little Gao Jinmings." Teng quietly subverted the Center's April 13, 1967, decision that had declared Husansi, Gao Jinming and Quan Xingyuan the victors in their struggle with loyalist Party leaders Wang Yilun and Wang Duo and the generals.

The May 22 Directive, from 1969, which faulted the *wasu* campaign for having gone too far, however, breathed some life into people formerly associated with Husansi and other rebel organizations. Coordination Offices to

Criticize Teng Haiqing cropped up in organizations such as the Inner Mongolia Printing Factory and Inner Mongolia Publishing House. As mentioned, our fifty-two college graduates at the Baotou Electric Machinery Plant also quickly established a Pi-Teng Station. We mounted numerous posters, distributed leaflets, and drove sound trucks denouncing Teng Haiqing's crimes. The rebels' challenge to Teng was based both on a call for sympathy for Mongol victims of the *wasu* campaign and defense of their own revolutionary credentials in having overturned Ulanhu and his loyalist Party successors.

But with the Red Guards disbanded, most rebels dispersed to the countryside, and their former leaders divided into new factions (Hao Guangde, Huo Daoyu, Wang Zhiyou and Nasanbayar as Pi-Teng leaders; Wang Jinbao and Yang Wanxiang as May 22 faction leaders; and Gao Shuhua tilting toward the latter), Husansi could not mount an effective challenge to Teng Haiqing and his military backers.

A forum, signaling a resurgence of rebel activism, was held in Hohhot on June 12, 1969, convened by university-based rebel organizations, the Pi-Teng Station of the Public Security Department, and the Pi-Teng Station of Inner Mongolia government units.[5]

The criticism from the Public Security Department hit Teng hardest. A spokesman mocked the conspiratorial charges made by Teng Haiqing of Case 206 of 1963, the origin of the claim that a New Neirendang posed a direct challenge to national unity. If the New Neirendang had been a secret counterrevolutionary organization, how could it have recruited hundreds of thousands of members from the ranks of PLA soldiers, CCP cadres, workers, and poor herders with no one the wiser? If it were in fact a highly disciplined secret organization based on one-point contact, how could Neirendang members credibly confess to knowing hundreds of party members? He firmly stated, "The New Inner Mongolia People's Revolutionary Party recruited several hundred thousand members, and not a single person split, as if the organization was made of steel; such a claim completely negated the high prestige of Chairman Mao and the strength of the Party's policies, contradicting the law of class struggle and struggle against enemies."[6]

The central question critics asked was whether the so-called New Neirendang existed. If it did, then they demanded that Teng prove it. The editorial note introducing the proceedings commented: "This meeting seized on the key issue of the New Neirendang, and critically analyzed the evidence for the existence of the New Neirendang and its 'offshoot organizations' that had been dug up by Teng Haiqing. They concluded that it was impossible to believe in the existence of a New Neirendang that Teng Haiqing targeted—a gigantic region-wide, international espionage organization with a central committee, grassroots branches and several hundred thousand members."[7]

This verdict was courageous, given the fact that Mao, Zhou, and the Center continued to insist that the New Neirendang existed and commended the "contributions" of Teng Haiqing in exposing it even while criticizing certain "excesses." It was also far-sighted in a double sense: not only did it accurately depict the tragedies that unfolded in the region; it astutely anticipated that the Center, attempting to bring order to the country and being particularly sensitive to border areas like Inner Mongolia, could no longer ignore the mounting voices of critics who exposed the devastating effects of the pogrom on the people.

Teng Haiqing retained his primacy in Inner Mongolia and long refused to make a public self-criticism. His belated apology on June 24, 1969, prompted a rebuke from the Pi-Teng Liaison Station of the whole region that asked fifty questions, demanding clarification and "honest, soul-searching, earnest answers." The rebuke was widely distributed in the *Dongzong* newspaper but ignored in the *Inner Mongolia Daily*.[8]

Inner Mongolia was in virtual anarchy. Every unit had victims, some including once-powerful people. Some surviving victims returned to their posts after rehabilitation. But who was in charge? And what policies would they implement? Some who had pressed the *wasu* campaign had disappeared. But quarrels erupted between victims and their remaining persecutors. Chaos reigned.

I felt strongly that those who had invented stories for personal gain should be punished for their crimes. Those who had refused to obey orders to commit torture or fabricate evidence, and those who doubted and challenged the whole fantastic story of a New Neirendang plot, should be recognized and promoted. But with no official statement from Beijing indicating that the entire New Neirendang story was a hoax and a travesty, and above all with Teng Haiqing still in power, who dared to openly question the policies passed down from the Center? The only powerful pressure that the poor victims could sometimes bring to bear was by appealing their suffering to the public.

Under mounting pressure, in the end, even as strong a warrior as Teng, by then seventy years old, could not withstand the attack. After days of public humiliation and nights of isolation from the majority of standing committee members, Teng lost his previous arrogance and, his face lined, head bald, and back bent, suddenly aged fifteen years. A strange illness started to torment him, later diagnosed as Ménière's disease. In July 1969 he sought medical treatment at the PLA's prestigious 301 Military Hospital in Beijing. Once the Center approved his medical treatment, Teng promptly disappeared, never to return to Inner Mongolia. After being assigned to a marathon Tangshan study class for one and a half years, he resumed his former position as deputy commander of the Beijing Military Region.

The rehabilitation in Inner Mongolia was led by Wu Tao and Gao Jinming, the two most important political survivors. Although both had supported the New Neirendang witch hunt, with Gao having been one of its earliest architects, their victimization by Teng in the later stage of the campaign made them heroes to many. However, Teng's supporters counterattacked, charging that the new leadership had gone too far in rehabilitating victims, tantamount to liberating the black gang of Ulanhu, who continued to be branded the No. 1 enemy of the region. The fallen founder of the Inner Mongolia Autonomous Region, who had been safely hidden away by the Center in Hunan province,[9] continued to loom large in the eyes of many in Inner Mongolia as a sword of Damocles.

The Autonomous Region Dismembered

Like the April Decision of April 13, 1967, by the Center, which plunged Inner Mongolia into turmoil that only military intervention could stop, the Center's May 22 Directive, from 1969, also failed to restore order. Again, the Center intervened. Following the worsening factional struggle throughout Inner Mongolia during Teng Haiqing's absence for medical treatment, the Center ordered one thousand key Inner Mongolian figures from both Pi-Teng and Bao-Teng (or May 22) factions to return to Beijing to participate in a Mao Zedong Thought study class. The class at the Beijing Air Force Institute ran from late July to mid-October.[10]

On July 23, 1969, the Center made a shocking decision in response to the turmoil: it dismembered Inner Mongolia, transferring the three eastern leagues (Hulunbuir, Juu'uda, and Jirim) to, respectively, the three northeastern Chinese provinces of Heilongjiang, Jilin, and Liaoning. In addition, Ejine and Alasha Right banners were transferred to Gansu province, and Alasha Left banner to the Ningxia Hui Autonomous Region. Military affairs in those areas were also transferred to different military regions—Shenyang in the northeast and Lanzhou in the northwest—severed from the Beijing Military Region.

As early as May 1967, the Inner Mongolia Military Region not only lost its status as a "Large Military Region" but was subordinated to the Beijing Military Region. Two years later, in one stroke, the Inner Mongolia Autonomous Region lost more than half its territory, the so-called three eastern leagues and three western banners, and about two-thirds of its population,

MAP 4 Map of China in 1969–1979, with Inner Mongolia in reduced size

while keeping its name. One of the biggest crimes Ulanhu's opponents, both rebels and loyalists, had charged him with was restoration of the historical Mongolian land, changes that adhered to Mao's 1935 promise.

It appears that the Center made but had not yet implemented the decision to dismember Inner Mongolia long before July 1969, as revealed in the minutes of the Central leaders' meeting in Beijing with Teng Haiqing on February 4, 1969:

> Comrade Xie Fuzhi: "Neirendang" are Communists in the open, but in the dark, they are nationalists. They must be destroyed.

> Kang Lao [Kang Sheng]: Even the army has "Neirendang," this question is very serious. Such an army must be reformed. Do you know which army has "Neirendang"?

> Comrade Jiang Qing: Your border defense line is so long, if the cavalry runs everywhere, it would be disastrous.

> Kang Lao: Inner Mongolia stretches like Chile in Latin America. How do you command it when war takes place?
>
> Premier: [We] have already made a decision to carve out the two ends.
>
> Kang Lao: Have [we] already made such a decision? I'm not aware of it.[11]

Clearly the decision rested on a profound distrust of the Mongols, its goal to forestall any threat the Mongols might pose. However, Document No. 206 issued by the Inner Mongolia Revolutionary Committee on August 1, 1969, presented it as something that would also benefit "all nationalities in Inner Mongolia": "This decision is Chairman Mao's great strategic deployment, to strengthen leadership and increase readiness for war in the service of anti-imperialism and anti–New Neirendang, therefore, having great political, military, and economic significance. It is fully consistent with the interests of the people of the whole country and the fundamental interests of all nationalities in Inner Mongolia. We resolutely support this wise decision."[12]

The 1969 territorial dismemberment simultaneously sought to strengthen preparation for war with the Soviet Union and the MPR and end three years of fierce internal turmoil. The immediate political impact of the changes, however, was to recast Han-Mongol relations at the expense of the Mongols. The transfer of eastern and western leagues to four different provinces and an autonomous region meant that grievances in these areas would no longer be addressed in the Mongol homeland. The authorities there had little knowledge of, and less sympathy for, problems that had arisen in Inner Mongolia, above all those with devastating impact on the Mongol population.

The dismemberment of Inner Mongolia would be maintained for a decade. Not until July 1979, three years after the deaths of Mao and Zhou, was Inner Mongolia restored to its original territory of 1969, reuniting the larger part of the Mongol population in a single "autonomous region." But it was a region in which political power remained firmly concentrated in Han hands.

Simultaneous with the dismemberment of Inner Mongolia, the rehabilitation of Mongol victims that had barely begun was denounced, in yet another pendulum shift, as having "gone too far." Victims were warned yet again not to go to Hohhot or to league centers to demand solutions to their cases. Those who were murdered would be treated as "having died while on duty," but they would not be recognized as "martyrs" as demanded by victims' families. Nor would their families receive compensation. Those who had been dispersed to other provinces had no prospect of receiving a hearing.

The scale of the turmoil in Inner Mongolia after partition can be gauged from the frequent meetings between the Central authorities and Inner Mongolia leaders, who were attending a special Mao Zedong Thought study class in Beijing. From August 1 to September 14, 1969, accompanied by Zheng Weishan and Chen Xianrui, commander and political commissar of the Beijing Military Region, most members of the newly elected Politburo, including Zhou Enlai, Chen Boda, Kang Sheng, Jiang Qing, Yao Wenyuan, Huang Yongsheng, Wu Faxian, Qiu Huizuo, Li Zuopeng, Ji Dengkui, and Li Desheng, received Inner Mongolia leaders as many as eight times. The Center prioritized bringing order to Inner Mongolia at a time of continuing military friction on the border.

During the second meeting on August 12, after Zhou Enlai and Kang Sheng's criticism of the Inner Mongolia leadership's mishandling of nationality policies, Zhou mentioned having received two letters from a sent-down Beijing-educated teenager in Shiliingol league. Zhou did not mention the girl's name, but people realized that it was his niece Zhou Bingjian, who had been dispatched to Shine brigade, Yehegol commune, Abaga banner. Zhou said:

> A junior middle school graduate, a teenage girl, was sent to the border region in Shiliingol league. During her time there, the campaign to oppose Gao Jinming and the digging up of the Neirendang had not yet begun.
>
> Later, however, she sent me a letter, saying that there were a dozen households in her production team, all but three of whom were labeled as members of a "Traitor's Party." None of them ran away but continued to work as normal. Some militia members had also been labeled as Neirendang members, but still stood guard. The broad masses in Inner Mongolia are good, most herdsmen are good, the same is also true of the majority of the cadres, and the Mongol-Han relationship! . . .
>
> I received another letter from this girl, saying that, after the 5.22 Directive, local people have been deeply moved and are very supportive. They cheer the great leader Chairman Mao who has liberated them, and the national relationship is now much better. The mistakes of excesses were serious, but there is always a bright side!. . . .
>
> The Han comrades should take the major responsibility for the nationality problem. Because Han are the majority, they are also the majority in the Revolutionary Committee, the Core Group, and the whole of the Inner Mongolia Autonomous Region, therefore, they should be more conscious. . . . Those responsible should apologize to the minority nationality victims.[13]

Zhou Enlai's speech is often quoted to show the importance of Zhou Bingjian's first letter to the Center's decision for stopping the *wasu* and the anti–New Neirendang suppression, thereby saving the Mongolian victims. However, such a claim is not sustainable. Zhou Bingjian's first letter reached Zhou Enlai before October 1, 1968, but Zhou did not publicly mention the letter until the fall of 1969, almost one year later. Zhou had the power to stop the "excesses" of Teng Haiqing's *wasu* campaign in Inner Mongolia. Instead, he merely passed this message to Chen Xianrui, the political commissar of the Beijing Military Region. Chen's office notified Tengban in Hohhot by phone, asking that it prevent torture and excesses. One of Teng Haiqing's secretaries received the phone call, and reportedly tried to pass the message to *wasu* teams in Shiliingol league at the end of 1968, but the message seemed to have been ignored.[14] The "excesses" continued.

Zhou Enlai mentioned his niece's letters at this 1969 meeting not to issue a genuine apology for the atrocity committed against the Mongols but to inform the bickering Inner Mongolia leaders of the looming prospect of war with the Soviet Union and the MPR, and to show that they should be thankful for the fact that, despite the pogrom, the Mongols in the border areas had not lost faith in the CCP and China. He urged them to prioritize preparing for war. But the premier was whistling in the wind. The *wasu* continued.

On September 10, 1969, directed by the Center, the members of the Inner Mongolia class of the Mao Zedong Thought study class at the Beijing Air Force Institute prepared the "Urgent Telegram to the Whole Region's Revolutionary People of Various Nationalities." Issued on October 4, with Mao's imprimatur *Zhaofa* (Distribute as is), it urged people to be alert to the possibility of Soviet-Mongolian invasion and warned of anarchy.

Two points were particularly significant. First was the demand for the immediate dismantling of all coordination offices, fighting corps, and other mass organizations that cut across trades and professions (*kua hangye*). This reflected the Center's concern that rebels who had been dispersed and confined to individual work units might again unite to form alliances to seize power. Second, it endorsed the revolutionary three-in-one combinations that had co-opted rebels into revolutionary committees, a process that subordinated them to the leadership selected by the Center and dominated by Party and army. Reiterating Mao's words, "Revolutionary Committees are good," it rejected "any pretext to storm the Revolutionary Committees, beat up Revolutionary Committee staff, occupy Revolutionary Committee offices, loot, smash, or steal Revolutionary Committee documents, seals, property, and equipment."

The result was to restrict independent protest and resistance or to establish effective channels for airing grievances. The Center, ignoring military and state violence that stemmed directly from Teng Haiqing and the Tengban leadership, continued its efforts to bring a fractious Inner Mongolia under its control by warning of violence on the part of rebels whose only potential strength lay in the ability to join with aggrieved citizens in protest.

The Inner Mongolia leadership remained divided. Wu Tao and Gao Jinming tried to act on Mao's concern about *wasu* excesses to rehabilitate those who had been falsely accused and arrested. But Teng Haiqing (hiding in Beijing) and his military allies, far from initiating rehabilitation, transferred many jailed leaders, including Cholmon, Hao Fan, Chen Bingyu, and other close associates of Ulanhu who had been victims of the *wasu* campaign from Hohhot to labor camps in Yekejuu league under PLA control. In addition, *wasu* activists in the western coal city Wuda in Bayannuur league organized the Protect Teng Haiqing Corps and attacked the Pi-Teng organizations in Hohhot, smashing, and looting their offices, kidnapping their staff members, robbing vehicles, and besieging the Inner Mongolia Revolutionary Committee. They beat Huo Daoyu, deputy chair of the Revolutionary Committee, a rebel leader of the North China Construction, and leading member of the Criticize Teng Haiqing faction. Teng Haiqing remained officially in charge, but from a distance in Beijing, he was unable to overcome the deep divisions that had been exacerbated by the *wasu* campaign and the post-*wasu* mass cleansing.

When the marathon Mao Zedong Thought study class at the Beijing Air Force Institute concluded in mid-October 1969, all were sent back to Inner Mongolia to resume their original jobs. However, from October to December 1969, the situation in Inner Mongolia remained chaotic. Teng Haiqing had lost the ability to rule Inner Mongolia. Gao Jinming's ambitions to replace him focused not on rehabilitating victims and restoring people's trust and social order but on winning support among divided officials and mass organizations.

The Shiguai Coal Mine Strike: "The Biggest Economic Evil Wind"

In the summer of 1969, I received a letter from my friend Ji Kuan, a skilled carpenter working in Pit No. 3 of the Shiguai Coal Mine. He was a country boy who migrated from Xinghe county of Ulaanchab league to Baotou city in 1959, the same year that I arrived in Hohhot. He was a middle school classmate of my friend Zhao Lu, who migrated to Baotou from the same county that year. After we established our Pi-Teng Station in Baotou, Ji Kuan visited, asking us to look into the strike in Shiguai that had shut down the mines. I showed Ji Kuan's letter to Jin Feng, who urged me to investigate: "Go to Shiguai and write an internal report. Although we cannot report the strike publicly, the authorities need timely information."

The next day, I returned to Baotou, and Zhao Lu joined me. Shiguai was fifteen miles northeast of the East River district of Baotou and connected to Baotou by train.

Ji Kuan met us at Shiguai Station the following morning. Wearing a new blue uniform with the Coal Mine's logo, with a short hairstyle and a round smiling face, he looked happy. "Welcome to Shiguai!"

Named for the Mongolian word *shugui*, meaning "forest," Shiguai is Baotou's major supplier of coal and other minerals. More than twelve thousand miners were working three pits, nine thousand of them working underground. Of the workers, 95 percent were Han. Like many small towns in Inner Mongolia, Shiguai was dusty, with only one paved road.

The central square, where the demonstration took place, was about the size of two soccer fields, with the Coal Mine Bureau headquarters (a four-story red-brick building) facing the center of the square. Arriving at 10 a.m., we found thousands of workers and family members gathered under the hot morning sun. Two sound trucks, each with four loudspeakers facing the headquarters, were parked at each end of the square. They blasted: "To rebel is justified. Demand wage justice!" "The working class is the master; supplemental wages must be paid!" "Without paying our blood and sweat money, the strike will never end!" "Those who harm the working class will end badly!" "Down with Liu Shaoqi!" "Down with Ulanhu!" "Down with Teng Haiqing!"

Ji Kuan told us that the miners initiated the strike spontaneously, their numbers gradually growing from dozens to hundreds and eventually thousands of participants. Recently, Yang Xiu and Lü Hua, the two leading members of the Mine's Revolutionary Committee, had begun to support the strikers. Rebel workers patrolled the major facilities and equipment of the mines around the clock, preventing sabotage and attempts to crush the strike.

At the entrance to the office building, I showed my *Daily* ID to the two guards and asked to interview the leading comrades of the Coal Mine Bureau. While one guard went inside to check with the leadership, I asked the other guard what they would do if some workers wanted to continue working. The young man looked at me seriously and said: "Do you mean scabs? So far, we have not seen one. If we do, we'll break his legs!"

The guard returned quickly, inviting us to enter the meeting room on the second floor. Negotiations between the leaders and the workers' representatives were going on. About twenty people were sitting in a circle surrounded by clouds of smoke. Ji Kuan introduced us: Cheng Tiejun as an *Inner Mongolia Daily* reporter and Zhao Lu as director of the Baotou East River Pi-Teng Station. We shook hands with the three leaders, Yang Yongchang, Yang Xiu, and Lü Hua. Yang Yongchang was the director of the Shiguai Coal Mine Bureau Revolutionary Committee. Formerly the political commissar of the Baotou Military Subdistrict, he came to the revolutionary committee as a military representative. Yang Xiu, the deputy director, also a former soldier, had become a thirteenth-level senior cadre. He had been the mine's labor union chair before the Cultural Revolution. Lü Hua, an electrician in his early thirties, was a member of the standing committee of the bureau's revolutionary committee. As the former leader of a rebel organization, he had become the director of the mass dictatorship command office. Although enjoying a high position, as a three-in-one element, his status remained that of a worker.[15]

Yang Xiu said, "Today, we're having an all-day meeting of the bureau leaders and the worker representatives, so, we can only give you thirty minutes." Tall and in his late fifties, he had white hair. Wearing a dark-gray Mao suit, he appeared refined and highly educated.

The origins of the strike, he told us, lay in a 1966 directive by the Coal Ministry in Beijing to increase wages for all coal miners. The directive stipulated a subsidy of 8.15 yuan per month for underground workers and 6.15 yuan for aboveground workers in light of the difficult working conditions, retroactive for the previous thirty-eight months. The directive clearly stated that there would be no subsidy for officials, but Lü Hua (the rebel worker who joined the revolutionary committee) was entitled to the back pay because he retained a worker's status.

However, the Shiguai Coal Mine was a local state-managed enterprise (*difang guoying qiye*). It was not directly controlled by the Ministry of Coal in Beijing, but was managed through the Inner Mongolia Coal Management Bureau. Ulanhu unilaterally decided not to implement the wage hike in light of the difficult financial situation the region faced at the time. Workers and officials, at the point of production, never even learned about the decision.

Three years after Ulanhu's fall, in the summer of 1969, rebel activists discovered the Coal Ministry's 1966 letter in the files of the Inner Mongolia Coal Management Bureau. They branded the decision to deprive the workers of the subsidy one of Ulanhu's towering crimes. When a poster reproduced the letter throughout Inner Mongolia, the Shiguai workers launched a wildcat strike.

Following Yang Xiu's introduction, rebel leader Lü Hua spoke:

Many people think I am the leader of the strike, but in fact I am not. Those black [soot-covered] coal diggers [Chinese, *meiheizi*] initiated the strike spontaneously. After weeks passed when no one paid any attention to their demand, they came to ask my opinion . . . I should stand on the side of the workers, representing their interests, not only because I am a worker myself, but because their demand is just.

Look at the workers in the Wuda Coal Mines. Why don't they demonstrate? It is because their salary has increased since 1966 in accord with the Center's directive. . . . I am trying to persuade Chairman Yang and Deputy Chairman Zhou to support us, but Zhou has still not agreed to do so.

After Lü Hua finished, the worker representatives cheered. Yang Xiu then introduced Political Commissar Yang Yongchang, saying, "As director of our Bureau Revolutionary Committee, he has not yet endorsed the workers' demands."

Yang Yongchang, in his midforties, with a square red face, wearing a green PLA uniform with two red-flag collar badges, then spoke: "I am a simple PLA man, knowing little of policies and theories, just following orders from above. Now, our national economy is facing difficulties. Strikes and requests for salary increase will make things worse. Our working class, and all other comrades, should learn from Comrade Lei Feng and be less concerned about our personal interests. Without an order from above, I will not support this strike. This is a serious evil wind of economism."

"Shut up!" some workers shouted angrily. "You cadres, with high incomes and a better life, know nothing of how hard our life is. The money we are fighting for was earned by our blood and sweat."

It was time for us to leave. Yang Xiu asked everyone to calm down to continue their discussion.

On our way back to Ji Kuan's home he told me that "only a few officials share the view of Commissar Yang Yongchang, but all workers agree with Lü Hua and Yang Xiu."

During lunch at Ji's home, I learned that because of the high incidence of death and injury, no urban woman would marry a miner. Nearly half the miners had married rural women but left them in their native villages. Many others were unable to marry. Public housing was in short supply. Ji Kuan had to wait five years to be assigned his little house. After bringing his rural wife to the mines, he had to buy high-priced grain on the black market because his wife had no urban *hukou* (household registration) that would entitle her to government-subsidized grain. Ji Kuan told us that these harsh conditions led many miners to addictions to drink and gambling.

We learned that smaller strikes had occurred in a few enterprises in Kundulun district and Qingshan district, where most of the arsenal factories were located. There were protests in front of the city government almost every day. Some protesting workers demanded salary increases; others equal treatment for temporary and contract workers; most protesters sought compensation and rehabilitation of the New Neirendang victims.

I submitted my long telegram on the strike to our editorial office in Hohhot and returned to Baotou by train the next day.

In late July 1969, I reported to Jin Feng in Hohhot on my trip to Baotou and Shiguai. It seemed to him that the strike had gone on too long and would cause long-term economic, social, and political damage to Inner Mongolia.

"We have to send more reporters to observe the situation," he said. "I hope that coal production can resume soon. Otherwise, the Center will definitely intervene."

I later learned from Zhao Lu in Baotou and Ji Kuan in Shiguai that in mid-August 1969 the miners had won: 3.5 million yuan owed to them was distributed and work resumed.

However, the Party Center subsequently denounced the Shiguai strike as the "evil wind of economism" that emerged during the early stage of the Cultural Revolution. In December 1966, encouraged by rebellious Red Guards, temporary and contract workers in Shanghai who had the lowest wages and poorest benefits launched strikes demanding job security and equal pay for equal work. They formed their own organizations criticizing class privilege and social injustice under "capitalist roaders." Although initially supported by Jiang Qing, Chen Boda, Kang Sheng, and other members of the Central Cultural Revolution Group, the multiple crises the economy faced at the time of the strike prompted Zhou Enlai to denounce their demands for higher wages as economism.[16] At the beginning of 1967, the Center banned the national organization of temporary and contract laborers as well as national organizations of demobilized soldiers, sent-down educated youths and railroad workers. With major leaders arrested, one of the most powerful and principled challenges to emerge from the working class during the Cultural Revolution was suppressed.

Whether stimulated by the victory of the strikers in the Shiguai Coal Mine or encouraged by the chaotic fighting in some southern Chinese provinces including Hubei, Hunan, Guangxi, and Sichuan, increasing numbers of workers in Inner Mongolia staged actions demanding protection of worker rights. On August 14, 1969, only one week after the Shiguai strike victory, workers in the Baotou Second Machinery Tool Plant (one of the largest antiaircraft artillery manufacturers in China) demonstrated, demanding increased supplementary wages. Encircling the Military Control Commission, workers rushed into the meeting room and beat the military representatives and revolutionary committee members. When the news reached Beijing, the Central leadership criticized the leading cadres of Inner Mongolia in the study class at Beijing Air Force Institute: "You even have problems ensuring payment of the regular salary in Inner Mongolia, let alone increasing the supplementary salary! If you don't implement the Center's 'July 23 Notice' and instead permit economism and anarchy everywhere, if Soviet and Mongolian revisionism advances, you will perish together!"[17]

In response to the growing protests in Inner Mongolia, the Center ordered Teng Haiqing and Wu Tao to organize an emergency telephone conference: "Resolutely Implement the July 23 Notice, Maintain Stability, and Prepare for

War" in the early morning of August 21, in Beijing, where the marathon study class was still going on. Wu Tao criticized the Shiguai strikers: "The demonstrators forced the coal mine leaders to sign a paper, beat and wounded people and forced the withdrawal of 3.5 million yuan from the bank. This is an evil wind of economism. . . . These actions have been criticized by the Central leaders, so we must resolutely deal with them."[18]

The Shiguai strike and the Baotou workers' demonstration were not the only concern on the minds of the leaders. Teng Haiqing warned of growing economic and political chaos:

> Public security organs and military control commissions have lost their way, and don't fulfill their responsibilities . . .
>
> Shiliingol and Bayannuur leagues have made some achievements in confiscating guns, but there are still a lot of herdsmen making appeals in Shiliingol Military Subdistrict. You should mobilize them to go home . . .
>
> What are the Pi-Teng Stations? What are the Warbands of May 22? Why organize Widows Appeal Groups? Those things must be quickly dissolved . . .
>
> There are hundreds of trucks in Shiliingol league, but the roads are not open, and the trucks are not moving. Coal cannot be transported out of Inner Mongolia, and food cannot be brought in.[19]

After completion of the study class at the Beijing Air Force Institute, more than two thousand leading cadres were sent back to Inner Mongolia, charged with maintaining stability, but to little effect.

Martial Law

On December 19, 1969, the Center intervened directly to control a fractious Inner Mongolia. Proclaiming *fenqu quanmian junguan* (zoning and comprehensive martial law), it replaced the Teng leadership with a powerful new military leadership headed by General Zheng Weishan (commander of the Beijing Military Region), a close associate of Lin Biao and Chen Boda, and Zheng's deputy, Du Wenda (deputy commander of the Beijing Military Region). Zheng was not new to Inner Mongolia. In the wake of the May 22, 1967, directive, his army units had moved into Hohhot and controlled railroad, radio stations, newspapers, and public security. Now Zheng strengthened his grip on power as commander of the Beijing Military Region by assuming personal control over the Inner Mongolia Front Line Command Headquarters, subordinating it to the Beijing Military Region (Beijing junqu Neimenggu qianxian zhihui suo, for short, Neimeng qianzhi). A new martial law–run military regime was imposed throughout Inner Mongolia.

Zhang Lu, former Standing Committee member and director of the Office of the Inner Mongolia Revolutionary Committee, illuminated the situation in 1969 thus:

> When the December 19 Order was approved by the Center, Teng Haiqing, Wu Tao, Gao Jinming, Quan Xingyuan, Li Shude, Li Zhi, Lei Daifu, Zhang Ping, and Zhang Lu of the Inner Mongolia Revolutionary Committee, were immediately summoned to Beijing where Zhou Enlai, Kang Sheng and others met them at the Great Hall of the People and announced the imposition of martial law on Inner Mongolia. . . . Afterwards, the Inner Mongolia Revolutionary Committee flew back to Hohhot in the same plane with the leaders of the Front Command Post, Zheng Weishan, Du Wenda, Huang Zhentang, and Zhang Zhengguang.[20]

On December 21, 1969, before taking up his post in Inner Mongolia, Zheng Weishan asked his political boss Chen Boda for instructions. Chen told him: "You are going to the IMAR to implement martial law with the sword of the state in your hand. You are the conquerors, not the winners."[21] Meaning that Zheng was not a local winner in a factional struggle, but the representative of the Center sent to impose order.

Zheng set up military headquarters in the Inner Mongolia Party School in Hohhot. The compound was also the regional headquarters for the militarized production corps of sent-down youth, whose numbers would peak in 1972 at 170,000. In addition to the semimilitary production corps, formal military forces were dispatched from nearby provinces to Inner Mongolia with tanks, artillery, armored vehicles, and other heavy equipment. Four field armies moved into Inner Mongolia within days. The revolutionary committees, military subdistricts (garrisons) of Baotou, Hohhot, and also the leagues of Bayannuur, Shiliingol, Ulaanchab, and Yekejuu were controlled by the Sixty-Third, Sixty-Fifth, Sixty-Ninth, and Twenty-Seventh field armies.[22]

Deputy Commander Cao Buchi and Deputy Commissar Tian Yindong of the Sixty-Third Army were in charge of Baotou city, the Inner Mongolia Railway Bureau, the Wuda and Shiguai coal mines, and the Hexi (River West) Company. Deputy Commander Yu Hongxin of the Sixty-Third Amy and Deputy Commissar Wang Xue of the 187th Division controlled Bayannuur.[23]

The average size of a PLA field army at that time was thirty thousand to fifty thousand men. Thus, a total of 120,000 to 200,000 soldiers were deployed to Inner Mongolia in the name of preparing for war. With the Center preoccupied with the threat of war on the border of Inner Mongolia, MPR, and the Soviet Union, the army moved to take direct control not only of the government but also the Party and local armies. From late December 1969 to early January 1970, the Center ordered most Inner Mongolia cadres (approximately ten thousand) to attend study classes in Tangshan in northern Hebei. Their positions were filled by sent-in cadres from outside Inner Mongolia. The Center simultaneously broke the power of Teng Haiqing and took direct control of Inner Mongolia through the introduction of new military units carrying out martial law.

Martial Law and Marriage

The declaration of martial law, which divided Inner Mongolia along League lines and restricted movement among them, created a marriage crisis among college graduates, especially those who were facing job assignment. People rushed to register marriages in the hope of being assigned to the same locality as their spouse. Zhao Zongzhi and Guo Zhuping, Zhang Daren and Luan Zhenping, Sun Panshi and Sechen—all quickly married.

I, too, married on December 31, 1969. After my marriage, my roommate Sun Panshi temporarily moved back to his home in New Town. With no home, no furniture, not even new clothes, our wedding was a simple one. I wore my Baotou factory uniform and Qingxian's mother gave her a hand sewn flower smock to wear over her old quilted jacket. We invited a dozen close friends from Teachers' College, the Medical College, and the *Inner Mongolia Daily*, to "eat wedding candies" on New Year's Eve. Unfortunately, however, a ferocious wind was blowing and it was bitter cold, with heavy snow, so only ten students and six colleagues were able to join us.

It was January 3, 1970, Sunday, before the snow finally stopped and the sky cleared. My father and stepmother insisted on having a family wedding banquet at home, so we invited six friends. My father provided his best wine. After lunch, the four men continued drinking until early evening.

Liu Dongsheng got drunk as a lord and suddenly yelled: "Damn Lin Biao! Why choose him as Mao's successor? And even write it into the Party's Constitution at the Ninth Party Congress? Maybe it was his idea to put Inner Mongolia under fucking martial law!" Zhang Daren, afraid that neighbors would hear, hastily pushed Dongsheng onto the *kang*, picked up a pillow and pressed his head down, saying: "Drunk, drunk, no longer able to speak human language. Go to sleep!" The incident reflected the growing alienation of many of the young generation at a time of deepening conflict between IMAR and Beijing.

From January 15 to January 31, 1970, Qingxian and I visited my home village in Raoyang county, Hebei. My mother, brother, sister-in-law, and their two-year old daughter were happy about my return with a bride. Our ex-

FIGURE 21 Cheng Tiejun with his fiancée Wang Qingxian, June 17, 1969

tended family and the Cheng lineage held several parties to celebrate our marriage. My mother used her German sewing machine to make a new suit for Qingxian. According to rural custom, a new daughter-in-law had to kowtow to my mother. But Qingxian was an urban educated youth, so mother waived this protocol as one of the four olds.

Returning to Hohhot at the end of January, Qingxian went to Medical College to complete paperwork for her job assignment. That year the Center strictly applied Mao's June 26 Directive, requiring that all medical graduates be sent down to the lowest levels, meaning medical clinics at the township and people's commune level.[24] Not a single doctor could be assigned to county- or higher-level hospitals. Fortunately, she was assigned to Xi'nan Commune Community Hospital in Urad Front banner, Bayannuur league, one hour by bus or train from Baotou city. We traveled to Baotou together and after the Lunar New Year holiday (February 6–8, 1970), she took up her hospital job, and I continued as a lathe operator in the machinery plant.

Revolutionary Justice under Martial Law: Ten Death Sentences

In the early winter of 1970, I visited Hohhot and met Zhai Ximin, my former classmate and colleague during the student Long March, who was teaching English at the No. 3 Railroad Middle School. He angrily told me that the teachers had met that afternoon to study official documents issued by the Inner Mongolia Front Line Command Headquarters. The documents announced the death sentence of ten counterrevolutionary criminals, including Jin Xigu, a teacher in our Foreign Languages Department at Teachers' College; Ye Rong, a rebel temporary worker; Sun Fengcai, a rebel leader in the River West Company; Zhong Lun, a teacher at the Xinhua Primary School; and a husband-wife couple, Fan Yusheng and Lin Xiumei, in the Hohhot Railroad Bureau.

The news was like a thunderclap from a clear sky. Among the ten people, I knew Teacher Jin and Ye Rong; I was also familiar with the story of the couple.

Ximin said: "The public trial is scheduled for tomorrow morning in Xinhua Square. All teachers and students in our school are ordered to attend! The sons of bitches among the military authorities are killing innocents! What fucking crimes did they commit? They are all good people!"

The next day was a bitter cold Sunday. Putting on a fur coat, I stood at the steps of the cinema palace across Xinhua Boulevard from the front entrance of the *Daily*. I wanted to honor my friend Ye Rong and Teacher Jin Xigu, and to see them for the last time. They were highly educated talents who contributed to their country with honesty and hard work. Now their loyalty and honesty were leading to execution!

Following a public trial, a motorcade of ten trucks brought the ten who were sentenced to death to the execution ground in the northern suburb of Hohhot. Around 11:30 a.m., the motorcade slowly passed the cinema palace. Ye Rong was on the first truck surrounded by two armed soldiers. Passing just three yards from me, I saw that his arms were tied. Still, he tried to lift his head and looked around, perhaps hoping to catch a last glimpse of his wife and the two boys.

I got to know Ye Rong and his wife, Qin Ping, during the military and loyalist siege of Teachers' College in spring 1967 in the wake of Han Tong's death. At that time, Ye and many rebels in Hohhot who had been driven out of their units and homes by loyalists sought refuge in Teachers' College. Gao Shuhua, who was a friend of Ye, offered Ye and his family his own dormitory and asked me to bring the family there.

Ye Rong was in his late thirties, slight and in poor health, always wearing a pair of dirty blue work pants and worn leather construction boots. An architecture graduate from Nanjing Industrial College, he had been assigned to the Beijing Institute of Architectural Design in the early 1950s. But during the Anti-Rightist Campaign of 1957, he was exiled to the Inner Mongolia Architectural Design Institute on suspicion that he hid his father's pistol.

His wife, Qin Ping, was an accountant with the Inner Mongolia Song and Dance Troupe. In June 1966, with inside information about sexual scandals involving high leaders with the young singers and dancers in her unit, she provided information for her husband to write posters criticizing Wang Yilun. Both became rebels. Ye was a temporary laborer without a work unit, and Qin had been driven out of her unit. In winter 1969 Ye was arrested for holding a placard asking for a job in front of the headquarters of the Inner Mongolia Revolutionary Committee. A year later, he was executed for that "crime."[25]

Teacher Jin Xigu was on the second truck. Since his imprisonment, his wife and children had refused to visit him. That might be why he did not open his eyes but instead stood erect, his head high. Like Ye Rong, there was no sign of fear on his face.[26]

Teacher Jin Xigu was fifty-one years old, a native of Shanghai and a graduate of Zhendan University (a.k.a. Aurora University, a leading Catholic university in Shanghai from 1903 to 1952). An English major, he later taught himself Russian. In the 1950s, he was promoted to senior interpreter in the Communist Party's Central Bureau of Translating and Editing Marxist-Leninist Works. During the 1957–1958 Anti-Rightist Campaign, however, he was labeled a rightist and sent to Inner Mongolia to teach in the Foreign Languages Department at Teachers' College. Among the faculty in our department, only Teacher Jin was able to teach both English and Russian. His real nightmare started with the *wasu* campaign. Most victims just tried to bear the unbearable insults and attacks, both mental and physical. But he refused to curse himself or to kneel down before Mao's portrait begging for forgiveness. "A gentleman would rather die than suffer humiliation!" (*Shi kesha buke ru*), he said. This forthrightness led him to embark on a path from which there was no exit.

Activists put him under house arrest, then moved him to our student dormitory, taking over my empty bed as his cell. Two student guards often beat him to display their revolutionary credentials. Teacher Jin responded by shouting "reactionary" slogans, such as "Lin Biao is a traitor" (*jianchen*) or "Mao is a fatuous ruler" (*hunjun*). These slogans, reported to higher authorities, accumulated as evidence of his crimes.

One day I returned to the dormitory and found him alone writing self-criticism. I asked why he shouted slogans guaranteed to bring him more trouble.

He said: "Tiejun, the students beat me every day, so I shout those slogans to make my case serious enough for them to hand me over to the police. I think the state has law, and they should treat me according to the law!"

The authorities at Teachers' College finally handed him over to the Inner Mongolia Public Security Bureau in early 1969, and in winter 1970, the military sentenced him to death as part of the One-Strike Three-Anti campaign.[27]

Teacher Jin appealed to "law" for justice. The authorities served him their brand of justice by executing him.

Fan Yusheng was on the third truck, and his wife, Lin Xiumei, on the fourth. Both were in their late thirties. Graduates of Changsha Railroad College, they had come to work as engineers at the Hohhot Railroad Bureau in 1959 after being labeled as rightists for criticizing the Great Leap Forward. During the Cultural Revolution, the couple often discussed issues at home ranging from Mao to Jiang Qing. Unbeknownst to them, the railroad's military authorities were seeking evidence of apostasy in the midst of *wasu*, and they collected it from their two young daughters who had been promised Mao badges and red scarves of Young Pioneers, a huge enticement for kids with rightist parents. The girls' report on their parents' conversations led to the arrest of the couple as "active counterrevolutionaries" in winter 1968 and then to their executions.[28]

The girls were paraded everywhere and hailed as youthful heroines.

Headlines in the *Inner Mongolia Daily* and the *Hohhot Daily* proclaimed: "Two Young Girls Expose Parents' Reactionary Crimes."

I had heard of their stories when the two little girls came to the *Daily* to expose their "reactionary parents" in the winter of 1968 at the beginning of the *wasu*, but I had never seen them. After being jailed for two years, both were pale and gaunt. The parents looked around the street carefully, perhaps hoping to glimpse their beloved daughters.

Not wanting to see the other six convicts on the trucks, I turned and walked away. At home I lay down and cried under my quilt, their faces and stories flashing through my mind.

The Tangshan Study Class

Under martial law, between January 1970 and May 1971, 11,106 Inner Mongolia cadres were detained and dispatched for "rectifying thought and unifying understanding" to various locations in Hebei, Shanxi, and Beijing, collectively known as the Tangshan Study Class. To ensure that the Center kept full control, classes were held outside of Inner Mongolia under the auspices of the Beijing Military Region. Of these, 7,769 cadres were from IMAR-level units, including organization leaders, all dispatched to Tangshan, Hebei. The other 3,337 people from cities and leagues were distributed to Yanggao in Shanxi province, and Chaigoubu, Huolu, and Tangshan in Hebei province. A smaller group of high-ranking cadres was sent to the Beijing Air Force Institute and later to Tangshan.[29]

The main locations were the Tangshan Railroad College and Tangshan Coal Mining College. Its organization and schedule were highly militarized. For instance, Gao Shuhua was registered in the No. 1 Team, No. 3 Company, No. 3 Platoon, No. 13 Class. The company commander and platoon leader were active PLA officers. Everyone, even such senior cadres as Teng Haiqing and Gao Jinming, attended morning drills and lined up to wash, eat, and watch movies.

The authorities imposed militarized discipline with phone calls, visiting and communication in minority languages banned. All letters, including those to and from family members and colleagues, had to be submitted for inspection.

Study materials included Mao's works, official documents from the Center and the IMAR, including the Revolutionary Committee and the Front Command Post, and two booklets prepared by the Study Class leading group: *100 Mistakes Made by Teng Haiqing* and *100 Crimes Committed by Gao Jinming*. The former focused on Teng's excesses in the *wasu* and anti–New Neirendang campaigns, and the latter on Gao's more serious excesses in implementing Mao's May 22 Directive. All members were required to criticize Teng and especially Gao as well as Ulanhu.

The climax of the Tangshan Study Class was the Center's presentation of conclusions about the *wasu* or anti–New Neirendang campaign. These were laid out in speeches by Zhou Enlai, Kang Sheng, Chen Boda, and Huang Yongsheng on behalf of the Central Cultural Revolution Group in Beijing on April 16, 1970. The hourlong reception at the Capital Stadium was attended by twenty-one thousand Mao Zedong Thought study class members from Shanxi, Guizhou, Sichuan, Hubei, Xinjiang, and Inner Mongolia. All these provinces and autonomous regions had fractured as a result of factional infighting, which the Center tried to overcome through sending regional cadres to the study classes. Gao Shuhua recorded the speeches in his notebook:

> Premier Zhou said: "It is more than a year since last April when Chairman Mao called on us to prepare for war. . . . Inner Mongolia is a border region, but it isn't doing a good job as a result of two excesses. It went too far in digging out the Neirendang, but another excess occurred in rectifying deviations, so we had to send PLA troops there. . . . Now the situation in Inner Mongolia is good. Do you say 'Yes' or 'No'? (All reply: 'Yes!')"
>
> Other central leaders said: "Is there a Neirendang? Yes, there is. There are its roots, both old and new, but not that many members . . . The Neirendang maintains contact with Outer Mongolia, therefore it is counterrevolutionary."[30]

Zhou and the Center continued to insist on the existence of an underground Inner Mongolian nationalist party conniving with Outer Mongolia to divide

China. They only regretted that the scope of attack in the *wasu* and anti–New Neirendang campaigns was too large, and too many people were hurt. This was the first excess mentioned by Zhou, who blamed Teng Haiqing for this. The second excess referred to the rehabilitation of victims led by Gao Jinming after Chairman Mao's May 22 Directive in 1969. However, there was a difference between the two excesses or mistakes: Teng Haiqing committed a mistake of degree. By contrast, Gao Jinming's error was a mistake of direction or line, one that could call into question the core policies of Mao, Zhou Enlai, and the Center. The former "leftist mistake" would be lightly punished; the latter "rightist mistake" would incur heavy punishment.

Reeducation in Tangshan involved public humiliation and self-criticism. But unlike the *wasu* campaign, the predominantly Han military and political cadres faced no torture or killing. They were being groomed for return to cadre positions. Although living under virtual prison conditions, they continued to receive their regular salaries throughout. Nevertheless, protracted internment and reeducation led to mental derangement and in some cases suicide. One Baotou veteran cadre, after many interrogations and struggles, was finally "liberated," only to die of a heart attack soon after.[31]

At the end of April 1971, after a year and a half, classes became more relaxed. In May, the leaders outlined the next stage: each participant would write a self-evaluation. After each level, beginning with class and continuing up to platoon and company, had finished collective summary and evaluation of each individual, job assignments would be made.

From early to mid-May 1971, the Center arranged several meetings to receive the Inner Mongolia class. At one meeting attended by Zhou Enlai, Kang Sheng, Jiang Qing, and Wang Hongwen, Kang Sheng repeatedly asked the assembled cadres: "After one and a half years of study, do you still want to petition? Does anyone wish to pass a note to the Center?" Receiving no answer, Kang was satisfied, the Center was satisfied. Mao Zedong Thought had achieved another "great victory." Zhou Enlai even sharpened four pencils himself and passed them to the four former rebel leaders (Gao Shuhua, Hao Guangde, Wang Jinbao, and Nasanbayar) as gifts, encouraging them: "You are still young, you should listen to Chairman Mao and study very hard."[32]

By late May 1971, the class members faced different fates following completion of their study. According to Mao'aohai (or Muunohoi in Mongolian), there were five categories for assignment.[33] Category 1, those having good family background, hewing to Mao Zedong's revolutionary line, and clearly breaking with Ulanhu, were assigned jobs in government agencies, either returning to their original units or transferring to other units with promotion to higher leading positions. None of my friends or colleagues was in this category.

Category 2, those who performed satisfactorily in the study classes, were transferred to other government units in Inner Mongolia at the same administrative level as previously. Gao Shuhua, Hao Guangde, Wang Jinbao, Nasanbayar, and Zhang Peiren were in this category.

Category 3, those who did not perform particularly satisfactorily were sent to lower government agencies, at league or banner levels, as deputy heads. My colleagues at the *Daily*, Li Zhiguo and Zhong Bayuan were in this category.

Category 4, those whose cases remained unresolved, either with historical background to be checked or political attitude to be corrected, were sent to one of the Inner Mongolia May 7 Cadre Schools in Bayannuur league or Tumed Right banner or to other farms and factories for further study and labor reeducation, including further background checks. Category 5, those who were deemed politically unreliable, were sent down to the countryside for labor reform. Mao'aohai alone was in this category.

What about the highest leaders of the Inner Mongolia Revolutionary Committee? Teng Haiqing was dispatched to the Beijing Military Region, where he resumed his previous position as deputy commander. Clearly, he belonged to Mao'aohai's first category. In 1975, he transferred to the Jinan Military Region as deputy commander and retired in 1980.

Gao Jinming was sent to a military farm for labor reform for two more years. Punished for committing a mistake of political line, he belonged to Mao'aohai's fifth category. In the mid-1970s, he was assigned as deputy director of the Luoyang Tractor Plant in Henan Province. He retired from that position in 1978, never returning to Inner Mongolia and never having secured a post of comparable responsibility to his previous leadership position.

Quan Xingyuan was sent to a factory for labor reform, then posted as deputy chair of the Gansu Provincial Revolutionary Committee, retiring in 1980.

The worst fate befell Li Zhi, a standing committee member of the Inner Mongolia Revolutionary Committee. Because Kang Sheng suspected him of having been a Guomindang spy in the 1930s, he remained in the study class for further checks. After years in which nothing was discovered, he was sent to a small factory for labor reform in Fengzhen county, Ulaanchab league, eventually dying there.

Li Shude alone was restored to his position as standing committee member of the IMAR Revolutionary Committee following his release. Chair of a special group in charge of investigating the Neirendang in the IM Revolutionary Committee formed in January 1968, Li was one of Teng Haiqing's staunch supporters in the *wasu*. He died of illness in 1976.

Only one major Inner Mongolia figure was not assigned to the Tangshan Study Class: Wu Tao. He remained in Hohhot as political commissar of the

Inner Mongolia Military District and was later promoted to deputy political commissar of the Beijing Military Region. He died in 1983 at age seventytwo, virtually the lone Mongol elevated to high position during the Cultural Revolution. He enjoyed the patronage of Zhou Enlai and other leaders of the Central Cultural Revolution Group, but he apparently exercised little power throughout his years in Inner Mongolia.

From May 13 to May 18, 1971, a few weeks before the Tangshan Study Class members returned, the Third Party Congress of IMAR was held in Hohhot. You Taizhong, commander of the Twenty-Seventh Army and deputy commander of the Beijing Military Region, was elected first secretary concurrently serving as director of the Revolutionary Committee. In fact, two months earlier, You had become the commander of the Inner Mongolia Front Line Command, replacing Zheng Weishan, who had been purged by Mao in January 1971 to weaken Lin Biao and Chen Boda.[34] You would stay in Inner Mongolia for almost eight years until October 1978, during which time he served also as commander and political commissar of the Inner Mongolia Military District. Among the four secretaries elected were Wu Tao and Zhao Ziyang, the latter a newly rehabilitated cadre transferred from Guangdong province, where he was Party secretary from 1965 to 1967 and in detention until 1971, when Zhou Enlai liberated him and dispatched him to Inner Mongolia.[35] Once again, Wu Tao was the only Mongol in a leadership position in Inner Mongolia until February 1975 when Boroldoi was enlisted to serve until October 1976. Boroldoi was a shepherdess promoted from a model production team in Yekejuu league renowned as "Dazhai in the Pastoral Area." She was first identified by Ulanhu in 1963.

By the time military officers and revolutionary committee members completed reeducation in Tangshan in 1971, their original units had appointed new staff members to replace them. The new appointees, many from other provinces, had long since settled in Inner Mongolia with their families. When the officers and cadres returned to work, the total number of staff doubled. The result was that the call for "simplification of administration" actually produced a large increase in personnel on state payrolls. This process was replicated in the revolutionary committees of many other provinces.

The Impact of Martial Law in Inner Mongolia

On June 6, 1971, the marathon Tangshan Study Class ended. Chartered trains brought the class members back to Inner Mongolia. Martial Law in Inner Mongolia was terminated on January 12, 1972, but the withdrawal of military personnel proceeded slowly, in some areas dragging on to the summer of 1972.[36] In summarizing the impact of martial law in Inner Mongolia, three points stand out. First is the large size and lasting impact of the Tangshan Study Class, attended by more than eleven thousand Inner Mongolian cadres of all nationalities, the majority being Han. Not only would there be no rehabilitation of *wasu* victims, but Zheng Weishan undermined even the minimal reconciliation efforts that the Inner Mongolia Revolutionary Committee had begun after the May 22 Directive. Under Zheng and You Taizhong, the *wasu* campaign, though reduced in scope, continued, and new victims were locked up. For example, Tenghe, the former deputy director of the Inner Mongolia Public Security Bureau, was tortured to death.[37] In short, Zheng Weishan continued many of the repressive policies of Teng Haiqing without Teng Haiqing.

Second, under martial law the influx of Han from other provinces accelerated, including hundreds of thousands of sent-down educated youth, and a similar number of active and demobilized soldiers, officers, and family members. This latest wave of migrants intensified the population and job competition in Inner Mongolia. For instance, in the summer of 1970, the military authorities ordered the Baotou Electric Machinery Plant to accept more than three hundred demobilized soldiers from rural Hebei and Shanxi, dramatically increasing both the payroll of the plant and the Han presence in the workforce. The soldiers had not only transferred their rural *hukou* to urban *hukou*; they also changed the *hukou* status of family members. This was the only large-scale rural-to-urban *hukou* change in all of China during the Cultural Revolution. It was made possible by martial law. At the same time, Zheng Weishan and the Center transferred some four hundred Mongolian PLA officers at or above regimental level from Inner Mongolia to inland provinces—Hebei, Shanxi, Tianjin, and Shaanxi province—including both anti–New Neirendang activists and victims.[38] The process completed the virtual elimination of Mongols from positions of authority in the Party, government, and army in Inner Mongolia. The problem of Han immigrants was especially serious in ecologically fragile grassland regions. Excessive land reclamation by the Construction Corps in an attempt to realize self-reliance in food grains resulted in pasture degradation, desertification, and salinization, leading to serious sandstorms throughout North China.

Third is the effect of violent suppression. Of course, massive arrests, public trials, and executions were hardly new, or limited to Inner Mongolia. They remained widespread throughout China from 1970 to 1972 in the name of the One-Strike and Three-Anti campaign. To take a single example, in spring

1970, the army, which controlled the Shiguai Coal Mine, attacked an assembly of workers, and arrested Yang Xiu, Lü Hua and other worker representatives. The army announced Zhou Enlai's verdict on the coal-mine strike, which branded it "the biggest evil wind of economism since the founding of the country, a serious counterrevolutionary incident." The arrested workers were sentenced to death with reprieve, and the retroactive pay that all other workers had received was gradually deducted from their salaries.

The Lin Biao Incident and
My Farewell to Inner Mongolia

Repercussions of the Lin Biao Incident in Inner Mongolia

In Baotou in the fall of 1970, the military authorities, applying massive political pressure, arrests, torture and executions, had crushed the labor unrest though not eliminated its sources. We were then notified that our labor assignment at the Baotou Electric Machinery Plant would end and we would be reassigned to teach in middle schools. After a Lunar New Year farewell party with workers, we college graduates moved out. Four of us (Liu Dongsheng, Zhang Daren, Jia Zhicun, and I) transferred to the Baotou No. 19 Middle School to begin new lives as teachers.

Middle schools throughout the country had closed in December 1966, "stopping classes to make revolution." From late 1967, the Center repeatedly ordered schools to "resume classes while carrying out the revolution" (*fuke nao geming*), but as late as 1970, few schools had resumed regular classes. In Baotou, most schools stood empty. My English-language class that was to have had fifty students had only a dozen, and because there were no English textbooks, the class hardly met. My daily work mainly consisted of reading newspapers, Mao's works, and drinking tea. I was earning a salary for doing nothing.

Moreover, I was living in Baotou alone, separated from my family. My first son, Peng, was born in Hohhot on December 12, 1970. After the Spring Festival of 1971, Qingxian took the infant with her to Xi'nan Commune Hospital when she went back to work. Facing this impasse in our personal lives, I began to think about leaving Inner Mongolia to return to my hometown in Hebei. But it was easier said than done. An easier option would be for Qingxian to transfer to Baotou, where we could work in the same city and bring up the child together. Living conditions in the midsize city were certainly superior to those in my poor hometown in rural Raoyang.[1] However, Qingxian's rural assignment was part of the national response to Mao's June 26 Directive of 1965, designed to improve rural health care both by transferring urban physicians to the countryside and launching the barefoot doctors movement by providing short-term medical training to rural medics. This made it impossible for professionally trained medical personnel to move from the countryside to the city. As a last resort, I decided to seek work at the middle school in Xi'nan commune, where Qingxian's hospital was located, and to wait for opportunities to transfer to Raoyang. The Xi'nan commune personnel department promptly approved my application to teach because the school was preparing to open English classes. I brought my aging mother to Xi'nan, thinking that, as her eldest son, I should look after her. Mother was happy to see and care for her ten-month-old grandson, and Qingxian was pleased to have Mother with us. For the first time since marrying in late 1969, Qingxian and I were able to share a small home. Four people of three generations lived in a two-room adobe bungalow assigned by Qingxian's hospital.

The middle school where I taught dated to 1905, when it was established as a primary school by the Belgian missionary Father Verlinden Remi to educate Mongol and Han children. Initially consisting of a Mongol and a Han school, the Mongol school was disbanded in 1934, when Han settlers took over. It was run by Suiyuan governor Fu Zuoyi's army from 1939.[2] After 1949 it expanded to include a primary school and a junior and senior middle school, eventually totaling more than two thousand students, mostly from surrounding villages, as well as a few hundred children of cadres and workers from the neighboring Twelfth Regiment of the Second Inner Mongolia Production Corps. The principal wanted to open English classes quickly. But we had no textbooks or teaching materials, so he asked me to teach Chinese, history, and political science. I taught twelve classes a week, two classes a day, with Sunday off.

The Lin Biao incident, a key turning point in the Cultural Revolution, took place on September 13, 1971, but most people learned of it only weeks, or even months, later. Thanks to my high-quality Red Flag shortwave radio, I learned of it almost immediately. The news came around 11 p.m. in a Voice of America special program, in English, a few days after Lin's death. It said that Mongolian People's Republic authorities had confirmed that a British-built Trident 1E, with Chinese Aviation number 256 painted on its wings, had crashed, killing a high-ranking Chinese military leader, his wife, and son, as well as crew members. This leader was most likely Lin Biao, China's No. 2. I could not believe it, initially thinking that it must be an American or Soviet attempt to smear China. How could Mao's "closest comrade-in-arms," "good student," and officially designated "successor" betray him by attempting to flee the country? Switching to other channels, I found that Japan's NHK, Radio Moscow, Australia, and Taiwan were all broadcasting the same news. The official mainland Chinese radio station remained silent. I then tried three Chinese underground radio stations (Red Star Radio, Red Guard Radio, and Chinese Communist Party Radio).[3] They too reported Lin's death. The underground station calling itself Chinese Communist Party Radio eventually reported that Mao and Zhou Enlai had organized Lin Biao's assassination. Assessing the multiple reports, it seemed likely that Lin Biao had died, yet many questions remained.

The news that Mao's successor had been assassinated was so shocking that I could not sleep. I could not decide whether to rejoice or mourn and feared the worst. The next morning, after Qingxian had gone to work, I told Mother what I had heard. She replied: "Whether the news is true or not, say nothing about it to anyone, including Qingxian. That could ruin your life!"

Behind mother's worry lurked some bloody lessons. In Xuzhangbao village, Wugong commune, in our home county Raoyang, Xu Laige, a woman in her late fifties, had been sentenced to death in the One-Strike and Three-Anti campaign of 1970 for merely saying that Lin Biao looked like a treacherous court official (*jianchen*) and Jiang Qing looked like Delilah. My teacher Jin Xigu at Teachers' College had also been executed, mainly for voicing critical comments about Lin Biao and Jiang Qing.

While China's official media remained silent, leading cadres were gradually learning about the Lin Biao incident. In mid- to late October, 1971, about five weeks after Lin's death, the news finally reached Party secretaries in grassroots units. Teachers and staff members were not told of the Central documents until December.

In mid-January 1972, on orders from Urad Front banner, our middle school closed for a week for teachers and staff to study the documents. School then resumed for half-day classes, the rest of the time used for faculty and staff meetings and discussions for more than a month. Our study and discussion focused on two documents. One was the CCP's Central notice. The other was an attached document titled "'571 Project' Summary," the outline of Lin Biao's planned anti-Mao military coup, allegedly written by Lin Biao's son Lin Liguo.[4] It was a bombshell. The notice directed the cadres and the masses throughout the nation to study the attached materials and criticize Lin Biao and his anti-Party counterrevolutionary clique.

In the summary, Lin Biao called Mao "B-52," describing him as a contemporary incarnation of the book-burning emperor Qin Shihuang and suggesting that the Cultural Revolution was above all about "burning books and burying Confucians" (*fenshu kengru*). Sending cadres and intellectuals for thought reform in so-called May Seventh Cadre Schools (*wuqi ganxiao*) through hard agricultural labor and studying Mao's works was tantamount to being "sent into exile," and sending educated youth to the countryside was "labor reform."

Everyone had to take turns criticizing Lin Biao and his group of military and Party leaders (Chen Boda, Huang Yongsheng, Wu Faxian, Lin's wife Ye Qun, Li Zuopeng, and Qiu Huizuo).

During the study sessions, teachers repeatedly discussed a Tang dynasty poem entitled *Fenshu Keng* (Pits for Book Burning), written by Zhang Jie (836–905):

> As the smoke from burning bamboo and silk clears,
> > the empire is weakened.
> The Hangu Pass and the Yellow River guard
> > the domain of Qin Shi Huang in vain.
> Pits of ash were not yet cold,
> > disorder reigned east of the Xiao Mountains.
> As it turned out,
> > Liu Bang and Xiang Yu could not read.[5]

The reason for attention to the poem was that Lin Biao clique member, chief of staff Huang Yongsheng, had recited the last line in a meeting, likening Mao to China's infamous book-burning first emperor.

Mao included the poem in the Central document with the attached "'571 Project' Summary" for reference and criticism. Thus, this Tang poem became widely known throughout China.

However, the Central documents provided no instruction on how to understand the poem. Teacher Wang Zhanfu, the chair of the Chinese literature group, was asked to explain the poem. Being only a high school graduate, however, he dared not offer an explanation and encouraged me to do so. I agreed, but stating that my major was English not Chinese, I asked others to correct my possible errors.

I first translated the classical poem into modern Chinese, and then explained that it described the unrest following Qin Shihuang's book burning and the persecution of Confucian scholars. Qin Shihuang attempted to burn books and kill Confucian scholars to prevent the overthrow of his empire. But soon after the book burning and killing, two illiterate leaders of peasant uprisings, Liu Bang and Xiang Yu, overthrew the Qin dynasty.[6] My explanation impressed those attending the meeting.

After that, whenever literary questions arose, they would ask me, and I would answer when I could. One day the official *Reference News* (*Cankao Xiaoxi*), which translated foreign news for cadre study, carried an article in which the wife of the American president was called "the first lady" (*diyi furen*).

One teacher asked Headmaster Wang Yu what "first lady" meant. Wang said, "First lady means the first wife of the president; he could have a second or third wife."

Hearing this nonsense, I immediately corrected him: "No. First lady means the wife of the supreme leader of a country. Not only referring to the United States, it also could be said of China. For example, foreign newspapers call Jiang Qing, Chairman Mao's wife, China's first lady. Besides, US law, like Chinese law, prohibits bigamy, so a president could not have more than one wife, though secret affairs were possible."

My explanation embarrassed the headmaster. With a dark red face, he refuted me: "Teacher Cheng, what you said is not necessarily right, is it? Those capitalist countries are so decadent—how is it possible that a president can't have several wives?"

Teacher Wang Zhanfu quickly came to his aid: "We have to investigate this matter. If Teacher Cheng is wrong, that would risk beautification of US imperialism!" At that, the teachers burst out laughing. I thought that he was just joking, too. But this was not a laughing matter.

As the campaign of criticism against Lin Biao deepened, we were asked to search for examples from teachers and cadres to expose sympathizers of Lin Biao. Headmaster Wang Yu used the opportunity to avenge his humiliation.

Wang Zhanfu and I had casually chatted about the Lin Biao incident, and for the most part we were in agreement. Learning that we had privately discussed the Lin Biao incident, Wang Yu pressed him to report on our conversation. With a set of "black materials" submitted by Wang Zhanfu labeling me an "active reactionary," Wang Yu prepared a summary of my remarks and submitted it to the Party Committee of the Commune to secure approval for a meeting to criticize me.

The commune's leadership proposed holding an open staff meeting on the issue. The original proposal for a meeting to "expose and criticize" was downgraded into a meeting to "criticize and help." I was to criticize myself, after which other staff members would help me to correct my errors.

One day, Wang Yu, and the school's Party Secretary Li informed me that some teachers had reported that I had some unhealthy, and even incorrect, opinions about the Lin Biao incident and that the commune Party Committee had approved holding a school meeting to criticize and help me. I was dumbfounded. I was given one day to prepare a response to their charges.

After the notification, my faculty colleagues suddenly became cold. Those who often talked and laughed now pretended not to see me. Some, not daring to say a word, hurried away, reminding me of my situation as a struggle object during the Socialist Education Movement seven years earlier. Without years of struggle throughout the Cultural Revolution, I would have been terrified by the prospect of this public intimidation. But having experienced political storms at college and the *Inner Mongolia Daily*, I went to the meeting prepared to fight.

The venue was a classroom. The desks were set in a circle, surrounded by the entire faculty and leaders, including two leaders from the commune, the director of education and the commune office secretary Wan Jisheng representing the commune Party secretary who was attending a meeting in the banner. (I later heard that, since the Banner Education Bureau had not endorsed the meeting, the commune Party secretary decided to make himself absent and send two lower-level officials.) I took a seat opposite Wang Zhanfu so that I could see him face-to-face.

The classroom was silent. I looked out at grim faces. A few teachers who ordinarily were very cordial toward me were smoking, filling the air with cigarette smoke. Headmaster Wang Yu, without stating the charges, ordered me to "confess." He said that the purpose of the meeting was not to interrogate class enemies but was an internal criticism so that faculty members could help one another. After Wang's introduction, I spoke for about two hours. Using skills honed in years of debates, I turned the charges against me into criticism of Wang Zhanfu, closely following the official propaganda of the time.

After giving details of what had been discussed in our private conversation, I dissected Wang Zhanfu's viewpoint: "The '571 Project Summary' looks like a combination of miscellaneous charges, not a well-prepared plan for a military coup. It might have been invented by other people seeking to justify Lin Biao's death." I said that the summary, whether prepared by Lin Biao or by his son Lin Liguo, was a program to attack Chairman Mao. It could not have been concocted by someone else to discredit them. If this had been made up, why were there so many words slandering Chairman Mao, including the Tang poem that ostensibly mocked Qin Shihuang but actually mocked Chairman Mao? If we doubted the truth of this document, like Wang Zhanfu, how could we teach our students?

While speaking, I observed Wang Zhanfu's face turn red then white and then back to red again. When it was his turn to speak, he panicked and was often tongue-tied. What he called the "mistakes of Cheng Tiejun" were mainly copied from my speech, mimicking my earlier statements. The only difference was that I said they were Wang Zhanfu's mistaken words, and Wang Zhanfu attributed them to me. But he was unable to criticize me in the categories of the official media. The result left many to shake their heads and sigh.

Wang Yu had not anticipated this outcome. His plan was to mobilize other teachers to attack me following Wang Zhanfu's speech. But after hearing the two speeches, most teachers sympathized with me, finding Wang's speech unconvincing.

After Wang Zhanfu spoke, Wang Yu repeatedly called on others to speak, but there was no response. Wang Yu then hastily announced the end of the meeting, urging everyone to further think about the issues, and saying that the school would arrange other meetings.

Seeing that Wang Yu wanted to shelve the matter without conclusion, I raised my hand and said loudly: "Teacher Wang has made allegations about me. I haven't replied yet. I request five minutes to reply." Wang Yu hesitated and looked toward the commune office secretary, who nodded and said, "Let Teacher Cheng reply." I stood up and thanked everyone. The following were my major points:

First, I think this meeting is a little bit unusual, because, in the campaign to criticize Lin Biao, everyone expresses similar views, whether inside or outside of meetings. The Lin Biao incident, after all, is hardly a normal situation. If we don't think about it and don't talk about it, that would be self-deception. But our school did not arrange meetings like this for everyone to engage in self-criticism or to criticize one another. It only singled me out, as if I were different from other people and my ideas needed to be taken seriously. I feel deeply honored. So I especially want to thank Headmaster Wang Yu for making careful arrangements and thank all the teachers and commune leaders for spending valuable time to give me special help.

Second, I regret that, at this important and carefully prepared meeting, only Wang Zhanfu spoke on his own behalf. I have not yet heard others' criticisms of me. If there is not sufficient time today, I hope that there will be another chance for others to speak. The recently completed *wasu* and anti-Neirendang campaign also caused havoc in our Xi'nan commune. Many detained victims have only recently been released. Their release was made possible by Chairman Mao's May 25 Directive and the Central documents. We need to bear in mind historical lessons to avoid making the same mistake of too easily suspecting, interrogating, and criticizing good colleagues and comrades.

Third, I hope we can learn from this meeting and create a new working environment in our school. I came here less than three months ago, but have received special care from Headmaster Wang Yu. Why? After reflection, the only reason I've been able to come up with is my correction of his explanation of the English term "first lady" in a public meeting, leading him to seek revenge so as to tame me in the future. Perhaps, as in the case of Wang Zhanfu, I could be used by him as a mad dog to bite whomever he chooses. Today's meeting has shown our school's abnormal political life. I reserve the right to appeal to higher levels of government to send a representative here to investigate whether the situation is in accord with Party policy.

Finally, a few words of advice to Teacher Wang and Headmaster Wang. The campaign to criticize Lin Biao should touch everyone's soul and improve our ability to distinguish true and false Marxism by looking at real life to see what we need to be vigilant about or need to change. Using this standard of analysis, I have to say that what Headmaster Wang Yu and Teacher Wang Zhanfu have done are in essence of the same nature as Lin Biao's behavior, "a good man in front, but a demon behind." Today, as we criticize Lin Biao, we should act to change the social environment that created Lin Biao's behavior so that Xi'nan Middle School can become a great school of Mao Zedong Thought.

With the end of my speech, the audience applauded. Even the two commune officials clapped. Wang Yu and Wang Zhanfu, blushing like roosters, hurriedly left the classroom.

I was fearless then because I was angered by the two Wangs' immoral behavior. Of course, I was encouraged by the presence of the commune officials serving as judges. I might have had second thoughts had they not been there. Although I was a rebel, I was after all an outsider and alone. As an old Chinese adage goes, *qianglong buya ditoushe*: a powerful dragon cannot crush a snake in its old haunts.

A few weeks later, the commune Party Committee and the banner's Education Department ruled that criticizing me was wrong and Wang Yu should take responsibility for it. He was transferred to the remote commune of Dashetai deep in the mountains of Urad Front banner. Party Secretary Li was appointed acting headmaster. After that, the atmosphere of the school improved, and people started talking and laughing at meetings more frequently.

Hunting Warlord Yu Hongxin

The Chinese saying *yibo weiping, yibo youqi*—one wave has not yet calmed while a new wave is rising—well describes the situation in Inner Mongolia in the early 1970s. The Lin Biao incident was not yet resolved when the Yu Hongxin incident occurred in late spring 1972.

After the termination of martial law in Inner Mongolia in May 1971, most military officers were gradually withdrawn from the border's front lines. Yu Hongxin remained in Bayannuur league as head of the military control committee until the late summer of 1971 when he was ordered to return to the headquarters of the Sixty-Third Army in Taiyuan, Shanxi province, to join a campaign to criticize Chen Boda (and later Lin Biao).

One day after school, all teachers and staff were called to an emergency meeting. We learned only that an important criminal had run away from an inland province and might sneak into Inner Mongolia and attempt to escape to the MPR. Strangely, the criminal was not named. We received only a description.

Two weeks later, when a printed *Tong ji ling* (most-wanted order) was posted on the school bulletin board, we were surprised to find that the target was Yu Hongxin, our Bayannuur league's military overlord![7] The order from the Ministry of Public Security dated May 29, 1972, said that "active counter-revolutionary Yu Hongxin, on May 18, 1972, at 2 a.m., committed murder and absconded." Warning that Yu was armed, it ordered a nationwide hunt to apprehend him.

All teachers and staff were divided into small groups, each having five people, supplied with three rifles and two handguns, and assigned particular spots to guard. We were all experienced in using weapons having been trained as militia. Our spot was a small bridge on the northern side of Xi'nan commune, with an unpaved road leading toward the MPR. To guard the road around the clock seven days a week, we were equipped with weapons and heavy army fur coats. Each shift was four hours. We stopped all trucks, tractors, buses, cars, and motorcycles. After showing them the poster with Yu Hongxin's picture and searching their vehicles, we let them go.

Yu was the leader of Bayannuur league under martial law. He had impeccable military credentials. Having risen through the ranks as an anti-Japanese war hero in Wuqiang county, Hebei, he fought in the Korean War, commanding the 187th Division of the Sixty-Third Army, which was said to have won a fierce battle over the British.[8]

After the Korean War, Yu was sent to Nanjing Artillery Academy for training (previously he had had little education). His research article on combining artillery and infantry attracted the attention of Zheng Weishan and Lin Biao who appointed him deputy commander of the Sixty-Third Army under Xu Xin. When Xu Xin and Yu Hongxin were sent to Inner Mongolia to implement martial law, Xu took charge of Baotou and Yu commanded most of the military units in Bayannuur and the Construction Corps with 150,000 educated youths and 30,000 PLA men.[9] Yu was a rising star.

But rumors about Yu Hongxin quickly spread. Although the official media gave no hint as to whom he had killed or why, a picture of him as a modern warlord emerged in gossip. Bayannuur league cadres described Yu as a skilled boxer who was quick to use his fists, beating his bodyguards, his secretary, and even his wife.

A story circulated that Yu Hongxin had once exploded in anger at a mass assembly of thousands of Wuda coal miners. He took out his pistol, threw it on the table, and shouted: "*Cao ni ma* [fuck your mother]! Listen, *Laozi* [I] is coming here to carry out martial law, to control you sons of bitches. You want economism, asking for a bonus and benefits, right? Let me tell you, if you want money, the answer is no! If you want peanuts [bullets], yes, we have plenty of them. Tomorrow we'll give you a public trial." Soon after, he opened a series of mass trials, each time executing a group of alleged active counter-revolutionaries without any judicial process.

Yu Hongxin was also known for avarice and extortion. During martial law, he grabbed whatever caught his fancy. Among local products, he particularly liked "Wallace" honeydew melons, for which western Inner Mongolia was famous, and the traditional medicines *suoyang* (Chinese cynomorium) and *roucongrong* (desert broomrape), as well as *tanyangpi* (tan goat fur) and cashmere.[10] These were collected at very low prices and shipped to inland provinces for profit or given to his superiors as gifts. Local people described Yu as having "arrived with one suitcase, and left with truckloads."

Yu Hongxin was well known as a lothario, keen to "inspect" any place that had large numbers of young women, such as hospitals, song and dance troupes, textile mills, and female companies of sent-down educated youth. Whenever the commander arrived for inspection, the staff would line up to welcome him. He would then order the leadership to send the woman he desired to his office or his hotel room to "report her thoughts" (*huibao sixiang*); there she would be raped.

His victims in Bayannuur league sent many letters of complaint to the martial law authorities in Hohhot and the Central government in Beijing to no avail. All were returned with an official seal: "transfer to the original unit for investigation and handling."

But he finally tripped himself up. Yu Hongxin had an old friend named Xie, who had some power, although his rank was lower than Yu's. On hearing that his friend was the boss in Bayannuur league, Xie told Yu that his daughter had been sent down to the Construction Corps in Bayannuur, and he hoped that Yu would take care of her. Yu arranged a comfortable job in the league's fertilizer plant for her. When she returned to Beijing during the Spring Festival, her parents asked whether Uncle Yu took good care of her. The girl broke into tears, saying, "He's a beast." Yu had repeatedly raped her. She wrote a report on the rape, and her father handed it to Deng Yingchao, who headed China's Women's Association. She passed it to her husband, Zhou Enlai. Many looked to Zhou as a kind of ombudsman.

After verifying Yu's crime, Zhou ordered him to return immediately to the Sixty-Third Army headquarters in Taiyuan to join a Mao Zedong Thought study class. Yu left for Taiyuan suspecting that Political Commissar Cao Buchi, with whom he had many conflicts, had reported him.

The reeducation camp was for army officers, about fifteen in number under the command of the Beijing Military Region. Cao Buchi was in charge. One day, after being severely criticized in class following his wife's report about his beating, Yu took two guns and went after Cao. Walking into his dormitory at midnight, he fired three shots. Cao covered his head and didn't move. His wife, however, sat up in bed and was shot. By the time Cao's bodyguards arrived, the wife and a bodyguard were dead. Yu raced off in his jeep.

A huge manhunt was organized across Shanxi, northern Hebei, and western Inner Mongolia. Finally, after his jeep ran out of gas, Yu abandoned it, sending it over a cliff in the Taihang Mountains, then walked to a wheat field in Yuci county, Shanxi province, and shot himself with a pistol. His body was found by two farmers in mid-June 1972.

Yu Hongxin's case was indicative of the scale of violence carried out with impunity by the army against civilians under martial law. It also pointed to a larger issue of the PLA, one exemplified by Lin Biao's planned coup. If the PLA could be used by Mao to control the nation, reining in the factional fighting he had unleashed during the early stages of the Cultural Revolution, after 1970 the army posed a threat to Mao's very rule. By then, Mao had become increasingly concerned about the atrocities committed by the army sent in to support the "revolutionary leftist masses" in January 1967. Nowhere were these dangers greater than in Inner Mongolia during the *wasu* and anti–New Neirendang campaigns on the MPR and Soviet borders. In August 1972, Mao decided to end military control as soon as new Party Committees were established to strengthen the Party's control of the army. The termination of martial law in Inner Mongolia in May 1971 anticipated this momentous change in China's politics. However, occupation forces did not leave Inner Mongolia in toto until August 1972.[11]

External Investigations

Soon after the Yu Hongxin case ended, I received some unexpected good news. One day in summer 1972 I went to the commune's food grain station to pick up our monthly ration supply, mainly wheat flour and cornmeal. The manager, Lao Wu, looked at my ration booklet and asked "Why do you only have rations for three people?" I told him that because my mother had a rural *hukou* (household registration) in Hebei, she was ineligible to receive grain from the state.

Lao Wu said, "Just last week we received a new document allowing your mother to change her rural *hukou* into an urban *hukou*." The document issued by the Inner Mongolia Revolutionary Committee stipulated that direct dependents (spouse, parents, and children) of a state cadre with rural *hukou* who had lived with the cadre for more than one year could obtain an urban one. Mother was delighted: "At last I don't need to fear famine, as in 1960. The state will guarantee my grain supply."

Given the ease with which mother was able to change her *hukou* from rural to urban, I thought this might reflect a new national policy. In late 1972, however, I learned that the policy was implemented only in Inner Mongolia to facilitate changing the *hukou* of hundreds of thousands of PLA family members who had moved there during martial law. This was a rare case of household registration flexibility that allowed a large group of military dependents to get urban jobs in Inner Mongolia. I recalled my own *hukou* change—catching the "last bus" from Raoyang to Hohhot in 1959, in the wake of famine before the state crackdown.

One day soon after, two men came from the Inner Mongolia Revolutionary Committee to Xi'nan Middle School to conduct a *waidiao* (external investigation) on Gao Shuhua in connection with the One-Strike and Three-Anti campaign.[12] Party Secretary Li called me to his office to answer their questions. The two men, one in military uniform, were from the Political Department where Gao had worked before the Tangshan Study Class. Their attitude toward me was good; they did not try to bully me like many officials did. I asked them how they knew I was working in this small school. With a smile, the military cadre said: "Wherever you are, we can find you."

Their investigation had two goals. The first was to locate a book published for internal circulation among high-ranking officials: a Chinese edition of Boccaccio's *Decameron*, which was regarded as an erotic novel. Gao Shuhua had borrowed it from the internal collection of the Inner Mongolia Party Committee Library before going to Tangshan Study Class. After finishing it, he lent it to me. But having no time to read when working at the *Inner Mongolia Daily*, I brought it back to the Baotou Electric Machinery Plant. In the factory dormitory, someone took it and never returned it. I told the two investigators that I had borrowed it from Gao Shuhua and I was responsible for its loss. I offered to have the price deducted from my salary.

Their real goal, however, was to learn about our relationship. They raised many questions: Why did you personally join the rebellion sparked by Gao Shuhua at Teachers' College? Why did he recommend you to work at the *Inner Mongolia Daily*? Why did you entrust him to submit your poster manuscript to Zhou Enlai's office to criticize Teng Haiqing and the anti-Neirendang campaign? What was Gao Shuhua's attitude toward Teng Haiqing and Gao Jinming? After Gao Shuhua returned from Tangshan, were you often in contact? Did you ever hear Gao speak about Chairman Mao, Jiang Qing, and other Central leaders? Do you know of his activities related to the May 16 Counterrevolutionary Conspiracy Group in Beijing, Hohhot, or other places? May 16 referred to an ultraleft Red Guard organization in Beijing that used Mao's notice from May 16, 1966, that launched the Cultural Revolution to oppose Zhou Enlai in 1967. Mao had ordered an investigation of the organization in September 1967 and in 1971 again organized a May 16 Special Case Joint Group and launched a nationwide investigation.

Their questions suggested two possible purposes for the investigation of Gao Shuhua's recent political activities since the Tangshan Study Class: one was to purge him, the other to promote him. In either case, it was necessary to clarify his political history so that the personnel office could file a report—and most likely promote him, as I sensed from the attitudes of the two cadres. After this investigation, Gao was appointed by the Inner Mongolia Revolution ary Committee to head the General Education Group in the Inner Mongolia Bureau of Education (June 1972), then deputy Party secretary of the Tumed Left banner (March 1973), and finally deputy Party secretary of Hohhot (March 1976–December 1977), the zenith of his career.

Before this there were several investigations of friends and colleagues during my tenure at the *Inner Mongolia Daily* in Hohhot and the Electric Machinery Plant in Baotou. I followed three cardinal principles for handling such investigations: be neither too polite nor supercilious but show mutual respect; seek truth from facts, and fabricate nothing; and only discuss publicly known or open content, not anything that could not be verified by a third party. Following these principles, I told them how I had joined Gao Shuhua's revolt at Teachers' College. As for our criticism of Teng Haiqing's anti–New Neirendang campaign, I simply repeated the content of our poster. Concerning other things about Gao Shuhua and my personal views, including the evaluation of Teng Haiqing and his opponents, martial law in Inner Mongolia and the future of the Cultural Revolution, I said nothing.

That afternoon they came again, showing me their draft summary of the interview and giving me a chance to confirm that it was what I had told them. I carefully read their draft, signed it, and attached my fingerprint. Using fingerprints for verification was widely practiced in China, dating back to ancient China's pre-Qin era (200s BC).

A week after their departure, two other cadres came to see me at the middle school. The older one, in his late forties, was a Han. The younger was a Mongol in his late twenties. They came from Shiliingol league to investigate my good friend Ma Shuqi, a Han biologist who had graduated from Inner Mongolia University and become the chair of the Revolutionary Committee of the Grassland Research Institute of Inner Mongolia in Abaganar banner, Shiliingol league.

From the start, their hostility toward me was clear. After handing over a sheet of more than twenty questions, the older man said: "Look at Ma Shuqi's confession. You can then testify whether he really voiced those reactionary opinions." I hastily looked over the list, surprised that Ma Shuqi would have confessed to having said things that we had discussed privately such as criticizing Teng Haiqing when he visited me at the *Inner Mongolia Daily* in the summer of 1969. If known, any of the views expressed could have led to arrest or even execution during the One-Strike and Three-Anti campaign. Although martial law had been lifted, the lightest punishment he would have received in 1972 was expulsion from public office. A heavier punishment could have been imprisonment. Ma's views included the following:

1. The purpose of *wasu* and uprooting the New Neirendang was to strengthen autocratic rule, not only to instill fear in minority nationalities, but also to crack down on any independent thought, especially among intellectuals.
2. Teng Haiqing's goal was to suppress the Mongolian people and intellectuals of all nationalities who express independent thought.
3. Gao Jinming and other local Inner Mongolia cadres could not defeat Teng Haiqing because of Teng's position in the Beijing Military Region and his ties to the Center.
4. Mao incorrectly labeled Ulanhu and his Mongol cronies as separatists. Basically, Mao never truly trusted minority cadres. Han emperors throughout Chinese history never trusted minority nationalities.
5. Although we support the rebels, we also need to examine the purpose of the Cultural Revolution: has it benefited the country and people, or has it brought disaster?
6. Mao Zedong, Lin Biao, Kang Sheng, and Jiang Qing belong to the extreme left; Liu Shaoqi and Deng Xiaoping belong to the conservative bureaucratic class which wants to negate Mao's authority and follow the revisionist road of the Soviet Union and Eastern Europe. Zhou Enlai is a centrist who wants to mediate between the Cultural Revolution left and the bureaucratic right. China's future is uncertain. We need to be calm to observe, not blindly support one faction or another.

We had in fact discussed these issues, but I couldn't imagine that Shuqi would confess to such opinions or that outsiders could have known of them. Recognizing the serious nature of the charges, I decided to deny everything, even if threatened with imprisonment or death. I stood up and angrily protested:

These "confessions" are completely fabricated. I suspect that Lao Ma was tortured to force such confessions. He comes from a poor peasant family, is a

Party member, and the Cultural Revolution has placed him in a leadership position as deputy director of your research institute. So why would he have any doubts about Chairman Mao and the Communist Party? Why would he oppose the Cultural Revolution? Besides, if he really had those reactionary thoughts, why would he come to the *Inner Mongolia Daily* to talk to me? Wouldn't he be afraid that I might expose him? If he had told me such things and I did not report him to the Military Control Committee at the *Daily*, would I not become an active counterrevolutionary element?

The older cadre repeatedly nodded his head but said nothing. The young man said sternly, "Our questions are drawn from private conversations between you and Ma Shuqi. We merely came to verify whether they are true. He said you expressed these views. Do you deny it?"

Listening to our argument, Party Secretary Li realized that the situation was serious. He interjected: "Teacher Cheng, you needn't be upset. If your friend really has these problems, please don't hide anything. It is better to seek truth from facts."

I retorted: "Secretary Li, this is not a small thing. Look at this list, each item would be enough to qualify someone as a counterrevolutionary. If we had really discussed these questions, how could I forget them?"

The older cadre responded: "Teacher Cheng, you say that nothing on this outline occurred. If so, we cannot summarize this investigation report. Can you draft a report describing how you got to know each other, the nature of your conversations, the time, place and content of your talks? Tomorrow, we will come back for it."

Secretary Li gave me the day off, arranging for another faculty member to teach my classes. I wrote describing how Ma Shuqi and I got to know each other starting from the early 1960s, how he visited me at the *Inner Mongolia Daily* in the summer of 1969. But I said little about the content of our conversations. I mainly emphasized Ma Shuqi's poor family background, his Party membership, and our long friendship. Stressing the fact that Ma Shuqi was a fine revolutionary comrade, I hoped that the leadership of his unit would implement the Party's policy, "not to wrong a good man, but don't let a bad man escape either," restore his Party membership, and allow him to resume his work.

The next morning, after carefully rereading the draft, I signed my name and pressed my fingerprint. In the afternoon the two cadres reviewed my statement and left.

A few years later, I met Ma Shuqi in Hohhot, where his research institute had moved. When I asked him about that "external investigation," he said that after detention for more than a month, he nearly collapsed under fierce interrogation. With his head muddled, he thought I might have confessed about our talk in Manduhai Park. If so, the result would be serious if Ma then refused to confess. This case illustrates the theory of the prisoner's dilemma. In attempting to avoid punishment, he eventually handed over the full content of our private conversation, which resulted in a situation in which both of us could receive extreme punishment.

I cursed him, asking why he did not realize that the most dangerous course was to confess and to implicate both of us. Fortunately, I had recognized the danger and was able to deny the charges. Following investigation, he resumed his Party membership and office work. He said to me emotionally: "I was really naive. Had you not written that report, I might still be behind bars!"

Goodbye, Inner Mongolia

The two external investigations went no further, but increased my anxiety about the dangerous situation in Inner Mongolia. With the political tide turning against the former rebels, it seemed best to leave Inner Mongolia, both because I had been deeply involved in the Cultural Revolution and because, during my service at the *Inner Mongolia Daily*, I came to know many high-ranking government and military officials. If any of them got into political trouble, I could be implicated.

I was also concerned about my mother's health. Mother loved the outgoing character and hospitality of the local people, but she could not adapt to the cold coming from Mongolia and Siberia. Temperatures plummeted far below zero in winter, which worsened her asthma and emphysema. Watching her cough and gasp all night, and being unable to help her, we determined to move, either to our hometown in Hebei or to a warm place in southern China.

My job transfer application to Raoyang was approved by the Education Bureau of Urad Front banner. After bidding farewell to family and friends, I boarded the No. 90 express train from Hohhot Station in September 1972, traveling east toward Beijing. On the train, I reflected on the thirteen years I had lived in Inner Mongolia, the most exciting, and also the most painful, period of my life. Many of my Mongol and Han friends had been tortured. Some had lost their lives. From a junior middle school student to a college graduate, having gone through the storms of the Cultural Revolution and observed developments as a journalist, a worker, and a teacher, I began to gain an understanding of society and prepared to face serious tests in the years ahead.

As the train accelerated on the Ulaanchab plain, with sirens blaring and the rails rumbling rhythmically, I gazed at the scenery, trying to devour the picturesque landscape: the Daqing Mountains rolling as in a Chinese ink painting in the distance, villages scattered beneath white clouds and blue sky, cows grazing in the rolling meadows, and sheep scattered like pearls across green velvet. Recalling thirteen cold winters and hot summers of Inner Mongolia with a blend of thankfulness and anger, I couldn't help but shed tears.

Closing the Page on Inner Mongolia's Rebel History

When I returned to Raoyang county in 1972, there was little discernible trace of the Cultural Revolution; all leading officials and teachers who had been criticized or jailed in the early stages of the Cultural Revolution had been rehabilitated and resumed their pre–Cultural Revolution positions.[13] Raoyang Middle School had become the Comprehensive Technical School of Raoyang county. Its mission was to train rural teachers, barefoot doctors, mechanical engineers, and other technicians for village brigades and production teams. I was asked to teach English language and Chinese literature to future English teachers for the twelve middle schools in the county. Qingxian began to teach medical science to village barefoot doctors, commune members who had received short-term first aid and medical education in the Raoyang hospital.

The deaths of Mao Zedong, Zhou Enlai, and Zhu De in 1976, and the coup d'état that led to the arrest of the Gang of Four in the same year, punctuating the end of the decade-long Cultural Revolution, were momentous events that shook the nation. Raoyang, though a rural backwater, pulsated along with the nation, and I could not sit idle content simply with teaching English. My passion for observing, studying, and participating in social and political developments remained strong. When higher education resumed throughout China in 1977, I decided to return to university to pursue an academic career. In the following year I passed an examination to enter the Chinese Academy of Social Sciences in Beijing to study for a master of arts degree in world economy and politics, graduating in 1981.

Following a brief stint as a lecturer at the Hebei University of Economy and Finance in Shijiazhuang, in 1982 I went to the United States on a scholarship from the Economics Department at the University of Massachusetts at Amherst. Two years later, in 1984, I transferred to the Department of Sociology of Binghamton University to conduct doctoral research on China's household registration (*hukou*) system that had been introduced in 1959, the year I arrived in Inner Mongolia, dividing the country along rural and urban lines and turning rural residents into second-class citizens, a status hierarchy that continues to this day despite repeated efforts to reform the system.

The death of Party General Secretary Hu Yaobang in April 1989 led to the rise of a democracy movement followed by social turmoil and bloodshed culminating in the Tiananmen Square massacre on June 4. As president of the Chinese Student Association at Binghamton, I was active in collecting signatures on petitions drafted by Chinese student groups at Harvard, Columbia, and other American universities. I obtained my PhD degree in 1991 and started part-time teaching in the Department of Sociology and a full-time research job in the Institute of Multiculturalism and International Labor at Binghamton, from the fall of 1991 to the summer of 1997. After a short stint at Radio Free Asia, in 1999, I accepted a teaching position at the University of Macau in its newly established program on contemporary China studies. When I retired in 2010, my wife and I returned to the States to live with my sons in California.

Over the four decades since leaving Hohhot, I have closely followed developments in Inner Mongolia. It is, after all, Qingxian's hometown, a place where I spent my formative years and where my best friends live. The fate of Gao Shuhua, Inner Mongolia's most famous rebel and my political mentor, provides a fruitful way to close the page on Inner Mongolia's rebel history.

Rebels began to face trouble soon after Zhou Enlai and Mao Zedong died, and in October 1976, the Party leadership denounced the Gang of Four of Cultural Revolution radicals who had ridden high during the Cultural Revolution, headed by Mao's wife Jiang Qing, holding them responsible for the excesses of the era. With the rise of Hua Guofeng and Deng Xiaoping to power at the highest level of the Party, the decade-long Cultural Revolution was brought to a close. But a new movement was immediately launched throughout the country to cleanse the Gang of Four and its associates.

In Inner Mongolia, this movement began on November 12, 1976, with the arrest of rebel leader Liu Litang from the Hohhot Railroad Bureau. Gao Shuhua later called that day the Doomsday of the Rebels. In short order, all former rebel leaders were arrested, regardless of their positions, including many who had gone into hiding in other provinces. For example, Li Feng (leader of the Inner Mongolia Party Committee Work Unit Red Flag Headquarters) was arrested in Heilongjiang, Wang Zhiyou (8.18 leader from River West Company) in Nanjing, and Huo Daoyu (leader of Huajian Jinggangshan) in Hubei. Later that month, Hao Guangde and Nasanbayar, two former rebels and ranking members of the Inner Mongolia Revolutionary Committee, were detained by the Cleansing the Gang of Four Office.

May 1, 1977, was the thirtieth anniversary of the founding of the IMAR. One week later, Hohhot held the first mass rally to expose and criticize the Gang of Four and "their followers." Most rebel leaders holding positions in Inner Mongolia, including Gao Shuhua, Hao Guangde, Wang Jinbao, Wang Zhiyou, Nasanbayar, as well as *wasu* and anti–New Neirendang activists such as Ulaanbagan and Erdeni-Uul, faced public denunciation. Among the targets, only one was a high-ranking cadre at that time, Guo Yiqing, former Party secretary of Inner Mongolia University, who became an ardent supporter of *wasu* while serving as a senior member of the Inner Mongolia Revolutionary Committee. All other high-ranking leaders, such as Teng Haiqing, Gao Jinming, and Quan Xingyuan had either been protected or transferred to safety in other provinces by the Center. Gao Shuhua was detained in early December 1977.[14]

The following year, Zhou Hui became Party secretary of Inner Mongolia. A Jiangsu native, he was acting Party secretary of Hunan province in 1959 when he was punished by Mao for supporting Marshal Peng Dehuai's criticism of Mao's Great Leap Forward policy. In his nine-year tenure as Party secretary of Inner Mongolia, he was instrumental in introducing the household contract system that replaced the collectives with family farming and markets throughout rural China, boosting agricultural productivity and rural incomes in subsequent years. But the logic of agriculture and animal husbandry were profoundly different. Dividing the grasslands into minuscule plots of fenced land with hundreds of sheep and goats eliminated the possibility of the seasonal migration that was the heart of the pastoral economy. The result was massive desertification of the grasslands, with devastating impacts on the pastoral economy and herder incomes. Zhou's failure to appreciate both the imperatives of agriculture and pastoral production and the ethnic complexity of Inner Mongolia precipitated a new round of ethnic conflict.

During this period, two major political events occurred in Beijing, each heavily affecting Inner Mongolia. One was the Center's decision on Kang Sheng; the other was the trial of the two "reactionary cliques" of Lin Biao and the Gang of Four. On October 19, 1980, the CCP center denounced Kang Sheng's crimes, expelled him from the Party, withdrew the eulogy to him (at his death on December 16, 1975), and labeled him as one of the sixteen key members of "the Lin Biao–Jiang Qing Reactionary Clique." Kang Sheng, together with Zhou Enlai (who escaped the backlash against the Cultural Revolution), had played decisive roles in the rise of Teng Haiqing and the anti–New Neirendang campaign in Inner Mongolia.

On November 12, 1980, a special tribunal opened in Beijing for a public trial of the Lin Biao and Jiang Qing "reactionary cliques." Article 28 of the indictment stated, "At the instigation of Kang Sheng and Xie Fuzhi, the IMAR had launched the unjust and false Neirendang case, during which 346,000 cadres and masses were persecuted, and 16,222 died."[15]

In this way, total responsibility for the Neirendang pogrom was laid at the feet of Kang Sheng and Xie Fuzhi while all other leading members of the Chinese Communist Party and the military in Beijing, notably Zhou Enlai and Mao Zedong, and in the IMAR, above all Teng Haiqing, were exonerated. Zheng Weishan, the commander of the Beijing Military Region who implemented martial law in Inner Mongolia, had already been punished as early as January 1971 because of his association with Chen Boda. There was no apology from the Center to the large number of Mongol and other victims in Inner Mongolia; the Party was always "great, glorious, and correct" even in this hour during which many of its leading figures were denounced.

In the summer of 1981, a year before my departure to the United States, we returned to Inner Mongolia. Not knowing how long it would take to complete my studies, we decided that it would be best for my wife and two sons, Peng and Hui, to join her family in Hohhot.

"Many rebel leaders were sentenced to five to ten years of imprisonment," Zhang Peiren told me over dinner at his place with rebel friends in the *Inner Mongolia Daily* compound. "But I've heard that Zhou Hui has been unable to find any solid evidence to prosecute Gao Shuhua, because, as we know, he did nothing wrong."

I asked, "Then, he has lost his freedom for more than three years without trial? When do you think he might be tried or set free?"

All friends at the table shook their heads, saying, "He was detained for investigation in 1977, but only formally arrested in December 1979 and charged with being a key gangster element [*bangpai gugan fenzi*]."

After dinner, I went to Gao Shuhua's home to see his wife. Zong Fuhua told me that, during his detention, many friends, including those working in the government, tried to help him. Gao first sought help from Lishake, the son of Ulanhu in light of their long friendship and particularly because, during Lishake's detention in 1966 to 1967, Gao had secretly helped him to escape. After Ulanhu and his children resumed power in the mid-1970s, they promised to help if Gao encountered trouble. Gao asked his wife to visit Lishake in Beijing to see whether he could help him. But Lishake refused to see her, saying over the phone that, in such sensitive times, referring to the new campaign "to cleanse three kinds of Cultural Revolution activists" launched by the Center, it was not possible for him to meet her.[16]

Hearing this, I exploded, "That son of a bitch has no human heart!"

Teacher Zong tried to calm me. "Don't worry, Tiejun, Shuhua has confidence that this can be resolved." Two years later, in summer 1983, Gao wrote a letter to Hu Yaobang, the former head of the Youth League and a rising Central leader. Gao reminded Hu that he was the Red Guard that he met and discussed Youth League issues with during the Ninth Party Congress in 1969.

After reading Gao's letter, Hu called Zhou Hui saying, "If no criminal evidence could be found in Gao's case, set him free and give him some admin-

FIGURE 22 Gao Shuhua visiting Khrushchev's tomb at Moscow's Novodeichy Cemetery to rethink the issue of revisionism he criticized in his youthful years, 1990s

istrative responsibility." Gao Shuhua was released on July 25, 1983, five and a half years after being detained.[17]

After moving to Macau, where I taught at the University of Macau, Qingxian and I spent more than a month traveling in China in summer 2001. Upon visiting my home village and brother Ruijun's family in Raoyang county, we visited my stepmother and stepsister's family in Hohhot (my father had passed away in 1997). I asked my sister to call Gao Shuhua to ensure there was no problem for him to see me. Gao responded that we could meet anywhere except at his home or mine. So, on a hot Sunday afternoon, we met in a private VIP room on the second floor of a Mongolian restaurant.

Teacher Gao still looked youthful if slightly thinner. He had just returned from a business trip to Russia and Eastern Europe. After release from prison, he had lost his Party membership and his salary as a cadre. Ordered to undertake another year of labor reform at the Inner Mongolia Electronic Instrument Plant, he received just forty yuan per month as a stipend. Eventually, making use of his Russian-language skills, he went to Russia, Eastern Europe, and Mongolia to purchase metals needed by Inner Mongolian military-industrial enterprises.

Over roast lamb and liquor, we toasted our reunion after a long separation; the memories of Han Tong and Ouyang Ruchen, rebel martyrs of an earlier era; and finally, the timeless friendship among revolutionary rebels.

"I hear that you made good money abroad, is it true?" I asked.

"Don't believe Zhao Zongzhi and Huang Zhigao," he smiled. "They like to exaggerate. We are all involved in foreign trade with Russia. It is true that we can earn a decent living by trading with countries that have recently opened to the world market. We sell Chinese consumer goods and import raw materials (mainly energy and lumber). But only a few people connected to higher officials get the windfall. Not us ordinary traders. By the way, Tiejun, having accumulated some savings, I decided to stop doing business and write a book about the Cultural Revolution in Inner Mongolia. For security reasons, I don't want to discuss this with any friends here. You are the only person who might help. What do you think?"

I was excited by Gao's plan, and we immediately set to work, drafting an outline and setting the themes of the book. Our discussion lasted from lunch to dinner and continued into the night. In the following days, we agreed that the coauthored book would center on his reminiscence of the Cultural Revolution in Inner Mongolia. He would prepare the first draft and I would finalize it, checking key documents and important historical events, collecting data and conducting interviews. It would be an oral history, aiming to rescue the forgotten, or distorted history while avoiding factional prejudice and subjective judgments.

After returning to Macau, preoccupied with teaching and administrative duties I had no opportunity to visit Inner Mongolia for two years. In June 2003 I received a call from Hohhot. It was Teacher Zong Fuhua.

"Tiejun, I have to tell you that your Teacher Gao has gone three days ago," she said.

"What? Where has he gone? Russia again?"

"No. To a faraway place, and forever . . . His funeral was yesterday."

I was stunned and soon started to sob, recalling my teacher and friend whose poster in June 1966 changed the course of my life. He was sixty-two, only two years older than me.

"Teacher Gao was confident that you would keep your word to him. Before losing consciousness, he entrusted a Hong Kong friend to personally deliver a package to you."

One week later, a large yellow envelope arrived containing many handwritten pages, in different sizes and colors, and many black-and-white photos. It was the complete manuscript and related data, including a one-page note:[18]

Dear Tiejun:

I might be gone to meet with Han Tong and Ouyang by the time you see this note. My minor heart problem seems to have developed into a bigger problem.

My family members insist that I stay here in the Inner Mongolian Hospital for observation and medical treatment. I put everything I've done in this envelope, and this is all I can do. It is my best effort. I hope that you will be able to continue my unfinished work and have the book published as we planned . . .

Gao Shuhua in Hohhot

Early June 2003

The two-thousand-plus page manuscript was handwritten. Glancing over the pages, I found most of them written cursorily. Some pages were tea stained or marked with tears. Facing his manuscript, my heart sank and I could not sleep. I wondered whether the effort of the thousands of pages might have been the cause of his sudden death. At the same time, his vigorous handwriting conveyed his strong personality and his refusal to bow to injustice.

His example energized me, and after three years of hard work using my spare time amid heavy teaching, ongoing research, and administrative duties, the manuscript was ready. *The Cultural Revolution in Inner Mongolia: The Oral History of a Rebel Leader* was published in 2007 by Mirror Books in New York and Hong Kong.

Since all books published by Mirror Books were banned in Mainland China, I had to find a way to present the book as a gift to rebel friends to rescue history from the distortions of the regime. I eventually sent three hundred copies of the six-hundred-page book to individuals and libraries, in Hohhot, Baotou, Beijing, Shijiazhuang, and Hulunbuir. To protect the recipient from being punished for "illegally doing business in China," I stamped the inside of each book with a certificate containing my name and email address, adding a sentence in Chinese: *Cangtian youyan, mingjing gaoxuan, benshu zuozhe zengyue*: "Heaven has eyes, and the mirror is hung high, book donated by the authors," followed by my signature.

Meeting Teacher Zong Fuhua in Beijing, I handed her the book. She flipped through the pages of finely printed photos and text, carefully perusing the photos of Han Tong, Ouyang Ruchen, and Gao Shuhua, her hands trembling. She grasped my hands tightly, with tears in her eyes, and said: "Tiejun, thank you so much for completing Gao Shuhua's last wish. I will present this book, and the certificate, in front of Shuhua's tomb."

Later, in Hohhot, the Mongolian owner of a small bookstore that specialized in books about Mongolian culture in the market between Inner Mongolia University and Teachers University (it was upgraded from college in 1983), asked me whether I was interested in some nonofficially (that is, illegally) published books. I said, "Of course." Then he opened a box under the table and took out two books authored by Mao'aohai (Muunohoi) and

FIGURE 23 Cheng Tiejun (right) and his wife, Wang Qingxian (left), on the grasslands with Mongol and Chinese friends summer 2004

Alatengdelihai (Altandelhii, a.k.a. Bayantai). Mao'aohai was the leading Mongol dissident intellectual who had been persecuted for his support of Mongol student demonstrations in 1981. His book *Bingdian Wenti* (Freezing-Point Questions, 2001) was a scathing indictment of China's autonomous region system. Alatengdelihai was the pen name of Bayantai, one of the few Mongol rebels in the Inner Mongolia Party Committee. His 1999 samizdat *Nei Menggu Wasu Zainan Shilu* (Veritable Records of the Wasu Catastrophe in Inner Mongolia) provided a Mongol perspective on the anti–New Neirendang movement.

After purchasing these two precious books, I gave him two copies of our own book as a gift. Two days later, he called, saying many people wanted to buy the book and asking whether I could provide more copies. I told him that the book was not for sale. "If people want to buy it, you can pirate it. But please keep the price low." The interest of Mongols in our book, which presented a rebel perspective on Inner Mongolia's Cultural Revolution, gave me enormous satisfaction.

In the following years, friends told me that pirated copies were available in the underground book market in Hohhot reasonably priced at thirty-five yuan. On a recent trip, I bought a copy for fifty yuan.

★

I hope that this current book, which covers my own political memoir and a history of three-quarters of a century of historical change in Inner Mongolia and the borderland, will be viewed by both Han and Mongols as a record of the struggle of another rebel, who spent his youth in Inner Mongolia and participated in important movements during the region's most tumultuous years. I did not rise politically high as Gao Shuhua did, but as a Red Guard activist and a journalist at the *Inner Mongolia Daily*, I was able to see things in a wider context.

Thinking back, this experience as a journalist distinguished me from the majority of rebels who later became instruments of the *wasu* movement with such tragic consequences for the Mongols and for China. The scapegoating of the rebels alone after the Cultural Revolution, holding them responsible for all the atrocities of that tumultuous era, was, however, an attempt to mask the fact that it was the Party and the military that launched and directed those movements, divided as they were among themselves, with the result that loyalists and rebels all became pawns in a deadly political game. What made Inner Mongolia stand out was that the Mongols, who had staunchly supported the Chinese Communist Party and made enormous contributions to the founding and early development of the People's Republic, were subjected to a systematic witch hunt and massive pogrom based on their alleged anti-Han nationalism. In the *wasu* pogrom, the Chinese state mobilized its military and paramilitary resources as well as "the people" to attack an unarmed and loyal ethnic minority.

I deeply regret that the Chinese state has never issued a public apology, let alone examined the failures of the system, merely scapegoating a few fallen officials for errors while exempting the highest leaders, notably Mao Zedong and Zhou Enlai. A state that does not rethink its history is destined to repeat the same wrongs.

Today, political repression is taking place in the borderlands, especially in Tibet, Xinjiang, Inner Mongolia, and even Hong Kong, and Han are being mobilized to fight against alleged splittism. Much of what is happening in China in the Xi Jinping era, particularly in its borderlands north and south, evokes the tragedy of Inner Mongolia during the Cultural Revolution that I personally experienced.

Settler Colonialism, Minority Nationalities, and Politicide: Reassessing the Cultural Revolution from the Borderlands

This book has presented a history of a troubled Chinese borderland region—the Inner Mongolia Autonomous Region (IMAR)—whose torment was experienced and witnessed by Cheng Tiejun and assessed in light of the historical geopolitics of the region and the People's Republic of China's (PRC) minority nationality politics. Like millions of famine refugees from the North China plain settling in the Steppe beyond the Great Wall in the late nineteenth and twentieth centuries, his odyssey might have been an unremarkable account of toiling in stark circumstances. But he lived in a tumultuous epoch that not only transformed the politics, society, and geopolitics of China and its borderlands; it also upended—and in many cases took—the lives of many. Caught up in the whirlwind of the Great Proletarian Cultural Revolution (1966–1976), like many others, he attempted to reshape the nation in response to Mao Zedong's call to rebel against a corrupt Party leadership. In the process, he became a staunch rebel Red Guard as the nation polarized into warring camps of loyalists and rebels, each convinced of its correct understanding of Mao's injunctions, and each styling itself as "revolutionaries" while denouncing opponents as enemies of Mao and revolution.

The dominant Chinese interpretation of the Cultural Revolution—one widely shared in Anglophone scholarship—is that of a ten-year period of chaos and destruction stemming from Mao's call for a class war to "continue the revolution." After Mao's death in 1976, the leadership repudiated the Cultural Revolution, rejecting in toto its class struggle imperative and anticapitalist political mobilizing practices, though neither repudiating Mao nor holding him responsible for its excesses. It embarked on a national revitalization drive prioritizing the market economy and economic and political cooperation between China and the West while emphasizing domestic social harmony, social control, and the growth imperative, and holding out for the promise of common prosperity. These became core premises of China's subsequent state capitalism, or what its leaders call "socialism with Chinese characteristics." In just thirty years after embarking in 1978 on economic reform and opening to the outside world under Deng Xiaoping and his successors, China became the world's second-largest economy and the world's leading trading nation while achieving rapid growth rates and eliminating the most extreme manifestations of poverty. At least until the growing US-China conflict, which peaked during the Trump and Biden administrations, China was widely expected within the decade to overtake the United States to become the world's largest economy.

Many contemporary international scholars pinpoint the disasters of the Cultural Revolution era as precipitating China's subsequent economic reform and unparalleled economic growth. Roderick MacFarquhar and Michael Schoenhals put it succinctly: "No Cultural Revolution, no economic reform. The Cultural Revolution was so great a disaster that it provoked an even more profound cultural revolution, precisely the one that Mao intended to forestall."[1]

Like any epochal movement, the Cultural Revolution has a contested legacy. With the Chinese Party-state exonerating itself of responsibility for the disasters associated with the Cultural Revolution, claiming that it too was the victim of a "handful of bad elements" (notably the Gang of Four, Lin Biao, and Kang Sheng), few Chinese then or since have accepted responsibility for the consequences of that movement.[2] While many Confucian culturalists would brand the Cultural Revolution as a decade-long ideological holocaust (*haojie*) that destroyed a great civilization and ravaged the Chinese soul,[3] former rebel activists, including many in exile in the United States and the Anglophone world, would contend that, whatever its liabilities, it paved the way for China's pro-democracy movements since the 1980s.[4] Scores of millions devoted their youth to struggles, many of which were launched on foundations of high principles of revolutionary justice, yet they often descended into mass violence, scapegoating, torture and murder. For its part, the Chinese Party-state remains unwilling to publicly engage the numerous challenges the era poses for its legitimacy, suppressing all documentation and public discussion of the Cultural Revolution epoch.

Viewed from the borderlands, especially from Inner Mongolia, however, a distinctive picture of the Cultural Revolution emerges of the nature of the Chinese state and of Han-minority relations. There a pogrom took place that cost more than sixteen thousand lives, the overwhelming majority being Mongols, with more than five times that number crippled by official count.

The attack was rooted in grassroots mobilization directed from the highest levels of the military and the Party, with the support of multiple mass organizations of Red Guards, and urban Han Chinese (hereafter Han) sent-down youth targeting the Mongol population—all to devastating effect. The result was to shatter a core premise of Chinese governance: autonomy for minority peoples. Was this an aberration skewing the objective of the Cultural Revolution? Was it simply an ethnic conflict beyond the control of the Party-state? And what explains the violence of the Han attack on the Mongols in the IMAR, long the national model of a successful autonomous region under the leadership of Ulanhu?

The tragedies of Inner Mongolia raise sensitive questions about nationality politics that have been largely buried in assessing the Cultural Revolution. However, reflection on the Mongol experience, as well as the experience of minority nationalities during and since the Cultural Revolution, poses fundamental questions about the entire legacy of Chinese rule. Particularly important is the question of legitimacy of an autonomy long promoted by the official ideology governing borderlands and other regions with substantial minority populations and the prioritization of national security concerns centered on control of minority nationalities in sensitive borderland areas from the Cultural Revolution to the present. The issues are of singular urgency today, as China's borderlands, notably those of Tibet, Xinjiang, and Inner Mongolia, all experience heightened securitization and social control, as well as assaults on minority languages, cultures, and religions. Increasing Han chauvinism calls into question the fundamental principles of regional autonomy and equal rights for Han and minority people.

This coda addresses two fundamental issues that are essential for understanding both the tragedies in Inner Mongolia during the Cultural Revolution and the current Chinese onslaught against borderland minorities. Together they provide a new perspective on China's minority nationality politics. First and foremost, we address the question of settler colonialism, the essential precondition for Chinese-minority conflict in general and the attack on minority nationalities which has long been neglected in academic analysis of China's ethnic politics both in the PRC and internationally.

The borderlands of Tibet, Xinjiang, and Inner Mongolia were historically the homelands of non-Han peoples, and their full incorporation into China was a pivotal event of the transition from empire to nation-state as the Qing Empire (1636–1912) was replaced by the Republic of China (1912–1949) and its Communist successor the PRC (1949–present) in the long twentieth century. This was a story of Chinese conquest and colonization predicated on large-scale state-sponsored settlement of Han, a process that continues today.

While the Qing dynasty sought to separate Mongols from Chinese, restricting migration to protect the imperial enclave of the Manchus and their Mongol allies in the borderland, in the course of the Qing, Chinese agrarian settlement increased in a number of areas, reaching 80 percent of the population of Inner Mongolia by the mid-twentieth century as large areas of grassland were replaced by agrarian communities and large cities.

Second, the recent Chinese crackdown on the Uyghurs and other Muslim minorities in Xinjiang that many international observers have denounced as "genocide" as well as other attacks on minority rights invites comparison with the Han-led pogrom in Inner Mongolia during the Cultural Revolution recorded in this book. A salient fact is that both were committed by a regime led by the Chinese Communist Party (CCP), which long promoted itself as the "savior" of the minorities. Indeed, many of the Mongol victims during the Cultural Revolution were CCP members or activists. A recognition of this fact compels us to develop an alternative perspective on both the pogrom and contemporary Han-minority relations taking seriously the CCP definition of minority nationalities and their place in China's history and its future and recognizing certain profound difference between the two cases.

Inner Mongolia as a Chinese Settler Colony

THE SETTLER COLONIAL LEGACY AND COMPETING NATIONALISMS

The concept of the autonomous region was first implemented in 1949 with the creation of the Inner Mongolia Autonomous Region on the foundation of the Inner Mongolia Autonomous Government established two years before the founding of the PRC. Between 1949 and 1966, under the Mongol-centered leadership of Ulanhu, Inner Mongolia was the model of a constitutionally enshrined system of governance of the PRC's minority nationalities. Despite repudiation of the Cultural Revolution and formal reinstatement of the system after Mao's death in 1976, key elements of Party policies that led to the violence against the Mongols and the destruction of the relative autonomy of the earlier era continue today. Stated differently, the Cultural Revolution established a pattern of explicit if not constitutionally certified Han hegemony that would subsequently prevail not only in Inner Mongolia but in all regions with significant minority nationality populations. Whatever the internal differentiation and cleavage among the Han, such as Cantonese, Shanghainese, Fujianese, and many others with distinctive language and cultural characteristics, in Inner Mongolia, the critical clash involved a bifurcation between the

Han majority and the Mongol minority. We emphasize that the two categories of people were not simply "invented" in modernity, still less in the People's Republic; they were rooted in the long historical interaction and confrontation between China and its frontiers in Inner Asia.

While noting the legacy of the Cultural Revolution, we suggest that the subsequent tragedies of Inner Mongolia cannot be understood solely with reference to intra-Party ideological struggles among warring factions. Rather we highlight the ineluctable transformation of Inner Mongolia from a homeland of the Mongols to a Chinese settler colony from the twilight years of the Qing Empire at the turn of the twentieth century to the history of Mongol struggles for independence from China during the Republican era (1912–1949). As Penelope Edmonds observes, the "central dynamic of settler colonialism was supersession, that is, the displacement of indigenous peoples and their replacement with settlers," or, in Patrick Wolfe's memorable phrase, it was a "structure not an event."[5] Discussing white settler control of the land of indigenous peoples in North America, Audra Simpson suggests that the resulting structure was one of possession and dispossession.[6] Dispossession of Mongol land accompanied by violence and war in this Chinese settler colony has been endemic since the beginning of the twentieth century.

Settler colonialism is not simply territorial conquest of a land by an alien people but is predicated on permanent occupation and settlement that displaces and/or dispossesses the natives of their land and or attacks on the culture and language of the original inhabitants as in the case of Mongols, Tibetans, and Uyghurs in their historical homelands. In doing so, it establishes a relationship between the natives and the occupiers in a power hierarchy accompanied by attempts to alter, assimilate or destroy the polity, religious belief system, culture, languages, economy, society, and even the landscape of the natives.[7] However, the story of Chinese settler colonialism in Inner Mongolia is not one of simple subjugation of a weak people by an overwhelming power in the long twentieth century. It has to be understood both in the longer historical power dynamics between China and Inner Asia and, more importantly, in the context of China's modern geopolitical and ideological transformation.

Two points about the special historical circumstances of Inner Mongolia bear particular emphasis. The first concerns its position as China's northern frontier, a perspective long emphasized by Owen Lattimore in reflecting on Mongol history in the aftermath of the 1911 Revolution. Writing in 1935, Lattimore noted that the Mongol declaration of independence from China, culminating in the formation of the Mongolian People's Republic in 1924, "was merely an assertion of the historical principle that Mongolia is not part of

China. . . . The idea that a Chinese republic could claim to inherit the Manchu overlordship in Mongolia was historically a *non-sequitur*."[8] Lattimore points to the multiethnic Qing imperial polity with its five major officially classified groups (Manchu, Mongol, Tibetan, Muslims, and Han), each occupying different positions in the empire and for the most part separate from one another administratively, demographically and territorially. Above all, this is a repudiation of the Chinese nationalist claim, made by both the Chinese Nationalist Party (Guomindang) and the CCP, of natural Chinese entitlement to the Qing imperial heritage, specifically to that of its non-Han populations and territories whose incorporation was the product of Manchu diplomacy and conquest. We might add that during the Qing Empire from the seventeenth to the early twentieth century, while the Mongols became subordinate allies of the Manchus in conquering China, the Chinese were themselves a conquered people. Thus, the primary Chinese nationalist impulse culminating in the revolution in 1911 was an anticolonial one directed against the Manchu rulers and their Mongol allies, as manifest in the clarion call "Expel the barbarians, recover China" (*quchu dalu, huifu zhonghua*).

This does not mean that Manchu-Mongol relations during the Qing were entirely cordial or that they shared common interests in all realms. If the Mongols were beneficiaries of two and a half centuries of Qing rule during which a collective "Mongol" identity was forged out of disparate warring groups,[9] they also lost their independence and became subordinate to the Manchu rulers. Indeed, those who defied the Qing, such as the Junghar Mongols, were annihilated in the mid-eighteenth century.[10] In the mid-nineteenth century, moreover, the majority of Mongol armies perished while serving as the last military bulwark of the crumbling Qing, deployed to suppress the Chinese rebellions of the Taiping and Nian as well as Hui Muslim rebellions, and to fight the British and French at Tianjin and Beijing during the Second Opium War.[11] In the end, the Mongols, who had played a pivotal role in the Manchu conquest of China and subsequent challenges to it, were unable to protect their own interests in the face of multiple challenges from the Manchus, the Chinese and the international powers.

Second, the roots of transformation of the historical homeland of the Mongol people can be traced to the seventeenth century, when Mongolia underwent two forms of colonization, starting with the Qing conquest and ending with Chinese settler colonization from the late nineteenth century and continuing to the present. These were two discrete but interrelated sequential processes. In the first case, despite, and perhaps precisely because of, the challenge by some Mongol groups to Qing imperial ambitions, as well as heavy reliance on Mongol military power to expand and pacify the empire, the

Manchus took steps to assure that the Mongols would be incapable of forming an independent polity capable of challenging Qing authority. The Qing divided the Mongols into numerous mutually exclusive communities (banners and leagues) while bringing them under a single administrative system controlled by the Manchus. The Qing's Lifan Yuan, the Board for the Administration of Outlying Regions, was originally designed to govern the Mongols.[12] This was achieved through alternating processes of alliance and conquest, including cutting off Mongol relations with both the Chinese and the Russians. To be sure, the borders between the Mongols and the Chinese were never impenetrable, as Chinese farmers, many escaping famine or sometimes at the invitation of Mongol princes, found their way into Mongolia from the mid-Qing period.[13]

In the late nineteenth and early twentieth centuries, in the face of increasing Russian and Japanese encroachment on Mongolia and Manchuria, and with the weakening of Mongol military power, the Qing rulers began to rely on the Han to sustain their regime. This led to the abandonment of the long-standing ethnic segregation policy. With Mongolia and even the homeland of Manchuria open to Chinese settlement, millions of land-hungry Chinese poured in, quickly occupying the most fertile land and vastly outnumbering the native Mongols and Manchus. This resulted in a change of status of Han settlers "from illegal but tolerated to controlled and temporary, and finally to legally sanctioned and state-sponsored migrants."[14]

The scale of Chinese migration into Inner Mongolia can be gauged from the following: in the early 1800s, there were 2.15 million people in Inner Mongolia, of which Mongols were about 1.03 million and Chinese 1 million, with the Manchu, Hui, Daur, Ewenki, and Orochon making up the balance. Many of the Chinese at that time were seasonal migrants, tilling Mongol land in spring and summer and returning home in the fall and winter. By 1912, however, the Mongol population had dropped to 828,977 as a result of casualties in the wars of the late nineteenth century, while the Chinese population shot up to 1.55 million, many of whom became permanent settlers. In 1937, while the Mongol population remained stagnant at 864,429, the Chinese population more than doubled, reaching 3.72 million. By 1949, the Mongol population dropped further to 835,000, whereas the Chinese increased to 5.15 million.[15] These settlers took up the most fertile land of Inner Mongolia, forcing Mongol herders to subsist in a marginal environment. The banner and league system—the linchpin of the Qing divide and rule policy toward the Mongols—ultimately failed to protect the Mongols against this existential settler colonial threat.

In quick succession between 1911 and 1945, the borderland experienced Chinese occupation, a pan-Mongol independence movement, the collapse of the Qing dynasty, establishment of the Mongolian People's Republic with Soviet support, Japanese invasion, ultimately becoming what Lattimore aptly called a "cradle of conflict."[16] As the region that would become known as Inner Mongolia rapidly became a Chinese settler colony, various Mongol and Chinese forces developed clashing political ideologies and took up arms to fight for their own blood and soil in this troubled land: Mongol nationalist consciousness was predicated on opposition to Chinese settler colonialism, whereas Chinese nationalism justified control of the frontier as protecting China's national territory against both "barbarians" (Mongol and Manchu) and foreign imperialists (especially Russians and Japanese) bent on dividing up China territorially.[17] In Chinese nationalist thinking, ethnic Chinese settlers were the bulwark of the nation's defense, whereas barbarians-turned-minorities always were and would remain potential separatists. This binary oppositional structure was, however, complicated by the advent of the Communist Revolution, which swept across the Mongolian Steppe and China after 1921, eventually leading to an international and interethnic alliance between Mongols and Chinese. The formation of the CCP-led Inner Mongolia Autonomous Government in 1947 was a landmark event en route to the formation of the PRC, one predicated on the Communist ideology of national self-determination and colonial liberation. In this ideology, Mongols were recognized by the CCP as a weak and small people, colonized, exploited, and oppressed by the Han but also as potential revolutionary allies.

Let's first look at the emergence of Inner Mongolia as a territorial entity under the Qing and the post-Qing Chinese settler colonization.

THE COLONIAL FORMATION OF INNER MONGOLIA

Qing rule of the Mongols was implemented primarily through two colonial technologies: population categorization and territorial administration. It started with dividing Mongolia into two large but opposing categories: Gadaad Mongol (Tülergi Monggo in Manchu, or Waifan Menggu in Chinese), meaning "External Mongolia," and Dotood Haria Mongol, meaning "Internal Affiliated Mongolia." The former comprised groups led by hereditary ruling princes who enjoyed autonomous power, whereas the latter consisted of groups controlled directly by the Qing government. External Mongolia was further divided into Outer Mongolia and Inner Mongolia, the difference based on organizational proximity of the ruling princes to the Qing imperial center, with the former retaining greater autonomy while the latter enjoyed privileges associated with access to the Qing power center. From the early twentieth century the latter two entities began to be organized "territorially," a product of Mongolian nationalism and great power rivalry between Russia and Japan which carved up Mongolia into two separate spheres of influence: Outer Mongolia dominated by Russia and Inner Mongolia and Manchuria by Japan.[18]

The partitioning of Mongolia was institutionalized by the Treaty of Kyakhta, a tripartite agreement signed in 1915 between Russia, Mongolia, and China, that rescinded the independence of Mongolia that had been declared in December 1911 from the crumbling Qing Empire and turned the northern part into an autonomous Outer Mongolia together with recognition of the suzerainty of the Republic of China as the successor state to the Qing.[19] The Mongolian Revolution of 1921 with the assistance of the Soviet Red Army once again set Outer Mongolia on a path of independence from China, eventually winning de jure independence in January 1946. The southern part of Mongolia—that is, Inner Mongolia—however, did not come into being as a polity simultaneously. Instead, its western part was carved up into several "special administrative regions"—Ningxia, Suiyuan,[20] Chahar, and Rehe—while the eastern part was incorporated into three northeastern provinces of Heilongjiang, Jilin, and Fengtian (Liaoning). In 1928, the newly established Nationalist government in Nanjing, upon defeating the Beijing government through its northern expedition in the name of fighting warlords, turned these "special administrative regions" into provinces.[21] Chinese nation-building meant nation destruction for the Mongols and other non-Han groups on China's northern border.

Deprived of collective territorial administration, Mongol territories under Chinese provincial control were simply referred to as *mengqi*—Mongol banners, the banner is equivalent to county, the highest administrative unit permitted to exercise local self-governance under a province during the Nationalist period.[22] But county-level autonomy remained a rare luxury to the Mongols. Chinese warlords-turned-Nationalists such as Fu Zuoyi and Song Zheyuan, governors of Suiyuan and Chahar provinces, pushed for further colonization by setting up Chinese counties on banner territories under their control. This provoked an unprecedented Mongol nationalist movement for autonomy led by Prince Demchudongrob starting from 1929, a time of increasing Japanese aggressiveness toward China.[23]

Japanese occupation of Manchuria from 1931, and the establishment of Manchuguo in 1932 as a nominally independent state under Japanese control, stirred Mongol hopes for liberation from Chinese colonialism.[24] Under Japanese control, however, Mongols were divided into two regional groups:

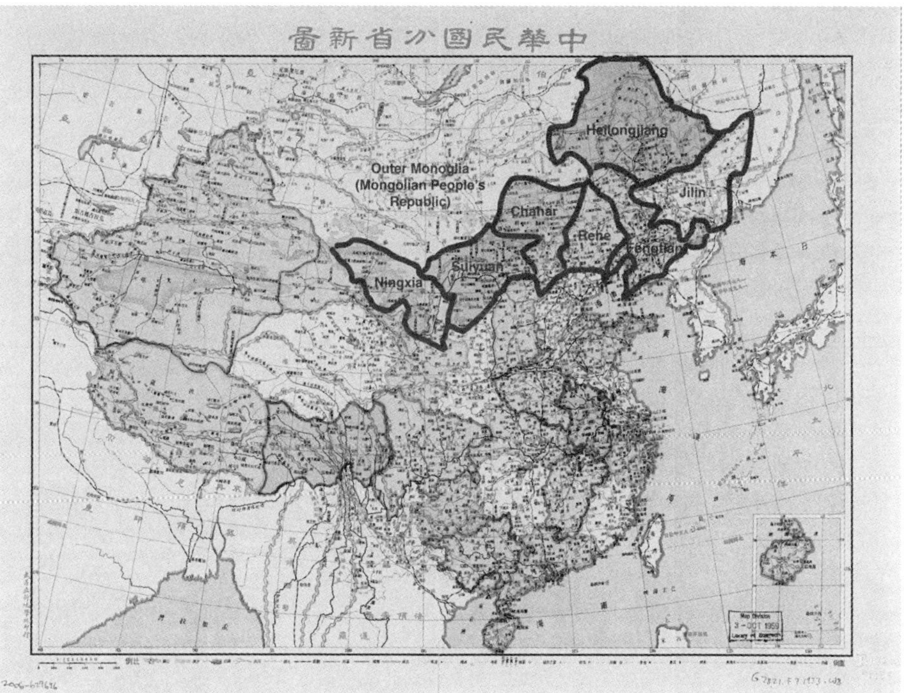

MAP 5 Map of the Republic of China, showing the four western provinces established on Inner Mongolian territories in 1928 and the three northeastern provinces occupying the eastern part of Inner Mongolia

Eastern Mongols and Western Mongols. The former, consisting of the three leagues of Josotu, Jirim and Juu'uda, and the Hulunbuir region, were organized by Manchuguo into the newly created Hingan (Xing'an) province. The latter, with three leagues of Shiliingol, Ulaanchab, and Yekejuu (primarily its two eastern banners), led by Prince Demchugdongrob and his princely allies, came to be organized into a Japanese-supported Mongolian borderland (Mengjiang) government in 1937, and in 1942 it expanded to become a Mongolian Autonomous State (Menggu Zizhi Bang).

While Mongols advanced in the years 1931–1945, crucially in organizing separate autonomous polities through collaborations with Japan, the Mongol nationalist vision for territorial unification was dashed. A unified Inner Mongolian polity had no place either in the Republic of China or Japan's Greater East Asia Co-Prosperity Sphere. It would have to be imagined in the interstices of the Mongol and Chinese Communist movements.

The founding of the Soviet- and Comintern-supported Mongolian People's Republic (MPR) in 1924 was little noted in twentieth-century world history, but it was the world's first "people's republic." In expunging the name

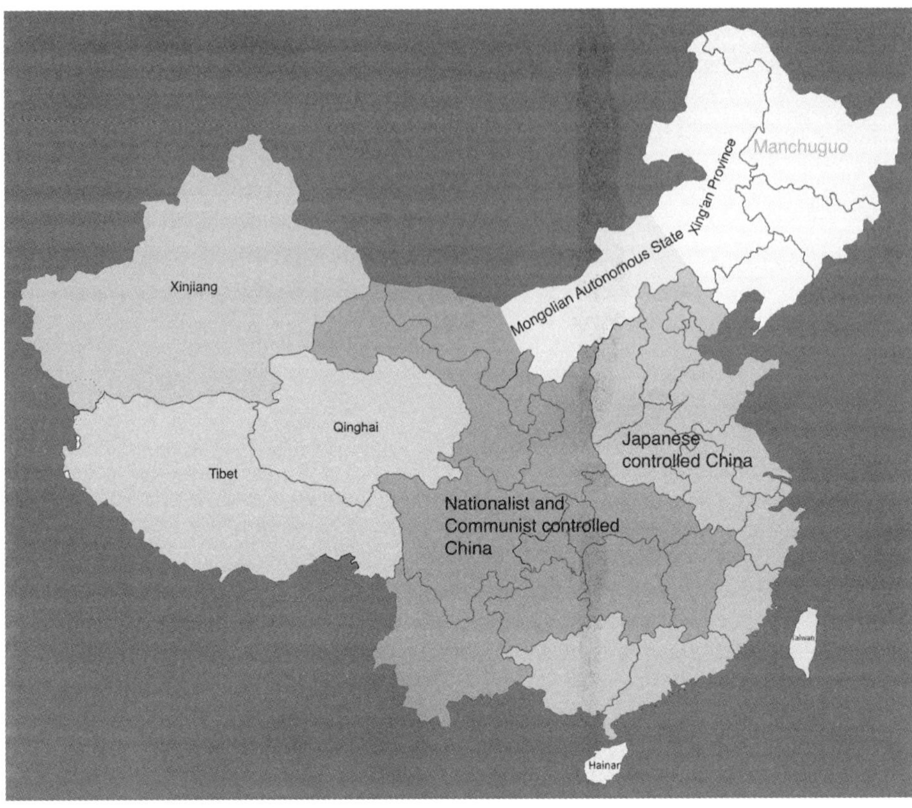

MAP 6 Map of China showing Mongol areas controlled by the Mongolian Autonomous State and Man-chuguo's Xing'an Province, 1942–1945

Outer Mongolia, which suggested a tributary relationship to China,[25] this people's republic proclaimed independence from China. In the same year, the Inner Mongolia People's Revolutionary Party (Nei Menggu Renmin Geming-dang, or Neirendang for short) was founded under Comintern leadership, initially with support of the Mongolian People's Revolutionary Party and both the Guomindang and the CCP, in response to Lenin's call for colonial liberation.[26] In 1924 the Neirendang became the first to use Inner Mongolia (Mongolian, Dotood Mongol; Chinese, Nei Menggu) to imagine a new Inner Mongolian entity. However, the Neirendang's aim was pan-Mongolian uni-fication of all Mongols in China with the MPR and the Buryat Autonomous Soviet Socialist Republic (founded in 1923) into a single Mongolian nation allied with the Soviet Union. This international experiment collapsed in 1928 after the Guomindang unified much of China including Mongol territories through military conquest.

Seven years later, Inner Mongolia was mentioned again, this time by the CCP, a fugitive party on the run from Guomindang annihilation after being driven out of its central China territorial base, the Jiangxi Soviet Republic. In December 1935, soon after arriving in Yan'an in Northwest China close to the Mongol Steppe after surviving the Long March, Mao Zedong made a proclamation to the Inner Mongolian people (*Nei Menggu Renmin*, sometimes referring to the Inner Mongolian nation, or *Nei Menggu Minzu*) on behalf of the government of the Chinese Soviet. Mao promised abolition of Chinese counties and provinces and restoration of all former Inner Mongolian territories to the Mongols in a bid for their support for the CCP's struggle against Japan and its domestic nemesis, the Guomindang. The proclamation even allowed for independence.[27] This is to say that Inner Mongolia as a polity with a clear territorial and administrative boundary was first proposed or rather promised by the CCP on condition that the Mongols side with them at a time when the greater part of Inner Mongolia was under Japanese control. A decade later, Ulanhu, a Tumed Mongol Communist, would emerge as the highest-ranking Mongol CCP leader tasked to deliver that promise.

The year 1945 provided a historic opportunity for Mongols to contemplate afresh the possibility of unifying the MPR and war-torn Inner Mongolia in the postwar settlement. But it was not to be. The Yalta deal negotiated by Stalin, Roosevelt and Churchill, and Chiang Kai-shek's decision to recognize the MPR's independence through a plebiscite (held on October 20, 1945) in exchange for Soviet recognition of Chinese control of Manchuria and Inner Mongolia, ensured that Inner Mongolia would remain part of China and be excluded from the MPR.[28]

On May 1, 1947, the Inner Mongolia Autonomous Government was founded, with Ulanhu as its leader and Hafenga, a Mongol from the former Manchuguo, as his deputy. For the first time, Inner Mongolia became a territorial political entity, emerging as the CCP and Guomindang scrambled to control Manchuria and other territories with Mongol populations. The Chinese name for this entity was Nei Menggu (meaning Inner Mongolia), but the Mongol name was changed from Dotood Mongol (Inner Mongolia) to Övör Mongol (Front or Southern Mongolia). The term *Övör* follows the indigenous toponymic tradition, and it is always paired with *Ar*, together referring to the front and rear sides of a mountain. Thus, in this linguistic imagination, *Övör Mongol* (Southern or Inner Mongolia) joins *Ar Mongol* (the MPR) surreptitiously to become a single geobody.

The "Mongolian Question" in China was finally resolved in 1949, when Inner Mongolia became an autonomous region of the newly founded PRC. It was also made possible by a new international situation in which the PRC

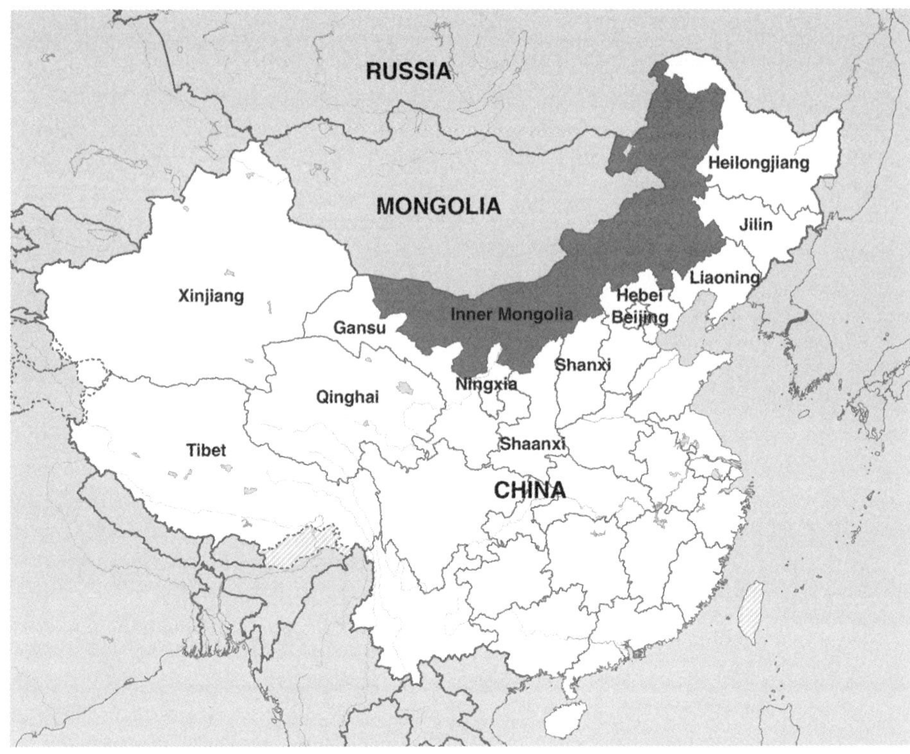

MAP 7 Present-day map of China, with Inner Mongolia marked in dark gray

for the first time joined the same ideological camp as the Soviet Union and the MPR. The system of autonomy embodied by the Inner Mongolia Autonomous Region (IMAR) was premised on three "unifications": the unification of Inner Mongolia with China, with Mongols exercising some rights in China; the Chinese and Mongols unified within a single polity; and the unification of most Mongol groups under one administration within China, the IMAR. It took six years for this unified Inner Mongolia to take shape in territorial terms, consummated by the incorporation of Alasha and Ejine banners in 1956. Hohhot became the capital of the IMAR in 1954, when Suiyuan province was abolished, five years before Cheng Tiejun settled there in 1959.[29]

But what was the nature of this autonomy of Inner Mongolia comprising both communism and ethnic nationalism amid conflicting forces of the era? Would the settler colonial legacy and competing nationalisms fade from consciousness after Inner Mongolia was incorporated into the PRC in 1949 as an autonomous region with the Mongols holding a leadership position in the borderland where Chinese were the majority population? How would

Mongol-Chinese ethnic relations play out in Inner Mongolia under CCP rule? At issue was not only a region with a complex history of colonial and nationalist entanglements but also the question of how to exercise nationality autonomy by a Mongol population vastly outnumbered by Chinese settlers in a Communist state at a time when "class struggle" was the overriding political imperative in the PRC.

PROBLEMS OF ETHNIC AUTONOMY IN A COMMUNIST SETTLER COLONIAL BORDERLAND

The history of the formation of Inner Mongolia shows that the region was not a simple frontier beyond the pale of civilization awaiting conquest or enlightenment. Rather, what was once the imperial center of the steppe and a springboard for regional and global conquest at the height of the Mongol world empire in the thirteenth century, and a central element during the expansion of Manchu power in the eighteenth century, was gradually pushed to the political margins of the Qing Empire before being thrown into a whirlwind of conflicting visions of empire, competing nationalisms, territorial and ethnic conflicts, modernizing visions and ideological struggles and perpetual warfare in the late nineteenth and much of the long twentieth century. However, to account for the intensity of the violence during the Cultural Revolution, a violence that destroyed the accomplishments of the IMAR over two decades and revealed the structural problems of the autonomy concept, we need to look at the ethnic structure, the institutional arrangements, and the ideology of Maoism premised on the application of a class struggle approach to interethnic relations.

From the formation of the Inner Mongolia Autonomous Government in 1947, a debate raged among Mongols, and between Chinese and Mongols, about Inner Mongolia's autonomy in general and its leadership in particular. Would it be led by the Neirendang, the left-leaning Mongol nationalist party that was revived in 1945 as an independence party and established a short-lived Eastern Mongolian Autonomous Government in January 1946? Or would it be led by the CCP through its Mongol agents who organized the Federation for the Autonomous Movement of Inner Mongolia in late 1945? At issue was the question whether Inner Mongolia should be envisaged as an autonomous Mongol polity or a polity open to both Mongols and Chinese settlers and accepting the numerical preeminence of the Chinese and prioritizing the harmonizing of interethnic relations. The latter view prevailed, leading to the acceptance of Neirendang members into the CCP, the transformation of its army into units of the PLA, and the abolition of the Neirendang.

CCP leadership meant that Inner Mongolia was perforce not fully "autonomous" since the Mongol leaders who held power between 1947 and 1966, like other regional leaders, were subject to CCP control and were not answerable exclusively to the Mongol people.

The interethnic violence in the land reform carried out in 1947 in areas under the control of the Inner Mongolia Autonomous Government, namely, the so-called liberated region, punctured the Communist promise of interethnic friendship. Applying the class struggle approach to a biethnic region of eastern Inner Mongolia in which Han farmers were predominantly tenants tilling Mongol lands, many Mongols were classified as landlords and subjected to class struggle and redistribution of their land. Mongols were also accused of collaborating with the Japanese invaders in Manchuguo. With this bloody rite of passage, and in an effort to stabilize the strategic rear that Inner Mongolia was and to win Mongol loyalty at the height of the Chinese Civil War, in 1948 Ulanhu introduced the CCP's first nationality policy—the "three nos and two benefits" policy (no class struggle, no class designation, and no land redistribution; herdlords and herders benefit each other). The policy, applied to pastoral regions, shielded Mongol pastoralists from Chinese land seizures and redistribution.[30]

Benedict Anderson, in his pathbreaking study of nationalism, puzzled over the violent conflicts between Communist countries.[31] He attributed this to the rise of nationalism but without explaining its ferocity. Nor did he address the suppression of minorities in a number of Communist countries. Both the Soviet Union and the PRC attempted to build socialism on a foundation of multinational empires. And as historians, sociologists and anthropologists document, both the incorporation and transformation of peripheral regions and peoples were violent processes, often privileging the Russian and Han majorities through a merger of class struggle and nationality struggle.[32] We trace the origins of Cultural Revolution violence in Inner Mongolia to the built-in tension between nationalism and communism, and above all, between divergent ethnic interests embedded in the embrace of communism, a tension manifest in Mongol membership in the CCP, a Chinese political party. In particular, we seek clues to the virulent exercise of Chinese nationalism in the wake of the deepening conflict between China and the Soviet Union with its MPR ally, which made the existence of Inner Mongolia as an autonomous region a national security liability to China.

Founded in May 1947, initially with jurisdiction over Mongol regions (i.e., Hingan or Xing'an province) in former Manchuguo and Shiliingol league and Chahar league of the former Mongolian Autonomous State, the Inner Mongolia Autonomous Government with Mongol leadership was created as an autonomous Mongolian polity. In October 1949, however, the autonomous government was incorporated as an autonomous region into the newly founded PRC. It thereby lost its "national autonomy" to become a multiethnic "nationality regional autonomy" with the Mongols as the titular nationality (*zhuti minzu*, literally "core nationality") and the Han as the majority nationality.[33] The IMAR subsequently expanded westward, subsuming Mongol territories in Rehe, Chahar, Suiyuan, and Ningxia provinces over the following six years, resulting in a territory the size and shape that presently exists.[34] In the process, most of the Chinese counties built on Mongol banner lands were dismantled, with Han residents coming under the newly constituted Mongol banners. If this suggests realization of Mao's 1935 promise to the Mongols, problems would subsequently emerge. The abolition of provinces and counties and their amalgamation into the IMAR—a product of both Mongol nationalist aspiration to restore their lost land and the Chinese Communist institutional design—created a new interethnic dynamic that might have initially privileged the Mongols, but ultimately undermined their "ethnic sovereignty" by weakening Mongol "self-government" in a territory with a substantial Chinese majority population.[35]

Modernity, in both capitalist and Communist societies, has privileged majority over minority as a matter of "democracy" or "people's democracy." In the PRC, the Han majority, deemed by Party leaders to be more advanced culturally and ideologically, was charged with uplifting minorities during their advance to socialism and communism. Ethnic autonomy in the PRC, defined as "nationality regional autonomy," was designed as a transitional stage to transform the social structure and political consciousness of minorities to facilitate their integration into Chinese society.[36] In such a conception of autonomy, the Chinese were privileged as "the advanced people," agents of the Chinese state in the transformation of the borderlands. Their language—Mandarin Chinese—prevailed in Inner Mongolia, especially in urban centers whose populations were overwhelmingly Han, although Mongols were able to develop a Mongolian-medium education system that sustained a new Mongolian culture in Mongol-inhabited rural areas which was "nationality in form, but socialist in content." Mongol Party and government cadres and educators who moved to Hohhot, the region's capital, or to banner or league centers, which had grown around Mongol monastic centers surrounded by Han traders or former Chinese settlements, were divorced from Mongolian culture, and their children or the second generation rapidly lost their Mongolian language competence.[37]

The rapid economic development of the IMAR and accelerated inward migration of the Chinese population in the 1950s were two sides of a coin with contradictory implications for the Mongol population. Between 1950 and 1957, more than 1.5 million Han migrated to Inner Mongolia, and in the next three years 1.9 million more poured in. By 1960, the Mongol population in Inner Mongolia (1.2 million) had declined to only 10 percent of the total population of the region (11.9 million). Han constituted 87 percent of Inner Mongolia's population, vastly outnumbering the Mongols and other minority nationalities.[38] The notable industrial progress in Inner Mongolia, achieved with Soviet support in the 1950s, highlighted the shortage of skilled industrial and technological labor among both Mongols and local Han, hence substantial skilled Han labor was imported from North and Northeast China's cities. Communist internationalism and the integration of Inner Mongolia into the Chinese political-economic system thus accelerated Chinese population flow into the relatively prosperous urbanizing and industrializing autonomous region throughout the 1950s.[39] The new settlers also included large numbers of refugees, including Cheng Tiejun, desperate to escape the famine induced by the Great Leap Forward.[40]

Mongols and Han in Inner Mongolia today both recall the first decade of the PRC as the golden era of interethnic relations. However, in the late 1950s, interethnic tensions increased, despite Ulanhu's skillful management in the service of interethnic harmony, national unity and economic development. This was a conflict between two populations, each of which viewed itself and the other through the prisms of class and nationality, one seeing itself as a "small and weak people" whose land was colonized by Han settlers, the other both as an absolute majority and as an advanced class that was entitled to leadership in a region it now called its own while feeling threatened by a minority which enjoyed the status of the titular nationality. Mongols, experiencing the loss of their land through administrative merger and increasing marginalization in the face of growing Han population concentration—not only in urban centers, factories, and universities but also in rural areas—felt that they had sacrificed too much for outsiders or settlers.

Han settlers, for their part, resented the loss of their power in the dissolution of counties and provinces. Chinese resistance to the Mongol "takeover" of power was both ideological and practical: why did the Mongols have to exercise "autonomy" when the Chinese no longer "oppressed" or "exploited" the Mongols in a country in which everyone was "liberated"? Wasn't Mongolian autonomy a form of Mongol nationalism treating the Han as oppressors and exploiters of the Mongols? Such questions, rooted in Communist understanding of nationalism as an issue embedded in class relationships, were deeply hurtful to the moral sensibility of the Han who deemed themselves to be good people. Ultimately the answers privileged the Han, who would challenge Mongol calls for autonomy as a manifestation of nationalism that had no place in a socialist country marching toward communism.[41]

How can we characterize such a history and such a zone? Neither national, transnational, or imperial perspectives can capture the distinctive character of Inner Mongolia as an ethnic, cultural, national, and transnational borderland, still less explain the wave of violence this book documents through the perceptions of Cheng Tiejun and his generation of Chinese and Mongols swept up in the Cultural Revolution. It is a settler colonial borderland saga with unique characteristics. If the promise of autonomy was useful in winning Mongols to the CCP in 1947 during a civil war pitting Communists against the Guomindang, nineteen years later, the CCP leadership began to see Mongol discontent at their diminished rights in their own autonomous region as a threat to China's sovereignty at a time of heightened international tensions on the China MPR Soviet border. Developing a profound paranoia with respect to the Mongol cadres and soldiers the CCP had nurtured and trained, during the Cultural Revolution, the Chinese Party, state, and army mobilized the Han majority, cracked down on the Mongols and eliminated the autonomy system in all but name.

Politicide

GENOCIDE OR POLITICIDE?

In the early 1960s, the debacle of the Great Leap Forward plunged the nation into famine, fractured China's leadership, and heightened pressures from above to reaffirm the revolutionary agenda in the form of a nationwide attack on "revisionism," both Soviet and domestic variants. Beginning in 1963, the new class struggle drive promoted by Mao and initially directed by Liu Shaoqi under the rubric of the Socialist Education Movement, threatened to repeat the pitting of Chinese against Mongol of the land reform era in Inner Mongolia. As the architect of the original nationality policy that eased class struggle to facilitate harmony between Mongols and Chinese, Ulanhu was acutely aware of the dangers of a movement spinning out of control. However, his repeated warning that a class-nation approach would rupture Mongol-Han relations prompted suspicions of his Mongol nationalism at the highest levels of Party power.

Li Xuefeng, first secretary of the North China Bureau (Ulanhu was second secretary), led the attack on Ulanhu during the Socialist Education Movement. Desperate to blunt the attack, Ulanhu reissued Mao's 1935 proclamation to the Mongols offering high levels of autonomy and restructured the Party and government administration. His goal was to thwart the challenge to the system of nationality autonomy in Inner Mongolia and legitimatize his leadership position. However, at a time of deepening international tensions on the borderland some in the Central leadership perceived his action as a coup d'état on behalf of Mongol independence.

With deepening conflicts between China and the Soviet Union in the early 1960s, on January 15, 1966, the MPR and the Soviet Union signed a new treaty of friendship, cooperation, and mutual assistance that included secret protocols allowing the Soviets to station troops, aircraft, and missiles in Mongolia.[42] The Cultural Revolution was thus launched both to solve an ideological dispute centered on class struggle and to confront a Soviet-MPR military threat to the borderlands.

The purge of Ulanhu and the Mongol generals in the Inner Mongolia Military Region in June 1966, together with the transfer to the IMAR of hundreds of Han military cadres from Shanxi and Hebei provinces, consolidated the Center's, particularly the military's, grip on Inner Mongolia at a time of tensions on the Soviet-MPR border. This was a critical step in the destruction of Mongol power in the autonomous region. The process would be completed in three stages beginning with the appointment by Beijing of a new Han leadership of IMAR under General Teng Haiqing brought in from the Beijing Military Area in 1967. This was followed by an onslaught against the Mongols led by General Teng in the course of the military-led cleansing (*wasu*) campaign of 1967–1969 to eliminate Ulanhu's influence in Inner Mongolia and that of a so-called New Neirendang. It was a trumped-up charge claiming the rebirth of an organization that had been dissolved in the late 1940s and allegedly emerged in 1961 to pursue secession and reunification of Mongols in IMAR and the MPR. The campaign ended with a 1969 declaration of martial law and dismembering of the IMAR that placed the eastern part under the jurisdiction of Heilongjiang, Jilin and Liaoning provinces, and the western part under Gansu province and the Ningxia Hui Autonomous Region. All this was carried out with the support of the Central Cultural Revolution Group controlled by Zhou Enlai. In short, the Cultural Revolution destroyed the last vestige of Inner Mongolia's tenuous autonomy, eliminated Mongol primacy in the IMAR, and unleashed a reign of terror conducted by Han at the expense of the Mongols.

The Cultural Revolution in Inner Mongolia thus differed fundamentally from the national pattern, even from developments in Tibet and Xinjiang. In their pioneering study of the Cultural Revolution in Tibet, Goldstein and colleagues conclude that violence in Tibet was part of a struggle between rival revolutionary groups and was not ethnically based.[43] Tsering Woeser's monumental study of Tibet during the Cultural Revolution based on her father's photographs shows that some of the bloodiest fighting in Lhasa was between Tibetan rebel Red Guards and the PLA, but there is little indication that the violence was a product of nationalism or ethnic hatred. The Cultural Revolution in Tibet by and large afforded an opportunity for Tibetan "emancipated serfs" to take revenge on former nobles and high lamas and to destroy Buddhist temples as vestiges of the old hierarchy. In contrast to Inner Mongolia, some of the bloodiest conflicts took place among Tibetans.[44]

The Cultural Revolution in Xinjiang unfolded on two fronts: one among the Han and the other among minorities. These two Cultural Revolutions ran parallel to each other. According to James Millward, Uyghurs and other minorities in Xinjiang were largely spared the violent factional struggles and even fighting among the Han: "It appears that of the Beijing leadership, Premier Zhou Enlai at least was anxious to keep Xinjiang's 'minority nationalities' from becoming politicized or embroiled in the factional fighting."[45] Consequently, the Cultural Revolution among minorities, especially the Uyghurs and various Muslim peoples, was carried out in the cultural and religious fields targeting their customs, burning Qur'ans, and shutting down and desecrating mosques, mazars, madrasas, and cemeteries. The biggest insult Uyghurs remember of the era was being forced to raise pigs in mosques. If, as Morris Rossabi observes, during the Cultural Revolution Xinjiang was hardly immune from violence directed at the Uyghurs and Islam, the level of violence, particularly Han violence directed at the Uyghurs, never approached the level of the pogrom in Inner Mongolia.[46]

The Cultural Revolution conflict in Inner Mongolia was quintessentially ethnic. Han spearheaded the violence against Mongols who suffered massive casualties. Pressed by Party and army activists as well as sent-down Han youth from late 1967, the *wasu* campaign was finally halted in mid-1969. In two years, the pogrom had taken the lives of 16,222 people, crippled or maimed 87,188, and persecuted 346,653 by official tabulation. The overwhelming majority of victims were from among the 1.4 million Mongols.[47] The death toll of 11.5 deaths per thousand Mongols was by far the largest recorded for a single nationality in any province or autonomous region during the Cultural Revolution.

Andrew Walder estimated deaths in China from Cultural Revolution violence in the years 1966 to 1971 at 1.6 million, or 2.2 deaths per thousand population. He found five counties in a Chinese national database whose reported death rates exceeded 1 percent, or ten deaths per thousand: "Three of them are in Inner Mongolia, and their death rates, based on published records, ranged from 14 to 17 per thousand. . . . These were localities where the intensity of the violence would have ranked high among the most notorious cases in recent world history."[48]

A number of Mongols have recorded a far larger scale of violence against the Mongols in Inner Mongolia than that provided by the official data. In a letter dated August 1, 1981, addressed to General Huang Kecheng, Ting Mao, the Mongol second Party secretary of Inner Mongolia, called for the prosecution of Teng Haiqing, who masterminded the *wasu* campaign, stating that during the Cultural Revolution more than 20,000 people were killed, 170,000 people crippled, and over one million persecuted.[49] Ting's plea fell on deaf ears. A semiofficial book entitled *History of the Inner Mongolia Autonomous Region*, edited by Mongol scholar Hao Weimin, raised the figure of total deaths to 27,900, with more than 120,000 people crippled.[50] The death toll was 19.9 per thousand. Yang Haiying, a Mongol-Japanese scholar who charged ethnic genocide, based on a Mongol source, estimated Mongol deaths at 300,000. The figure combined those who were murdered on the spot with those who died after being released from prison and returned home.[51] This would push the death toll to a staggering 214 per thousand, slightly lower than the 224 deaths per thousand in Cambodia under the Khmer Rouge but much higher than the 133 deaths per thousand in the 1994 massacre of Tutsi in Rwanda, as reported by Walder. The number of injuries and deaths cannot, of course, be estimated with confidence under conditions of closed archives and politicized reports. The available evidence nevertheless suggests that the heaviest toll of deaths and injuries anywhere during the Cultural Revolution occurred among the Mongols and that many of those tortured, injured and killed had played no role in the Cultural Revolution clashes of rebels and loyalists. They included many with no known political involvement, people largely scapegoated for their Mongol identity. There is no evidence, moreover, that the Party ever conducted a serious investigation of perhaps the largest ethnic massacre in the course of the PRC, still less that it issued an official apology.

Arrest, torture, and death were far from the only consequences of the Cultural Revolution for Mongols and for the region. The fate of Inner Mongolia, the preeminent model of an autonomous region in the years 1949–1966, exemplified the fragility of the position of the Mongols. Mongols' ability to exercise significant leadership over their historic homeland was permanently broken in the course of the Cultural Revolution. Small numbers of Mongol officials subsequently served in cadre and leadership positions in Party, government, and army, but with sharply diminished authority and scant opportunity to defend Mongol interests. Indeed, throughout China, in the more than half a century since 1966, no titular minority official would hold the top position of Party secretary—the highest authority of the Party-state—in their provincial-level autonomous region.[52] Though barely mentioned in the literature in Chinese or English, the Cultural Revolution strengthened the foundation for Han domination of the Party, state, and army at the national and provincial levels.

Perhaps the most formidable challenge this book confronts is how to characterize the pogrom that is a lasting legacy of the Cultural Revolution in Inner Mongolia and the entire minority-majority nationality structure on which the PRC polity rests. While the Chinese term *haojie*, or catastrophe, is often used to refer to Cultural Revolution disasters, it is ultimately a bland descriptive term that prescribes no moral or political responsibility and eludes analytical rigor. Western scholarship has for the most part refrained from characterizing the ethnic pogrom in Inner Mongolia as genocide, although in recent years, some have advanced notions of cultural genocide or ethnocide for contemporary Chinese policies toward Tibetans and Uyghurs.[53] However, a recent campaign launched in the Mongol diaspora characterizes the pogrom as genocide.[54] It is a view that has gained currency since former US secretary of state Mike Pompeo denounced Chinese genocide against the Uyghurs in Xinjiang on January 19, 2021, his final day in office, a position subsequently adopted by the Biden administration and a number of Western countries, including Belgium, the Netherlands, Canada, and the United Kingdom.

However reprehensible the pervasive torture and killing in Inner Mongolia during the *wasu* campaign based essentially on ethnicity, the concept of genocide—"intent to destroy, in whole or in part, a national, ethnical, racial or religious group as such," as defined by the authoritative 1951 UN resolution on genocide—misconstrues both the motivation and the consequences for what transpired in Inner Mongolia during the Cultural Revolution and in Xinjiang in recent years. The problem is to prove unequivocally the "intent to destroy"— whether by killing or by forced migration—the goals of such classical genocides as Nazi elimination of the Jews and Roma, Turkish elimination of the Armenians, and more recently the Tutsi in Rwanda and the Rohingya in Burma.[55]

The *wasu* and the anti–New Neirendang campaigns employed a definition of apostasy so broad, and so conspiratorial, that in practice virtually the entire Mongol population was targeted including many who had never participated in a political movement and others with lifelong loyalty to the CCP. Tens of thousands of deaths and many more injuries occurred in the course of screening suspected New Neirendang members using torture to extract confessions and force victims to name traitors. This was a crime against humanity, yet we nevertheless distinguish the Inner Mongolian case both from classical genocides and from other violent episodes of the Cultural Revolution and after.

We conceptualize the Inner Mongolian pogrom as politicide. The term *politicide* was coined by Barbara Harff and Ted Gurr in 1988 to refer to mass killing of political enemies, defined "primarily in terms of their hierarchical position or political opposition to the regime and dominant groups."[56] Moreover, as Clark McCauley argues, "politicide is killing by category. The targets of politicide are not determined by any individual characteristics or individual behaviors but by their link or membership to a social group."[57] However, scholarship on politicide inspired by Harff and Gurr often fails to distinguish it from genocide, the only difference being that politicide is a politically motivated genocide.[58] Our usage is different; it is more akin to Baruch Kimmerling's application of the term to describe the Israeli destruction of Palestinian capacity to build an independent state. Politicide, for Kimmerling, involves "a wide range of social, political, and military activities whose goal is to destroy the political and national existence of a whole community of people and thus deny it the possibility of self-determination."[59]

The key differences between genocide and politicide, we emphasize, lie in the conceptualization of the target and the goals of the campaign. The subject of genocide is a people broadly defined as a national, ethnic, racial, or religious group, and as such it could be an identity either achieved or ascribed, such as Catholics or Jews, or Latinos or Blacks in contemporary American society, or other national, racial, religious, or political characteristics of a people elsewhere. The Mongols, the targets of politicide, were not simply an ethnically distinct people; they also embodied an "idea," "institutional expression," and "physical base" that officially inscribed them as a nationality with an autonomous region in their name.[60]

We show that the pogrom in Inner Mongolia during the Cultural Revolution, which proclaimed the goal of eliminating Mongol "traitors," actually destroyed the foundations for regional national autonomy and subordinated the Mongols to a repressive Chinese regime—politically, socially, and culturally—resulting in a heavy toll in human life. In this process, the first targets were Mongol CCP members who were accused of being national splittists (members of a "New Neirendang") and subjected to torture and killing to force confessions of their alleged treasonous activities and to name fellow Neirendang members. In contrast to genocide, the goal was not elimination of the Mongol people as a whole or their forced removal from China. Rather, it was the taming of the Mongols, especially their politically active members, and destruction of their capacity and will to organize "politically" in opposition to the Chinese state. Stated differently, the goal was to assure Mongol loyalty to China. This was a violent process, accompanied with the arrest, torture, and death of numerous people. It was politicide.[61] The cruelest irony is that the charge of a mass Mongol secessionist movement led by the Neiren-dang was pure fabrication.

There is, however, a crucial dimension to the destruction of Mongol autonomy during the Cultural Revolution. Unlike, for example, the Palestinians who the Israeli leadership and many Israeli citizens view as an alien and dangerous Other and a threat to annihilate the Israeli state and its people, Mongol autonomy after 1947 in Inner Mongolia was the institutional expression of CCP policy with the goal of winning over the Mongols. Successive PRC constitutions define the role of minority nationalities in autonomous regions, prefectures and counties, a distinctive system that was created and administered from Beijing. That is, if the Mongols were no longer an independent people, they were a constitutionally recognized minority nationality of the PRC and, from 1949 to 1966, the titular nationality of Inner Mongolia led by a cohesive group of Mongol Communists. Moreover, the targets for destruction in the subsequent politicide included many loyal CCP members and activists, who were attacked as hidden nationalists and separatists threatening both Mao's political line and China's national sovereignty.

THE ART OF CHINESE POLITICIDE

The initial Cultural Revolution attacks on revisionism and illegitimate authority in Inner Mongolia were made without explicit reference to ethnicity. The call to arms was issued by Chinese and Mongols alike against enemies they accused of "taking the capitalist road," that is rejecting the revolutionary path, framed primarily in terms of China's domestic social class structure and secondarily in terms of threats of revisionism from the Soviet Union and the MPR whose troops massed in the borderlands at a time of rising tensions between China and its two neighbors.

The Center's purge of Ulanhu at the Qianmen Hotel Conference in Beijing in June and July 1966, however, reoriented the Cultural Revolution agenda to attacking the power held by Mongols in Inner Mongolia. As a result, the entire political spectrum of Inner Mongolia's revolutionary activists, both self-styled rebels and loyalists, converged to denounce not only the former leader but his "black gang" of associates. Within a few weeks of the fall of Ulanhu, almost the entire Mongol leadership of the IMAR was deposed, as well as many of Ulanhu's Chinese associates in leadership ranks.

In attacking Ulanhu and his associates, criticizing Mongol nationalism was pinpointed as the moral high ground, on a par with loyalty to Mao and fealty to revolution. While abstract principles of socialism and capitalism were difficult to grasp, in Inner Mongolia's Cultural Revolution, they were personified. Both the loyalist camp and the rebel camp were equally scathing in attacking Mongol nationalism framed as splittism (*minzu fenlie zhuyi*) through links initially to Ulanhu and then to a fictitious New Neirendang with Ulanhu presented as the face of Mongol nationalist separatism. This attack inaugurated a campaign to "dig up Ulanhu's black line and cleanse his pernicious influence," that is, *wasu*, meaning to dig out all those who had supported Ulanhu or whom Ulanhu promoted or protected, especially hidden members of the New Neirendang. This was accomplished by torture, starting with suspect Mongol cadres, to force confessions of their crimes and naming of their associates in a New Neirendang. One way to stay alive, the only hope for ending the torture, was to deny one's own Mongol nationalism by naming (i.e., inventing) alleged New Neirendang conspirators.

That the anti-Ulanhu and anti-Mongol nationalism movement lasted so long in the absence of a single documented incident of Neirendang activity, with mounting casualties and deaths from 1966 to 1969, may be explained in part by a ploy used by Mao. Ulanhu was stripped of his positions in several stages, leaving those who denounced him uncertain about the Center's, and Mao's, real intention. Even after the announcement that he had been deprived of all his Party and military positions, setting off a wave of attacks on Ulanhu's associates throughout Inner Mongolia, on August 31, 1966, Ulanhu appeared on the Tiananmen rostrum with Mao and Lin Biao, suggesting the possibility of a political comeback at the precise moment when the Red Guards were launched nationwide.

Mao, the Central Cultural Revolution Group controlled by Zhou Enlai, and the military, continued to encourage open denunciation of Ulanhu as a feudal prince (*wangye*) of Inner Mongolia and a nationalist separatist. These were crimes worthy of capital punishment, but unlike President Liu Shaoqi, who was thrown to the mercy of the angry masses in successive struggle meetings, Ulanhu remained protected in Beijing, and later in Hunan province. He was never sent back to Inner Mongolia to face the iron fists of "the revolutionary masses" or public struggle meetings. No other high-ranking leader except Deng Xiaoping received such a privilege following his fall. With this Mao effectively turned Ulanhu into a sword of Damocles hanging above his accusers. With their political future in suspended animation, attacks on Ulanhu morphed into an all-out witch hunt for New Neirendang conspirators.

Among the enigmatic aspects of the pogrom was the absence of a publicly articulated anti-Mongol intent. This was a deliberate strategy, one that distinguishes politicide from genocide. As early as the Qianmen Hotel Conference of June and July 1966, the critical moment in the campaign to topple Ulanhu, the Center took pains to ensure that the movement not be perceived as one of Han attempting to annihilate Mongols. Chinese leaders cultivated Mongol opponents of Ulanhu to denounce the leader. The most virulent anti-Mongol expression was that of the writer and cultural official Ulaanbagan, himself a Mongol whose public lectures stoked Han fear of Mongols by portraying them as plotting to kill Han and betray China by creating a new Mongolian nation uniting the MPR and Inner Mongolia.

Kang Sheng, one of the leaders of the Central Cultural Revolution Group, astutely instructed Teng Haiqing that there must be Mongol voices criticizing Mongol nationalism and Mongol crimes. In the *wasu* campaign, General Teng was paired with Political Commissar Wu Tao, a Mongol general, Teng's second in command, and the only prominent Mongol leader to emerge from the campaign unscathed. This search for Mongol faces and voices to frame the charges, however few and powerless, gave Mongols a hope that they could exonerate themselves. This produced waves of Mongol anti-Ulanhu and anti–New Neirendang heroes, but each in turn was quickly suspected of concealing ties to Ulanhu or the New Neirendang. Even Wu Tao was eventually accused of being a covert New Neirendang member. The evidence was compelling: if he was not a member, why was he unenthusiastic about leading the movement?

The logic of competition in this kaleidoscopic triangular struggle—Mongol and Han, rebel and loyalist, leftist and rightist, with the meaning of the terms shifting in the course of the struggle—is that everyone risked being labeled a traitor and New Neirendang, but everyone could also be saved. For instance, even Gao Jinming (a Manchu who passed as Han), an IMAR secretary of the Party Secretariat who rose to power as a rebel supporter to become the highest civilian leader in the Inner Mongolia Revolutionary Committee and promulgated the earliest theory of alleged New Neirendang conspiracy, was eventually accused of being a New Neirendang member. Gao was finally saved by Zhou Enlai, the Central leader who closely monitored and brokered the outcomes in Inner Mongolia through the Central Cultural Revolution Group during and after the fall of Ulanhu.

We have shown that the campaign required exposing everyone with whom one had personal relationships as members of the New Neirendang. It meant naming names, including family members, friends, and colleagues, eventually engulfing almost the entire Mongol population as well as some Han collateral victims. This resulted in a classical witch hunt, in which every Mongol, especially those two-faced Mongols—CCP members who were accused of being New Neirendang—would be required to prove their innocence by naming names. Providing names, revealing the true face of a hidden enemy pretending to be a friend, was the only way to end the torture.

This mechanism worked in a way fundamentally different from classical genocide, which, rather than target an entire group for destruction, suggested that anyone could be saved. Suspects had a chance to redeem themselves by naming others. In the *wasu* campaign, with massive numbers of people tortured mentally as well as physically, with many left crippled and thousands dead, no one but Mao could call a halt to the slaughter by admitting, at long last in May 1969, that the Cultural Revolution had "gone too far," without, of course, accepting his own responsibility for that outcome.

Many of the survivors would live the rest of their lives not only in fear of Chinese torture but also in guilt for having capitulated to the demand of the torturers, in numerous cases subjecting colleagues, friends, or relatives to torture. This complicity through torture explains why few in the troubled borderland were subsequently willing to pursue justice for the victims, another contrast to the classical genocides. The relative silence after suffering the largest pogrom anywhere in China is a testimony to the success of China's politicide in Inner Mongolia, a success that has extended to the relative inattention to the Mongolian pogrom both in China and in global understanding of China's revolutionary trajectory.

A REVOLUTIONARY WAR WITHOUT OPPONENTS

Consider this conundrum. Given the massive Chinese assault on the Mongolian polity and Mongol bodies in the years 1966–1969, why didn't Mongols stand and fight as they had successfully just twenty years earlier in rallying to the Communist side under Ulanhu's leadership in the Chinese Civil War, leading to the formation of the Inner Mongolia Autonomous Government in 1947 and the People's Republic of China in 1949? We suggest that an answer lies in the CCP power structure.

By the late 1950s all Mongols were organized within the CCP and the state system, leaving no alternative social power structures external to the CCP. "Mongol bandits," that is, anyone who resisted incorporation, had been eliminated or imprisoned; most monks and nuns at monasteries and temples had been sent home and, with the exception of a small number of temples that remained open as historical monuments, others were closed; and the Mongol princes had been co-opted or sidelined. Ulanhu commanded a large number of Mongol troops, the majority of forces in Inner Mongolia, but they had been integrated into the PLA under the leadership of Lin Biao and ultimately Mao. A Mongol leader might have been able to utilize the opportunity structure of the Party to protect core Mongol interests, as brilliantly illustrated by Ulanhu in the decades prior to 1966, but ultimately, was subject to its disciplinary power. Even he was incapable of protecting the Mongol people from the life-or-death threat posed by the pogrom. Ulanhu best exemplified this paradox: long powerful as the leading official in Inner Mongolia and the highest-ranking and most influential minority official in China, in the end, he too was powerless in the face of the anti–New Neirendang pogrom.[62]

The CCP structure was and is such that only its highest authority, Mao and later Deng Xiaoping and Xi Jinping, could rule with exception, exemplifying Carl Schmitt's recognition that the sovereign, the leader who creates the law, alone has the power to decide the state of exception.[63] Mao controlled the Party through his mode of periodically "stepping aside," placing his subordinates in positions of power, and sometimes threatening to "return to the Jinggangshan base" to fight his own comrades from the maquis if his will was defied. The Mongol mimicry, in the form of abortively calling for a return to the "Daqingshan mountains to fight a guerrilla war" at the 1966 Qianmen Hotel Conference that dethroned Ulanhu, provoked immediate arrest and disarming of large numbers of Mongol army officers. To the extent that Ulanhu and his Mongol associates exercised power within the Party's changing opportunity structure, they could be removed at any time. Their only recourse to redress wrongs was to appeal to the Party, and ultimately to Mao, to change its judgment.

"If the Cultural Revolution should be called a revolution at all," wrote Hu Ping, a dissident Chinese scholar in exile in the United States and editor of the journal *Beijing Spring*, "it was a revolution without real opponents."[64] This was because the revolution was orchestrated by one paramount leader, and it was a revolution to stamp out what the leader proclaimed to be deviant. The struggle among the population, divided as it was into opposing camps, was not a struggle between orthodoxy and heterodoxy; rather, the two camps competed for orthodoxy, a struggle for recognition by the supreme leader.

Hu Ping's analysis can be extended to ethnic relations. During and after the Cultural Revolution, no Mongol movement emerged within China to proclaim a nationalist agenda such as unifying Inner Mongolia with the MPR (renamed Mongolia in 1992) or establishing an independent Inner Mongolia. This did not mean that no Mongols favored autonomous rights, rights to receive education in Mongolian or to maintain a Mongolian identity and culture. Ironically, facing the pogrom implemented during the Cultural Revolution, their sincere denial of nationalism could lead only to more severe torture to force them to admit to having harbored nationalist thoughts against China and the Han. The following account given by Tumen and Zhu Dongli of the most bloodstained protests by Mongols speaks volumes about how those who were branded enemies of Mao mounted their resistance:

> A herder in Shiliingol league living close to the border, after being accused of Neirendang membership, did not flee to Outer Mongolia, even though it was only several miles away. Instead, riding his camel, he went to Beijing hundreds of miles away, to lodge his complaint to the Party Center and Chairman Mao. A young man called Bilig from a border police station, after being accused of Neirendang membership, stabbed a Chairman Mao badge into his chest muscle and walked to Beijing from the distant Gobi.
>
> A soldier named Guo Qijian of the No. 5 Cavalry Division suffered heavy torture during interrogation. After being whipped more than 1,600 times, he averred, "I am not a Neirendang member! If you don't believe me, I will pull out my heart to show you!" Sure enough, availing of the opportunity to go to the toilet, he cut open his abdomen and pulled out his own red still pulsating heart.[65]

The point is not whether the stories are credible in their excruciating detail, but that they circulated widely in an effort to demonstrate militant Mongol denial of their anti-China nationalism.

Conclusion: Rebellion and Democracy in the Settler Colonial Borderland

We would like to end this book by considering the implications of Inner Mongolia's Cultural Revolution experience for social justice and democratization, which were among the ideals many rebels fought for. Our starting point is the observation that pro-democracy movements in China in the late 1970s and 1980s, particularly the June 4 movement of 1989, were crushed and subsequently banished abroad, principally to the United States but also to Europe, East and Southeast Asia, and elsewhere. There, former rebels during the Cultural Revolution and democracy movement activists of 1989 subsequently provided support for pro-democracy movements in China. Their influence also extended to subsequent democracy movements in Taiwan and Hong Kong and throughout the world Chinese diaspora.

Cheng Tiejun, a rebel activist during the Cultural Revolution, became a pro-democracy and human rights activist in the 1980s and 1990s in the United States. Interestingly, some US-based democracy activists trace the origin of China's democracy movement to the sixteen points in the "Decision concerning the Great Proletarian Cultural Revolution" of August 8, 1966, which later gave rise to the "four great rights" inscribed in the 1975 and 1978 PRC Constitutions. These principles of direct democracy were the right to speak out freely, to air one's views fully, to write big-character posters, and to hold great debates. Democracy advocates in China and abroad condemned the elimination of these constitutional rights, also known as Great Democracy (*da minzhu*), through a 1980 amendment of the 1978 Constitution following Deng Xiaoping's 1979 suppression of the Democracy Wall movement, and intensified suppression of these and other citizenship rights under Xi Jinping.[66]

These concepts of democracy transcended narrow emphasis on the vote, emphasizing the right of all people to directly challenge authority and empower the powerless. At the same time, this left open the possibility that a mobilization style of democratic politics might sweep aside the rights of a minority, precisely the outcome that produced such tragic results during the Cultural Revolution, notably in the IMAR but also today in Xinjiang, Tibet, Inner Mongolia, and elsewhere with substantial minority populations, even without comparable mobilization from below in these or other regions.

The Cultural Revolution in Inner Mongolia thus poses distinctive questions pertaining to the fundamental structure of Han-minority relations and constitutional rights, which are core principles of Chinese governance. In early 1967, Inner Mongolia's rebel forces were on the brink of being crushed by powerful loyalist forces backed by the army with its monopoly on weapons and state organizational, economic and political resources. However, with Mao calling for an attack on capitalist roaders in the Party, and in the wake of the first recorded shooting of a student rebel by a military officer in Inner Mongolia, the Central Cultural Revolution Group led by Zhou Enlai, and ultimately Mao, supported the rebels. This led to a reorganization of the region's Party, government, and army. Suddenly, rebels in Inner Mongolia found themselves close to the center of power in the Autonomous Region. Cheng Tiejun, not yet a college graduate and barred from Youth League and Party membership, was then tapped, along with other rebel student activists, to become a reporter for the *Inner Mongolia Daily* newspaper, the mouthpiece of the Party in the region. Two of his fellow rebels from Teachers' College, a faculty member and a student, became Standing Committee members of the Inner Mongolia Revolutionary Committee, the leading new authority in IMAR. Nevertheless, power remained firmly concentrated in the hands of the military and the Party apparatus.

We have noted that in 1966 rebels joined loyalists in denouncing Ulanhu and his "black gang," criticizing them for nationalism, splittism and other heinous crimes, seeking to outdo their rivals in the ferocity of denunciation and in distancing themselves from the enemy. More telling, with the military taking the lead in pressing the *wasu* campaign that targeted Mongols for torture and killing, Mongols in the ranks of the rebels became prime targets, while Han rebels in positions of power, with very few exceptions, actively supported the pogrom. The results point to the depth of a political culture of victimization embedded in China's mobilizational politics directed against the Mongols. In Inner Mongolia, for the two decades before 1966, Mongols played an active political role in all spheres of Ulanhu's administration. But in the wake of the Cultural Revolution pogrom, they found themselves helpless. Not unique to one camp, the politics of scapegoating would pose a challenge to achieving a democratic polity open to political mediation of deep social differences. Put differently, the former rebels in exile in the 1980s and after may lay claim to being among the original democrats in the People's Republic, not in the sense of championing the right to vote, but in expanding the politically relevant strata that could play a role in shaping political outcomes. However, the role of rebels in the IMAR politicide directed against the Mongols warns of the possibility that democrats could be equally repressive when confronting the Other—be they ethnic minorities, Communists, landlords, intellectuals, or religious believers. The fact is that Chinese Communists, who had sympathized with ethnic minorities, denounced Guomindang brutality toward them in the 1930s and 1940s and pioneered a system of autonomous regions to protect minority rights, eventually spearheaded a pogrom against the Mongols during the Cultural Revolution as well as large-scale repression of Tibetans and especially Uyghurs in the new millennium.

Democracy as a political institution and culture is routinely presented as a remedy to ethnocide, genocide and other mass killings in the dominant discourse in democratic societies. However, this book has drawn attention to the challenge that any future democracy will have to address, and not only in China. This is a question of the rights of minority nationalities. Under which circumstances, if any, should constitutional limits be placed on the majority in a multinational polity, especially if the majority happens to be an ethnic, racial, or religious group that enjoys absolute dominance in numerical and in power terms in a locality or the nation? How can the tension between democratic premises of majority rule and the need to protect the rights of minorities be reconciled? These are issues of global relevance in our times, not least in China, but also in the United States and Europe and their present and former colonies or semicolonies. One need look only at deeply entrenched white discrimination and police brutality directed at African Americans, native Americans, Asian Americans and other citizens of color in the United States and far-right populist attacks on immigrants across European countries. The educational system in the Global North is engaged in a bitter conflict between proponents of decolonization and those attacking critical race theory, which highlights the pernicious influence of racism in US society and beyond.

At issue is the question whether China's internal ethnic or cultural diversity should be understood through the lens of Western, especially American categories. William Kymlicka suggests a useful distinction between national minorities and ethnic groups. These are two categories whose formations are related to the history of nation-building. By national minorities he refers to previously self-governing, territorially concentrated cultures which were later incorporated into a larger state whose dominant culture and/or racial composition differs. Ethnic groups, for him, are defined as loose associations formed by individuals and families that migrate and settle in a new country or region. These two categories of groups have different aspirations and expectations in relation to the state. While national minorities "typically wish to maintain themselves as distinct societies alongside the majority culture, and demand various forms of autonomy or self-government to ensure their survival as distinct societies," ethnic groups "typically wish to integrate into the larger society, and to be accepted as full members of it."[67]

This distinction is often elided both by progressive politicians and scholars as well as human rights activists, especially those in the United States and a number of other Western nations. They also tend to ignore or even reject the category "minority nationality" as Communist constructions or inventions and insist on calling them "ethnic groups." The distinctions are critical in comparing, for example, Mongols, Uyghurs, and Tibetans in regions of China native to them, with Han who migrate to regions of China previously inhabited by non-Han peoples with distinctive languages, cultures and religions. Failure to distinguish the two categories, or unwittingly applying the political morality associated with polyethnicity, we argue, will misunderstand and do injustice to national minorities even when the intention is to help them.[68] For example, criticism of the Chinese state or Han discrimination against minorities is frequently predicated on an ideal of national unity and interethnic equality that ignores and therefore rejects the aspiration of minority nationalities for cultural and political autonomy in their own homeland. The resulting outcome may be complicity with the Chinese suppression of alleged minority separatism and enforcement of assimilation.

The dismal record of some Han rebels during the Cultural Revolution in attacking alleged Mongol nationalism and separatism in the name of democracy and equality is sobering in light of the pogrom that resulted. It alerts us to the fact that Inner Mongolia, the historical homeland of the Mongols, had become a Chinese settler colony posing a formidable structural obstacle for the Mongols either to exercise rights autonomous of the Han or establish and maintain a position as the titular nationality in a territory in which they were the absolute minority vis-à-vis the Han majority.

Inner Mongolia's population in 2022 was 18 percent Mongol and 79 percent Han, with other minority nationalities comprising the balance.[69] We have traced Chinese settler colonization of Inner Mongolia to the late Qing and the Republic, with subsequent waves of migration throughout the People's Republic and political dominance squarely in the hands of Han in the five decades since the fall of Ulanhu and his Mongol associates in 1966. In the first half of the twentieth century, frontier Han settlers repressed local people in ways that invite comparison with the fate of Native Americans at the hands of the inexorable westward movements of ranchers and farmers, but without the latter's tradition of "rugged democracy." Many Han on the northwestern and southwestern frontiers were themselves refugees in the wake of Japanese invasion in the 1930s and 1940s. Indeed, Chinese violence committed against indigenous locals in the name of fighting foreign imperialism and minority separatism was so great that the CCP leadership eventually made a rare apology for it delivered by Chinese premier Zhou Enlai in 1950:

> In this history of our country, contradictions among nationalities have been big. In terms of relations between the Han and minority nationalities, it is the Han who have been unfair [*dui bu qi*] to minority nationalities. From now on, our Han comrades should take the blame for these wrongs on behalf of the Chinese [*dai ren shou guo*], and apologize to them [*pei bu shi*]. [We] should do more explanation, clarifying that today's China is different from the past, that [we] will not oppress minority nationalities anymore. If saying [apologizing] once is not sufficient, say it one more time, don't be afraid of saying more. Eventually they will understand that what you have said is right.[70]

The CCP's effort to distinguish itself from the Han in general and the Guomindang and the warlords in particular, and its apology to minorities, paved the way for initial ethnic reconciliation resulting in significant minority identification with the PRC in the early years of the People's Republic. In the decades of Ulanhu's rule in Inner Mongolia from 1947 to 1966, Mongols not only played leading roles in governance and society but also made economic gains while the rights of Han migrants were also respected. However, the CCP apology was not accompanied by withdrawal of Han settlers from areas native to minority nationalities.[71] Rather, it was a strategic calculation designed to achieve Party objectives of consolidating the borderlands with further Han settlement while mitigating minority resistance. With the Cultural Revolution, and especially with the *wasu* repression in Inner Mongolia, all pretense of remorse was gone. The Party-state then ruthlessly conducted politicide using as pretext a fabricated threat of Mongol treason and separatism. After brutalizing the Mongol population, killing and maiming many, and leaving the survivors in deep psychological trauma, and with autonomy emptied of all politically viable components, Mao finally called a halt to the pogrom with nothing more than the offhand comment: "Inner Mongolia has gone too far."

The heart of the matter is whether minority rights, a political issue that confronts all nations if in varying degrees, can be protected in contemporary China. The political history of Inner Mongolia during the Cultural Revolution, and contemporary developments in minority regions, notably Xinjiang, Tibet, and Inner Mongolia, in diverse ways highlight the obstacles to securing minority rights. The politicide carried out during the Cultural Revolution has left a lasting legacy in which minorities may be perceived by the majority and by the authorities not as victims of Chinese exploitation or oppression, but as a potentially treasonous fifth column while Han are perceived as stalwart defenders of the Chinese nation (*Zhonghua minzu*) under CCP leadership.

In this light, Inner Mongolia's experience during the Cultural Revolution set a precedent for recent events in Xinjiang. Since 2017 in Xinjiang, the Chinese state has implemented a draconian policy of incarcerating hundreds of thousands or more Uyghurs and other Muslim citizens claiming to reeducate them to become "better" Chinese citizens.[72] Cultural norms associated with Uyghur life, language, religion, foodways, music, and art have been targeted for destruction, and numerous iconic cultural figures have disappeared and been arrested and silenced.[73] The current policy was preceded by Chinese intellectuals' criticism of the state's preferential treatment of minorities, such as providing a special allowance for minority children in the college entrance examinations or exemption from the one child policy. Above all, some prominent Chinese scholars criticized the nationality policy, especially the system of autonomy, for nurturing Uyghur separatism.[74] These criticisms closely resonate with denunciations during the Cultural Revolution, the only time that the Chinese state openly supported attack on its nationality policy.[75] As in Inner Mongolia earlier, Chinese settlers in almost all minority regions, especially the borderlands, today express grievances at feeling unwelcomed by indigenous minorities who claim the right to be masters of their homeland. As in Inner Mongolia during the Cultural Revolution, the Chinese state has deployed this settler sentiment to crush alleged minority nationalism in the name of fighting separatism and minority violence.

There are both differences and similarities between the treatment of Mongols in the *wasu* and New Neirendang campaigns of 1967–1969 and the repression in Xinjiang since 2017. Significant differences include the facts that in Xinjiang the Uyghurs are the majority, they are Muslims, and they are far less assimilated in language and cultural terms than the Mongols. By contrast, the Mongols in the 1960s and today account for less than 18 percent of the Inner Mongolia population, and far lower percentages in the cities. This may explain the Chinese mass incarceration of the Uyghur population but also what some international critics call the "slow genocide" of the Uyghurs by driving down the fertility rate through sterilization and abortion and accelerating Han migration to Xinjiang in the effort to make Han settlers the majority.[76] What is similar in the two borderland regions is the wide-scale mobilization of Han settlers, many of whom have taken the law into their own hands, convinced that they are fighting an existential war. In both cases, the Chinese state has set the agenda and directed the attack rather than mediating among communities in conflict. We have called the pogrom in Inner Mongolia a politicide, initiated and carried out by the CCP to destroy the capacity of the Mongols to organize themselves politically. The historian James Millward, likewise, holds the Chinese Party-state responsible for the atrocities committed in recent years against the Uyghurs and other Muslims in Xinjiang, calling it an "institutionalized ethnocide" comprising surveillance, mass internments, demographic suppression, and forced labor.[77]

In 2020, the issue of minority rights surfaced again throughout the country, including in Inner Mongolia, a land where little Mongol autonomy remains and a high degree of linguistic, cultural, and social assimilation has occurred. A substantial majority of Mongols speak Chinese, most exclusively or as their first language. Only a small minority of Mongols, notably those in the countryside, still send their children to Mongolian-medium schools, a right guaranteed by the Chinese Constitution. This right to education in one's "mother tongue" is arguably the only remaining right of self-governance, or the right to run the "internal affairs" of a minority nationality. Weakening this constitutional right in late August 2020, the Chinese government introduced a Chinese-medium teaching program to phase out Mongolian-medium teaching in three significant programs over three years. What this means is that the Mongolian language, long in decline, is being pushed out of the public domain.[78] In the new public sphere, which is a community of the Chinese nation (*Zhonghua minzu gongtongti*), as promoted by Xi Jinping, a linguistic community is being created whose members must communicate in the "National Common Language," Mandarin Chinese (*Putonghua*). In short, the place reserved for minority languages, not only Mongolian, is narrowing. Minorities are no longer nationalities with territorial, political, and cultural as well as linguistic rights, rights granted and protected by the constitution. Instead, they are ethnic (*zuqun*) minorities whose mission is to melt into the community of "the Chinese nation."[79]

We thus point to a central challenge to achieve significant gains in democracy and equality in a multinational context such as Inner Mongolia,

Xinjiang, and Tibet. The Cultural Revolution in Inner Mongolia culminating in a destructive politicide followed by the onslaught against the Uyghurs in Xinjiang and the broad attack on minority language education in IMAR and other autonomous regions in recent years may be a harbinger of what lies ahead for diverse minority nationalities in China's volatile borderlands and beyond. China now, as during the Cultural Revolution, is entering an era in which policies applied in the borderlands become central to China's national and international politics, thereby placing minority nationality policies at the center of the state's agenda and the nation's future. At the same time we are entering a brave new world in which the United States and China, the world's two most powerful nations, have moved from wide-ranging cooperation to bitter confrontation. The two superpowers have started trading criticism of each other's human rights records, the United States and its allies fiercely condemning China's treatment of its borderland minoritics as genocide, while China reminds the United States of its own history of genocide against Native Americans as well as slavery and racial discrimination targeting African Americans, Latinos, and Asian Americans, among other immigrants. We can only hope that the politicide story we have documented and the analytical insights we have advanced will help prepare us to confront the uncertainty ahead in China, the United States, and other nations with multinational populations.

Glossary

B

Ba bai qi 拔白旗: Pull out the White Flag

ban zhuren 班主任: head teacher

banda jiao 半大脚: half-bound feet

bangong ting 办公厅: general office

bangpai gugan fenzi 帮派骨干分子: a key gangster element

baodangpai 保党派: loyalist faction, literally meaning "Protect the Party Faction"

Baogang Erye 包钢二冶: Baotou Steel Mill and Baotou Second Metallurgical Construction Company

baohuangpai 保皇派: loyalist faction, literally meaning "Protect the Emperor Faction"

baoshoupai 保守派: loyalist or conservative faction

Baotoushi Donghequ Piteng Lianluo Zongzhan 包头市东河区批腾联络总站: the General Liaison Station of Baotou East River District for Criticizing Teng Haiqing

bi ma wen 弼马温: the title given the Monkey King in the classical novel Journey to the West when he was demoted to take care of the Jade Emperor's horses

biaoxian 表现: performing one's attitude and behavior

bigong 逼供: extortion

Bingdian Wenti 冰点问题: Freezing-Point Questions

Bupa panxing zuojian, jiupa hushi qunzhuan 不怕判刑坐监，就怕呼市群专: Unafraid of being sentenced and imprisoned, but afraid of dealing with the Hohhot mass dictatorship

buzhong 不忠: disloyal

C

Cankao Xiaoxi 参考消息: Reference News

Cangtian youyan, mingjing gaoxuan, benshu zuozhe zengyue 苍天有眼，明镜高悬，本书作者赠阅: Heaven has eyes, and the mirror is high, book donated by the authors

cao ni ma 操你妈: Fuck your mother

Caoyuan Fenghuo 草原烽火: The Flames of War on the Grassland

changwu shuji 常务书记: Executive Party secretary

chelun 车轮: interrogators taking turns to wear down a single target

Cheng Ye Xiao He, Bai Ye Xiao He 成也萧何，败也萧何: the key to one's success is also one's undoing

chezhi 撤职: dismissed from post

chifan 吃饭: eating

chuanlian 串联: make liaison, connections

chusheng niudu bupa hu 初生牛犊不怕虎: newborn calves are unafraid of tigers

chuzhong 初中: junior middle school

D

da banzhang 大班长: senior class monitor

dachuanlian 大串联: great liaison; to exchange experiences

da junqu 大军区: large military region

da ming, da fang, dazibao, da bianlun 大鸣，大放，大字报，大辩论: speaking freely, airing views freely, writing big-character posters and holding great debates

da minzhu 大民主: great democracy

Da Shu 大树: big tree

Da Zhao 大召: Yekejuu Monastery

dadao jiayang guizi 打倒假洋鬼子: Down with the Bogus Foreign Devils

dailiren 代理人: agent

dangdai wangye 当代王爷: current prince

di tai 敌台: enemy radio

diaocha yanjiu 调查研究: investigation and research

difang guoying qiye 地方国营企业: local state-managed enterprise

diguozhuyi 帝国主义: imperialism

diyi furen 第一夫人: the first lady

Dongfanghong Hongweibing 东方红红卫兵: The East Is Red Red Guards

Dongfanghong Lianshe 东方红联社: East Is Red Associated Organizations

Dongfanghong Zaofan Zongbu 东方红造反总部: The East Is Red Rebel Headquarters

Dongfanghong Zhanbao 东方红战报: The East Is Red War Bulletin

Dongfanghong Zhandou Zongdui 东方红战斗纵队: The East Is Red Fighting Column

Dong Meng Zizhi Fa 东蒙自治法: Eastern Mongolia Autonomy Law

Dong Zong 东纵: abbreviation of Dongfanghong Zhandou Zongdui

dou, pi, gai 斗批改: struggle, criticism, and transformation

duoshu guandian 多数观点: majority view

duoshupai 多数派: majority faction

E

Erzhong 二中: No. 2 Middle School

er dizhu 二地主: Han Chinese land merchant, literally "second landlord"

er mao zi 二毛子: literarily "second hairy," refers to people of mixed Chinese and Russian descent

erdai wangye 二代王爷: second generation prince

Er'rentai 二人台: a two-person opera form popular in Shanxi and western Inner Mongolia

Er yue ni liu 二月逆流: the February adverse current

F

fandong jishu quanwei 反动技术权威: reactionary technological authority

fandongpai 反动派: reactionary

fangxiang luxian cuowu 方向路线错误: mistake of a political line and directional nature

fei nongye renkou 非农业人口: nonagricultural population

fenshu keng 焚书坑: pits for book burning

fenshu kengru 焚书坑儒: burning books and burying Confucians

fenqu quanmian junguan 分区全面军管: zoning and comprehensive martial law

fu mishuzhang 副秘书长: deputy secretary-general

fudao duiwu 辅导队伍: team of instructors

fu ke nao geming 复课闹革命: return to school ostensibly to carry out revolution there

fuwu dalou 服务大楼: service building

G

Gaoxiao Shejiao Yundong 高校社教运动: Socialist Education Movement in Higher Education Institutions

gaozhong 高中: senior middle school

Geming Zaofan Zhandoudui 革命造反战斗队: Revolutionary Rebel Fighting Corps

geming zhanshi 革命战士: Revolutionary Soldier

geming zuopai 革命左派: a revolutionary leftist

gong xuan dui 工宣队: workers' propaganda team

gongsi heying 公私合营: joint ventures of public and private enterprises

gongxiaoshe 供销社: supply and marketing cooperative

gongzuo zu 工作组: work team

gongzuo dui 工作队: work team

gouzaizi 狗崽子: son of a bitch

guojia lingdao ren 国家领导人: state leader

guancha 观察: observation

guangzhong boshou 广种薄收: plant widely and harvest thinly

Guilin shanshui jia tianxia 桂林山水甲天下: Guilin's landscape is the best in the world

H

Haishi jiao geming weiyuanhui hao 还是叫革命委员会好: it would be better renamed a revolutionary committee

Han shan yi, han jiefangjun nan 撼山易，撼解放军难: It's easy to move the mountain; it's hard to move the PLA

hanhou 憨厚: honest and direct

hanjian 汉奸: Chinese traitors

Hao siling 郝司令: Commander Hao

heibang 黑帮: black gang

Hexi gongsi 河西公司: the River West Company

hexin xiaozu 核心小组: core group

Hongdaihui 红代会, abbreviation of 红卫兵代表大会: Red Guard Congress

Hongqi 红旗: Red Flag

Hongse gongren 红色工人: Red Workers Alliance

Hongse Zaofanzhe Lianmeng 红色造反者联盟 Red Rebels Alliance

Hongse Zaofantuan 红色造反团: Red Rebel Corps

Hongtie Zhanshi 红铁战士: Red Railway Worker Fighters

Hongqi 红旗: Red Banner

Hongweibing huodongri 红卫兵活动日: Red Guard Action Days

Hong Zong 红总: Red Guard Headquarters

Hu'ersi 呼二司: Hohhot Second Headquarters

Huhehaote Qunzhong Zhuanzheng Zhihuibu 呼和浩特群众专政指挥部: Hohhot Mass Dictatorship Headquarters

Huhehaote shi dazhuan yuanxiao Mao Zedong zhuyi hongweibing linshi zongbu 呼和浩特市大专院校毛泽东主义红卫兵临时总部: Hohhot City University and College Maoist Red Guard Provisional Headquarters

hukou 户口: household registration

hukoudi 户口地: household land

hukou qianyi zheng 户口迁移证: household registration transfer

Hulang dangdao; zhongguo xiuyi 虎狼当道，中国休矣: Tigers and wolves block our way, China is dying

hunjun 昏君: fatuous ruler

Huochetou 火车头: Locomotive

Hushi dazhongzhuan yuanxiao Mao Zedong sixiang hongweibing silingbu 呼市大中专院校毛泽东思想红卫兵司令部: The Mao Zedong Thought Red Guard Headquarters of the Colleges and Schools of Hohhot

Huhehaote Dazhongzhuan Yuanxiao Hongweibing Geming Zaofan Silingbu 呼和浩特大专院校红卫兵革命造反司令部: the Revolutionary Rebel Headquarters of Red Guards of Colleges and Schools of Hohhot

huibao sixiang 汇报思想: report one's thought to authorities

Husansi 呼三司: Hohhot Third Headquarters

Huyisi 呼一司: Hohhot First Headquarters

J

jianchen 奸臣: traitor

jiao'ao 骄傲: arrogant

jiaodao zhuren 教导主任: academic director

jiben zhidu 基本制度: basic systems

jieji douzheng ximie lun 阶级斗争熄灭论: theory of "the dying out of class struggle"

jiekai dangwei de gaizi 揭开党委的盖子: lift the cover of the Party Committee

jiguan 籍贯: native place

jimao suanpi, popomama 鸡毛蒜皮，婆婆妈妈: chicken feathers and garlic skins, that is old wives' tales

Jingxi Binguan 京西宾馆: Western Guesthouse

Jinggangshan 井冈山: Jinggang Mountains

Jinggangshan Hongweibing 井冈山红卫兵: Jinggangshan Red Guard.

Jiu heishou lianluo zhan 揪黑手联络站: Ferreting Out the Black Hands Liaison Station

Jiu pantu jituan lianluo zhan 揪叛徒集团联络站: Ferreting Out the Traitor Clique Liaison Office

Jiu Wu liandui 揪乌联队: United Team to Ferret out Ulanhu

Jiucheng nan chaihuo shi 旧城南柴火市: the Southern Firewood Market in the old city

Jiushi yao qunzhong zhuanzheng 就是要群众专政: What we want is exactly the Mass Dictatorship

Jiuyue anliu 九月暗流: Secret Current of September

jun xuan dui 军宣队: military propaganda team

junwei batiao 军委八条: Eight-Point Order from the Central Military Commission

K

kang 炕: heated brick bed

kao bian zhan 靠边站: stand aside

kongbu 恐怖: terror

kua hangye 跨行业: cut across trades and professions

kuaiban 快板: performance recited to the rhythm of bamboo clappers

L

lao mao zi 老毛子: literally "old hairy," refers to Russians

laodong banzhang 劳动班长: class monitor for physical labor

laodong duanlianke 劳动锻炼课: labor training class

laohudeng 老虎凳: the tiger bench

laojia 老家: hometown

laozi 老子: I (literally meaning "father," a reference to oneself, showing contempt for the addressee)

lengjing sikao 冷静思考: thinking it over while cooling off

lian'ai 恋爱: dating

Liandong 联动: United Action

Lianhe Zhanbao 联合战报: Joint Battle Report

Lianying Shangdian 联营商店: Joint-Venture Shop, Hohhot's largest department store

Lifan Yuan 理藩院: Board for the Administration of Outlying Regions

luxian cuowu 路线错误: a mistake of line

M

mangliu 盲流: blindly flowing population

mantou 馒头: steamed bun

Mao Zedong Zhuyi Hongweibing Zongbu 毛泽东主义红卫兵总部: Mao Zedong Thought Red Guard General Headquarters

meiheizi 煤黑子: black coal digger

Menggu Zizhi Bang 蒙古自治邦: Mongolian Autonomous State

Mengjiang 蒙疆: Mongolian borderland government

Mengjian 蒙奸: Mongol traitors

Mengqi 蒙旗: Mongol banners

minzu ban 民族班: nationality classes

minzu fenlie zhuyi 民族分裂主义: nationality separatism

Minzu lüshe 民族旅社: Nationality Hotel

minzu tuanjie 民族团结: (1) national unity; (2) interethnic amity

minzhu buke 民主补课: make up for the missed democratic lesson

muhou zhihui 幕后指挥: backstage director

N

Nei Menggu 内蒙古: Inner Mongolia

Nei Menggu Junda Eryuan 内蒙古军大二院: the Second College of Inner Mongolia Military University

Nei Menggu Minzu 内蒙古民族: Inner Mongolian Nation

Nei Menggu Renmin 内蒙古人民: Inner Mongolian People

Nei Menggu Renmin Geming Dang 内蒙古人民革命党: Inner Mongolia People's Revolutionary Party

Nei Menggu Ribao, Dongfanghong Dianxun 内蒙古日报，东方红电讯: Inner Mongolia Daily, East Is Red Dispatch

Nei Menggu Shiyuan Mao Zedong Zhuyi Hongweibing 内蒙古师院毛泽东主义红卫兵: The Inner Mongolia Teachers' College Maoist Red Guards

Nei Menggu Zizhiqu Gongnongbing Geming Weiyuanhui 内蒙古自治区工农兵革命委员会: Inner Mongolia Autonomous Region Workers, Peasants and Soldiers Revolutionary Committee

Nei Menggu Zizhiqu Zhigong Hongweijun Lianhehui 内蒙古自治区职工红卫军联合会: Inner Mongolia Autonomous Region Staff Workers Red Guard Army Association

Nei Menggu Zizhiqu Wuchanzhe Geming Zongbu 内蒙古自治区无产者革命总部: The Proletarian Revolutionary Headquarters

Nei Menggu Zhujingban 内蒙古驻京办: The Inner Mongolia Liaison Office in Beijing

Nei Menggu Zizhi Zhengfu 内蒙古自治政府: Inner Mongolia Autonomous Government

Nei Menggu Zizhi Qu 内蒙古自治区: Inner Mongolia Autonomous Region

neibu faxing 内部发行: internal distribution

neidi 内地: interior or inland China

Neirendang 内人党: Inner Mongolia People's Revolutionary Party

Neirentuan 内人团: the Inner Mongolia People's Revolutionary Youth League

ni jiu gan 你就干: Just do it

ni pusa guo jiang, zishen nanbao 泥菩萨过江，自身难保: a clay Bodhisattva fording a river can't guarantee his own safety

ning zuo wu you 宁左勿右: would rather be on the left than on the right

niugui sheshen 牛鬼蛇神: cow monsters and snake spirits

Nongcun Gongzuodui Bao 农村工作队报: Bulletin of the Agricultural Village Work Team

nongye renkou 农业人口: agricultural population

P

Paoda Dongzong, Xuexi Sansi 炮打东纵，血洗三司: Bombard Dongzong; Flood Husansi with blood

pidou 批斗: criticism and struggle

pin xuan dui 贫宣队: poor and lower middle peasant propaganda teams

Piteng lianluozhan 批腾联络站: Liaison Stations for Criticizing Teng Haiqing

Q

qi gou ba liang yimian po 七沟八梁一面坡: the seven ditches, eight gorges and one hillside

qian ren zhong shu, hou ren cheng liang 前人种树，后人乘凉: previous generations plant trees, later generations enjoy the shade

qianzhi 前指: advance command

qinwu zu 勤务组: leading group

qingdui 清队: abbreviation of *qingli jieji duiwu*

qingli jieji duiwu 清理阶级队伍: cleansing the class ranks

Qingsong bulao, sansi budao 青松不老，三司不倒: Green pine, never aging; Third Headquarters never overturned

qingxi 清洗: sacking or cleansing someone

Qingzhen dasi 清真大寺: Grand Mosque

qiumao 屄毛: pubic hair

quanwudi 全无敌: Without peer

quchu dalu, huifu zhonghua 驱除鞑虏，恢复中华: Expel the Barbarians, Recover China

quedian cuowu 缺点错误: error or shortcoming

R

renmin neibu maodun 人民内部矛盾: contradictions among the people

ren qiong, zhi bu qiong 人穷志不穷: although financially poor, we were not spiritually poor

Renren yaoguo Wasu guan; shengchan biding fanyifan 人人要过挖肃关，生产必定翻一番: If everyone was to pass the gate of Wasu, it would mean doubling the production quota

reqing bangzhu 热情帮助: warmly help

roucongrong 肉苁蓉: desert broomrape

S

sanbu liangli 三不两利: Three Nos and Two Benefits. A policy adopted in 1948 for governing ethnic and class relations in Inner Mongolia: no class struggle, no redistribution of property, and no class labeling of Mongols; mutual benefit for herders and herdlords

San De Xiaozu 三德小组: Three Virtues Group

san jia cun 三家村: the three-family village

san jie he 三结合: Three-in-One Combination

san nian zao zhidao 三年早知道: knowing three years in advance

san tong 三同: "three togethers": live together, eat together, and work together

sandai wangye 三代王爷: third-generation prince

sanfan fenzi 三反分子: three-anti element (anti-Party, anti-socialism, and anti–Mao Zedong Thought).

sangu shili 三股势力: three sets of forces

Sanqingtuan 三青团: Three People's Principles Youth Corps

Sansi budao, yonghuo shao. Qingsong bulao, yong gaopao 三司不倒，用火烧。青松不老，用镐刨: If the Third Headquarters can't be overturned, we'll burn it. If the green pine doesn't age, we'll use shovels to uproot it

sha huimaqiang 杀回马枪: a horseback rider races forward and suddenly veers back to strike his enemies

shangfang tuan 上访团: petition group

shanghai er yida hongse zaofan tuan 上海二医大造反团: Red Rebels from Shanghai No. 2 Military Medical University

shangshan xiaxiang 上山下乡: "Up to the Mountains and Down to the Countryside" movement

shanyu yulai feng man lou 山雨欲来风满楼: the wind blows before the approaching storm

shaomai 烧麦: small hot lamb mince-filled pastry

shaoshu guandian 少数观点: minority viewpoint

shaoshupai 少数派: minority faction

shaxue weimeng 歃血为盟: perform a blood covenant

shifan 师范: teacher training

Shijian 实践: Practice

shudao husun san 树倒猢狲散: When the tree falls, all the monkeys flee

si da 四大: Four Bigs

si jia dian 四家店: the four-family shop

sige mianxiang 四个面向: Four-Facing Principles

silingbu 司令部: military headquarters

Songwenshen 送瘟神: Away with All Pests

soyang 锁阳: Chinese cynomorium

suqing 肃清: cleanse and eliminate

Suiyuan Sili Fendou Zhongxue 绥远私立奋斗中学: Suiyuan Private Struggle Middle School

suku 诉苦: speaking bitterness

3.18 zhuan an zu 3.18 专案组: March 18 Case Group

12 yue huibao tigang 十二月汇报提纲: December Report Outline

T

Taitou wangjian beidouxing, xinzhong xiangnian Mao Zhuxi 抬头望见北斗星，心中想念毛主席: Raising our heads to look at the Big Dipper, We Miss Chairman Mao in our heart

tequ 特区: special zone

Teng Wu Shou Zhang 腾吴首长: Chief leaders Teng Haiqing and Wu Tao

Tengban 腾办: Teng Haiqing's Office

tianxia daluan dadao tianxia dazhi 天下大乱达到天下大治: create great chaos under heaven in order to achieve great order and peace under heaven

tikai dangwei nao geming 踢开党委闹革命: push aside Party Committees to carry on the revolution

tiedan 铁蛋: iron egg

tingzhi 停职: stop work

Tong ji ling 通缉令: Most-Wanted Order

Tongyi zizhi 统一自治: unified autonomy

tu gu na xin 吐故纳新: spit out the old and take in the new

Turan yipian tongyun zhi, yuda yuanyang daochu fei 突然一片彤云至，雨打鸳鸯到处飞: Black clouds arrive suddenly and rainfall drives the love birds everywhere

W

Wa Xin Neirendang Tujidui 挖新内人党突击队: Shock Brigades for Uprooting New Neirendang

waidiao 外调: external investigation

Waifan Menggu 外藩蒙古: Mongolia on the Outside

wasu 挖肃: dig up and eliminate

Wasu Zainan Shilu 挖肃灾难实录: True Record of the Tragedy caused by Wasu

weihu tuanjie, shishi qiushi, chengqian bihou, zhibing jiuren 维护团结，实事求是，惩前毖后，治病救人: Uphold unity, seek truth from facts, learn from past mistakes to avoid future ones, and cure the disease to save the patient

wendou 文斗: civilized struggle

Wenwei 文委: Cultural Committee

wenyi banzhang 文艺班长: class monitor for cultural activities

wowotou 窝窝头: corn meal bread

wudou 武斗: violent struggle

Wulanfu fandang panguo jituan 乌兰夫反党叛国集团: Ulanhu Anti-Party Treasonous Group

Wuqi ganxiao 五七干校: May Seventh Cadre School

wushang 误伤: mistakenly hurt

Wushi guafu shangfangtuan 五十寡妇上访团: fifty widows appeal group

wuxian shanggang 无限上纲: to exaggerate somebody's mistakes to the maximum

wuzhuang bu 武装部: Department of the People's Armed Forces

X

xi dang zongzhi 系党总支: Department Party general branch

xi tuan zongzhi shuji 系团总支书记: Department Youth League Secretary

xiafang 下放: sent down

xian tuan ji 县团级: county/regiment level

xiangdang jiaoxin 向党交心: hand in your heart to the Party

Xiangjiang fenglei 湘江风雷: the Xiang River Storm,

xiao fangdui 消防队: firefighters

Xichu Jiayuguan, Liangyan leibugan, qianwang dagebi, houwang guimenguan 西出嘉峪关，两眼泪不干，前看戈壁滩，后望鬼门关: Once going west of the Jiayu Pass, tears won't dry in the eyes; ahead is the great Gobi, behind is the gate of hell

xiexie zhengfu 谢谢政府: Thank the government

Xilitu Zhao 席力图召: Shireetjuu Monastery

Xin Neirendang 新内人党: New Inner Mongolia People's Revolutionary Party

Xincheng Bingguan 新城宾馆: New Town Guest House,

Xiongmei Kaihuang 兄妹开荒: Brother and Sister Open the Wasteland

xinyong 信用: credit

xuetong lun 血统论: blood pedigree theory

xuesheng dang zongzhi 学生党总支: Student Party general branch

Y

yezhu 业主: business owners

yibo weiping, yibo youqi 一波未平, 一波又起: one wave has not yet calmed while a new wave is rising

yidasanfan yundong 一打三反运动: the One-Strike and Three-Anti campaign

yike hongxin, liangzhong zhunbei 一颗红心，两种准备: one red heart and two preparations yiku sitian 忆苦思甜: recalling bitterness and reflecting on sweetness

yiliang weigang 以粮为纲: take grain as the key link

yitan sishui 一潭死水: a pool of stagnant water

Yizhong 一中: No. 1 Middle School

youhui zhengce 优惠政策: preferential policies

youmai mian 莜麦面: flour made of naked oat (avena nuda)

Z

zai qingli jieji duiwu zhong, nei menggu yijing kuoda hua le 在清理阶级队伍中，内蒙古已经 扩大化了: Inner Mongolia has gone too far during the cleansing of the class ranks

zaofan youli 造反有理: to rebel is justified

zhandoudui 战斗队: fight team

zhandou zhuanye duiwu 战斗专业队伍: professional fighting teams

zhandui 站队: queue up

zhaoban 照办: act accordingly

zhaofa 照发: distribute as is

zhenya qunzhong 镇压群众: suppression of the masses

zhengzhi bianfang 政治边防: political border defense

zhengzhi chu 政治处: Political Office

zhilaohu 纸老虎: paper tiger

zhiren zhimian bu zhixin 知人知面不知心: You know a man but don't understand his mind, or Fair without, foul within

zhongdian xuexiao 重点学校: key point school

Zhonghua minzu 中华民族: Chinese nation

Zhonghua minzu gongtongti 中华民族共同体: community of the Chinese nation

zhongyang ba tiao 中央八条: Eight Central Points

zhongyang wenhua geming xiaozu 中央文化革命小组: Central Cultural Revolution Group (CCRG)

zhuti minzu 主体民族: main nationality, titular nationality

zhua geming, cu shengchan 抓革命促生产: Grasp revolution, promote production

zhuan'an ban 专案办: special case office

zhuan'an yundong 专案运动: special investigation movement

zhuan liang zheng 转粮证: grain transfer certificate

Zhuan xue zheng 转学证: certification of school transfer

zibenjia 资本家: capitalist

zichan jieji de duo zhongxin lun 资产阶级的多中心论: bourgeois multicentrism

zidong tuituan 自动退团: abandoning the Youth League

zidong tuodang 自动脱党: giving up Party membership of one's own accord

ziyou zhuyi 自由主义: liberalism

zong toumu 总头目: general chief

zongdui 纵队: column

zuqun 族群: ethnic group

zuigao zhishi 最高指示: Mao's supreme directive

zuopai 左派: leftist

zuopai shuji 左派书记: leftist Party secretaries

Notes

Chapter 1

1. For the history of Suiyuan and Inner Mongolia, see Justin Tighe, *Constructing Suiyuan: The Politics of Northwestern Territory and Development in Early Twentieth-Century China* (Leiden: Brill, 2005). Xiaoyuan Liu, *Frontier Passages. Ethnopolitics and the Rise of Chinese Communism, 1921–1945* (Washington, DC: Woodrow Wilson Center Press, 2006), 129–57.

2. The standard Western account of Fu's career remains Donald G. Gillin, *Warlord: Yen Hsi-shan in Shansi Province 1911–1949* (Princeton, NJ: Princeton University Press, 1967).

3. Philippe Forêt, *Mapping Chengde: The Qing Landscape Enterprise* (Honolulu: University of Hawai'i Press, 2000).

4. On Hohhot, see Piper Rae Gaubatz, *Beyond the Great Wall: Urban Form and Transformation on the Chinese Frontiers* (Stanford, CA: Stanford University Press, 1996); William R. Jankowiak, *Sex, Death, and Hierarchy in a Chinese City: An Anthropological Account* (New York: Columbia University Press, 1993); Li Narangoa, "Nationalism and Globalization on the Inner Mongolia Frontier: The Commercialization of a Tamed Ethnicity," *Asia-Pacific Journal*, November 15, 2007, http://japanfocus.org/-Li-Narangoa/2575.

5. Foot binding was long a marker of Chinese "civility" vis-à-vis non-Chinese. See Dorothy Ko, *Cinderella's Sisters: A Revisionist History of Footbinding* (Berkeley: University of California Press, 2005), esp. ch. 5, "The Erotics of Place: Male Desires and the Imaginary Geography of the Northwest."

6. The temples were the material embodiment of the close historical bonds between Mongols and Tibetan Buddhism. Da Zhao (*Yekejuu*), the oldest monastery in Inner Mongolia, was built in 1579. But perhaps the most important monastery was Xilitu Zhao (*Shireetjuu*). Built in 1585 by the Tumed Mongol chieftain Altan Khan for the Gelugpa Buddhist leader Sodnam Gyatso, whom he recognized in 1578 as the Third Dalai Lama, the monastery housed over one thousand lamas at its height during the Qing. See Robert James Miller, *Monasteries and Culture Change in Inner Mongolia* (Wiesbaden, Germany: Harrassowitz, 1959). See also Gaubatz Chi Li, *Huhehaote xiancun simiao kao* (A survey of the existing monasteries in Hohhot) (Huhehaote: Yuanfang Chubanshe, 2016).

7. Within Inner Mongolia, grain rations differed not only by cities and leagues but also by age and profession. For example, in 1960, workers were classified into nine categories according to their physical labor: light, heavy and superheavy, with each further divided into three

subcategories. Cadres were divided into two groups: those at district and township level and those (including mental workers) at and above banner and county level. *Nei Menggu Zizhiqu Liangshizhi* (Inner Mongolia Autonomous Region grain annals) (Huhehaote: Nei Menggu Renmin Chubanshe, 1997), 65–66.

8. Cheng Tijie, "Neimeng Dongbu 'Wenhe Tugai' yu Wulanfu de Wenge Daotai" ("Gentle land reform" in Eastern Inner Mongolia and the fall of Ulanhu in the Cultural Revolution), in *Chongshen Mao Zedong de Tugai Zhengce: Zhonggong Jianzheng Chuqi de Zhengzhi Yundong 70 Zhounian de Lishi Huigu (Xia)* (Reassessing Mao's land reform: Critical perspectives on Communist China's first wave of political campaigns), ed. Song Yongyi (Xianggang: Tianyuan Shuwu, 2019), 2:352–83.

9. Wang Duo, *Wushi Chunqiu* (Fifty years of spring and autumn) (Hohhot: Inner Mongolia People's Publishing House, 1992), 462–63, describes mobilization for iron and steel production in Inner Mongolia during the Leap.

10. Song Naigong et al., eds., *Zhongguo Renkou: Nei Menggu Fence* (Chinese population: Inner Mongolia volume) (Beijing: Caizheng Jingji Chubanshe, 1987), 83.

11. For studies of urban Mongols educated in Mongolian and Chinese schools in the 1950s and 1960s, see Wurlig Bao, "When Is a Mongol? The Process of Learning in Inner Mongolia" (PhD diss., University of Washington, 1994).

12. During the Great Leap Forward, the Party launched a "five good" campaign (five good teachers, commune members, soldiers, cadres, women, and workers and staff). Liu Yee-fui, Ho Wan-yee, Yeung Sai-cheung, *Glossary of Chinese Political Phrases* (Hong Kong: Union Research Institute, 1977), 460–65.

13. Sentries used wolf droppings for fuel to give off heavy smoke that could be seen from afar.

14. The personal dossier, *dang'an*, including comprehensive evaluation reports, is kept on every individual in China. Available to the authorities, its content is kept secret from the people concerned. Andrew Jacobs, "A Rare Look into One's Life on File in China," *New York Times*, March 15, 2015.

15. A secondary or middle school in China is usually divided into two levels: junior (*chuzhong*, three years) and senior (*gaozhong*, three years, except for 1971–1982, when it was two years), equivalent to the American middle or junior high school and high school.

16. See "Huhehaote Shi Di'er Zhongxue" (Hohhot No. 2 Middle School), in "Nei Menggu Jiaoyu Congshu," ed. Bianweihui, *Nei Menggu Zizhiqu Xiaoshi Xuanbian* (Huhehaote: Neimenggu Jiaoyu Chubanshe 1987).

17. "Huhehaote Shi Di'er Zhongxue," 22.

18. *Nei Menggu Zizhiqu Menggu Yuwen Gongzuo Zanxing Tiaoli (Cao'an)* (Provisional regulations on the work of the Mongolian language in the Inner Mongolia Autonomous Region [draft]), in *Wei Fazhan Fanrong Menggu Yuwen Zuochu Xin de Gongxian* (Make new contributions to developing and promoting the Mongolian language) (Huhehaote: Nei Menggu Renmin Chubanshe, 1962).

19. In 1947, Hohhot had only 1,328 Mongols (local Tumed Mongols), constituting barely 2 percent of the total; they were outnumbered even by the Hui (9,046) and the Manchu (3,428). The overwhelming majority were Han (72,825). By 1964, the Han population had soared to 729,172, or about 91 percent of the total, and the Mongols became the second-largest group, numbering 44,484, but still just under 6 percent of the total. Huhehaoteshi Difangzhi Bianxiu Bangongshi, *Huhehaote Zhi (Shang)* (Huhehaote: Nei Menggu Renmin Chubanshe, 1999), 234–35.

20. "Huhehaote Shi Di'er Zhongxue" (Hohhot No. 2 Middle School).

21. In 1960–1961, Inner Mongolia was subject to a large military campaign, Opening the Wasteland, in Hulunbuir league, organized by Wang Zhen, the general who had gained fame for opening wasteland at Nanniwan. The operation was scaled back the following year due to strong Mongol protest against a policy that dealt heavy blows to the pastoral economy as pastureland turned into wasteland when the topsoil blew off.

22. Wang, *Wushi Chunqiu*, 470.

23. Wang, 472.

24. Nicholas Lardy, "The Chinese Economy Under Stress, 1958–1965," in *The Cambridge History of China: Volume 14, The People's Republic, Part I: The Emergence of Revolutionary China, 1949–1965*, ed. Roderick MacFarquhar and John K. Fairbank (Cambridge: Cambridge University Press, 1987), 383; *Zhonghua renmin gongheguo jingji da shi dian* (Economic almanac of the People's Republic of China) (Changchun: Jilin renmin chuban she, 1987), p. 317.

25. Siu-lun Wong, *Sociology and Socialism in Contemporary China* (London: Routledge, 1979), 65.

26. Ann Anagnost, *National Past-times: Narrative, Representation, and Power in Modern China* (Durham, NC: Duke University Press, 1997), esp. ch. 1, "Making History Speak"; Uradyn E. Bulag, "Can the Subalterns Not Speak?" *Inner Asia* 12, no. 1 (2010): 95–111.

27. Uradyn E. Bulag, *The Mongols at China's Edge: History and the Politics of National Unity* (Lanham, MD: Rowman and Littlefield, 2002), ch. 4.

28. Li Rui, *Mao Zedong tongzhi de chuqi geming huodong* (Comrade Mao Zedong's early revolutionary activities) (Beijing: Zhongguo qingnian, 1957); Anthony W. Sariti and James C. Hsiung, trans., *The Early Revolutionary Activities of Mao Tse-tung* (White Plains, NY: M. E. Sharpe, 1977).

29. Mao Tsetung, *A Critique of Soviet Economics*, trans. Moss Roberts (New York: Monthly Review Press, 1977). Mao's 1960–1962 critique targeted two Soviet works: *Political Economy: A Textbook* and Stalin's *Economic Problems of Socialism in the Soviet Union.*

Chapter 2

1. Nei Menggu Shifan Daxue, "Fazhan minzu gaodeng jiaoyu, dali peiyang minzu jiaoyu rencai" (Develop nationality higher education and vigorously train nationality educational talent) *Nei Menggu Zizhiqu Minzu Jiaoyu Wenji* (Huhehaote: Nei Menggu Daxue Chubanshe, 1987), 459–65.

2. League (Mongolian, *aimag*; Chinese, *meng*) is the prefecture-level administrative unit in Inner Mongolia. Below it is the banner (Mongolian, *hoshuu*; Chinese, *qi*) which is equivalent to county.

3. Hao Weimin, ed., *Nei Menggu Zizhiqu Shi (History of the Inner Mongolia Autonomous Region)* (Huhehaote: Nei Menggu Renmin Chubanshe, 1991), 217–26.

4. Uradyn E. Bulag, *The Mongols at China's Edge: History and the Politics of National Unity* (Lanham, MD: Rowman & Littlefield, 2002), ch. 4.

5. For primary sources on this policy, see volumes 56 and 59 of *Nei Menggu Wenshi Ziliao* (Inner Mongolia cultural and historical materials): *"Sanbu Liangli" yu "Wenkuanchang" Wenxian yu Shiliao* (2005); *"Sanbu Liangli" yu "Wenkuanchang" Huiyi yu Sikao* (2006).

6. Xu Lili, "Tudi gaige zhong shaoshu minzu diqu de jieji huafen zhengce tanxi: Yi yuan Suiyuan sheng weili" (An analysis of the policy of class designation in minority nationality regions

during the land reform: Taking the former Suiyuan province as an example)," *Nei Menggu Minzu Daxue Xuebao* 47, no. 2. (2021): 98–105.

7. The CCP North China Bureau was established in 1948 and abolished in 1954. Reinstated in November 1960 with Li Xuefeng as first secretary, Ulanhu as second secretary, and Lin Tie as third secretary, it was disbanded again in 1966 soon after the launch of the Cultural Revolution.

8. Wang Duo, *Wushi Chunqiu* (Fifty years of spring and autumn) (Hohhot: Inner Mongolia People's Publishing House, 1992), 488. On Xie Xuegong and Li Xuefeng in the Great Leap Forward and Socialist Education Movement, see Edward Friedman, Paul Pickowicz, and Mark Selden, *Revolution, Resistance and Reform in Village China* (New Haven, CT: Yale University Press, 2005), 4, 26–27, 32, and 46.

9. The people's commune was the township level administration in rural China from 1958 to 1983. Below a commune were production brigades, further subdivided into production teams.

10. Zhang Shusheng and Shi Rui, "Kaishi quanmian jianshe shehui zhuyi shiqi Wulate Qianqi de zhengzhi yundong" (Political movements in the Urad Front banner during the period when all-out socialist construction unfolded), in *Nei Menggu Shehui Fazhan yu Bianqian* (Social development and transformation in Inner Mongolia), ed. Si Ping (Huhehaote: Nei Menggu Daxue Chubanshe, 1991), 299–300.

11. Li Gui, *Li Gui Fandong Yanlun Zhaibian* (Extracts of Reactionary Words of Li Gui) (Huhehaote: Nei Menggu Zizhiqu Geming Bangongshi Ziliaozu, 1966); Huhehaote Geming Zaofan Lianluo Zongbu, Pidou Wulanfu Fandang Jituan Lianluozhan, eds., *Du Caoji: Wulanfu Fangeming Yanlun Xuanbian* (Poisonous Weeds: Select Counterrevolutionary Remarks of Ulanhu), vol. 3 (n.p., 1967).

12. Hudalagu, *Temu'erbagen de Yisheng* (Tömörbagan's Life) (Huhehaote: Nei Menggu Renmin Chubanshe, 2007).

13. For list of presidents and Party secretaries and other information about Inner Mongolia Teachers' College (University), see the website http://www.imnu.edu.cn/chn/general/lrld.htm.

14. Lishake, Ulanhu's third son, currently goes by Wu Jie. Born in 1935, he studied engineering physics at the Leningrad Chemical-Pharmaceutical Institute from 1956 to 1960. His political career took off after 1983, when he was appointed deputy mayor of Chifeng city, and later mayor of Baotou city. From 1989 to 1993, he served as deputy governor of Shanxi province, and in 1993, he was appointed vice minister of the State Commission for Economic Restructuring of the PRC. He is also an eminent philosopher, having published numerous books.

15. Panchen Lama, *A Poisoned Arrow: The Secret Report of the 10th Panchen Lama* (London: Tibet Information Network, 1997).

16. The most detailed source on the events in Tibet is Tsering Shakya, *The Dragon in the Land of Snows: A History of Modern Tibet since 1947* (New York: Columbia University Press, 1999), 242–13. See also Tom Grunfeld, *The Making of Modern Tibet*, rev. ed. (Armonk, NY: M. E. Sharpe, 1996), 163–64.

17. Over Ulanhu's objection, Mao deployed the Fifth Cavalry Division of the Inner Mongolian Military Region to Qinghai and Tibet to suppress the Tibetan rebellion in 1958. For an account of the role of Mongol forces in the military suppression and its consequences, see Yang Haiying, *Menggu Qibing zai Xizang Huiwu Riben Dao: Meng Zang Minzu de Shidai Beiju* (Mongol cavalry wielding Japanese swords in Tibet: Mongolian-Tibetan tragedy of the age) (Taibei: Dakui Wenhua, 2017).

18. Tsering Shakya states in *Dragon in the Land of Snows* that when the Panchen Lama submitted his seventy-thousand-word petition to Zhou Enlai on May 18, 1962, Ulanhu was among

the leaders at the meeting to discuss it (272). Significant concessions were made at that time to the Panchen Lama.

19. See his memoir Dawaʾaosiʾer (Dawa Odsor), "Wo de jingli jianwen" (My experiences and what I saw and heard), *Wo de jingli jianwen, Nei Menggu Wenshi Ziliao* 31 (1988): 104–85.

20. Dawa Odsor, "Nashun Menghe de Yisheng" (The life of Nasan Mönkh), unpublished ms.

21. There were two Party branches in the Foreign Languages Department. One was the department's Party general branch (*xi dang zongzhi*) chaired by Wang Lüʾan. The other was the student Party general branch (*xuesheng dang zongzhi*) chaired by Liu Pu with Gao Shuhua as deputy chair. Gao was also the Department Youth League secretary (*xi tuan zongzhi shuji*).

Chapter 3

1. Roderick MacFarquhar, *The Origins of the Cultural Revolution*, vol. 3, *The Coming of the Cataclysm 1961–1966* (Oxford: Oxford University Press, 1997), 456–65; Harry Harding, "The Chinese State in Crisis, 1966–9," in *The Politics of China, 1949–1989*, ed. Roderick MacFarquhar (Cambridge: Cambridge University Press, 1993), 162–72.

2. Roderick MacFarquhar and Michael Schoenhals, *Mao's Last Revolution* (Cambridge, MA: Harvard University Press, 2006), 12.

3. Tala, *Ping Fan de Rensheng: Tala Geming Huiyilu* (An ordinary life: Tala's reminiscences of the revolutionary times) (Huhehaote: Nei Menggu Renmin Chubanshe, 2001), 364.

4. In Hohhot, Li Gui, a trusted Han associate of Ulanhu, was the Party secretary; Baotou was controlled by Han Feng (a Han), who was Ulanhu's nephew by marriage, and Mo Zhiqing, a Tumed Mongol; Ulaanchab league by Li Wenjing, a Tumed Mongol, and two trusted local Han, Yan Yaoxian and Hao Xiushan; Jirim league by Shi Guanghua, a Han and his son-in-law, and Yun Shubi, his eldest daughter, Shi's wife; Hulunbuir by Qi Junshan, a Tumed Mongol.

5. In the 1990s, Tegusi, the former deputy director of the Propaganda Department of the Inner Mongolia Party Committee, who headed the Socialist Education Movement in the pastoral region, confided to Bulag that his report that Mongol pastoralist communities were ridden with class conflicts was a slap in the face to Ulanhu, and he deeply regretted this (personal communication).

6. *Mao Zedong Wenji*, 1:374–75; Stuart Schram, ed., *Mao's Road to Power: Revolutionary Writings 1912–1949* (Armonk, NY: M. E. Sharpe, 1999), 71–72. The proclamation was issued following the arrival of Communist forces in northern Shaanxi at the end of the Long March. Translation slightly edited for clarity.

7. This proclamation was made by Mao on behalf of the Chinese Soviet Government in December 1935, shortly after the arrival of the Chinese Red Army at Yanʾan having survived the Long March from central China.

8. "Xie Xuegong tongzhi guanyu Nei menggu qu dangwei yinfa 1935 nian 'zhonghua suweiai zhongyang zhengfu dui Nei menggu renmin xuanyan,' 'Mao zhuxi he zhongyang fuze tongzhi guanyu Nei Meng gongzuo he minzu wenti de zhishi' wenjian de diaocha baogao," in *Documents Related to the Mongolian Genocide during the Cultural Revolution in Inner Mongolia*, vol. 3, *Down with Ulanhu*, ed. Yang Haiying (Tokyo: Fukyosha Publishing, 2011), 126.

9. Wolfgang Bartke, *Who's Who in the People's Republic of China* (Armonk, NY: M. E. Sharpe, 1987), 353.

10. Qi Zhi, *Nei Meng Wenge Shilu: "Minzu Fenlie" yu "Wasu" Yundong* (Veritable records of the Cultural Revolution in Inner Mongolia: "Nationality splittism" and the "Wasu" movement) (Xianggang: Tianxingjian Chubanshe, 2010), 120.

11. Edward Friedman, Paul Pickowicz, and Mark Selden, *Chinese Village, Socialist State* (New Haven, CT: Yale University Press, 1991), 217–19.

12. Edward Friedman, Paul Pickowicz, and Mark Selden, *Revolution, Resistance, and Reform in Village China* (New Haven, CT: Yale University Press, 2005), 84–85.

13. Harding, "Chinese State in Crisis," 170.

14. MacFarquhar, *Origins of the Cultural Revolution*, 3:458–60; Harding, "Chinese State in Crisis," 170–72.

15. Gao Shuhua and Cheng Tiejun, *Neimeng Wenge Fenglei: Yiwei Zaofanpai Lingxiu de Koushushi* (Cultural Revolution in Inner Mongolia: Oral history of a rebel leader) (New York: Mirror Books, 2007), 39–43.

16. See Gao and Cheng, 37–39. The account of Gao's actions at this time and later draw on this book and Cheng Tiejun's discussions and interviews with Gao.

17. Gao's poster, written on June 2 but not posted until June 3, was not the first to appear in Inner Mongolia. On June 2, several second-year students, including Jia Guotai, at Inner Mongolia University posted "What has our university's Party committee done during the Cultural Revolution?" (*Jinggangshan*, no. 4, 1967, 38). But it was Gao's poster that ignited the movement in Inner Mongolia.

18. David Milton, Nancy Milton, and Franz Schurmann, eds., *People's China: Social Experimentation, Politics, Entry onto the World Scene 1966 to 1972* (New York: Vintage Books, 1974), 269; Harding, "Chinese State in Crisis," 173.

19. Gao and Cheng, *Neimeng Wenge Fenglei*, 40.

20. *Jinggangshan*, no. 4, 1967, 38–39.

21. *Wuchan Jieji Wenhua Da Geming Jishi Cankao Ziliao, di yi ji (6/3–6/30)*, ed. Nei Meng Shiyuan Dongfanghong Hongweibing/Nei Meng Shiyuan Dongfanghong Zhandou Zongdui Liaoyuan Zhandou Zu (Beijing, June 1966), 1.

22. Mao Tse-tung, "Speech at a Meeting of All Circles in Yan'an to Commemorate Stalin's Sixtieth Birthday," in *Mao's Road to Power: Revolutionary Writings 1912–1949: New Democracy (1939–1941)*, by Stuart R. Schram and Nancy Jane Hodes (Armonk, NY: M. E. Sharpe, 2004), 7:310.

23. *Wuchan Jieji Wenhua Da Geming Jishi Cankao Ziliao, di yi ji (6/3–6/30)*, 3.

24. *Jinggangshan*, no. 4, 1967, 40.

25. Harding, "Chinese State in Crisis," 174.

26. "Huabei Ju 'Qianmen Fandian' Huiyi Jiudou Wulanfu Dashiji," *Wenge Ziliao*, no. 25, October 1967, comp. Nei Menggu Dangwei Jiguan Hongqi Lianhe Zongbu, 2.

27. Tumen and Zhu Dongli, *Kang Sheng yu Neirendang Yuan'an* (Kang Sheng and the trumped-up case of the Neirendang) (Beijing: Zhonggong Zhongyang Dangxiao Chubanshe, 1995), 14.

28. "Huabei Ju 'Qianmen Fandian' Huiyi Jiudou Wulanfu Dashiji," 3.

29. *Long Live Mao Zedong Thought*, internal materials compiled by Wang Chaoxing and printed and distributed by Gangersi Wuhan Daxue Zongbu, 1968 (see https://www.marxists.org/chinese/maozedong/1968/4-018.htm).

30. "Huabei Ju 'Qianmen Fandian' Huiyi Jiudou Wulanfu Dashiji," 5.

31. Tumen and Zhu, *Kang Sheng*, 13.

32. "Huabei Ju 'Qianmen Fandian' Huiyi Jiudou Wulanfu Dashiji," 5.

33. Tumen and Zhu, *Kang Sheng*, 17.

34. Qi, *Nei Meng Wenge Shilu*, 110.

35. Qi, 6.

36. Gucheng Li, *A Glossary of Political Terms of the People's Republic of China* (Hong Kong: Chinese University Press, 1995), 148.

37. Gao and Cheng, *Neimeng Wenge Fenglei*, 51–55.

38. *Wuchan Jieji Wenhua Da Geming Jishi Cankao Ziliao, di yi ji (6/3–6/30)*, 7–8.

39. *Wuchan Jieji Wenhua*, 44.

40. *Wuchan Jieji Wenhua*, 12.

41. *Jinggangshan*, no. 4, 1967, 43. Gao and Cheng, *Neimeng Wenge Fenglei*, 81–84.

42. Gao and Cheng, *Neimeng Wenge Fenglei*, 564–66.

43. *Jinggangshan*, no. 4, 1967, 48; Gao and Cheng, *Neimeng Wenge Fenglei*, 95–98.

44. *Wuchan Jieji Wenhua Da Deming Jishi Cankao Ziliao, di er ji (7/1–8/31)*, 5–6.

45. "Huhehaote Diqu Wuchan Jieji Wenhua Da Geming Da Shiji, Bianxie Zu 1967, Huhehaote Diqu Wuchan Jieji Wenhua Da Geming Da Shiji (Chugao)," *Jinggangshan*, no. 4, 1967, 48; *Nei Menggu Shifan Xueyuan Wuchan Jieji Wenhua Da Geming Jishi Cankao Ziliao*, vol. 2 (1966, 7, 1–8, 31), comp. Nei Menggu Shifan Xueyuan Dongfanghong Hongweibing Dongfanghong Zhandou Zongdui Liaoyuan Zhandou Zu (Beijing, 1966), 10:7.

46. "Liu Shaoqi Tongzhi Tong Wulanfu Tongzhi Tanhua Jilu" (Record of the conversation between Comrade Liu Shaoqi and Comrade Ulanhu), *Wenge Ziliao*, no. 2, August 1967.

47. "Liu Shaoqi," 121–22.

48. *Nei Menggu Shifan Xueyuan Wuchan Jieji Wenhua Da Geming Jishi Cankao Ziliao*, 9.

49. *Luxian cuowu*, or "mistake of line," refers to a wrong political ideology or principle in the CCP lexicon. The histories of the CCP are understood in terms of sequences of "line struggles," with Mao's line established in 1945 as the absolutely correct line. Any deviation from that would be denounced as a mistake and would have profound political implications for its adherents. See Yoshihiro Ishikawa and Craig A. Smith, "Line Struggle," in *Afterlives of Chinese Communism: Political Concepts from Mao to Xi*, ed. Christian Sorace, Ivan Franceschini, and Nicholas Loubere (Canberra: ANU Press and Verso Books, 2019), 115–19.

50. Ishikawa and Smith, 11.

51. Gao and Cheng, *Neimeng Wenge Fenglei*, 143.

52. Jerome Chen, ed., *Mao Papers: Anthology and Bibliography* (London: Oxford University Press, 1970), 26–30; Harding, "Chinese State in Crisis," 176–77.

53. *Nei Menggu Shifan Xueyuan Wuchan Jieji Wenhua Da Geming Jishi Cankao Ziliao*, 16–17.

54. *Nei Menggu Shifan*, 19.

55. "Bombard the Headquarters: My First Big Character Poster," August 5, 1966, https://www.marxists.org/reference/archive/mao/selected-works/volume-9/mswv9_63.htm.

56. On the CCP's personnel dossier system, see Hong Yung Lee, *From Revolutionary Cadres to Party Technocrats in Socialist China* (Berkeley: University of California Press, 1991), ch. 13.

Chapter 4

1. Nei Menggu Shifan Xueyuan Dongfanghong Hongweibing Dongfanghong Zhandou Zongdui Liaoyuan Zhandou Zu, ed., *Nei Menggu Shifan Xueyuan Wuchan Jieji Wenhu Da Geming Jishi Cankao Ziliao (1966, 7, 1–8, 31)* (Reference Materials about the Great Proletariat Cultural Revolution at the Inner Mongolia Teachers' College), vol. 2 (n.p., 1966).

2. *Baoshoupai* (literally conservatives) was not a self-appellation as was *zaofanpai* (rebels); it was a term of abuse used by rebels to brand their opponents as supporting the capitalist roaders,

or Mao's enemies in the Party. They would sometimes be called *baohuangpai* (lit. "royalists," or "loyalists," as rendered in most English studies). Over the years, there would be frequent crossovers between the two categories. After the Cultural Revolution, popular usage often treated those who had joined any Red Guard organizations or mass organizations as rebels. These were thus politically contentious terms. In this book, for the sake of convenience, we use *loyalist* and *rebels* to describe these two opposing factions.

3. "The Sixteen Points: 'Decision of the CCP Central Committee concerning the Great Proletarian Cultural Revolution," *Studies in Comparative Communism* 3, nos. 3–4 (July–October 1970): 178.

4. In Carma Hinton's documentary film *Morning Sun*, Song Binbin denied that she had ever beaten or killed anyone. After a few years in Inner Mongolia as a sent-down youth, Song went to the United States and received a doctorate in atmospheric and planetary sciences at Massachusetts. She returned to China in 2003 and in the following year participated with fellow students in a ceremony apologizing for the violence that took the lives of their vice principal and others without acknowledging her personal role in the killing. Raymond Li, "Song Binbin's Cultural Revolution Apology Sparks National Remorse Call," *South China Morning Post*, January 19, 2014.

5. Mao Tse-tung, "Report on an Investigation of the Peasant Movement in Hunan (March 1927)," *Selected Works of Mao Tse-tung*, vol.1, https://www.marxists.org/reference/archive/mao/selected-works/volume-1/mswv1_2.htm#n4.

6. Nei Menggu Shifan Xueyuan Dongfanghong Hongweibing, 20.

7. *Jinggangshan*, no. 4, July 1967, 54–56.

8. Nei Menggu Shifan Xueyuan Dongfanghong Hongweibing, 24.

9. Wang Youqin, *Wenge Shounanzhe: Guanyu Pohai, Jianjin he Shalu de Xunfang Shilu* (Victims of the Cultural Revolution: An investigative account of persecution, imprisonment, and murder) (Hong Kong: Kaifang Zazhi Chubanshe, 2004), 229–30.

10. Wang, 228.

11. Pu Sheng, "Mianhuai Jiang Longji xiansheng, huiyi dangnian de Li Guizi shijian" (In memory of Mr. Jiang Longji, and reminiscences of the Li Guizi incident), 2013, http://m.wendangku.net/doc/49a45068f5335a8102d2209c.html#.

12. *Dangdai Zhongguo de Gansu* (Gansu of contemporary China) (Beijing: Dangdai Zhongguo Chubanshe, 1992), 115.

13. Xiao Ming 2018, "Zai fengkuang, huangtang yu beican, xuexing de rizi li" (During the crazy, ridiculous, miserable and bloody days), https://yibaochina.com/?p=237766.

14. Nei Menggu Shifan Xueyuan Dongfanghong Hongweibing, 26.

15. *Jinggangshan*, no. 4, July 1967, 59.

16. Tang Shaojie, "Tsinghua Jinggangshan Bingtuan de Xingshuai" (The rise and fall of Tsinghua University's Jingganshan Corps), in *The Cultural Revolution: Facts and Analysis*, ed. Liu Qingfeng (Hong Kong: Chinese University of Hong Kong, 1996), 49–64. See Mi Hedou and Zhang Qi, "Suiyue Liusha: Kuai Dafu Zishu" (Time passing by like moving sand: Kuai Dafu's personal account), 2011, http://beijingspring.com/bj2/2010/170/201121220435.htm.

17. Gao Shuhua and Cheng Tiejun, *Neimeng Wenge Fenglei: Yiwei Zaofanpai Lingxiu de Koushushi* (Cultural Revolution in Inner Mongolia: Oral history of a rebel leader) (New York: Mirror Books, 2007), 175.

18. *Huhehaote shi dazhuan yuanxiao Mao Zedong zhuyi hongweibing linshi zongbu.*

19. *Hushi dazhongzhuan yuanxiao Mao Zedong sixiang hongweibing silingbu.*

20. *Yingzhe Geming de Baofengyu Zhandou Chengzhang: Hushi Sansi Douzheng Jianshi (di yi juan)* (A brief history of the struggles of the Hohhot Third Headquarters), Neimenggu dangxiao "Jinggangshan" Bingtuan Xuanchuanzu Fanying, May 1967, 5.

21. *Jinggangshan*, no. 4, July 1967, 63.

22. Gao and Cheng, *Neimeng Wenge Fenglei*, 170–74.

23. Gao and Cheng, 176–79.

24. Wang Duo, *Wushi Chunqiu* (Fifty years of spring and autumn) (Hohhot: Inner Mongolia People's Publishing House, 1992), 508.

25. Wang Duo, 508–9.

26. *Jinggangshan*, no. 7, 1967, 28.

27. Gao and Cheng, *Neimeng Wenge Fenglei*, 180–83.

28. *Jinggangshan*, no. 7, 1967, 30; Gao and Cheng, *Neimeng Wenge Fenglei*, 186–87.

29. *Huhehaote Dazhongzhuan Yuanxiao Hongweibing Geming Zaofan Silingbu.*

30. *Yingzhe Geming de Baofengyu Zhandou Chengzhang*, 5–6.

31. Qi, *Nei Meng Wenge Shilu: "Minzu Fenlie" yu "Wasu" Yundong* (Veritable records of the Cultural Revolution in Inner Mongolia: "Nationality splittism" and the "Wasu" movement) (Xianggang: Tianxingjian Chubanshe, 2010), 127. See also "Seventh Ministry of Machine Building" (Ministry of Astronautics Industry), https://www.globalsecurity.org/space/world/china/moai.htm.

32. *Nei Menggu Zizhiqu Gongnongbing Geming Weiyuanhui* (Inner Mongolia Autonomous Region Workers, Peasants and Soldiers Revolutionary Committee); *Nei Menggu Zizhiqu Zhigong Hongweijun Lianhehui* (Inner Mongolia Autonomous Region Staff Workers Red Guard Army Association); and *Nei Menggu Zizhiqu Wuchanzhe Geming Zongbu* (The Proletarian Revolutionary Headquarters).

33. Qi, *Nei Meng Wenge Shilu*, 127–32.

34. *Jinggangshan*, no. 7, 1967, 31.

35. *Jinggangshan*, 34–35.

36. *Jinggangshan*, 37. Wang allocated ten thousand yuan to Hongweijun, which comprised Kangda Bingtuan of Teachers' College, Hanwei Mao Zedong Sixiang Zhandou Zongdui of the Light Industry and Chemical Industry Department of Inner Mongolia, and other loyalist organizations.

37. *Jinggangshan*, 39–40.

38. See also Gao and Cheng, *Neimeng Wenge Fenglei*, 190–201.

39. The order was repeated in March 13, but *dachuanlian* did not completely stop until 1968.

Chapter 5

1. Yang Jisheng, *Tianfan Difu: Zhongguo Wenhua Dageming Shi* (The world turned upside down: A history of China's Great Cultural Revolution) (Hong Kong: Tiandi Tushu, 2018), 309–12.

2. Jiang Yihua, "Mao Zedong Wannian Gaige Zhengzhi Tizhi de Gouxiang yu Shijian" (Mao Zedong's conception and practice of reforming the political system in his later years), 2018, http://www.aisixiang.com/data/107578.html.

3. Roderick MacFarquhar and Michael Schoenhals, *Mao's Last Revolution* (Cambridge, MA: Harvard University Press, 2006), 162–68.

4. *Jinggangshan*, no. 7, 1967, 40.

5. In Inner Mongolia, factional fighting was carried out with fists and boots but both sides exercised restraint on the use of firearms, hence casualties were low at this time.

6. *Jinggangshan*, no. 7, 1967, 45.

7. The twelve large military regions created in 1955 were Shenyang, Beijing, Jinan, Nanjing, Guangzhou, Wuhan, Chengdu, Kunming, Lanzhou, Xinjiang, Inner Mongolia, and Xizang (Tibet). In 1956, Fuzhou Military Region was added to the list, making thirteen.

8. In late June 1966, alarmed at a possible revolt on the tense Mongolian-Soviet border, the military leadership in Beijing sent several dozen leading Mongol military officers to a study class at the Military Region's infantry school in a suburb of Hohhot. All were Tumed Mongols. Tala, *Ping Fan de Rensheng: Tala Geming Huiyilu* (An ordinary life: Tala's reminiscences of the revolutionary times) (Huhehaote: Nei Menggu Renmin Chubanshe, 2001), 417.

9. Tala, 426–30; Amulan, *Kongfei Fengyu Kanke 60 Nian: Xin Zhongguo Kaiguo Menggu Zu Jiangjun Kongfei Zhubanji* (Sixty rough years of Kongfei: Biography of Kongfei, the Mongolian founding general of New China) (Huhehaote: Nei Menggu Chubanshe, 2012), 356–60.

10. Gao and Cheng, *Neimeng Wenge Fenglei*, 216–17.

11. Qi, *Nei Meng Wenge Shilu*, 134–38.

12. The directives in the "Decision concerning the People's Liberation Army's Resolute Support of the Revolutionary Masses of the Left" include the following: "1. The previous directives concerning the army's noninvolvement in the Cultural Revolution on the local level and other directives that violate its spirit are all nullified. 2. Actively support the broad revolutionary masses' struggle to seize power. Whenever genuine proletarian leftists ask the army to come to their aid, the army should dispatch a unit to actively support them. 3. Resolutely suppress counterrevolutionary elements and counterrevolutionary organizations that oppose the proletarian revolutionary left. If the counterrevolutionaries take up arms, the army should resolutely counterattack." The full document is in Ying-mao Kau, *The People's Liberation Army and China's Nation-Building* (New York: Routledge, 1973), 317–19.

13. Wu Di, "'Wenge' zhong jundui xiang xuesheng kai de diyiqiang" (The first shot fired by the army at students during the "Cultural Revolution"), *Dangdai Zhongguo Yanjiu*, no. 3 (2002): 155. See also Tumen and Zhu, *Kang Sheng*, 28.

14. Wu Di, "'Wenge.'"

15. *Jinggangshan*, no. 8, 1967, 44.

16. The Central authorities apparently did not take note of the absence of the Mongolian masthead until two years later on February 4, 1969, at a meeting supporting Teng Haiqing's strategy of eliminating Ulanhu's influence in Inner Mongolia and rooting out alleged Mongol nationalists that it claimed had organized a New Neirendang. After Zhang Chunqiao noted, "I saw that the masthead of the *Inner Mongolia Daily* has no Mongolian words whereas the *Xinjiang Daily* has Uyghur words," Zhou Enlai said, "Don't make people feel that after Ulanhu was struck down, we don't want Mongolian language anymore." Zhou would have been particularly sensitive to both the domestic and international repercussions of such a radical de-Mongolization at a time of international conflict in the borderland. Bayantai, *Wasu Zainan Shilu* (Veritable records of the *wasu* catastrophe), unpublished ms., collated by the Southern Mongolian Human Rights Information Center, n.d.), 36, https://www.smhric.org/IMPRP.pdf.

17. Kerry Brown, *The Purge of the Inner Mongolian People's Party in the Cultural Revolution, 1967–1969: A Function of Language, Power and Violence* (London: Global Oriental, 2006).

18. Tumen and Zhu, *Kang Sheng*, 26–27.

19. Qi, *Nei Meng Wenge Shilu*, 169.

20. *Jinggangshan*, No. 8, 1967, 45.

21. Gao and Cheng, *Neimeng Wenge Fenglei*, 213.

22. *Jinggangshan*, no. 8, 1967, 45.

23. *Yingzhe Geming de Baofengyu Zhandou Chengzhang*, 15–16.

24. See Wu Di, "'Wenge' Zhong,"157; Tumen and Zhu, *Kang Sheng*, 31.

25. MacFarquhar and Schoenhals, *Mao's Last Revolution*, 174–77.

26. Gao and Cheng, *Neimeng Wenge Fenglei*, 221.

27. Gao and Cheng.

28. *Jinggangshan*, no. 8, 1967, 48.

29. Gao and Cheng, *Neimeng Wenge Fenglei*, 224.

30. Qi, *Nei Meng Wenge Shilu*, 178.

31. Gao and Cheng, *Neimeng Wenge Fenglei*, 225–26.

32. The Qinghai incident remains disputed. In 1978, Zhao Yongfu was released and restored to his original post as division commander. For the official government narrative of the incident, see Di Jiu and Zhi Wu, *Xue yu Huo de Jiaoxun: "Wenge" Zhuming Wudou Can'an Jishi* (A lesson of blood and fire: True records of famous feuding tragedies during the Cultural Revolution) (Wulumuqi: Xinjiang Daxue Chubanshe, 1993), ch. 7; Cheng Yunfeng, ed., *Dangdai Qinghai Jianshi* (Brief history of contemporary Qinghai) (Beijing: Dangdai Zhongguo Chubanshe, 1996), ch. 10. Opposing views can be found in Xian Henghan, *Fengyu Bashi Zai* (Eighty years of wind and rain), 2009, http://blog.116.com.cn/?uid-618-action-viewspace-itemid-57647; Yu Ruxin, "'Zhao Yongfu Shijian' Qianxi: Xian Henghan Huiyilu Buzheng zhi'er" (Brief analysis of the "Zhao Yongfu Incident": Additions and corrections to Xian Henghan's memoir), *China News Digest, Chinese Magazine*, no. 649, 2008, http://hx.cnd.org/2008/05/20/.

33. Bianxie Zu, "Huhehaote Diqu Wuchan Jieji Wenhua Da Geming Da Shiji" (Chronicles of the Great Proletarian Cultural Revolution in the Hohhot area), vol. 2, October 1967, 1.

34. Qi, *Nei Meng Wenge Shilu*, p.181.

35. Bianxie Zu, "Huhehaote," 2.

36. The Inner Mongolia Party Committee sent Wang Duo, Li Shude, Li Zhi, Zhang Lu, and Guo Yiqing. The military representatives were Huang Hou, Jiang Wenqi, Zhang Runzi, Chu Fangyu, and Ao Changsuo. Loyalist Hongweijun representatives were Zhang Sanlin, Fan Junzhi, Du Fan, Zhang Qisheng, and Cheng Jilong. Bianxie Zu, "Huhehaote," 3. Subsequently, each delegation increased in size. For example, at the fifth meeting on April 12, 1967, fourteen leaders represented the Center; the Inner Mongolia Party Committee had seven representatives (Wang Duo and Wang Yilun had been expelled); IMMR had twelve representative and twenty-four military rebels attended; Husansi had fifty-seven representatives; and the Hongweijun loyalists had nine. See *Zhongyang Guanyu Chuli Nei Meng Wenti de Youguan Wenjian he Zhongyang Fuze Tongzhi Jianghua Huibian* (Central documents and speeches of the Central leaders for handling Inner Mongolia issues) (Huhehaote Geming Zaofan Lianluo Zongbu, May 30, 1967), 1:83.

37. Gao and Cheng, *Neimeng Wenge Fenglei*, 231.

38. Gao and Cheng, 226.

39. Gao and Cheng, 232–33.

40. *Zhongyang Guanyu Chuli Nei Meng Wenti*, 1:7.

41. He was the father of Zeng Qinghong, China's vice president from 2003 to 2008.

42. Tumen and Zhu, *Kang Sheng*, 35.

43. The other five rebel delegates were Zhou Wenxiao (peasant), Liu Shuli (worker), Liu Litang (locomotive driver), Yang Wanxiang (worker), and Shao Zhongkang (military rebel).

44. Bianxie Zu, "Huhehaote," 5.

45. *Zhongyang Guanyu Chuli Nei Meng Wenti*, 1:24.

46. Bianxie Zu, "Huhehaote," 2.

47. Gao and Cheng, *Neimeng Wenge Fenglei*, 240–41.

48. Gao and Cheng, 242–43.

49. Bianxie Zu, "Huhehaote," 16.

50. Bianxie Zu.

51. Bianxie Zu, 20.

52. Bianxie Zu.

53. Bianxie Zu, 21.

54. Bianxie Zu, 23.

55. *Zhongyang Guanyu Chuli Nei Meng Wenti*, 1:42.

56. *Zhongyang Guanyu Chuli Nei Meng Wenti*, 1:96.

Chapter 6

1. Paul Joscha Kohlenberg, "The Use of 'Comrade' as a Political Instrument in the Chinese Communist Party, from Mao to Xi," *China Journal* 77 (2017): 72–92.

2. See detail from *Zhongyang Guanyu Chuli Nei Meng Wenti*, 1:73–74.

3. *Zhongyang Guanyu Chuli Nei Meng Wenti*, 1:107.

4. According to Yu Ruxin, the eight provinces put under military control in 1967 were Jiangsu, Guangdong, Zhejiang, Yunnan, Anhui, Qinghai, Fujian, and Tibet. By September 1968, military commanders led revolutionary committees in all twenty-nine provinces and autonomous regions. Yu Ruxin, "Jundui yu Wenge (Shang)" (The Army and the Cultural Revolution), http://museums.cnd.org/CR/ZK19/cr1019.gb.html#1.

5. MacFarquhar and Schoenhals, *Mao's Last Revolution*, 98–99.

6. For the fullest discussion of Zhou's role in the CCRG, see Yang Jisheng, *Tianfan Difu: Zhongguo Wenhua Dageming Lishi* (Upside down: A history of the Chinese Cultural Revolution) (Xianggang: Tiandi Tushu, 2018).

7. Bianxie Zu, "Huhehaote," 33.

8. *Zhongyang Guanyu Chuli Nei Meng Wenti*, 1:109–10.

9. Teng Haiqing, Wu Tao, Gao Jinming, Quan Xingyuan, Kang Xiumin, Hao Guangde, Gao Shuhua, Li Shude, Nasanbayar, Zhou Wenxiao, Wang Zhiyou, Liu Litang, Li Zhi, Shao Zhongkang, Yang Wanxiang, and Huo Daoyu.

10. Bianxie Zu, "Huhehaote," 43.

11. *Zhongyang Guanyu Chuli Nei Meng Wenti*, 2:5.

12. *Zhongyang Guanyu Chuli Nei Meng Wenti*, 2:28.

13. *Zhongyang Guanyu Chuli Nei Meng Wenti*, 2:53–58.

14. *Zhongyang Guanyu Chuli Nei Meng Wenti*, 2:62.

15. *Zhongyang Guanyu Chuli Nei Meng Wenti*, 2:58–61.

16. Qi, *Nei Meng Wenge Shilu*, 209.

17. "Military district" is used here to reflect IMMR's reduced status as a provincial level military district. The Chinese term for both provincial and supraprovincial levels is the same: *junqu*.

18. Qi, *Nei Meng Wenge Shilu*, 204.

19. In 1976, after Mao's death and the fall of the "Gang of Four," Han Tong and Ouyang Ruchen were stripped of their status as revolutionary martyrs. Han Tong's grave, erected by the Inner Mongolia Revolutionary Committee, was destroyed.

Chapter 7

1. Christopher Atwood, *Young Mongols and Vigilantes in Inner Mongolia's Interregnum Decades, 1911–1931*, 2 vols. (Leiden: Brill, 2002).

2. The Nomonhan incident has been studied extensively, but often from Soviet or Japanese perspectives. Alvin D. Cox, *Nomonhan: Japan Against Russia, 1939*, 2 vols. (Stanford: Stanford University Press, 1985); Katsuhiko Tanaka and Borjigin Husel, eds., *Haruhagawa Nomonhan Senso To Kokusai Kankei* (Khalkhyn Gol–Nomonhan War and international relations) (Tokyo: Sangensha, 2013). See also Uradyn E. Bulag, "The Nomonhan Incident and the Politics of Friendship on the Russia-Mongolia-China Border," *Asia-Pacific Journal*, November 30, 2009.

3. Butegeqi, *Zai Lu Shang* (On the road) (Shenzhen: Shenzhen Baoye Jituan Chubanshe, 2010), 93; Butegeqi, *Fengyu Jiancheng Wushi Nian* (Fifty years of trials and hardship) (Huhehaote: Nei Menggu Renmin Chubanshe, 1997), 144–45.

4. Su Yong, *Hulunbei'er Meng Minzu Zhi* (Annals of nationalities in Hulunbuir league) (Huhehaote: Nei Menggu Renmin Chubanshe, 1997), 621.

5. In the 1980s the site was turned into a major world memorial site against Japanese aggression.

6. The train from Moscow to Beijing via Hulunbuir followed route 2. Route 1 connected Moscow with Beijing via Mongolia (Ulaanbaatar). The train from Beijing was route 3, and the return train from Moscow was route 4.

7. The reference is to efforts by a group of PLA veterans, including generals Tan Zhenlin, Chen Yi, Ye Jianying, and Xu Xiangqian, to oppose the radicalism promoted by Lin Biao, Jiang Qing, and others of the CCRG in February 1967. They were particularly critical of the incitement of radical insurgency against the troops. In Inner Mongolia, the term was also applied to the confrontation between rebels and the Inner Mongolia Military Region during the same period.

8. The Center institutionalized this action on February 5, 1968, in "Report about the Work of Deep Ferreting Out of Traitors" from the Heilongjiang Provincial Revolutionary Committee. It instructed the entire Party "to adhere to the mass line to make a thorough investigation and study of the archives of the enemy and puppet governments, so as to uncover the renegades, secret agents, persons having illicit relations with a foreign country and all kinds of counter-revolutionaries hidden in every locality, every unit and every corner." See the Chinese original in Zhongguo Renmin Jiafangjun Guofang Daxue Dangshi Dangjian Zhenggong Jiaoyanshi, ed., 'Wenhua Da Geming' Yanjiu Ziliao (Research materials on 'the Great Cultural Revolution') (Beijing: Guofang Daxue Chubanshe, 1988), 2:16.

9. Merigen, *Wode aba Hafenga: Jiyi Zhong de lishi* (My father Hafenga: History in memory) (Xianggang: Yanhuang Chubanshe, 2015), 103–15.

10. This story was repeated many times by my *Daily* colleagues, many of whom attended Ulaanbagan's lectures, although most people thought it was a joke or a novelist's tale.

11. Qi, *Nei Meng Wenge Shilu*, 235–37.

12. Qi, 226–27.

13. Jiang Qing, "Talk at the Peking Forum on Literature and Art," https://www.marxists.org /archive/jiang-qing/1967/november/09.htm.

14. "Jiang Qing tongzhi zai Beijing Gongren Zuotanhui shang de jianghua" (Jiang Qing's speech at the Workers' Forum in Beijing), in 'Wenhua Da Geming' Yanjiu Ziliao, 1:635–36.

15. Ding Shu, "Wenge zhong 'qingli jieji duiwu' yundong: Sanqian wan ren bei dou, wushi wan ren siwang" (The "Cleansing the Class Ranks" movement during the Cultural Revolution:

30 million people were denounced, half a million died," 2004, http://www.cnd.org/HXWZ/ZK04/zk408.gb.html.

16. MacFarquhar and Schoenhals, *Mao's Last Revolution*, 254.

17. Gao and Cheng, *Neimeng Wenge Fenglei*, 289–90.

18. Quoted in Qi, *Nei Meng Wenge Shilu*, 232–33.

19. Qi, 242–48.

20. For the post–Cultural Revolution representation of the prince, see Nasan Bayar, "History and Its Televising: Events and Narratives of the Hoshuud Mongols in Modern China," *Inner Asia* 4, no. 2 (2002): 241–76.

21. Gao and Cheng, *Neimeng Wenge Fenglei*, 290.

22. Gao and Cheng, 290–91.

23. Mao Tse-tung, "On the People's Democratic Dictatorship," 1949, https://www.marxists.org/reference/archive/mao/selected-works/volume-4/mswv4_65.htm.

24. Yang Jisheng, *Tianfan Difu: Zhongguo Wenhua Dageming shi* (The world upside down: A history of China's Great Cultural Revolution) (Xianggang: Tiandi Tushu, 2018), 152.

25. Translated from the Chinese original at https://www.marxists.org/chinese/maozedong/1968/5-350.htm.

26. MacFarquhar and Schoenhals, *Mao's Last Revolution*, 215.

27. Michael Schoenhals, "Outsourcing the Inquisition: 'Mass Dictatorship' in China's Cultural Revolution," *Totalitarian Movements and Political Religions* 9, no. 1 (2008): 3.

28. Gao and Cheng, *Neimeng Wenge Fenglei*, 117–20.

29. Qi, *Nei Meng Wenge Shilu*, 255.

30. Tumen and Zhu, *Kang Sheng*, 61–62.

31. MacFarquhar and Schoenhals, *Mao's Last Revolution*, 101.

32. Tumen and Zhu, *Kang Sheng*, 137.

33. Readers may have noted that we list the names of all the key players repeatedly. The presence or absence of certain figures was a thermometric indicator of their political fortune or misfortune or factional alignment or realignment.

34. Bayantai, *Wasu Zainan Shilu* (Veritable records of the *wasu* catastrophe), unpublished ms., collated by the Southern Mongolian Human Rights Information Center, n.d.), 11, https://www.smhric.org/IMPRP.pdf.

35. Tumen and Zhu, *Kang Sheng*, 137–38.

36. Gao and Cheng, *Neimeng Wenge Fenglei*, 319–28.

Chapter 8

1. Gao and Cheng, *Neimeng Wenge Fenglei*, 310.

2. See the original document in *Documents Related to the Mongolian Genocide during the Cultural Revolution in Inner Mongolia*, vol. 2, *The Purge of the Inner Mongolian People's Party*, ed. Yang Haiying (Tokyo: Fukyosha Publishing, 2010), 108–13. See also Tumen and Zhu, *Kang Sheng*, 142; Bayantai, *Wasu Zainan Shilu*, 17.

3. Full texts of the two documents can be found in *Documents Related to the Mongolian Genocide*, 2:126–38.

4. In *Documents Related to the Mongolian Genocide*, 2:56–57.

5. Full text in *Documents Related to the Mongolian Genocide*, 2:139–45.

6. Hao Weimin, ed., *Nei Menggu Zizhiqu Shi 1947–1987* (History of the Inner Mongolia Autonomous Region from 1947 to 1987) (Huhehaote: Nei Menggu Daxue Chubanshe, 1991), 315.

7. Tumen and Zhu, *Kang Sheng*, 178.

8. Cheng Tiejun interview with Chasu in Raoyang, 1973.

9. The new higher education experiment began at Peking University and Tsinghua University in June 1970. After Mao's death, Deng Xiaoping resumed entrance examinations beginning in 1977.

10. Full text in *Documents Related to the Mongolian Genocide*, 2:423–25.

11. *Peking Review*, August 30, 1968.

12. During this period Mao and the Center cracked down on most rebel organizations in Beijing and major cities. Yang Xiaokai, a rebel theorist in Hunan province, was sentenced to ten years in prison for criticizing Mao and Zhou. For subsequent rebel discussions of Mao's politics, see Yang Xiaokai's autobiography: "My Whole Life," in *Where Is China Going? Memorial for Yang Xiaokai*, ed. Chen Yizi (New York: Mirror Books, 2004), 39. For Yao Wenyuan's article, see *People's Daily*, August 26, 1968. On the meeting of Gao Shuhua with his rebel friends, see Gao and Cheng, *Neimeng Wenge Fenglei*, 341–42.

13. Full text in *Documents Related to the Mongolian Genocide*, 2:198–205.

14. Gao and Cheng, *Neimeng Wenge Fenglei*, 344.

15. Gao and Cheng, 353.

16. Qi, *Nei Meng Wenge Shilu*, 324–26.

17. Qi.

18. Gao and Cheng, *Neimeng Wenge Fenglei*, 354.

19. Harding, "Chinese State in Crisis," 225–27.

20. The full text is in *Documents Related to the Mongolian Genocide*, 2:174; also in Tumen and Zhu, *Kang Sheng*, 149–51.

21. *Documents Related to the Mongolian Genocide*, 1:441–54.

22. *Documents Related to the Mongolian Genocide*, 1:455–68.

23. See more detail from Gao and Cheng, *Neimeng Wenge Fenglei*, 357.

24. Full text in *Documents Related to the Mongolian Genocide*, 1:176–94.

25. *Documents Related to the Mongolian Genocide*.

26. Bayantai, *Wasu Zainan Shilu*, 140.

27. The full text in *Documents Related to the Mongolian Genocide*, 2:175.

28. Full text in *Documents Related to the Mongolian Genocide*, 2:216–29.

Chapter 9

1. *Husansi*, No. 152, *Wenge Ziliao*, n.d., 4.

2. Tumen and Zhu, *Kang Sheng*, 147.

3. *Inner Mongolia Daily*, January 22, 1969, 1, quoted in Bayantai, *Wasu Zainan Shilu*, 144.

4. Bayantai, *Wasu Zainan Shilu*, 144.

5. *Central Leaders' Directions When Received Teng Haiqing on Feb. 4, 1969*, cited in Bayantai, *Wasu Zainan Shilu*, 84.

6. Qi, *Nei Meng Wenge Shilu*, 352–53.

7. Tumen and Zhu, *Kang Sheng*, 227.

8. In *Husansi*, August 4, 1969.

9. Bayantai, *Wasu Zainan Shilu*, 84.

10. Based on my memory and Gao and Cheng, *Neimeng Wenge Fenglei*, 364.

11. Torghut is one of the four Oirat Mongolian groups. In the 1620s, the Torghuts moved from today's Xinjiang and western Mongolia to the Volga region. Some returned in 1771, settling mostly in Xinjiang. The Torghuts in Ejine are descendants of a small group which came on pilgrimage to Tibet in 1698. For their suffering during the Cultural Revolution, see Bayantai, *Wasu Zainan Shilu*, 62.

12. See Qi, *Nei Meng Wenge Shilu*, 319–20. Zhou Enlai reportedly received a letter from his niece Zhou Bingjian (a sent-down youth dispatched from Beijing to Shiliingol league) about torture of Mongols prior to National Day (October 1) in 1968. He passed the information to Chen Xianrui, deputy commander of the Beijing Military Region, who conveyed Zhou's warning to Teng, to no avail. Mo Ran and Nima, "Zhou Enlai's Niece Zhou Bingjian and Her Mongol Husband," in *Zhonghua Ernü* (Chinese Sons and Daughters), no. 1, 1991, 16. See also Qi, *Nei Meng Wenge Shilu*, 321.

13. Steven M. Watt, "Afghan and Iraqi Victims of Torture by U.S. Military Seek Justice from International Human Rights Tribunal," *ACLU 100 Years*, https://www.aclu.org/blog/national-security/torture/afghan-and-iraqi-victims-torture-us-military-seek-justice.

14. Liu Xiaomeng, *Zhongguo Zhiqing Shi: Dachao (1953–1968)* (History of sent-down youth in China: The spring tide [1953–1968]) (Beijing: China Social Sciences Press, 1998).

15. Weijian Shan, *Out of the Gobi: My Story of China and America* (New York: Wiley 2019), recalls the harsh lives of sent-down Beijing youth in the Inner Mongolia Production and Construction Corps, remote from the local Mongol population and the *wasu* campaigns.

16. Tumen and Zhu, *Kang Sheng*, 202–3.

17. The Yekejuu league is the home of Bulag, coauthor of this book. For local memories of that time, see Yang Haiying, *Meiyou Mubei de Caoyuan: Menggu Ren yu Wenge Datusha* (Grassland without tombstones: Mongols and the Cultural Revolution massacre) (Taibei: Baqi Wenhua, 2014). Yang provides graphic details of torture of his family and relatives in Ushin banner.

18. Qi Fengyuan, *Batubagan zai yimeng* (Batubagen in Yekejuu league) (Haila'er: Nei Menggu Wenhua Chubanshe, 1997), 14.

19. Qi, 15.

20. Quoted in Gao and Cheng, *Neimeng Wenge Fenglei*, 369–71.

21. Gao and Cheng, 374–75.

22. For more graphic accounts of torture and the scale of the pogrom, see Yang, *Meiyou*.

23. Qi, *Nei Meng Wenge Shilu*, 382.

24. Mao Zedong, "The Situation and Our Policy after the Victory in the War of Resistance against Japan," August 13, 1945, http://www.marxists.org/reference/archive/mao/selected-works/volume-4/mswv4_01.htm.

25. Gao Jinming's resumption of power is mentioned in Teng Haiqing and Wu Tao's second letter from Beijing to Quan Xingyuan in Hohhot (undated), quoted in Qi, *Nei Meng Wenge Shilu*, 386.

26. Full text in *Documents Related to the Mongolian Genocide*, 2:612–13.

27. Gao and Cheng, *Neimeng Wenge Fenglei*, 387.

28. Gao and Cheng, 388.

29. The full text in Qi, *Nei Meng Wenge Shilu*, 399–401.

30. The Central leaders included Zhou Enlai, Chen Boda, Kang Sheng, Jiang Qing, Xie Fuzhi, Huang Yongsheng, Wu Faxian, and Ye Qun. There were two new faces: Zheng Weishan

(commander of the Beijing Military Region) and Chen Xianrui (political commissar of Beijing Military Region).

31. Full text of the May 22 Central Document in *Documents Related to the Mongolian Genocide during the Cultural Revolution in Inner Mongolia*, vol. 1, *The Discourse of General Teng Haiqing*, ed. Yang Haiying (Tokyo: Fukyosha Publishing, 2009), 625–40.

32. Tumen and Zhu, *Kang Sheng*, 242.

33. Hao Weimin, *Nei Menggu Zizhiqu Shi*, 316–20. Also see Teng Haiqing's "Self-Criticism on June 23, 1969," in *Documents Related to the Mongolian Genocide*, 1:683–86.

Chapter 10

1. This letter was entitled "What Comrade Teng Has Done behind the Back of the Center: A Letter to the Center." See *Documents Related to the Mongolian Genocide*, 1:703–10.

2. Qi, *Nei Meng Wenge Shilu*, 408–9.

3. Bayantai, *Wasu Zainan Shilu*, 53.

4. The full text is in *Documents Related to the Mongolian Genocide*, 1:680–82. The document ends with the following: "This document can be put on walls but not published in newspapers or broadcast."

5. For the three keynote speeches presented at the forum, see *Documents Related to the Mongolian Genocide*, 1:740–55.

6. *Documents Related to the Mongolian Genocide*, 1:752–53.

7. *Documents Related to the Mongolian Genocide*, 1:742.

8. In *Documents Related to the Mongolian Genocide*, 1:762–72.

9. Ulanhu stayed in Beijing under house arrest from 1966 to 1969, when he was put in military custody in Changsha, capital of Hunan province. Released in winter 1971, Ulanhu returned to Beijing and gradually resumed political life from August 1973 when he was elected a member of the CCP Central Committee. See Wang Shusheng and Hao Yufeng, eds., *Wulanfu Nianpu* (Ulanhu's biographical chronology) (Beijing: Zhongyang Wenxian Chubanshe, 2013), 481–90.

10. Gao and Cheng, *Neimeng Wenge Fenglei*, 399–400.

11. Bayantai, *Wasu Zainan Shilu*, 36.

12. Qi, *Nei Meng Wenge Shilu*, 418.

13. Tumen and Zhu, *Kang Sheng*, 268.

14. Qi, *Nei Meng Wenge Shilu*, 321 and 424; Tumen and Zhu, *Kang Sheng*, 267.

15. In Chinese enterprises, salary scales and welfare follow two separate employee systems: cadre and worker. China at this time had twenty-three levels in the cadre ranks. A thirteen-level cadre was a senior cadre (*gaoji ganbu*), equivalent to the level of prefectural governor in the government system or division commander in the military.

16. Elizabeth Perry, *Proletarian Power: Shanghai in the Cultural Revolution* (Boulder, CO: Westview, 1997), 100–03; Yang Jisheng, *Tianfan Difu: Zhongguo Wenhua Da Geming Shi* (The world upside down: A history of the Chinese Cultural Revolution) (Xianggang: Tiandi Tushu, 2018), 317–33.

17. Qi, *Nei Meng Wenge Shilu*, 428. "The July 23 Notice" sought to halt violent factional fighting in Shanxi province.

18. Full text of Wu Tao's speech in *Documents Related to the Mongolian Genocide*, 1:692–97.

19. *Documents Related to the Mongolian Genocide*, 1:687–90.

20. Zhang Lu's reminiscences summarized in Tumen and Zhu, *Kang Sheng*, 271.

21. Bayantai, *Wasu Zainan Shilu*, 164.

22. Zhonggong Nei Menggu Zizhiqu Weiyuanhui Zuzhibu et al., *Zhongguo Gongchandang Nei Menggu Zizhiqu Zuzhishi Ziliao: 1925.3–1987.12* (Historical data of the organization of the CCP in IMAR) (Huhehaote: Nei Menggu Renmin Chubanshe, 1995), 240.

23. Zhonggong Nei Menggu Zizhiqu Weiyuanhui Zuzhibu et al.

24. Mao's "Directive on Public Health," issued on June 26, 1965, stated, "In medical and health work put the emphasis on the countryside!" The directive led to the system of "barefoot doctor" training and its role in the rural health-care system. Mao Tse-tung, "Directive on Public Health" (June 26, 1965), in *Selected Works of Mao Tse-tung*, vol. 9, https://www.marxists.org/reference /archive/mao/selected-works/volume-9/mswv9_41.htm; Chunjuan Nancy Wei, "Barefoot Doctors," in *Mr. Science and Chairman Mao's Cultural Revolution: Science and Technology in Modern China*, ed. Nancy Wei Chunjuan and Darryl E. Brock (Lanham, MD: Lexington Books, 2012), 251–80.

25. For more on Ye Rong, see Gao and Cheng, *Neimeng Wenge Fenglei*, 574–80.

26. For more on Jin Xigu see Cheng Tiejun, *Xin Pai'an Jingqi* (New amazing tales) (Morrisville, NC: Lulu Press, 2019), 56–66.

27. Launched in February 1970, "one strike" targeted "counterrevolutionary destructive activities," and "three anti" aimed at "graft and embezzlement," "profiteering," and "extravagance and waste." See Andrew Walder, *China Under Mao: A Revolution Derailed* (Cambridge, MA: Harvard University Press, 2015), 283.

28. For more on the couple, see Cheng, *Xin Pai'an Jingqi*, 66–77.

29. Qi, *Nei Meng Wenge Shilu*, 441–42.

30. Gao and Cheng, *Neimeng Wenge Fenglei*, 414–15.

31. Qi, *Nei Meng Wenge Shilu*, 450.

32. Qi.

33. Mao'aohai, *Menghuan Rensheng* (A dreamful life) (Xianggang: Tianma Youxian Gongsu, 2003), 212–13.

34. For Mao's purge of Zheng Weishan, see Xia Wei, *Jianzheng: Yiduan Xianwei Renzhi de Lishi* (Witness: A little-known episode of history) (Beijing: Zhongguo Qingnian Chubanshe, 2015), 101–22.

35. Zhao left Inner Mongolia in March 1972. He later became first Party secretary in Sichuan, China's premier in 1980, and general secretary of the CCP in 1987. His clash with Deng Xiaoping over the 1989 student movement cost him his political career. He remained thereafter under house arrest, the highest-ranking political prisoner, until his death in 2005.

36. Bianweihui, *Nei Menggu Zizhiqu Zhi: Zhengfu Zhi* (Gazetteers of the IMAR: Government) (Beijing: Fangzhi Chubanshe, 2001), 514.

37. See details from Bayantai, *Wasu Zainan Shilu*, 98. Neirendang suspects, including Wang Zaitian, Buyanjab, Batu, Mörön, Tegusi, Biligbaatar, Ting Mao, Kong Fei, Cholmon, and Gombojab, among others, were transferred to the Yekejuu league for continued detention until the spring of 1973.

38. Tumen and Zhu, *Kang Sheng*, 272.

Chapter 11

1. According to the 1964 census, the population of Baotou municipality was 1,075,700, of which 581,500 people lived in the urban districts, the others in the suburbs and rural banners

and counties. *Baotou Shizhi* (Annals of Baotou Municipality) (Huhehaote: Yuanfang Chuban-she, 2001), 1:352.

2. Chen Jiansheng, "Xi'nan Xiaoxue Xiaoshi" (History of Xi'nan Primary School), *Wulate Qianqi Wenshi Ziliao* (Urad Front banner culture and history materials), 1986, 2:62–76.

3. These underground radio stations mainly operated from 1967 to 1972. Some continued into the 1980s. Their broadcasts mainly criticized Mao Zedong, Jiang Qing, and Zhou Enlai. For a list of stations, see Jonny14's YouTube page, "Chinese Clandestine Radio Station Intervals (1966–1989)," January 13, 2015, https://www.youtube.com/watch?v=3UFS6kHBv5w Their location and provenance has not been conclusively determined, but strong candidates include the Soviet Union, the United States, and the Republic of China on Taiwan.

4. Stephen Uhalley Jr. and Jin Qiu, "The Lin Biao Incident: More Than Twenty Years Later," *Pacific Affairs* 66, no. 3 (1993): 386–98.

5. "Burning of books and burying of scholars: 213–212 BCE philosophical purge in ancient China," https://www.wikiwand.com/en/Burning_of_books_and_burying_of_scholars.

6. Liu Bang and Xiang Yu overthrew the Qin Dynasty (221–206 BC). Liu eventually defeated Xiang and established the Han Dynasty (206 BC–AD 220).

7. "Yu Hongxin bei jubao wuru funü duoren, zou jiduan shesha zhengwei airen, weizui hou shuangqiang zisha" (Yu Hongxin reported insulting numerous women, going to the extreme by shooting the wife of a political commissar, and killing himself with two guns to escape punishment), https://www.mdeditor.tw/dl/1gaVw/zh-hk.

8. For the battles of the 187th Division of the 63rd Army in Korea, see "Chaoxian Zhanchang: Yingguo jundui yu zhiyuanjun jiaozhan sanzhan sanbai" (Korean Battlefield: British troops lost three out of three battles against the Volunteer Army), http://news.ifeng.com/history/1/jishi/200811/1124_2663_892034.shtml.

9. For the divisions and locations of the semi-military Construction Corps in Inner Mongolia, see "Nei Menggu shengchan jianshe bingtuan" (Inner Mongolia Production and Construction Corps) https://baike.baidu.com/item/内蒙古生产建设兵团/4807468.

10. *Soyang* (Chinese cynomorium) and *roucongrong* (desert broomrape) are regarded as boosting male hormones, much like Viagra.

11. Gao Yuan, "Neimeng Quanmian Junguan yu Yu Hongxin Shijian" (The total military occupation of Inner Mongolia and the Yu Hongxin incident), *Jiyi* (Memory), no. 56, August 30, 2010, https://difangwenge.org/forum.php?mod=viewthread&tid=5016&extra=page%3D1.

12. *Waidiao* was a term referring to checking people's political behavior, social connections, and family background during a cadre's personnel promotion or punishment, especially during campaigns such as One-Strike and Three-Anti.

13. On the Cultural Revolution in Raoyang and Hebei, see Edward Friedman, Paul G. Pickowicz, and Mark Selden, *Revolution, Resistance and Reform in Village China* (New Haven, CT: Yale University Press, 2005).

14. Gao and Cheng, *Neimeng Wenge Fenglei*, 473.

15. Tumen and Zhu, *Kang Sheng*, 2.

16. See Gao's reminiscences of his relations with Ulanhu's family in Gao and Cheng, *Neimeng Wenge Fenglei*, 564–70.

17. For details of Gao Shuhua's life and career, see Gao and Cheng, *Neimeng Wenge Fenglei*.

18. His note was reproduced in "Foreword: My Last Wish," in Gao and Cheng, *Neimeng Wenge Fenglei*, 25–28.

Coda

1. Roderick MacFarquhar and Michael Schoenhals, *Mao's Last Revolution* (Cambridge, MA: Belknap Press of Harvard University Press, 2006), 3.

2. Only a handful of former Red Guards such as Song Binbin have apologized for their actions, in the case of Song, half a century later. Tylor Roney, "Famous Chinese Princeling Apologizes for Cultural Revolution," *The Diplomat*, January 16, 2014, https://thediplomat.com/2014/01 /famous-chinese-princeling-apologies-for-cultural-revolution/. Song Binbin, famed for pinning an armband on Mao Zedong in Tiananmen Square in 1966 at the launch of the Red Guard movement, was subsequently criticized for concealing her own involvement in Cultural Revolution violence, including the killing of the deputy principal of her high school. On the controversy, see Chris Buckley, "Bowed and Remorseful, Former Red Guard Recalls Teacher's Death," *New York Times*, January 13, 2014. See also Timothy Ma, "Rethinking Apology in Chinese Culture," in *Doing Integrative Theology: Word, World, and Work in Conversation*, ed. Philip Halstead and Myk Habets (Auckland: Archer Press, 2015), 176–94.

3. Tu Wei-ming, "Destructive Will and Ideological Holocaust: Maoism as a Social Source of Suffering in China," in *Social Suffering*, ed. Arthur Kleinman, Veena Das and Margaret Lock (Berkeley: University of California Press, 1997), 149–80.

4. Luo Siling, "An Exiled Editor Traces the Roots of Democratic Thought in China," *New York Times*, October 28, 2016.

5. Penelope Edmonds, "Unpacking Settler Colonialism's Urban Strategies: Indigenous Peoples in Victoria, British Columbia, and the Transition to a Settler-Colonial City," *Urban History Review* 38, no. 2 (2010): 5; Patrick Wolfe, "Settler Colonialism and the Elimination of the Native," *Journal of Genocide Research* 8, no. 4 (2006): 388.

6. Audra Simpson, *Mohawk Interruptus: Political Life across the Borders of Settler States* (Durham, NC: Duke University Press, 2014).

7. A number of scholars have recently begun to apply this perspective to studies of Tibet: Carole McGranahan, "Afterword: Chinese Settler Colonialism: Empire and Life in the Tibetan Borderland," in *Frontier Tibet: Patterns of Change in the Sino–Tibetan Borderlands (517–540)*, ed. S. Gros (Amsterdam: Amsterdam University Press, 2019), 517–39; Gerald Roche, James Leibold, and Ben Hillman, "Urbanizing Tibet: Differential Inclusion and Colonial Governance in the People's Republic of China," *Territory, Politics, Governance* (2020): https://doi.org/10.1080/2 1622671.2020.1840427.

Xinjiang (New Frontier), as its name indicates, is a settler colony par excellence. The region was brought under Qing rule in the mid-eighteenth century when the Mongol Junghar Khanate was annihilated. It was turned into a province in 1884 after the Qing reconquered the region. In 1954, a year before the province was turned into a Uyghur autonomous region, the CCP established a settler colony called the Xinjiang Construction and Production Corps (*Xinjiang Bingtuan*), manned by Han Chinese soldiers transferred from inland China. For studies of Qing/ Chinese conquest and colonization of Xinjiang, see Peter C. Perdue, *China Marches West: The Qing Conquest of Central Eurasia* (Cambridge, MA: Harvard University Press, 2010); James A. Millward, *Eurasian Crossroads: A History of Xinjiang* (London: Hurst & Company, 2021); James D. Seymour, "Xinjiang's Production and Construction Corps, and the Sinification of Eastern Turkestan," *Inner Asia* 2, no. 2 (2000): 171–93; James Leibold, "Beyond Xinjiang: Xi Jinping's Ethnic Crackdown," *The Diplomat*, May 28, 2021. For an early application of the settler colonial concept in Inner Mongolia, see Uradyn E Bulag, "From Yekejuu League to Ordos Municipality: Settler Colonialism and Alter/Native Urbanization in Inner Mongolia," *Provincial China* 7, no. 2 (2002): 196–234; Uradyn E. Bulag, "From Inequality to Difference: Colonial Contradictions of Class and Ethnicity in 'Socialist' China," in *The Mongols at China's Edge: History and the Politics of National Unity* (Lanham, MD: Rowman and Littlefield, 2002), ch. 6.

8. Owen Lattimore, "Prince, Priest and Herdsman in Mongolia," *Pacific Affairs* 8, no. 1 (1935): 35–47, at 44. See Xiaoyuan Liu, *Reins of Liberation. An Entangled History of Mongolian Independence, Chinese Territoriality, and Great Power Hegemony, 1911–1950* (Washington, DC: Woodrow Wilson Center, 2006), 9–11.

9. Christopher P. Atwood, "'Worshipping Grace': Guilt and Striving in the Mongolian Language of Loyalty," *Late Imperial China* 21 (2000): 86–139; Johan Elverskog, *Our Great Qing: The Mongols, Buddhism and the State in Late Imperial China* (Honolulu: University of Hawai'i Press, 2006); Pamela Crossley, "Making Mongols," in *Empire at the Margins: Culture, Ethnicity, and Frontier in Early Modern China*, ed. Pamela Crossley, Helen Siu, and Donald Sutton (Berkeley: University of California Press, 2006), 58–82.

10. Peter Perdue, *China Marches West*; Christopher P. Atwood, *Encyclopedia of Mongolia and the Mongol Empire* (New York: Facts on File, 2004), 621–24; Fred W. Bergholz, *The Partition of the Steppe: The Struggle of the Russians, Manchus, and the Zunghar Mongols for Empire in Central Asia, 1619–1758* (New York: Peter Lang, 1993).

11. Zhuo Bohai, "Senggelinqin Ruogan Wenti Yanjiu" (Several questions concerning Senggerinchen) (PhD diss., Minzu University of China, 2012); Uradyn E. Bulag, "Senggelinqin yu Yingguo Erdengbing: Ying Diguozhuyi shi ruhe aiguo de" (Senggerinchen and an English private: On British imperialist patriotism), in Xin Xueheng, ed. Zhu Qingbao and Sun Jiang (Nanjing: Nanjing Daxue Chubanshe, 2018), vol. 3. The impact of the Hui Muslim rebellion (1862–1873) on Mongol society can be gauged in the dramatic reduction of the Mongol population among the Ordos. The total population of five banners of Ordos in 1839 was 162,233; the number dropped to 110,995 in 1885, a nearly 32 percent reduction. Daixiao, "Tongzhi Nianjian Xibei Huimin Qiyi dui Yikezhaomeng Renkou de Yingxiang" (The impact of the Northwestern Hui uprising on the population of Yekejuu league), *Yinshan Xuekan* 33, no. 2 (2020): 33–36.

12. Uradyn E. Bulag, "Clashes of Administrative Nationalisms: Banners and Leagues vs. Counties and Provinces in Inner Mongolia," in *Managing Frontiers in Qing China: The Lifanyuan and Libu Revisited*, ed. Dittmar Schorkowitz and Chia Ning (Leiden: Brill, 2016), 349–88; Nicola Di Cosmo, "Qing Colonial Administration in Inner Asia," *International History Review* 20, no. 2 (1998): 287–309.

13. While all major groups within the Qing were segregated from one another throughout the Qing dynasty, the Manchus were particularly keen to keep the Mongols and the Chinese apart so as to prevent Mongol conquest of China and/or Mongol alliance with the Chinese to challenge Manchu supremacy. The Manchus also built the Willow Palisade, a system of embankments and ditches planted with willows, to prevent movement of Mongols and Koreans into Manchuria in the late seventeenth century. James Reardon-Anderson, "Land Use and Society in Manchuria and Inner Mongolia during the Qing Dynasty," *Environmental History* 5, no. 4 (2000): 503–30. Uradyn E. Bulag, "Rethinking Borders in Empire and Nation at the Foot of the Willow Palisade," in *Frontier Encounters: Knowledge and Practice at the Russian, Chinese and Mongolian Border*, ed. Franck Billé, Caroline Humphrey, and Grégory Delaplace (Cambridge, UK: Open Book Publishers, 2012), 33–53.

14. Ki Yip Yee, "Han Migrant Farmers in Qing Inner Mongolia Reluctant Pioneers or Human Great Wall?" *Central Asiatic Journal* 62, no. 1 (2019): 119–40.

15. Song Naigong et al., eds., *Zhongguo Renkou: Nei Menggu Fence* (Population of China: Inner Mongolia) (Beijing: Zhongguo Caizheng Jingji Chubanshe, 1987), 50–57; Yi Wang, *Transforming Inner Mongolia. Commerce, Migration and Colonization on the Qing Frontier* (Lanham, MD: Rowman and Littlefield, 2021), 25.

16. Owen Lattimore, *Manchuria: Cradle of Conflict* (New York: Macmillan, 1932).

17. For Chinese territorial thinking on Mongolia and the frontier in general, see Liu Xiaoyuan, *Reins of Liberation: An Entangled History of Mongolian Independence, Chinese Territoriality, and Great Power Hegemony, 1911–1950* (Stanford, CA: Stanford University Press, 2006); Sudebilige, *Wan Qing Zhengfu dui Xinjiang, Menggu he Xizang Zhengce Yanjiu* (Studies on late Qing policies toward Xinjiang, Mongolia, and Tibet) (Huhehaote: Nei Menggu Renmin Chubanshe, 2005).

18. Cai Fenglin, *Ri'E Sici Miyue: Jindai Riben "Manmeng" Zhengce Yanjiu zhiyi* (Four Russo-Japanese secret treaties: A study of the modern Japanese policy on "Manchu-Mongolia") (Beijing: Zhongyang Minzu Daxue Chubanshe, 2008).

19. Chang Chi-hsiung, *Waimeng Zhuquan Guishu Jiaoshe: 1911–1916* (Disputes and negotiations over Outer Mongolia's national identity, unification or independence, and sovereignty, 1911–1916) (Taibei: Zhongyang Yanjiuyuan Jindaishi Yanjiusuo, 1995).

20. Suiyuan (1928–1954) was the most powerful of the frontier provinces with the largest concentration of Chinese settlers. See Justin Tighe, *Constructing Suiyuan: The Politics of Northwestern Territory and Development in Early Twentieth-Century China* (Leiden: Brill, 2005).

21. In the same year, Qinghai province was established in the Kokonuur region inhabited by Amdo Tibetans, Mongols, and Hui Muslims. The Kham region of historical Tibet was turned into Xikang province in 1939. The same concept of special administrative region was applied to Hong Kong and Macau after they were returned to the PRC in 1997 and 1999, respectively. During the Republican period, special administrative region was a preparatory stage for full direct provincial-cum-Chinese control of a non-Han region.

22. The official remit of the Mongolian and Tibetan Affairs Commission established by the Nationalist government in 1928 was Outer Mongolia (i.e., the MPR) and Tibet, and its mission was to conquer and colonize the two "regions" by establishing provinces.

23. Sechin Jagchid, *The Last Mongol Prince: The Life and Times of Demchugdongrob, 1902–1966* (Bellingham: Center for East Asian Studies, Western Washington University, 1999).

24. James Boyd, *Japanese-Mongolian Relations, 1873–1945: Faith, Race and Strategy* (Folkestone, UK: Global Oriental, 2011).

25. For a recent Chinese reflection on the division of "all under heaven" into the interior and the exterior as a constantly changing process, see Ge Zhaoguang, "The 'Interior' and the 'Exterior' in Historical China: A Re-clarification of the Concepts of 'China' and the 'Periphery,'" *Chinese Studies in History* 51, no. 1 (2018): 4–28. This perspective allows the author to depart from the dominant Chinese narrative and acknowledge that the incorporation of the periphery—frontier regions inhabited by non-Han peoples during the Qing—was a process of colonization.

26. Christopher P. Atwood, *Young Mongols and Vigilantes in Inner Mongolia's Interregnum Decades, 1911–1931*, 2 vols. (Leiden: Brill, 2002); Liu, *Frontier Passages*, 47–49.

27. The first two items of the proclamation read:

We maintain that the six leagues, twenty-four sections, and forty-nine banners of Inner Mongolia, Chahar, the two sections of Tumute, as well as the whole area of the three special banners in Ningxia, whether they have changed their status into *xian* or have been designated as grassland, should be returned to the Inner Mongolian people as part of their territory. The titles of the three administrative provinces of Re[he], Cha[har], and Sui[yuan] and their de facto administrative offices should be abolished. Under no circumstances should other nationalities be allowed to occupy the land of the Inner Mongolian nation or expropriate it under various excuses.

We maintain that the Inner Mongolian people have the right to solve all their internal problems themselves, and no one else is entitled to interfere by force with the life, customs, religion, morality, and other rights of the Inner Mongolian nation. At the same time, the Inner Mongolian nation can organize in whatever way it pleases. It has the right, in accordance with the principle of independence, to shape its own life and set up its own government; it has the right to form federal ties with other nations, and it also has the right to remain completely separate. In a word, a nation is deserving of respect, and at the same time all nations are equal.

Stuart Schram, ed., *Mao's Road to Power. Revolutionary Writings 1912–1949*, vol. 5, *Toward the Second United Front January 1935–July 1937)* (Armonk, NY: M. E. Sharpe, 1999), 71–72.

28. Christopher P. Atwood, "Sino-Soviet Diplomacy and the Second Partition of Mongolia, 1945–1946," in *Mongolia in the Twentieth Century: Landlocked Cosmopolitan*, ed. Bruce A. Elleman and Stephen Kotkin (Armonk, NY: M. E. Sharpe, 1999), 137–61; Sergey Radchenko, "The Truth about Mongolia's Independence 70 Years Ago: A Referendum in Mongolia Seventy Years Ago Sheds Light on the Country's Path Since," *The Diplomat*, October 22, 2015.

29. See Uradyn E. Bulag, *Mongols at China's Edge*; Uradyn E. Bulag, *Collaborative Nationalism: The Politics of Friendship at China's Mongolian Frontier* (Lanham, MD: Rowman and Littlefield, 2010).

30. Uradyn E. Bulag, "From Inequality to Difference: Colonial Contradictions of Class and Ethnicity in 'Socialist' China," in *Mongols at China's Edge*.

31. Benedict R. O'G. Anderson. *Imagined Communities: Reflections on the Origin and Spread of Nationalism* (1991; London: Verso, 2006); see also Benedict Anderson, *Spectre of Comparisons: Nationalism, Southeast Asia and the World* (London: Verso, 1998).

32. Terry Martin, *The Affirmative Action Empire: Nations and Nationalism in the Soviet Union, 1923–1939* (Ithaca, NY: Cornell University Press, 2001); Francine Hirsch, *Empire of Nations: Ethnographic Knowledge and the Making of the Soviet Union* (Ithaca, NY: Cornell University Press, 2005); Dru C. Gladney, *Dislocating China: Muslims, Minorities, and Other Subaltern Subjects* (Chicago: University of Chicago Press, 2004). Uradyn E. Bulag, *Mongols at China's Edge*.

33. A useful comparison is Tibet's relations with China in the early years of the People's Republic. Before 1959, Tibet had a Tibetan government that signed a seventeen-point agreement with the PRC government in 1951. China's repudiation of the agreement in 1959 in the wake of the Dalai Lama's flight to India led to China's abolition of the Local Government of Tibet. A preparatory government with officials appointed by the Chinese government established the Tibet Autonomous Region in 1965, with power firmly held by Chinese officials. In contrast to Inner Mongolia, which reclaimed most of the historical Mongol territories, Tibet lost its Kham and Amdo regions to Sichuan and Qinghai, respectively. This meant that substantial Tibetan populations were subsequently located in other provinces, in several cases as Tibetan autonomous prefectures or counties.

34. Chahar was abolished in 1952, Suiyuan in 1954, and Rehe in 1955. Chahar and Rehe had been formed in 1928 with Mongol and Chinese populations. After their abolition, territories

under Mongol banner administrations were allocated to Inner Mongolia, whereas Chinese territories were transferred to Liaoning and Hebei provinces. Suiyuan was the only province established entirely on Mongol territory, so there was less territorial dispute with neighboring provinces after its incorporation into Inner Mongolia. Ningxia was merged with Gansu province in 1954. In 1956, the Mongol territories under the enlarged Gansu province were allocated to Inner Mongolia, and in 1958, a Ningxia Hui Autonomous Region was carved out of Mongol areas of Gansu.

35. The concept of ethnic sovereignty was introduced by Mark Elliott to understand Manchu anxiety during the Qing dynasty concerning maintaining their identity while ruling a large territory in which they were vastly outnumbered by conquered subjects. Mark C. Elliott, *The Manchu Way: The Eight Banners and Ethnic Identity in Late Imperial China* (Stanford, CA: Stanford University Press, 2001).

36. This challenges recent Chinese scholarly views that the system of nationality regional autonomy and nationality policies strengthened minority nationalism and encouraged their separatist tendency. Such a diagnosis has led to new Chinese government policies in Tibet, Xinjiang, and Inner Mongolia. The foundational text of this new policy is Hu Angang and Lianhe Hu, "Di'erdai Minzu Zhengce: Cujin Minzu Jiaorong Yiti He Fanrong" (Second generation Minzu policies: Promoting ethnic mingling and prosperity), *Xinjiang Shifan Daxue Xuebao* 32, no. 5 (2011): 1–13.

37. Uradyn E. Bulag, "Mongolian Ethnicity and Linguistic Anxiety in China," *American Anthropologist* 105, no. 4 (2003): 753–63.

38. Song Naigong et al., eds., *Zhongguo Renkou: Nei Menggu Fence* (Chinese population: Inner Mongolia volume) (Beijing: Caizheng Jingji Chubanshe, 1987), 82; Tian Xueyuan, *Zhongguo Minzu Renkou* (Ethnic Populations of China) (Beijing: Zhongguo Renkou Chubanshe, 2002), 1:117.

39. Uradyn E. Bulag, *Collaborative Nationalism*, esp. ch. 5.

40. Frank Dikötter, *Mao's Great Famine: The History of China's Most Devastating Catastrophe, 1958–1962* (New York: Walker, 2010). Yang Jisheng, in arguably the definitive account of the Great Famine, suggests a more moderate figure of thirty-six million. Yang Jisheng, *Mubei: Zhongguo liushi niandai da jihuang jishi* (Tombstone: A chronicle of the Great Famine in China in the 1960s) (Hong Kong: Tiandi tushu, 2008). An abridged English translation of the book was published in 2012: *Tombstone: The Great Chinese Famine, 1958–1962*, trans. Stacy Mosher and Guo Jian (New York: Farrar, Straus & Giroux, 2012).

41. Uradyn E. Bulag, "Good Han, Bad Han: The Moral Parameters of Ethnopolitics in China," in *Critical Han Studies: The History, Representation, and Identity of China's Majority*, ed. Thomas S. Mullaney, James Leibold, Stéphane Gros, and Eric Vanden Bussche (Berkeley: University of California Press, 2012), 92–109, 282–85.

42. Sergey Radchenko, "The Soviets' Best Friend in Asia: The Mongolian Dimension of the Sino-Soviet Split," CWIHP Working Paper No. 42, Cold War International History Project, Washington, DC, 2003.

43. Melvyn C. Goldstein, Ben Jiao, and Tanzen Lhundrup, *On the Cultural Revolution in Tibet: The Nyemo Incident of 1969* (Berkley: University of California Press, 2009).

44. Tsering Woeser, *Forbidden Memory: Tibet during the Cultural Revolution* (Lincoln, NE: Potomac Books, 2020).

45. Millward, *Eurasian Crossroads*, 267.

46. Morris Rossabi, *China and the Uyghurs. A Concise Introduction* (Lanham, MD: Rowman and Littlefield, 2021), 60–61.

47. Census taken by the end of 1964. Song Naigong et al. (eds.), *Zhongguo Renkou*, 349.

48. Andrew G. Walder, *Agents of Disorder: Inside China's Cultural Revolution* (Cambridge, MA: Harvard University Press, 2019), 192

49. Quoted in Bayantai, *Wasu Zainan Shilu* (Veritable records of the *wasu* catastrophe), unpublished ms., collated by the Southern Mongolian Human Rights Information Center, n.d.), 136, https://www.smhric.org/IMPRP.pdf.

50. Hao Weimin, ed., *Nei Menggu Zizhiqu Shi* (History of the Inner Mongolia Autonomous Region) (Huhehaote: Nei Menggu Daxue Chubanshe, 1991), 313–14.

51. Yang Haiying, "The Truth about the Mongolian Genocide during the Chinese Cultural Revolution," *Asian Studies* (Shizuoka University), March 2017, 1.

52. A number of minority cadres have taken up top positions in provinces and regions other than their own. Wu Jinghua, an ethnic Yi, served as Party secretary in the Tibet Autonomous Region from May 1985 to December 1988, and Bayanchuluu, a Mongol, was Party secretary of Jilin Province from August 2014 to November 2020. The only exception to this rule today appears to be Shen Yiqin, a Bai woman from Guizhou Province, serving as Party secretary in her home province Guizhou since November 2020. She is the third woman to serve as a Provincial Party secretary in the PRC. Guizhou, though multiethnic, is not an autonomous region.

53. Adrian Zenz, a German anthropologist, has spearheaded the use of *cultural genocide* to characterize China's human rights violations in Xinjiang starting with his 2019 article "Break Their Roots: Evidence for China's Parent-Child Separation Campaign in Xinjiang." *Journal of Political Risk* 7, no. 7 (2019): https://www.jpolrisk.com/break-their-roots-evidence-for-chinas-parent-child-separation-campaign-in-xinjiang/. His work has been widely cited in media reports and furnished crucial evidence for international sanctions against Chinese officials responsible for human rights abuses in Xinjiang and the US ban on imports of cotton from Xinjiang. Joanne Smith Finley used *genocide* in her article "Why Scholars and Activists Increasingly Fear a Uyghur Genocide in Xinjiang," *Journal of Genocide Research* (2020): https://doi.org/10.1080/14623528.2020.1848109. However, the terms *genocide* or *cultural genocide* have been avoided by many influential researchers on Xinjiang, such as Darren Byler, who prefer to refer to camps, terror capitalism, and so on. See Darren Byler, Ivan Franceschini, and Nicholas Lobere, eds., *Xinjiang Year Zero* (Canberra: ANU Press, 2022); Darren Byler, *Terror Capitalism: Uyghur Dispossession and Masculinity in a Chinese City* (Durham, NC: Duke University Press, 2022).

54. The foundational text for the genocide charge is the Mongol-Japanese scholar Yang Haiying's Japanese study, *Bohyo Naki Sogen: Uchi Mongoru ni okeru Bunkadaikakumei, gyakusatsu no kiroku* (Grassland without tombstones: Records of the massacre during Inner Mongolia's Cultural Revolution (Tokyo: Iwanami Shoten, 2009). It describes in detail the experience of a dozen Mongol victims, from various backgrounds—Party leaders, PLA officers, intellectuals, and herders, including the author's family members—graphically portraying the tortures, both mental and physical, and accusing Han Chinese and the CCP of inflicting ethnic genocide on the Mongols.

55. Robert Barnett has cautioned against an easy equivalence of Tibet with Xinjiang, and the application of concepts such as genocide or annihilation used in Xinjiang to situations in Tibet. In contrast to his concerns centered on the difference in degree of intensity of Chinese oppression in these two regions, we argue, for a different conceptualization that we suggest can more precisely characterize the nature of Chinese policy in these and other autonomous regions. Robert Barnett, "China's Policies in Its Far West: The Claim of Tibet-Xinjiang Equivalence," March 29, 2021. https://www.cfr.org/blog/chinas-policies-its-far-west-claim-tibet-xinjiang-equivalence. For a

critique of Barnett's discussion of Chinese policies in Xinjiang and Tibet see Tenzin Dorjee, "The Question of Tibet-Xinjiang Equivalence: China's Recent Policies in Its Far West," *Asia Unbound*, Council on Foreign Relations, June 3, 2021, https://www.cfr.org/blog/question-tibet -xinjiang-equivalence-chinas-recent-policies-its-far-west.

56. Barbara Harff and Ted R. Gurr, "Toward Empirical Theory of Genocides and Politicides: Identification and Measurement of Cases since 1945," *International Studies Quarterly* 32, no. 3 (1988): 360. See also their "Victims of the State: Genocides, Politicides and Group Repression since 1945," *International Review of Victimology* 1 (1989): 23–41.

57. Clark McCauley, "'Killing Them to Save Us': Lessons from Politicide for Preventing and Countering Terrorism," in *Handbook of Terrorism Prevention and Preparedness*, ed. Alex P. Schmid (The Hague: ICCT Press, 2020), 146.

58. For instance, in their recent survey of genocide and politicide during civil war, Uzony and Demir use *genocide* and *politicide* in juxtaposition without differentiating them. Gary Uzony and Burak Demir, "Excluded Ethnic Groups, Conflict Contagion, and the Onset of Genocide and Politicide during Civil War," *International Studies Quarterly* 64 (2020): 857–66.

59. Baruch Kimmerling, *Politicide: Sharon's War against the Palestinians* (London: Verso, 2003), 4.

60. In principle, and in law, these are quintessential properties of political security, which, according to Buzan, "concerns the organizational stability of states, systems of government, and the ideologies that give them legitimacy." B. Buzan, "New Patterns of Global Security in the Twenty-First Century," *International Affairs* 67, no. 3 (1991): 433.

61. For an early application of the concept of politicide in Inner Mongolia, see Uradyn E. Bulag, "Twentieth Century China: Ethnic Assimilation and Inter-Group Violence," in *The Oxford Handbook of Genocide Studies*, ed. Donald Bloxham and A. Dirk Moses (Oxford: Oxford University Press, 2010), 426–44.

62. Uradyn E. Bulag, "The Cult of Ulanhu: History, Memory, and the Making of an Ethnic Hero," in *Mongols at China's Edge*.

63. Carl Schmitt, *Political Theology: Four Chapters on the Concept of Sovereignty*, trans. George Schwab (Chicago: University of Chicago Press, 2005). See Giorgio Agamben, *State of Exception*, trans. Kevin Attell (Chicago: University of Chicago Press, 2005).

64. Hu Ping, "Bisai Geming de Geming: Dui Wenhua Geming the Zhengzhi Xinlixue Fenxi" (A revolution of competing for revolution: A political psychological analysis of the Cultural Revolution), *Beijing Zhi Chun* (Beijing Spring), no. 6 (1996), https://sites.google.com/site/hupin gwenji/wenge/wenhuageming. See also Luo Siling, "An Exiled Editor Traces the Roots of Democratic Thought in China," *New York Times*, October 28, 2016.

65. Tumen and Zhu Dongli, *Kang Sheng yu Neirendang Yuan'an* (Kang Sheng and the trumped-up case of the Neirendang) (Beijing: Zhonggong Zhongyang Dangxiao Chubanshe, 1995), 225.

66. Robert L. Worden, Andrea Matles Savada, and Ronald E. Dolan, eds., "The Government," in *China: A Country Study* (Washington, DC: GPO for the Library of Congress, 1987).

67. William Kymlicka, *Multicultural Citizenship* (Oxford, UK: Clarendon, 1995), 10–11. To be sure, some ethnic or religious groups, such as orthodox Jews in the United States and globally and Muslims in many countries, are intent on preserving their dress code, foodways, or other distinctive features, but this is characteristically expressed in terms of multiculturalism rather than associated with territorial autonomy or independence.

68. For an early application of Kymlicka's distinction in discussing ethnic politics in Inner Mongolia, see Uradyn E. Bulag, *Mongols at China's Edge*, especially the introduction. Mark

Elliott was among the first to make a case for recognizing the territorial, hence indigenous, dimension of China's minority groups: "The Case of the Missing Indigene: Debate over a 'Second-Generation' Ethnic Policy," *China Journal*, no. 73 (January 2015): 186–213.

69. According to the Seventh National Census conducted in 2020, Inner Mongolia's permanent population was approximately 24 million, of which the Mongols were 4,247,000 and the Han Chinese 18,935,000. See "Nei Menggu changzhu renkou wei 2404.9 wan ren, pingjun meige jiatinghu 2.35 ren" (The permanent population of Inner Mongolia is 24,049,000, each household having 2.35 persons), *China News*, https://www.chinanews.com/gn/2021/05-20/9481795 .shtml#:~:text=中新网呼和浩特5,的人口为2.35人%E3%80%82.

70. Zhou Enlai, "Guanyu Xibei Diqu de Minzu Gongzuo" (On nationality work in the Northwestern Region), June 26, 1950, https://www.marxists.org/chinese/zhouenlai/234.htm/

71. In April 1980, Hu Yaobang, general secretary of the CCP, made an inspection tour of Tibet, where he apologized to Tibetans and ordered the withdrawal of thousands of Han cadres from Tibet. But this was not to grant national autonomy to Tibetans. Rather, it was to increase the ratio of Tibetan cadres in a region that remained under CCP rule. The result was that a more moderate nationality policy was briefly introduced leading to some revitalization of minority cultures.

72. Darren Byler, "Violent Paternalism: On the Banality of Uyghur Unfreedom," *Asia-Pacific Journal* (2018), https://apjjf.org/2018/24/Byler.html; Bethany Allen-Ibrahimian, "Exposed: China's Operating Manuals for Mass Internment and Arrest by Algorithm," *China Cables*, 2019, https:// www.icij.org/investigations/china-cables/exposed-chinas-operating-manuals-for-mass-intern ment-and-arrest-by-algorithm/; Linda Maizland, "China's Repression of Uighurs in Xinjiang," *Council on Foreign Relations*, 2020 https://www.cfr.org/backgrounder/chinas-repression -uighurs-xinjiang.

73. Magnus Fiskesjo, "Bulldozing Culture: China's Systematic Destruction of Uyghur Heritage Reveals Genocidal Intent," *Cultural Property News*, June 23, 2021, https://culturalproperty news.org/bulldozing-culture-chinas-systematic-destruction-of-uyghur heritage-reveals -genocidal-intent/. For a comprehensive documentation of the Chinese repression in Xinjiang, see the Xinjiang Documentation Project database at https://xinjiang.sppga.ubc.ca/.

74. The most vehement attack came from Tsinghua University scholars in 2011. Hu Angang and Lianhe Hu, "Dierdai Minzu Zhengce: Cujin Minzu Jiaorong Yiti He Fanrong" (Second generation Minzu policies: Promoting organic ethnic blending and prosperity), *Xinjiang Shifan Daxue Xuebao* 32, no. 5 (2011): 1–13.

75. David Brophy, "The Minorities: Civilised Yet?" in *China Story Yearbook 2013: Civilising China*, ed. Geremie R. B. Barmé and Jeremy Goldkorn (Canberra: Australian Centre on China in the World, Australian National University, 2013), 309, https://www.thechinastory.org/content /uploads/2013/10/Civilising-China-Geremie-R.-Barme_sml.pdf

76. Adrian Zenz and Erin Rosenberg, "Beijing Plans a Slow Genocide in Xinjiang: Chinese Officials' Own Words Speak to Plans to Reduce Uyghur Births," *Foreign Policy*, June 8, 2021, https://foreignpolicy.com/2021/06/08/genocide-population-xinjiang-uyghurs/; Adrian Zenz, "End the Dominance of the Uyghur Ethnic Group": An Analysis of Beijing's Population Optimization Strategy in Southern Xinjiang," *Central Asian Survey* 40, no. 3 (2021): 291–312; Nathan Ruser and James Leibold, "Family De-planning: The Coercive Campaign to Drive Down Indigenous Birth-Rates in Xinjiang," Australian Strategic Policy Institute Policy Brief Report, no. 44 (2021), https:// www.aspi.org.au/report/family-deplanning-birthrates-xinjiang.

77. Millward, *Eurasian Crossroads*, 393.

78. Christopher Atwood, "Bilingual Education in Inner Mongolia: An Explainer," *Made in China Journal*, August 30, 2020, https://madeinchinajournal.com/2020/08/30/bilingual-education-in-inner-mongolia-an-explainer/; Antonio Graceffo, "China's Crackdown on Mongolian Culture: A New Policy Promoting Mandarin-Language Education Has Sparked Protests in Inner Mongolia and Outrage across the Border," *The Diplomat*, September 4, 2020, https://thediplomat.com/2020/09/chinas-crackdown-on-mongolian-culture/.

79. Uradyn E. Bulag, "Minority Nationalities as Frankenstein's Monsters? Reshaping 'the Chinese Nation' and China's Quest to Become a 'Normal Country,'" *China Journal* 86, no. 2 (2021): 46–67; Uradyn E. Bulag, "Mandarin Chinese as the National Language and Its Discontents," in *Southernizing Sociolinguistics: Colonialism, Racism, and Patriarchy in Language in the Global South*, ed. Bassey E. Antia and Sinfree Makoni (London: Routledge, 2023), 186–205.

Index

Qinghai incident: Cheng Tiejun and, 131–33; dispute over, 369n32

Qinghai province, 370n4; Amdo region and, 381n33; defense of, 10; establishment of, 380n21

Qinghai University, 131

Qin Ping, 278

Qin Shihuang, 289, 290, 292

Qin Weixian, 195, 199, 243, 257, 259

Qiu Huizuo, 267, 290

Qi Zhi, 187

Quan Jiafu, 80

Quanwudi (Invincible), 105, 106

Quan Xingyuan: April 13th Decision and, 261; detention of, 129; Gao Shuhua and, 198–99; Hohhot campus monitoring by, 74; as Hohhot mass rally, 87; Husansi and, 111, 112, 121, 143; IMMR and, 125; IMMR's arrest of, 149; Inner Mongolia Party Committee and, 73, 93, 108, 109, 129; labor reform, 275, 283; Li Tanyou and, 146–47; loyalists' attack on, 139, 228; Mao on, 245; May 22 verdict and, 251; at negotiations in Beijing, 147; Neirendang issue and, 232; on Preparatory Group of Revolutionary Committee of IMAR, 150, 154, 163, 184, 370n9; rebel support by, 111, 112, 121, 123, 140; resumption of power, 249; secret reports of, 59; on Standing Committee of Inner Mongolia Revolutionary Committee, 186, 197, 249; at Teachers College, 83, 84, 109, 140; Teng Haiqing and, 155, 231; Third Headquarters and, 108; Ulanhu and, 57, 71, 144; Wu Tao and, 123, 125; Zhou Enlai's order to free, 136; Zhou Enlai's summons to, 161

racism, global aspects of, 7

radical insurgency, against military, 371n7

radicalism, PLA veteran opposition to, 371n7

radical redistribution, 42

radicals: responsibility born by, 7. See also Gang of Four; Kang Sheng

radio, underground radio stations, 377n3

Raoyang: Cheng family's return to, 11, 302, 303, 307; famine in, 3, 13, 17, 21–22, 32, 298; Japanese occupation of, 30, 71; land reform in, 12; Liu Wang in, 30, 31; middle school education in, 13–14, 19–20, 201, 303; as paternal ancestral place, 10; Zhangcun village, 1, 12, 162, 276, 287

Rash, 197

reactionaries, revolutionaries (term) and, 21

rebellion: as ethnic targeting, 6; social justice framing of, 6–7. See also Husansi (Hohhot Third Headquarters)

rebel(s): on antiestablishment activities, 7; Cheng as, 3, 4, 312; complex position of, 4; confrontation between IMMR and, 371n7; on Cultural Revolution, 313; death sentences, 277–80;

in Hunan province, 373n12; rebel delegates, 369nn36–41; rebel dispersement, 215–18; responsibility born by, 7; term usage, 365–66n2; *wasu* movement and, 204–30. See also Dongzong (Dongfanghong Zhandou Zongdui) (The East Is Red Fighting Column); Gao Shuhua; Ouyang Ruchen; Red Guard; revolutionary leftists (*gemin zuopai*); Yang Xiaokai

rebel victory/military takeover of Inner Mongolia, 147–74

Red Flag (*Hongqi*) of the Party Committee, 110, 128, 135, 158, 179, 304

Red Flag (journal), 56, 110, 131, 133, 235

Red Guard, 86–91; activism in North China cities, 4; apologies from former, 378n2; assessments of role of, 7; attack on the Four Olds, 87–91; Cheng as member of, 103–4, 312; Cheng Tiejun and, 4, 103–4; Han Tong as, 130; Lanzhou Incident, 91–97; Mao's call to, 3; Mao's inspection, 100–103; on march, 86–118; members as rebels, 366n2; murder of a, 119–21; Red August, 86–91; support of, 314. See also Dongzong (Dongfanghong Zhandou Zongdui) (The East Is Red Fighting Column)

Red Guard Action Days, 89

Red Guard Headquarters ("Hong Zong"), 120, 128

Red Guards. See Dongzong (Dongfanghong Zhandou Zongdui) (The East Is Red Fighting Column)

Red Railway Worker Fighters (Hongtie Zhanshi), 159

Red Rebel Corps (Hongse Zaofantuan), 128, 130, 140

reeducation camps, 8, 213, 216, 217, 282, 283, 284, 297. See also labor reform

refugees, experience of, 312

regional autonomy: Han chauvinism and, 314; minority people and, 314

Rehe province, 320, 327, 381n27; abolishment of, 381n34

religions. See minority religions

Ren Zuolin, 115

"Report about the Work of Deep Ferreting Out of Traitors," 371n8

reporting: by Cheng Tiejun, 7; from grasslands, 175–78; under partial military control, 164–67

repression, responsibility for, 7

Republic of China (ROC), 314; formal recognition of independence of MPR, 2; special administrative regions during, 380n21; Treaty of Kyakhta, 320; underground radio stations and, 377n3

"Resolution concerning the Question of Qinghai," 146

revisionists, as enemies of Cultural Revolution, 3

revolt(s), in Mongolian-Soviet borderland, 368n8